Secure PHP Development: Building 50 Practical Applications

Secure PHP Development: Building 50 Practical Applications

Mohammed J. Kabir

Wiley Publishing, Inc.

Secure PHP Development: Building 50 Practical Applications

Published by
Wiley Publishing, Inc.
10475 Crosspoint Boulevard
Indianapolis, IN 46256
www.wiley.com

Copyright © 2003 by Wiley Publishing, Inc., Indianapolis, Indiana

Published by Wiley Publishing, Inc., Indianapolis, Indiana

Published simultaneously in Canada

ISBN: 0-7645-4966-9

Manufactured in the United States of America

10 9 8 7 6 5 4 3 2 1

1B/SU/QU/QT/IN

For general information on our other products and services or to obtain technical support, please contact our Customer Care Department within the U.S. at (800) 762-2974, outside the U.S. at (317) 572-3993 or fax (317) 572-4002.

Wiley also publishes its books in a variety of electronic formats. Some content that appears in print may not be available in electronic books.

Library of Congress Cataloging-in-Publication Data

Library of Congress Control Number: 2003101844

WILEY is a trademark of Wiley Publishing, Inc.

Credits

SENIOR ACQUISITIONS EDITOR
Sharon Cox

ACQUISITIONS EDITOR
Debra Williams Cauley

PROJECT EDITOR
Sharon Nash

DEVELOPMENT EDITORS
Rosemarie Graham
Maryann Steinhart

TECHNICAL EDITORS
Richard Lynch
Bill Patterson

COPY EDITORS
Elizabeth Kuball
Luann Rouff

EDITORIAL MANAGER
Mary Beth Wakefield

VICE PRESIDENT & EXECUTIVE GROUP
PUBLISHER
Richard Swadley

VICE PRESIDENT AND EXECUTIVE
PUBLISHER
Bob Ipsen

VICE PRESIDENT AND PUBLISHER
Joseph B. Wikert

EXECUTIVE EDITORIAL DIRECTOR
Mary Bednarek

PROJECT COORDINATOR
Dale White

GRAPHICS AND PRODUCTION
SPECIALISTS
Beth Brooks
Kristin McMullan
Heather Pope

QUALITY CONTROL TECHNICIANS
Tyler Connoley
David Faust
Andy Hollandbeck

PROOFREADING AND INDEXING
TECHBOOKS Production Services

About the Author

Mohammed J. Kabir is CEO and founder of EVOKNOW, Inc. His company (www.evoknow.com) develops software using LAMP (Linux, Apache, MySQL, and PHP), Java, and C++. It specializes in custom software development and offers security consulting services to many companies around the globe.

When he is not busy managing software projects or writing books, Kabir enjoys riding mountain bikes and watching sci-fi movies. Kabir studied computer engineering at California State University, Sacramento, and is also the author of *Apache Server 2 Bible*, *Apache Server Administrator's Handbook*, and *Red Hat Server 8*. You can contact Kabir via e-mail at kabir@evoknow.com or visit the book's Web site at http://www.evoknow.com/publications/books/phpbook.php.

Preface

Welcome to **Secure PHP Development: Building 50 Practical Applications**. PHP has come a long way since its first incarnation as a Perl script. Now PHP is a powerful Web scripting language with object-oriented programming support. Slowly but steadily it has entered the non-Web scripting arena often reserved for Perl and other shell scripting languages. Arguably, PHP is one of the most popular Web platforms. In this book you will learn about how to secure PHP applications, how to develop and use an application framework to develop many useful applications for both Internet and intranet Web sites.

Is This Book for You?

This is not a PHP language book for use as reference. There are many good PHP language books out there. This book is designed for intermediate- to advanced-level PHP developers who can review the fifty PHP applications developed for this book and deploy them as is or customize them as needed. However, it is entirely possible for someone with very little PHP background to deploy the applications developed for this book. Therefore, even if you are not currently a PHP developer, you can make use of all the applications with very little configuration changes.

If you are looking for example applications that have defined features and implementation requirements, and you want to learn how applications are developed by professional developers, this book a great starting point. Here you will find numerous examples of applications that have been designed from the ground up using a central application framework, which was designed from scratch for this book.

The book shows developers how PHP applications can be developed by keeping security considerations in focus and by taking advantage of an object-oriented approach to PHP programming whenever possible to develop highly maintainable, extensible applications for Web and intranet use.

How This Book Is Organized

The book is organized into seven parts.

Part 1: Designing PHP Applications

Part I is all about designing practical PHP applications while understanding and avoiding security risks. In this part, you learn about practical design and implementation considerations, best practices, and security risks and the techniques you can take to avoid them.

Part II: Developing Intranet Solutions

Part II introduces you to the central application framework upon which almost all the Web and intranet applications designed and developed for this book are based. The central application framework is written as a set of object-oriented PHP classes. Using this framework of classes, you are shown how to develop a set of intranet applications to provide central authentication, user management, simple document publishing, contact management, shared calendar, and online help for your intranet users. Because all of the applications in this part of the book are based on the core classes discussed in the beginning of the book, you will see how that architecture works very well for developing most common applications used in modern intranets.

Part III: Developing E-mail Solutions

Part III deals with e-mail applications. These chapters describe a suite of e-mail applications such as Tell-a-Friend applications, e-mail-based survey applications, and a MySQL database-driven e-mail campaign system that sends, tracks, and reports e-mail campaigns.

Part IV: Using PHP for Sysadmin Tasks

Part IV focuses on demonstrating how PHP can become a command-line scripting platform for managing many system administration tasks. In these chapters, you learn to work with many command-line scripts that are designed for small, specific tasks and can be run automatically via Cron or other scheduling facilities. Applications developed in this part include the Apache virtual host configuration generator, the BIND zone generator, a multi-user e-mail reminder tool, a POP3 spam filtering tool, a hard disk partition monitoring tool, a system load monitoring tool, and more.

Part V: Internet Applications

In Part V, you learn how to develop a generic Web form management application suite and a voting (poll) application for your Web site. Because Web form management is the most common task PHP performs, you will learn a general-purpose design that shows you how PHP can be used to centralize data collection from Web visitors, a critical purpose of most Web sites.

Part VI: Tuning and Securing PHP Applications

In this part, you learn ways to fine-tune your PHP applications for speed and security. You will learn how to benchmark your applications, and cache your application output and even application opcode. You will also learn to protect your applications using various security measures involving PHP development and the Apache Web server platform.

Part VII: Appendixes

The four appendixes in Part VII present a detailed description of the contents and structure of the CD-ROM, and help on PHP, SQL and Linux. The CD-ROM contains full source code used in the entire book.

The SQL appendix introduces you to various commands that enable you to create and manage MySQL databases, tables, and so on, from the command line and via a great tool called phpMyAdmin.

Linux is one of the most popular PHP platforms. In the Linux appendix, you learn how you can install PHP and related tools on a Linux platform.

Tell Us What You Think

I am always very interested in learning what my readers are thinking about and how this book could be made more useful. If you are interested in contacting me directly, please send e-mail to `kabir@evoknow.com`. I will do my best to respond promptly. The most updated versions of all the PHP applications discussed in this book can be found at `http://www.evoknow.com/phpbook.php`.

Acknowledgments

I'd like to thank Debra Williams Cauley, Sharon Cox, Sharon Nash, Rosemarie Graham, Maryann Steinhart, Elizabeth Kuball, Luann Rouff, Richard Lynch, and Bill Patterson for working with me on this book.

I would also like to thank Asif, Tamim, Ruman, and the members of the EVO-KNOW family, who worked with me to get all the development work done for this book. Thanks, guys!

Finally, I would also like to thank the Wiley team that made this book a reality. They are the people who turned a few files into a beautiful and polished book.

Contents at a Glance

Contents

Part III   **Developing E-mail Solutions**

Part I

Designing PHP Applications

Chapter 1

Features of Practical PHP Applications

IN THIS CHAPTER

♦ Exploring the features of a practical PHP application

♦ Putting the features to work in applications

PHP BEGAN AS A PERSONAL home page scripting tool. Today PHP is widely used in both personal and corporate worlds as an efficient Web application platform. In most cases, PHP is introduced in a corporation because of its speed, absence of license fees, and fast development cycle.

The last reason (fast development cycle) is often misleading. There is no question that PHP development is often faster than other Web-development platforms like Java. However, the reasons for PHP development's faster cycle are often questioned by serious non-PHP developers. They claim that PHP development lacks design and often serves as a glue logic scripting platform—thrown together in a hurry. Frankly, I've seen many such scripts on many commercial engagements. In this book, I introduce you to a PHP application design that is both well planned and practical, therefore, highly maintainable.

Features of a Practical PHP Application

When developing a practical PHP application you should strongly consider the following features:

♦ **An object-oriented code base:** Granted, most freely available PHP applications are not object oriented, but hopefully they will change soon. The benefits of object-oriented design outweigh the drawbacks. The primary benefits are a reusable, maintainable code base. You'll find that there are similar objects in every application you develop, and reusing previously developed, tested, and deployed code gives you faster development time as you develop more and more applications.

I developed all the applications in this book using a single object framework (discussed in Chapter 4). Being able to develop more than 50 applications using the same framework means that I can easily fix any bugs, because the framework object code base is shared among almost all the applications.

♦ **External HTML interfaces using templates:** Having user interface elements within an application makes it difficult to adapt to the changing Web landscape. Just as end users like to change their sites' look and feel, they also like to make sure the application-generated screens match their sites' overall design. Using external HTML templates to generate application screens ensures that an end user can easily change the look and feel of the application as frequently as he or she wants.

♦ **External configuration:** When designing a practical application, the developer must ensure that end-user configuration is not within the code. Keeping it in an external-configuration-only file makes it very easy for end users to customize the application for their sites. The external configuration file should have site configuration data such as database access information (host name, username, password, port, etc.), path information, template names, etc.

♦ **Customizable messages:** The messages and error messages shown by the application should be customizable, because a PHP application could find its way into many different locales. A basic internationalization scheme would be to keep all the status and error messages in external files so that they can be customized per the local language.

♦ **Relational data storage:** Storing data on flat files or comma-separated value (CSV) files is old and a lot less manageable than storing data in a fast relational database such as MySQL. If the Web application collects lots of data points from the Web visitors or customers, using a relational database for storing data is best. Using a database can often increase your data security, because proper database configuration and access control make it difficult for unauthorized users to access the stored data.

♦ **Built-in access control:** If a Web application has sensitive operations that are to be performed by only a select group of people and not the entire world of Web visitors, then there has to be a way for the application to control access to ensure security.

♦ **Portable directory structure:** Because most PHP applications are deployed via the Web, it's important to make the applications easy to install by making the required directory structure as portable as possible. In most cases, the PHP application will run from a directory of its own inside the Web document root directory.

Employing the Features in Applications

Now let's look at how you can implement those features in PHP applications.

Creating object-oriented design

The very first step in designing a practical application is to understand the problem you want the application to solve and break down that problem into an object-oriented design.

For example, say you're to develop a Web-based library check-in/checkout system. In this situation, you have to identify the objects in your problem space. We all know that a library system allows its members to check in and check out books. So the objects that are immediately visible are members (that is, users) and books. Books are organized in categories, which have certain attributes such as name, description, content-maturity ratings (adults, children), and so on. A closer look reveals that a category can be thought of as an object as well. By observing the actual tasks that your application is to perform, you can identify objects in the system. A good object-oriented design requires a great deal of thinking ahead of coding, which is always the preferred way of developing software.

After you have base object architecture of your system, you can determine whether any of your previous work has objects that are needed in your new application. Perhaps you have an object defined in a class file that can be extended to create a new object in the new problem space. By reusing the existing proven code base, you can reduce your application's defects probability number significantly.

Using external HTML templates

Next, you need to consider how user interfaces will be presented and how can you allow for maximum customization that can be done without changing your core code. This is typically done by introducing external HTML templates for interface. For example, instead of using HTML code within your application, you can use HTML templates.

HTML templates are used for all application interfaces in this book so that the applications are easy to update in terms of look and feel. To understand the power of external HTML user-interface templates, carefully examine the code in Listing 1-1 and Listing 1-2.

Listing 1-1: A PHP Script with Embedded User Interface

```php
<?php

// Turn on all error reporting
error_reporting(E_ALL);
```

Continued

Listing 1-1 *(Continued)*

```php
// Get name from GET or POST request
$name = (! empty($_REQUEST['name'])) ? $_REQUEST['name'] : null;

// Print output
print <<<HTML

<html>
<head><title>Bad Script</title></head>
<body>
<table border=0 cellpadding=3 cellspacing=0>

<tr>
<td> Your name is </td>
<td> $name </td>
</tr>

</table>
</body>
</html>

HTML;

?>
```

Listing 1-1 shows a simple PHP script that has HTML interface embedded deep into the code. This is a very unmaintainable code for an end user who isn't PHP-savvy. If the end user wants to change the page this script displays, he or she has to modify the script itself, which has a higher chance of breaking the application. Now look at Listing 1-2.

Listing 1-2: A PHP Script with External User Interface

```php
<?php

    // Enable all error reporting
    error_reporting(E_ALL);

    // Set PHPLIB path
    $PHPLIB_DIR  = $_SERVER['DOCUMENT_ROOT'] . '/phplib';

    // Add PHPLIB path to PHP's include path
     ini_set( 'include_path', ':' . $PHPLIB_DIR . ':'
                               . ini_get('include_path'));

    // Include the PHPLIB template class
    include('template.inc');
```

```php
// Setup this application's template
// directory path
$TEMPLATE_DIR = $_SERVER['DOCUMENT_ROOT'] .
               '/ch1/templates';

// Setup the output template filename
$OUT_TEMPLATE = 'listing2out.html';

// Get name from GET or POST request
$name = (! empty($_REQUEST['name'])) ? $_REQUEST['name'] : null;

// Create a new template object
$t = new Template($TEMPLATE_DIR);

// Set the template file for this object to
// application's template
$t->set_file("page", $OUT_TEMPLATE);

// Setup the template block
$t->set_block("page", "mainBlock" , "main");

// Set the template variable = value
$t->set_var("NAME", $name);

// Parse the template block with all
// predefined key=values
$t->parse("main", "mainBlock", false);

// Parse the entire template and print the output
$t->pparse("OUT", "page");

?>
```

This application looks much more complex than the one shown in Listing 1-1, right? At first glance, it may look that way, but it's really a much better version of the script. Let's review it line by line:

```php
$PHPLIB_DIR  = $_SERVER['DOCUMENT_ROOT'] . '/phplib';
```

The first line of the script sets a variable called $PHPLIB_DIR to a path where PHPLIB library files are stored. The path is set to PHPLIB (phplib) subdirectory document root (hereafter %DocumentRoot%). This means if your Web document root is set to /usr/local/apache/htdocs, the script assumes your PHPLIB directory is

/usr/local/apache/htdocs/phplib. Of course, if that is not the case, you can change it as needed. For example:

```
$PHPLIB_DIR  = '/www/phplib';
```

Here the PHPLIB path is set to /www/phplib, which may or may not be within your document root. As long as you point the variable to the fully qualified path, it works. However, the preferred path is the %DocumentRoot%/somepath, as shown in the script.

The next bit of code is as follows:

```
ini_set( 'include_path', ':' . $PHPLIB_DIR . ':'
                              . ini_get('include_path'));
```

It adds the $PHPLIB_DIR path to PHP's include_path setting, which enables PHP to find files in PHPLIB. Notice that we have set the $PHPLIB_DIR path in front of the existing include_path value, which is given by the ini_get('include_path') function call. This means that if there are two files with the same name in $PHPLIB_DIR and the original include_path, the $PHPLIB_DIR one will be found first.

Next, the code sets the $TMEPLATE_DIR variable to the template path of the script:

```
$TEMPLATE_DIR = $_SERVER['DOCUMENT_ROOT'] .
                    '/ch1/templates';
```

The path is set to %DocumentRoot%/ch1/templates. You can change it to what-ever the exact path is. Again, the ideal path setting should include $_SERVER ['DOCUMENT_ROOT'] so that the script is portable. If an exact path is hard coded, such as the following, then the end user is more likely to have to reconfigure the path because the %DocumentRoot% may vary from site to site:

```
$TEMPLATE_DIR = '/usr/local/apache/htdocs/ch1/templates';
```

The next line in Listing 1-2 sets the output template file name to $OUT_TEMPLATE:

```
$OUT_TEMPLATE = 'listing2out.html';
```

This file must reside in the $TEMPLATE_DIR directory.

The code then sets $name variable to the 'name' value found from an HTTP GET or POST request:

```
$name = (! empty($_REQUEST['name'])) ? $_REQUEST['name'] : null;
```

The script creates a template object called $t using the following line:

```
$t = new Template($TEMPLATE_DIR);
```

The Template class is defined in the `template.inc` file, which comes from the PHPLIB library.

The $t template object will be used in the rest of the script to load the HTML template called $OUT_TEMPLATE from $TEMPLATE_DIR, parse it, and display the resulting contents. The HTML template file `listing2out.html` is shown in Listing 1-3.

Notice that in creating the object, the $TEMPLATE_DIR variable is passed as a parameter to the Template constructor. This sets the $t object's directory to $TEMPLATE_DIR, which is where we are keeping our `listing2out.html` HTML template.

The following line is used to set the $t object to the $OUT_TEMPLATE file. This makes the $t object read the file and internally reference the file as "page".

```
$t->set_file("page", $OUT_TEMPLATE);
```

The following line defines a template block called "mainBlock" as "main" from the "page" template:

```
$t->set_block("page", "mainBlock" , "main");
```

A block is a section of template contents that is defined using a pair of HTML comments, like the following:

```
<!-- BEGIN block_name -->

HTML CONTENTS GOES HERE

<!-- END block_name -->
```

A block is like a marker that allows the template object to know how to manipulate a section of an HTML template. For example, Listing 1-3 shows that we have defined a block called mainBlock that covers the entire HTML template.

Listing 1-3: The HTML Template (`listing2out.html`) for Listing 1-2 Script

```
<!-- BEGIN mainBlock -->
<html>
<head><title>Bad Script</title></head>
<body>
<table border=1>
```

Continued

Listing 1-3 *(Continued)*

```
<tr>
<td> Your name is </td>
<td> {NAME} </td>
</tr>

</table>
</body>
</html>
<!-- END mainBlock -->
```

You can define many blocks; blocks can be nested as well. For example:

```
<!-- BEGIN block_name1 -->

HTML CONTENTS GOES HERE

<!-- BEGIN block_name2 -->

    HTML CONTENTS GOES HERE

    <!-- END block_name2 -->

<!-- END block_name1 -->
```

block_name1 is the block that has block_name2 as a nested block. When defining nested blocks, you have to use set_block() method carefully. For example:

```
$t->set_block("page", "mainBlock" , "main");
$t->set_block("main", "rowBlock" , "rows");
```

The mainBlock is a block in "page" and rowBlock is a block within "main" block. So the HTML template will look like this:

```
<!-- BEGIN mainBlock-->

HTML CONTENTS GOES HERE

<!-- BEGIN rowBlock -->

    HTML CONTENTS GOES HERE

    <!-- END rowBlock -->

<!-- END mainBlock -->
```

You cannot define the embedded block first.

The next line in Listing 1-2 sets a template variable NAME to the value of $name variable:

```
$t->set_var("NAME", $name);
```

In Listing 1-3, you will see a line such as the following:

```
<td> {NAME} </td>
```

Here the template variable is {NAME}. When setting the value for this template variable using the set_var() method, you didn't have to use the curly braces, as it is automatically assumed.

Now that the script has set the value for the only template variable in the template, you can parse the block as done in the next line:

```
$t->parse("main", "mainBlock", false);
```

This line calls the parse() method of the $t template object to parse the mainBlock, which is internally named as "main." The third parameter is set to false, because we don't intend to loop through this block. Because nested blocks are often used in loops, you'd have to set the third parameter to true to ensure that the block is parsed properly from iteration to iteration.

Finally, the only remaining thing to do is print and parse the entire page:

```
$t->pparse("OUT", "page");
```

This prints the output page.

What all this additional code bought us is an implementation that uses an external HTML template, which the end user can modify without knowing anything about the PHP code. This is a great achievement, because most of the time the end user is interested in updating the interface look and feel as his or her site goes through transitions over time.

Using external configuration files

An external configuration file separates code from information that is end-user configurable.

By separating end-user editable information to a separate configuration file we reduce the risk of unintentional modification of core application code. Experienced commercial developers will tell you that this separation is a key timesaver when customers make support calls about PHP applications. As a developer, you can instruct the end user to only modify the configuration file and never to change anything in the core application files. This means any problem created at the end-user site is confined to the configuration file and can be identified easily by the developer.

In Listing 1-2, we had the following lines:

```
$PHPLIB_DIR  = $_SERVER['DOCUMENT_ROOT'] . '/phplib';

ini_set( 'include_path', ':' . $PHPLIB_DIR . ':'
                              . ini_get('include_path'));
include('template.inc');

include('template.inc');

$TEMPLATE_DIR = $_SERVER['DOCUMENT_ROOT'] .
                '/ch1/templates';

$OUT_TEMPLATE = 'listing2out.html';
```

These lines are configuration data for the script. Ideally, these lines should be stored in an external configuration file. For example, Listing 1-4 shows a modified version of Listing 1-2.

Listing 1–4: Modified Version of Listing 1–2

```php
<?php

  require_once('app_name.conf');

  // Enable all reporting
  error_reporting(E_ALL);

  // Get name from GET or POST request
  $name = (! empty($_REQUEST['name'])) ? $_REQUEST['name'] : null;

  // Create a new template object
  $t = new Template($TEMPLATE_DIR);

  // Set the template file for this object to
  // application's template
  $t->set_file("page", $OUT_TEMPLATE);

  // Setup the template block
  $t->set_block("page", "mainBlock" , "main");

  // Set the template variable = value
  $t->set_var("NAME", $name);
```

```
// Parse the template block with all
// predefined key=values
$t->parse("main", "mainBlock", false);

// Parse the entire template and print the output
$t->pparse("OUT", "page");

?>
```

Notice that all the configuration lines from the Listing 1-2 script have been removed with the following line:

```
require_once('app_name.conf');
```

The `require_once()` function loads the configuration file. The configuration lines now can be stored in the `app_name.conf` file, as shown in Listing 1-5.

Listing 1-5: Configuration File for Listing 1-4 Script

```
<?php

    // Set PHPLIB path
    $PHPLIB_DIR  = $_SERVER['DOCUMENT_ROOT'] . '/phplib';

    // Add PHPLIB path to PHP's include path
    ini_set( 'include_path', ':' . $PHPLIB_DIR . ':'
                                . ini_get('include_path'));
    // Include the PHPLIB template class
    include('template.inc');

    // Setup this application's template
    // directory path
    $TEMPLATE_DIR = $_SERVER['DOCUMENT_ROOT'] .
                    '/ch1/templates';

    // Setup the output template filename
    $OUT_TEMPLATE = 'listing2out.html';

?>
```

Another great advantage of a configuration file is that it allows you to define global constants as follows:

```
define(YOUR_CONSTANT, value);
```

For example, to define a constant called VERSION with value 1.0.0 you can add the following line in your configuration file:

```
define(VERSION, '1.0.0');
```

Because constants are not to be modified by design, centralizing then in a configuration file makes a whole lot of sense.

Using customizable messages

To understand the importance of customizable messages that are generated by an application, let's look at a simple calculator script.

Listing 1-6 shows the script, called calc.php. The configuration file used by calc.php is calc.conf, which is similar to Listing 1-5 and not shown here. This script expects the user to enter two numbers (num1, num2) and an operator (+ for addition, – for subtraction, * for multiplication, or / for division). If it doesn't get one or more of these required inputs, it prints error messages which are stored in an $errors variable.

Listing 1-6: calc.php

```php
<?php

    // Enable all error reporting
    error_reporting(E_ALL);

    require_once('calc.conf');

    // Get inputs from GET or POST request
    $num1 = (! empty($_REQUEST['num1'])) ? $_REQUEST['num1'] : null;
    $num2 = (! empty($_REQUEST['num2'])) ? $_REQUEST['num2'] : null;

    $operator = (! empty($_REQUEST['operator'])) ?
                $_REQUEST['operator'] : null;

    // Set errors to null
    $errors = null;

    // If number 1 is not given, error occurred
    if ($num1 == null)
    {
        $errors .= "<li>You did not enter number 1.";
    }
```

```php
// If number 2 is not given, error occurred
if ($num2 == null) {
    $errors .= "<li>You did not enter number 2.";
}

// If operator  is not given, error occurred
if (empty($operator)) {
    $errors .= "<li>You did not enter the operator.";
}

// Set result to null
$result = null;

// If operation is + do addition: num1 + num2
if (!strcmp($operator, '+'))
{
   $result = $num1 + $num2;

// If operation is - do subtraction: num1 - num2
} else if(! strcmp($operator, '-')) {
   $result = $num1 - $num2;

// If operation is * do multiplication: num1 * num2
} else if(! strcmp($operator, '*')) {
   $result = $num1 * $num2;

// If operation is / do division: num1 / num2
} else if(! strcmp($operator, '/')) {

    // If second number is 0, show divide
    // by zero exception
    if (! $num2) {
        $errors .= "Divide by zero is not allowed.";
    } else {
       $result = sprintf("%.2f", $num1 / $num2);
    }
}

// Create a new template object
$t = new Template($TEMPLATE_DIR);

// Set the template file for this
// object to application's template
$t->set_file("page", $OUT_TEMPLATE);
```

Continued

Listing 1-6 *(Continued)*

```
// Setup the template block
$t->set_block("page", "mainBlock" , "main");

// Set the template variable = value
$t->set_var("ERRORS", $errors);
$t->set_var("NUM1", $num1);
$t->set_var("NUM2", $num2);
$t->set_var("OPERATOR", $operator);
$t->set_var("RESULT", $result);

// Parse the template block with all
// predefined key=values
$t->parse("main", "mainBlock", false);

// Parse the entire template and
// print the output
$t->pparse("OUT", "page");

?>
```

The script can be called using a URL such as the following:

```
http://yourserver/ch1/calc.php?num1=123&operator=%2B&num2=0
```

The calc.php script produces an output screen, as shown in Figure 1-1, using the
`calc.html` template stored in `ch1/templates`.

Figure 1-1: Output of the `calc.php` script.

If the script is called without one or more inputs, it shows error messages. For
example, say the user forgot to enter the operator, in such a case the output looks
as shown in Figure 1-2.

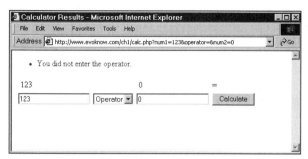

Figure 1-2: Output of the `calc.php` script (calling without an operator).

Similarly, if the operator is division (/) and the second number is 0, then the divide by zero error message is shown, as in Figure 1-3.

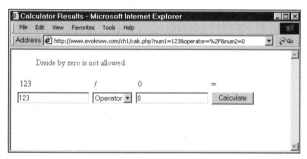

Figure 1-3: Output of `calc.php` script (divide by zero error message).

So this script is able to catch input errors and even a run-time error caused by bad user input (divide by zero). But, sadly, this script is violating a design principle of a practical PHP application. Notice the following lines in the script:

```
$errors .= "<li>You did not enter number 1.";
// lines skipped

$errors .= "<li>You did not enter number 2.";
// lines skipped

$errors .= "<li>You did not enter the operator.";
// lines skipped

$errors .= "Divide by zero is not allowed.";
```

These error messages are in English and have HTML tags in them. This means if the end user wasn't fond of the way the messages were shown, he or she would have to change them in the code and potentially risk modification of the code that may result in bugs. Also, what if the end user spoke, say, Spanish, instead of English? This also means that the end user would have to change the code. A better solution is shown in Listing 1-7 and Listing 1-8.

Listing 1-7: `calc2.php`

```php
<?php

// Enable all error reporting
error_reporting(E_ALL);

require_once('calc2.conf');
require_once('calc2.errors');

// Get inputs from GET or POST request
$num1 = (! empty($_REQUEST['num1'])) ? $_REQUEST['num1'] : null;
$num2 = (! empty($_REQUEST['num2'])) ? $_REQUEST['num2'] : null;

$operator = (! empty($_REQUEST['operator'])) ?
            $_REQUEST['operator'] : null;

// Set errors to null
$errors = null;

// If number 1 is not given, error occurred
if ($num1 == null)
{
    $errors .= $ERRORS[LANGUAGE]['NUM1_MISSING'];
}

// If number 2 is not given, error occured
if ($num2 == null) {
    $errors .= $ERRORS[LANGUAGE]['NUM2_MISSING'];
}

// If operator  is not given, error occured
if (empty($operator)) {
    $errors .= $ERRORS[LANGUAGE]['OPERATOR_MISSING'];
}

// Set result to null
$result = null;
```

```php
// If operation is + do addition: num1 + num2
if (!strcmp($operator, '+'))
{
    $result = $num1 + $num2;

// If operation is - do subtraction: num1 - num2
} else if(! strcmp($operator, '-')) {
    $result = $num1 - $num2;

// If operation is * do multiplication: num1 * num2
} else if(! strcmp($operator, '*')) {
    $result = $num1 * $num2;

// If operation is / do division: num1 / num2
} else if(! strcmp($operator, '/')) {

    // If second number is 0, show divide by zero exception
    if (! $num2) {
        $errors .= $ERRORS[LANGUAGE]['DIVIDE_BY_ZERO'];
    } else {
        $result = sprintf("%.2f", $num1 / $num2);
    }
}

// Create a new template object
$t = new Template($TEMPLATE_DIR);

// Set the template file for this object to application's template
$t->set_file("page", $OUT_TEMPLATE);

// Setup the template block
$t->set_block("page", "mainBlock" , "main");

// Set the template variable = value
$t->set_var("ERRORS", $errors);
$t->set_var("NUM1", $num1);
$t->set_var("NUM2", $num2);
$t->set_var("OPERATOR", $operator);
$t->set_var("RESULT", $result);

// Parse the template block with all predefined key=values
$t->parse("main", "mainBlock", false);

// Parse the entire template and print the output
$t->pparse("OUT", "page");

?>
```

The difference between `calc.php` and `calc2.php` is that `calc2.php` doesn't have any error messages hard-coded in the script. The `calc.php` error messages have been replaced with the following:

```
$errors .= $ERRORS[LANGUAGE][NUM1_MISSING];
$errors .= $ERRORS[LANGUAGE][NUM2_MISSING];
$errors .= $ERRORS[LANGUAGE][OPERATOR_MISSING];
$errors .= $ERRORS[LANGUAGE][DIVIDE_BY_ZERO];
```

The `calc2.php` script loads error messages from the `calc2.errors` file using the following line:

```
require_once('calc2.errors');
```

The `calc.errors` file is shown in Listing 1-8.

Listing 1-8: `calc2.errors`

```php
<?php

    // US English
    $ERRORS['US']['NUM1_MISSING']     = "<li>You did not enter number 1.";
    $ERRORS['US']['NUM2_MISSING']     = "<li>You did not enter number 2.";
    $ERRORS['US']['OPERATOR_MISSING'] = "<li>You did not enter the operator.";
    $ERRORS['US']['DIVIDE_BY_ZERO']   = "Divide by zero is not allowed.";


    // Spanish (translated using Google
    // Uncomment the following lines to get Spanish error messages
    // Also, set LANGUAGE in calc2.conf to ES
    // $ERRORS['ES']['NUM1_MISSING']     = "<li>Usted no incorporo el numero 1";
    // $ERRORS['ES']['NUM2_MISSING']     = "<li>Usted no incorporo el numero 2.";
    // $ERRORS['ES']['OPERATOR_MISSING'] = "<li>Usted no inscribio a operador..";
    // $ERRORS['ES']['DIVIDE_BY_ZERO']   = "Dividase por cero no se permite.";

?>
```

The `calc2.errors` file loads a multidimensional associative array called `$ERRORS`. The first dimension is the language and the second dimension is error code. For example:

```
$ERRORS['US']['NUM1_MISSING']     = "<li>You did not enter number 1.";
```

`'US'` is shorthand code for the U.S. English language. The `NUM1_MISSING` is a code that has the `"<li>You did not enter number 1."` error message associated with it. When the `calc2.php` script executes a line such as the following:

```
$errors .= $ERRORS[LANGUAGE]['NUM1_MISSING'];
```

The $errors string is set to the value of given code (NUM1_MISSING) for the chosen language (set using LANGUAGE in the calc2.conf configuration file).

Since we have defined LANGUAGE constant as follows in calc2.conf:

```
define(LANGUAGE, 'US');
```

The U.S. language versions of error messages are selected. However, if you wanted to choose the Spanish language (ES) version of error messages, all you have to do is set LANGUAGE to ES in calc2.conf and uncomment the ES version of error codes in calc2.errors file. To save memory you can comment out the U.S. version of the error code or remove them if wanted.

In most applications in this book we define $DEFAULT_LANGUAGE as the language configuration for applications.

So you see how a simple configuration change can switch the language of a script from English to Spanish. You can access a large number of major languages using this method.

We translated the U.S. English to Spanish using Google's language translation service and therefore the accuracy of the translation is not verified.

In larger application, you will not only have error messages but also messages that are shown in dialog windows or status screens. In such case you can use the exact same type of configuration files to load messages. In most of the applications throughout the books we use app_name.messages for dialog/status messages and app_name.errors for error messages.

Using relational database

If you need to store data, strongly consider using a relational database. My experience shows that, in the beginning of most projects, developers decide whether to use a database based on available data, complexity of managing data, and expected growth rate of data. Initially, all of these seem trivial in many projects and, therefore, a flat file or comma-separated values (CSV) files–based data store is elected for quick and dirty jobs.

If you have access to a fast database such as MySQL, strongly consider storing your application data in the database. The benefits of a database like MySQL are almost unparalleled when compared with other data-storage solutions.

Using portable directory structure

When designing the directory structure of your application, consider a portable one. A portable directory structure is one that is easy to deploy and avoids hard-coded fully qualified paths whenever possible. Almost all the applications in this book use the following portable directory structure:

```
%DocumentRoot%
|
+---app_name
    |
    +--apps
        |
        +---class
        |
        +---templates
```

For example, the calendar application in Chapter 10 uses the following:

```
%DocumentRoot%
|
+---framework
|
+---pear
|
+---phplib
|
+---calendar
    |
    +--apps
        |
        +---class
        |
        +---templates
```

This directory structure can be created using the following PHP code

```
// If you have installed PEAR packages in a different
// directory than %DocumentRoot%/pear change the setting below.
$PEAR_DIR        = $_SERVER['DOCUMENT_ROOT'] . '/pear' ;

// If you have installed PHPLIB in a different
// directory than %DocumentRoot%/phplib, change the setting below.
$PHPLIB_DIR      = $_SERVER['DOCUMENT_ROOT'] . '/phplib';
```

```
// If you have installed framewirk directory in a different
// directory than %DocumentRoot%/framework, change the setting below.
$APP_FRAMEWORK_DIR  = $_SERVER['DOCUMENT_ROOT'] . '/framework';

//If you have installed this application in a different
// directory than %DocumentRoot%, chance the settings below.
$ROOT_PATH          = $_SERVER['DOCUMENT_ROOT'];
$REL_ROOT_PATH      = '/calendar';

$REL_APP_PATH       = $REL_ROOT_PATH . '/apps';
$TEMPLATE_DIR       = $ROOT_PATH    . $REL_APP_PATH . '/templates';
$CLASS_DIR          = $ROOT_PATH    . $REL_APP_PATH . '/class';
$REL_TEMPLATE_DIR   = $REL_APP_PATH . '/templates/';
```

The key point is that you should avoid hard-coding a fully qualified path in the application so that deployment of your application is as hassle-free as it can be. For example, say you have developed the application on your Web server with the following directory structure:

```
/usr/local/apache/htdocs
            |
        +---your_app
            |
            +---templates
```

If /usr/local/apache/htdocs is your Web server's document root (%DocumentRoot%), make sure that you haven't hard-coded it in the configuration. If you use $TEMPLATE_DIR to point to your template directory in your_app.conf, you should use the following:

```
$ROOT_PATH          = $_SERVER['DOCUMENT_ROOT'];
$REL_ROOT_PATH      = '/your_app;
$TEMPLATE_DIR       = $ROOT_PATH    . '/templates';
```

Instead of:

```
$TEMPLATE_DIR       =
'/usr/local/apache/htdocs/your_app/templates';
```

The benefit of the non-hard-coded version is that if you created a tar ball or a zip file of your entire application and gave it to another user whose Web document root is set to something else, she doesn't have to change your application configuration for fixing paths as long as she installs the application in the %DocumentRoot%/your_appsee directory.

Using access control

If your PHP application is deployed on a site where unauthorized use is possible, you have to implement access control. Access control can be established using two methods:

◆ Authentication, such as restriction using username/password. You can learn more about this in detail in Chapter 5.

◆ Authorization, such as IP/network address allow/deny control. You can learn more about this in detail in Chapter 22.

You can deploy one or both of these techniques in developing a comprehensive access control for sensitive applications.

Summary

In this chapter, you learned about the features of a practical PHP application. When you write an application that uses external configuration files, template-based interface, and database for storage in an object-oriented manner, you are likely to have a well-structured, maintainable application.

Chapter 2

Understanding and Avoiding Security Risks

IN THIS CHAPTER

◆ Identifying sources of risks

◆ Minimizing user-input risks

◆ Running external programs safely

◆ Acquiring user input in a safe manner

◆ Protecting sensitive information

BEFORE YOU CAN DESIGN secure PHP applications, you have to understand the security risks involved and know how to deal with them. In this chapter, we will discuss the most common risks involved with Web-based PHP applications.

Identifying the Sources of Risk

The sources of most security problems are user input, unprotected security information, and unauthorized access to applications.

Among these risk factors, user input stands out the most, and it is also the most exploited to make unauthorized, unintended use of applications. A poorly written PHP application that handles user input as safe data provides ample opportunity for security breaches quite easily.

Sensitive data is often made available unintentionally by programs to people who should not have any access to the information. Such exposure can result in disaster if the information falls in the hands of a malicious hacker.

Unauthorized access is difficult to deal with if users can't be authenticated using user names and passwords and/or hostname/IP address based access control cannot be established. User authentication and access control are covered in detail in Chapter 5 and Chapter 22 so we will not discuss them here.

In the following sections, we discuss these risks and potential solutions in detail.

Minimizing User-Input Risks

As previously mentioned, user input poses the most likely security risk to your Web applications. Let's look at a few scenarios for how seemingly harmless and simple programs can be made to do malicious tasks.

Running external programs with user input

Listing 2-1 shows a simple PHP script called bad_whois.php (bad_ has been added so that you think twice before actually putting this script in any real Web site).

Listing 2-1: bad_whois.php

```php
<?php

// Set error reporting to all
error_reporting(E_ALL);

// Get domain name
$domain = (! empty($_REQUEST['domain'])) ?
          $_REQUEST['domain'] : null;

// The WHOIS binary path
$WHOIS = '/usr/bin/whois';

// Execute WHOIS request
exec("$WHOIS $domain", $output, $errors);

// Initialize output buffer
$buffer = null;

while (list(,$line)=each($output))
{
    $buffer .= $line . '<br>';
}

echo $buffer;
```

```
if (! empty($errors))
{
    echo "Error: $errors when trying to run $WHOIS<br>";
}


?>
```

This simple script displays the whois database information for a given domain. It can be run like this:

```
http://server/bad_whois.php?domain=evoknow.com
```

The output is shown in Figure 2-1.

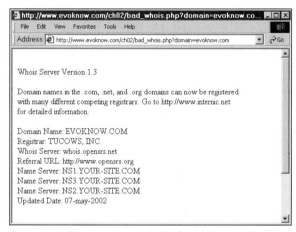

Figure 2-1: Harmless output of bad_whois.php script.

Now what's wrong with this output? Nothing at all. domain=evoknow.com is used as an argument to execute the /usr/bin/whois program. The result of the script is the way it was intended by the programmer: It displays the whois database query for the given domain.

But look what happens when the user runs this same script as follows:

```
http://server/bad_whois.php?domain=evoknow.com;cat%20/etc/passwd
```

The output is shown in Figure 2-2.

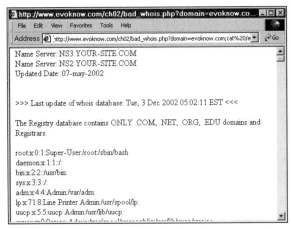

Figure 2-2: Dangerous output of `bad_whois.php` script.

The user has supplied `domain=evoknow.com;cat%20/etc/passswd`, which is run by the script as

```
$runext = exec("/usr/bin/whois evoknow.com;cat /etc/passwd", $output);
```

The user has not only supplied a domain name for the whois program but also inserted a second command using the semicolon separator. The second command is `cat /etc/passwd`, which displays the `/etc/passwd` file. This is where this simple script becomes a tool for the malicious hackers to exploit system information or even do much more harmful activities such as running the `rm -rf` command to delete files and directories.

Now, what went wrong with the simple script? The script programmer trusted user input and will end up paying a big price for such a misplaced trust. You should never trust user input when you have no idea who the next user is. Listing 2-2 shows an improved version of `bad_whois.php` script called `better_whois.php`.

Listing 2-2: `better_whois.php`

```php
<?php

// Set error reporting to all
error_reporting(E_ALL);


// Get domain name
```

```php
$secureDomain  = (! empty($_REQUEST['domain'])) ?
        escapeshellcmd($_REQUEST['domain']) : null;

// The WHOIS binary path
$WHOIS = '/usr/bin/whois';

echo "Running whois for $secureDomain <br>";

// Execute WHOIS request
exec("$WHOIS $secureDomain", $output, $errors);

// Initialize output buffer
$buffer = null;

while (list(,$line)=each($output))
{
    if (! preg_match("/Whois Server Version/i", $line))
    {
        $buffer .= $line . '<br>';
    }
}

echo $buffer;

if (! empty($errors))
{
   echo "Error: $errors when trying to run $WHOIS<br>";
}


?>
```

If this script is run as

```
http://server/bette_whois.php?domain=evoknow.com;cat%20/etc/passwd
```

it will not run the cat /etc/passwd command, because the escaping of shell characters using the escapeshellcmd() function makes the given domain name evoknow.com\;cat /etc/passwd. Because this escaped version of the (illegal) domain name does not exist, the script doesn't show any results, which is much better than showing the contents of /etc/passwd.

So why didn't we call this script great_whois.php? Because it still has a user-input-related problem, which is discussed in the next section.

Getting user input in a safe way

In the preceding example, we had user input returned to us via the HTTP GET method as part of the URL, as in the following example:

```
http://server/bette_whois.php?domain=evoknow.com
```

When better_whois.php is called, it automatically gets a variable called $domain created by PHP itself. The value of the $domain variable is set to evoknow.com.

This automatic creation of input variables is not safe. For an example, take a look at Listing 2-3.

Listing 2-3: bad_autovars.php

```php
<?php

    error_reporting(E_ALL);

    // This bad example will only work
    // if you have register_globals = Off
    // in your php.ini.

    // This example is for educational
    // purpose only. It will not work in
    // sites with register_globals = On

    global $couponCode;

    if (is_coupon($couponCode))
    {
        $is_customer = isCustomer();

    }

    if ($is_customer)
    {
        echo "You are a lucky customer.<br>";
        echo "You won big today!<br>";

    } else {
        echo "Sorry you did not win!<br>";
    }

    function is_coupon($code = null)
    {
```

```
      // some code to verify coupon code
      echo "Check if user given coupon is valid or not.<br>";
      return ($code % 1000 == 0) ? TRUE : FALSE;

   }

   function isCustomer()
   {
      // a function to determine if current user
      // user is a customer or not.
      // not implemented.
      echo "Check if user is a customer or not.<br>";
      return FALSE;
   }


?>
```

When this script is run as

```
http://server/bad_autovars.php?couponCode=2000
```

it checks to see if the coupon code is valid. The is_coupon() function takes the user given coupon code and checks if the given code is completely divisible by 1000 or not. Code that are divisible by 1000 are considered valid and the function returns TRUE else it returns FALSE. If the coupon code is valid, it checks whether the current user is a customer. If the current user is a customer, it shows a message indicating that the customer is a winner. If the current user is not a customer, it shows the following:

```
Check if user given coupon is valid or not.
Check if user is a customer or not.
Sorry you did not win!
```

Because we didn't implement the isCustomer() function, we return FALSE at all times, so there's no way we should ever show a message stating that the current user is a winner. But alas! Look at the following request:

```
http://server/bad_autovars.php?couponCode=1001&is_customer=1
```

Even with an invalid coupon, the user is able to see the following message:

```
Check if user given coupon is valid or not.
You are a lucky customer.

You won big today!
```

Do you know why the user is able to see the preceding message? Because this user has supplied is_customer=1, which became an automatic variable and forced the winner message to appear. This type of trick can be done only with strong knowledge of the application being used. For example, if this was a free script widely used by many sites, a malicious hacker could force it to get what he wants.

This example demonstrates that automatic variables can be tricked into doing things that are not intended by the programmers, so we need to have a better way of getting user data. Thankfully, PHP 4.2 or above by default do not create automatic variables. Creating automatic variables is turned off in the php.ini configuration file using the following configuration parameter:

```
register_globals = Off
```

When register_globals is off by default, PHP does not create automatic variables. So how can you get data from the user? Very easily using $_GET, $_POST, $_REQUEST, $_SERVER, $_SESSION, $_ENV, and $_COOKIE. Table 2-1 shows which of these variables correspond to what input of a request.

TABLE 2-1 PHP GLOBAL-REQUEST-RELATED AUTOMATIC VARIABLES

Variable	Description
$_GET	Used for storing data passed via HTTP GET method. For example, http://server/any.php?a=1&b=2 will result in $_GET['a'] = 1; $_GET['b'] = 2;
$_POST	Used for storing data passed via HTTP POST method. For example: <form action="any.php" method="POST"> <input type=text name="email"> <input type=hidden name="step" value="2"> </form> When this form is submitted, the any.php will have $_POST['email'] = user_supplied_email $_POST['step'] = 2
$_REQUEST	Works for both GET and POST. This variable is the best choice because it will work with your application whether data is submitted via the GET method or the POST method.
$_SESSION	Stores session data.
$_COOKIE	Stores cookie data.

Variable	Description
$_ENV	Stores environment information.
$_FILES	Stores uploaded file information.
$GLOBALS	All global variables that are stored in this associative array.

Now let's implement bad_autovars.php without the automatic field variables as shown in Listing 2-4.

Listing 2-4: autovars_free.php

```php
<?php

  // Enable all error reporting
  error_reporting(E_ALL);

  // Initialize
  $is_customer = FALSE;

  // Get coupon code
  $couponCode = (! empty($_REQUEST['couponCode'])) ?
                $_REQUEST['couponCode'] : null;

  if (is_coupon($couponCode))
  {
      $is_customer = isCustomer();
  }

  if ($is_customer)
  {
      echo "You are a lucky customer\n";
      echo "You win big today!\n";

  } else {
      echo "Sorry you do not win!\n";
  }

  function is_coupon($code = null)
  {
      // some code to verify coupon code
      echo "Check if user given coupon is valid or not <br>";
      return ($code % 1000 == 0) ? TRUE : FALSE;
```

Continued

Listing 2-4 *(Continued)*

```php
    }

    function isCustomer()
    {
        // a function to determine if current user
        // user is a customer or not.
        // not implemented.
        echo "Check if user is customer <br>";
        return FALSE;
    }


?>
<?php
    // Enable all error reporting
    error_reporting(E_ALL);
    // Initialize
    $is_customer = FALSE;
    // Get coupon code
    $couponCode = (! empty($_REQUEST['couponCode'])) ?
                    $_REQUEST['couponCode'] : null;
    if (is_coupon($couponCode))
    {
        $is_customer = isCustomer();
    }
    if ($is_customer)
    {
        echo "You are a lucky customer\n";
        echo "You win big today!\n";

    } else {
        echo "Sorry you do not win!\n";
    }

    function is_coupon($code = null)
    {
        // some code to verify coupon code
        echo "Check if user given coupon is valid or not <br>";
        return ($code % 1000 == 0) ? TRUE : FALSE;
    }
    function isCustomer()
    {
        // a function to determine if current user
        // user is a customer or not.
```

```
      // not implemented.
      echo "Check if user is customer <br>";
      return FALSE;
   }
?>
```

Here $is_customer is first initialized to FALSE, which makes it impossible for the user to set it using the GET or POST method. Next, improvement is made by using the $_REQUEST['couponCode'] to get the coupon data. With this version, the user can't force $is_customer to any value and, therefore, the code works as intended.

Using validation code

In addition to getting user data from $_REQUEST, you also need to validate user input, because it may contain unwanted patterns that cause security problems. Sometimes programmers confuse validation with cleanup. Earlier, in Listing 2-2 (better_whois.php), we used escapeshellcmd() to escape any user-provided shell characters. This would qualify as a cleanup or quarantine operation. A validation operation checks the validity of the data and, if it's invalid, the script rejects it instead of fixing it.

For example, say you have a PHP script that expects a data field called num1. You can do a test like the following:

```
if (!is_numeric($_REQUEST['num1']))
{
    // User supplied num1 not a number!
}
```

There are many built-in functions, such as is_numeric(), is_int(), is_float(), is_array(), and so forth, that you can use to perform validation. However, often you want to validate a number or string from a different prospective. For example, e-mail addresses are strings, but not all strings are e-mail addresses. To validate e-mail addresses, you need a validation function for e-mail address. Similarly, ZIP codes are special type of numbers with nnnnn or nnnnn-nnnn formats. For validating ZIP codes, you would need to create custom validation functions. Your validation functions should return TRUE for valid data and FALSE for invalid data. The following is a simple structure of a validation function:

```
function isValidFIELDNAME($fieldValue = null)
}
    // Perform validation code here
    // You must return TRUE here if valid.

    // Default is false
    return FALSE;
}
```

Validation can be done not only on data types but also on other aspects of the user input. However, the type validation is more of a security concern than the actual meaning of the value in your application context. For example, say the user fills out a form field called "age" with a value of 3000. Because we have yet to find a person anywhere (on Earth or anywhere else) who lived 3,000 years, the age value is invalid. However, it isn't an invalid data type. In this case, you may want to combine all your validity checking in a single `isValidAge()` function.

One of the best ways to validate data is to use regular expressions. Following are some of the regular expression functions PHP provides:

- `preg_match()`. This function takes a regular expression and searches for it in the given string. If a match is found, it returns `TRUE`; otherwise, it returns `FALSE`. The matched data can also be returned in an array. It stops searching after finding the first match. For example, say you want to find out if a user data field called `$userData` contains anything other than digits. You can test it with `preg_match("/[^0-9]/", $userData)`. Here, the regular expression `/[^0-9]/` tells `preg_match` to find anything but the digits.

- `preg_match_all()`. This function is just like `preg_match()`, except it continues searching for all regular expression patterns in the string. For example: `preg_match("/[^0-9]/", $userData, $matches)`. Here the regular expression `/[^0-9]/` tells `preg_match_all` to find anything but the digits and store them in $matches.

- `preg_quote()`. You can use this function to escape a regular expression that contains regular expression characters. For example, say you want to find out if a string called `$userData` contains a pattern such as `"[a-z]"`. If you call the `preg_match()` function as `preg_match("/[a-z]/", $userData)`, it will return wrong results because `"[a-z]"` happens to be a valid regular expression itself. Instead, you can use `preg_quote()` to escape `"[a-z]"` and then use it in the `preg_match()` call. For example, `preg_match('/' . preg_quote("[a-z]") . '/' , $userData)` will work.

There are other functions such as `preg_grep()`, `preg_replace()`, and so forth, that are also useful. For example, you can access information on these functions via `http://www.evoknow.com/preg_grep` and `http://www.evoknow.com/preg_replace`. Instead of writing validation routines for common data types, you can find free validation classes on the Web. One such class is called `Validator`, which can be found at `www.thewebmasters.net/php/Validator.phtml`.

After you download and install the `Validator` class per its author's instructions, you can use it very easily. For example, Listing 2-5 shows a simple Web form script called `myform.php` that uses this validation class to validate user data.

Listing 2-5: `myform.php`

```php
<?php
  error_reporting(E_ALL);
  define('DEBUG', FALSE);
  include("class.Validator.php3");

  // Create a Validator object
  $check = new Validator ();

  // Get User data
  $email = (! empty($_REQUEST['email'])) ? $_REQUEST['email'] : null;
  $state = (! empty($_REQUEST['state'])) ? $_REQUEST['state'] : null;
  $phone = (! empty($_REQUEST['phone'])) ? $_REQUEST['phone'] : null;
  $zip =   (! empty($_REQUEST['zip']))   ? $_REQUEST['zip']   : null;
  $url =   (! empty($_REQUEST['url']))   ? $_REQUEST['url']   : null;
  DEBUG and print "Debug Code here \n";

  // Call validation methods
  if (!$check->is_email($email))  { echo "Invalid email format<br>\n";}
  if (!$check->is_state($state))  { echo "Invalid state code<br>\n";  }
  if (!$check->is_phone($phone))  { echo "Invalid phone format<br>\n";}
  if (!$check->is_zip($zip))      { echo "Invalid zip code<br>\n";    }
  if (!$check->is_url($url))      { echo "Invalid URL format<br>\n";  }

  // If form data has errors show error and exit
  if ($check->ERROR)
  {
      echo "$check->ERROR<br>\n";
      exit;
  }

  // Process form now
  echo "Form processing not shown here.<br>";
?>
```

The class `Validator.php3` is included in the script. The `$check` variable is a `Validator` object, which is used to validate user-supplied data. If there is any error in any of the validation checks — that is, if any of the validation methods return false — the script displays an error message. If no error is found, the script continues to process the form, which is not shown in this sample code. To learn more about the validation methods that are available in this class, review the documentation supplied with the class.

Not Revealing Sensitive Information

Another major source of security holes in applications is unnecessary disclosure of information. For example, say you have a script called `mysite.php` as follows:

```php
<?php
   phpinfo();
?>
```

This script shows all the PHP information about the current site, which is often very useful in finding various settings. However, if it is made available to the public, you give malicious hackers a great deal of information that they would love to explore and potentially exploit.

Such a harmless script can be a security hole. It reveals too much information about a site. For security purposes, it is extremely important that you don't reveal your system-related information about your site to anyone. We recommend that you use `phpinfo()` in only development systems which should not be allowed to be accessed by everyone on the Web. For example, you can use $_SERVER['REMOTE_ADDR'] value to restrict who has access to a sensitive script. Here is an example code segment:

```php
<?php

   // Enable all error reporting
   error_reporting(E_ALL);


   // Create a list of valid IP addresses that can access
   // this script
   $validIPList = array('192.168.1.1', '192.168.1.2');

   // If current remote IP address is not in our valid list of IP
   // addresses, do not allow access
   if (! in_array($_SERVER['REMOTE_ADDR'], $validIPList))
   {
      echo "You do not access to this script.";
      exit;
   }

   // OK, we have a valid IP address requesting this script
   // so show page
   phpinfo();

?>
```

Here the script exists whenever a request to this script comes from a remote IP address that is not in the valid IP list ($validIPList).

Let's take a look at some other ways in which you can safely conceal information about your application:

♦ **Remove or disable any debugging information from your application.** Debugging information can provide clues about your application design (and possibly its weaknesses) to others who may take the opportunity to exploit them. If you add debugging code, use a global flag to enable and disable debugging. For example:

```php
<?php

  define('DEBUG', FALSE);

  DEBUG and print "Debug message goes here.\n";

?>
```

Here DEBUG constant is set to FALSE and, therefore, the print statement is not going to print anything. Setting DEBUG to TRUE enables debug messages. If all your debug code is enabled or disabled in this manner, you can easily control DEBUG messages before you put the script in the production environment.

♦ **Don't reveal sensitive paths or other information during Web-form processing.** A common misunderstanding that hidden fields are secret, often causes security-novice developers to reveal sensitive path or other information during Web-form processing. For example:

```
<input type=hidden name="save_path"
value="/www/secret/upload">
```

This line in a HTML form is not hidden from anyone who has a decent Web browser with the View Source feature. So do not ever rely on hidden field for security. Use hidden fields only for storing information that are not secret.

♦ **Never store sensitive information on the client side.** If you must store sensitive data, consider using a database or at least a file-based session, which will store data on the server side. If you must store data on the client side for some special reason, consider encrypting the data (not just encoding it). See Chapter 22 for details on data encryption.

Summary

In this chapter, you learned about the common security risks for PHP applications and how to deal with them. Most of the security risks are related to user input and how you handle them in your scripts. Expecting all users will behave politely and will not try to break your code is not at all realistic. Let's face it, there are a lot of people (of all ages) with too much free time and Internet bandwidth these days, which means there is a lot out there with intents to hack, deface Web sites just for the sake of it. So do not trust user input to be just what you need to run your application. You need to deal with unexpected input as well.

Revealing sensitive information such as software version, server environment data, etc., can also have a major ill effect on your overall security as such information can be used in building attack tools or techniques. The best practice is to reveal as little as necessary.

Chapter 3

PHP Best Practices

IN THIS CHAPTER

- ◆ Best practices for naming variables and functions or methods
- ◆ Best practices for functions or methods
- ◆ Best practices for database
- ◆ Best practices for user interface
- ◆ Best practices for documentation
- ◆ Best practices for configuration management

THE APPLICATION CODE PRESENTED in this book uses a set of programming practices that qualify as best practices for any PHP application development. This chapter discusses these practices. Familiarizing yourself with them will ease the learning curve for the applications discussed in the rest of the book.

Best Practices for Naming Variables and Functions

Top software engineers know that good variable, function (or method), and class names are necessary for the maintainability of the code. A good name is one that conveys meaning related to the named function, object, class, variable, etc. Application code becomes very difficult to understand if the developers don't use good, meaningful names. Take a look at the following code sample:

```php
<?php
    error_reporting(E_ALL);
    $name = (! empty($_REQUEST['field1'])) ? $_REQUEST['field1'] : "Friend";
    outputDisplayMsg("Hello $name");
    exit;
```

```php
    function outputDisplayMsg($outTextMsgData = null)
    {
        echo $outTextMsgData;
    }
?>
```

Now look at the same code segment with meaningful names for variables and functions:

```php
<?php

    error_reporting(E_ALL);

    $name = (! empty($_REQUEST['field1'])) ? $_REQUEST['field1'] : "Friend";

    showMessage("Hello $name");

    exit;

    function showMessage($outTextMessageData = null)
    {
        echo $outTextMessageData;
    }

?>
```

The second version is clearly easier to understand because showMessage is a better name for the outputDisplayMsg function.

Now let's look at how you can use easy-to-understand names for variables, functions (or methods), and classes.

When creating a new variable or function name (or method), ask yourself the following questions:

♦ What is the purpose of this variable? In other words, what does this variable hold?

♦ Can you use a descriptive name that represents the data the variable holds?

♦ If the descriptive name appears to be too long, can you use meaningful abbreviations? For example, $textMessage is as good as $txtMsg. Names exceeding 15 characters probably need to be reconsidered for abbreviation.

After you determine a name, follow these rules:

♦ **Use title casing for each word in multiword names.** However, the very first word should be lowercase. For example, $msgBody is a better name then $msgbody, $messageBODY, or $message_body. Single word names should be kept in lowercase. For example, $path and $data are single word variables.

♦ **Use all capital letters to name variables that are "constant like" – in other words, variables that do not change within the application.** For example, if you read a variable from a configuration file, the name of the variable can be in all uppercase. To separate uppercase words, use underscore character (for example, use $TEMPLATE_DIR instead of $TEMPLATE-DIR). However, when creating constants it is best to use define() function. For example, define(PI, 3.14) is preferred over $PI = 3.14. The defined constant PI cannot be changed once defined whereas $PI can be changed.

♦ **Use verbs such as get, set, add, delete, modify, update, and so forth in naming your function or method.** For example, getSomething(), setSomething(), and modifySomething() are better function names than accessSomething(), storeSomething(), and editSomething(), respectively.

Best Practices for Function/Method

In this section I discuss a set of practices that will improve your function or method code.

Returning arrays with care

When your function (or method) returns an array, you need to ensure that the return value is a defined array because the code from which the function is called is expecting an array. For example, review the following bad code segment.

```
// BAD

function getData()
{

    $stmt = "SELECT ID, myField1, myField2 from myTable";

    $result = $this->dbi->query($stmt);
```

```
if ($result != NULL)
{
   while($row = $result->fetchRow())
   {
      $retArray[$row->ID] = $row;
   }

}

return $retArray;

}
```

In this example, the function called `getData()` returns an array called `$retArray` when the SQL statement executed returns one or more rows. The function works fine if the SQL `select` statement always returns at least one row. However, it returns nothing when the SQL statement returns no rows. In such a case, the following code segment, which calls the function, produces a PHP warning message:

```
error_reporting(E_ALL);

$rowObjectArray = $this->getData();

while(list($id, $rowObject) = each($rowObjectArray))
{
   // do something here
}
```

`$rowObjectArray` causes `each()` to generate a warning when the `myFunction()` method fails to return a real array. Here's a better version of the `getData()` method:

```
// GOOD

function getData()
{

   $retArray = array();

   $stmt = "SELECT ID, myField1, myField2 from myTable";

   $result = $this->dbi->query($stmt);

   if ($result != null)
```

```
    {
        while($row = $result->fetchRow())
        {
            $retArray[$row->ID] = $row;
        }

    }

    return $retArray;

}
```

The second version of getData() function initializes $retArray as an array, which ensures that functions such as each() do not complain about it.

 You can avert PHP warning messages by initializing arrays using array().

Simplifying the function or method argument list order issue

When a function or method has many arguments, as shown in the following code, bugs are more likely to appear because of data mismatches in function calls.

```
// Not So Good

function myFunction($name  = null,
                    $email = null,
                    $age   = null,
                    $addr1 = null,
                    $addr2 = null,
                    $city  = null,
                    $state = null,
                    $zip   = null
                    )
{

    echo "Name      = $name\n";
    echo "Email     = $email\n";
    echo "Age       = $age\n";
    echo "Address 1 = $addr1\n";
```

```php
    echo "Address 2 = $addr2\n";
    echo "City      = $city\n";
    echo "State     = $state\n";
    echo "ZIP       = $zip\n";

}

// First call
myFunction($name,
           $email,
           $age,
           $addr1,
           $addr2,
           $city,
           $state,
           $zipcode
           );

// Second call
myFunction($name,
           $email,
           $age,
           $addr2,
           $addr1,
           $city,
           $state,
           $zipcode
           );
```

In this example, the function myFunction() expects a list of arguments. The code segment also shows two calls to this function. Notice that the second call has $addr1 and $addr2 misplaced. This type of argument misplacement is very common and is the cause of many bugs that take a great deal of time to fix.

When you have a function that requires a large number of parameters to be passed, use an associative array, as shown in the following code segment:

```php
$params = array(
                'NAME'  => $name,
                'EMAIL' => $email,
                'AGE'   => $age,
                'ADDR1' => $addr1,
                'ADDR2' => $addr2,
                'CITY'  => $city,
                'STATE' => $state,
                'ZIP'   => $zipcode
           )
```

```
myFunction($params);

function myFunction($params = null)
{

    echo "Name      = $params['NAME']\n";
    echo "Email     = $params['EMAIL']\n";
    echo "Age       = $params['AGE']\n";
    echo "Address 1 = $params['ADDR1']\n";
    echo "Address 2 = $params['ADDR2']\n";
    echo "City      = $params['CITY']\n";
    echo "State     = $params['STATE']\n";
    echo "ZIP       = $params['ZIP']\n";

}
```

$params is an associative array, which is set up using key=value pairs. The function is called with only one argument. The order of the key=value does not matter as long as the right key is used with the right value. This position-independent way of passing values to the function is much less likely to cause parameter bugs in your code.

Best Practices for Database

Most applications require database connectivity and, therefore, you need to know about some best practices that will help you make your code more efficient and bug-free. Here, I discuss the techniques that relate to relational database access. I assume that you're using the DBI class (class.DBI.php), which is part of our application framework discussed in Chapter 4. The DBI class is really a database abstraction layer that allows applications to access a set of database methods used to perform operations such as connect, query, etc. Since this class hides the database behind the scene, it provides a very easy way to change database backends from MySQL to Postgres or vise versa when needed. By changing the DBI class code to connect to a new database, an application can be easily ported from one database to another.

Writing good SELECT statements

SELECT is the most commonly used SQL statement that applications use to get data from databases. Unfortunately, a large number of SELECT statements that you will find in many applications use it in a way that can cause serious problems. For example, look at the following code segment:

```
// Bad SELECT statement
$statement = "SELECT * FROM myTable";
```

```
$result = $dbi->query($statement);
$result->fetchRow();
```

This SELECT statement gets all the columns (field values) from the named table (myTable). If the table is changed to have new fields, the SELECT statement will also get values for the new fields. This is a side effect that can be good or bad.

It is a good side effect only if your code is smart enough to handle the new data. Most codes are not written to do so. The bad effect could be that your code can become slower due to additional memory requirements to hold the new data, which is never used. For example, say that myTable has two fields, ID and NAME. The example code segment works just fine until the DBA adds a new field called COMMENTS (large text field) in the table to allow another application to work with comments. Our example code is adversely affected by this database change because it now wastes memory loading COMMENTS when there's no use for this data in our application. Using named fields in the SELECT statement is the solution.

```
// Good SELECT statement
$statement = "SELECT ID, NAME FROM myTable";
$result = $dbi->query($statement);
$result->fetchRow();
```

Dealing with missing data

When accessing data via SELECT statements, be prepared to handle situations resulting from no data or missing data. For example:

```
// Bad
// no data or missing data
$statement = "SELECT myField1 FROM myTable";
$result = $dbi->query($statement);
$result->fetchRow();
```

If myTable doesn't have any data when this code executes, the fetchRow() method causes PHP to throw an exception. This can be easily avoided by ensuring that the $result object is not null before calling the fetchRow() method of the $result object, as the following code shows:

```
// Good
$statement = "SELECT myField1 FROM myTable";
$result = $dbi->query($statement);

if ($result != null)
{
    $result->fetchRow();
}
```

Handling SQL action statements

There are several best practices that make using SQL action statements such as INSERT, UPDATE, and DELETE most effective. Here I will explain those practices.

Quoting and protecting against slashes

Quote database fields that are `char` or `varchar` types, and escape for slashes. Quoting character or varchar fields is important because these data types can have keywords or punctuation marks that can be interpreted as part of an SQL statement and thus producing wrong results. Escaping slashes in these data types is also very important since data stored in these data types can be easily misinterpreted by the SQL engine. Often I see code segments that are as shown here:

```php
$params['FNAME'] = 'Jennifer';
$params['LNAME'] = 'Gunchy';
$params['SCHOOL'] = 'CSUS, Sacramento';
$params['YEAR'] = 4;


$this->myFunction($params);



// BAD
function myFunction($params = null)
{

    $values  = "'" . $params['FNAME'] . "',";
    $values .= "'" . $params['LNAME'] . "',";
    $values .= "'" . $params['SCHOOL'] . "',";
    $values .=       $params['YEAR'];

    $stmt = "INSERT INTO myTable VALUES($values)";

    $result = $this->dbi->query($stmt);

    return ($result == DB_OK) ? TRUE : FALSE;

}
```

In this example, the `myFunction()` method is called with `$params` argument. Some of the data fields stored in the `$params` variable are `char` or `varchar` fields and, therefore, hard-coded quotations are used as they are stored in `$values`. This type of hard-coded quotation can easily break if the data value include the quotation character. Here's a better approach:

```php
// GOOD

function myFunction($params = null)
{

    $fields = array('FNAME'  => 'text',
                    'LNAME'  => 'text',
                    'SCHOOL' => 'text',
                    'YEAR'   => 'number'
                    );

    $fieldList = implode(',', array_keys($fields));

    while(list($fieldName, $fieldType) = each($fields))
    {
        if (strcmp($fieldType, 'text'))
        {
            $valueList[] =
            $this->dbi->quote(addslashes($params[$fieldName]));
        } else {
            $valueList[] = $params[$fieldName];
        }
    }

    $values = implode(',', $valueList);

    $stmt = "INSERT INTO myTable ($fieldList) VALUES($values)";

    $result = $this->dbi->query($stmt);

    return ($result == DB_OK) ? TRUE : FALSE;

}
```

In this example, an associative array called $fields is used to store field and field type information. A comma-separated value list called $fieldList is created using the keys from the $fields array.

A while loop is used to loop through each of the fields in the $fields array and fields of type 'text' are quoted using the quote() method in our DBI class. Before quoting the field value the char/varchar value is escaped for slashes using the addslashes() function.

The quoted, slash-escaped char/varchar values are stored in $valueList array. Similarly, non-quoted numeric values are stored in $valueList.

The comma-separated values are stored in $values by imploding the $valueList. The INSERT statement is then composed of $fieldList and $values, which is very clean and free from quote and slash issues.

Returning error condition

When using SQL action statements, you cannot assume that your query is always successful. For example:

```
// BAD
$statement = "UPDATE myTable SET myField1 = 100 WHERE ID = 1";
$result = $dbi->query($statement);
```

Here the $result object needs to be checked to see if the SQL action operation was successful. The following code takes care of that:

```
// GOOD
$statement = "UPDATE myTable SET myField1 = 100 WHERE ID = 1";
$result = $dbi->query($statement);

return ($result == DB_OK) ? TRUE : FALSE;
```

This segment returns TRUE if $result is set to DB_OK; otherwise, it returns FALSE. The DB_OK constant is set in the DB.php package used by class.DBI.php discussed in Chapter 4. For our discussion, what is important is that you should test the result of a query to see if database operation was successful or not.

Naming fields in INSERT statements

When inserting data in tables, many developers do not use field names in the INSERT statement, as the following code shows:

```
$params[1] = 30;
$params[2] = 500000;

myFunction($params);


// BAD
function myInsertFunction($params = null)
{

    $stmt = "INSERT INTO myTable VALUES($params[1], $params[2])";

    $result = $this->dbi->query($stmt);

    return ($result == DB_OK) ? TRUE : FALSE;

}
```

In this example, the INSERT statement is dependent on the ordering of the parameters and fields in the database. If the database administrator adds a new field before any of the existing fields, the INSERT statement might fail. To remove such a chance, use the following INSERT statement:

```
// GOOD
function myInsertFunction($params = null)
{

    $stmt = "INSERT INTO myTable (AGE, INCOME) VALUES("
            "$params[1], $params[2])";

    $result = $this->dbi->query($stmt);

    return ($result == DB_OK) ? TRUE : FALSE;

}
```

Now the INSERT statement uses field list (AGE, INCOME) to identify which fields are being inserted in a row.

Efficient update statement

When updating data using the UPDATE statement, you need to create a list of key=value pairs to set database fields to respective values. Here's an example of how not to do this:

```
// BAD
function myUpdateFunction($params = null)
{
    $values =      "FNAME  = '" . $params['FNAME']  . "'," .
                   "LNAME  = '" . $params['LNAME']  . "'," .
                   "SCHOOL = '" . $params['SCHOOL'] . "'," .
                   "YEAR = " .    $params['YEAR'];

    $stmt =  "UPDATE myTable SET $values WHERE ID = $params['ID']";
    $result = $this->dbi->query($stmt);

    return ($result == DB_OK) ? TRUE : FALSE;

}
```

This example is "bad" because the code is not clean or easy to manage if the database field list grows or reduces. Here is the better version of the code:

```
// GOOD:
function myUpdateFunction($params = null)
{

    $fields = array('FNAME'  => 'text',
                    'LNAME'  => 'text',
                    'SCHOOL' => 'text',
                    'YEAR'   => 'number'
                    );


    while(list($k, $v) = each($fields))
    {
        if (!strcmp($v, 'text'))
        {
            $params[$k] = $this->dbi->quote(addslashes($params[$k]));
        }

        $valueList[] = $k . '=' . $params[$k];
    }

    $values = implode(',', $valueList);

    $stmt =  "UPDATE myTable SET $values WHERE ID = $params['ID']";

    $result = $this->dbi->query($stmt);

    return ($result == DB_OK) ? TRUE : FALSE;

}
```

In this example, the field list is stored in $fields as a field_name=field_type pair. The string data is first slash-escaped and quoted and all data are stored in $valueList as field_name=field_value pairs. A comma-separated list called $values is created from the $valueList. The UPDATE statement then becomes quite simple and is very readable and easy to maintain. If a new field is added to the database, you simply update the $fields array; similarly, if a field is removed, removing it from the $fields array takes care of it all.

Best Practices for User Interface

A user interface (UI) is a big part of the applications that we're going to design and develop throughout this book. Here are some very good practices that you should consider when developing code that has UI.

Avoiding HTML in application code

Don't use HTML tags in PHP code. HTML tags make the code very unmanageable. For example:

```
echo "<html>";
echo "<head><title>My Document</title></head>";
echo "<body bgcolor='#ffffff'>";
echo "<h1>Hello $user</h1>";
echo "</body>";
echo "</html>";
```

If the above code is in a PHP script, the HTML can only be changed by modifying the PHP code itself. This means the person changing the code needs to know PHP, which means someone with good HTML skill but no PHP skill cannot change the interface, which is very common. This is why it is not manageable.

When generating HTML interface for Web application, you should use HTML template object. For example, below I show you how to use the PHPLIB Template class (found in template.inc) to create HTML template objects to display HTML page where page is external to the code.

```
$TEMPLATE_DIR = '/some/path';
$MY_TEMPLATE  = 'screen.ihtml';

$template = new Template($TEMPLATE_DIR);
$template->set_file('fh', $MY_TEMPLATE);
$template->set_block ('fh', 'mainBlock', 'main');
$template->set_var('USERNAME', $user);

$template->parse('main','mainBlock', false);
$template->pparse('output', 'fh');
```

This example code does the following:

- ◆ Assigns a variable called $TEMPLATE_DIR to /some/path and $MY_TEMPLATE variable to screen.ihtml.
- ◆ Creates a Template object that points to $MY_TEMPLATE file (shown in Listing 3-1) in the $TEMPLATE_DIR directory.

- ◆ Uses the set_block() method to assign the variable name 'main' to a block called mainBlock, which is identified in the template using <!-- BEGIN mainBlock --> and <!-- END mainBlock --> tags.

- ◆ Uses the set_var() method to replace a template tag called {USERNAME} with data from $user variable.

- ◆ Uses the parse() method to parse mainBlock within the template.

- ◆ Parses the template to insert the contents of the already parsed mainBlock in the output, and uses the pparse() method to print all the contents of the template.

Listing 3-1: screen.ihtml

```
<html>
<head><title>My Document</title></head>

<!-- BEGIN mainBlock -->
<body bgcolor="#ffffff">
<h1>Hello {USERNAME} </h1>
</body>
<!-- END mainBlock -->
</html>
```

Generating HTML combo lists in application code

When using HTML interface, especially Web forms to collect input data from users, it is often necessary to display drop-down combo list (select) boxes. Ideally, the PHP code responsible for generating the combo boxes should be free from HTML tags so that total interface control remains within the HTML template. Here is a code segment that creates a combo list using PHP but includes HTML tags:

```
//BAD:

$TEMPLATE_DIR = '/some/path';
$MY_TEMPLATE  = 'bad_screen.ihtml';

$cmdArray = array(
                   '1' => 'Add',
                   '2' => 'Modify',
                   '3' => 'Delete'
                 );
```

```
while(list($cmdID, $cmdName) = each($cmdArray))
{
  $cmdOptions .= "<option value=$cmdID>$cmdName</option>";
}

$template = new Template($TEMPLATE_DIR);
$template->set_file('fh', $MY_TEMPLATE);
$template->set_block ('fh', 'mainBlock', 'main');

$template->set_var('USERNAME', $user);
$template->set_var('CMD_OPTIONS', $cmdOptions);
$template->parse('main','mainBlock', FALSE);
$template->pparse('output', 'fh');
```

This example uses bad_screen.ihtml, shown in Listing 3-2, as the HTML interface file. A while loop is used to create $cmdOptions. Notice that some HTML tags are embedded in the following line:

```
$cmdOptions .= "<option value=$cmdID>$cmdName</option>";
```

This violates the principle of keeping all HTML out of the code. There are situations in which it isn't possible to keep the HTML out, but in creating combo boxes you can.

Listing 3-2: bad_screen.ihtml

```
<html>
<head><title>My Document</title></head>
<!-- BEGIN mainBlock -->

<body bgcolor="#ffffff">
<h1>Hello {USERNAME} </h1>
<form>
<select name="cmd">
{CMD_OPTIONS}
</select>
<input type=submit>
</form>
</body>
<!-- END mainBlock -->
</html>
```

Listing 3-3 shows a modified version of Listing 3-2. Here the combo box (select list) is shown as an embedded block called optionBlock within the mainBlock in the template. The <option value="{CMD_ID}">{CMD_NAME}</option> line is looped when the block is populated.

Listing 3-3: good_screen.ihtml

```
<html>
<head><title>My Document</title></head>
<!-- BEGIN mainBlock -->

<body bgcolor="#ffffff">
<h1>Hello {USERNAME} </h1>
<form>
<select name="cmd">

 <!-- BEGIN optionBlock -->
   <option value="{CMD_ID}">{CMD_NAME}</option>
<!-- BEGIN optionBlock -->

</select>
<input type=submit>
</form>
</body>
<!-- END mainBlock -->
</html>
```

To generate the combo box without having any HTML code inside the PHP application, we modify the last code segment as follows:

```
$TEMPLATE_DIR = '/some/path';
$MY_TEMPLATE  = 'bad_screen.ihtml';

$cmdArray = array(
                  '1' => 'Add',
                  '2' => 'Modify',
                  '3' => 'Delete'
                 );

$template = new Template($TEMPLATE_DIR);
$template->set_file('fh', $MY_TEMPLATE);
$template->set_block ('fh', 'mainBlock', 'main');
$template->set_block ('mainBlock', 'optionBlock', 'options');

while(list($cmdID, $cmdName) = each($cmdArray))
{
  $template->set_var('CMD_ID', $cmdID);
  $template->set_var('CMD_NAME', $cmdName);
  $template->parse('options','optionBlock', TRUE);
}
```

```
$template->set_var('USERNAME', $user);
$template->parse('main','mainBlock', FALSE);
$template->pparse('output', 'fh');
```

The embedded block optionBlock is populated using the while loop, which replaced the CMD_ID, and CMD_NAME inside the loop. The parse() method that is called to parse the optionBlock has the append flag set to TRUE. In other words, when the block is parsed, the output of the last parsed block is appended to the current one to make the list of options.

Finally, the mainBlock is parsed as usual and the combo box is generated completely from the interface template, without needing HTML tags in the PHP code.

Reducing template code

When using the Template object to display a user interface, you may think that many calls to the set_var() method are needed to replace template tags. For example:

```
// OK - could be better
$TEMPLATE_DIR = '/some/path';
$MY_TEMPLATE  = 'screen.ihtml';

$template = new Template($TEMPLATE_DIR);
$template->set_file('fh', $MY_TEMPLATE);
$template->set_block ('fh', 'mainBlock', 'main');

$template->set_var('FIRST',  $first);
$template->set_var('LAST',   $last);
$template->set_var('EMAIL',  $email);
$template->set_var('AGE',    $age);
$template->set_var('GENDER', $gender);

$template->parse('main','mainBlock', false);
$template->pparse('output', 'fh');
```

If you are assigning a lot of template variables to values like in the previous code segment, you can reduce the number of set_var() calls by combining all of the calls into a single call. This will speed up the application since a single call is faster than many calls to a method. An improved version of this script is shown below.

```
// BETTER

$TEMPLATE_DIR = '/some/path';
$MY_TEMPLATE  = 'screen.ihtml';
```

```
$template = new Template($TEMPLATE_DIR);
$template->set_file('fh', $MY_TEMPLATE);
$template->set_block ('fh', 'mainBlock', 'main');

$template->set_var( array(
                        'FIRST'  => $first,
                        'LAST'   => $last,
                        'EMAIL'  => $email,
                        'AGE'    => $age,
                        'GENDER' => $gender
                        )
               );

$template->parse('main','mainBlock', false);
$template->pparse('output', 'fh');
```

In this example, a single instance of set_var() method is used to pass an unnamed associative array with template tags as keys and appropriate data as values.

Best Practices for Documentation

When you decide to develop software, you should create design and implementation documentations. Design documentations include block diagrams that describe the system, flow charts that describe a specific process, class diagrams that show the class hierarchy, and so on.

Implementation documentation also has flow charts to describe specific implementation processes. Most importantly, though, you use inline code comments to describe what your code does.

You can use single-line or multiple comments such as:

```php
<?php

    // This is a single-line comment
    $myName = 'Joe Gunchy';

  /*
      This is a multi-line comment that can span
      over multiple lines.
  */
  $mySchool = 'CSUS';

?>
```

All the code for this book is commented, although the inline code comments have been stripped out of the code listings printed in the book to reduce the number of lines and because the book covers each method in detail. However, you can get the commented version of the code on the accompanying CD-ROM and/or on the Web site for the book at www.evoknow.com/phpbook.php.

Best Practices for Web Security

In this section I will discuss a set of best practices that if practiced will result in better security for your Web applications.

Keep authentication information away from prying eyes

Many Web applications use authentication information to allow restricted access to the application using username/password or IP addresses. Similarly, all applications using databases use database access information (host name, username/password, port, etc.) that should never be revealed to any Web visitors. You should keep these authentication data away from prying eyes by using one of these methods:

◆ Store authentication data way from the Web document tree. Make your applications read authentication related files from outside the Web document tree so that these files are not browseable via Web. This will require that your Web server has read access to these files. No other user (other than the root) should have access to these files.

◆ If you cannot store authentication files outside your Web document tree for some reason, you need to make sure the authentication files are not browseable via the Web. This can be done by using file extensions and restricting these extensions from being served by the Web server.

When using databases with applications always create a limited privilege user by following your database administration guide. This user should be allowed to only access the specific database that your application needs access to. You should never use a privileged database user account to access database from Web applications. Consult your database documentation for details on how to create limited privilege database users.

See your errors before someone else does

Often malicious hackers use debugging or error information to take advantage of a broken application. This is why it is critical that you perform extensive tests on your Web applications before you deploy it on production servers.

The best way to test and find problems is to have all levels of error reporting enabled using the `error_reporting(E_ALL)` function. This function should be used as the very first line in your application code. For example:

```php
<?php

    // Enable all error reporting
    error_reporting(E_ALL)

    // Your code goes below.

?>
```

During development you should set error_reporting() to E_ALL, which enables all types of errors to be reported. There are many error reporting levels. You can find all about these error reporting levels in `http://www.php.net/manual/en/ref.errorfunc.php#errorfunc.constants`

Once you have thoroughly tested your application, you can reduce the error reporting level or even disable it. However, if you do the latter, make sure you enable error logging using the `error_log()` function. You can learn about this function at http://www.php.net/manual/en/function.error-log.php.

Restrict access to sensitive applications

When you have an application that should be used by only a restricted set of users, you need to control access to the application from either PHP code or using Web server access control mechanism. This is covered in great detail in Chapter 22.

Best Practices for Source Configuration Management

When developing any software, use a version-control system to manage changes. We used Concurrent Version System (CVS) when developing applications discussed in this book. CVS allows you to create versions of your software by creating a source repository from which you check out and check in code changes. CVS maintains all version information automatically so that you can retrieve an older version with a single command. It is also the de-facto version control mechanism for many large-scale Open Source software.

You can learn more about CVS at `www.gnu.org/software/cvs` or at `http://www.cvshome.org.`

Summary

In this chapter I have discussed various best practices for functions/methods, database, user interface, documentation, security, and version control. Getting used to these best practices is often very difficult since many programmers are often under great time pressure to produce workable applications. However, it is very important to get started with these practices as early in the development as possible so that they become second nature in future projects. This is particularly true for getting used to version control tools such as CVS. Many developers find version control as an "additional task" that does not relate directly to the deadline and simply wait till the very end to place code in version control. This type of practices often leads to big code maintenance problem in the long run. The key issue is early adoption of best practices so that you get used to it from the beginning.

Part II

Developing Intranet Solutions

Chapter 4

Architecture of an Intranet Application

INTRANET APPLICATIONS ARE PRIMARILY focused on automating an organization's daily business processes. A modern company has many intranet applications that are available to its employees to help them be more productive and efficient. For example, a group calendar system or task-tracking system can save a great deal of time and resources for most companies with more than five employees. This chapter focuses on the underlying architecture of intranet applications and discusses an open-source framework that enables you to develop intranet PHP applications in a rapid manner.

Understanding Intranet Requirements

To develop intranet applications, you need to understand how a typical intranet is deployed. A company with two employees can have an intranet, but the average intranet application is deployed in an organization with tens to hundreds of users. Figure 4-1 shows how an intranet "connects" employees in multiple departments of a company that uses an intranet application server to manage its daily internal business functions.

A company generally uses its intranet server to automate interdepartment communication activities such as a shared calendar, shared contact database, document management, project/task tracking, and so forth.

Before you develop the framework that will enable you to create intranet applications in PHP, you need to understand the intranet user requirements. Figure 4-2 shows how a single department within an organization appears from an intranet-requirements point of view.

Users in organizations work in teams. A team usually has a team leader and a project assignment. The projects are managed by the department head. This type of hierarchical user base is very common in modern organizations.

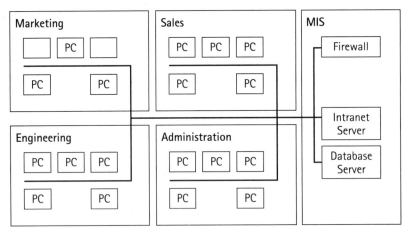

Figure 4-1: A typical intranet-enabled company.

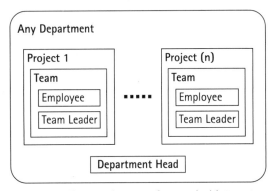

Figure 4-2: User requirements for a typical intranet-enabled company.

Each intranet application you develop must be able to authenticate and authorize different types of users. For example, an employee vacation management application has to incorporate the hierarchical chain of command that enables employee vacation requests to be reviewed and approved first by team leaders and then by the department head. So far, our intranet application framework has the following requirements:

♦ **Central authentication:** Users need to be authenticated to access intranet applications. There are likely to be many intranet applications within an organization and therefore user authentication should be done such that a user logs in only once to access any application. A session should be created that allows all applications to identify an authenticated user. When a user attempts to access an intranet application without logging in first, the application should automatically redirect the user to the login application. When the user is successfully authenticated via the login application, she should be automatically forwarded back to the application she had been attempting to access. The login process should be seamless. Similarly, a central, seamless logout facility should be provided to allow the users to log out from the intranet.

♦ **Application-specific authorization:** Different types of users exist in an intranet and, therefore, intranet applications must discriminate when authorizing users. Employee access to an intranet application will vary. Because each application will have different requirements for authorizing the user, the task of authorization should be left to the application itself.

♦ **A shared database:** Most intranet activity involves collaboration or group efforts. For example, users working in a team within a project might need to report the status of the project tasks individually, but the team leader or department head needs to access the information from the entire team to make technical or business decisions. A shared database is therefore the solution to store data.

Based on these requirements, let's go ahead and build an intranet application framework.

Building an Intranet Application Framework

An intranet consists of many applications. It is a good idea to create an application framework that provides a set of commonly needed objects and services to implement applications. Typical intranet applications have user authentication requirements, database access requirements, user interfaces requirements, and business logic requirements. Each application's business logic, which is the work done by the application, is unique and must be implemented in the application code itself. However, each application can benefit from using a standard application framework consisting of objects that standardize authentication, database access, user interface, etc. The framework I will build here will do just that.

Figure 4-3 shows the high-level design diagram for an intranet application that will use our application framework.

Now let's discuss the components of this architecture.

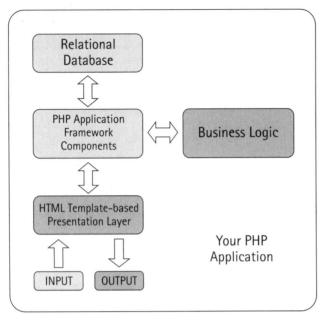

Figure 4-3: High-level architecture diagram of an intranet application using our framework.

Using an HTML template-based presentation layer

All input and output to and from the application is handled via a template-driven HTML presentation layer. When the application needs input from the user, it presents an HTML page generated from an appropriate HTML template. Similarly, when the application needs to display output, it generates an HTML page by replacing special application-specific tags within the template. This ensures that cosmetic changes to the input or output interfaces can be done without requiring help from the application developer. For example, an application that uses the template-based presentation layer can have its interface modified by an HTML writer or graphics artist.

Using PHP Application Framework components

The components in the PHP Application Framework (PHPAF) layer implement the base application by providing the following services:

- **Database abstraction support:** See the "Relational database" section later in this chapter for details.

- **Centralized authentication support:** All applications defer the login and logout to the central authentication facility, as discussed earlier in this chapter.

- ◆ **Override authorization support:** Each application using the intranet application defines its own authorization method.

- ◆ **Debugging support:** An application needs to be debugged many times during the development process. Because debugging is a core part of the development process, the framework includes a built-in debugger. The current implementation is very simple yet useful.

- ◆ **Internationalized error and status message handling support:** Each application using the framework must use a central error message and status message repository. Both error and status messages can be internationalized.

Business logic

Each application has its own business-logic requirements. The business-logic objects will be given database connectivity from the application framework. This ensures that database abstraction is maintained.

Relational database

The relational database access is abstracted from the application using an abstraction layer, which is part of the application framework. This ensures that application database requirements can change without drastically affecting the application. For example, an application can be developed with this framework such that it works with the widely used, high-performance MySQL database and then deployed in an environment where the database is Oracle. Of course, the developers have to be careful not to use any vendor-specific features.

Figure 4-4 shows a block diagram of an application that uses the previously mentioned application framework.

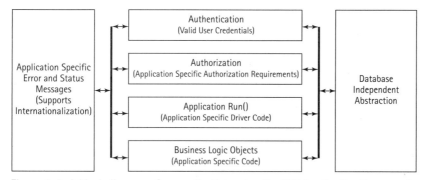

Figure 4-4: A block diagram of an application using the PHP Application Framework.

The application checks for valid user credentials in the authentication phase, which is already supplied by the framework's login application for valid users.

The authorization step involves application-specific privilege management. Not all valid (authenticated) users are likely to have the same privilege based on the type of application. For example, an Employee Information System (EIS) application in an engineering firm can assign different privileges to executive management, department heads, team leaders, and engineers. This is why the authorization code is specific to the instance of the application and should be written by the application developer and should not be provided by the framework.

When an application has gone through the authentication and authorization phases, it will run the application. This code will involve invoking application specific business objects and database interaction.

The application will have database access via the database-independent abstraction and also will produce status messages and errors using the facilities provided by the framework.

Figure 4-5 shows a real-world application framework that we will create in this chapter.

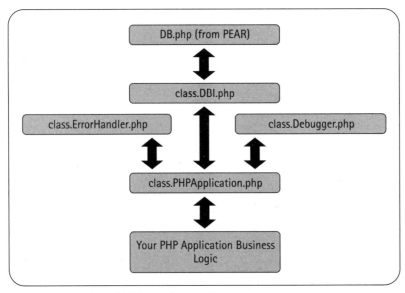

Figure 4-5: A real-world PHP Application Framework.

The core of this framework is the class.PHPApplication.php. This class provides an abstract PHP application that you can extend to incorporate facilities provided by the error handler (class.ErrorHandler.php), the debugger (class.Debugger.php), and the database abstraction (class.DBI.php).

This framework is provided with the CD-ROM. You don't need to create it from scratch. Also note that the database abstraction uses DB.php from the PEAR.

Now let's create the classes needed to implement this application framework.

Creating a Database Abstraction Class

Accessing a database using its own API is common in the PHP world. For example, most PHP developers use PHP with MySQL and, therefore, they write code that is specific to the MySQL API found in PHP.

There is nothing wrong with this approach if you know that your PHP applications will be used only for the MySQL database server. However, if there is a chance that your applications will be used with other databases such as Oracle, Postgres, and so forth, you need to avoid MySQL-specific API. A developer who has abstracted the database API in a level above the vendor-specific API can enjoy the speed of porting the application to different relational databases. Here, we will create a class called class.DBI.php that will implement a database abstraction layer for our application framework. Listing 4-1 shows `class.DBI.php`, which implements the database abstraction using PEAR DB.

 See `http://pear.php.net/manual/en/core.db.php` for details on PEAR DB, a unified API for accessing SQL-databases.

Listing 4-1: `class.DBI.php`

```
<?php

    /*

    Database abstraction class

    Purpose: this class provides database abstraction using the PEAR
    DB package.
```

Continued

Listing 4-1 *(Continued)*

```
*/
define('DBI_LOADED', TRUE);

class DBI {

    var $VERSION = "1.0.0";

    function DBI($DB_URL)
    {

        $this->db_url = $DB_URL;

        $this->connect();

        if ($this->connected == TRUE)
        {
            // set default mode for all resultset

            $this->dbh->setFetchMode(DB_FETCHMODE_OBJECT);
        }
    }

    function connect()
    {

        // connect to the database
        $status = $this->dbh = DB::connect($this->db_url);

        if (DB::isError($status))
        {
            $this->connected = FALSE;

            $this->error = $status->getMessage();

        } else {

            $this->connected = TRUE;
        }

        return $this->connected;

    }

    function isConnected()
```

```
{

   return $this->connected;

}


function disconnect()

{


   if (isset($this->dbh)) {

       $this->dbh->disconnect();

       return 1;

   } else {

       return 0;

   }

}



function query($statement)

{


   $result = $this->dbh->query($statement);


   if (DB::isError($result))

   {


      $this->setError($result->getMessage());


      return null;


   } else {


      return $result;

   }

}
function setError($msg = null)

{

   global $TABLE_DOES_NOT_EXIST, $TABLE_UNKNOWN_ERROR;


   $this->error = $msg;


   if (strpos($msg, 'no such table'))

   {

      $this->error_type = $TABLE_DOES_NOT_EXIST;


   } else {
```

Continued

Listing 4-1 *(Continued)*

```
                $this->error_type = $TABLE_UNKNOWN_ERROR;
        }
    }

    function isError()
    {
       return (!empty($this->error)) ? 1 : 0;
    }

    function isErrorType($type = null)
    {
        return ($this->error_type == $type) ? 1 : 0;
    }

    function getError()
    {
        return $this->error;
    }

    function quote($str)
    {
        return "'" . $str . "'";
    }

    function apiVersion()
    {
       return $VERSION;
    }
   }
?>
```

Here are the functions the DBI class implements:

◆ DBI(): This is the constructor method, which creates the instances of the
   DBI object. For example, here is a script called test_dbi.php that creates a
   DBI object.

```
<?php

// Turn on all error reporting
error_reporting(E_ALL);

// If you have installed PEAR packages in a different
// directory than %DocumentRoot%/pear change the
```

```php
// setting below.
$PEAR_DIR = $_SERVER['DOCUMENT_ROOT'] . '/pear' ;

// If you have installed PHPLIB in a different
// directory than %DocumentRoot%/phplib, change
// the setting below.
$PHPLIB_DIR = $_SERVER['DOCUMENT_ROOT'] . '/phplib';

// If you have installed framework directory in
// a different directory than
// %DocumentRoot%/framework, change the setting below.
$APP_FRAMEWORK_DIR=$_SERVER['DOCUMENT_ROOT'] . '/framework';

// Create a path consisting of the PEAR,
// PHPLIB and our application framework
// path ($APP_FRAMEWORK_DIR)
$PATH = $PEAR_DIR . ':' .
        $PHPLIB_DIR . ':' .
        $APP_FRAMEWORK_DIR;

// Insert the path in the PHP include_path so that PHP
// looks for our PEAR, PHPLIB and application framework
// classes in these directories
ini_set( 'include_path', ':' .
        $PATH . ':' .
        ini_get('include_path'));

// Now load the DB.php class from PEAR
require_once 'DB.php';

// Now load our DBI class from application framework
// directory
require_once('class.DBI.php');

// Set the database URL to point to a MySQL
// database. In this example, the database is
// pointing to a MySQL database called auth on
// the localhost server, which requires username
// (root) and password (foobar) to login
$DB_URL = 'mysql://root:foobar@localhost/auth';

// Create a DBI object using our DBI class
// Use the database URL to initialize the object
// and make connection to the database
$dbi = new DBI($DB_URL);
```

```
// Dump the contents of the DBI object to
// see what it contains.
echo "<pre>";
print_r($dbi);
echo "</pre>";

?>
```

Here, $dbi is an instance of the DBI object created from class.DBI.php. The constructor method has to be passed a database URL which has the following syntax:

```
database_type://username:password↓tabase_host/database_name
```

The $DB_URL variable was set to create a database URL that pointed to a MySQL database (mysql) named mydb on host called localhost The database can be accessed using the root user account and foobar password.

The DBI() method sets the DB URL passed to itself as db_url member variable and calls the connect() method to connect to the given database. The constructor sets the fetch mode to DB_FETCHMODE_OBJECT, which allows us to fetch database rows as objects.

◆ connect(): By default, the DBI() constructor method calls the connect() function directly to establish the connection, so you don't need to. connect() connects to the database specified in db_url member variable of the object. It sets a member variable dbh to the database handle object created by the DB::connect() method, which is found in the PEAR DB package. connect also sets a member variable called connected to Boolean TRUE or FALSE and returns that value.

◆ disconnect(): The disconnect() function disconnects the DBI object from the database.

The terminate() function in PHPApplication class (class.PHPApplication.php) calls the disconnect() function if the application is connected to a database. See terminate() function in PHPApplication class for details.

◆ query(): This function performs a SQL query on the connected database. The result of the query is stored in a result object called $result. If the query returns SQL error(s), a member variable called $this->dbi->error is set to the error message and null is returned.

If the query is successful, it returns the result object. The result object can be used to fetch rows. For example, the test_query.php script tries to fetch data from a table called PROD_TBL using a database URL such as mysql://root:foobar@localhost/products.

```php
<?php

// Turn on all error reporting
error_reporting(E_ALL);

// If you have installed PEAR packages in a different
// directory than %DocumentRoot%/pear change the
// setting below.
$PEAR_DIR = $_SERVER['DOCUMENT_ROOT'] . '/pear' ;

// If you have installed PHPLIB in a different
// directory than %DocumentRoot%/phplib, change
// the setting below.
$PHPLIB_DIR = $_SERVER['DOCUMENT_ROOT'] . '/phplib';

// If you have installed framework directory in
// a different directory than
// %DocumentRoot%/framework, change the setting below.
$APP_FRAMEWORK_DIR=$_SERVER['DOCUMENT_ROOT'] . '/framework';

// Create a path consisting of the PEAR,
// PHPLIB and our application framework
// path ($APP_FRAMEWORK_DIR)
$PATH = $PEAR_DIR . ':' .
        $PHPLIB_DIR . ':' .
        $APP_FRAMEWORK_DIR;

// Insert the path in the PHP include_path so that PHP
// looks for our PEAR, PHPLIB and application framework
// classes in these directories
ini_set( 'include_path', ':' .
        $PATH . ':' .
        ini_get('include_path'));

// Now load the DB.php class from PEAR
require_once 'DB.php';

// Now load our DBI class from application framework
require_once('class.DBI.php');
```

```
// Setup the database URL
$DB_URL = 'mysql://root:foobar@localhost/products';

// Create a DBI object that connects to the
// database URL
$dbi = new DBI($DB_URL);

if (! $dbi->isConnected())
{
    echo "Connection failed for $DB_URL<br>";
    exit;
}

// Create a SQL statement to fetch data
$statement = 'SELECT ID, NAME FROM PROD_TBL';

// Execute the statement using DBI query method
$result = $dbi->query($statement);

// If the result of query is NULL then show
// database error message
if ($result == NULL)
{
    echo "Database error:" . $dbi->getError() . "\n";

// Else check if there are no data available or not
} else if (! $result->numRows()){

    echo "No rows found.";

// Now data is available so fetch and print data
} else {

    echo "<pre>ID\tNAME<br>";

    while ($row = $result->fetchRow())
    {
        echo $row->ID, "\t", $row->NAME, "<br>";
    }
    echo "</pre>";
}

?>
```

The SQL statement `SELECT ID, NAME FROM PROD_TBL` is stored in `$statement` variable and passed to the `DBI::query()` method. The result is tested first for null. If the result is null, the database error is printed using the `DBI::getError()` method.

If there are no database errors, the next check is made to see if there are any rows using the `numRow()` method from the `$result` object. If there are no rows, an appropriate message is printed.

If there are data in the returned `$result` object, the result is printed in a loop using the `fetchRow()` method.

The row data is fetched in `$row` object. The `$row->DATA_FIELD` method is used to get the data for each field. For example, to retrieve the `NAME` field data, the `$row->NAME` value is accessed.

◆ `quote()`: This is a utility function that puts a pair of single quotes around a string to protect the string from being passed without quotation. Here's an example in which the `$name` field is single-quoted using `$this->dbi->quote($name)` call:

```php
<?php

// Turn on all error reporting
error_reporting(E_ALL);

// If you have installed PEAR packages in a different
// directory than %DocumentRoot%/pear change the
// setting below.
$PEAR_DIR = $_SERVER['DOCUMENT_ROOT'] . '/pear' ;

// If you have installed PHPLIB in a different
// directory than %DocumentRoot%/phplib, change
// the setting below.
$PHPLIB_DIR = $_SERVER['DOCUMENT_ROOT'] . '/phplib';

// If you have installed framework directory in
// a different directory than
// %DocumentRoot%/framework, change the setting below.
$APP_FRAMEWORK_DIR=$_SERVER['DOCUMENT_ROOT'] . '/framework';

// Create a path consisting of the PEAR,
// PHPLIB and our application framework
// path ($APP_FRAMEWORK_DIR)
$PATH = $PEAR_DIR . ':' .
        $PHPLIB_DIR . ':' .
        $APP_FRAMEWORK_DIR;
```

```php
// Insert the path in the PHP include_path so that PHP
// looks for our PEAR, PHPLIB and application framework
// classes in these directories
ini_set( 'include_path', ':' .
         $PATH . ':' .
         ini_get('include_path'));

// Now load the DB.php class from PEAR
require_once 'DB.php';

// Now load our DBI class from application framework
require_once('class.DBI.php');

// Setup the database URL
$DB_URL = 'mysql://root:foobar@localhost/foobar';

// Create a DBI object that connects to the
// database URL
$dbi = new DBI($DB_URL);

if (! $dbi->isConnected())
{
    echo "Connection failed for $DB_URL<br>";
    exit;
}

$id = 100;
$name = "Joe Gunchy";

$name = $dbi->quote($name);

$statement = "INSERT INTO PROD_TBL (ID,NAME) " .
             "VALUES($id, $name)";

$result = $dbi->query($statement);

if ($result == NULL)
{
    echo "Database error:" . $dbi->getError() . "<BR>\n";

} else {

    echo "Added $name in database.<BR>\n";

}

?>
```

◆ `apiVersion()`: This is a utility method that returns the version number of the DBI object. The DBI abstraction class enables you to connect to any database and perform any SQL query, such as `SELECT`, `INSERT`, `UPDATE`, `DELETE`, and so forth. Because it hides the database vendor-specific details from your application, porting to other databases become a much easier task.

Now let's look at how we can develop an error handler class.

Creating an Error Handler Class

Every application needs to display error messages. In the old days, error messages were usually hard-coded in the executable programs and were very difficult to understand, let alone modify!

Now, in the days of Web interface, we should not resort to the old way of showing hard-coded error messaging because the application can be used in so many parts of the world. Error messages written in English are just not friendly enough for the world in this Internet age. So applications that have internationalizable error message support will have broader reach.

Listing 4-2 shows an error message handler, which loads and displays error messages in the application's default language. Because an application's default language can be changed in the configuration file, it becomes very easy to display error messages in different languages.

Listing 4-2: `class.ErrorHandler.php`

```php
<?php
/*
* CVS ID: $Id$
*/
/*
* Centalizes all error messages.
* Supports internationalization of error messages.
*
* @author EVOKNOW, Inc. <php@evoknow.com>
* @access public
*/
  define('ERROR_HANDLER_LOADED', TRUE);
  class ErrorHandler
  {
     function ErrorHandler($params = null)
     {
        global $DEFAULT_LANGUAGE;
        $this->language = $DEFAULT_LANGUAGE;
```

Continued

Listing 4-2 *(Continued)*

```php
        $this->caller_class = (!empty($params['caller'])) ? $params['caller'] :
null;

        $this->error_message = array();
        //error_reporting(E_ERROR | E_WARNING | E_NOTICE);
        $this->load_error_code();
    }


    function alert($code = null, $flag = null)
    {
        $msg = $this->get_error_message($code);
        if (!strlen($msg))
        {
            $msg = $code;
        }
        if ($flag == null)
        {
            echo "<script>alert('$msg');history.go(-1);</script>";
        } else if (!strcmp($flag,'close')){
            echo "<script>alert('$msg');window.close();</script>";
        } else {
            echo "<script>alert('$msg');</script>";
        }
    }
    function get_error_message($code = null)
    {

        if (isset($code))
        {
            if (is_array($code))
            {
                $out = array();
                foreach ($code as $entry)
                {
                    array_push($out, $this->error_message[$entry]);
                }
                return $out;
            } else {
                return (! empty($this->error_message[$code])) ? $this-
>error_message[$code] : null;
            }
        } else {
            return (! empty($this->error_message['MISSING'])) ? $this-
>error_message['MISSING'] : null;
        }
```

```
   }
   function load_error_code()
   {
      global $ERRORS;
      if (empty($ERRORS[$this->language]))
      {
         return FALSE;
      }
      while (list($key, $value) = each ($ERRORS[$this->language])) {
         $this->error_message[$key] = $value;
      }
      return TRUE;
   }
 }
?>
```

The class.ErrorHandler.php class assumes that the application has all its error messages defined in an application-specific configuration file and all error messages are stored in a multidimensional array called $ERRORS. For example:

```
<?php

// US English
$ERRORS['US']['SAMPLE_ERR_CODE'] = "This is an error message.";

// Spanish
$ERRORS['ES']['SAMPLE_ERR_CODE'] = "Esto es un mensaje de error.";

//German
$ERRORS['DE']['SAMPLE_ERR_CODE'] = "Dieses ist eine Fehlermeldung.";

?>
```

If this code is stored in *appname*.errors file and loaded by an application using require_once('*appname*.errors'), then the ErrorHandler class can print the SAMPLE_ERR_CODE error message in any of the three languages, depending on the default language settings.

You can translate your error messages in multiple languages using Language Translation Tools provided by Google at http://translate. google.com/translate_t. Be aware that not all automatic translations are perfect.

You can set an application's default language using the $DEFAULT_LANGUAGE variable in a configuration file for your application. For example,

```php
<?php

  // appname.conf

  // Default language for
  $DEFAULT_LANGUAGE = 'US';

?>
```

If this configuration is loaded by an application using the ErrorHandler class, all error messages will be displayed in U.S. English.

ErrorHandler() is the constructor function for the class.ErrorHandler.php. This function sets the default language of the error handler to what is set in the application configuration as global $DEFAULT_LANGUAGE variable.

This method can be passed an associative array as a parameter. If the parameter array has a *key=value* pair called caller=*class_name*, then it sets the member variable called caller_class to the *value*.

The constructor also initializes a member array called error_message and loads the error code for the default language by calling the load_error_code() method.

The error handler class ErrorHandler is automatically invoked by the PHPApplication class so you don't need to create an error handler manually in your application code.

Now let's look at the other functions available in ErrorHandler class.

◆ alert(): This function displays an internationalized error message using a simple JavaScript pop-up alert dialog box. It is called with the error code. The get_error_message() method is used to retrieve the appropriate error message in default application language from the application's error configuration file.

◆ get_error_message(): This function retrieves the error messages for given error code. If an array of error codes is supplied as parameter, the function returns an array of error messages. If no error code is supplied, the function returns a default error message using the MISSING error code.

◆ load_error_code(): This function loads the application's error code in from the global $ERRORS array to its own member array variable error_message. This function is called from the constructor method and does not need to be called manually, unless you want to reload error messages from $ERRORS.

Creating a Built-In Debugger Class

When developing applications, each developer uses at least some form of debugging. Although PHP-supported Integrated Development Environments (IDEs) are becoming available, they're still not the primary development tools for most PHP developers, who are still using `echo`, `print`, and `printf` functions to display debugging information during development.

The debugging class called `class.Debugger.php` is a bit more advanced than the standard `echo`, `print`, and `printf` messages.

It provides a set of facilities that include

- Color-coding debug messages

- Automatically printing debug line numbers

- Optionally buffering debug messages

- Prefixing debug messages with a given tag to make it easy to identify messages in a large application

Listing 4-3 shows the debugger class that is part of our application framework. It can be used to perform basis application debugging.

Listing 4-3: `class.Debugger.php`

```php
<?php


/*
* CVS ID: $Id$
*/
   define('DEBUGGER_LOADED', TRUE);
   class Debugger {

      var $myTextColor = 'red';

      function Debugger($params = null)
      {

         // Debugger constructor method
         $this->color  = $params['color'];
         $this->prefix = $params['prefix'];
         $this->line = 0;
         $this->buffer_str = null;
         $this->buffer = $params['buffer'];
         $this->banner_printed = FALSE;
```

Continued

Listing 4-3 *(Continued)*

```
    }


function print_banner()
{

    if ($this->banner_printed == TRUE)
    {
        return 0;
    }

    $out = "<br><br><font color='$this->myTextColor'>" .
           "<strong>Debugger started for $this->prefix</strong>" .
           "</font><br><hr>";

    if ($this->buffer == TRUE ){
        $this->buffer_str .= $out;
    } else {
        echo $out;
        $this->banner_printed = TRUE;
    }

    return 1;
}

function write($msg)
{
    $out = sprintf("<font color='%s'>%03d  </font>" .
                   "<font color=%s>%s</font><br>\n",
                   $this->myTextColor,
                   $this->line++,
                   $this->color,
                   $msg);


    if ($this->buffer == TRUE)
    {
        $this->buffer_str .= $out;
    } else {
        echo $out;
    }
}
```

```php
function debug_array($hash = null)
{
    while(list($k, $v) = each($hash))
    {
        $this->write("$k = $v");
    }
}

function set_buffer()
{
    $this->buffer = TRUE;
}

function reset_buffer()
{
    $this->buffer = FALSE;
    $this->buffer_str = null;
}

function flush_buffer()
{
    $this->buffer = FALSE;
    $this->print_banner();
    echo $this->buffer_str;
}

}

?>
```

The debugger class has the following methods:

♦ Debugger(): This is the constructor function for the debugger class
(class.Debugger.php). This function initializes the color, prefix, line, and
buffer_str, banner_printed member variables. The color is used to
display the debug information in a given color. The prefix variable is used
to prefix each debug message displayed, which allows for easier identifi-
cation of messages.

The line variable is initialized to zero, which is automatically incremented
to help locate debug information quickly. The buffer_str variable is used
to store buffered debug information. The banner_printed variable, which

controls the banner printing, is set to FALSE. The debugger can be invoked in an application called test_debugger1.php as follows:

```php
<?php

// Turn on all error reporting
error_reporting(E_ALL);

// If you have installed framewirk directory in
// a different directory than
// %DocumentRoot%/framework, change the setting below.
$APP_FRAMEWORK_DIR=$_SERVER['DOCUMENT_ROOT'] . '/framework';

// Insert the path in the PHP include_path so that PHP
// looks for our PEAR, PHPLIB and application framework
// classes in these directories
ini_set( 'include_path', ':' .
         $APP_FRAMEWORK_DIR . ':' .
         ini_get('include_path'));

// Now load our Debugger class from application framework
require_once('class.Debugger.php');

$myDebugger = new Debugger(array(
                          'color'  => 'red',
                          'prefix' => 'MAIN',
                          'buffer' => FALSE)
                         );


// Define an array of fruits
$fruits = array('apple', 'orange', 'banana');

// Show the array contents
$myDebugger->debug_array($fruits);

?>
```

In this example, a new Debugger object called $myDebugger is created, which will print debug messages in red color and use 'MAIN' as the prefix for each message. The buffering of debug messages is disabled as well.

◆ print_banner(): This function prints a banner message as follows:

Debugger started for *PREFIX*

The *PREFIX* is set when the object is created.

◆ `write()`: This function displays a debug message using the chosen color and automatically prints the debug message line number. If debug buffering is on, then the message is written to the buffer (`buffer_str`).

◆ `debug_array()`: This function allows you to debug an associative array. It prints the contents of the associative array parameter using the `write()` method.

◆ `set_buffer()`: This function sets the buffering of debug messages.

◆ `reset_buffer()`: This function resets the buffering of debug messages.

◆ `flush_buffer()`: This function prints the buffer content along with the debug banner.

Now let's look at how an application called test_debugger2.php can use this debugging facility:

```php
<?php

// Turn on all error reporting
error_reporting(E_ALL);

// If you have installed framewirk directory in
// a different directory than
// %DocumentRoot%/framework, change the setting below.
$APP_FRAMEWORK_DIR=$_SERVER['DOCUMENT_ROOT'] . '/framework';

// Insert the path in the PHP include_path so that PHP
// looks for our PEAR, PHPLIB and application framework
// classes in these directories
ini_set( 'include_path', ':' .
         $APP_FRAMEWORK_DIR . ':' .
         ini_get('include_path'));

// Now load our Debugger class from application framework
require_once('class.Debugger.php');


// Create a variable
$name = 'M. J. Kabir';

$myDebugger = new Debugger(array(
                          'color'  => 'blue',
                          'prefix' => 'MAIN',
                          'buffer' => 0)
                          );
```

```
// Write the variable out using debugger write() method
$myDebugger->write("Name = $name");
?>
```

This will print a message such as the following:

```
<font color='red'>000  </font>
<font color=blue>Name = M. J. Kabir</font><br>
```

Buffering debug messages enables you to print all debug messages together, which is often very beneficial in identifying a flow sequence. For example, here an application called test_debugger3.php buffers debugging information and prints the information when the buffer is flushed using `flush_buffer()` method found in the Debugger class.

```php
<?php
// Turn on all error reporting
error_reporting(E_ALL);
// If you have installed framewirk directory in
// a different directory than
// %DocumentRoot%/framework, change the setting below.
$APP_FRAMEWORK_DIR=$_SERVER['DOCUMENT_ROOT'] . '/framework';
// Insert the path in the PHP include_path so that PHP
// looks for our PEAR, PHPLIB and application framework
// classes in these directories
ini_set( 'include_path', ':' .
         $APP_FRAMEWORK_DIR . ':' .
         ini_get('include_path'));
// Now load our Debugger class from application framework
require_once('class.Debugger.php');
// Create a variable
$name  = 'M. J. Kabir';
$email = 'kabir@evoknow.com';
$myDebugger = new Debugger(array(
                            'color'  => 'blue',
                            'prefix' => 'MAIN',
                            'buffer' => TRUE)
                            );
$myDebugger->write("Name = $name");
$myDebugger->write("Email = $email");
echo "This will print before debug messages.\n\n";
$myDebugger->flush_buffer();
?>
```

In this example, the first two debug messages ("`Name = $name`" and "`Email = $email`") will be printed after the "`This will print before debug messages. \n\n`" message.

In the next section, we look at how we can incorporate all of these classes to create an abstract PHP application class.

Creating an Abstract Application Class

The code in Listing 4-4 uses `class.DBI.php`, `class.ErrorHandler.php`, and `class.Debugger.php` to create an abstract PHP application class.

Listing 4-4: `class.PHPApplication.php`

```php
<?php
/*
*
* PHPApplication class
*
* @author <php@evoknow.com>
* @access public
*
* Version 1.0.1
*/


  if (defined("DEBUGGER_LOADED") && ! empty($DEBUGGER_CLASS))
  {
      include_once $DEBUGGER_CLASS;
  }


  //require_once 'lib.session_handler.php';


  class PHPApplication {

     function PHPApplication($param = null)
     {

        global $ON, $OFF, $TEMPLATE_DIR;
```

Continued

Listing 4-4 *(Continued)*

```
        global $MESSAGES, $DEFAULT_LANGUAGE,
               $REL_APP_PATH,
               $REL_TEMPLATE_DIR;

        // initialize application
        $this->app_name  = $this->setDefault($param['app_name'], null);
        $this->app_version      = $this->setDefault($param['app_version'],
null);
        $this->app_type  = $this->setDefault($param['app_type'], null);
        $this->app_db_url        = $this->setDefault($param['app_db_url'],
null);
        $this->debug_mode= $this->setDefault($param['app_debugger'], null);

        $this->auto_connect      = $this->setDefault($param['app_auto_connect'],
TRUE);
        $this->auto_chk_session  = $this-
>setDefault($param['app_auto_chk_session'], TRUE);
        $this->auto_authorize    = $this-
>setDefault($param['app_auto_authorize'], TRUE);

        $this->session_ok        = $this-
>setDefault($param['app_auto_authorize'], FALSE);

        $this->error             = array();
        $this->authorized= FALSE;
        $this->language          = $DEFAULT_LANGUAGE;
        $this->base_url          = sprintf("%s%s", $this->get_server(),
$REL_TEMPLATE_DIR);
        $this->app_path          = $REL_APP_PATH;
        $this->template_dir      = $TEMPLATE_DIR;
        $this->messages          = $MESSAGES;

        // If debuggger is ON then create a debugger object

        if (defined("DEBUGGER_LOADED") && $this->debug_mode == $ON)
        {
            if (empty($param['debug_color']))
            {
                $param['debug_color'] = 'red';
            }
            $this->debugger = new Debugger(array('color'  =>
$param['debug_color'],
                                            'prefix' => $this->app_name,
                                            'buffer' => $OFF));
        }
```

```
// load error handler
$this->has_error = null;

$this->set_error_handler();

// start session

if (strstr($this->get_type(), 'WEB'))
{

    session_start();

    $this->user_id          = (! empty($_SESSION["SESSION_USER_ID"]))  ?
$_SESSION["SESSION_USER_ID"] : null;
    $this->user_name        = (! empty($_SESSION["SESSION_USERNAME"]))  ?
$_SESSION["SESSION_USERNAME"]: null;;
    $this->user_email       = (! empty($_SESSION["SESSION_USERNAME"]))  ?
$_SESSION["SESSION_USERNAME"]: null;;
    $this->set_url();

    if ($this->auto_chk_session) $this->check_session();

    if (! empty($this->app_db_url) && $this->auto_connect && ! $this-
>connect())
    {
        $this->alert('APP_FAILED');

    }

    if ($this->auto_authorize && ! $this->authorize())
    {
        $this->alert('UNAUTHORIZED_ACCESS');
    }

    }
}

function getEMAIL()
{
    return $this->user_email;
}
```

Continued

Listing 4-4 *(Continued)*

```php
function getNAME()
{
    list($name, $host) = explode('', $this->getEMAIL());
    return ucwords($name);
}

function check_session()
{

    if ($this->session_ok == TRUE)
    {
        return TRUE;
    }

    if (!empty($this->user_name))
    {

        $this->session_ok = TRUE;

    } else {

        $this->session_ok = FALSE;

        $this->reauthenticate();
    }

    return $this->session_ok;
}

function reauthenticate()
{
    global $AUTHENTICATION_URL;
    header("Location: $AUTHENTICATION_URL?url=$this->self_url");

}

function getBaseURL()
{
    return $this->base_url;
}
```

```php
function get_server()
{
   $this->set_url();
   return $this->server;
}

function getAppPath()
{
   return $this->app_path;
}

function getFQAP()
{
   // get fully qualified application path

   return sprintf("%s%s",$this->server, $this->app_path);
}

function getFQAN($thisApp = null)
{
   return sprintf("%s/%s", $this->getFQAP(), $thisApp);
}

function getTemplateDir()
{
   return $this->template_dir;
}

function set_url()
{

    $row_protocol = $this->getEnvironment('SERVER_PROTOCOL');

    $port  = $this->getEnvironment('SERVER_PORT');

    if ($port == 80)
    {
        $port = null;
    } else {
        $port = ':' . $port;
    }

    $protocol = strtolower(substr($row_protocol,0,
strpos($row_protocol,'/')));
```

Continued

Listing 4-4 *(Continued)*

```
        $this->server = sprintf("%s://%s%s",
                                $protocol,
                                $this->getEnvironment('HTTP_HOST'),
                                $port);

        $this->self_url = sprintf("%s://%s%s%s", $protocol,
                                  $this->getEnvironment('HTTP_HOST'),
                                  $port,
                                  $this->getEnvironment('REQUEST_URI'));


    }

    function getServer()
    {
        return $this->server;
    }

    function terminate()
    {
        if (isset($this->dbi))
        {
            if ($this->dbi->connected) {
              $this->dbi->disconnect();
            }
        }
        //Asif Changed
        session_destroy();
        exit;
    }

    function authorize($username = null)
    {

        // override this method
        return FALSE;

    }

    function set_error_handler()
    {
        // create error handler
        if (defined("ERROR_HANDLER_LOADED"))
            $this->errHandler = new ErrorHandler(
```

```php
                           array ('name' => $this->app_name));
}

function getErrorMessage($code)
{
    return $this->errHandler->error_message[$code];
}

function show_popup($code)
{
    return $this->errHandler->alert($code, 0);
}

function getMessage($code = null, $hash = null)
{
    $msg = $this->messages[$this->language][$code];

    if (! empty($hash))
    {
        foreach ($hash as $key => $value)
        {
            $key = '/{' . $key . '}/';
            $msg = preg_replace($key, $value, $msg);
        }
    }

    return $msg;
}

function alert($code = null, $flag = null)
{
    return (defined("ERROR_HANDLER_LOADED")) ?
            $this->errHandler->alert($code, $flag) : false;
}


function buffer_debugging()
{
    global $ON;

    if (defined("DEBUGGER_LOADED") && $this->debug_mode == $ON)
    {
        $this->debugger->set_buffer();
    }
}
```

Continued

Listing 4-4 *(Continued)*

```php
function dump_debuginfo()
{
    global $ON;

    if (defined("DEBUGGER_LOADED") && $this->debug_mode == $ON)
    {
        $this->debugger->flush_buffer();
    }
}

function debug($msg)
{
    global $ON;
    if ($this->debug_mode == $ON) {
        $this->debugger->write($msg);
    }
}

function run()
{
    // run the application
    $this->writeln("You need to override this method.");
}

function connect($db_url = null)
{
    if (empty($db_url))
    {
        $db_url = $this->app_db_url;
    }

    if (defined('DBI_LOADED') && ! empty($this->app_db_url))
    {
        $this->dbi = new DBI($db_url);
        return $this->dbi->connected;
    }

    return FALSE;

}

function disconnect()
{
    $this->dbi->disconnect();
    $this->dbi->connected = FALSE;
```

```
        return $this->dbi->connected;
}

function get_error_message($code = null)
{
    return $this->errHandler->get_error_message($code);

}

function show_debugger_banner()
{
    global $ON;

    if ($this->debug_mode == $ON)
    {
        $this->debugger->print_banner();
    }

}

function get_version()
{
    // return version
    return $this->app_version;
}

function get_name()
{
    // return name
    return $this->app_name;
}

function get_type()
{
    // return type
    return $this->app_type;
}

function set_error($err = null)
{
    // set error condition
    if (isset($err))
    {
        array_push($this->error, $err);
        $this->has_error = TRUE;
```

Continued

Listing 4-4 *(Continued)*

```php
            return 1;
        } else {
            return 0;
        }
    }


    function has_error()
    {
        return $this->has_error;
    }


    function reset_error()
    {
        $this->has_error = FALSE;
    }


    function get_error()
    {
        // return error condition
        return array_pop($this->error);
    }


    function get_error_array()
    {
        return $this->error;
    }


    function dump_array($a)
    {
        if (strstr($this->get_type(), 'WEB'))
        {
            echo '<pre>';
            print_r($a);
            echo '</pre>';
        } else {
            print_r($a);
        }


    }


    function dump()
    {
        if (strstr($this->get_type(), 'WEB'))
```

```
    {
      echo '<pre>';
      print_r($this);
      echo '</pre>';
    } else {
      print_r($this);
    }


  }

  function checkRequiredFields($fieldType = null, $fieldData = null,
$errorCode = null)
    {
      $err = array();

      while(list($field, $func) = each ($fieldType))
      {
        $ok = $this->$func($fieldData[$field]);

        if (! $ok )
        {
          $this->alert($errorCode[$field]);
        }

      }
      return $err;
    }

  function number($num = null)
    {
      if (is_array($num))
      {
        foreach ($num as $i)
        {
          if (! is_numeric($i))
          {
            return 0;

          }

        }

        return 1;
```

Continued

Listing 4-4 *(Continued)*

```php
        } else if (is_numeric($num))
        {
            return 1;
        } else {
            return 0;
        }
    }

    function name($name = null)
    {

        if (!strlen($name) || is_numeric($name))
        {
          return 0;
        } else {
          return 1;
        }
    }

    function email($email = null)
    {
        if (strlen($email) < 5 || ! strpos($email,''))
        {
            return 0;
        } else {
            return 1;
        }

    }

    function currency($amount = null)
    {
        return 1;
    }

    function month($mm = null)
    {
        if ($mm >=1 && $mm <=12)
        {
            return 1;
        } else {
            return 0;
        }
    }
```

```
// ASIF what is thie method doing in this class???
function comboOption($optVal = null)
{

  if ($optVal != 0)
  {
   return 1;
  }else {
   return 0;
  }


}

function day($day = null)
{
   if ($day >=1 && $day <=31)
   {
      return 1;
   } else {
      return 0;
   }
}

function year($year = null)
{
   return ($this->number($year));
}

function one_zero_flag($flag = null)
{
   if ($flag == 1 || $flag == 0)
   {
       return 1;

   } else {

       return 1;
   }
}

function plain_text($text = null)
{
   return 1;
}
```

Continued

Listing 4-4 *(Continued)*

```
function debug_array($hash = null)
{
   $this->debugger->debug_array($hash);
}


function writeln($msg)
{
   // print
   global $WWW_NEWLINE;
   global $NEWLINE;
   echo $msg ,(strstr($this->app_type, 'WEB')) ? $WWW_NEWLINE :  $NEWLINE;
}



function show_status($msg = null,$returnURL = null)
{
   global $STATUS_TEMPLATE;
   $template = new Template($this->template_dir);
   $template->set_file('fh', $STATUS_TEMPLATE);
   $template->set_block('fh', 'mainBlock', 'mblock');
   $template->set_var('STATUS_MESSAGE', $msg);

   if (!preg_match('/^http:/', $returnURL) && (!preg_match('/^\//',
$returnURL)))
      {
         $appPath = sprintf("%s/%s", $this->app_path, $returnURL);

      } else {

         $appPath = $returnURL;
      }

   $template->set_var('RETURN_URL', $appPath);

   $template->set_var('BASE_URL', $this->base_url);
   $template->parse('mblock', 'mainBlock');
   $template->pparse('output', 'fh');
 }

function set_escapedVar($hash)
{
    while(list($key, $value) = each ($hash))
      {
```

```php
        $this->escapedVarHash{$key} = preg_replace("/\s/","+",$value);
    }
}

function get_escapedVar($key)
{
    return $this->escapedVarHash{$key};
}

function setUID($uid = null)
{
    $this->user_id = $uid;
}

function getUID()
{
    return $this->user_id;
}

//To Kabir: I added this -- Asif
function getUserName()
{
    return $this->user_name;
}

function emptyError($field, $errCode)
{
  if (empty($field))
  {
      $this->alert($errCode);
  }
}

function getRequestField($field, $default = null)
{
    return (! empty($_REQUEST[$field] )) ? $_REQUEST[$field] : $default;
}

function getSessionField($field, $default = null)
{
    return (! empty($_SESSION[$field] )) ? $_SESSION[$field] : $default;
}
```

Continued

Listing 4-4 *(Continued)*

```php
    function setDefault($value, $default)
    {
        return (isset($value)) ? $value : $default;
    }

    function fileextension($filename)
    {
        return substr(basename($filename), strrpos(basename($filename), ".") +
1);
    }

    function outputTemplate(&$t)
    {
        $t->parse('main', 'mainBlock', false);
        return $t->parse('output', 'fh');

    }

    function showScreen($templateFile = null, $func = null, $app_name)
    {

        $menuTemplate = new Template($this->getTemplateDir());

        $this->doCommonTemplateWork($menuTemplate, $templateFile, $app_name);

        if ($func != null)
        {
            $status = $this->$func($menuTemplate);
        }

        if ($status)
        {
            return $this->outputTemplate($menuTemplate);

        } else {

            return null;
        }

    }

    function doCommonTemplateWork(&$t, $templateFile, $app_name)
    {
```

```
        $t->set_file('fh', $templateFile);

        $t->set_block('fh','mainBlock', 'main');

        $t->set_var(array(
                        'APP_PATH'      => $this->getAppPath(),
                        'APP_NAME'      => $app_name,
                        'BASE_URL'      => $this->getBaseURL()
                    )
                );
    }

function getEnvironment($key)
{
    return $_SERVER[$key];
}

function showPage($contents = null)
{

    global $THEME_TEMPLATE;
    global $THEME_TEMPLATE_DIR, $REL_TEMPLATE_DIR;
    global $REL_TEMPLATE_DIR;
    global $PHOTO_DIR, $DEFAULT_PHOTO, $REL_PHOTO_DIR;

    $themeObj = new Theme($this->dbi, null,'home');

    $this->themeObj = $themeObj;
    $this->theme = $themeObj->getUserTheme($this->getUID());

    $themeTemplate = new Template($THEME_TEMPLATE_DIR);

    $themeTemplate->set_file('fh', $THEME_TEMPLATE[$this->theme]);
    $themeTemplate->set_block('fh', 'mmainBlock', 'mmblock');
    $themeTemplate->set_block('mmainBlock', 'contentBlock', 'cnblock');
    $themeTemplate->set_block('mmainBlock', 'printBlock', 'prnblock');
    $themeTemplate->set_var('printBlock', ' ');
    $themeTemplate->parse('prnblock', 'printBlock',false);
    $themeTemplate->set_block('mmainBlock', 'pageBlock', 'pblock');
    $themeTemplate->set_var('pblock', null);
    $photoFile = sprintf("%s/photo%003d.jpg",$PHOTO_DIR, $this->getUID());
    $defaultPhoto = sprintf("%s/%s",$REL_PHOTO_DIR,$DEFAULT_PHOTO);
    $userPhoto = sprintf("%s/photo%003d.jpg",$REL_PHOTO_DIR,$this->getUID());
    $photo = file_exists($photoFile) ? $userPhoto : $defaultPhoto;
```

Continued

Listing 4-4 *(Continued)*

```
    $themeTemplate->set_var('PHOTO', $photo);
    $themeTemplate->set_var('TEMPLATE_DIR', $REL_TEMPLATE_DIR);
    $themeDir = $THEME_TEMPLATE_DIR . '/' . dirname($THEME_TEMPLATE[$this-
>theme]);
    $leftNavigation = $this->themeObj->getLeftNavigation($themeDir);
    $themeTemplate->set_var('LEFT_NAVIGATION', $leftNavigation);

    $themeTemplate->set_var('SERVER_NAME', $this->get_server());
    $themeTemplate->set_var('BASE_HREF', $REL_TEMPLATE_DIR);
    $themeTemplate->set_var('CONTENT_BLOCK', $contents);
    $themeTemplate->parse('cnblock', 'contentBlock');
    $themeTemplate->parse('mmblock', 'mmainBlock');
    $themeTemplate->pparse('output', 'fh');


  }


}


?>
```

The methods in the class.PHPApplication.php class, which implements the base application in our framework, are discussed in detail in Table 4-1.

TABLE 4-1 METHODS IN CLASS.PHPAPPLICATION.PHP

Function	Description
PHPApplication()	The constructor function for PHPApplication (class.PHPApplication.php) class. Sets app_name, app_version, app_type, debug_mode, error, authorized, and has_error member variables.
	If debug_mode is set to $ON (1), a debugger object called debugger is created. It also creates an error handler from ErrorHandler class.
	The constructor starts the session using session_start(), and also sets self_url by calling set_url().
check_session()	Checks if the session username variable is set, or calls the reauthenticate() function method.

Function	Description
reauthenticate()	Redirects the application user to the authentication application pointed by the global $AUTHENTICATION_URL variable.
set_url()	Creates a URL that points to the application itself.
terminate()	Terminates the application. If the application is connected to a database, the database connection is first closed and then the application session is destroyed.
authorize()	A blank authorized function method that should be overridden by the application. The abstract application object cannot authorize access to the application itself.
set_error_handler()	Creates an error handler object and stores the object in errHandler member variable.
alert()	Calls the alert function method from the ErrorHandler class.
get_error_message()	Gets the error message from the ErrorHandler class.
show_debugger_banner()	Displays the debug banner if debugging is enabled. (The banner display is done by the debugger class.)
buffer_debugging()	Sets the debug message buffering in the built-in Debugger object if the debugging is turned on.
dump_debuginfo()	Flushes the debug buffer if debugging was turned on.
debug()	Provides a wrapper for the write() method in the built-in debugger.
run()	Should be overridden by the instance of the PHPApplication to run it.
connect()	Creates a DBI object and connects the application to the desired relational database.
disconnect()	Disconnects the application from the database.
get_error_message()	Returns the error message for a given error code (calls the get_error_message of the ErrorHandler).
show_debugger_banner()	Prints the debugger banner if debugging is turned on.
buffer_debugging()	Enables you to buffer debugging so that it can be printed later.

Continued

TABLE 4-1 METHODS IN CLASS.PHPAPPLICATION.PHP *(Continued)*

Function	Description
dump_debuginfo()	Dumps all debug information if it was buffered in the built-in debugger object.
debug()	Writes the debug message using the debugger object's write() function method.
run()	A dummy function method that must be overridden by each application to run the application. An application usually has its business logic driver in this method.
connect()	Creates a DBI object and connects the application to a given database. The database URL is passed as a parameter, and the DBI object is stored as a member variable called dbi in the PHPApplication class.
disconnect()	Disconnects the database connection for the application by calling the DBI disconnect()method.
get_version()	Returns the version of the application. The version is supplied as a parameter during PHPApplication object creation.
get_name()	Returns the name of the application (supplied as a parameter during PHPApplication object creation).
get_type()	Returns the type of the application (supplied as a parameter during PHPApplication object creation).
set_error()	Sets error code for the application and also sets the has_error flag to TRUE. (When used to set error code, the error codes are stored in an array called error.) When application needs to generate an error message, you use this function method to set the error code first, and then call get_error_message().
has_error()	Returns TRUE if the application has error(s); otherwise it returns FALSE.
reset_error()	Resets has_error flag to FALSE.
get_error()	Returns an error code from the error array.
get_error_array()	Returns the entire error code array. You can get the error code array and use the get_error_message() method to return the appropriate error messages.

Function	Description
dump()	Prints the entire application object without the methods. This is a very powerful debugging feature.
checkRequiredFields()	Performs minimal required field type validation.
number()	Returns 1 if the parameter is a number or a number array; otherwise, it returns 0.
name()	Returns 1 if the parameter is not empty and not a number; otherwise, it returns 0.
email()	Returns 1 if the parameter is an e-mail address; otherwise, it returns 0.
currency()	Returns 1 if the parameter is a currency number; otherwise, it returns 0.
month()	Returns 1 if the parameter is a number between 1 and 12; otherwise, it returns 0.
day()	Returns 1 if the parameter is a number between 1 and 31; otherwise, it returns 0.
year()	Returns 1 if the parameter is a number; otherwise, it returns 0.
one_zero_flag()	Returns 1 if the parameter is either 1 or 0; otherwise, it returns 0.
plain_text()	Returns 1 if the parameter is plain text; otherwise, it returns 0.
debug_array()	Enables you to print out key=value from an associative array.
writeln()	Prints a message with either ' ' or '\n' at the end, depending on application type. For example, when the application type is set to WEB, it uses ' ' to end the message, and when the application type is set to anything else, it uses the new line character instead.
show_status()	Displays a status message screen using an HTML template. It requires global variables called $TEMPLATE_DIR and $STATUS_TEMPLATE to be set to template directory and HTML status template file name.
	It is called with two parameters: $msg and $returnURL. The $msg variable is used to display the actual message and the $returnURL is used to create a link back to the application that displays the status screen.

The checkRequiredFields() takes three associative arrays as parameters: field type array, field data array, and corresponding error code array. For example:

```
$fieldType = array('mm'  => 'month',
                   'dd'  => 'day',
                   'yy'=> 'year'
                  );

reset($fieldType);

$errCode = array();

while (list($k, $v) = each($fieldType))
{
    $fields{$k} = (! empty($_REQUEST[$k])) ? $_REQUEST[$k] : null;

    $errCode{$k} = 'MISSING_' . strtoupper($k) ;
}

// Check required fields
$err = $this->checkRequiredFields($fieldType, $fields, $errCode);

$this->dump_array($err);
```

In this code segment, the $fieldType is an associative array with three elements: mm, dd, and yy. This array defines which field is what type of data and then an $errCode array is created in the loop to set each field-specific error code. For example, for the $_REQUEST['mm'] field, the error code is MISSING_START_MM. Next the checkRequiredFields() method is called to check each field for type and minimal range validation. The range validation is limited to type. For example, $_REQUEST['mm'] field is set to type month so the value of this variable must not be out of the 1 to 12 range. Similarly, the $_REQUEST['dd'] variable is set to type day and, therefore, the valid range of values for this variable is between 1 and 31.

Now let's take a look at an example application that uses this framework.

Creating a Sample Application

Before you can create an application that uses the framework discussed in this chapter, you need to install the framework on your Web server running PHP. From the CDROM, copy the framework.tar.gz file which is stored in author's folder under CH4 directory. Extract the source code into %DocumentRoot% directory which will create framework directory. Make sure your Web server has read and execution permission for files in this directory.

Listing 4-5 shows a sample application called `sample.php` that uses the framework we just developed.

Listing 4-5: `sample.php`

```php
<?php
    // Turn on all error reporting
    error_reporting(E_ALL);

    require_once 'sample.conf';
    require_once 'sample.errors';
    require_once 'sample.messages';

    $thisApp = new sampleApp(
                        array(
                            'app_name'=> 'Sample Application',
                            'app_version'           => '1.0.0',
                            'app_type'              => 'WEB',
                            'app_db_url' =>
                            $GLOBALS['SAMPLE_DB_URL'],
                            'app_auto_authorize'    => FALSE,
                            'app_auto_chk_session' => FALSE,
                            'app_auto_connect'      => FALSE,
                            'app_type'              => 'WEB',
                            'app_debugger'          => $ON
                        )
                    );

    $thisApp->buffer_debugging();
    $thisApp->debug("This is $thisApp->app_name application");
    $thisApp->run();
    $thisApp->dump_debuginfo();

?>
```

First, this application loads the `sample.conf` file shown in Listing 4-6.

Listing 4-6: `sample.conf`

```php
<?php
    // Turn on all error reporting
    error_reporting(E_ALL);

    // If you have installed PEAR packages in a different
    // directory than %DocumentRoot%/pear change the
    // setting below.
    $PEAR_DIR = $_SERVER['DOCUMENT_ROOT'] . '/pear' ;

    // If you have installed PHPLIB in a different
    // directory than %DocumentRoot%/phplib, change
    // the setting below.
    $PHPLIB_DIR = $_SERVER['DOCUMENT_ROOT'] . '/phplib';

    // If you have installed framewirk directory in
    // a different directory than
    // %DocumentRoot%/framework, change the setting below.
    $APP_FRAMEWORK_DIR=$_SERVER['DOCUMENT_ROOT'] . '/framework';

    // Relative URL to login script
    $AUTHENTICATION_URL='/login/login.php';


    //Default language
    $DEFAULT_LANGUAGE = 'US';


    // Create a path consisting of the PEAR,
    // PHPLIB and our application framework
    // path ($APP_FRAMEWORK_DIR)
    $PATH = $PEAR_DIR . ':' .
            $PHPLIB_DIR . ':' .
            $APP_FRAMEWORK_DIR;

    // Insert the path in the PHP include_path so that PHP
    // looks for our PEAR, PHPLIB and application framework
    // classes in these directories
    ini_set( 'include_path', ':' .
            $PATH . ':' .
            ini_get('include_path'));
```

```
// Now load the DB.php class from PEAR
require_once 'DB.php';

// Now load our DBI class from application framework

require_once $APP_FRAMEWORK_DIR . '/' . 'constants.php';
require_once $APP_FRAMEWORK_DIR . '/' . $DEBUGGER_CLASS;
require_once $APP_FRAMEWORK_DIR . '/' . $APPLICATION_CLASS;
require_once $APP_FRAMEWORK_DIR . '/' . $ERROR_HANDLER_CLASS;
require_once $APP_FRAMEWORK_DIR . '/' . $AUTHENTICATION_CLASS;
require_once $APP_FRAMEWORK_DIR . '/' . $DBI_CLASS;
require_once $APP_FRAMEWORK_DIR . '/' . $USER_CLASS;
require_once $TEMPLATE_CLASS;

// Load the Sample Application class
require_once 'class.sampleApp.php';
// Setup the database URL
$SAMPLE_DB_URL = 'mysql://root:foobar@localhost/testdb';

?>
```

This configuration file sets the path for the framework classes using $APP_FRAMEWORK_DIR. It sets the application name using $APPLICATION_NAME, the default language using $DEFAULT_LANGUAGE, the application's database URL using $SAMPLE_DB_URL, the application's authenticator URL using $AUTHENTICATION_URL.

The configuration file also sets the include path for PHP to include application framework path, PHPLIB, and PEAR path needed to load various classes. The classes needed to run the application are loaded using :require_once() function.

The sample application shown in Listing 4-5 then loads the sample.errors configuration shown in Listing 4-7.

Listing 4-7: sample.errors

```
<?php

// Errors for Sample appliction

$ERRORS['US']['UNAUTHORIZED_ACCESS'] = "Unauthorized access.";
$ERRORS['US']['MISSING']             = "Missing or invalid.";

?>
```

This configuration file creates a multidimensional array called $ERRORS and sets two error codes to appropriate error messages in U.S. English. If the sample application is to be used in a different language region, say in Spain, then this file can be modified to create the ES (shorthand for Spanish) language-specific errors by replacing US as ES and also translating the actual error messages.

When internationalizing the error messages, the error code such as UNAUTHORIZED_ACCESS should not be translated because that code name is the key to locate the "Unauthorized access" error message. Only the error message should be translated, and the appropriate language identifier needs to be set.

The sample application then loads the sample.messages file, which is shown in Listing 4-8.

Listing 4-8: sample.messages

```php
<?php
    $MESSAGES['US']['APP_FAILED']   = "Application Failed.";
    $MESSAGES['US']['DEFAULT_MSG'] = "Hello World";
?>
```

Like the error message files, this file loads a multidimensional array called $MESSAGES with language support for each message.

The sample.conf file also loads the constants.php file, which defines a set of constants needed by the framework classes. The same sample configuration file also loads the framework classes along with a class called class.sampleApp.php, which is shown in Listing 4-9.

This class extends the PHPApplication class and overrides the run() and authorize() function. It implements another function called doSomething(), which is specific to itself. We will discuss the details of this class in the next section. Now let's look at the rest of the sample.php code.

Once the class.sampleApp.php class is loaded, the session is automatically started by the sampleApp object, which extends the PHPApplication object.

Next the application creates an instance of the sampleApp object called $thisApp. This is the application object. The application name, version, type, and debugger ON or OFF flag are set when creating this object.

After the $thisApp object has been created, the sample application enables debug message buffering by calling the buffer_debugging() method in class. PHPApplication.php class.

It then calls the run() function, which has been overridden in class. sampleApp.php. This is the main function that runs the application.

After the application has run, more debugging information is buffered and the debug information is dumped:

```
$thisApp->buffer_debugging();
$thisApp->run();
$thisApp->debug("Version : " . $thisApp->get_version());
$thisApp->dump_debuginfo();
```

Figure 4-6 shows what is displayed when the sample.php application is run after a user has already logged in.

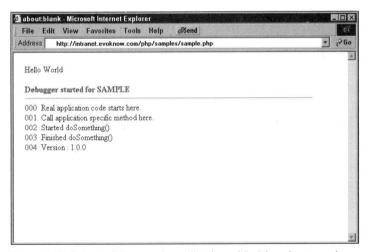

Figure 4-6: Output of the sample application with debugging turned on.

You have to have the application framework created in this chapter installed on your system and at least one user created to run this application. To learn about how to create a user, see Chapter 5.

Figure 4-7 shows the application with the debug flag turned off.

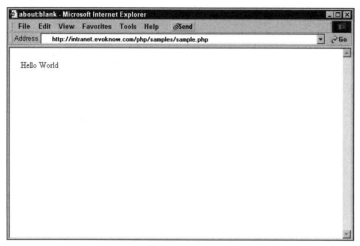

Figure 4-7: Output of the sample application with debugging turned off.

Listing 4-9 shows the `class.sampleApp.php`, which extends the `PHPApplication` class from our framework.

Listing 4-9: `class.sampleApp.php`

```php
<?php

    class sampleApp  extends PHPApplication {

        function run()
        {
            // At this point user is authorized
            // Start business logic driver
            $this->debug("Real application code starts here.");
            $this->debug("Call application specific function here.");
            $this->doSomething();
        }

        function authorize($email = null)
        {
            return TRUE;
        }

        function doSomething()
        {
            global $MESSAGES, $DEFAULT_LANGUAGE;
```

```
        $this->debug("Started doSomething()");
        echo $MESSAGES[$DEFAULT_LANGUAGE]['DEFAULT_MSG'];
        $this->debug("Finished doSomething()");
    }
} // Class

?>
```

This sampleApp class has only three functions: run(), authorize(), and doSomething(). The run() function overrides the abstract run() method provided in class.PHPApplication.php and it is automatically called when the application is run. Therefore, sampleApp run() method is needed to application logic in sample.php.

In the example, the authorization check always returns TRUE, because this isn't a real-world application and the run() function calls the doSomething() function, which simply prints a set of debug messages along with a status message. Notice that although the application status message $MESSAGES[$DEFAULT_LANGUAGE]['DEFAULT_MSG'] is internationalized, the debug messages are in English.

As you can see the application framework makes writing new applications quite easy; development time is greatly reduced, because you can build onto the framework instead of starting from scratch every time.

Summary

In this chapter I have shown you how to develop a complete application framework consisting of a few object-oriented classes. These classes provide a set of facilities for writing applications that use a standard approach to writing PHP applications for both intranet and the Web.

The application framework developed in this chapter allows you to develop a new application by simply extending the primary class, PHPApplication class, of the framework. Immediately your application inherits all the benefits of the new framework, which includes a database abstraction, an error handler, and a debugging facility.

This application framework is used throughout the rest of the book for developing most of the applications discussed in this book. The latest version of this framework is always available from http://www.evoknow.com/phpbook/.

Chapter 5

Central Authentication System

A CENTRAL AUTHENTICATION SYSTEM consists of two applications: login and logout. The login application allows users to login and the logout application is used to terminate the login session. This chapter shows you how to build and implement such a system.

How the System Works

First, let's take a look at how such a system will work with any of your PHP Application Framework–based applications. Figure 5-1 shows a partial flow diagram for a PHP application that requires authentication and authorization.

When such an application starts up, it checks to see if the user is already authenticated. This is done by checking for the existence of a user session. If such a user session is found, the user is authenticated and the application then performs the authorization check itself. If the user is not authenticated already, she is automatically redirected to the authentication system. Similarly, in the authorization phase, if the user is found to be incapable of running the application due to lack of privilege, she is redirected to the authentication system.

In our PHP Application Framework (PHPAF) model, the authentication application is called login.php. Figure 5-2 shows how this application works.

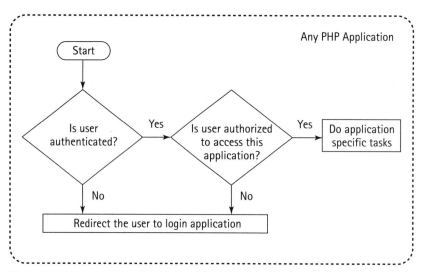

Figure 5-1: How an application works with the authentication system.

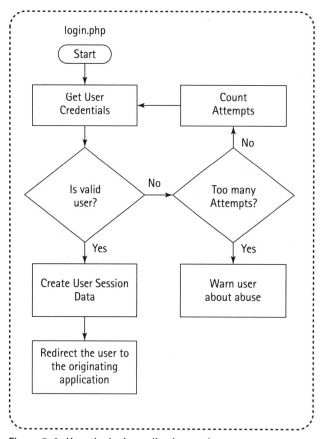

Figure 5-2: How the login application works.

The login application gets the user credentials (username and password) from the GUI and checks the validity of the credentials with a user table in the authentication database. If the user has supplied valid credentials, a user session is created and the user is directed to the application that made the login request.

A user is given a set number of chances to log in, and if she doesn't succeed in providing valid credentials, the login application automatically directs the user to an HTML page which should warn the user about abuse.

Like the login application, the central logout application can be linked from any application interface to allow a user to immediately log out. The logout application works as shown in Figure 5-3.

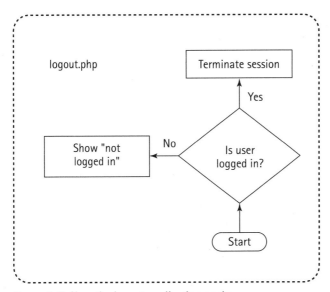

Figure 5-3: How the logout application works.

The logout application checks if the user is really logged in. If she is logged in, the user session is removed, and if she isn't, a "Not Logged In" message is displayed.

The class level architecture of the central authentication system is shown in Figure 5-4.

Here you can see that the login.php application uses a class called class.Authentication.php and a framework class called class.PHPApplication.php to implement its services. The latter class provides database access to the login application via another framework class called class.DBI.php. Both of these framework classes have been developed in Chapter 4. The session management aspect of login and logout is provided by PHP's built-in session functionality.

Similarly, the logout application uses the class.PHPApplication to implement its logout service.

In the rest of the chapter we will create necessary classes and develop the login/logout applications to implement the above-mentioned central authentication system.

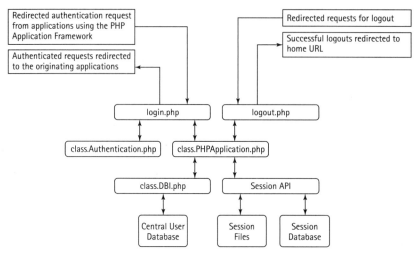

Figure 5–4: Class Level Architecture of the central authentication system.

Creating an Authentication Class

Listing 5-1 shows the authentication class called `class.Authentication.php`, which will implement the central authentication system.

Listing 5-1: `class.Authentication.php`

```php
<?php

/*
 *
 * Application class
 *
 * @author EVOKNOW, Inc. <php@evoknow.com>
 * @access public
 * CVS ID: $Id$
 */

    include_once $DEBUGGER_CLASS;

    class Authentication {

        function Authentication($email = null, $password = null, $db_url = null)
        {
```

```
        global $AUTH_DB_TBL;

        $this->status = FALSE;
        $this->email = $email;
        $this->password = $password;
        $this->auth_tbl = $AUTH_DB_TBL;

        $this->db_url = ($db_url == null) ? null : $db_url;

        if ($db_url == null)
        {
            global $AUTH_DB_TYPE, $AUTH_DB_NAME;
            global $AUTH_DB_USERNAME, $AUTH_DB_PASSWD;
            global $AUTH_DB_HOST;

            $this->db_url = sprintf("%s://%s:%s@%s/%s",$AUTH_DB_TYPE,
                                                $AUTH_DB_USERNAME,
                                                $AUTH_DB_PASSWD,
                                                $AUTH_DB_HOST,
                                                $AUTH_DB_NAME);

        }

        $this->status = FALSE;
    }

    function authenticate()
    {

        $dbi = new DBI($this->db_url);

        $query  = "SELECT USER_ID, PASSWORD from " . $this->auth_tbl;
        $query .= " WHERE EMAIL = '" . $this->email . "' AND ACTIVE = '1'";

        $result = $dbi->query($query);

        if ($result != null)
        {

            $row = $result->fetchRow();

            $salt = substr($row->PASSWORD,0,2);
            if (crypt($this->password, $salt) == $row->PASSWORD)
            {
```

Continued

Listing 5-1 *(Continued)*

```
                $this->status  = TRUE;
                $this->user_id = $row->USER_ID;

          } else {
              $this->status = FALSE;
          }
      }

      $dbi->disconnect();

      return $this->status;
    }

    function getUID()
    {
        return $this->user_id;
    }


    }

?>
```

The following are the functions in this class:

♦ Authentication(): This is the constructor method, which sets the default values of the authentication object. First it sets the status variable to FALSE to signify that authentication is not successful yet. The e-mail variable is set to the e-mail address supplied as part of the parameter. (The authentication system uses e-mail address as the username and, therefore, it is a required item in the user-supplied credential.) The password parameter is stored in the password variable.

The function also sets the auth_tbl and db_url variables to authentication table name and the fully qualified database name of the central authentication database.

♦ authenticate(): This function performs the authentication. It retrieves active UID and PASSWORD fields for the given e-mail address. If the user account has been deactivated (ACTIVE = 0), then the method returns default authentication status (FALSE), and if the user account is active and the encrypted version of the given password matches the stored cryptographic password, then the method returns TRUE status, which indicates successful authentication.

Now using this class (`class.Authentication.php`) and our existing application framework, let's create central login and logout applications.

Creating the Central Login Application

The purpose of the login application is to present a username and password entry interface using an HTML template, and then to authenticate the user.

If the user is successfully authenticated by the `class.Authentication.php` object, the login application creates the session data necessary to let other applications know that the user is already authenticated and has valid credentials.

If the user doesn't supply valid credentials, the login application should allow the user to try a few times (say three times) and, if she fails after retrying for a configurable number of times, then she is taken to an HTML page showing a warning about potential abuse of the system. This is to stop non-users from abusing the system.

 Valid users who have forgotten their passwords can run another login helper application to send new passwords via e-mail. This helper application is discussed in Chapter 6.

Listing 5-2 shows the login application `login.php`, which implements these features.

Listing 5-2: `login.php`

```php
<?php

    require_once "login.conf";
    require_once "login.errors";

    /*
        Session variables must be defined before session_start()
        method is called
    */

    $count = 0;

    class loginApp extends PHPApplication {
```

Continued

Listing 5-2 *(Continued)*

```
function run()
{
   global $MIN_USERNAME_SIZE, $MIN_PASSWORD_SIZE, $MAX_ATTEMPTS;
   global $WARNING_URL, $APP_MENU;


   $email = $this->getRequestField('email');
   $password = $this->getRequestField('password') ;
   $url = $this->getRequestField('url');

   $emailLen = strlen($email);
   $passwdLen = strlen($password);

   $this->debug("Login attempts : " . $this-
>getSessionField('SESSION_ATTEMPTS'));


   if ($this->is_authenticated())
   {
      // return to caller HTTP_REFERRER
      $this->debug("User already authenticated.");
      $this->debug("Redirecting to $url.");
      $url = (isset($url)) ? $url : $this->getServer();
      header("Location: $url");

   } else if (strlen($email) < $MIN_USERNAME_SIZE ||
         strlen($password) < $MIN_PASSWORD_SIZE) {
      // display the login interface
      $this->debug("Invalid Email or password.");
      $this->display_login();
      $_SESSION["SESSION_ATTEMPTS"] = $this-
>getSessionField("SESSION_ATTEMPTS") + 1;

   } else {

      // Prepare the email with domain name
      if (!strpos($email, ''))
      {
         $hostname = explode('.', $_SERVER['SERVER_NAME']);

         if (sizeof($hostname) > 1)
         {
            $email .= '' . $hostname[1] . '.' . $hostname[2];
         }
      }
```

```
        // authenticate user

        $this->debug("Authenticate user: $email with password $password");

        if ($this->authenticate($email, $password))
        {
            $this->debug("User is successfully authenticated.");
            $_SESSION["SESSION_USERNAME"] = $email;
            $_SESSION["SESSION_PASSWORD"] = $password;
            $_SESSION["SESSION_USER_ID"]  = $this->getUID();

            if (empty($url))
            {
                $url = $APP_MENU;
            }

            // Log user activity
            $thisUser = new User($this->dbi, $this->getUID());
            $thisUser->logActivity(LOGIN);

            $this->debug("Location $url");
            header("Location: $url");

            $this->debug("Redirect user to caller application at url =
$url.");

        } else {
            $this->debug("User failed authentication.");
            $this->display_login();
            $_SESSION["SESSION_ATTEMPTS"] = $this-
>getSessionField("SESSION_ATTEMPTS") + 1;
        }
    }
}

function warn()
{
    global $WARNING_URL;
    $this->debug("Came to warn the user $WARNING_URL");
    header("Location: $WARNING_URL");
}

function display_login()
{
```

Continued

Listing 5-2 *(Continued)*

```
        global $TEMPLATE_DIR;
        global $LOGIN_TEMPLATE;
        global $MAX_ATTEMPTS;
        global $REL_TEMPLATE_DIR;
        global $email, $url;
        global $PHP_SELF,
               $FORGOTTEN_PASSWORD_APP;


        $url = $this->getRequestField('url');

        if ($this->getSessionField("SESSION_ATTEMPTS") > $MAX_ATTEMPTS)
        {
            $this->warn();
        }

        $this->debug("Display login dialog box");
        $template = new Template($TEMPLATE_DIR);
        $template->set_file('fh', $LOGIN_TEMPLATE);
        $template->set_block('fh', "mainBlock");
        $template->set_var('SELF_PATH', $PHP_SELF);
        $template->set_var('ATTEMPT', $this-
>getSessionField("SESSION_ATTEMPTS"));
        $template->set_var('TODAY', date("M-d-Y h:i:s a"));
        $template->set_var('TODAY_TS', time());
        $template->set_var('USERNAME', $email);
        $template->set_var('REDIRECT_URL', $url);
        $template->set_var('FORGOTTEN_PASSWORD_APP', $FORGOTTEN_PASSWORD_APP);
        $template->parse("fh", "mainBlock");
        $template->set_var('BASE_URL', sprintf("%s",$this->base_url));
        $template->pparse("output", "fh");
        return 1;
    }


    function is_authenticated()
    {
        return (!empty($_SESSION["SESSION_USERNAME"])) ? TRUE : FALSE;
    }

    function authenticate($user = null, $passwd = null)
    {
        $authObj = new Authentication($user, $passwd, $this->app_db_url);
```

```
        if ($authObj->authenticate())
        {
            $uid = $authObj->getUID();
            $this->debug("Setting user id to $uid");
            $this->setUID($uid);
            return TRUE;
        }

        return FALSE;
    }

}

global $AUTH_DB_URL;

$thisApp = new loginApp(
                    array(
                        'app_name'            => $APPLICATION_NAME,
                        'app_version'         => '1.0.0',
                        'app_type'            => 'WEB',
                        'app_db_url'          => $AUTH_DB_URL,
                        'app_auto_authorize'  => FALSE,
                        'app_auto_chk_session' => FALSE,
                        'app_auto_connect'    => TRUE,
                        'app_type'            => 'WEB',
                        'app_debugger'        => $OFF
                        )
                    );


$thisApp->buffer_debugging();
$thisApp->debug("This is $thisApp->app_name application");
$thisApp->run();
$thisApp->dump_debuginfo();

?>
```

Figure 5-5 shows the flow diagram of login.php. When the login application is run, it goes through the following steps:

1. It determines if the user is already authenticated. It calls the is_authen-ticated() method to determine if the user has a session already. If the user has a session, the is_authenticated() method returns TRUE or else FALSE.

2. If the user is authenticated already, the user is redirected to the application that called the login application.

3. If the user is not already authenticated, the `login.php` application determines whether the user supplied a username (e-mail address) and whether the password passes the minimum-size test. If either the username (e-mail address) or password does not pass the test, the login attempt is counted and the login menu or the warning page is displayed according to the allowed number of login attempts per `login.conf` file.

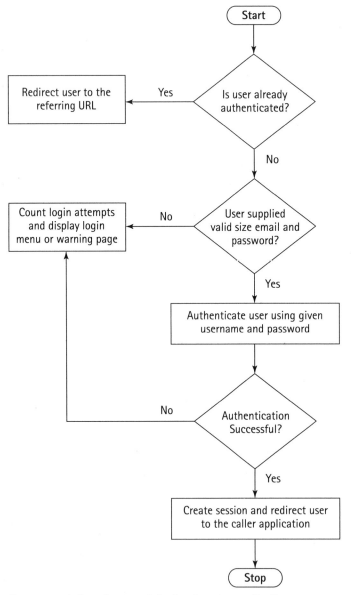

Figure 5-5: A flow diagram of the `login.php` application.

4. If the user credentials (username and password) passes the minimum-size test, the actual authentication is done using the user record stored in the authentication database via the `authenticate()` method found in the `class.Authentication.php` object.

5. If the `authenticate()` method returns `TRUE`, the user is valid and a session variable called `SESSION_USERNAME` is registered with the supplied username (e-mail address).

6. If the `authenticate()` method returns `FALSE`, the user login attempt is counted and the login menu or the warning page is displayed according to the allowed number of login attempts per `login.conf` file.

Now that you know how `login.php` works, let's take a look at what configuration it gets from `login.conf` as shown in Listing 5-3.

Listing 5-3: `login.conf`

```php
<?php
   // login.conf

   // Turn on all error reporting
   error_reporting(E_ALL);

   // If you have installed framework directory in
   // a different directory than
   // %DocumentRoot%/framework, change the setting below.
   $APP_FRAMEWORK_DIR=$_SERVER['DOCUMENT_ROOT'] . '/framework';
   $PEAR            =$_SERVER['DOCUMENT_ROOT'] . '/pear';
   $PHPLIB          =$_SERVER['DOCUMENT_ROOT'] . '/phplib';

   // Insert the path in the PHP include_path so that PHP
   // looks for PEAR, PHPLIB and our application framework
   // classes in these directories
   ini_set( 'include_path', ':' .
        $PEAR .   ':' .
        $PHPLIB . ':' .
        $APP_FRAMEWORK_DIR . ':' .
        ini_get('include_path'));

   $PHP_SELF = $_SERVER["PHP_SELF"];

   $LOGIN_TEMPLATE   = 'login.html';

   $APPLICATION_NAME = 'LOGIN';
   $DEFAULT_LANGUAGE = 'US';
```

Continued

Listing 5-3 *(Continued)*

```
    $AUTH_DB_URL        = 'mysql://root:foobar@localhost/auth';
    $ACTIVITY_LOG_TBL = 'ACTIVITY';
    $AUTH_DB_TBL        = 'users';

    $MIN_USERNAME_SIZE= 5;
    $MIN_PASSWORD_SIZE= 8;
    $MAX_ATTEMPTS = 5;
    $FORGOTTEN_PASSWORD_APP = '/user_mngr/apps/user_mngr_forgotten_pwd.php';

    $APP_MENU          = '/';

    $TEMPLATE_DIR       = $_SERVER['DOCUMENT_ROOT'] . '/login/templates';
    $REL_TEMPLATE_DIR  = '/login/templates/';
    $WARNING_URL        = $TEMPLATE_DIR . '/warning.html';

    require_once "login.errors";
    require_once "login.messages";
    require_once 'DB.php';
    require_once $APP_FRAMEWORK_DIR . '/' . 'constants.php';

    require_once $APP_FRAMEWORK_DIR . '/' . $DEBUGGER_CLASS;


    require_once $APP_FRAMEWORK_DIR . '/' . $APPLICATION_CLASS;
    require_once $APP_FRAMEWORK_DIR . '/' . $ERROR_HANDLER_CLASS;
    require_once $APP_FRAMEWORK_DIR . '/' . $AUTHENTICATION_CLASS;
    require_once $APP_FRAMEWORK_DIR . '/' . $DBI_CLASS;
    require_once $APP_FRAMEWORK_DIR . '/' . $USER_CLASS;
    require_once $TEMPLATE_CLASS;
?>
```

The configuration details are explained in Table 5-1.

TABLE 5-1 LOGIN.CONF **EXPLANATIONS**

Variable	Description
$APP_FRAMEWORK_DIR	Sets the framework directory to %DocumentRoot%framework.
$TEMPLATE_DIR	Sets /evoknow/intranet/php/login/templates (same as $APP_FRAMEWORK_DIR).

Variable	Description
$LOGIN_TEMPLATE	Sets the name of the login menu file to login.ihtml. This file has to be stored in /evoknow/intranet/php/login/templates/login.ihtml.
$APPLICATION_NAME	Sets the name of the application to LOGIN.
$DEFAULT_LANGUAGE	Sets the default language of the application to US.
$AUTH_DB_TYPE	Sets the database type to mysql.
$AUTH_DB_HOST	Sets the database server location to localhost.
$AUTH_DB_NAME	Sets the authentication database name to auth, which must have the table specified by $AUTH_DB_TBL fields.
$AUTH_DB_TBL	Sets the name of the user information table to users.
$AUTH_DB_USERNAME	Sets the username required to access the database. Since sensitive database information is stored in login.conf file make sure either store it outside the Web document tree or use Apache configuration that disallows Web visitors from retrieving .conf files. See Chapter 22 for details.
$AUTH_DB_PASSWD	Sets the password required to access the database. Since sensitive database information is stored in login.conf file make sure either store it outside the Web document tree or use Apache configuration that disallows Web visitors from retrieving .conf files. See Chapter 22 for details.
$MIN_USERNAME_SIZE	Sets the minimum username size to 5. Usernames smaller than five characters can be guessed too easily and therefore at least five character name is preferred.
$MIN_PASSWORD_SIZE	
$MAX_ATTEMPTS	Sets the maximum number of tries to 3.
$WARNING_URL	Sets the warning page URL to /php/login/templates/warning.html.
$DEFAULT_DOMAIN	Sets the default name to evoknow.com.
$APP_MENU	Sets the name of the application menu to /php/menu.php. If the login application was directly called, the successfully authenticated user is redirected to this menu.

All the error messages that the `login.php` application generates are taken from the `login.errors` file shown in Listing 5-4.

Listing 5-4: `login.errors`

```php
<?php

  // Errors for Login application

    $ERRORS['US']['MISSING_CODE'] = "No error message found";
    $ERRORS['US']['INVALID_DATA'] = "Invalid data.";


?>
```

The `login.php` application displays the login menu using the `login.ihtml` file, which is shown in Listing 5-5. The `$LOGIN_TEMPLATE` is set to point to `login.ihtml` in the `login.conf` file.

Listing 5-5: `login.ihtml`

```html
<html>
<head><title>Login</title></head>
<body>
<!-- BEGIN mainBlock -->
<center>
<form action="{SELF_PATH}" method="POST">
<table border=0 cellpadding=3 cellspacing=0 width=30%>
<tr>
    <td bgcolor="#cccccc" colspan=2>Login</td>
</tr>

<tr>
    <td>Email</td>
    <td><input type=text
            name="email"
            value="{USERNAME}"
            size=30
            maxsize=50>
    </td>
</tr>

<tr>
    <td>Password</td>
    <td><input type=password name="password" size=30 maxsize=50></td>
</tr>

<tr>
    <td align=center colspan=2>
```

```
    <input type=submit value="Login">
     
    <input type=reset value="Reset">
    </td>
</tr>

</table>

<input type=hidden name="url"
        value="{REDIRECT_URL}">
</form>

<font size=2>Login attempt {ATTEMPT}.</font>
</center>
<!-- END mainBlock -->
</body>
</html>
```

The `login.ihtml` template has a set of template tag variables that are replaced by the `login.php` application. These template tag variables are explained in Table 5-2.

TABLE 5-2 TEMPLATE TAG VARIABLES IN LOGIN TEMPLATE

Template Tag	Explanation
{SELF_PATH}	Set as a form action. The login application replaces this with the relative path to the login application itself. This allows the login menu form to be submitted to the login application itself.
{USERNAME}	Replaced with the username previously entered when the user failed to successfully authenticate the first time. This saves the user from having to type the username again and again when she doesn't remember the password correctly. This is a user-friendly feature.
{REDIRECT_URL}	Set to the URL of the application that redirected the user to the login application.
{ATTEMPT}	Displays the number of login attempts the user has made.

When the login attempts exceed the number of attempts set in the $MAX_ATTEMPTS variable in the `login.conf` file, the user is redirected to the $WARNING_URL page, which is shown in Listing 5-6.

Listing 5-6: `warning.html`

```
<html>
<head>
<title>Invalid Login Attempts</title>
</head>
<body>
<h1>Excessive Invalid Login Attempts</h1>
<hr>
You have attempted to login too many times.
</body>
</html>
```

 The warning page can be any page. For example, you can set $WARNING_URL to your privacy or network usage policy page to alert the user of your policies on resource usage.

Creating the Central Logout Application

The central logout application terminates the user session. A flowchart of such an application is shown in Figure 5-6.

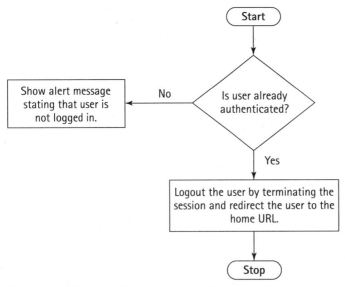

Figure 5-6: A flowchart for the logout application.

The logout application checks to see whether the user is logged in. If the user is not logged in, she is warned of her status. If the user is logged in, her session is terminated and the user is redirected to a home URL. Listing 5-7 implements this flowchart in `logout.php`.

Listing 5-7: `logout.php`

```php
<?php

    require_once "login.conf";
    require_once "login.errors";

    /*
        Session variables must be defined before session_start()
        method is called
    */

    $count = 0;

    class loginApp extends PHPApplication {

        function run()
        {
            global $MIN_USERNAME_SIZE, $MIN_PASSWORD_SIZE, $MAX_ATTEMPTS;
            global $WARNING_URL, $APP_MENU;

            $email = $this->getRequestField('email');
            $password = $this->getRequestField('password') ;
            $url = $this->getRequestField('url');

            $emailLen = strlen($email);
            $passwdLen = strlen($password);

            $this->debug("Login attempts : " .
            $this->getSessionField('SESSION_ATTEMPTS'));


            if ($this->is_authenticated())
            {
                // return to caller HTTP_REFERRER
                $this->debug("User already authenticated.");
                $this->debug("Redirecting to $url.");
                $url = (isset($url)) ? $url : $this->getServer();
                header("Location: $url");
```

Continued

Listing 5-7 *(Continued)*

```
    } else if (strlen($email) < $MIN_USERNAME_SIZE ||
            strlen($password) < $MIN_PASSWORD_SIZE) {
        // display the login interface
        $this->debug("Invalid Email or password.");
        $this->display_login();
        $_SESSION["SESSION_ATTEMPTS"] =
        $this->getSessionField("SESSION_ATTEMPTS") + 1;

    } else {

        // Prepare the email with domain name
        if (!strpos($email, ''))
        {
            $hostname = explode('.', $_SERVER['SERVER_NAME']);

            if (sizeof($hostname) > 1)
            {
                $email .= '' . $hostname[1] . '.' . $hostname[2];
            }
        }

        // authenticate user

        $this->debug("Authenticate user: $email with password $password");

        if ($this->authenticate($email, $password))
        {
            $this->debug("User is successfully authenticated.");
            $_SESSION["SESSION_USERNAME"] = $email;
            $_SESSION["SESSION_PASSWORD"] = $password;
            $_SESSION["SESSION_USER_ID"]  = $this->getUID();

            if (empty($url))
            {
                $url = $APP_MENU;
            }

            // Log user activity
            $thisUser = new User($this->dbi, $this->getUID());
            $thisUser->logActivity(LOGIN);

            $this->debug("Location $url");
            header("Location: $url");
```

```
                    $this->debug("Redirect user to caller application at url =
$url.");

            } else {
                $this->debug("User failed authentication.");
                $this->display_login();
                $_SESSION["SESSION_ATTEMPTS"] =
                $this->getSessionField("SESSION_ATTEMPTS") + 1;
            }
        }
    }

    function warn()
    {
        global $WARNING_URL;
        $this->debug("Came to warn the user $WARNING_URL");
        header("Location: $WARNING_URL");
    }

    function display_login()
    {

        global $TEMPLATE_DIR;
        global $LOGIN_TEMPLATE;
        global $MAX_ATTEMPTS;
        global $REL_TEMPLATE_DIR;
        global $email, $url;
        global $PHP_SELF,
               $FORGOTTEN_PASSWORD_APP;

        $url = $this->getRequestField('url');

        if ($this->getSessionField("SESSION_ATTEMPTS") > $MAX_ATTEMPTS)
        {
            $this->warn();
        }

        $this->debug("Display login dialog box");
        $template = new Template($TEMPLATE_DIR);
        $template->set_file('fh', $LOGIN_TEMPLATE);
        $template->set_block('fh', "mainBlock");
        $template->set_var('SELF_PATH', $PHP_SELF);
        $template->set_var('ATTEMPT',
               $this->getSessionField("SESSION_ATTEMPTS"));
```

Continued

Listing 5-7 *(Continued)*

```
        $template->set_var('TODAY', date("M-d-Y h:i:s a"));
        $template->set_var('TODAY_TS', time());
        $template->set_var('USERNAME', $email);
        $template->set_var('REDIRECT_URL', $url);
        $template->set_var('FORGOTTEN_PASSWORD_APP', $FORGOTTEN_PASSWORD_APP);
        $template->parse("fh", "mainBlock");
        $template->set_var('BASE_URL', sprintf("%s",$this->base_url));
        $template->pparse("output", "fh");
        return 1;
    }


    function is_authenticated()
    {
        return (!empty($_SESSION["SESSION_USERNAME"])) ? TRUE : FALSE;
    }


    function authenticate($user = null, $passwd = null)
    {
        $authObj = new Authentication($user, $passwd, $this->app_db_url);

        if ($authObj->authenticate())
        {
            $uid = $authObj->getUID();
            $this->debug("Setting user id to $uid");
            $this->setUID($uid);
            return TRUE;
        }

        return FALSE;
    }

}

global $AUTH_DB_URL;

$thisApp = new loginApp(
                    array(
                        'app_name'           => $APPLICATION_NAME,
                        'app_version'        => '1.0.0',
                        'app_type'           => 'WEB',
                        'app_db_url'         => $AUTH_DB_URL,
                        'app_auto_authorize' => FALSE,
                        'app_auto_chk_session' => FALSE,
```

```
                                   'app_auto_connect'     => TRUE,
                                   'app_type'             => 'WEB',
                                   'app_debugger'         => $OFF
                                 )
                      );
    $thisApp->buffer_debugging();
    $thisApp->debug("This is $thisApp->app_name application");
    $thisApp->run();
    $thisApp->dump_debuginfo();
?>
```

The `logout.php` application calls the `is_authenticated()` method of the `class.PHPApplication.php` object and, if the user is authenticated, it calls its own logout method. This method calls the `session_unset()` and `session_destroy()` methods, which are part of PHP's built-in session management API. The `session_unset()` method simply makes the session variables as if they were never set before. The effect of `session_unset()` in our login scenario is that session variables such as `SESSION_USERNAME` and `SESSION_ATTEMPTS` are unset. Similarly, the `session_destroy()` method removes the entire session (file or database record) from the session storage. The full effect is that the user loses her session and will need a new login session to work with applications that require the central login facility.

The `logout.php` application uses the `logout.conf` file shown in Listing 5-8. This configuration file is very similar to the `login.conf` and requires no further explanation except that the `$HOME_URL` is a new entry. This variable sets the URL, which is used to redirect the logged out user to a central page. Typically this URL would be set to the home page of the intranet or Internet site.

Listing 5-8: `logout.conf`

```
<?php


    // login.conf

    //extract($_GET);
    //extract($_POST);


    // Turn on all error reporting
    error_reporting(E_ALL);

    // If you have installed framewirk directory in
    // a different directory than
    // %DocumentRoot%/framework, change the setting below.
```

Continued

Listing 5-8 *(Continued)*

```
$APP_FRAMEWORK_DIR=$_SERVER['DOCUMENT_ROOT'] . '/framework';
$PEAR            =$_SERVER['DOCUMENT_ROOT'] . '/pear';
$PHPLIB          =$_SERVER['DOCUMENT_ROOT'] . '/phplib';

// Insert the path in the PHP include_path so that PHP
// looks for PEAR, PHPLIB and our application framework
// classes in these directories
ini_set( 'include_path', ':' .
      $PEAR .    ':' .
      $PHPLIB . ':' .
      $APP_FRAMEWORK_DIR . ':' .
      ini_get('include_path'));

$PHP_SELF = $_SERVER["PHP_SELF"];

$LOGIN_TEMPLATE    = 'login.html';

$APPLICATION_NAME = 'LOGIN';
$DEFAULT_LANGUAGE = 'US';

$AUTH_DB_URL       = 'mysql://root:foobar@localhost/auth';
$ACTIVITY_LOG_TBL = 'ACTIVITY';
$AUTH_DB_TBL       = 'users';

$MIN_USERNAME_SIZE= 3;
$MIN_PASSWORD_SIZE= 3;
$MAX_ATTEMPTS = 250;
$FORGOTTEN_PASSWORD_APP =
'/user_mngr/apps/user_mngr_forgotten_pwd.php';

$APP_MENU        = '/';

$TEMPLATE_DIR      = $_SERVER['DOCUMENT_ROOT'] .
'/login/templates';
$REL_TEMPLATE_DIR  = '/login/templates/';
$WARNING_URL       = $TEMPLATE_DIR . '/warning.html';

require_once "login.errors";
require_once "login.messages";
require_once 'DB.php';
require_once $APP_FRAMEWORK_DIR . '/' . 'constants.php';
```

```
require_once $APP_FRAMEWORK_DIR . '/' . $DEBUGGER_CLASS;


require_once $APP_FRAMEWORK_DIR . '/' . $APPLICATION_CLASS;
require_once $APP_FRAMEWORK_DIR . '/' . $ERROR_HANDLER_CLASS;
require_once $APP_FRAMEWORK_DIR . '/' . $AUTHENTICATION_CLASS;
require_once $APP_FRAMEWORK_DIR . '/' . $DBI_CLASS;
require_once $APP_FRAMEWORK_DIR . '/' . $USER_CLASS;
require_once $TEMPLATE_CLASS;
?>
```

The logout application also has a `logout.errors` file, shown in Listing 5-9, and `logout.messages` file, shown in Listing 5-10.

Listing 5-9: `logout.errors`

```php
<?php

  // Errors for Logout application

  $ERRORS['US']['MISSING_CODE'] = "No error message found";

  $ERRORS['US']['INVALID_DATA'] = "Invalid data.";

?>
```

The logout messages are displayed using the `alert()` method found in the `class.PHPApplication.php` object.

Listing 5-10: `logout.messages`

```php
<?php

  // Messages for logout applications

  $MESSAGES['US']['LOGOUT_SUCCESSFUL']      = "You are logged out.";
  $MESSAGES['US']['LOGOUT_FAILURE']         = "You are not logged in.";
  $MESSAGES['US']['LOGOUT_NOT_LOGGED_IN']   = "You are not logged in.";

?>
```

Now let's test our central login and logout applications.

Creating the Central Authentication Database

Before you can use the login and logout applications, you need to create the central authentication database and then add a user to it. The central authentication database information is stored in both `login.conf` and `logout.conf` files using the following configuration variables:

```
$AUTH_DB_TYPE     = 'mysql';
$AUTH_DB_HOST     = 'localhost';
$AUTH_DB_NAME     = 'auth';
$AUTH_DB_TBL      = 'users';
$AUTH_DB_USERNAME = 'root';
$AUTH_DB_PASSWD   = 'foobar';
```

In our example, the database type is `mysql` and the database host name is `local-host`, which means we're implementing the database on the same server as a MySQL database. If you want to use a different database host or a different database server such as Postgres or Oracle, you have to change these variables. For our example, I assume that you're using the given sample values for `$AUTH_DB_TYPE`, `$AUTH_DB_HOST`, `$AUTH_DB_NAME`, and `$AUTH_DB_TBL`. However, I strongly suggest that you use different `$AUTH_DB_USERNAME` and `$AUTH_DB_PASSWD` values for your database.

Make sure that the user you specify in `$AUTH_DB_USERNAME` has the privilege to access (`select`, `insert`, `update`, and `delete`) `$AUTH_DB_NAME` on `$AUTH_DB_HOST`. You should test the user's ability to access this database using your standard database-access tools. For example, if you're using MySQL, you can run the command-line MySQL client as `mysql -u root -p -D auth` to access the authentication database.

Assuming that you're using the given settings, you can create a MySQL database called `auth` using the `mysqladmin create auth` command. You'll require appropriate permission to run `mysqladmin` or equivalent commands to create the `auth` database. Please consult your MySQL documentation for details.

Now to create the `$AUTH_DB_TBL` (users) table you can run the `users.sql` script using `mysql -u AUTH_DB_USERNAME -p -D AUTH_DB_NAME < auth.sql` command. The `auth.ddl` script is shown in Listing 5-11.

Listing 5-11: `auth.sql`

```
# phpMyAdmin MySQL-Dump
# version 2.2.5
# http://phpwizard.net/phpMyAdmin/
```

```
# http://phpmyadmin.sourceforge.net/ (download page)
#
# Host: localhost
# Generation Time: May 14, 2002 at 01:55 PM
# Server version: 3.23.35
# PHP Version: 4.1.0
# Database : `auth`
# --------------------------------------------------------


#
# Table structure for table `users`
#

CREATE TABLE users (
  UID int(11) NOT NULL auto_increment,
  EMAIL varchar(32) NOT NULL default '',
  PASSWORD varchar(128) NOT NULL default '',
  ACTIVE tinyint(4) NOT NULL default '0',
  TYPE tinyint(4) NOT NULL default '0',
  PRIMARY KEY  (UID),
  UNIQUE KEY EMAIL (EMAIL)
) TYPE=MyISAM COMMENT='User Authentication Table';
```

The table created using this script is described in Table 5-3.

TABLE 5-3 THE USER TABLE FIELDS

Field	Details
UID	This is the user ID field. This is automatically generated.
EMAIL	This is the username field. We use e-mail as the username in the login because e-mail is easy to remember and always unique for each person in an organization.
PASSWORD	This is the encrypted password.
ACTIVE	This is the active (1 or 0) field. If the value is 1, then the user is active and can log in. Otherwise, she cannot log in.
TYPE	The type of user is specified using this field. The type can be a number. Currently, we assume that the number 9 is the highest-ranking user, such as the administrator.

After this table is created, you can add a user, as explained in the following section, to test your login/logout applications.

Testing Central Login and Logout

To test the authentication system, you need to create users in the database. (User management applications are discussed Chapter 6.)

To create a user using the MySQL command-line tool you can run commands such as the following:

```
mysql -u root -p -D auth;
Enter password: *****
mysql> insert into users (EMAIL, PASSWORD, ACTIVE, TYPE)
values('admin@example.com', ENCRYPT('mysecret'), 1, 9);
```

Here the first line tells mysql to connect you to the auth database using username root and a password which you have to enter when asked. Of course if you are not using root account for this database, you should replace the username as appropriate.

Next at the mysql prompt, you can enter an INSERT statement as shown. Here the insert statement creates a user account called admin@example.com with password mysecret. You should change both the username and password to what you desire. The ACTIVE field is set to 1 to turn on the user and TYPE field is set to 9 to make this user an administrator. To create a regular user the TYPE field has to be set to 1.

The insert statement inserts a user named "admin@example.com" with a password called "mysecret" and sets the user's status to active. The user type is set to 9, which is the highest-ranking user type. If you want to create new users using this script, then you have to change the username and password and run the script to produce the insert statement.

After the user is added in the database you can run the login application from a Web browser. For example, Figure 5-7 shows the login application being called using the `http://intranet.evoknow.com/php/login/login.php` URL.

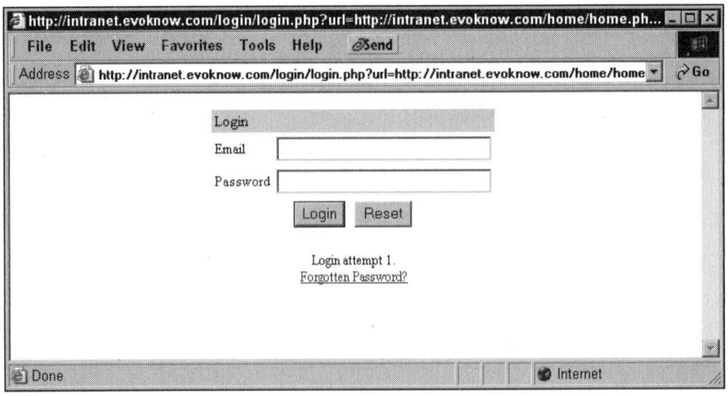

Figure 5-7: The login application menu.

Enter the newly created username and password and log in. If you cannot login, check to see if the user exists in the authentication database. Also, if the user is not active, the user cannot log in. You can check whether the active flag is working by toggling it using `update` statements such as follows from your MySQL database command line. The following code shows a MySQL command-line session, which sets the active flag to 0 (`ACTIVE = 0`) and again activates the admin user (`ACTIVE = 1`).

```
$ mysql -u AUTH_DB_USERNAME -p -D AUTH_DB_NAME

mysql> update users set ACTIVE = 0 where USERNAME =
'admin@example.com';
mysql> exit;

$ mysql -u AUTH_DB_USERNAME -p -D AUTH_DB_NAME

mysql> update users set ACTIVE = 1 where USERNAME =
'admin@example.com';
mysql> exit;
```

You can test the logout application by simply calling it directly using the appropriate URL. For example, `http://intranet.evoknow.com/php/logout/logout.php` will log out a user session.

Making Persistent Logins in Web Server Farms

Organizations with Web server farms will have to use site-wide persistent logins to ensure that users are not required to log in from one system to another. Figure 5-8 shows a typical Web server farm.

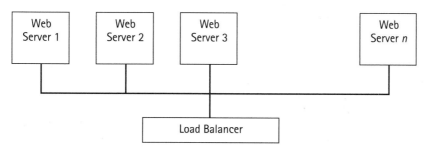

Figure 5-8: A typical Web server farm balances an organization's server workload.

Web server farms are often used to increase scalability and redundancy for the application services the organization provides. Such a farm usually implements all the applications in each server node so that any one of the servers can go down or become busy at any time but the user is directed to a server that is able to service the application request.

In such an environment, the session data cannot be stored in local files in each server node. Figure 5-9 shows what happens when file-based user sessions are used in a Web server farm.

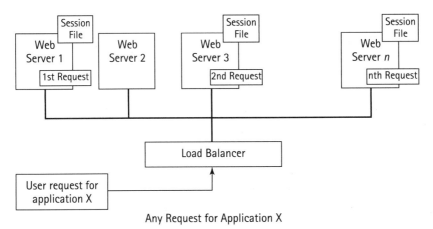

Figure 5-9: Why file-based sessions are not persistent in Web server farms.

When a user logs into a system using a file-based session, the file is stored in a single server and, in the next request, the user might be sent to a different server due to load or server failure. In such a case the next system will not have access to the session and will simply redirect the user to the login application to create a new login session. This can annoy and inconvenience the user, so a central database-based session solution is needed, which is shown in Figure 5-10.

To implement this solution, we need to define seven session management functions that PHP will use to implement sessions.

The functions are session_open(), sess_close(), sess_read(), sess_write(), sess_destroy(), sess_gc(), and session_set_save_handler(). The sess_open() function is called to start the session, the sess_close() function called when session is closed, the sess_read() function is called to read the session information, the sess_destroy() function is called when session is to be destroyed, the sess_gc() function is called when garbage collection needs to be done, and finally session_set_save_hander() is used to tell PHP the names of the other six session functions.

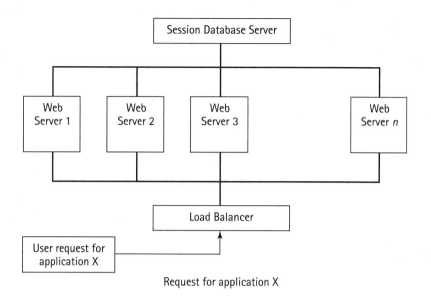

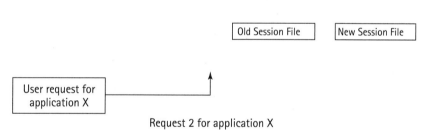

Figure 5-10: How database-based sessions persist in Web server farms.

Listing 5-12 shows libsession_handler.php which implements all these functions.

Listing 5-12: `lib.session_handler.php`

```php
<?php

error_reporting(E_ALL);
require_once('constants.php');
require_once('class.DBI.php');
require_once 'DB.php';

$DB_URL = "mysql://root:foobar@localhost:/sessions";

$dbi = new DBI($DB_URL);
```

Continued

Listing 5-12 *(Continued)*

```
$SESS_LIFE = get_cfg_var("session.gc_maxlifetime");

    function sess_open($save_path, $session_name) {
        return true;
    }

    function sess_close() {
        return true;
    }

    function sess_read($key) {
            global $dbi, $DEBUG, $SESS_LIFE;

            $statement = "SELECT value FROM sessions WHERE " .
                         "sesskey = '$key' AND expiry > " . time();

            $result = $dbi->query($statement);

            $row = $result->fetchRow();
            if ($row) {
                return $row->value;
            }

            return false;
    }

    function sess_write($key, $val) {
            global $dbi, $SESS_LIFE;

            $expiry = time() + $SESS_LIFE;
            $value = addslashes($val);

            $statement = "INSERT INTO sessions ".
                         "VALUES ('$key', $expiry, '$value')";
            $result = $dbi->query($statement);

            if (! $result) {
                    $statement = "UPDATE sessions SET " .
                                 " expiry = $expiry, value = '$value' " .
                                 " WHERE sesskey = '$key' AND expiry > " .
                                 time();
                    $result = $dbi->query($statement);
            }
```

```
            return $result;
    }

    function sess_destroy($key) {
            global $dbi;

            $statement = "DELETE FROM sessions WHERE sesskey = '$key'";
            $result = $dbi->query($statement);
            return $result;
    }

    function sess_gc($maxlifetime) {
            global $dbi;

            $statement = "DELETE FROM sessions WHERE expiry < " . time();
            $qid = $dbi->query($statement);
            return 1;
    }

    session_set_save_handler(
            "sess_open",
            "sess_close",
            "sess_read",
            "sess_write",
            "sess_destroy",
            "sess_gc");
?>
```

Here the sess_open(), sess_close(), sess_read(), sess_destory(), and sess_gc() methods use a DBI object from our class.DBI.php class to implement database-based session management. To implement this database-based session management in our framework, we need to do the following:

1. Place the lib.session_handler.php in the framework directory. For example, if you're keeping the class.PHPApplication.php in the /usr/php/framework directory, then you should put the lib.session_handler.php in the same directory.

2. Create a database called sessions using mysqladmin command such as mysqladmin -u root -p create sessions. You will need to know the username (here root) and password that is allowed to create databases. Next create a table called sessions using the sessions.ddl script with the mysql -u root -p -D sessions < sessions.sql command. Here's the sessions.sql:

```
CREATE TABLE sessions (
  sesskey varchar(32) NOT NULL default '',
  expiry int(11) NOT NULL default '0',
  value text NOT NULL,
  PRIMARY KEY  (sesskey)
) TYPE=MyISAM;
```

3. Modify the following line in lib.session_handler.php to reflect your user name, password, and database host name:

```
$DB_URL = "mysql://root:foobar@localhost:/sessions";
```

Here user name is root, password is foobar, and database host is local-host. You should change them if they're different for your system.

4. Add the following line at the beginning of the class.PHPApplication.php file.

```
require_once 'lib.session_handler.php';
```

After you've completed these steps, you can run your login application and see that sessions are being created in the sessions table in the sessions database. To view sessions in your sessions database, run mysql -u root -p -D sessions. When you're logged into the sessions database, you can view sessions using queries such as the following:

```
mysql> select * from sessions;
+----------------------------------+------------+----------------------+
| sesskey                          | expiry     | value                |
+----------------------------------+------------+----------------------+
| 3b6c2ce7ba37aa61a161faafbf8c24c7 | 1021365812 | SESSION_ATTEMPTS|i:3; |
+----------------------------------+------------+----------------------+
1 row in set (0.00 sec)


After a successful login:

mysql> select * from sessions;
+----------------------------------+------------+------------------------------
-+
| sesskey                          | expiry     | value
|
+----------------------------------+------------+------------------------------
-+
| 3b6c2ce7ba37aa61a161faafbf8c24c7 | 1021365820 |
SESSION_ATTEMPTS|i:3;SESSION_USERNAME|s:15:"joe@evoknow.com"; |
+----------------------------------+------------+------------------------------
-+
```

```
1 row in set (0.00 sec)
After logging out:

mysql> select * from sessions;
Empty set (0.00 sec)
```

You can see that the session is started after login.php and the session is removed once the user runs logout.php.

Summary

In this chapter you learned about a central authentication system which involves a login and logout application and a central authentication database. All PHP applications in your intranet or Web can use this central authentication facility. When an application is called directly by entering the URL in the Web browser, it can check for the existence of a session for the user and if an existing session is found, she is allowed access or else she is redirected to the login form. The logout application can be linked from any PHP application to allow the user log out at any time. Once logged out the session is removed. Having a central authentication system such as this helps you reduce the amount of code and maintenance you need to do for creating a seamless authentication process throughout your entire Web or intranet environment.

Chapter 6

Central User Management System

A CENTRAL USER MANAGEMENT system is a set of applications that enables you to manage users for your PHP applications in a central manner. Using the applications developed in this chapter you will be able to manage user accounts that are stored in the central authentication database created in the previous chapter.

Identifying the Functionality Requirements

First, let's define the functionality requirements for the user management system. The user manager must provide the following functionality:

♦ **Central user database:** The user manager must use a central user database. This is a requirement because of our central authentication architecture. If the user database is not central, we can't centrally authenticate the users.

♦ **Root user support:** A user should be identified as the root user, which cannot be deleted or deactivated by anyone including the root user itself.

♦ **Administrative user support:** The root user should be able to create other administrative users.

♦ **Standard user support:** A root or administrative user can create, modify, or delete a standard user account.

157

◆ **User password support:** A standard user can change her password at any time after logging in.

◆ **Password recovery support:** If a user forgets her password, she can recover it.

To implement these features we need a User object that can permit all of these operations on a user account.

Creating a User Class

The very first class that we need to build here is the User class, which will provide methods to add, modify, delete user accounts and also return various other information about an user.

User() is the constructor method for the User class. It sets the variables shown in Table 6-1.

TABLE 6-1 MEMBER VARIABLES SET IN User() **METHOD**

Member Variable	Value
user_tbl	Set to $USER_TBL, which is a global variable set in the user_mngr.conf file to point to the user table in the central authentication database.
dbi	Set to the DBI object passed as a parameter to the constructor.
minimum_username_size	Set to the user_mngr.conf configuration file variable, $MIN_USERNAME_SIZE, which sets the minimum size of the username allowed.
min_pasword_size	Set to the user_mngr.conf configuration file variable, MIN_PASSWORD_SIZE, which sets the minimum size of the password allowed.
USER_ID	Set to null or the user ID passed as parameter (if any).
user_tbl_fields	Set to an associative array, which creates a key value pair for each of the fields and field types (text or number) for the user table.

If the user ID is set in the constructor then it loads the user information by calling the getUserInfo() method in the class. The status of the getUserInfo()

method is stored as `is_user`, which can be `TRUE` or `FALSE` depending on whether user information was retrieved from the database.

A User class needs the following methods to implement all the operations needed for user management:

Methods	Description
isUser()	Returns `TRUE` if the current `user_id` number is really a user ID. If no user ID was supplied to the constructor method or the supplied-user ID does not point to a real user, this method returns `FALSE`.
getUserID()	Returns the current user ID.
setUserID()	Sets the current user ID if it is supplied or else it returns the current user ID set by the constructor method.
getUserIDByName()	Returns the user ID by given user name. When a valid username is given as the parameter, the method queries the user table to retrieve the appropriate user ID.
getUserTypeList()	Returns an associative array called `$USER_TYPE`, which is loaded from the `user_mngr.conf` file. The array defines the types of users allowed in the central user management system, and appears as follows: `$USER_TYPE = array('1' => 'Administrator', '2' => 'Standard User');`
getUID()	Returns the user ID (`USER_ID`) for the current User object.
getEMAIL()	Returns the e-mail address (`EMAIL`) for the current User object.
getPASSWORD()	Returns the password (`PASSWORD`) for the current User object.
getACTIVE()	Returns the active flag status of a User object.
getTYPE()	Returns the user type of the User object.
getUserFieldList()	Returns the array of user table fields.

Continued

Methods	Description
getUserInfo()	Returns user fields for a given or current user ID.
getUserList()	Returns a list of users in the current user table. The associative array returned contains each user's ID (USER_ID) as the key and username (EMAIL) as the value.
makeUpdateKeyValuePairs()	This is a utility method that returns a comma separated list of key =>value pairs, which can be used to update a user record.
updateUser()	Updates an user data. User data is passed to this method as an associative array called $data. This array is passed to the makeUpdateKeyValuePairs() method which returns a comma separated list of key=>value pairs used in SQL update statement inside the updateUser() method. This method returns TRUE if the update is successful and returns FALSE otherwise.
addUser()	Adds a new user in the user table in the central authentication database. New user record is passed to the method using the $data variable. The method first escapes and quotes the textual data and makes a list of key=>value pairs to be used in the insert statement. This method returns TRUE if the update is successful and returns FALSE otherwise.
deleteUser()	Returns the chosen (or current) user from the database.
getReturnValue()	Returns TRUE if the result parameter ($r) is set to DB_OK or else it returns FALSE. This method is used to see if a database query was successful or not.

Listing 6-1 shows a User class that provides the methods to implement all the operations needed for user management.

Listing 6-1: `class.User.php`

```php
<?php

   class User
   {
      function User($dbi = null, $uid = null)
      {

         global $AUTH_DB_TBL,
                $MIN_USERNAME_SIZE,
                $MIN_PASSWORD_SIZE,
                $ACTIVITY_LOG_TBL;


         $this->user_tbl          = $AUTH_DB_TBL;
         $this->user_activity_log = $ACTIVITY_LOG_TBL;
         $this->dbi               = $dbi;

         //print_r($this->dbi);

         $this->minmum_username_size = $MIN_USERNAME_SIZE;
         $this->minmum_pasword_size  = $MIN_PASSWORD_SIZE;

         $this->USER_ID  = $uid;

         //$this->debugger = $debugger;

         $this->user_tbl_fields = array('EMAIL'    => 'text',
                                        'PASSWORD' => 'text',
                                        'TYPE'     => 'number',
                                        'ACTIVE'   => 'number'
                                        );

         if (isset($this->USER_ID))
         {
            $this->is_user = $this->getUserInfo();
         } else {
            $this->is_user = FALSE;
         }
      }
```

Continued

Listing 6-1 *(Continued)*

```
function isUser()
{
    return $this->is_user;
}

function getUserID()
{
    return $this->USER_ID;
}

function setUserID($uid = null)
{
    if (! empty($uid))
    {
        $this->USER_ID = $uid;
    }

    return $this->USER_ID;
}

function getUserIDByName($name = null)
{

    if (! $name ) return null;

    $stmt   = "SELECT USER_ID FROM $this->user_tbl WHERE EMAIL = '$name'";

    $result = $this->dbi->query($stmt);

    if ($result != null)
    {
        $row = $result->fetchRow();

        return $row->USER_ID;
    }

    return null;

}

function getUserTypeList()
{
    global $USER_TYPE;

    return $USER_TYPE;
```

```
    }

    function getUID()
    {
        return (isset($this->USER_ID)) ? $this->USER_ID : NULL;
    }

    function getEMAIL()
    {
        return (isset($this->EMAIL)) ?  $this->EMAIL : NULL;
    }

    function getPASSWORD()
    {
        return (isset($this->PASSWORD)) ? $this->PASSWORD : NULL;
    }

    function getACTIVE()
    {
        return (isset($this->ACTIVE)) ? $this->ACTIVE : NULL;
    }

    function getTYPE()
    {
        return (isset($this->TYPE)) ? $this->TYPE : NULL;
    }

    function getUserFieldList()
    {
        return array('USER_ID', 'EMAIL', 'PASSWORD', 'ACTIVE', 'TYPE');
    }

    function getUserInfo($uid = null)
    {

        $fields   = $this->getUserFieldList();

        $fieldStr = implode(',', $fields);

        $this->setUserID($uid);

        $stmt    = "SELECT $fieldStr FROM $this->user_tbl " .
                   "WHERE USER_ID = $this->USER_ID";

        //echo "$stmt <P>";
```

Continued

Listing 6-1 *(Continued)*

```
        $result = $this->dbi->query($stmt);


        if ($result->numRows() > 0)
        {
            $row = $result->fetchRow();

            foreach($fields as $f)
            {
                $this->$f  = $row->$f;
            }

            return TRUE;

        }

        return FALSE;
    }



    function getUserIDbyEmail($email = null)          // needed for EIS
    {
        $stmt   = "SELECT USER_ID FROM $this->user_tbl " .
                  "WHERE EMAIL = '$email'";

        $result = $this->dbi->query($stmt);

        if($result->numRows() > 0)
        {
            $row = $result->fetchRow();

            return $row->USER_ID;

        } else {

            return 0;
        }
    }



    function getUserList()
    {
```

```
$stmt    = "SELECT USER_ID, EMAIL FROM $this->user_tbl";


$result = $this->dbi->query($stmt);

$retArray = array();

if ($result != null)
{
    while($row = $result->fetchRow())
    {
        $retArray[$row->USER_ID] = $row->EMAIL;
    }
}

return $retArray;

}


function makeUpdateKeyValuePairs($fields = null, $data = null)
{
    $setValues = array();

    while(list($k, $v) = each($fields))
    {

        if (isset($data[$k]))
        {
            //echo "DATA $k = $data[$k] <br>";

            if (! strcmp($v, 'text'))
            {
                $v = $this->dbi->quote(addslashes($data[$k]));

                $setValues[] = "$k = $v";

            } else {

                $setValues[] = "$k = $data[$k]";
            }
        }
    }
```

Continued

Listing 6-1 *(Continued)*

```
        return implode(', ', $setValues);
    }


    function updateUser($data = null)
    {

        $this->setUserID();

        $fieldList = $this->user_tbl_fields;

        $keyVal = $this->makeUpdateKeyValuePairs($this->user_tbl_fields,
$data);

        $stmt = "UPDATE $this->user_tbl SET $keyVal WHERE USER_ID = $this-
>USER_ID";

        $result = $this->dbi->query($stmt);

        return $this->getReturnValue($result);


    }

    function addUser($data = null)
    {

        $fieldList = $this->user_tbl_fields;
        $valueList = array();

        while(list($k, $v) = each($fieldList))
        {
           if (!strcmp($v, 'text'))
           {
              $valueList[] = $this->dbi->quote(addslashes($data[$k]));
           } else {
              $valueList[] = $data[$k];
           }
        }

        $fields = implode(',', array_keys($fieldList));
        $values = implode(',', $valueList);

        $stmt   = "INSERT INTO $this->user_tbl ($fields) VALUES($values)";
        //echo $stmt;
        $result = $this->dbi->query($stmt);
```

```
        return $this->getReturnValue($result);

    }

    function deleteUser($uid = null)
    {

        $this->setUserID($uid);


        $stmt = "DELETE from $this->user_tbl " .
                "WHERE USER_ID = $this->USER_ID";

        $result = $this->dbi->query($stmt);

        return $this->getReturnValue($result);
    }



    function getReturnValue($r = null)
    {
        return ($r == DB_OK) ? TRUE : FALSE;

    }

    function logActivity($action = null)
    {

        $now = time();

        $stmt = "INSERT INTO  $this->user_activity_log SET " .
                "USER_ID     = $this->USER_ID, ".
                "ACTION_TYPE = $action, " .
                "ACTION_TS = $now";

        // echo "$stmt <P>";

        $result = $this->dbi->query($stmt);

        return $this->getReturnValue($result);
    }
}
?>
```

User Interface Templates

Throughout the user management system, many user interface templates are needed to allow users and administrators to interact with the system. These templates are simple HTML forms with embedded tags, which are dynamically replaced to create the desired look and feel of the applications. These templates are supplied with the CD-ROM and are very simple in nature. These templates are:

◆ usermngr_menu.html - this template displays the user manager menu

◆ usermngr_user_form.html - this template is the user add/modify form

◆ usermngr_status.html - this template shows status of add/modify/delete etc.

◆ usermngr_pwd_change.html - this template is used for password changes

◆ usermngr_pwd_reset.html - this template is used to reset passwords

◆ usermngr_forgotten_pwd.html - this template is used as forgotten password request form.

◆ usermngr_forgotten_pwd_email.html - this template is used in e-mailing password reset request for those who have forgotten passwords

Creating a User Administration Application

The primary application in the central user management system is the user administration application. It enables the user administrator to do the following tasks:

◆ Add new user accounts

◆ Modify user accounts

◆ Toggle user account active flags

◆ Change user passwords

◆ Upgrade or downgrade users

◆ Delete user accounts

user_mngr.php is a user manager application that implements these features. Let's look at some of its main methods:

◆ run(): This method is used to run the application. It acts as a driver and performs the following tasks:

   ■ It checks to see if the user is authorized to run the application.

■ If the application is called with $cmd set to add, run() calls addDriver() to handle user add operation.

  If the application is called with $cmd set to modify, run() calls modifyDriver() to handle user modification operation.

  If the application is called with $cmd set to delete, run() calls deleteUser() to handle user delete operation.

  If the $cmd variable is not set, run() calls showScreen() to show the user management menu.

◆ addUser(): This method adds a user as follows:

1. It calls checkInput() to check user input supplied in add user interface.

2. It adds the default domain to the user's e-mail address if the username entered by the user does not include a domain name. For example, if the user enters carol as the username, addUser() sets the username to carol@evoknow.com assuming $DEFAULT_DOMAIN is set to evoknow.com.

3. It generates a two-character random string to be used as a salt for the crypt() function used to encrypt the user-supplied password.

4. It lowercases the username and creates a User object. An associative array is defined to hold the user-supplied data in a key=value manner. The keys are database field names for respective user data.

5. It uses the User object, $userObj, to call addUser(), which in turn adds the user in the database.

6. It displays a success or failure status message accordingly.

◆ modifyUser(): This method modifies a user account as follows:

1. It uses checkInput() to check user-supplied input.

2. If the user is trying to modify the root user account (identified by the $ROOT_USER variable loaded from the user_mngr.conf file), then the user is not allowed to deactivate the root user. Also, the root user account cannot be lowered to a standard account. This check is also performed and an appropriate alert message is displayed when such attempts are made by the administrator user.

3. It enters the user-supplied user type (TYPE), active flag (ACTIVE), and user ID (USER_ID) into an associative array called $hash.

4. If the user-supplied password does not match the dummy password (identified by the $DUMMY_PASSWD variable loaded from the user_mngr.conf file), modifyUser() encrypts the password using a random two-character-based salt string.

5. It uses $userObj to call getUserInfo() to load current user data into the object.

6. It stores modified username (EMAIL) in the $hash variable.

7. It uses the $uesrObj object's updateUser() method to update the user in the database.

8. It displays a success or failure status message as appropriate.

◆ **deleteUser():** This method, used to delete the chosen user, works as follows:

1. It displays an error message if the user ID is not supplied from the user interface.

2. It creates a User object, $userObj, and uses getUserInfo() to load the current user data.

3. It compares the chosen user's username (EMAIL) with the $ROOT_USER specified user's name to avoid deleting the root user account.

4. It uses $userObj's deleteUser() to perform the actual delete operation, removing the user from the database.

5. It displays a success or failure status message accordingly.

The following are the other functions/methods used in the user manager application:

Function	Description
modifyDriver()	This is the modify driver. It uses the form variable $step to control how the modify operation is implemented. When $step is not set, showScreen() is used to display the modify user interface. The user modify interface sets $step to 2, which is used to call modifyUser(). modifyUser() uses the User object's updateUser() method to modify the user account.
addDriver()	This is the add driver. It uses the form variable $step to control how an add operation is implemented. When $step is not set, showScreen() is used to display the add user interface. The user add interface sets $step to 2, which is used to call modifyUser(). modifyUser() uses the User object's addUser() method to add the user account.
menu()	Called by showScreen() to display the user management menu. It uses a User object called $userObj to get a list of existing users using the getUserList() function. The user list is displayed in the user interface for modification and deletion operation.

Function	Description
modify_screen()	Called by showScreen() to display the user modification interface. modify_screen() also uses a User object called $userObj to get current user information and display it on the interface.
add_screen()	Called by showScreen() to display the user add interface.
checkPassword()	Checks the user-entered password for length and confirmation tests.
checkInput()	Checks if the user has entered the username (EMAIL), user type (TYPE), and password (PASSWORD) information correctly from user interfaces displayed in user management.
authorize()	Determines if the user is authorized to run the application. If the user is not $ADMINISTRATIVE_USER, then the method returns FALSE. Otherwise, it returns TRUE.

Listing 6-2 shows the user manager application called user_mngr.php.

Listing 6-2: user_mngr.php

```php
<?php

   require_once "user_mngr.conf";

   require_once $USER_CLASS;

   class userManagerApp extends PHPApplication {

      function run()
      {
         global $USERMNGR_MNGR;

         $cmd = $this->getRequestField('cmd');


         if (! $this->authorize())
         {
            $this->alert('UNAUTHORIZED_ACCESS');
         }
```

Continued

Listing 6-2 *(Continued)*

```
        // At this point user is authorized

        $cmd = strtolower($cmd);

        if (!strcmp($cmd, 'add'))
        {
            $this->addDriver();

        } else if (!strcmp($cmd, 'modify')) {

            $this->modifyDriver();

        } else if (!strcmp($cmd, 'delete')) {

            $this->deleteUser();

        } else {

            global $USERMNGR_MENU_TEMPLATE;

            print $this->showScreen($USERMNGR_MENU_TEMPLATE,
                            'menu',
                            $USERMNGR_MNGR);

        }
    }


    function modifyDriver()
    {
        $step = $this->getRequestField('step');

        if ($step == 2)
        {
            $this->modifyUser();

        } else {

            global $USERMNGR_USER_TEMPLATE, $USERMNGR_MNGR;

            print $this->showScreen($USERMNGR_USER_TEMPLATE,
                            'modify_screen',
                            $USERMNGR_MNGR);
```

```
     }
}

function addDriver()
{
    $step = $this->getRequestField('step');

    if ($step == 2)
    {
        $this->addUser();

    } else {

        global $USERMNGR_USER_TEMPLATE, $USERMNGR_MNGR;

        print $this->showScreen($USERMNGR_USER_TEMPLATE,
                                'add_screen',
                                $USERMNGR_MNGR);
    }
}

function addUser()
{
    $username = $this->getRequestField('username');
    $password1 = $this->getRequestField('password1');
    $password2 = $this->getRequestField('password2');
    $user_type = $this->getRequestField('user_type');
    $active = $this->getRequestField('active');

    global $DEFAULT_DOMAIN,
           $USERMNGR_MNGR;

    $this->checkInput();

    if (!strstr($username,''))
    {
        $username = $username . '' . $DEFAULT_DOMAIN;
    }

    $salt = chr(rand(64,90)) . chr(rand(64,90));

    $cryptPassword = crypt($password1, $salt);
```

Continued

Listing 6-2 *(Continued)*

```php
$hash = array(
                'EMAIL'    => strtolower($username),
                'PASSWORD' => $cryptPassword,
                'TYPE'     => $user_type,
                'ACTIVE'   => $active
            );

$userObj = new User($this->dbi);

$status = $userObj->addUser($hash);

if ($status)
{
    $this->show_status($this->getMessage('USER_ADD_SUCCESSFUL'),
                    $USERMNGR_MNGR);
} else {
    $this->show_status($this->getMessage('USER_ADD_FAILED'),
                    $USERMNGR_MNGR);
}

}


function modifyUser()
{
    $username = $this->getRequestField('username');
    $password1 = $this->getRequestField('password1');
    $password2 = $this->getRequestField('password2');
    $user_type = $this->getRequestField('user_type');
    $active = $this->getRequestField('active');
    $user_id = $this->getRequestField('user_id');

    global $USERMNGR_MNGR,
           $ADMINISTRATIVE_USER,
           $ROOT_USER,
           $DUMMY_PASSWD;

    $this->checkInput();

    // If user is ROOT USER then she cannot be deactivated
    if ( ! strcmp($username, $ROOT_USER))
```

```
{
    if (! $active )
    {
      $this->alert('INACTIVE_NOT_OK');
      return;
    }

    if ($user_type != $ADMINISTRATIVE_USER)
    {
      $this->alert('OPERATION_NOT_ALLOWED');
      return;
    }

}

$hash = array(
                'TYPE'    => $user_type,
                'ACTIVE'  => $active,
                'USER_ID' => $user_id
            );

if (strcmp($password1, $DUMMY_PASSWD))
{

    $salt = chr(rand(64,90)) . chr(rand(64,90));
    $cryptPassword    = crypt($password1, $salt);
    $hash['PASSWORD'] = $cryptPassword;
}



$userObj = new User($this->dbi, $user_id);

$userObj->getUserInfo();

$hash['EMAIL'] = (strcmp($username,
                  $userObj->getEMAIL())) ? strtolower($username) :
null;

$status = $userObj->updateUser($hash);
```

Continued

Listing 6-2 *(Continued)*

```
         if ($status)
         {
            $this->show_status($this->getMessage('USER_MODIFY_SUCCESSFUL'),
                               $USERMNGR_MNGR);
         } else {
            $this->show_status($this->getMessage('USER_MODIFY_FAILED'),
                               $USERMNGR_MNGR);
         }
      }

      function deleteUser()
      {
         global $USERMNGR_MNGR,
                $ROOT_USER;

         $user_id = $this->getRequestField('user_id');

         $this->emptyError($user_id, 'USER_ID_MISSING');


         $userObj = new User($this->dbi, $user_id);

         $userObj >getUserInfo();

         $email = $userObj->getEMAIL();

         if (! strcmp($email, $ROOT_USER))
         {
            $this->alert('USER_DELETE_NOT_ALLOWED');

         } else {

            $status = $userObj->deleteUser();
         }

         if ($status)
         {
            $this->show_status($this->getMessage('USER_DELETE_SUCCESSFUL'),
                               $USERMNGR_MNGR);
         } else {
            $this->show_status($this->getMessage('USER_DELETE_FAILED'),
                               $USERMNGR_MNGR);
         }

      }
```

```
function menu(&$t)
{
    $userObj = new User($this->dbi);
    $users = $userObj->getUserList();

    $t->set_block('mainBlock','userBlock', 'ublock');

    while(list($uid, $email) = each($users))
    {
        $t->set_var( array(
                            'USER_ID'   => $uid,
                            'USER_NAME' => $email,
                            )
                    );

        $t->parse('ublock', 'userBlock', true);
    }


    return TRUE;
}


function modify_screen(&$t)
{

    global $DUMMY_PASSWD;

    $user_id = $this->getRequestField('user_id');

    $userObj = new User($this->dbi, $user_id);

    $status = $userObj->getUserInfo();

    if (! $status)
    {

        $this->alert('USER_INFO_MISSING');

    } else {

        $userType = $userObj->getTYPE();

    }
```

Continued

Listing 6-2 *(Continued)*

```
$userTypes = $userObj->getUserTypeList();

$t->set_block('mainBlock','typeBlock', 'tblock');

$chosen = '';

while(list($tid, $typeName) = each($userTypes))
{

    $chosen = ($tid == $userType) ? 'selected' : '';

    $t->set_var(
                array(
                        'TYPE_ID'   => $tid,
                        'USER_TYPE' => $typeName,
                        'CHOSEN'    => $chosen
                        )
                );

    $t->parse('tblock', 'typeBlock', true);

}

$fields = $userObj->getUserFieldList();

foreach ($fields as $f)
{
   $t->set_var($f, null);
}

$activeON  = ( $userObj->getACTIVE()) ? 'checked' : null;
$activeOFF = (!$userObj->getACTIVE()) ? 'checked' : null;

$t->set_var(array(
                'EMAIL'      => $userObj->getEMAIL(),
                'PASSWORD'   => $DUMMY_PASSWD,
                'ACTIVE_ON'  => $activeON,
                'ACTIVE_OFF' => $activeOFF,
                'ACTION'     => 'modify',
                'USER_ID'    => $user_id
                )
            );

    return TRUE;

}
```

```
function add_screen(&$t)
{
   $userObj = new User($this->dbi);
   $userTypes = $userObj->getUserTypeList();

   $t->set_block('mainBlock','typeBlock', 'tblock');

   $chosen = '';

   while(list($tid, $typeName) = each($userTypes))
   {
      $t->set_var( array(
                         'TYPE_ID'   => $tid,
                         'USER_TYPE' => $typeName,
                         'CHOSEN'    => $chosen
                         )
                 );

      $t->parse('tblock', 'typeBlock', true);
   }

   $fields = $userObj->getUserFieldList();

   foreach ($fields as $f)
   {
      $t->set_var($f, null);
   }

   $t->set_var('ACTIVE_ON', 'selected');
   $t->set_var('ACTIVE_OFF', null);
   $t->set_var('ACTION', 'add');

   return TRUE;

}

function checkPassword($pwd1, $pwd2)
{

   global $MIN_PASSWORD_SIZE, $DUMMY_PASSWD;

   $this->emptyError($pwd1, 'PASSWORD1_MISSING');
   $this->emptyError($pwd2, 'PASSWORD2_MISSING');
```

Continued

Listing 6-2 *(Continued)*

```
        if (strcmp($pwd1, $pwd2))
        {
           $this->alert('PASSWORD_MISMATCH');

        } else if (strlen($pwd1) < $MIN_PASSWORD_SIZE) {

           $this->alert('INVALID_PASSWORD');

        }

    }

    function checkInput()
    {
        $username = $this->getRequestField('username');
        $password1 = $this->getRequestField('password1');
        $password2 = $this->getRequestField('password2');
        $user_type = $this->getRequestField('user_type');

        $this->emptyError($username, 'USERNAME_MISSING');
        $this->emptyError($user_type, 'USER_TYPE_MISSING');
        $this->checkPassword($password1, $password2);

    }

    function authorize()
    {
        global $ADMINISTRATIVE_USER;

        $userObj = new User($this->dbi, $this->getUID());

        $type = $userObj->getTYPE();


        return ($type == $ADMINISTRATIVE_USER) ? TRUE : FALSE;

    }

}//class

$SESSION_USERNAME = null;
$SESSION_USER_ID  = null;
global $APP_DB_URL;
```

```
$thisApp = new userManagerApp(
                        array( 'app_name'     => $APPLICATION_NAME,
                               'app_version'  => '1.0.0',
                               'app_type'     => 'WEB',
                               'app_db_url'   => $APP_DB_URL,
                               'app_auto_authorize' => FALSE,
                               'app_auto_connect' => TRUE,
                               'app_auto_chk_session' => FALSE,
                               'app_debugger' => $ON
                               )
                        );

    //$thisApp->buffer_debugging();
    $thisApp->run();
    //$thisApp->dump_debuginfo();
?>
```

Configuring user administration applications

The user manager application and all the other applications in the user management system require configuration information that is stored in user_mngr.conf. Table 6-2 shows the configuration settings.

TABLE 6-2 USER MANAGER CONFIGURATION

Variable	Purpose
$PEAR_DIR	Set to the directory containing the PEAR package; specifically the DB module needed for class.DBI.php in our application framework.
$PHPLIB_DIR	Set to the PHPLIB directory, which contains the PHPLIB packages; specifically the template. inc package needed for template manipulation.
$APP_FRAMEWORK_DIR	Set to our application framework directory.

Continued

TABLE 6-2 USER MANAGER CONFIGURATION *(Continued)*

Variable	Purpose
$PATH	Set to the combined directory path consisting of the $PEAR_DIR, the $PHPLIB_DIR, and the $APP_FRAMEWORK_DIR. This path is used with the ini_set() method to redefine the php.ini entry for include_path to include $PATH ahead of the default path. This allows PHP to find our application framework, PHPLIB, and PEAR-related files.
$AUTHENTICATION_URL	Set to the central login application URL.
$LOGOUT_URL	Set to the central logout application URL.
$APPLICATION_NAME	The internal name of the application.
$DEFAULT_LANGUAGE	Set to the default (two character) language code.
$DEFAULT_DOMAIN	Set to the default domain of the user. This domain is appended when the user does not specify the fully qualified username (user@host) during interaction with the user management applications.
$ROOT_PATH	Set to the parent directory within the Web server's document root where the user-manager-specific directory exists as a subdirectory.
$REL_APP_PATH	The relative application path as seen from Web browser.
$TEMPLATE_DIR	Set to the template directory containing the ihtml template files needed for the user management applications.
$CLASS_DIR	Set to the class directory where user-management-related class files are stored.
$USER_CLASS	Fully qualified pathname for the User class.
$MIN_USERNAME_SIZE	Minimum user name (EMAIL) size.
$MIN_PASSWORD_SIZE	Minimum password size.

Variable	Purpose
$DUMMY_PASSWD	Dummy password used during account modification step.
$ROOT_USER	Fully qualified username of the root user
$SECRET	A secret random number used in checksum generation, which is used when forgotten password URL links are sent via e-mail.
$CHAR_SET	Default character set to be used in e-mail content type header.
$USERMNGR_MNGR	Name of the user manager application.
$USERMNGR_FORGOTTEN_APP	Name of the forgotten password application.
$USERMNGR_CHANGE_PWD_APP	Name of the change password application.
$REL_TEMPLATE_DIR	Relative path to the template directory as seen from the Web.
$APP_DB_URL	The fully qualified database URL needed to access the user database.
$USER_TBL	Name of the user table.
$STATUS_TEMPLATE	Name of the status information display template.
$USERMNGR_MENU_TEMPLATE	Name of the user management menu template.
$USERMNGR_USER_TEMPLATE	Name of the user add/modify form template.
$USERMNGR_PWD_REQUEST_TEMPLATE	Name of the password change template.
$USERMNGR_PWD_EMAIL_TEMPLATE	Name of the e-mail template, which is used to send the e-mail message for forgotten passwords.
$USERMNGR_PWD_RESET_TEMPLATE	Name of the forgotten password reset template.
$USERMNGR_PWD_CHANGE_TEMPLATE	Name of the password change template.
$ADMINISTRATIVE_USER	Numeric type value for administrative user.
$STANDARD_USER	Numeric type value for standard user.
$USER_TYPE	Associative array defining the relationship between the numeric user type and user type labels.

Listing 6-3 shows the configuration file (`user_mngr.conf`).

Listing 6-3: `user_mngr.conf`

```php
<?php

    // Turn on all error reporting
    error_reporting(E_ALL);

    // If you have installed framework directory in
    // a different directory than
    // %DocumentRoot%/framework, change the setting below.
    $APP_FRAMEWORK_DIR=$_SERVER['DOCUMENT_ROOT'] . '/framework';
    $PEAR            =$_SERVER['DOCUMENT_ROOT'] . '/pear';
    $PHPLIB          =$_SERVER['DOCUMENT_ROOT'] . '/phplib';

    // Insert the path in the PHP include_path so that PHP
    // looks for PEAR, PHPLIB and our application framework
    // classes in these directories
    ini_set( 'include_path', ':' .
        $PEAR .   ':' .
        $PHPLIB . ':' .
        $APP_FRAMEWORK_DIR . ':' .
        ini_get('include_path'));

    $AUTHENTICATION_URL = "/login/login.php";
    $LOGOUT_URL        = "/logout/logout.php";

    $APP_MENU          = '/home/home.php';

    $APPLICATION_NAME  = 'USER_MNGR';

    $XMAILER_ID        = 'Example User Manager Version 1.0';

    $DEFAULT_LANGUAGE  = 'US';
    $DEFAULT_DOMAIN    = 'example.com';
    $ROOT_PATH         = $_SERVER['DOCUMENT_ROOT'];
    $REL_ROOT_PATH     = '/user_mngr';
    $REL_APP_PATH      =  $REL_ROOT_PATH . '/apps';

    $TEMPLATE_DIR      = $ROOT_PATH      . $REL_APP_PATH . '/templates';
    $CLASS_DIR         = $ROOT_PATH      . $REL_APP_PATH . '/class';
    $REL_TEMPLATE_DIR  =  $REL_APP_PATH . '/templates/';
```

```
require_once "user_mngr.errors";
require_once "user_mngr.messages";
require_once 'DB.php';
require_once $APP_FRAMEWORK_DIR . '/' . 'constants.php';
require_once $APP_FRAMEWORK_DIR . '/' . $APPLICATION_CLASS;
require_once $APP_FRAMEWORK_DIR . '/' . $ERROR_HANDLER_CLASS;
require_once $APP_FRAMEWORK_DIR . '/' . $AUTHENTICATION_CLASS;
require_once $APP_FRAMEWORK_DIR . '/' . $DBI_CLASS;
require_once $APP_FRAMEWORK_DIR . '/' . $USER_CLASS;
require_once $TEMPLATE_CLASS;

$MIN_USERNAME_SIZE= 3;
$MIN_PASSWORD_SIZE= 3;
$DUMMY_PASSWD = '1234567890';
$ROOT_USER      = 'kabir@evoknow.com';
$SECRET         = 916489;
$CHAR_SET       = 'charset=iso-8859-1';

// Application names

$USERMNGR_MNGR              = 'user_mngr.php';
$USERMNGR_FORGOTTEN_APP     = 'user_mngr_forgotten_pwd.php';
$USERMNGR_CHANGE_PWD_APP    = 'user_mngr_passwd.php';


/* -------------START TABLE NAMES --------------------- */
$APP_DB_URL        = 'mysql://root:foobar@localhost/auth';
$AUTH_DB_TBL       = 'users';



/* -------------END TABLE NAMES --------------------- */

$STATUS_TEMPLATE               = 'usermngr_status.html';
$USERMNGR_MENU_TEMPLATE        = 'usermngr_menu.html';
$USERMNGR_USER_TEMPLATE        = 'usermngr_user_form.html';
$USERMNGR_PWD_REQUEST_TEMPLATE= 'usermngr_forgotten_pwd.html';
$USERMNGR_PWD_EMAIL_TEMPLATE   = 'usermngr_forgotten_pwd_email.html';
$USERMNGR_PWD_RESET_TEMPLATE   = 'usermngr_pwd_reset.html';
$USERMNGR_PWD_CHANGE_TEMPLATE = 'usermngr_pwd_change.html';

$ADMINISTRATIVE_USER = 9;
$STANDARD_USER = 1;
$USER_TYPE = array('9' => 'Administrator', '1' => 'Standard User');

?>
```

Make sure you change this file to adjust the file and directory path information
as needed.

Configuring user administration application messages

Like any other application in our application framework, all user management applications need to have an external message file that contains all the internationalized messages printed from applications. Listing 6-4 shows such a message file, called `user_mngr.messages`.

Listing 6-4: `user_mngr.messages`

```php
<?php

    $MESSAGES['US']['USER_ADD_SUCCESSFUL']      = "User added.";
    $MESSAGES['US']['USER_ADD_FAILED']          = "User not added.";

    $MESSAGES['US']['USER_MODIFY_SUCCESSFUL']   = "User modified.";
    $MESSAGES['US']['USER_MODIFY_FAILED']       = "User not modified.";

    $MESSAGES['US']['USER_DELETE_SUCCESSFUL']   = "User deleted.";
    $MESSAGES['US']['USER_DELETE_FAILED']       = "User not deleted.";

    $MESSAGES['US']['USER_INFO_MISSING']        = "Cannot locate user
information.";

    $MESSAGES['US']['PWD_EMAIL_SENT']           = "An email with password reset
link has been sent to you.";
    $MESSAGES['US']['PWD_EMAIL_NOT_SENT']       = "Could not send email due to
mail problem. Try later.";

?>
```

Configuring user administration application error messages

Again, like any other application in our application framework, all user management applications need to have an external error message file that contains all the internationalized error messages printed from applications. Listing 6-5 shows such an error message file, called `user_mngr.errors`.

Listing 6-5: `user_mngr.errors`

```php
<?php

    // Errors for user manager apps

    $ERRORS['US']['APP_FAILURE']                = "Application failure";
```

```
    $ERRORS['US']['UNAUTHORIZED_ACCESS']       = "You do not have privilege to
access this application.";
    $ERRORS['US']['INVALID_REQUEST']           = "Invalid request.";

    $ERRORS['US']['USERNAME_MISSING']          = "Please enter email as the
username.";
    $ERRORS['US']['PASSWORD1_MISSING']         = "Please enter password.";
    $ERRORS['US']['PASSWORD2_MISSING']         = "Please enter confirmation
password.";
    $ERRORS['US']['USER_TYPE_MISSING']         = "Please select user type.";
    $ERRORS['US']['PASSWORD_MISMATCH']         = "Passwords do not match.";
    $ERRORS['US']['PASSWORD_MISMATCH']         = "Password and confirmation password
do not match.";
    $ERRORS['US']['INVALID_PASSWORD']          = "This password is too short or
invalid .";

    $ERRORS['US']['USER_DELETE_NOT_ALLOWED'] = "This (root) user cannot be
deleted.";
    $ERRORS['US']['USER_NOT_FOUND']            = "User not found.";
    $ERRORS['US']['INACTIVE_NOT_OK']           = "This (root) user cannot be
deactivated.";
    $ERRORS['US']['OPERATION_NOT_ALLOWED']     = "You cannot reduce privilege of a
root user.";

?>
```

Testing the user management application

After you've created class.User.php, user_mngr.php, user_mngr.conf,
user_mngr.messages, and user_mngr.errors files in the appropriate directories
as configured in user_mngr.conf, you can test the application. In this section, I
will assume that the user manager application is installed in the following directory
structure and accessible by http://php.evoknow.com/ /user_mngr/apps/
user_mngr.php.

```
    (%DOCUMENT_ROOT)
      +---user_mngr
          |
          +---apps
              |
              +---templates
```

To access the user manager application for the first time, you need the admin account created in Chapter 5.

When you try to access the `user_mngr.php` application it will redirect you to the central login application unless you're already logged in. Enter the admin username and password created in Chapter 5.

You should now see the main user management interface, as shown in Figure 6-1.

Figure 6-1: The user management menu.

This menu enables you to add, modify, and delete users in the entire system. To create a new user, click on the Add User button, which displays the interface shown in Figure 6-2.

Enter new user information and click on Add User button to create the new user. If you choose to make a new user inactive, the new user cannot log in until you change his account to active.

 When creating a new user, you don't need to enter the host name part of the username (EMAIL) if the user's host name matches the $DEFAULT_DOMAIN setting specified in the `user_mngr.conf` file.

When you've added the user, her username (EMAIL) appears in the list of existing users that you can modify or delete. To modify a user, select the username from the drop-down list on the user manager interface (refer to Figure 6-1), click the Modify User button, and change information as needed on the modify-user interface, shown in Figure 6-3.

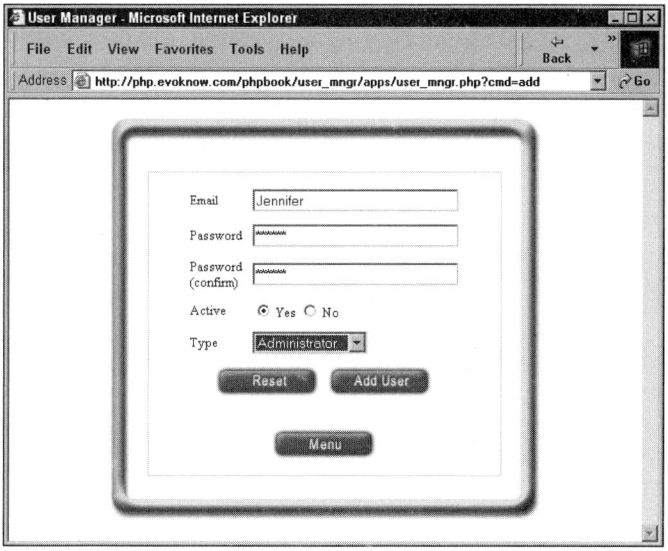

Figure 6-2: Adding a new user.

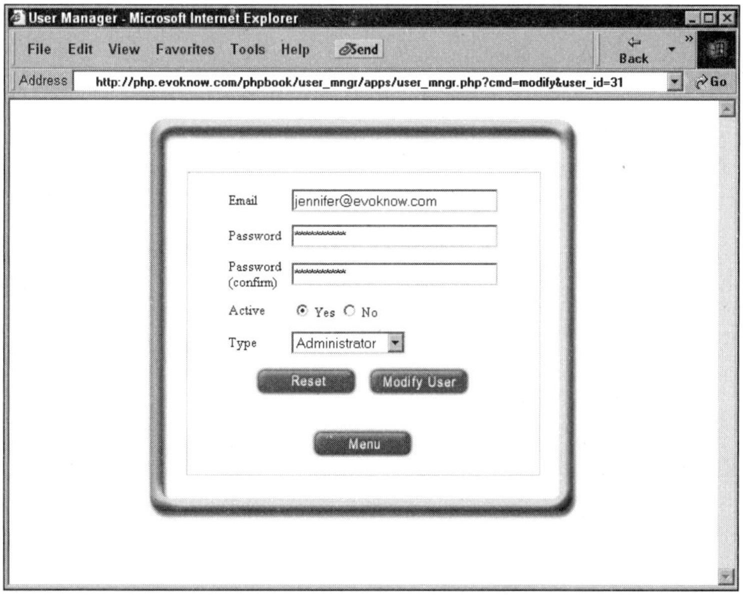

Figure 6-3: Modifying an existing user.

You can delete a user other than the root user at any time. To delete a user, select the username from the drop-down list on the user manager interface, and click the Delete User button. Be warned that the delete operation is irreversible. However, you cannot delete the root user, which is set in the $ROOT_USER variable in the configuration file.

Don't attempt to deactivate the root user or downgrade a root user's type from administrator to standard. This will create a problem since you will not be able to manage users until you manually fix this.

Creating a User Password Application

Users should be able to change their passwords without the need to inform the user administrator, so the central user management system needs a user password-changing tool. We'll use a user password application called user_mngr_passwd.php.

Let's look at the methods implemented in this application.

changePassword() is the method used to actually implement the password change, and it:

1. Uses checkPassword() to check the new password against the confirmation password and makes sure they are same. If they are not same, the method shows an alert message.

2. Generates a random two-character salt string to encrypt the new password.

3. Uses $userObj to call the updateUser() method to change the current password with the new password.

4. Displays the success or failure status of the updateUser() operation on the screen.

Following are the other methods used in the user password application:

Method	Description
run()	Calls the changePasswordDriver() method to change the password.
changePasswordDriver()	Uses the form variable $step to manage the password-change process. If $step is not set, showScreen() is used to display the password-change request form. If $step is set to 2 in the change request form, changePassword() is used to change the password.

Method	Description
checkPassword()	Checks the user-supplied new password. If the new password is empty, does not match the confirmation password, violates the minimum length limit, or matches the dummy password, it displays the appropriate alert message.
change_pwd()	This method is called by showScreen() to display the password-change interface.
authorize()	Checks if the current user is authorized to run the application. Because anyone can run this application, this method uses the isUser() method with a User object called $userObj to return TRUE or FALSE status accordingly.

Listing 6-6 shows the user password application user_mngr_passwd.php.

Listing 6-6: user_mngr_passwd.php

```php
<?php

// Turn on all error reporting
error_reporting(E_ALL);

// If you have installed framewirk directory in
// a different directory than
// %DocumentRoot%/framework, change the setting below.
$APP_FRAMEWORK_DIR=$_SERVER['DOCUMENT_ROOT'] . '/framework';
$PEAR           =$_SERVER['DOCUMENT_ROOT'] . '/pear';
$PHPLIB         =$_SERVER['DOCUMENT_ROOT'] . '/phplib';

// Insert the path in the PHP include_path so that PHP
// looks for PEAR, PHPLIB and our application framework
// classes in these directories
ini_set( 'include_path', ':' .
    $PEAR .   ':' .
    $PHPLIB . ':' .
    $APP_FRAMEWORK_DIR . ':' .
    ini_get('include_path'));
```

Continued

Listing 6-6 *(Continued)*

```php
$AUTHENTICATION_URL = "/login/login.php";
$LOGOUT_URL         = "/logout/logout.php";


$APP_MENU           = '/home/home.php';


$APPLICATION_NAME   = 'USER_MNGR';


$XMAILER_ID         = 'Example User Manager Version 1.0';


$DEFAULT_LANGUAGE   = 'US';
$DEFAULT_DOMAIN     = 'example.com';
$ROOT_PATH          = $_SERVER['DOCUMENT_ROOT'];
$REL_ROOT_PATH      = '/user_mngr';
$REL_APP_PATH       =  $REL_ROOT_PATH . '/apps';


$TEMPLATE_DIR       = $ROOT_PATH    . $REL_APP_PATH . '/templates';
$CLASS_DIR          = $ROOT_PATH    . $REL_APP_PATH . '/class';
$REL_TEMPLATE_DIR   =  $REL_APP_PATH . '/templates/';



require_once "user_mngr.errors";
require_once "user_mngr.messages";
require_once 'DB.php';
require_once $APP_FRAMEWORK_DIR . '/' . 'constants.php';
require_once $APP_FRAMEWORK_DIR . '/' . $APPLICATION_CLASS;
require_once $APP_FRAMEWORK_DIR . '/' . $ERROR_HANDLER_CLASS;
require_once $APP_FRAMEWORK_DIR . '/' . $AUTHENTICATION_CLASS;
require_once $APP_FRAMEWORK_DIR . '/' . $DBI_CLASS;
require_once $APP_FRAMEWORK_DIR . '/' . $USER_CLASS;
require_once $TEMPLATE_CLASS;


$MIN_USERNAME_SIZE= 3;
$MIN_PASSWORD_SIZE= 3;
$DUMMY_PASSWD = '1234567890';
$ROOT_USER    = 'kabir@evoknow.com';
$SECRET       = 916489;
$CHAR_SET     = 'charset=iso-8859-1';

// Application names

$USERMNGR_MNGR             =  'user_mngr.php';
$USERMNGR_FORGOTTEN_APP    =  'user_mngr_forgotten_pwd.php';
$USERMNGR_CHANGE_PWD_APP   =  'user_mngr_passwd.php';
```

```
/*  -------------START TABLE NAMES ---------------------  */
$APP_DB_URL          = 'mysql://root:foobar@localhost/auth';
$AUTH_DB_TBL         = 'users';



/*  --------------END TABLE NAMES ---------------------  */

$STATUS_TEMPLATE              = 'usermngr_status.html';
$USERMNGR_MENU_TEMPLATE       = 'usermngr_menu.html';
$USERMNGR_USER_TEMPLATE       = 'usermngr_user_form.html';
$USERMNGR_PWD_REQUEST_TEMPLATE= 'usermngr_forgotten_pwd.html';
$USERMNGR_PWD_EMAIL_TEMPLATE  = 'usermngr_forgotten_pwd_email.html';
$USERMNGR_PWD_RESET_TEMPLATE  = 'usermngr_pwd_reset.html';
$USERMNGR_PWD_CHANGE_TEMPLATE = 'usermngr_pwd_change.html';

$ADMINISTRATIVE_USER = 9;
$STANDARD_USER = 1;
$USER_TYPE = array('9' => 'Administrator', '1' => 'Standard User');

?>
```

This application can be run after a user is logged in to the system. Its interface is shown in Figure 6-4.

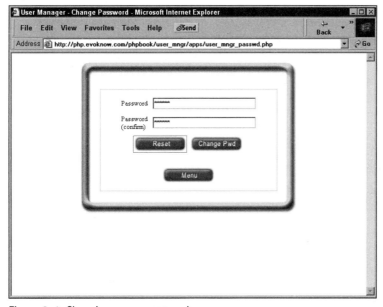

Figure 6-4: Changing a user password.

A user enters the new password in the Password field, confirms the new password in the Password (confirm) field, and clicks the Change Pwd button to submit the change request. The user is shown a status message stating that the password has been changed. From the next login, she will be required to enter the new password at the central login prompt.

Creating a Forgotten-Password Recovery Application

If Murphy were alive today, surely he would have added a new law about forgotten passwords in his famous "Murphy's Laws" list. It would probably go something like the following: *If a user is given a password, it will be forgotten.*

Passwords are often forgotten due to the "Remember my password" feature in many desktop applications — which caches the password for easy access, freeing the user from having to remember it — or because users have to try to remember several passwords, different ones for different applications.

In our application architecture, each user needs to know a single password. Forgetting the password will be very annoying because the user will not be able to access any applications until the password is reset.

Ideally, there should be a way for the user to recover the forgotten password. However, our central authentication system uses cryptographic (one-way hash) passwords, so there is no way for the system to determine what the original password is if the user fails to supply the correct one.

So instead of recovering the old password, we will allow the user to recover from the forgotten password state by replacing her forgotten password with a new one.

Figure 6-5 shows a functional diagram of this recovery process.

Here's how the recovery process works:

1. The user tries to log in using the wrong password.

2. The central login application rejects the login attempt.

3. The user clicks the link to the forgotten-password recovery application and enters her e-mail address and clicks on Send Mail button.

4. The forgotten-password recovery application sends the user an e-mail that includes a URL.

5. The user clicks the URL and is taken to a password-change form, which she fills out using a new password.

6. The user submits the form. The application stores the new password and returns a success message.

7. The user can now log in using the new password.

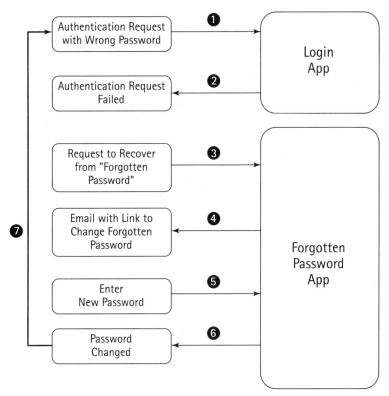

Figure 6-5: A user recovering from the "forgotten password" state.

In the following section, I discuss how to design, develop, and test a forgotten-password application that works with our central authentication framework.

Designing the forgotten-password recovery application

We know what we want the application to do, so now we need a flow diagram of the application, as shown in Figure 6-6.

As the flowchart indicates, when the application is starts (Step 1), it gets an e-mail address from the user. If the e-mail address belongs to an existing user, the application sends an e-mail to the user with a URL that has embedded information to allow the user to call the same application. The embedded URL in the e-mail has step=2 set so that the application can determine which step is next.

In Step 2 mode, the application verifies that the information supplied with the URL is valid and came from the e-mail sent earlier. It then allows the user to enter a new password.

If the new password is acceptable – that is, it meets the minimum password size requirement – it is encrypted and stored in the database.

Now let's look at how you can implement this flow diagram into an application.

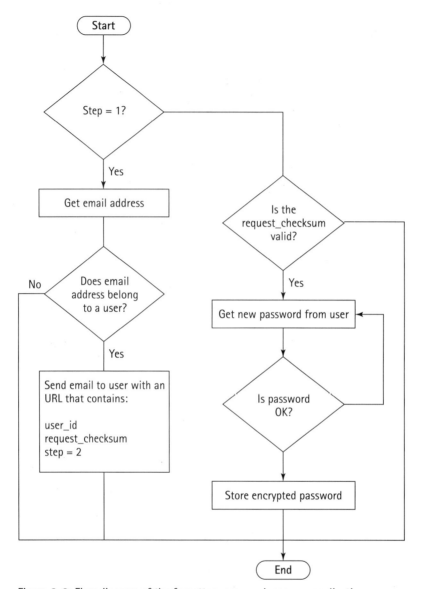

Figure 6-6: Flow diagram of the forgotten-password recovery application.

Implementing the forgotten-password recovery application

The forgotten-password recovery application implements the methods:

◆ resetPasswordDriver(): This method uses the global form variable, $step, to determine phases of the forgotten password recovery process. The tasks performed by this method are as follows:

1. When $step is unset, the first step in the process is assumed and the user is provided an interface to enter her username (EMAIL) address.

2. When the user has entered the username, the interface supplies a new value (2) for $step, which is embedded as a hidden field within the HTML form displayed in the first step.

3. In the second step, the method calls sendEmail() to send an e-mail to the user with a link that enables her to return to this application and enter the third step.

4. When the user clicks on the e-mailed link, a user interface that enables the user to change her password is presented. Submitting the new password with the confirmation password makes the method enter the final step.

5. In the final step, the method calls resetPassword() to reset the existing password with the newly entered password.

◆ resetPassword(): This method performs the actual task of resetting the existing password to the newly entered password. It works as follows:

1. It uses getCheckSum() to calculate the checksum of the request, and then compares it with the given checksum. If they don't match, the application shows an alert message and returns the user to the last screen.

2. It uses checkPassword() to check the password for length and dummy password issues.

3. It creates a two-character salt using two random characters, and then encrypts the user-entered password, adding it to an associative array called $hash.

4. It creates a User object, $userObj, and calls getUserInfo() to load the user information.

5. It calls updateUser() with $hash as the parameter. updateUser() performs the actual database operation of updating the password. It only updates the password because $hash contains only the password information.

6. It displays the appropriate success or failure status message.

◆ email(): This method is called by showScreen() to populate the e-mail template, which becomes the HTML message sent to the user who is requesting the change for a forgotten password. It works as follows:

1. It creates a User object, $userObj, and uses getUserIDByName() to retrieve the user's ID.

2. It returns FALSE if the user ID is not found.

   Otherwise, it uses getCheckSum() to generate a checksum for the current user ID.

3. It incorporates the checksum value in a URL along with the user ID and step value set to 3.

4. It embeds the forgotten password application URL into the HTML template by replacing the PASSWORD_URL tag with the URL value.

5. It returns TRUE status.

The following are other methods implemented in this application.

Method	Description
run()	Calls the resetPasswordDriver(), which is responsible for managing the entire forgotten-password process.
sendEmail()	Sends an e-mail link to the user, which she can use to return to the forgotten password application to enter a new password. The e-mail message is read as an HTML template, which is processed by the showScreen() method. The showScreen() method calls the email() method to create the actual message, which sendEmail() method sends to the user.
getCheckSum()	Creates a checksum value using the user ID and a secret random number loaded from the configuration file. The checksum number is used to protect the e-mailed link from being generated by an unfriendly user.

Method	Description
checkPassword()	Checks the user-entered password for length and confirmation tests.
get_username()	Called by showScreen() method when displaying the user name entry interface as the first step in resetting the forgotten password.
reset_pwd()	Called by showScreen() method when displaying the password entry interface as the third step in resetting the forgotten password.
authorize()	Because anyone can request to change her password, the authorization method always returns TRUE.

Listing 6-7 shows the code for the forgotten-password recovery application.

Listing 6-7: usermngr_forgotten_pwd.php

```php
<?php

    // Turn on all error reporting
    error_reporting(E_ALL);

    // If you have installed framewirk directory in
    // a different directory than
    // %DocumentRoot%/framework, change the setting below.
    $APP_FRAMEWORK_DIR=$_SERVER['DOCUMENT_ROOT'] . '/framework';
    $PEAR              =$_SERVER['DOCUMENT_ROOT'] . '/pear';
    $PHPLIB            =$_SERVER['DOCUMENT_ROOT'] . '/phplib';

    // Insert the path in the PHP include_path so that PHP
    // looks for PEAR, PHPLIB and our application framework
    // classes in these directories
    ini_set( 'include_path', ':' .
        $PEAR .   ':' .
        $PHPLIB . ':' .
        $APP_FRAMEWORK_DIR . ':' .
        ini_get('include_path'));

    $AUTHENTICATION_URL = "/login/login.php";
    $LOGOUT_URL         = "/logout/logout.php";
```

Continued

Listing 6-7 *(Continued)*

```php
$APP_MENU            = '/home/home.php';


$APPLICATION_NAME    = 'USER_MNGR';


$XMAILER_ID          = 'Example User Manager Version 1.0';


$DEFAULT_LANGUAGE    = 'US';
$DEFAULT_DOMAIN      = 'example.com';
$ROOT_PATH           = $_SERVER['DOCUMENT_ROOT'];
$REL_ROOT_PATH       = '/user_mngr';
$REL_APP_PATH        =  $REL_ROOT_PATH . '/apps';


$TEMPLATE_DIR        = $ROOT_PATH     . $REL_APP_PATH . '/templates';
$CLASS_DIR           = $ROOT_PATH     . $REL_APP_PATH . '/class';
$REL_TEMPLATE_DIR    =  $REL_APP_PATH . '/templates/';



require_once "user_mngr.errors";
require_once "user_mngr.messages";
require_once 'DB.php';
require_once $APP_FRAMEWORK_DIR . '/' . 'constants.php';
require_once $APP_FRAMEWORK_DIR . '/' . $APPLICATION_CLASS;
require_once $APP_FRAMEWORK_DIR . '/' . $ERROR_HANDLER_CLASS;
require_once $APP_FRAMEWORK_DIR . '/' . $AUTHENTICATION_CLASS;
require_once $APP_FRAMEWORK_DIR . '/' . $DBI_CLASS;
require_once $APP_FRAMEWORK_DIR . '/' . $USER_CLASS;
require_once $TEMPLATE_CLASS;


$MIN_USERNAME_SIZE= 3;
$MIN_PASSWORD_SIZE= 3;
$DUMMY_PASSWD = '1234567890';
$ROOT_USER    = 'kabir@evoknow.com';
$SECRET       = 916489;
$CHAR_SET     = 'charset=iso-8859-1';


// Application names

$USERMNGR_MNGR              = 'user_mngr.php';
$USERMNGR_FORGOTTEN_APP     = 'user_mngr_forgotten_pwd.php';
$USERMNGR_CHANGE_PWD_APP    = 'user_mngr_passwd.php';


/* --------------START TABLE NAMES --------------------- */
$APP_DB_URL          = 'mysql://root:foobar@localhost/auth';
$AUTH_DB_TBL         = 'users';
```

```
/*  --------------END TABLE NAMES ---------------------- */

$STATUS_TEMPLATE             =  'usermngr_status.html';
$USERMNGR_MENU_TEMPLATE      =  'usermngr_menu.html';
$USERMNGR_USER_TEMPLATE      =  'usermngr_user_form.html';
$USERMNGR_PWD_REQUEST_TEMPLATE=  'usermngr_forgotten_pwd.html';
$USERMNGR_PWD_EMAIL_TEMPLATE  =  'usermngr_forgotten_pwd_email.html';
$USERMNGR_PWD_RESET_TEMPLATE  =  'usermngr_pwd_reset.html';
$USERMNGR_PWD_CHANGE_TEMPLATE =  'usermngr_pwd_change.html';


$ADMINISTRATIVE_USER = 9;
$STANDARD_USER = 1;
$USER_TYPE = array('9' => 'Administrator', '1' => 'Standard User');


?>
```

To make it easy for users to reset forgotten passwords, you can add the forgotten-password application link in the login interface template. Figure 6-7 shows such a login interface.

Figure 6-7: Central login interface with forgotten-password link.

Testing the forgotten-password recovery application

To test the forgotten password application, simply click the forgotten-password link on the login interface. Submit a user's e-mail address and wait for an e-mail to appear in the user's mailbox. Click on the link in the e-mail and change the password. (See Figure 6-8.)

After you've changed the password, you can log in to any application that uses the central authentication system with the user's name and the new password.

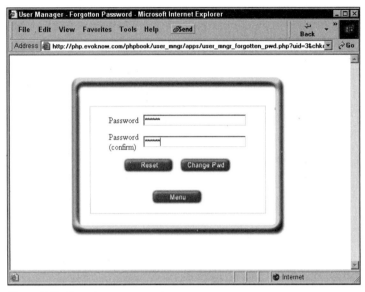

Figure 6-8: Changing a password.

Summary

In this chapter I discussed how you can manage users using a central user management system consisting of a few applications. This user management (create, modify, delete and forgotten password support) system works with the central Login/Logout system previously developed in the earlier chapter.

The very idea of having a central user authentication (login/logout) and a user management system is to ease user management and make access to various applications as seamless as possible. In the future chapters the applications we will develop will simply rely on these systems.

Chapter 7

Intranet System

IN THIS CHAPTER

◆ Developing a base intranet-application

◆ Using login/logout information to generate access reports

◆ Developing a simple messaging application

A BASE INTRANET APPLICATION is an application which is used to provide a home page for each user. This application shows links to other applications.

In this chapter, we will develop the base intranet application that shows each user a home page. When a user logs in, she sees a generated page with information, such as notes from other intranet users, or she can access other intranet tools that we will build in later chapters.

Identifying Functionality Requirements

The base intranet application system consists of the following features:

◆ **A central user authentication and user management facility:** We built this in the first two chapters in this section of the book. In this chapter, we will add a set of applications called Access Reporter, Admin Access Reporter, and Daily Logbook that will allow intranet users, administrations to access login/logout access information. Each regular user will be allowed to access only her own access report while administrators will have full access to all user access report and summaries. In a company environment, these access reports can serve as office attendance record.

◆ **A user home application:** Each user should be able to log in and view a dynamic home page that enables that user to access information and applications available on the intranet system. The home application will have two small utilities to display tips and handle user preferences related to screen themes.

◆ **A simple messaging application that enables users and administrators to send messages in the form of notes:** For example, a user should be able to send a note via the intranet to another user about a task deadline or a meeting. We will implement this messaging tool, which we named here as the Message of the Day (MOTD) tool.

◆ **A simple document-publishing application that enables intranet users to publish HTML documents in an organized manner:** This tool enables users to provide feedback to each posted document. Also, whenever a new document is added or an existing one is updated, users who have access to the document should be automatically notified via the messaging system previously mentioned. The applications for this suite are built in Chapter 8.

◆ **A simple central contact-manager application that enables intranet users to access common contact information such as that for vendors, customers, partners, and co-workers:** These applications are built in Chapter 9.

◆ **A simple central event-calendar application suite that enables users to publish and view important events:** These applications are built in Chapter 10.

◆ **A simple Internet resource manager application suite that allows users to share Internet resources such as Web and FTP sites:** These applications are built in Chapter 10.

The intranet applications that we develop here require the central login/logout and user-management components of the intranet discussed in the previous three chapters in this section.

You'll need to have those applications (login, logout, user-management) already implemented so that we can develop the base intranet home and access applications in this chapter.

Designing the Database

Since we are designing the intranet to support small to large number of users, we need a SQL server as the data storage. Like previous chapters and rest of he book, we will assume that you are going use MySQL for the database here as well.

The authentication database (auth) previously built for central authentication will still be used for storing user information such as username, password, active flag, and so on. Here we will develop a database that stores intranet messages, user details, preferences, theme choices, and user-access activity log data.

Figure 7-1 shows the database diagram for the intranet system.

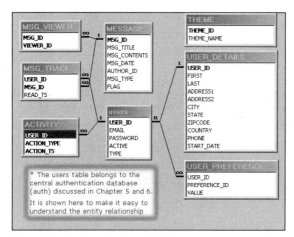

Figure 7-1: Intranet system ER diagram.

 The users table is shown in the ER diagram to clarify the relationship. It actually does not belong in the INTRANET database but in the central user-authentication database called auth discussed in Chapter 5. Users who appear in the auth database in the users table have access to the intranet.

Table 7-1 describes the details of each table in details.

TABLE 7-1 INTRANET DATABASE TABLES

Table	Description
MESSAGE	Holds the message title (MSG_TITLE), message number (MSG_ID), message contents (MSG_CONTENTS), message date (MSG_DATE), message type (MSG_TYPE), flag (FLAG), and ID of the author who created the message (AUTHOR_ID). The message number (MSG_ID) is automatically generated by the database.
MSG_TRACK	Contains the message tracking information. It holds the user ID (USER_ID) of the user who received the message, the message number (MSG_ID), and the time stamp when the message is read by the viewer user (READ_TS).

Continued

TABLE 7-1 INTRANET DATABASE TABLES *(Continued)*

Table	Description
MSG_VIEWER	Holds the message viewer data, the message number (MSG_ID), and the viewer ID (VIEWER_ID). It relates which message should be viewed by which user.
THEME	Holds information about the available intranet themes that can be used by the user. It contains the theme number (THEME_ID) and the name of the theme (THEME_NAME).
ACTIVITY	Holds information about the user login/logout activities, discussed in Chapter 5. It contains the user ID (USER_ID), action type (ACTION_TYPE), and action timestamp (ACTION_TS).
USER_DETAILS	This table contains detailed user information. This table holds the user ID (USER_ID), first name (FIRST), last name (LAST), address line #1 (ADDRESS1), address line #2 (ADDRESS2), city (CITY), state (STATE), zip code (ZIPCODE), country (COUNTRY), phone number (PHONE), and start date of the user in the intranet (START_DATE).
USER_PREFERENCE	Contains the user preference information: the user ID (USER_ID), preference ID (PREFERENCE_ID), and value (VALUE).

intranet.mysql is an implementation of the intranet database in MySQL. It's included on this book's CD-ROM (CDROM/ch07/sql/intranet.mysql). To use this database for these applications, create a database called INTRANET in your database server and run the following command:

```
mysql -u root -p -D INTRANET < INTRANET.sql
```

Make sure that you change the user name (root) to whatever is appropriate for your MySQL database system.

The INTRANET database must be set up before you start designing the PHP classes, which are needed to implement the intranet applications.

Designing and Implementing the Intranet Classes

Three new classes are needed to implement the intranet system: `Message`, `ActivityAnalyzer`, and `IntranetUser`. Figure 7-2 shows the system design that uses these classes.

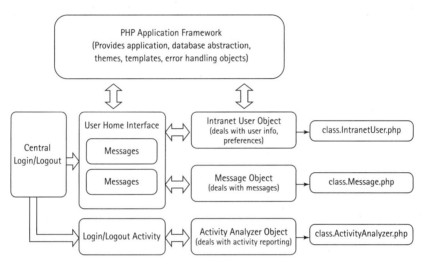

Figure 7-2: Intranet system diagram.

In the preceding design, you can see that central login/logout applications are used to access user home application. The user home application displays links to other intranet applications and allows users to create intranet messages. The home application and login/logout activity applications use `User` object, `Message` object, and `Activity Analyzer` objects to perform their operations. Notice also that all of the intranet applications are based on the PHP Application Framework that we developed earlier in the book. The following sections describe these classes.

Message class

The `Message` class is used to manipulate each message. It allows an application to create and delete messages. The `ch07/home/class/class.Message.php` file in the CD-ROM is an implementation of the Message class.

This class implements the following methods:

- ◆ Message(): This is the constructor method. It performs the following functions:

  - Sets an object variable named dbi to point to the class.DBI.php-provided object, which is passed to the constructor by an application. The dbi object variable holds the DBI object, which is used to communicate with the backend database.

  - Sets an object variable named msg_tbl to $MESSAGE_TBL, which is loaded from the configuration file (home.conf). The $MESSAGE_TBL holds the name of the MESSAGE table.

  - Sets an object variable named msg_track_tbl to $MSG_TRACK_TBL, which is loaded from the home.conf file. The $MSG_TRACK_TBL holds the name of the message tracking table.

  - Sets an object variable named msg_view_tbl to $MSG_VIEWER_TBL, which is loaded from the home.conf file. The $MSG_VIEWER_TBL holds the name of the message viewer table.

  - Sets an object variable called MSG_ID to the given message number (if any) by calling setMessageID().

  - Sets an object variable called fields to field names of the MESSAGE table. The fields variable is an associative array, which contains both field names and field types in a key = value format.

- ◆ loadMessageInfo(): This method loads all the message attributes, such as message number, message title, message contents, message publishing date, author ID, message type, and flag for a given message. Here's how it works:

  - First, the given message ID ($msg_id) is set as the current Message object's message ID using setMessageID().

  - A comma-separated list of MESSAGE table field names are created in the $fieldStr variable using the $this->fields value, which is set in the constructor.

  - A statement to select all the message fields for the given message ID is created in $stmt.

  - Using the DBI object ($this->dbi), the $stmt statement is run via $this->dbi->query() in DBI object. The result of the query is stored in the $result variable.

- If more than zero rows are in the $result object, each row is fetched in the $row variable.

- For each message field of type text, the data is stripped for embedded slash characters, which are used to escape quotation marks and slashes in the value of the field.

- Each message field data is stored as an object variable using the $this->$fieldname runtime variable.

◆ getMessages(): This method returns all messages for a given user where messages have been published on or earlier than a given timestamp or today. It works as follows:

- A variable called $fields is assigned a comma-separated list of message fields stored in $this->fields.

- If the method is called without a date ($lastDate), the $lastDate is set to the current timestamp.

- An SQL statement is created in $stmt, which queries the MESSAGE table for all messages that have been published on or earlier than the $lastDate. The returned rows are ordered using message type (MSG_TYPE) and message timestamp (MSG_DATE) in descending order.

- The query is performed using the $this->dbi->query() method of the DBI object embedded in $this->dbi. The result is stored in $result.

- If no rows are returned in the $result object, the method returns null. If there are matching rows, each row is stored in the $row object.

- For each row, a SQL statement is created in $stmt, which queries the message tracking table ($this->msg_track_tbl) for messages that have the same ID as the row's message ID ($row->MSG_ID) and the same user ID as the current user ID. The purpose of this query is to find out whether the current message in the row has already been tracked (that is, viewed by the current user). The statement is executed and the result is stored in the $finResult object.

- If no row is returned for the statement, the current message ($row->MSG_ID) has not been tracked (that is, viewed) by the current user and, therefore, it ($row) is pushed into an array called $retArr[].

- The $retArr[] array is returned after all rows in the first result set pointed by the $result object are checked. The resulting array, $retArr[] contains a list of message rows that the current user has not viewed yet.

◆ `getAllMessages()`: This method returns all messages in the MESSAGE table. It works as follows:

- A variable called `$fields` is assigned a comma-separated list of MESSAGE table fields, which are stored in `$this->fields`.

- A statement, `$stmt`, is created to select all data from the MESSAGE table in message type and date order.

- The query is performed using the `$this->dbi` object's `query()` method, and the result set is stored in `$result` object. If no message is found, the method returns null.

- On the other hand, if rows are in the `$result` object, an associative array called `$retArr` is populated using message ID (MSG_ID) as the key and `$row`, containing each message data, as the value.

- The `$retArr` array is returned.

◆ `addMessage()`: This method adds a new message in the MESSAGE table. The method is called with message title (`$title`), publication date (`$date`), contents (`$msg`), flag (`$flag`), author ID (`$auth`), and type (`$type`). It works as follows:

- A variable called `$fields` is assigned a comma-separated list of MESSAGE table fields stored in `$this->fields`.

- The given title (`$title`) and message body (`$msg`) are escaped for characters such as quotation marks and slashes using `$this->dbi->quote(addslashes())`.

- An SQL statement, `$stmt`, is created to insert the new message data into the MESSAGE table.

- The SQL statement is executed using `$this->dbi->query()` and the result of the query is stored in `$result` object.

- If the `$result` status is not okay, the method returns false to indicate insert failure. Otherwise, another SQL statement, `$stmt`, is created to query the database to return the newly created message row's message ID. This is done by setting the WHERE clause of the SELECT statement to AUTHOR_ID = `$auth`, MSG_TYPE = `$type`, MSG_DATE = `$date`, and FLAG = `$flag`, which uniquely identifies the new message.

- If the result of the select query does not return a row, the method returns null and, if it does, it returns the MSG_ID of the newly created message.

◆ modifyMessage(): This method updates an existing message in the database. It works as follows:

■ The method is called with message ID ($mid), title ($title), date ($date), body ($msg), and flag ($flag).

■ It sets the current message ID to the given message ID ($mid) using the setMessageID() method.

■ The given title ($title) and message body ($msg) are escaped for characters such as quotation marks and slashes using $this->dbi->quote(addslashes()).

■ An SQL statement, $stmt, is created to update the existing message data into the MESSAGE table. The statement uses MSG_ID in the WHERE clause to ensure that only the given message ($mid) is updated.

■ The SQL UPDATE statement is executed using $this->dbi->query(), and the result of the query is stored in the $result object.

■ If the update is successful, the method returns true; otherwise, it returns false.

◆ getViewers(): This method returns a list of the user IDs who have viewed a given message. It works as follows:

■ The method is called with a message ID ($mid).

■ It sets the current message ID to the given message ID ($mid) using setMessageID().

■ An SQL SELECT statement, $stmt, is created to return VIEWER_ID from all rows in the message view table that match the given message ID ($mid).

■ If the returned result set object, $result, has no rows, the method returns null. Otherwise, it creates an array called $retArr, with the user IDs that are returned per row in the $result object.

◆ addViewer(): This method adds users in the message view table who can view a given message. It works as follows:

■ The method is called with message ID ($mid) and an array of user IDs for the viewers ($views).

■ It sets the current message ID to the given message ID ($mid) using the setMessageID() method.

■ For each user (viewer), it inserts a row in the message view table.

- ◆ deleteViewers(): This method deletes all the viewers of a given message. It works as follows:

  - The method is called with the message ID ($mid).

  - It sets the current message ID to the given message ID ($mid) using the setMessageID() method.

  - Using a SQL DELETE statement, the method deletes all rows from the message view table for the given message.

- ◆ isViewable(): This method determines whether the given message can be viewed by the given user. It works as follows:

  - The method is called with message ID ($mid) and an user ID ($uid).

  - It sets the current message ID to the given message ID ($mid) using setMessageID().

  - An SQL SELECT statement, $stmt, is created and executed to return viewer IDs (VIEW_ID) for the given message and viewer ID. In other words, if one row for the given message has VIEWER_ID set to the given user ID ($vid), the statement returns a result object, $result, which has a nonzero row count.

  - The number of rows is returned. A positive number indicates that the current message has the given user ID as a viewer.

- ◆ getMsgIDbyMessageTitle(): This method returns the message ID for a given message title. It works as follows:

  - The method is called with the message title ($title).

  - The given title ($title) is escaped for characters such as quotation marks and slashes using $this->dbi->quote(addslashes()).

  - An SQL SELECT statement, $stmt, is created and executed to return the message ID (MSG_ID) for the given message title. The result of the query is stored in a result object called $result.

  - If the $result object has no rows, the method returns null.

  - Otherwise, the message ID (MSG_ID) is fetched from the row in the $result object and returned. This will always return the first message that has the matching title.

The following table describes the rest of the methods for this class:

Method	Description
getMessageContents()	Returns the contents of the given message while taking the message ID as input.
getMessageTitle()	Returns the title of the given message while taking the message ID as input.
getMessagePublishDate()	Returns the publishing date of the given message while taking the message ID as input.
setMessageID()	Sets the message ID of the message object if a message ID is passed as a parameter. It also returns the message ID.
updateTrack()	Updates a user's message tracking information by inserting a new row in the message track table. When this method is called with a user ID ($uid) and message ID ($mid), it inserts the current timestamp in the message track table.
deleteMessage()	Deletes a given message from the database, using the given message ID ($mid).
isRead()	Determines whether the given message has been read by querying the message track table for rows matching a given message ID.

ActivityAnalyzer class

Each time a user logs in or logs out of the intranet, a record is stored in the database. This record is called the *activity log*. We will develop a class called the ActivityAnalyzer, which will be used to determine login/logout statistics for one or more users.

This ActivityAnalyzer class provides the Activity Analyzer object. The list object is used to manipulate activities. There are two types of activities: login (ACTIVITY_TYPE = 1) and logout (ACTIVITY_TYPE = 2).

The class allows an application to create and delete actions or activities. The ch07/home/class/class.ActivityAnalyzer.php file on the CD-ROM is an implementation of this class, which is discussed in the following section.

This class implements the following methods:

- getDailyStartTS(): This method returns the first activity timestamp for a given timestamp range ($start, $end) for a given user. It works as follows:

  - The method is called using the action timestamp range ($start, $end) and is supplied a user ID ($uid).

  - An SQL SELECT statement, $stmt, is created to return the minimum (using SQL MIN() function) action timestamp ($ACTION_TS) as START_TIME from the activity table where the given user ID matches. The returned action timestamp is always within the given action timestamp range ($start, $end).

  - If the result of the SQL query returns no rows, the method returns null; otherwise, the row is fetched and the minimum action timestamp (as START_TIME) is returned from the result object.

- getDailyEndTS(): This method returns the last activity timestamp for a given timestamp range ($start, $end) for a given user. It works as follows:

  - The method is called using action timestamp range, which starts with $start, $end and is supplied a user ID ($uid).

  - An SQL SELECT statement, $stmt, is created to return the maximum (using the SQL MAX() function) action timestamp ($ACTION_TS) as END_TIME from the activity table where the given user ID matches. The returned action timestamp is always within the given action timestamp range ($start, $end).

  - If the result of the SQL query returns no rows, the method returns null. Otherwise, the row is fetched and the minimum action timestamp (as END_TIME) is returned from the result object.

- getDailyActivityInfo(): This method returns a list of activity records for a given user in a given start and end action timestamp. It works as follows:

  - The method is called using the action timestamp range, which starts with $start and ends with $end. The method is also supplied a user ID ($uid).

  - An SQL SELECT statement, $stmt, is created to return action type (ACTION_TYPE) and timestamp (ACTION_TS) from the activity table where the given user ID matches. The returned action timestamp is always within the given action timestamp range ($start, $end).

  - If the result of the SQL query returns no rows, the method returns null. Otherwise, the list of action records (activity type and timestamp) are returned in an array called $activityArr[].

◆ `analyzeDailyActivity()`: This method returns the total office hours and extra (overtime) hours logged by a given user for a given period of time. It works as follows:

  ■ The method is called with an associative parameter array called `$params`, which contains the current user ID (`$params['USER_ID']`), activity start timestamp (`$params['DAY_START']`), and end timestamp (`$params['DAY_END']`).

  ■ The method calls `getDailyActivityInfo()` to find a list of activities in the given range for the current user. The list is stored in `$activityArr`. If this list is empty, the method returns null.

  ■ The method breaks down each element of `$activityArr` into activity type (`$type`) and timestamp (`$ts`).

  ■ By looping through the list of activities, it finds the first instance of a login activity (`$type = 1`) and sets `$startcount` to the login time-stamp (`$ts`). It also finds the logout activity (`$type = 2`) for which login activity is already found (`$startcount` is set) and calls `getOfficeAndExtraBreakdown()` to find the total office and extra hours breakdown. `getOfficeAndExtraBreakdown()` returns the break-down into an associative array, which is stored in `$breakdown`.

  ■ The `$totalOffice` time is incremented using the breakdown informa-tion for each complete activity (login and logout) session.

  ■ Finally, the total office hours and the extra hours are returned in an associative array called `$analysis`.

◆ `getDailyLog()`: This method returns the activity log of given user for a day. It works as follows:

  ■ The method is called with an associative parameter array called `$params`, which contains the current user ID (`$params['USER_ID']`), activity start timestamp (`$params['DAY_START']`), and end timestamp (`$params['DAY_END']`).

  ■ The method calls `getDailyActivityInfo()` to find a list of activities in the given range for the current user. The list is stored in `$activityArr`. If this list is empty, the method returns null.

  ■ The method breaks down each element of `$activityArr` into activity type (`$type`) and timestamp (`$ts`).

  ■ By looping through the list of activities, it finds the first instance of a login activity (`$type = 1`) and sets `$startcount` to the login time-stamp (`$ts`). It also finds the logout activity (`$type = 2`) for which login activity is already found (`$startcount` is set) and calls `getLogs()` to find the office and extra hours breakdown. `getLogs()` returns the breakdown into an associative array, which is stored in an associative array called $breakdown. The breakdown contains login, logout, office hours, and extra hours.

♦ getLogs(): This method returns an associative array containing login, logout, office hours, and extra hours information for a given start and end timestamp of an activity log record. It works as follows:

■ The method is called with an associative array parameter called $params, which contains information from the configuration file (home.conf) regarding start of office hours (OFFICE_START), end of office hours (OFFICE_END), start of lunch hour (LUNCH_START), and end of lunch hour (LUNCH_END). These settings are found as follows in the default configuration file:

```
define('OFFICE_START_TIME', 10);  //24 HRS TIME FORMAT
define('LUNCH_START_TIME', 13);   //24 HRS TIME FORMAT
define('LUNCH_END_TIME', 14);     //24 HRS TIME FORMAT
define('OFFICE_END_TIME', 19);    //24 HRS TIME FORMAT
```

■ The method defines an associative array called $retArr, which is what it returns after inserting appropriate key = value parameters.

■ It stores the start ($start) parameter as the login time in the $retArr. Similarly, it stores the end ($end) parameter as the logout time in the $retArr.

■ Office hours are initialized in a method variable $office to be zero. Extra hours are initialized to a method variable called $extra to be zero.

■ A global parameter $WEEKEND is loaded. This parameter is set in the configuration file as an array. The default configuration in home.conf for this array is

```
$WEEKEND = array('Sat', 'Sun');
```

■ The method checks to see whether the day of $start timestamp is in the $WEEKEND array. If so, it sets the $office variable to zero, because only extra (overtime) hours are allowed on weekends. It calculates the $extra time by subtracting the $start from $end.

■ If the start ($start) timestamp does not represent a weekend day, the method calculates the office hours by excluding the lunch hours from the office hours. It also calculates any extra hours that are beyond the office hours.

■ The method returns $retArr with login, logout, total office, and total extra hour information.

♦ getOfficeAndExtraBreakdown(): This method returns an associative array containing total office hours and total extra hours information for a given start and end timestamp of an activity log record.

The method is called exactly as getLogs() is, and it performs the same way. The method returns total office and total extra hour information in an anonymous associative array.

The following table describes the rest of the methods for this class:

Method	Description
ActivityAnalyzer()	The constructor method. It sets an object variable named dbi to point to the class.DBI.php-provided object, which is passed to the constructor by an application. dbi is used to communicate with the backend database.
	It also sets an object variable called activity_tbl to $ACTIVITY_TBL, which is loaded from the configuration file (home.conf). The $ACTIVITY_TBL variable holds the name of the activity table.
logUserOut()	Records a logout activity (ACTIVITY_TYPE = 2) in the ACTIVITY table for a given user by inserting a new activity row for the user ($uid) at given time ($time). If the logout activity is successfully inserted into the database, the method returns true. Otherwise it returns false.
logUserIn()	Records a login activity (ACTIVITY_TYPE = 1) in the ACTIVITY table for a given user by inserting a new activity row for the user ($uid) at given time ($time). If the login activity is successfully inserted into the database, the method returns true; otherwise, it returns false.

Creating the IntranetUser class

This InternetUser class provides the intranet user object, which is used to retrieve and set user information. The ch07/home/class/class.IntranetUser.php file in the CD-ROM is an implementation of this class.

Following are the methods available in this class:

◆ IntranetUser(): This is the constructor method, which performs the following tasks:

■ Sets an object variable named dbi to point to the class.DBI.php-provided object, which is passed to the constructor by an application. The dbi object variable holds the DBI object, which is used to communicate with the backend database.

- ■ Sets an object variable called user_details_tbl to
  $USER_DETAILS_TBL, which is loaded from the home.conf file. The
  $USER_DETAILS_TBL variable holds the name of the users table.

- ■ Sets an object variable called user_pref_tbl to $USER_PREFERENCE_TBL,
  which is loaded from the home.conf file. The $USER_PREFERENCE_TBL
  variable holds the name of the user preference table.

- ■ If the constructor is called with a user ID ($uid), it is set to
  $this->uid.

◆ getContactInfo(): This method returns all information regarding a
given user ID ($uid) from the USER_DETAILS table. It works as follows:

- ■ This method is called with the user ID ($uid) parameter.

- ■ It calls the setIntranetUserID() method to set the current user ID to
  $uid.

- ■ It creates an SQL SELECT statement, $statement, to select all informa-
  tion from the USER_DETAILS table for the given user ID ($uid).

- ■ The result of the executed select statement is stored in the $this-
  >contactInfo object.

The following table describes the other methods of this class:

Method	Description
setIntranetUserID()	Sets the intranet user ID. If the intranet user ID ($uid) is provided as a parameter, it is set as the object's intranet user ID ($this->uid), or the current intranet user ID is returned.
getName()	Returns the first and last name of the current user. It gets this information from the $this->contactInfo object variable, which is a DBI result set object set by the getContactInfo() method.
getPreferences()	Returns the preferences for a given user in an associative array.
updateAutoTip()	Updates tool tip status for a given user.
addAutoTip()	Sets or resets the automatic tip preference. The method is called with the user ID ($uid) and the tip preference option ($tip). It creates an SQL INSERT statement, $statement, that inserts the tip option for preference ID (2), which is the preference number for the automatic tip. It returns true if the tip preference is inserted successfully; otherwise, it returns false.

Setting Up Application Configuration Files

Each of the applications in the intranet system uses a central configuration file called home.conf. For the given configuration file, the directory structure is shown here:

Here's the directory structure that the home.conf require:

```
+---htdocs ($ROOT_PATH same as %DocumentRoot%)
   |
   +---home (applications and configuration files go here)
   |   |
   |   +--class (class files go here)
   |   |
   |   +---templates (html templates go here)
   |       |
   |       +---themes (theme templates are stored here)
   |       |
   |       +---tips (tips are stored here)
   |
   +---photos (user photos are stored here)
   |
   +---login (central login application)
   |

        +---logout (central logout application)
```

Here the home directory is assumed to be a top-level directory in the %DocumentRoot% of the intranet Web site. The photos directory is also a top-level directory within the site; user photos are optional, however, and can be placed in the directory manually as long as the file names are *userid*.jpg. A default photo called default_photo.jpg is provided in the photos directory for users without any photo in this directory. The login/logout directories are part of the central authentication discussed earlier in the book.

To configure the applications for your directory structure, you have to change the settings as shown in Table 7-2.

The messages displayed by the intranet applications are stored in the home.message file, which you can copy from the ch7/home directory within the CD-ROM. You can customize each message by using a text editor.

The error messages displayed by the intranet applications are stored in error messages file called home.errors which can be found in ch7/home directory of the CD-ROM. You can customize each message by using a text editor.

TABLE 7-2 HOME.CONF SETTINGS

Variable	Values
$PEAR_DIR	Set to the directory where you have installed the PEAR packages. The DB class needs the class.DBI.php, which is part of the PEAR packages.
$PHPLIB_DIR	Set to the directory where the PHPLIB packages are stored, because the Template class (template.inc) is part of the PHPLIB packages.
$APP_FRAMEWORK_DIR	Point this to our application framework class directory.
$AUTHENTICATION_URL	Point the central authentication application (login.php), which is part of our application framework. The default value is /login/login.php, which should work if you have followed instructions in Chapter 5.
$LOGOUT_URL	Point the central logout application (logout.php), which is part of our application framework. The default value is /logout/logout.php, which should work if you have followed instructions in Chapter 5.
$ROOT_PATH	Point to the document root directory of your Web site where you host this application.
$REL_ROOT_PATH	Point to the relative path, which is the parent of the apps directory.
$INTRANET _DB_URL	Configure this to enable you to connect to the intranet database via the named host using the named username and password. For example, the default value mysql://root:foobar@localhost/INTRANET states that the intranet database called INTRANET is located in the localhost system and can be accessed by using the username root and password foobar.
$USER_DB_URL	Configure to enable you to connect to the user database. For example, the default value mysql://root:foobar@localhost/auth states that the authentication database called auth is located in the localhost system and can be accessed by using the username root and password foobar.

Variable	Values
$TIP_SCRIPT	Point the tip script (tip_script.js), which is needed to show tips.
$TIP_URL	Point to the relative path, which is the parent of the tips directory.
$DEFAULT_THEME	Set to the default theme ID. By default, the theme is set to 1.
$USER_DEFAULTS	Point to an array that contains default preferences of all users.
$MAX_AVAILABLE_TIP	Set to the maximum number of tips that are available in the tips directory within the templates directory.
$ADMIN_MSG_COLOR	Set the color shown to the viewers with administrative privileges.
$STANDARD_MSG_COLOR	Set the color shown to the standard viewers.
$OFFICE_START_TIME	Set to the expected office start time, such as 10 (for 10 a.m.).
$LUNCH_START_TIME	Set the expected start time for lunch, such as 13 (for 1 p.m.; remember, we're using a 24-hour format).
$LUNCH_END_TIME	Set to the expected lunch end time, such as 14 (for 2 p.m.).
$OFFICE_END_TIME	Set to the expected office end time, such as: 19 (for 7 p.m.).
$DEFAULT_REPORT_TYPE	Set the default report type: MONTHLY, WEEKLY, or DAILY.
$ACCESS_REPORT_ EVEN_ROW_COLOR	Set the color for the even rows of the report. The color value is in HTML color format (RGB).
$ACCESS_REPORT_ ODD_ROW_COLOR	Set the color for the odd rows of the report. The color value is in HTML color format (RGB).
$ACCESS_RPT_OFFICE_ HR_TEXT_COLOR_REGULAR	Set the text color for the regular office hours of the access report. The color value is in HTML color format (RGB).
$ACCESS_RPT_OFFICE_HR_ TEXT_COLOR_IRREGULAR	Set the text color for the extra office hours of the access report. The color value is in HTML color format (RGB).
$ADMIN_TYPE	Set the user type value that will indicate an administrative user level. The default value of 9 is okay.
$EXPECTED_OFFICE_HRS	Set to the daily office hours that are expected to be maintained by every employee. The default is set to 8 hours per day.

Continued

TABLE 7-2 HOME.CONF SETTINGS *(Continued)*

Variable	Values
$GRACE	Set to the grace period (in seconds). The default value is 600 seconds (10 minutes). This means that if an employee fails to meet the full office hours requirements by 10 minutes or less, the grace period is applied to make up her full office hours.
$WEEKEND	Set to the day(s) of the week that is/are considered as weekend. The default values ('Sat', 'Sun') should be standard for most places on this planet. Keep the default.

Setting Up the Application Templates

The HTML interface templates needed for the applications are included on the CD-ROM. These templates contain various template tags to display necessary information dynamically. The templates are named in the home.conf file. Table 7-3 explains the purpose of each template.

TABLE 7-3 HTML TEMPLATES

File Name	Purpose
home.html	Home page template of intranet.
home_status.html	Shows status messages when user performs an operation such as updating preference settings.
access_report.html	Used to display an access report.
add_msg.html	Used to add an intranet message.
msg_mngr.html	Shows message-management options to users.
msg_preview.html	Shows the preview of a message to users.
preference.html	Shows the theme preference page.
log_detail.html	Shows the log details for a day.
admin_access_report.html	Shows the access report to administrators.

These templates also use images that are stored in an image directory called images within the template directory pointed by the $TEMPLATE_DIR variable in the home.conf file.

Intranet Home Application

The home.php application is responsible for displaying an intranet home page to each user. The application is included on the CD-ROM in the ch07/apps directory. home.php implements the following functionality:

- ◆ It displays the intranet home page to each user after the user is logged in.

- ◆ It uses the home page to show any message(s) that the user needs to view.

- ◆ When the user clicks the OK button of a message (to indicate that he has read the message), the application updates the message-tracking table so that the same message is not displayed again.

This application has the following methods:

- ◆ run(): This method is responsible for running the application. This method does the following:

  - ■ If the user is not authenticated, it displays an alert message and returns the user to previous page. This effectively terminates the application.

  - ■ If the user is authenticated, it creates a theme object, $this->themeObj.

  - ■ The current user's theme choice is stored in $this->theme by calling the getUserTheme() method of the theme object created.

  - ■ When the user comes to the home application after clicking the OK button to indicate that she has read a message, this method calls the updateMsgTrack() method.

  - ■ Then the displayHome() method is called to display the intranet home page.

- ◆ displayHome(): This method displays the home page of the intranet system and also shows specific messages to specific users. Here is how it works:

  - ■ It applies the appropriate theme to the page.

  - ■ It checks whether tips are to be shown to the user and sets tip information accordingly.

  - ■ It sets the photo of the user who has requested this page.

- It sets the current date and time on the home page.

- It sets any new or unread messages for the user in appropriate places in the appropriate order.

- It parses or renders the page information and shows the page accordingly to the user.

Other methods for this application include those described in the following table:

Method	Description
authorize()	Authorizes everyone on the intranet to view the page and, therefore, always returns TRUE.
updateMsgTrack()	Takes the message ID that has been read by the user and updates the database accordingly.
getName()	Finds and returns the formatted first name of the user retrieved from the viewer's username (e-mail address).
popAutoTip()	Pops up a tip of the day. It is called from the displayHome() method if the user has the auto-tip option ON in her preference.
unhtmlentities()	The exact reverse of the htmlentities() method in the PHP API.

Now we will develop a set of mini applications that can be run from the home page of each user. They are as follows:

- ◆ **MOTDO manager application:** This application is used to send intranet messages from one user to another. It is ideally used by administrators to notify users of company-wide events, hence it is named the *MOTD* (*Message of the Day*) application.

- ◆ **Access reporter application:** This application is used to provide login/logout reports for intranet users. Each user can view her access log information in a nicely formatted manner to see how she is keeping her office hours. Users cannot view other user's access report.

- ◆ **Admin access reporter application:** This application allows intranet administrators to view anyone's access report in a daily, weekly, or monthly view.

- ◆ **Daily logbook application:** This application allows users to view the login/logout activities for a given day.

◆ **User preference application:** This application allows users to set their themes and automatic tip-preference settings.

◆ **User tip application:** This application shows an automatic tip from the tip directory when a user sets her preference to receive an automatic tip on each login.

The details of these applications are discussed in the following sections.

MOTD manager application

The MOTD manager application, `ln_msg_mngr.php`, is responsible for managing daily messages. It is included on the CD-ROM in the `ch07/apps` directory.
The application implements the following functionality:

◆ **It enables all users to create, modify, and delete messages.** Administrative users use a different message template than regular users so that admin messages can be easily identified.

◆ **It enables all users to select viewers for each message while adding or modifying messages.**

This application has the following methods:

◆ `run()`: When the application is run, this method is called. It does the following:

   ▪ Calls the `authorize()` method to see whether the user is allowed to access this application. If the user is not allowed, it displays an alert message and returns her to the home page.

   ▪ Creates a theme object called `$this->themeObj` and retrieves the theme selection for the current user by using the `getUserTheme()` method. The chosen theme is set to `$this->theme` variable of the application.

   ▪ Uses two query parameters, `cmd` and `step`, to determine which message operation (`add`, `modify`, `delete`) is requested and what step of the operation needs to be processed. When `cmd` is set to `add`, `step` can be null, which represents the start of the add message operation, and, therefore, `displayMsgAddModMenu()` is called to show the add message interface. After the user fills out the new message information, the interface submits a `step` parameter with a value of 2, indicating that the user has submitted a new message. Then `confirmMessage()` is called to display a confirmation page showing the message for the user to confirm. When the user confirms the message, the step parameter is

returned with a value of 3 from the user interface shown by
confirmMessage(). This indicates that the user has confirmed the new
message, which is then written to the database addMessage().

- Similarly, when the user decides to modify an existing message and
  run() is called with cmd set to modify, the step parameter value can be
  1, 2, or 3 — calling displayMsgAddModMenu(), confirmMessage(), and
  modifyMessage(), respectively — or null.

- If the user decides to delete an existing message and the run method is
  called with cmd set to delete, deleteMessage() is called.

- If the user does not specify any message operations (add, modify,
  delete), the user is shown the main message interface using
  displayMsgMngrMenu().

- In summary, run() decides which functionality is requested by the
  user and calls the appropriate message method to perform the desired
  operations.

◆ deleteMessage(): This method finds the message ID of the message to be
  deleted and deletes that message from the database. If this method is
  called without a proper message ID, it shows an error message. It works as
  follows:

- If it is called without a message ID ($mid) as a query parameter, it
  shows an alert message and returns null.

- Else, a message object called $msgObj is created and the deleteMessage()
  of the object is called with the $mid value to delete the message. The
  status of this operation is stored in $status variable.

- A theme template object called $themeTemplate is created and set up
  in the usual way to load the user-selected theme template file.

- A status message template ($STATUS_TEMPLATE) is loaded in a template
  object called $template as usual. If the $status is true, a status message indicating that the message is deleted is inserted into the $tem-
  plate content block. Also, deleteViewers() is called to remove all
  the users from the message's viewer table. This is done to ensure that,
  when a message is deleted, the system does not attempt to show the
  viewers a nonexistent message.

- If the message could not be deleted, $status is false, and a message
  indicating the failure is inserted in the $template object's content
  block.

- Finally, the contents of the $template object are inserted into the
  $themeTemplate object's content block, and the results are printed on
  the user's browser screen.

◆ `confirmMessage()`: This method shows a preview of the message after the user has added or modified one and gets his confirmation. It also confirms that the message is a valid one or shows appropriate error messages. If the user chooses to cancel from this screen, she is taken back to the add/modify menu, where she can edit her message and continue. This method works as follows:

- When the method is called, the user has either created a new message or modified an existing message. So the method receives the message title (`$title`), publication date (`$msgDate`), body (`$msg`), current timestamp (`$currentTS`), operation mode (`$mode`), message ID (`$mid`) (only if editing an existing message), and viewer list (`$viewers`).

- A local variable `$date` is created using the month (`$m`), day (`$d`), and year (`$y`) of the given publication date.

- If the given date is invalid or less than the current date, the method shows an alert message indicating a bad publication date and returns null.

- The method checks to see whether the title, body, or viewer list is empty. If any of them are not defined by the user in the previous step, an alert message is shown and the method returns null.

- Using a current timestamp from the `mktime()` function, a new timestamp containing the current hour, minute, and second, along with the user-given month, day, and year, is created in the `$realDate` variable.

- A theme template object called `$themeTemplate` is created and set up in the usual way to load the user-selected theme template file.

- Similarly, a message preview template (`$MSG_PREVIEW_TEMPLATE`) is loaded in a template object called `$template` as usual. All user-supplied data are embedded into the preview template.

- Finally, the contents of the `$template` object are inserted into the `$themeTemplate` object's content block, and the results are printed on the user's browser screen.

◆ `modifyMessage()`: This method gets the modified message information, such as message ID, message title, publish date, message contents, and viewer IDs, and updates the database. It shows the appropriate confirmation message if no error is found. Otherwise, it shows the appropriate error message. Here's how it works:

- If the method is called without a viewer list, it shows an alert message and returns.

- A message object called `$msgObj` is created with the current message ID (`$mid`), which is supplied to the method as a query parameter.

- The isRead() method of the $msgObj is called to determine whether the chosen message has already been read. The message cannot be modified if other users have already acknowledged reading it. Changing this message now would be unethical. The best approach is to add a new message using the modified content so that the users can see it again. Therefore, if the message is already read, addMessage() is called to add the modification as a new message.

◆ addMessage(): This method gets new message information, such as message title, publish date, message contents, and viewer IDs, and inserts the message data into the database. It shows the appropriate confirmation message if no error is found. Otherwise, it shows the appropriate error message. Here's how it works:

  - If the method is called without a viewer list, it shows an alert message and returns.

  - A message object called $msgObj is created.

  - We add the new message using the addMessage() method of the $msgObj. The status of this operation is stored in the $status variable.

  - If $status is true, a status message indicating that the message is added is inserted in the $template content block, and addViewers() is called to add the viewers of this message. If the message could not be added, $status is false, and a message indicating the failure is inserted in the $template object's content block.

  - The contents of the $template object are inserted into the $themeTemplate object's content block, and the results are printed on the user's browser screen.

◆ displayMsgMngrMenu(): This method displays the initial message manager options menu available only to administrators, because only administrators can modify or delete messages. This is how it works:

  - A message manager template ($MSG_MNGR_TEMPLATE) is loaded in a template object called $template.

  - A new message object called $msgObj is created.

  - The template includes buttons to add, modify, and delete messages and a list of messages from which the user can choose messages to modify or delete.

- The list is loaded using the `getAllMessages()` method of the `$msgObj` object.

- The contents of the `$template` object are inserted into the `$themeTemplate` object's content block, and the results are printed on the user's browser screen.

◆ `displayMsgAddModMenu()`: This method displays the add/modify message interfaces. This is how it works:

- Checks whether the message ID has been supplied when this method is called with the `'modify'` parameter. If the message ID has not been supplied, the method shows the appropriate error message and returns the user to the previous page. Otherwise, it creates the new message object, `$msgObj`, and stores the message contents, publish date, and title attributes of the message into variables for later use.

- A message add/modify template (`$MSG_ADD_TEMPLATE`) is loaded in a template object called `$template`.

- The template includes a Web form for taking input of the message title, message contents, publish date, and view rights. If this method is called with the `'modify'` parameter, it loads the specified message information into the Web form.

- The contents of the `$template` object are inserted into the `$themeTemplate` object's content block, and the results are printed on the user's browser screen.

◆ `unhtmlentities()`: This method is the exact reverse of the `htmlentities()` method in the PHP API.

◆ `authorize()`: This method authorizes access to this application. It works as follows:

- It uses `getUID()` to check whether the current user ID is positive. Because all valid user IDs are positive numbers, it creates a `DBI` object called `$user_dbi` that points to the central user-authentication database (`USER_DB_URL`).

- A user object called `$userObj` is created using the `$user_dbi` and current user ID.

- The current user type is tested using `getType()` to determine whether it is administrator (`ADMIN_TYPE`) or not. If the current user is of type administrator, the `$isAdmin` variable is set to `TRUE` and it returns `TRUE`. For nonadministrative users, this method will return `TRUE` if `cmd` = add; otherwise, it returns `FALSE`.

Access reporter application

The access reporter application, `access_reporter.php`, shows the access report of the current user. It is included on the CD-ROM in the `ch07/apps` directory.

It has the following methods:

♦ `run()`: When the application is run, this method is called. It basically decides which functionality is requested by the user and calls the appropriate method to perform the desired operations. It does the following:

- Creates a theme object, `$this->themeObj`.

- Stores the current user's theme choice in `$this->theme` by calling the `getUserTheme()` method of the theme object created.

- If the application is called with `cmd` = `"Force Login"`, `logUserIn()` is called. Similarly, `cmd` = `"Force Logout"` calls `logUserOut()`. These two operations are done when an administrator wants to manually log in or log out a user.

- Calls the `reportDriver()` method to show the access report.

♦ `logUserOut()`: This method logs out the specified user. It works as follows:

- Checks whether the administrator provided the given date and time is valid. Otherwise, it shows the appropriate error message to the user and returns to the previous page.

- Checks whether the given date and time correspond to the future. If they do, it shows the appropriate error message to the user and returns to the previous page.

- Creates a new `ActivityAnalyzer` object called `$analyzer`.

- Uses the `logUserOut()` method of the `$analyzer` object to log out the user.

- Calls the `reportDriver()` method to render the updated access report.

♦ `logUserIn()`: This method logs in the specified user. It works as follows:

- Checks whether the given date and time is valid. If they aren't, it shows the appropriate error message to the user and returns to the previous page.

- Checks whether the given date and time correspond to the future. If they do, it shows the appropriate error message to the user and returns to the previous page.

- Creates a new `ActivityAnalyzer` object called `$analyzer`.

- ■ Uses the `logUserIn()` method of the `$analyzer` object to log in the user.

- ■ Calls the `reportDriver()` method to render the updated access report.

◆ `authorize()`: This method authorizes access to this application. It works as follows:

- ■ It checks the current user ID using the `getUID()` method. Because all valid user IDs are positive numbers, it creates the `DBI` object called `$user_dbi` that points to the central user-authentication database (`USER_DB_URL`).

- ■ A user object called `$userObj` is created using the `$user_dbi` and the current user ID.

- ■ The `getType()` method is called to determine the user type of the current user. If the current user is of type administrator (`ADMIN_TYPE`), the `$isAdmin` variable is set to `TRUE`.

- ■ This method always returns `TRUE`, because everyone on the intranet can view this application.

◆ `reportDriver()`: This method generates and displays the user-access report. It works as follows:

- ■ Generates the appropriate report. For example, if the report type (`$rpt`) is a weekly report, the `generateWeeklyReport()` method is called to generate the weekly report.

- ■ Displays the report using the `displayReport()`.

◆ `generateDailyReport()`: This method generates the access report of a user for a specific day. This method works as follows:

- ■ If the user viewing the page has administrator privileges, this method shows her the admin block that includes a list of users from which she can select any user's daily report. This block also includes a link to the overall summary report and the buttons for force login and force logout.

- ■ It finds out the timestamp of the day to be shown. Because the user has the option to scroll through the days by using the >> and << buttons, this timestamp is not always the current day.

- ■ It finds out the starting and ending timestamps of the given day and uses the `ActivityAnalyzer` object to retrieve the office hours and the extra hours for the day for that user.

- ■ It returns the formatted information that includes the date, the day, the start time, the end time, the total office hours, and the total extra hours. It also includes a brief summary with totals and averages.

- `generateWeeklyReport()`: This method generates an access report of a user for a specific week. This method works as follows:

  - If the user viewing the page has administrator privileges, this method shows her the admin block that includes a list of users from which she can select any user's daily report. The block includes a link to the overall summary report and the buttons for force login and force logout.

  - It finds out the timestamp of the week to be shown. Because the user has the option to scroll through the weeks by using the >> and << buttons, this timestamp is not always the current week.

  - It finds out the starting and ending timestamps of the given week and uses the `ActivityAnalyzer` object to retrieve the office hours and the extra hours for each day of the given week for that user.

  - It returns the formatted information that includes the date, the day, the start time, the end time, the total office hours, and the total extra hours, as well as a brief summary with totals and averages.

- `generateMonthlyReport()`: This method generates an access report of a user for a specific month. This method works as follows:

  - If the user viewing the page has administrator privileges, this method shows him the admin block that includes a list of users from which he can select any user's monthly report. This includes a link to the overall summary report and the buttons for force login and force logout.

  - It finds out the timestamp of the month to be shown. As the user has the option to scroll through the months by using the >> and << buttons, this timestamp is not always the current month.

  - It finds out the starting and ending timestamps of the given month and uses the `ActivityAnalyzer` object to retrieve the office hours and the extra hours for each day of the given month for that user.

  - It returns the formatted information that includes the date, the day, the start time, the end time, the total office hours, and the total extra hours and includes a brief summary with totals and averages.

- `displayReport()`: This method displays user-access reports. It works as follows:

  - It uses the `Theme` class to find out the preferred theme for this user.

  - It creates a new `ThemeTemplate` object called `$themetemplate` and loads the preferred theme template.

  - The content block of the `$themeTemplate` is loaded with `$report`, which is passed to this method as a parameter.

  - It renders the contents of `$themeTemplate` to the user.

Other methods for this application include those in the following table:

Method	Description
convert()	Converts time stamp values as taken from the seconds as input into hours, minutes, and remaining seconds and returns the resultant string.
getWeeklyTSRange()	Returns the weekly time stamp range for a given day, in an array containing the starting and ending time stamps of the week with any time stamp as input.
getMonthlyTSRange()	Returns the monthly time stamp range for a given day, in an array containing the starting and ending time stamps of the month with any time stamp as input.
now()	Returns the time stamp corresponding to the current date and time.

Admin access reporter application

The admin access reporter application, admin_access_reporter.php, shows the overall access report of all the employees/users that can be viewed only by the administrators. It is included on the CD-ROM in the ch07/apps directory.

This application has the following methods.

◆ run(): When the application is run, this method is called. It checks whether the user has administrative privileges. If the user does not have administrative privileges, it exits from the application. If the user has administrative privileges, it calls the reportDriver() method.

◆ authorize(): This method authorizes only administrators to view the application. If the user has administrative privileges, it returns TRUE. Otherwise, it returns FALSE. It uses the $userObj object of User class to get the current user type; sets the isAdmin property of the application, depending on the type it finds; and returns the isAdmin property, which identifies whether the user is an administrator.

◆ generateDailyReport(): This method generates an access report of all users for a specific day. This method works as follows:

■ It finds out the timestamp of the day to be shown. Because the user has the option to scroll through the days by using the >> and << buttons, this timestamp is not always the current day.

- It finds out the starting and ending timestamps of the given day and then uses the `ActivityAnalyzer` object to retrieve the office hours and the extra hours for the day for all users.

- It returns the formatted information that includes the user name, total office hours, and total extra hours of all users for that day, as well as a brief summary with totals and averages.

- `generateWeeklyReport()`: This method generates an access report of a user for a specific week. This method works as follows:

  - It finds out the timestamp of the week to be shown. Because the user has the option to scroll through the weeks by using the >> and << buttons, this timestamp is not always the current week.

  - It finds out the starting and ending timestamps of the given week and uses the `ActivityAnalyzer` object to retrieve the office hours and the extra hours for each day of the given week for all users.

  - It returns the formatted information that includes the username, total office hours, and total extra hours of all users for that week, as well as a brief summary with totals and averages.

- `generateMonthlyReport()`: This method generates an access report of a user for a specific month. This method works as follows:

  - It finds out the timestamp of the month to be shown. Because the user has the option to scroll through the months by using the >> and << buttons, this timestamp is not always the current month.

  - It finds out the starting and ending timestamps of the given month and uses the `ActivityAnalyzer` object to retrieve the office hours and the extra hours for each day of the given month for all users.

  - It returns the formatted information that includes the username, total office hours, and total extra hours of all users for that month and a brief summary with totals and averages.

- `displayReport()`: This method is used to display user-access reports. It works as follows:

  - It uses the `Theme` class to find out the preferred theme for this user.

  - It creates a new `ThemeTemplate` object called `$themeTemplate` and loads the preferred theme template.

  - The content block of the `$themeTemplate` is loaded with `$report`, which is passed to this method as a parameter.

  - The contents of the `$themeTemplate` are rendered to the user.

The following tables describes the other methods for this application:

Method	Description
reportDriver()	Generates the appropriate report based on the type of report requested. (For example, if report type ($rpt) is weekly report (WEEKLY = 2), generateWeeklyReport() is called to generate the report.) It then calls displayReport() to display the report.
convert()	Converts timestamp values as taken from the seconds as input into hour, minute, and remaining seconds and returns the resultant string.
getWeeklyTSRange()	Returns the weekly timestamp range for a given day. This method returns an array containing the starting and ending timestamps of the week with any timestamp as input.
getMonthlyTSRange()	Returns the monthly timestamp range for a given day. This method returns an array containing the starting and ending timestamps of the month with any timestamp as input.
now()	Returns the timestamp corresponding to the current date and time.
toggleSortCriteria()	Toggles the sort criteria from ascending to descending and vice-versa. It takes the string 'reverse' or null as input and returns the other one of the two as output in an exclusive manner.
sortByExtra()	Sorts the report by extra hours of the users in descending order. It takes two arrays as parameters and returns 1 if the first one's extra hour value is less than the other one's; otherwise, it returns -1.
sortByOffice()	Sorts the report by office hours of the users in descending order. It takes two arrays as parameters and returns 1 if the first one's office hour value is less than the other one's; otherwise, it returns -1.
reversesortByExtra()	Sorts the extra hours of the users in ascending order. It takes two arrays as parameters and returns -1 if the first one's extra hour value is less than the other one's; otherwise, it returns 1.
reversesortByOffice()	Sorts the office hours of the users in ascending order. It takes two arrays as parameters and returns -1 if the first one's office hour value is less than the other one's; otherwise, it returns 1.

Daily logbook manager application

The daily logbook manager application is called `daily_logbook_mngr.php`, which shows a daily breakdown of login/logout for a particular user. This application is included on the CD-ROM in the `ch07/apps` directory.

It has the following methods:

- `run()`: When the application is run, this method is called. It does the following:

  - Checks whether the user has administrative privilege.

  - If the user has the administrative privilege and if she passes a user ID, she can view the access logs of that user as well. `run()` sets `$this->userID` as the passed user ID. Nonadministrative users are not allowed to view others' access logs. They can view only their own logs.

  - After setting the `userID`, it runs `reportDriver()`, which shows the daily activities of the intended user for the given date.

- `authorize()`: This method authorizes access to this application. It works as follows:

  - It creates the `DBI` object called `$user_dbi`, which points to the central user authentication database (`USER_DB_URL`).

  - A user object called `$userObj` is created using the `$user_dbi` and current user ID.

  - The `getType()` is used to determine the current user type. If the user is an administrator (`ADMIN_TYPE`), the `$isAdmin` variable is set to `TRUE`.

  - This method always returns `TRUE`, because everyone on the intranet can view this application.

- `reportDriver()`: This method generates and displays the user access report. It works as follows:

  - It finds out all the timestamps (Office start timestamp, Lunch start timestamp, Lunch end timestamp, and so on) that are necessary to retrieve the activities of the day.

  - It creates an object of the `ActivityAnalyzer` class and uses the `getDailyLog()` method of that object to get the daily activity log.

  - It generates the report using the `$LOG_DETAIL_TEMPLATE` template and shows it to the user.

- convert(): This method converts timestamp values as taken from the seconds as input into hours, minutes, and remaining seconds and returns the resultant string.

User tip application

The user tip application is called `tips.php` and shows a tip of the day. This application is included on the CD-ROM in the `ch07/apps` directory.

It has the following methods:

◆ `run()`: This method is responsible for running the application. It sets `$TIP_URL` to the URL of the tip to be shown by randomly choosing a tip template and then redirects the application to show the tip template.

◆ `authorize()`: This method authorizes everyone on the intranet to view the document access list and, therefore, always returns `TRUE`.

User preference application

Currently, the user can have two types of preferences: a specific theme ID or an automatic tip display on or off. A preference application (discussed later) asks the user to choose a theme and enable/disable automatic tip on login options.

A preference ID value of 1 indicates that the preference is for a theme; a value of 2 indicates that the user's preference is for an automatic tip display.

A *theme* is like a skin on the intranet interface that makes the intranet look different for different users. The themes are HTML templates that are loaded by intranet applications, and the application's own interface is embedded within the contents block area of the theme.

The user preference application is called `preference.php`, and is included on the CD-ROM in the `ch07/apps` directory.

This application enables users to choose a theme for their intranet home page and also allows them to toggle automatic tip display on login. It has the following methods:

◆ `run()`: When the application is run, this method is called. It decides which functionality is requested by the user and calls the appropriate method to perform the desired operations. It does the following:

  ■ Creates a theme object, `$this->themeObj`.

  ■ The current user's theme choice is stored in `$this->theme` by calling the `getUserTheme()` method of the theme object created.

  ■ If the application is called with `$pref = upd`, the preferences are updated. (At the first instance of preference change, if there is no previous preference to update, `run()` adds the new preferences to the database. Thereafter, it continues to update [and not insert] every time there is a request to change preference.)

  ■ `displayMenu()`is called to show the current preferences.

◆ `authorize()`: This method authorizes everyone on the intranet to view the document-access list and, therefore, always returns `TRUE`.

♦ `displayMenu()`: This method displays the menu shown in the preference page. This is how it works:

- A preference template ($`PREFERNCE_TEMPLATE`) is loaded in a template object called $`template`.

- The template contains a list of available themes that is loaded using the `getAllThemes()` method of the `Theme` class. The current theme for the user viewing the page is preselected.

- It also contains two radio buttons for the auto tip option (Yes/No); one of them is preselected based on the current user's auto tip preference.

- The user's preferences are retrieved using the `getPreferences()` method of the `intranetUser` class.

- The update button at the bottom of the template lets the user update her preferences, which she can change using the combo box and the radio buttons.

- The contents of the $`template` object are inserted into the $`themeTemplate` object's content block and the results are printed on the user's browser screen.

Installing Intranet Applications from the CD-ROM

The installation process assumes the following:

♦ You are using a Linux system with MySQL and Apache server installed.

♦ During the installation process, this directory is referred to as `%DocumentRoot%`.

♦ Your MySQL server is hosted on the intranet Web server and can be accessed via `localhost`. However, if this is not the case, you can easily modify the database URLs in each application's configuration files. For example, the `home.conf` file has MySQL database-access URLs such as the following:

```
$INTRANET_DB_URL='mysql://root:foobar@localhost/INTRANET'
$USER_DB_URL = 'mysql://root:foobar@localhost/auth'
```

If your database server is called `db.domain.com` and the username and password to access the `INTRANET` and `auth` databases (which you will create during this installation process) are `admin` and `db123`, you would modify the database access URLs throughout each configuration file as follows:

```
$INTRANET_DB_URL='mysql://admin:db123@db.domain.com/INTRANET'
$USER_DB_URL = 'mysql://admin:db123@db.domain.com/auth'
```

◆ You have installed the PHPLIB and PEAR libraries. Normally, these are installed during PHP installation. For your convenience, we have provided these in the lib/phplib.tar.gz and lib/pear.tar.gz directories on the CD-ROM. In the sample installation steps, we assume that these are installed in the /evoknow/phplib and /evoknow/pear directories. Because your installation locations for these libraries is likely to differ, make sure that you replace these paths in the configuration files.

Here is how to get your intranet applications up and running:

1. **Install the framework.** You need to extract the framework.tar.gz file from the ch4 directory on the CD-ROM. This file should be placed in your %DocumentRoot% directory and extracted.

   Once you extract it by using tar xvzf framework.tar.gz, the framework.tar.gz will install the PHP Application Framework in the %DocumentRoot%/framework directory.

2. **Install the central user-authentication applications.** If you have not yet installed ch5.tar.gz from the CD-ROM (in the ch05 directory), you should extract the ch5.tar.gz file using tar xvzf ch5.tar.gz command in your %DocumentRoot% directory.

   This installs central login/logout applications in the %DocumentRoot%/login and %DocumentRoot%/logout applications.

   Make sure that you create the auth database and an administrative user as discussed in Chapter 5. The quickest way to create this database, with an administrative user account called carol and password mysecret, is to run the following commands:

```
mysqladmin -u root -p create auth
mysql -u root -p -D auth < auth.sql

mysql -u root -p -D auth

mysql> insert into users (EMAIL, PASSWORD, ACTIVE, TYPE)
values('carol@example.com', ENCRYPT('mysecret'), 1, 9);

mysql> exit
```

   The auth.sql file can be found in the ch5/sql directory on the CD-ROM.

   Make sure that you configure the login and logout applications using %DocumentRoot%/login/login.conf and %DocumentRoot%/logout/logout.conf files, respectively. In most cases, you should need to change only paths and database access information.

3. **Install the central user-management system.** From the ch6 directory of the CD-ROM, extract the user_mngr.tar.gz file using tar xvzf user_mngr.tar.gz in your %DocumentRoot% directory.

This will install the central user-management application in the `%DocumentRoot%/user_mngr` directory. Make sure that you configure the user manager applications by using the `%DocumentRoot%/user_mngr/apps/user_mngr.conf` file. In most cases, you should need to change only paths and database access information.

4. **Install the home applications.** If you have an `index.php` file in your `%DocumentRoot%`, rename and back up this file. Then, from the `ch7` directory of the CD-ROM, extract `ch7.tar.gz` in `%DocumentRoot%`. This will create a home directory and photos directories in your document root, and it will also install `index.php` script. Configure `%DocumentRoot%/home/home.conf` for path and database settings.

   Make sure that you create the `INTRANET` database as discussed earlier in this chapter. The quickest way to create this database is to run the following commands:

   ```
   mysqladmin -u root -p create database INTRANET
   mysql -u root -p -D INTRANET < INTRANET.sql
   ```

   The `INTRANET.sql` file can be found in the `ch07/sql` directory.

5. **Set the file/directory permissions.** Make sure that you've changed the file and directory permissions so that your intranet Web server can access all the files. The path pointed to by the `$LD_CATEGORY_NAV_DIR` variable in `home.conf` must be writeable by the Web server, because this is the navigation file that gets generated whenever a new document is published using the simple publishing tool discussed in Chapter 8. You should keep this directory outside your Web document tree if possible.

After you've performed these steps, you're ready to test your applications.

Testing the Intranet Home Application

Log in to your intranet via `http://yourserver/index.php` using the username and password that you created in Chapter 6. If you used the database configuration steps described in the previous section, you should have at least a default user called `carol` (with password set to `mysecret`) that can log you into your intranet.

The `index.php` file installed in `%DocumentRoot%` during the installation process is nothing but a simple redirect to `/home/home.php` application. So if you did not install `index.php` in the previous installation section, you can access your intranet using `http://yourserver/home/home.php`. You'll be automatically redirected to the central login script (`/login/login.php`), and after you authenticate success-fully, you'll see an intranet home page, as shown in Figure 7-3.

Figure 7-3: An intranet user home page.

The user home shows a left navigation bar with applications that are available on your intranet. The navigation bar is a file that is loaded from `%DocumentRoot%/themes/%CurrentTheme%/home_left_nav.html`. For example, the default theme (`std_blue`) will load the navigation file `%DocumentRoot%/themes/std_blue/home_left_nav.html`.

If you install intranet applications anywhere beyond the `%DocumentRoot%` as suggested, you'll need to modify the navigation files (`home_left_nav.html, default_left_nav.html`) for each theme in the themes directory. You'll have to update the links to applications in these files to point to the application locations where you installed them.

Changing user preferences

To change your theme or auto tip preferences, click the Preferences link in the navigation bar. You'll see a screen similar to that shown in Figure 7-4.

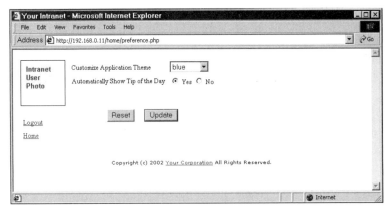

Figure 7–4: User preferences.

You can decide to view the automatic tip window at login by selecting the Automatically Show Tip of the Day option, and you can change the current theme by selecting a new theme from the drop-down list of themes.

After you submit your changes by clicking the Update button, the theme choice will take effect immediately. However, the auto tip is shown only once per login, so you'll have to log out to see a new tip.

The tips are stored in the %DocumentRoot%/home/templates/tips directory as number.html, where number is an integer. You can add as many tips as you want to show your users by creating new number.html files in sequential order and then updating the $MAX_AVAILABLE_TIP setting in home.conf to reflect the number of available tips in your intranet.

To return to the home page, click the Home link in the navigation bar.

Checking user access logs

To view your own access report, click the Access Report link, which shows a screen similar to that in Figure 7-5.

Because we're showing an administrative user (Carol) session in the sample screen, you see a great deal more than what a regular user sees.

As an administrator, our sample user, Carol, can force-login/logout anyone and also view other users' access logs. For example, Figure 7-6 shows Carol viewing another user's access log entries.

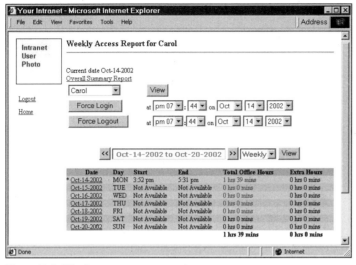

Figure 7-5: Viewing your own access log.

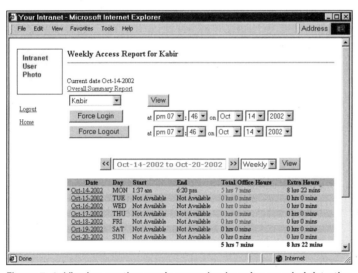

Figure 7-6: Viewing another user's access log by using an administrative account.

An administrative user, such as Carol, can also access a summary version of the access logs for all users by clicking the Overall Summary Report link. It shows a screen similar to that in Figure 7-7.

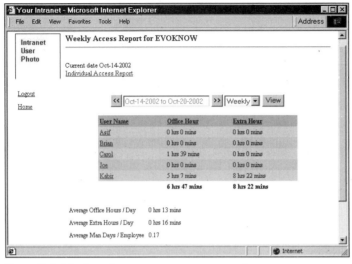

Figure 7-7: Viewing all user access summary reports.

As an administrative user, Carol can view weekly, daily, or monthly reports for all user access. The arrow buttons allow her to view previous months, weeks, or days.

Writing a message to other users

From the user home page, a user can send another user a message via the MOTD tool by clicking the MOTD Manager link on the navigation bar. Figure 7-8 shows the message screen.

Figure 7-8: Writing a message to other users.

A user can add a message and decide who can view it by selecting one or more users from the list or everyone. Clicking the Save Message link shows a confirmation page with the message shown on-screen for review. When the user confirms the message by clicking the Confirm button, the message is sent to the intended users and displayed on the day of the message.

Figure 7-9 shows the message being shown on Carol's home page.

Figure 7-9: A message from another user.

Carol must click the OK button to remove the message. The great thing about this type of messaging system is that all users must click OK to signify that they've read the message. This means that a company administrator is assured that all her messages are being read.

To log out from the intranet, click the Logout link at any time.

Summary

In this chapter, you explored a base intranet system that utilizes the central authentication and user-management systems discussed in the preceding chapters. Here you learned how to generate a user home page and how to enable a simple message delivery system that users can use to notify each other of company or personal events and issues.

Chapter 8

Intranet Simple Document Publisher

IN THIS CHAPTER

◆ Developing a simple intranet document publisher

◆ Installing the intranet document publisher

◆ Using the intranet document publisher

PUBLISHING DOCUMENTS ON THE WEB or on the intranet is a major task due to the complexity of the documents and how organizations manage their workflow. In this chapter, we'll develop a simple document publishing tool that is available to all users on the intranet and handles HTML documents only. Because most office word-processing applications these days can save files as HTML, this opens up the publisher to most organizations.

Let's look at the functionality requirements that this document publishing system will meet.

Identifying the Functionality Requirements

The document publisher will offer each user on the intranet the following:

◆ **Web forms to create new documents:** The Web form accepts both text and HTML data. However, the publisher itself does not support formatting. In other words, if a user wants to paste the contents of a Word document into the publisher form, she should save the Word document as an HTML file and copy the HTML contents instead of the text shown in Word's WYSIWYG editor. If text documents are to be submitted, a simple trick is needed to maintain formatting, which is discussed in the "Adding a new document" section later in this chapter.

◆ **Easy and simple category-based document organization:** Each document is published in a category. There can be only a single level of categories. Each category will have a defined set of users who can view documents and a defined set of publishers (i.e. users who can create/modify/delete documents).

♦ **User-level access control for viewing and creating documents:** Users can have view or publish (creation/modification/deletion) rights. Multiple users can have view or publish rights per category.

♦ **Automated announcements for document availability and updates:** When new documents are created, the users with view and publish rights are shown an MOTD announcement when they log in to the intranet. When an existing document is modified or removed, the appropriate users also are notified via MOTD. This notification is very useful because an important document change notice can be sent automatically to appropriate users who need to know about the changes. In fact, users will have to acknowledge that they know about the changes by clicking on the OK button of the MOTD document change notice message which gets displayed on their home pages.

Let's take a quick look at the prerequisites of such a publishing system.

The Prerequisites

This document publishing system builds on the intranet classes discussed in the previous chapters in this part of the book. For example, it uses the MOTD class (Chapter 6) to announce new documents and updates.

The applications that we develop here require the central login/logout applications (Chapter 5), user-management applications (Chapter 6), and the intranet home applications (Chapter 7).

In addition, administrative intranet users, who are defined in the intranet user table discussed in Chapter 6, are given full access to all aspects of the document and category management in this publishing tool.

Now let's look at the database design and implementation needed for creating this document publishing system.

Designing the Database

When designing the database for the document publisher we have consider the following data requirements:

♦ There will be multiple categories. Each category will have list of users who can view documents in that category. Each category will also have list of users who can publish documents in that category. So a category has many viewers and publishers.

◆ In each category there will be many documents. Each document will have tracking information and responses. Therefore each document has many tracking and response data.

Based on these requirements, we can create the database relationship as shown in Figure 8-1. Here the LD_CATEGORY table has one to many relationships with the LD_DOCUMENTS table because each category can have many documents. Similarly, LD_CATEGORY has one to many relationships with LD_CAT_VIEWER (viewer list) and LD_CAT_PUBLISHER (publisher list) tables. Since each document in LD_DOCUMENT table has many tracking and response records, it has one to many relationships with LD_TRACK (tracking data) and LD_RESPONSE (response data) tables.

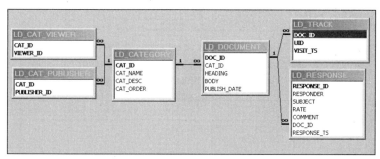

Figure 8-1: Intranet document publisher database diagram.

Table 8-1 describes each table in the database.

TABLE 8-1 DOCUMENT PUBLISHER DATABASE TABLES

Table	Description
LD_CATEGORY	This table is the integral part of this database. It holds the category number (CAT_ID), which is automatically generated by the database, and the category name (CAT_NAME), description (CAT_DESC), and order (CAT_ORDER).
LD_CAT_PUBLISHER	Contains the category publisher information: the category number (CAT_ID) and the ID of the publisher who can publish document in that category (PUBLISHER_ID).
LD_CAT_VIEWER	Holds the category viewer information: the category number (CAT_ID) and the viewer ID of the user who can view documents in that category (VIEWER_ID).

Continued

TABLE 8-1 DOCUMENT PUBLISHER DATABASE TABLES *(Continued)*

Table	Description
LD_DOCUMENT	Holds information about the document: the doc ID (DOC_ID), which is automatically generated when a new document is added to a category; the category number (CAT_ID) in which the document will be published; and the document heading (HEADING), body (BODY), and publishing date (PUBLISH_DATE).
LD_RESPONSE	Contains response(s) to a document published in a category. Each response consists of an ID (RESPONSE_ID), responder (RESPONDER), subject (SUBJECT), rate of the document (RATE), comment by the responder (COMMENT), document ID (DOC_ID), and time of response (RESPONSE_TS).
LD_TRACK	Stores information about when and who viewed the document. It contains the ID (DOC_ID) of the document that has been viewed, the ID (UID) of the users who viewed this page, and the time when the document was visited by the user (VISIT_TS).

I have provided the necessary SQL to create the document publisher database in the ch8/sql/ld_tool.sql file in the CDROM. You can create the database on your MySQL server using this file as follows:

```
mysql -u root -p -D INTRANET < ld_tool.sql
```

Make sure you change the user name (root) to whatever is appropriate for your system.

The Intranet Document Application Classes

With the intranet document publisher database designed, it's time to look at the PHP classes needed to implement the application. Figure 8-2 shows the system diagram for the publisher.

As shown in the system diagram, there are three new objects (Category, Doc, and Response) that are needed to implement the intranet document publisher. Let's discuss the classes that will provide these objects for your applications.

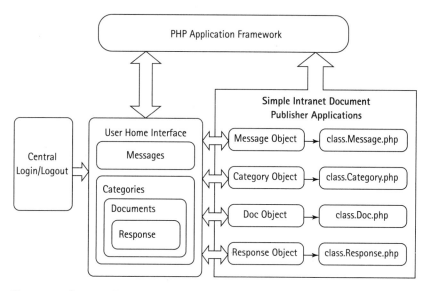

Figure 8-2: Intranet document publisher system diagram.

The Category class

The Category class is used to manipulate each category. It allows an application to create, modify, and delete a category. The `ch08/apps/class/class.Category.php` file in the CDROM an implementation of this class. This class uses the following methods:

- ◆ `Category()`: This is the constructor method. It performs the following functions:

    - Sets the object variable `cat_tbl` to `$LD_CATEGORY_TBL`, which is loaded with the category table name (LD_CATEGORY) from the `ld.conf` file.

    - Sets the object variable `doc_tbl` to `$LD_DOC_TBL`, which is loaded with the document table name (LD_DOCUMENT) from the `ld.conf` file.

    - Sets the object variable `cat_pub_tbl` to `$LD_CAT_PUB_TBL`, which is loaded with the category publisher table from the `ld.conf` file.

    - Sets the object variable `cat_view_tbl` to `$LD_CAT_VIEW_TBL`, which is loaded with the category viewer table name from the `ld.conf` file.

    - Sets the object variable `dbi` to point to the `class.DBI.php`-provided object that is passed to the constructor by an application. The `dbi` member variable holds the DBI object that is used to communicate with the back-end database.

    - Sets the object variable `CAT_ID` to the given category ID (if any).

    - Sets the object variable `std_fields`, which is an array that contains the `LD_CATEGORY` table attributes and their data type.

- ◆ `loadCatInfo()`: This method loads all attribute values into the category object from the `LD_CATEGORY` table by the specified category IDs. This is how it works:

  - ■ `setCatID()` is called to set the passed category ID to the current object. If no category ID is passed, the current `$this->cid` is taken.

  - ■ The `$this->dbi` object is used to retrieve all the attribute values of the given category from the `LD_CATEGORY` table.

  - ■ Each of the values is set to the current object so that they can be retrieved at any time using the other get methods of this class. For example `$this->CAT_NAME` is set to the value of the `CAT_NAME` of the given category.

- ◆ `getCategoryIDbyName()`: This method returns the category ID for the given category name. It works as follows:

  - ■ It takes the category name as parameter.

  - ■ The category name is quoted using the quote() method of the `$this->dbi` object and inserted into the SQL statement, which is needed to retrieve the category ID.

  - ■ The query executes, and the resultant category ID is returned. If no result is found, it returns null.

- ◆ `getCategories()`: This method returns all the category names along with their IDs from the `LD_CATEGORY` table. This is how it works:

  - ■ It executes a SQL query to retrieve all the field value of the `LD_CATEGORY` table ordered by descending `CAT_ORDER`.

  - ■ The result is stored in an array that contains the category ID and name.

  - ■ It returns the prepared array (or null, if the result set is empty).

- ◆ `getPublishers()`: This method returns the publisher IDs for a given category. This is how it works:

  - ■ It calls `setCatID()` to set the passed category ID.

  - ■ It executes a SQL query that retrieves all the publisher IDs from the `LD_CAT_PUBLISHER` table for the given category ID.

  - ■ It stores the result of the execution in an array (unless the result set is empty), and returns the array. It returns null if the result set is empty.

- ◆ `getViewers()`: This method returns the viewer IDs for a given category. It works as follows:

  - ■ It calls `setCatID()` to set the passed category ID.

  - ■ It executes a SQL query that retrieves all the viewer IDs from the `LD_CAT_VIEWER` table for the given category ID.

- It stores the result of the execution in an array (unless the result set is empty), and returns the array. It returns null if the result set is empty.

◆ addCategory( ): This method adds a new category into to the LD_CATE-GORY table. Category name, category ID, category order, and description are passed into an associative array as a parameter to the method. It works as follows:

  - The SQL statement is prepared using the $this->std_fields array that contains all the attributes of the LD_CATEGORY table and the values from the associative array that has been passed as parameter.

  - The values of the parameter are formatted using the quote( ) method of the $this->dbi object.

  - After executing the SQL statement, the newly added category's CAT_ID is retrieved using another SQL statement.

  - If the insertion query is successful, this method returns the category ID of the newly added category. Otherwise, it returns FALSE.

◆ modifyCategory( ): This method updates category information for a given category. Update information is passed in an associative array as a parameter to this method. It works as follows:

  - The SQL statement is prepared using the $this->std_fields array that contains all the attributes of the LD_CATEGORY table and the values from the associative array that has been passed as parameter.

  - The values of the parameter are formatted using the quote( ) method of the $this->dbi object.

  - If the update query is successful, this method returns TRUE. Otherwise, it returns FALSE.

◆ updateCategoryOrders( ): This method updates the orders of the categories. This takes an array of category ID and new order and assigns the new orders to each category. This is how it works for each category:

  - It updates the category by assigning it a temporary value (-1). This is done to avoid having the same order for two categories, which would forbid you to execute the query, because the ORDER attribute is unique.

  - After assigning the temporary value, the category is updated with the new order value for it.

  - The method returns TRUE upon successful update. Otherwise, it returns FALSE.

Method	Description
setCatID()	Sets the category ID of the category object. It takes a non-empty category ID as the parameter.
getCategoryName()	Returns the name of the category object from the LD_CATEGORY table. It calls loadCatInfo() to set all the field properties of the class and then returns $this->CAT_NAME.
getCategoryOrder()	Returns the order of the category object from the LD_CATEGORY table. It calls loadCatInfo() to set all the field properties of the class and then returns $this->CAT_ORDER.
getCategoryDesc()	Returns the description of the category object from the LD_CATEGORY table. It calls loadCatInfo() to set all the field properties of the class and then returns $this->CAT_DESC.
getHighestOrder()	Returns the highest order of the LD_CATEGORY table.
deleteCategory()	Deletes the category from the database. It deletes all data related to the category from the ld_tool database. It takes the category ID as a parameter and returns TRUE or FALSE depending on the status of the deletion operation.
deleteDocsByCatID()	Deletes all document records related to a category. It takes category ID as a parameter and returns TRUE or FALSE depending on the status of the deletion operation.
deleteCategoryViewers()	Deletes all viewer records related to a category. It takes category ID as a parameter.
deleteCategoryPublishers()	Deletes all publisher records related to a category. It takes category ID as a parameter.
isViewable()	Determines if a category is viewable by a specific viewer. It takes category ID and user ID as parameters and returns TRUE if the user is authorized to view documents under the given category; otherwise, it returns FALSE.

Method	Description
isPublishable()	Determines if the given publisher is allowed to publish in a specific category. It takes category ID and user ID as parameter and returns TRUE if the user is authorized to publish documents under the given category; otherwise, it returns FALSE.
addCategoryPublishers()	Adds publishers to a specific category. It takes category ID and user IDs as parameters and returns TRUE upon successful insertion of the data. It returns FALSE if it fails to add the publishers for the category.
addCategoryViewers()	Adds viewers to a specific category. It takes category ID and user IDs as parameters and returns TRUE upon successful insertion of the data. It returns FALSE if it fails to add the viewers for the category.

The Doc class

The Doc class provides the doc object, which is used to manipulate doc. It allows publishers to create and delete doc. The ch08/apps/class/class.Doc.php file in the CDROM is an implementation of this class. The following are the methods available in this class:

- ◆ Doc(): This is the constructor method, which performs the following tasks:

  - Sets the object variable cat_tbl, which holds the category table name, to $LD_CATEGORY_TBL, which is loaded from the ld.conf file.

  - Sets the object variable doc_tbl, which holds the LD_DOCUMENT table name, to $LD_DOC_TBL, which is loaded from the ld.conf file.

  - Sets the object variable resp_tbl, which holds the response table name, to $LD_RESPONSE_TBL, which is loaded from the ld.conf file.

  - Sets the object variable track_tbl, which holds the track table name, to $LD_TRACK_TBL, which is loaded from the ld.conf file.

  - Sets an object variable called std_fields, which is an array that contains the LD_DOCUMENT table attributes and their data type.

- Sets an object variable called fields, which holds a comma separated list of fields from the std_fields set earlier.

- Sets the object variable dbi to point to the class.DBI.php-provided object, which is passed to the constructor by an application. The dbi member variable holds the DBI object that is used to communicate with the back-end database.

- Calls setDocID()to set the document ID of the object.

- Sets an object variable called std_fields, which is an array that contains the LD_DOCUMENT table attributes and their data type.

- ◆ loadDocInfo(): This method loads all attribute values into the document object from the LD_DOCUMENT table by the specified document ID. This is how it works:

  - setDocID() is called to set the passed document ID to the current object. If no document ID is passed, the current object's document ID is taken.

  - The $this->dbi object is used to retrieve all the attribute values of the given document from the LD_DOCUMENT table.

  - Each of the values is set to the current object so that they can be retrieved at any time using the other get methods of this class. For example $this->DOC_NAME is set the value of the DOC_NAME of the given document. This method sets all the attributes such as document ID, category number, heading, body of the document, and publish date for a given document.

- ◆ addDoc(): This method adds new documents to the database. Attributes such as document ID, category number, heading, body of the document, and publish date are passed in an associative array as parameters to this method. It works as follows:

  - The SQL statement is prepared using the $this->std_fields array that contains all the attributes of the LD_DOCUMENT table and the values from the associative array that has been passed as parameter.

  - The values of the parameter are formatted using the quote() method of the $this->dbi object.

  - After executing the SQL statement, the newly added document's DOC_ID is retrieved using another SQL statement.

  - If the insertion query is successful, this method returns the category ID of the newly added category. Otherwise, it returns FALSE.

◆ `modifyDoc()`: This method updates document information in the database. Attributes such as document ID, category number, heading, body of the document, and publish date are passed in an associative array as parameters to this method. It works as follows:

  ■ The SQL statement is prepared using the `$this->std_fields` array that contains all the attributes of the `LD_DOCUMENT` table and the values from the associative array that has been passed as a parameter.

  ■ The values of the parameter are formatted using the `quote()` method of the `$this->dbi` object.

  ■ If the update query is successful, this method returns `TRUE`. Otherwise, it returns `FALSE`.

◆ `getDocsByCatID()`: This method returns all documents that are to be published until the current time related to the given category from the database. This method takes category ID as the parameter. It works as follows:

  ■ It executes a SQL statement that retrieves all the documents up to the current timestamp for the given category.

  ■ It stores the result into an array if the result set is not empty.

  ■ It returns the array, or, if the result is empty, it returns null.

◆ `getAllDocsByCatID()`: This method returns all documents that fall under the given category. This also takes category ID as a parameter. It works as follows:

  ■ It executes a SQL statement that retrieves all the documents for the given category.

  ■ It stores the result into an array if the result set is not empty.

  ■ It returns null if the result is empty. Otherwise, it returns the array.

◆ `getTrackDetails()`: This method returns all tracking information for the given document. It works as follows:

  ■ It executes a SQL query that retrieves all the user IDs and their visit timestamps for the given document ID.

  ■ The result is stored in an array if it is not empty.

  ■ The method returns null when the result set is empty. Otherwise, it returns the array.

The following are other methods of this class:

Method	Description
setDocID()	Sets the document ID. If the document ID is provided as a parameter, it is set as the object's document ID; otherwise, the current object's document ID is returned.
getHeading()	Returns the heading of the current document object. It takes document ID as a parameter.
getPublishDate()	Returns the publishing date of the current document object. It also takes document ID as a parameter.
getBody()	Returns the body of the current document object. Document ID is passed into this method as a parameter.
getCategory()	Returns the category of the current document object. It takes document ID as a parameter.
deleteDoc()	Deletes the document from the database. It will delete all data related to the document from the database. It takes the ID of the document to be deleted as the parameter.
deleteResponsesByDocID()	Deletes all responses related for any doc from the database. It takes document ID as the parameter.
trackVisit()	Tracks visits to the given document and enters new track information (document ID, user ID, and visit timestamp) into the LD_TRACK table of the database. It takes document ID, user ID, and the timestamp as parameters. It returns TRUE upon successful insertion; otherwise, it returns FALSE.

The Response class

The Response class provides the response object. The response object is used to manipulate response data. Applications can add or remove responses using the response object. The ch08/apps/class/class.Response.php file in the CDROM is an implementation of this class.

Following are the response class methods:

◆ `Response()`: This is the constructor method that creates the `response` object. This method does the following:

- Sets the object variable `cat_tbl`, which holds the category table name, to `$LD_CATEGORY_TBL`, which is loaded from the `ld.conf` file.

- Sets the object variable `doc_tbl`, which holds the document table name, to `$LD_DOC_TBL`, which is loaded from the `ld.conf` file.

- Sets the object variable `resp_tbl`, which holds the response table name, to `$LD_RESPONSE_TBL`, which is loaded from the `ld.conf` file.

- Sets the object variable `dbi` to point to the `class.DBI.php`-provided object, which is passed to the constructor by an application. The `dbi` member variable holds the DBI object that is used to communicate with the back-end database.

- Calls `setResponseID()` to set the response ID of the object. Sets the object variable `std_fields`, which is an array that contains the `LD_RESPONSE` table attributes and their data type.

◆ `loadResponseInfo()`: This method loads all attribute values into the response object from the `LD_RESPONSE` table by the specified response ID. This is how it works:

- It calls `setResponseID()` to set the passed response ID to the current object. If no response ID is passed, the current object's response ID is taken.

- The `$this->dbi` object is used to retrieve all the attribute values of the given response from the `LD_RESPONSE` table.

- Each of the values is set to the current object so that they can be retrieved at any time using the other get methods of this class. For example `$this->RESPONDER` is set the username who responded (i.e. provided feedback) to a document.

◆ `getResponsesByDocID()`: This method returns all responses for a given document ID. This is how it works:

- It executes a SQL query that retrieves all the attributes of the `LD_RESPONSE` table for a given document ID.

- It stores the result of the query in an array unless the result set is empty.

- The method returns null when there is no result found from the query; otherwise, it returns the array.

◆ addResponse(): This method adds new response to the LD_RESPONSE table of the database. The attributes such as response ID, category number, subject, document ID, rate, response time, and so on are passed into an associative array as parameters to this method. It works as follows:

- The SQL statement is prepared using the $this->std_fields array that contains all the attributes of the LD_RESPONSE table and the values from the associative array that has been passed as parameter.

- The values of the parameter are formatted using the quote() method of the $this->dbi object.

- After executing the SQL statement, the newly added response's RESPONSE_ID is retrieved using another SQL statement.

- If the insertion query is successful, this method returns the response ID of the newly added response. Otherwise, it returns FALSE.

Following are the other methods in this class:

Method	Description
setResponseID()	Sets the response ID. If the response ID is provided as the parameter, it is set as the object's response ID; otherwise, the current response ID is returned.
getResponseSubject()	Returns the subject of the current response. It takes the response ID as the parameter.
getResponseDocID()	Returns the document ID of the current response. It takes the response ID as the parameter.
getResponder()	Returns the responder of the current response. It takes response ID as the parameter.
getResponseBody()	Returns the body of the current response. Response ID is passed to this method as the parameter.
getAvgRatingByDocID()	Returns the average rating of a given document. It takes the document ID as the parameter.
getTotalResponseByDocID()	Returns the total number of responses for the given document. This method takes the document ID as the parameter.
deleteResponse()	Deletes the response from the database. It will delete all data related to the response from the database. It takes response ID as the parameter.

Setting up Application Configuration Files

Like all other applications we've developed in this book, the document publishing applications also use a standard set of configuration, message, and error files. These files are discussed in the following sections.

The main configuration file

The primary configuration file for the entire document publishing system is called ld.conf. Table 8-2 discusses each configuration variable.

TABLE 8-2 LD.CONF **VARIABLES**

Configuration Variable	Purpose
$PEAR_DIR	Set to the directory containing the PEAR package; specifically the DB module needed for class.DBI.php in our application framework.
$PHPLIB_DIR	Set to the PHPLIB directory, which contains the PHPLIB packages (specifically, the template.inc package needed for template manipulation).
$APP_FRAMEWORK_DIR	Set to our application framework directory.
$PATH	Set to the combined directory path consisting of $PEAR_DIR, $PHPLIB_DIR, and $APP_FRAMEWORK_DIR. This path is used with the ini_set( ) method to redefine the php.ini entry for include_path to include $PATH ahead of the default path. This allows PHP to find our application framework, PHPLIB, and PEAR-related files.
$AUTHENTICATION_URL	Set to the central login application URL.
$LOGOUT_URL	Set to the central logout application URL.
$HOME_URL	Set to the topmost URL of the site. If the URL redirection application does not find a valid URL in the e-campaign database to redirect to for a valid request, it uses this URL as a default.

Continued

TABLE 8-2 LD.CONF **VARIABLES** *(Continued)*

Configuration Variable	Purpose
$APPLICATION_NAME	Internal name of the application.
$DEFAULT_LANGUAGE	Set to the default (two-character) language code.
$ROOT_PATH	Set to the root path of the application.
$REL_ROOT_PATH	Relative path to the root directory.
$REL_APP_PATH	Relative application path as seen from the web browser.
$TEMPLATE_DIR	The fully qualified path to the template directory.
$THEME_TEMPLATE_DIR	The fully qualified path to the theme template directory.
$REL_PHOTO_DIR	The Web-relative path to the photo directory used to store user photos.
$PHOTO_DIR	The fully qualified path to the photo directory.
$DEFAULT_PHOTO	Name of the default photo file, which is used when a user does not have a photo in the photo directory.
$CLASS_DIR	The fully qualified path to the class directory.
$REL_TEMPLATE_DIR	The Web relative path to the template directory used.
$CATEGORY_CLASS	Name of the Category class file.
$DOC_CLASS	Name of the Doc class file.
$RESPONSE_CLASS	Name of the Response class file.
$MESSAGE_CLASS	Name of the Message class file. This class is developed for the MOTD application, discussed in the Chapter 7.
$LD_MNGR	Name of the application that shows document indexes for a given category or all categories.
$LD_DETAILS_MNGR	Name of the application that shows document details.

Configuration Variable	Purpose
$LD_RESPONSE_MNGR	Name of the application that manages responses to documents.
$LD_ADMIN_MNGR	Name of the application that allows administrative users to manage categories.
$LD_VISIT_LIST_MNGR	Name of the application that allows users to view document-tracking information.
$LD_DB_URL	The fully qualified URL for the database used to store the documents and categories.
$LD_CATEGORY_TBL	Name of the category table in the database.
$LD_DOC_TBL	Name of the document table in the database.
$LD_RESPONSE_TBL	Name of the response table in the database.
$USER_PREFERENCE_TBL	Name of the user preference table in the database.
$MESSAGE_TBL	Name of the MOTD message table in the database.
$LD_CAT_PUB_TBL	Name of the category publishers table in the database.
$LD_CAT_VIEW_TBL	Name of the category viewers table in the database.
$LD_TRACK_TBL	Name of the document tracking data table in the database.
$MSG_VIEWER_TBL	Name of the message viewer list table in the database.
$AUTH_DB_TBL	Name of the user authentication table in the database.
$STATUS_TEMPLATE	Name of the status template file used to display status messages.
$LD_HOME_TEMPLATE	Name of the document index template file.
$LD_DETAILS_TEMPLATE	Name of the document details template file.
$LD_RESPONSE_TEMPLATE	Name of the document response entry form template file.

Continued

TABLE 8-2 LD.CONF **VARIABLES** *(Continued)*

Configuration Variable	Purpose
$LD_VIEW_RESPONSE_TEMPLATE	Name of the document response view template file.
$ADD_MOD_DOC_TEMPLATE	Name of the add/modify document entry form template file.
$ADD_MOD_CATEGORY_TEMPLATE	Name of the add/modify category entry form template file.
$ANNOUNCE_LD_ADDED_TEMPLATE	Name of the new document announcement message template file.
$ANNOUNCE_LD_MOD_TEMPLATE	Name of the document modification announcement message template file.
$LD_VISIT_LIST_TEMPLATE	Name of the document track listing template file.
$LD_REORDER_CAT_TEMPLATE	Name of the category reordering entry form template file.
ODD_COLOR	Color defined for odd rows when displaying tabular data such as document track listing.
EVEN_COLOR	Color defined for even rows when displaying tabular data such as document track listing.
$ratings	Defines an associative array used to display response rating information.
USER_DB_URL	The fully qualified authentication database URL.
LD_ADMIN_TYPE	The administrative user type value.
CAT_PER_LINE	The number of categories per row to show in a navigation table, which is created in the navigation file.
SEPARATOR	The characters that separate each navigation entry (category) in the navigation, which is created in the navigation file.
LD_UPDATE_TITLE	The MOTD message header used to announce updated documents via MOTD.
LD_ADD_TITLE	The MOTD message header used to announce new documents via MOTD.

Configuration Variable	Purpose
$LD_CATEGORY_NAV_DIR	The fully qualified path for the category navigation file. Ideally, you should set this to a path that is outside your Web document tree and the files in this directory should have only read/write permissions for the Web server user which runs the PHP scripts.
$LD_CATEGORY_NAV_OUTFILE	The category navigation file created by the simple document publishing system.
$LD_CATEGORY_NAV_TEMPLATE	The category navigation template file used to generate the navigation file pointed by $LD_CATEGORY_NAV_OUTFILE.
$DEFAULT_THEME	The default theme index in the $THEME_TEMPLATE array.
$USER_DEFAULTS	A user's theme and auto tip default settings.
$TIP_SCRIPT	The name of the tip script.
$TIP_URL	The Web-relative path for the tip files.
$MAX_AVAILABLE_TIP	The maximum number of tips from which to display the tip.
$THEME_TEMPLATE[n]	The list of theme templates
$PRINT_TEMPLATE[n]	The list of print templates associative with the theme templates.

The directory structure used in the ld.conf file supplied in ch8 directory on the CD-ROM may need to be tailored to your own system's requirements. Here is what the current directory structure looks like:

```
htdocs ($ROOT_PATH same as %DocumentRoot%)
  |
  +---home (base intranet application discussed in chapter 7)
  |   |
  |   +---templates
  |        |
  |        +---themes (theme templates used by all intranet apps) <--+
  |                                                                  |
  +---photos (user photos used by all intranet apps)                |
```

```
    |                                                          |
 +---ld_tools (Intranet Simple Document Publisher Application) |
     |                                                         |
     +---apps (publisher apps and configuration files)         |
         |                                                     |
         +---class (publisher apps and configuration)          |
         |                                                     |
         +---templates (publisher HTML templates)              |
             |                                                 |
             +---themes ------------symbolically linked------------+
```

By changing the following configuration parameters in `ld.conf`, you can modify the directory structure to fit your site requirements.

```
$ROOT_PATH           = $_SERVER['DOCUMENT_ROOT'];

$REL_PHOTO_DIR       = '/photos';
$PHOTO_DIR           = $ROOT_PATH    . $REL_PHOTO_DIR;
$REL_ROOT_PATH       = '/ld_tool';
$REL_APP_PATH        = $REL_ROOT_PATH . '/apps';
$TEMPLATE_DIR        = $ROOT_PATH    . $REL_APP_PATH . '/templates';
$CLASS_DIR           = $ROOT_PATH    . $REL_APP_PATH . '/class';
$REL_TEMPLATE_DIR    = $REL_APP_PATH . '/templates/';
$THEME_TEMPLATE_DIR  = $TEMPLATE_DIR . '/themes';
```

The themes directory within the ld_tools/apps/templates should be a symbolic link pointing to the themes directory of the Intranet home application themes. For the given directory structure the ld_tools/apps/templates/themes can be created using the following command:

```
ln -s home/templates/themes ld_tools/apps/templates/themes
```

The above command assumes that it is being run from the %DocumentRoot% (htdocs) directory of the intranet Web site. If you cannot make symbolic links between two directories, you can simply copy the home/templates/themes directory as ld_tools/apps/templates/themes. Also, you can set the $THEME_TEMPLATE_DIR to $ROOT_PATH . '/home/templates/themes'.

The messages file

The messages displayed by the publisher applications are stored in the ch8/apps/ld.messages file in the CDROM. You can change the messages using a text editor.

The errors file

The error messages displayed by the document publishing applications are stored in the ch8/apps/ld.errors file in the CDROM. You can modify the error messages using a text editor.

Setting Up the Application Templates

The HTML interface templates needed for the applications are included on the CD-ROM. These templates contain various template tags to display necessary information dynamically. The templates are named in the ld.conf file. These templates are discussed in Table 8-3.

TABLE 8-3 HTML TEMPLATES

Configuration Variable	Template File	Purpose
$STATUS_TEMPLATE	ld_status.html	Shows status message.
$LD_HOME_TEMPLATE	ld_brief.html	Document index template.
$LD_DETAILS_TEMPLATE	ld_details.html	Shows the contents of the document.
$LD_RESPONSE_TEMPLATE	ld_response_input.html	Web form template to enter response information.
$LD_VIEW_RESPONSE_TEMPLATE	ld_response_view.html	Response viewer template.
$ADD_MOD_DOC_TEMPLATE	ld_add_mod_doc.html	Web form template to add or modify documents.
$ADD_MOD_CATEGORY_TEMPLATE	ld_add_mod_cat.html	Web form template to add or modify category.

Continued

TABLE 8-3 HTML TEMPLATES *(Continued)*

Configuration Variable	Template File	Purpose
$ANNOUNCE_LD_ADDED_TEMPLATE	ld_added_ announcement.html	Message template is shown when a new document is added.
$ANNOUNCE_LD_MOD_TEMPLATE	ld_modified_ announcement.html	Message that is shown when an existing document is modified.
$LD_VISIT_LIST_TEMPLATE	ld_visit_list.html	Lists the complete document-tracking information.
$LD_REORDER_CAT_TEMPLATE	ld_order_cat.html	Web form template that enables an administrator to modify the order of the categories.

The Document Publisher Application

The document publisher application, ld_admin_mngr.php, is responsible for managing documents and categories. This application is included on the CD-ROM in the ch8/apps directory.

It implements the following functionality:

◆ Enables administrative users to create, modify, and delete categories and documents.

◆ Enables administrative users to assign viewers (users who can view documents in a category) and publishers (users who can create, modify, or delete documents in a category) to each category.

◆ Enables users to create, modify, and delete documents.

◆ Does not allow non-administrative users to create, modify, or delete categories.

The ch8/apps/ld_admin_mngr.php in the CDROM an implementation of this application.

Here are the methods in this application:

◆ `run()`: When the application is run, this method is called. It decides which functionality is requested by the user and calls the appropriate driver method to perform the desired operations. Here's how it works:

   ■ Creates a theme object, `$this->themeObj`.

   ■ The current user's theme choice is stored in `$this->theme` by calling the `getUserTheme()` method of the theme object created.

   ■ If the application is called with the `cmd=del` query parameter, `deleteDriver()` is run. Similarly, `cmd=add` calls `addDriver()`, `cmd=mod` calls `modifyDriver()`, and `cmd=reo` calls `reorderDriver()`.

◆ `reorderDriver()`: This method is used to change the order of the categories in the system. Categories can be displayed in navigation displayed by the `home.php` (discussed in Chapter 7) in the given order set by this method.

   In addition, when the categories are listed in the document index page, the order of each category is determined by order information stored in the database. This method allows you to change the order. It is called when `cmd=reo` is passed as a query parameter to the application.

   Here is how it works:

   ■ The method checks to see if the application is being run by an administrator. If it isn't, the method returns a null.

   ■ The reordering of categories requires that first the user is given a chance to set the order and then apply the requested order. So the method uses the `$step` query parameter to control the application state.

   ■ If `step=1` is passed, the method displays the Web form that allows the user to reorder the categories. This Web form is created by calling `displayReorderMenu()`. If `step=2` is passed, the method updates the order of the category because the `step=2` is only passed from the Web form displayed by `displayReorderMenu()`, which is shown when `step=1` is passed.

◆ `deleteDriver()`: This method controls how delete operations are performed on documents, responses, and categories. It works as follows:

   ■ If the `obj=doc` query parameter is passed to this method when called, it calls `deleteDoc()` to start the document delete process.

   ■ If the `obj=response` query parameter is passed, it runs `deleteResponse()` to start the delete process for response for a document.

   ■ If the `obj=category` query parameter is passed, it runs `deleteCategory()` to start the category delete process.

◆ `addDriver()`: This method controls how add operations are performed on documents and categories. It works as follows:

■ If the `obj=doc` query parameter is passed to this method when called, it calls `addDoc()` to start the document creation process.

■ If the `obj=category` query parameter is passed, it runs `addCategory()` to start the category creation process.

◆ `modifyDriver()`: This method controls how modify operations are performed on documents and categories. It works as follows:

■ If the `obj=doc` query parameter is passed to this method when called, it calls `modifyDoc()` to start the document modification process.

■ If the `obj=category` query parameter is passed, it runs `modifyCategory()` to start the category modification process.

◆ `addDoc()`: This method controls how a new document is added. It works as follows:

■ If the `step=NULL` query parameter is passed, it calls the `displayAddModDocMenu()` method with `'add'` parameter to display the new document Web form.

■ If the `step=2` query parameter is passed, `storeDoc()` is called to store the new document.

◆ `modifyDoc()`: This method controls how documents are modified. It works as follows:

■ If the `step=NULL` and `nid` (document ID) query parameter is not empty, `displayAddModDocMenu()` is called with a `'Modify'` parameter, which loads the document referred by `$nid` and allows the user to modify it.

■ If the method is called without an `nid` (document ID), an error alert is shown.

■ If `step=2` parameter is passed, the document is updated using `updateDoc()`.

◆ `addCategory()`: This method controls how a new category is added. It works as follows:

■ If `step=NULL` query parameter is passed, it calls the `displayAddMod CategoryMenu()` method with the `'add'` parameter to display the new category Web form.

■ If `step=2` query parameter is passed, `storeCategory()` is called to store the new category.

◆ `modifyCategory()`: This method controls how categories are modified. It works as follows:

- If the `step=NULL` and `cid` (category ID) query parameter is not empty, `displayAddModCategoryMenu()` is called with the `'Modify'` parameter, which loads the category information referred by `$cid` and allows the user to modify it.

- If the method is called without a `cid` (category ID), an error alert is shown.

- If `step=2` parameter is passed, the document is updated using the `updateCategory()` method.

◆ `storeDoc()`: This method adds a document in the database. It works as follows:

- If the method is called with empty category ID (`$cid`) but a new category name (`$cat`), it creates the new category using a category object and retrieves the new category's ID using the `getCategoryIDByName()` method of the new category object.

- It creates a new document object called `$docObj`.

- It checks to see if there is a category ID (`$cid`) and whether or not the required document parts (subject called `$heading` and contents called `$body`) are provided. If any of this required information is missing, the method shows an alert message and returns null.

- It extracts the month, day, and year of the document's publish date (`$pub_date`), which has been supplied from the Web form.

- The publishing date is verified to be a future date using the `checkDate()` function. If it is not a future date, an alert message is shown to inform the user that documents cannot have a past publication date, and the method returns null.

- The current hour, second, and minutes are stored in `$curHr`, `$curSec`, and `$curMin` variables using the `date()` function.

- A parameter list array called `$params` is constructed using all the database fields needed to create the document, which is passed to the `addDoc()` method to create the document.

- If the `addDoc()` method of the document object returns `TRUE`, the document is added and a screen showing the success message is constructed using `showStatusMessage()`. To announce the new document, a `Message` object is created. The `addMessage()` method of the Message class (from Chapter 7) is used add the new document announcement message to appropriate viewers using the `addViewer()` of the `Message` object.

- If the document could not be added, a status message shows the failure notice.

◆ `displayReorderMenu()`: This method is used to display the category reordering Web form. It works as follows:

- It creates a template object to display the Web form on the browser.

- A category object called `$catObj` is created to get the list of available categories using the `getCategories()` method.

- The current order of categories is obtained using `getHighestOrder()`.

- Using a loop, the template tags are replaced to populate the Web form to show the categories and allow the user to change the category order.

◆ `updateOrders()`: This method is used to update the order of the categories. It works as follows:

- First, it checks to see if the order information passed as a query parameter from the Web form has no duplicates. It uses `array_unique()` to return a list of unique elements in the query parameter `$order`, which stores the category order given by the user. The result of `array_unique()` is passed to `count()` function to count the number of elements in the array. If the count is smaller than the count of the `$order` array (with possible duplication), an alert message is shown and the method returns null.

- If `$order` is a unique list of category order, a category object called `$catObj` is created. It calls `updateCategoryOrders()` to update the category order per user-supplied information.

- A status message is displayed using `showStatusMessage()`.

- Because category ordering has changed, the navigation file needed by `home.php` (used in Chapter 7 to display intranet home for each user) is updated using `generateCategoryNavigator()`.

◆ `storeCategory()`: This method is used to store a category in the database. It works as follows:

- A new category object called `$catObj` is created.

- The new category must have the required information: name, order, list of users who can publish, and list of users who can view documents to be published in the category. If any of this information is missing, an alert message is shown, and the method returns null.

- A parameter list, `$params`, is created with all the database fields for the category. `addCategory()` adds the new category.

- If the new category is added successfully, `addCategoryPublishers()` is called to add the publisher user list to the appropriate category database table, and `addCategoryViewers()` is called to add the viewer user list for the new category in the database table. A status message is shown using `showStatusMessage()` to inform the administrator about the successful creation of the category. Because the new category needs to be added to the navigation file used by `home.php` application, `generateCategoryNavigator()` is called to generate a new version of this file that includes the new category.

- If the new category is not added, `showStatusMessage()` informs the administrative user about the failure.

◆ `updateDoc()`: This method updates a document. Here's how it works:

- If the method is called with empty category ID (`$cid`) but a new category name (`$cat`), it creates the new category using a category object and retrieves the new category's ID using the `getCategoryIDByName()` method of the new category object.

- It creates a new document object called `$docObj`.

- It checks to see if there is a category ID (`$cid`) and whether or not the required document parts (subject called `$heading` and contents called `$body`) are provided. If any of this required information is missing, the method shows an alert message and returns null.

- It extracts the month, day, and year of the document's publish date (`$pub_date`), which has been supplied from the Web form.

- The publishing date is verified to be a future date using the `checkDate()` function. If it is not a future date, an alert message is shown to inform the user that documents cannot have a past publication date, and the method returns null.

- The current hour, second, and minutes are stored in the `$curHr`, `$curSec`, `$curMin` variables using the `date()` function.

- A parameter list array called `$params` is constructed using all the database fields needed to create the document, which is passed to the `modifyDoc()` method to modify the document.

- If the `modifyDoc()` method of the document object returns TRUE status, the document is added, and a screen showing the success message is constructed using `showStatusMessage()`. To announce the document modification, a `Message` object is created. The `addMessage()` method of the Message class (from Chapter 7) is used to add the new document announcement message to appropriate viewers using the `addViewer()` of the `Message` object.

- If the document could not be added, a status message shows the failure notice.

◆ `updateCategory()`: This method is used to update a category in the database. It works as follows:

■ A new category object called `$catObj` is created.

■ The new category must have required information: name, order, list of users who can publish, and list of users who can view documents published in this category. If any of this information is missing, an alert message is shown and the method returns null.

■ A parameter list, `$params`, is created with all the database fields for the category. `modifyCategory()` modifies the category.

■ If the category is modified successfully, `deleteCategoryPublishers()` and `deleteCategoryViewers()` are called to remove the existing publisher and viewer user lists. Then `addCategoryPublishers()` is called to add the current publisher user list to the appropriate category database table, and `addCategoryViewers()` is called to add the viewer user list for the new category in the database table. `showStatusMessage()` informs the administrator about the successful creation of the category. Because the modified category needs to be updated in the navigation file used by the `home.php` application, `generateCategoryNavigator()` is called to generate a new version of this file that includes the new category.

■ If the category is not modified, a status message informs the administrative user about the failure using the `showStatusMessage()` method.

◆ `generateCategoryNavigator()`: This method is used to create the category navigation file needed by the `home.php` application (discussed in Chapter 7). It works as follows:

■ It creates a new category object `$catObj`. `getCategories()` obtains a list of categories and stores it in `$categories`.

■ The category navigation template is loaded in a template object called `$template`.

■ If the number of categories is not zero, a maximum number of categories (configured in `ld.conf` file using `CAT_PER_LINE`) per line is written as an HTML table row by looping through the list of categories. Each category name is turned into a hyperlink that allows users to click on a category and view the documents available in that category.

◆ `displayAddModDocMenu()`: This method displays the add or modify document Web form as needed. It works as follows:

■ The user's theme template is loaded into the `$themeTemplate` object.

■ The add or modify document template called `$ADD_MOD_DOC_TEMPLATE` (configurable via `ld.conf`) is loaded in the `$template` object.

- A category object called $catObj is created. If the user has supplied the category name using a query parameter ($cat), the selected category name is used to retrieve the category ID ($selCid) using getCategoryIDbyName() of the $catObj Category object.

- The list of categories stored in $categories is used to populate an HTML drop-down list, but the user is not allowed to change the chosen category, so the menu is disabled.

- The publication date is stored as the current date using date("m/d/Y",mktime()).

- If the $nid query parameter, which is used to signify that the user is modifying an existing document (as $nid represent document ID), is not empty, the chosen document is loaded into the Web form using a document object called $docObj. Note that if multiple documents are selected by the user, an alert message is shown to inform the user that only a single document can be modified at any time.

- Unlike add, in case of modify the $categories list is used to create the HTML drop-down list, but this time the user is allowed to change the current category of the document. Therefore, the menu is not disabled.

- Finally, the user is presented with the filled out template with document data, which is embedded in the user's theme template.

- displayAddModCategoryMenu(): This method is responsible for displaying the add or modify category Web form. It works as follows:

  - It creates a theme template object called $themeTemplate and a template object called $template. These templates are populated with various template key=values.

  - It creates a category object called $cObj and retrieves the order of the categories in $lastOrder using the getHighestOrder() method.

  - If the method is called with a category ID ($cid), the method checks to see if more than one category is chosen. In case of more than one, it shows an alert message to state that only one category can be modified at any time and returns null.

  - In case a single category ID is provided in $cid, a new category object, $catObj, is used to get the publishers ($publishers) and viewers ($viewers) using the getPublishers() and getViewers() methods, respectively.

  - A DBI object called $authDBI is created to point to the central user database (USER_DB_URL). A user object called $userObj is created using the $authDBI object the database reference.

  - A list of current users is retrieved in $users using the getUserList() method of the $ userObj object.

- The user list is sorted and the sorted list is reset.

- The $pub_every is set to false to indicate that, by default, not everyone is allowed to publish. If the current publisher list ($publishers) is not empty and the publisher ID is 0 (zero), which indicates 'everyone' is in the list of $publishers, then the user list in the HTML template shows 'everyone' selected as the chosen list of publishers.

- The $view_every is set to false to indicate that, by default, not everyone is allowed to view. If the current viewer list ($viewers) is not empty and the viewer ID is 0 (zero), which indicates 'everyone' is in the list of $viewers, then the user list in the HTML template shows 'everyone' selected as the chosen list of viewers.

- The Web form is displayed using the standard template. The user fills out the Web form and submits the new or existing category for addition or modification, respectively.

◆ deleteDoc(): This method deletes an existing document. The document ID ($nid) must be supplied as a query parameter. It works as follows:

- If the document ID ($nid) is not found, the method returns NULL.

- If document ID is provided, a new document object called $docObj is created.

- Because the user is allowed to delete multiple documents, the $nid can be a list of document IDs, and a loop is used to delete each of the documents mentioned in the list.

- For each document, it retrieves the header ($heading) using getHeading() on the $docObj.

- Each document is deleted using deleteDoc().

- If a document is deleted successfully, all responses to the document are also deleted using deleteResponsesByDocID().

- If there are MOTD messages corresponding to the deleted document, they are removed using deleteMessage()on a Message object called $msgObj.

- A status message is displayed using showStatusMessage().

◆ deleteCategory(): This method is used to delete chosen categories. Here is how it works:

- If the category ID ($cid) list is not supplied as a query parameter, the method shows an alert message and returns null. Otherwise, it creates a Category object called $catObj and uses a loop to delete all the categories mentioned in the category ID list. For each to-be-deleted category, all the documents within the category are also deleted. A Doc object called $docObj is created, and getDocesByCatID() is used to retrieve the entire document IDs for a given to-be-deleted category. If there are documents in a category, `deleteDocsByCatID()` is used to delete all the documents in that category. In addition, for each document, all responses are deleted using the `deleteResponsesByDocID()` method.

- If the categories are successfully deleted, a status message is shown using `showStatusMessage()`. A new navigation file is created using `generateCategoryNavigator()`.

- If the categories could not be deleted, a status message stating the failure is shown using `showStatusMessage()`.

◆ `deleteResponse()`: This method is used to delete a response to a published document. It works as follows:

- If the response ID (`$rid`) list is not supplied as a query parameter, the method shows an alert message and returns null.

- It creates a `Response` object called `$respObj` and uses a loop to delete all the responses mentioned in the response ID list. Each response is deleted using `deleteResponse()`.

- If the responses are successfully deleted, a status message is shown using `showStatusMessage()`.

- If the responses could not be deleted, a status message stating the failure is shown using `showStatusMessage()`.

◆ `showStatusMessage()`: This method displays a message in a template. The method is called with the message (`$statusMessage`) and it simply loads a template object and displays the message in the template.

◆ `authorize()`: This method is used to authorize access to this application. It works as follows:

- It uses `getUID()` to check whether the current user ID is positive. Because all valid user ID are positive numbers, it creates a DBI object called `$user_dbi` that points to the central user authentication database (`USER_DB_URL`).

- A user object called `$userObj` is created using `$user_dbi` and the current user ID.

- `getType()` tests whether the current user type is administrator (`LD_ADMIN_TYPE`). If the current user is of type administrator, the `$isAdmin` variable is set to `TRUE` and the method returns true.

- If the application is called with category name (stored in `$cat` query parameter), a new `Category` object called `$catObj` is created. The category ID (`$cid`) for the supplied category (`$cat`) is retrieved by calling `getCategoryIDbyName()`.

- If the current user does not have publishing rights to the current category, the method returns `FALSE`. Otherwise, it returns `TRUE`.

The document index display application

The document index application, ld_mngr.php, shows document indexes for each category or all categories when the category is not specified. This application is included on the CD-ROM in the ch08/apps directory.

Here are its methods:

- ◆ run(): This method is responsible for running the application. It works as follows:

  - It creates a theme object called $themeObj and assigns it to $this->themeObj. The theme object identifies the user's preferred theme using getUserTheme().

  - It calls displayDocHome() to display the document index home page.

- ◆ authorize(): This method is called by the application to authorize the user. It works as follows:

  - It calls setUserType() to find out if the user is an administrator or a regular user. It returns TRUE if the user is an administrator.

  - If the user is not an administrator, it checks if the category name is passed as a query parameter called $cat. If the category name is passed, a Category object called $catObj is used to call getCategoryIDbyName() to get the category ID ($cid) by the category name ($cat).

  - Using the category ID, the Category object $catObject calls isViewable() to find if the user can view the category. Similarly, it uses isPublishable() to check whether the user can publish in the chosen category.

  - If the user can either view or publish, the method returns TRUE; otherwise, it returns FALSE.

- ◆ setUserType(): This method sets $this->isAdmin to TRUE if the user is administrator; otherwise, it sets it to FALSE. Here is how it works:

  - It sets the $this->isAdmin variable to FALSE. Therefore, the default is that user is not assumed an administrator.

  - If the current user's UID is greater than 0, which means valid, then it creates a DBI object called $user_dbi and passes that to the constructor of the User object called $userObj.

  - The $userObj calls getType() to find out if the current user's type matches LD_ADMIN_TYPE. If the user is an administrator, then $this->isAdmin is set to true.

- ◆ displayDocHome(): This method displays the document index page for a given category or shows all the categories with their document lists when a category is not provided. It works as follows:

- A theme template object called $themeTemplate loads the current user's template.

- A template object called $template loads the template file, $templateFile, passed to the method.

- A Category object called $catObj, a Doc object called $docObj, and a Response object called $resObj are created.

- If the user did not supply a category name in $cat as a query parameter to the application, the method loads all the available categories in the associative array called $categories by calling the getCategories() method of the $catObj.

- On the other hand, if a category name is supplied in $cat, getCategoryIDbyName() is used to retrieve the category ID in $cid. The $categories list is populated with the current category name and ID as an entry in the associative array.

- Now the category list $categories is looped to retrieve each category name $cname and category ID $cid.

- If the current user is not an administrator, the category list check box is set to NULL. This ensures that a regular user cannot select a category to modify or delete.

- If the current user is not an administrator and she cannot publish in the current category, then the method gets the document list, $docs, for the current category using the getdocsByCatID() method. Otherwise, it gets all the documents for the category by the getAlldocsByCatID() method.

- If the document list associative array ($docs) is not empty, then the method loops through each document.

- For each document, the method calls getTotalResponseByDocID() using the Response object $resObj.

- The total response per document is shown in a listing.

- If the current user is not an administrator or does not have publishing rights, the check box next to the document is disabled. Otherwise, it is enabled.

- Using the Category object $catObj, category description is retrieved using getCategoryDesc(). The description text is filtered for slashes using stripslashes() and shown in the template.

- If the user is an administrator or has publishing rights to the category being displayed, the category and the documents are shown with check boxes that the user can click on to modify or delete the category or document.

The document details application

The document details application, `ld_details_mngr.php`, shows the details of a document. This application is included on the CD-ROM in the `ch08/apps` directory. It has the following methods:

- ◆ `run()`: This method calls the `displayDocDetail()` to display the chosen document's contents.

- ◆ `authorize()`: This method sets `$this->isAdmin` to TRUE if the user is an administrator; otherwise, it sets it to FALSE. Here is how it works:

  - ■ It sets the `$this->isAdmin` variable to FALSE . Therefore, the default is that user is not assumed an administrator.

  - ■ If the current user's UID is greater then 0, which means valid, then it creates a DBI object called `$user_dbi` and passes that to the constructor of the `User` object called `$userObj`. If the current UID is less then 0, the method returns false and the PHP `Application` object `$DocDetailsMngr` aborts the application.

  - ■ The `$userObj` is used to call the `getType()` method to find out if the current user's type matches `LD_ADMIN_TYPE`. If the user is an administrator, then the `$this->isAdmin` is set to TRUE.

- ◆ `displayDocDetail()`: This method displays the contents of the chosen document. The chosen document ID is supplied by query parameter, `$nid`. It works as follows:

  - ■ If the `$nid` is not provided when the application is called, an alert message is shown and application is aborted by its `alert()` method.

  - ■ It creates a theme object called `$themeTemplate` and loads the current user's theme template.

  - ■ A template object called `$template` is loaded with the document details template (`$LD_DETAILS_TEMPLATE`).

  - ■ A document object called `$docObj` is created. The `trackVisit()` of the `Document` object is called to record that this user is visiting the document page.

  - ■ A `Response` object called `$resObj` is created. A response listing called `$responses` is created by calling the document's `getResponsesByDocID()` method.

  - ■ If there are one or more responses for this document, they are linked at the end of the document. Otherwise, the response block section of the template is set to null.

- If the current user is an administrator, the administrative block in the template is set; otherwise, it is set to NULL.

- The getTrackDetails() of the $docObj is called to retrieve the track count to display as number of visits.

- The document is displayed with the number of visits and responses.

The document response application

The document response application, ld_response _mngr.php, manages responses for each document. It's included on the CD-ROM in the ch08/apps directory. Users can create or view responses. It has the following methods:

- ◆ run(): This method is used to control how the application works. Here is how this method works:

  - A theme object called $this->themeObj is created. The theme used by the current user is set as the application's theme using the $this->theme variable.

  - The $cmd query parameter is used to determine if the user wants to create or view responses. If the $cmd is empty, displayResponseForm() is shown to allow the user to enter a new response. If the $cmd variable is set to 'submit', the user has submitted a new response, and using submitResponse() is used. Finally, if $cmd is set to 'view, the user wants to view a response, which is done using showResponse().

- ◆ showResponse(): This method is responsible for showing responses to documents. It works as follows:

  - It creates a theme template object called $themeTemplate, loads the current user's theme template, and sets theme-related template key values.

  - It creates a Response object called $respObj and retrieves the document's ID ($nid) using getResponseDocID() on the $resObj.

  - Using the $nid, it creates a document object called $docObj and retrieves the document's header ($heading) and publish date ($docPublishDate) using getHeading() and getPublishDate(), respectively, on the $docObj.

  - It retrieves the responder user name ($responderName), response heading ($responseHeading), and response ($responseBody) by calling the getResponder(), getResponseSubject(), and getResponseBody() methods, respectively, on the $resObj.

  - The response information is displayed using a template object called $template.

◆ submitResponse(): This method allows the application to write a new response of a chosen document. Here is how it works:

■ If the method is called without a document ID ($nid), empty response subject/header ($sub), or response body ($comment) as query parameters, it shows an alert message and returns NULL.

■ If all the required response data is supplied, an associative array called $params is created, which is passed to the addResponse() of a new Response object called $resObj to create the response in the database.

■ The status of the addition is displayed using the show_status() method.

◆ showStatusMessage(): This method displays a message in a template. The method is called with the message ($statusMessage) and it simply loads a template object and displays the message in the template.

◆ displayResponseForm(): This method is used to display the response entry Web form. It works as follows:

■ If a document ID ($nid) is not supplied as a query parameter, the method shows an alert message and returns null.

■ If a document ID is supplied, it creates a theme template object ($themeTemplate) and a template object ($template) and displays the response entry Web form.

The document view list application

The document view list application, ld_view_list_mngr.php, shows the list of users who have viewed this document. This application included on the CD-ROM in the ch08/apps directory. It has the following methods:

◆ run(): This method calls the displayDocVisitList() to display the list of users who have viewed the chosen document.

◆ authorize(): This method authorizes everyone on the intranet to view the document access list and, therefore, always returns TRUE.

◆ displayDocVisitList(): This method displays a list of users who have viewed the chosen document. It works as follows:

■ A template object called $template is created and various template variables are set.

■ If the document ID ($nid) is not supplied by the user as the query parameter, an alert message is shown and the application aborts.

- If `$nid` is supplied, a new document object called `$docObj` is created.

- The heading of the document is retrieved via the `getHeading()` method of the `$docObject` and inserted into the template after parsing for slashes by using `stripslashes()`.

- A list of document tracking information is stored in `$trackArr` by calling the `getTrackDetails()` method of the current document object.

- A DBI object called `$user_dbi` is created, which opens a connection to the user table specified by `USER_DB_URL`.

- For each track record for the document, the template is populated with a viewer's e-mail address by calling `getEMAIL()` of the `$userObj` object, which is created inside the loop for each track.

Installing Intranet Document Application

I assume that you're using a Linux system with MySQL and Apache server installed. The following installation process presumes the following:

◆ Your intranet web server document root directory is `/evoknow/intranet/htdocs`. Of course, if you have a different path, which is likely, you should change this path whenever you see it in a configuration file or instruction in this chapter. During the installation process, I will refer to this directory as `%DocumentRoot%`.

◆ You have installed the PHPLIB and PEAR library. Normally, these are installed during PHP installation. For your convenience, I have provided these in the `lib/phplib.tar.gz` and `lib/pear.tar.gz` directories on the CD-ROM. In these sample installation steps, I will assume that these are installed in the `/evoknow/phplib` and `/evoknow/pear` directories. Because your installation locations for these libraries are likely to differ, make sure you replace these paths in the configuration files.

Here is how you can get your intranet document publishing applications up and running:

1. **Install the base intranet applications.** If you haven't yet installed the base intranet user home application and the messaging system discussed in Chapter 7, you must do so before proceeding further.

2. **Install the intranet document publisher database tables.** You must already have installed the INTRANET database (see Chapter 7 for details). Once you have installed INTRANET database, you need to create the tables needed for the document publisher. The easiest way to do this is to use the `ch08/sql/ld_tools.sql` file found in the CDROM.

   To create the tables is to run the following commands:

   ```
   mysql -u root -p -D INTRANET < ld_tools.sql
   ```

3. **Install the intranet document publisher applications.** Now from the `ch8` directory of the CD-ROM, extract `ch8.tar.gz` in `%DocumentRoot%`. This creates `ld_tool` in your document root. Configure `%DocumentRoot%/ld_tool/apps/ld.conf` for path and database settings. The applications are installed in the `%DocumentRoot%/ld_tool/apps` directory and the templates are stored in `%DocumentRoot%/ld_tool/apps/templates`.

   Your MySQL server is hosted on the intranet web server and, therefore, it can be accessed via localhost. However, if this is not the case, you can easily modify the database URLs in each application's configuration files. For example, the `home.conf` file has a MySQL database access URLs such as the following:

   ```
   $LD_DB_URL='mysql://root:foobar@localhost/INTRANET'
   define('USER_DB_URL', 'mysql://root:foobar@localhost/auth');
   ```

   Say your database server is called `db.domain.com` and the user name and password to access the INTRANET and auth databases (which you will create during this installation process) are admin and db123. In this case, you will modify the database access URLs throughout each configuration file as follows:

   ```
   $LD_DB_URL='mysql://admin:db123@db.domain.com/INTRANET'
   define('USER_DB_URL',
   'mysql://admin:db123@db.domain.com/auth');
   ```

4. **Set file/directory permissions.** Make sure you have changed file and directory permissions such that your intranet web server can access all the files. The path pointed by `$LD_CATEGORY_NAV_DIR` variable in `home.conf` and `ld.conf` files must be writable by the web server, because this is the navigation file that gets generated whenever a new document is published. This directory should be outside your Web document tree and should be only writable by the Web server user running the PHP scripts.

The default theme template (std_blue) has links to the document publishing application. If you have installed the document publishing applications anywhere other than the %DocumentRoot%/ld_tool/apps directory (default), you will need to modify the %DocumentRoot%/themes/std_blue/home_left_nav.html file. Similarly, you have to modify the other (std_aqua, std_wheat) themes.

After you've performed these steps, you're ready to test your publishing applications.

Testing Intranet Document Application

Log in to your intranet via http://yourserver/index.php or http://yourserver/home/home.php using the user name and password you created in Chapter 6 and tested in Chapter 7.

Click on the Document Publisher link on the left navigation bar of your Intranet home page — or point your web browser to http://yourserver/ld_tool/apps/ld_mngr.php after you're logged in to the intranet — to see the primary document index, as shown in Figure 8-3.

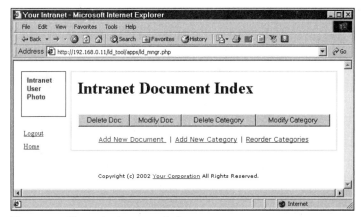

Figure 8-3: The main document index.

By default, the index is empty. Only administrator users can create, modify, and delete categories. An administrative user can also add, modify, or delete any documents in the system.

Creating a new category

The logged-in user in this example is an administrator, so she can add a new category by clicking on the Add a New Category link, which brings up a screen similar to the one shown in Figure 8-4.

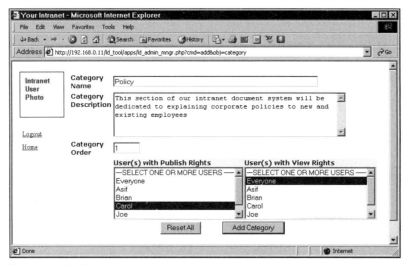

Figure 8-4: Adding a new category.

Adding category is a simple process. In Figure 8-4, the administrative user adds a new category called Policy to hold company policy documents and allows user Carol publishing rights and everyone in the company viewing rights.

After this category is added, it shows up in the home page of all users as a horizontal navigation bar, as shown in Figure 8-5.

Now when a user clicks on the Document Publisher (Doc Publisher) link on the left navigation bar, the document index shows the new category and its description as shown in Figure 8-6.

Figure 8-5: A new category in the user's home page.

Figure 8-6: A new category in the document index page.

Adding a new document

To add a new document in a category, click on the Document Publisher from the left navigation or the category itself on the horizontal navigation shown on top. You can then click on the Add a New Document link to add a document. Figure 8-7 shows a user adding a document in the Policy category.

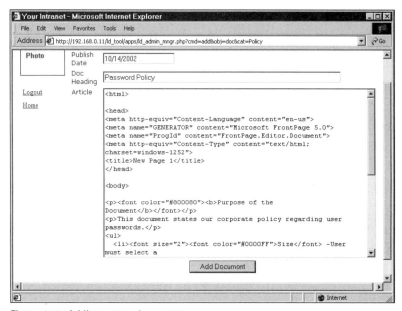

Figure 8-7: Adding a new document.

After the new document is added, the viewers of the category where the document is published receive a notice. An example of such a notice is shown in Figure 8-8.

When any user with viewing rights goes to the category index (by clicking the category link on the top) or by viewing the main document index using the Document Publisher link on the left navigation bar of her home page, she can view the document listed in the category as shown in Figure 8-9.

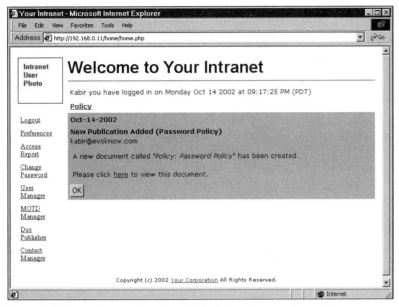

Figure 8-8: A new document notice via the intranet messaging system.

Figure 8-9: A new document in its category.

The user can click on the document title to view the document. The document appears as shown in Figure 8-10.

Figure 8-10: Viewing the document.

Notice that the document shows a View Visitors List which can be clicked on to see which users have already viewed this document. This link shows a screen similar to Figure 8-11.

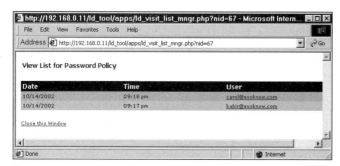

Figure 8-11: Viewing who else has seen this document.

Also, any user viewing this document can post comments by clicking on the Post Comments link, which shows a Web form as shown in Figure 8-12.

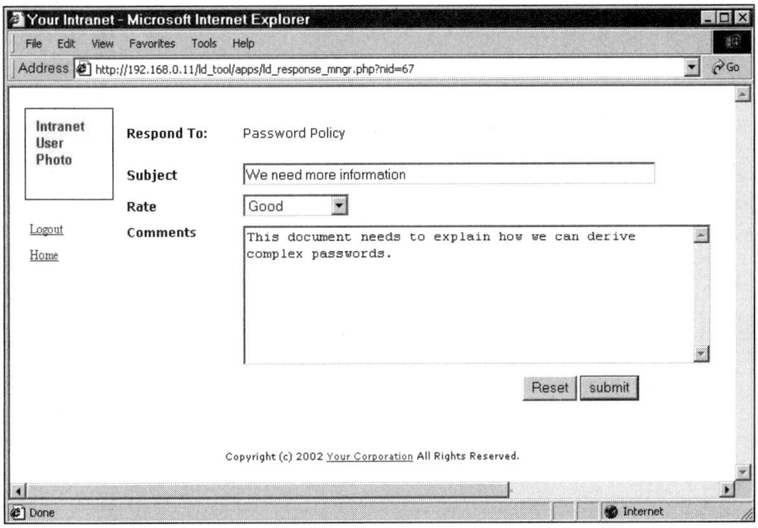

Figure 8-12: Adding feedback comments to published documents.

The posted comments appear along with document. Any other user can view the posted comment by clicking on the comment title shown in the Feedback section of the document, as shown in Figure 8-13.

Figure 8-13: A document with posted user feedback comments.

When you add a new category, the category name appears in the horizontal navigation bar. The number of categories shown per row is controlled in `ld.conf` using `define('CAT_PER_LINE', 5)` settings. To show more than five categories per navigation line in the horizontal top navigation, modify this setting. Figure 8-14 shows how multiple categories are shown in the user's home page using the horizontal navigation bar.

When you delete a category, the navigation file is automatically updated. Also, deleting a category deletes all the documents in that category.

Figure 8-14: The user's home page with multiple document categories.

Summary

In this chapter, you learned to create a simple document publishing system for your intranet. This system enables you to create categories and store documents within each category. The categories and documents are all stored in a database. You can extend this basic document publishing system to incorporate fancy features such as images, attachments, and so on.

Chapter 9

Intranet Contact Manager

IN THIS CHAPTER

♦ Developing an intranet contact manager

♦ Installing an intranet contact manager

♦ Using an intranet contact manager

EVERY OFFICE HAS A LIST OF contacts for vendors, customers, news/print/trade media, and so forth. These contacts are often managed in individual address books or in personal digital assistants (PDAs). In this chapter, you'll develop an intranet contact manager system that enables administrative users in the office to store any type of contact in a central contact database. All users can search the contact database without needing to move from their desk.

Functionality Requirements

The contact manager will have the following features:

♦ **Central contact database:** The database stores all contacts in a central back-end database, which can be backed up at any time by the system administrator.

♦ **Contact category hierarchy:** Each contact must be stored in a subcategory of a category. Only one-level subcategories are allowed. For example, a category called Vendors can have multiple one-level subcategories such as Telecommunication Vendors, Office Suppliers, Hardware Vendors, Food Suppliers, and so forth. In this version of the contact manager, a contact can only belong to a single category.

♦ **Contact management by administrative staff only:** The contact manager allows administrative users to add, modify, and delete contacts and categories.

♦ **Search interface for everyone:** Each administrative or regular user must be allowed to search the contacts stored in the database.

◆ **Automatic reminders:** When adding or modifying a contact, the administrator can set up reminders for future meeting/calls with the contact that will be shown via the intranet messaging interface when appropriate.

◆ **Easy e-mail interface:** Administrative users should be able to send e-mails to contacts by clicking on the contact e-mail address. The e-mail sent to the contact should be stored in the contact manager system, so that later the user can review the messages she sent to a contact. This is a good feature for lead management. For example, a user can add a new lead to the contact database, send an e-mail, and then pull up the e-mail from the contact database later when the lead calls or responses via email. Because the e-mail sent is stored with the central contact database, which can be very useful if a lead should call while the original user is unavailable, another administrator could easily pull up the lead's information and cover the situation (and the lead will feel very important because "everyone" in the company happens to know about the previous communications).

Understanding Prerequisites

This intranet contact manager system builds on the intranet classes discussed in Chapters 5, 6, and 7.

The applications that we develop here require the intranet central login/logout, user management, and home applications discussed in those earlier chapters.

Administrative intranet users, who are defined in the intranet user table discussed in Chapter 6, are given full access to all aspects of the contact management tool.

Let's look at the database design and implementation needed for creating this intranet contact management system.

The Database

Figure 9-1 shows the database diagram for the contact manager. The central table in this database is the CONTACT_INFO table, which stores the contact data. The CONTACT_CATEGORY table, which stores category information, has a one to many relationship with CONTACT_INFO since a category can have many contacts. Similarly the CONTACT_INFO table has a one to many relationship with the CONTACT_KEYWORD table. The latter stores one or more keywords per contact. The CONTACT_INFO table also has a one to many relationship with the CONTACT_REMINDER table, which stores reminders, and with the CONTACT_MAIL table, which stores emails sent to contacts.

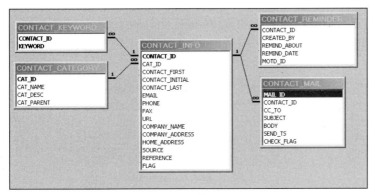

Figure 9-1: Contact manager database diagram.

Table 9-1 describes the details of the database tables.

TABLE 9-1 [NAME OF DATABASE] DATABASE TABLES

Table	Description
CONTACT_CATEGORY	This table holds the category ID (CAT_ID), category name (CAT_NAME), category description (CAT_DESC), and category parent (CAT_PARENT). The category number (CAT_ID) is automatically generated by the database.
CONTACT_INFO	Contains the contact information: the contact ID (CONTACT_ID), category ID (CAT_ID), contact first name (CONTACT_FIRST), contact middle initial (CONTACT_INITIAL), contact last name (CONTACT_LAST), contact e-mail (EMAIL), phone number (PHONE), fax (FAX), Web site URL (URL), company name (COMPANY_NAME), company address (COMPANY_ADDRESS), home address (HOME_ADDRESS), source (SOURCE), reference (REFERENCE), and a check flag (FLAG). The contact ID (CONTACT_ID) is automatically generated by the database.
	Since we are not allowing company or home address to be searchable in this version of contact manager, these fields are kept as text fields. Also, the source field is used to identify who provided the contact and reference field is used to identify who referred the contact.

Continued

TABLE 9-1 [NAME OF DATABASE] DATABASE TABLES *(Continued)*

Table	Description
CONTACT_KEYWORD	Holds the contact keyword information. The contact keyword consists of the contact number (CONTACT_ID) and keyword (KEYWORD).
CONTACT_MAIL	Holds information about the contact e-mail information: the e-mail ID (MAIL_ID), CONTACT_ID, CC To list (CC_TO), the subject of the e-mail (SUBJECT), body (BODY) of the e-mail, sending time stamp (SEND_TS), and the check flag (CHECK_FLAG). The e-mail ID (MAIL_ID) is automatically generated by the database.
CONTACT_REMINDER	Contains reminder(s) of contacts. A reminder can be set up during contact creation to remind the administrator to call/email the contact at a later date. For example, say you got a contact from a trade show and would like to contact the person after a week or so, in such case you can set up a reminder when you add the contact to the database. Each reminder consists of IDCONTACT_ID, reminder created by (CREATED_BY), reminder about (REMIND_ABOUT), reminder date (REMIND_DATE), and MOTD ID (MOTD_ID).

The ch9/sql/contact.sql file in the CDROM is a MySQL script to create the contact manager database. To create the contact manager database in MySQL, create a database called CONTACTS in your database server and run the following commands.

```
mysqladmin -u root -p create CONTACTS
mysql -u root -p -D CONTACTS < contact.sql
```

Make sure you change the user name (root) to whatever is appropriate for your system.

With the contact manager database ready, let's look at the PHP classes that will be needed to implement the applications.

The Intranet Contact Manager Application Classes

Now lets look at how we can design the contact manager system to work within our intranet. Figure 9-2 shows the system diagram for the objects needed to develop the contact manager. The category and contact objects are the only new objects in this diagram. All other objects and the framework have been already developed in earlier chapters.

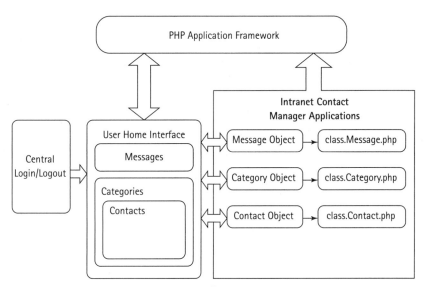

Figure 9-2: The contact manager system diagram.

The category and contact objects can be created with two new classes: the Category class and the Contact class.

The Message class needed for the contact manager has already been built in Chapter 7.

The `Category` class

The `Category` class is used to manipulate each category. It allows an application to create, modify, and delete a category. The `ch09/apps/class/class.Category.php` file on the CD-ROM implements this class. This class implements the following methods:

- ◆ `Category()`: This is the constructor method. It performs the following functions:

  - ■ Sets a member variable named `dbi` to point to the `class.DBI.php`-provided object, which is passed to the constructor by an application. `dbi` holds the DBI object that is used to communicate with the back-end database.

  - ■ Sets a member variable named `cat_tbl` to `$CONTACT_CATEGORY_TBL`, which is loaded from the `contact.conf` file. `$CONTACT_CATEGORY_TBL` holds the name of the category table.

  - ■ Sets a member variable named `std_fields`, which is an associative array to hold all the attributes of the `CONTACT_CATEGORY` table and their types.

  - ■ Sets a member variable named `fields`, which is a comma-separated list of `CONTACT_CATEGORY` table fields.

  - ■ Calls `setCatID()` to set a member variable called `cid` to the given category ID (if any).

- ◆ `loadCatInfo()`: This is the constructor method. It performs the following functions:

  - ■ Calls `setCatID()` to make sure that the passed category ID (if any) is set to the member variable.

  - ■ Creates in `$stmt` a statement to select all the table attribute values for the given category ID.

  - ■ Uses the DBI object (`$this->dbi`) to run the `$stmt` statement via the `$this->dbi->query()` method in the DBI object, and stores the result in `$result`.

  - ■ If there are more than zero rows in the `$result` object, each row is fetched in the `$row` variable. For each `CONTACT_CATEGORY` table field of type `text`, the data is stripped for embedded slash characters, which are used to escape quotation marks, and slashes in the value of the field. Each category field data is stored as an object variable using `$this->$fieldname` run-time variable.

◆ `getCategoryIDbyName()`: This method returns the category ID of the category object from the given category name. This is how it works:

- It formats the given category name to convert it to a SQL-capable string by adding slashes and quotes.

- It creates in `$stmt` a statement to select all category IDs for the given category name.

- It uses the DBI object `$this->dbi` to run the `$stmt` statement via the `$this->dbi->query()` method in the DBI object, and stores the result in `$result` variable.

- If there are no rows in the `$result` object, the method returns null. If the result set is not empty, the row is fetched in the `$row` variable, and the category ID from the row is returned.

◆ `addCategory()`: This method adds a new category into to the `CONTACT_CATEGORY` table. The category name, category ID, category parent, and description are passed in an associative array as a parameter to the method. It works in the following manner:

- From the given parameter all the values that are supposed to be of text type in the database are escaped for characters such as quotation marks and slashes using `$this->dbi->quote(addslashes())` methods.

- A variable called `$values` is assigned a comma-separated list of all the parameter values.

- A SQL statement, `$stmt`, is created to insert the new category data into the `CONTACT_CATEGORY` table using the member variable `'fields'` (contains attribute names) and `$values`.

- The SQL statement is executed using `$this->dbi->query()`, and the result of the query is stored in the `$result` object.

- If the `$result` status is not okay, the method returns `FALSE` to indicate insert failure. Otherwise, `getCategoryIDbyName()` is used to return the newly created category's ID.

◆ `getParentCategories()`: This method returns all the parent (main) categories. It works as follows:

- A statement to select all the table (CONTACT_CATEGORY) attribute values for the categories having parent ID as zero (the main categories) is created in `$stmt`.

- The DBI object `$this->dbi` runs the `$stmt` statement via the `$this->dbi->query()` method in the DBI object, and the result is stored in the `$result` variable.

- If there are more than zero rows in the $result object, each row is fetched in the $row variable.

- For each category, the category name and the category ID is stored in a single associative array. The method returns the array if the result set is not empty; otherwise, it returns null.

◆ getSubCategories(): This method returns all the children (subcategories) of a given parent category. This works as follows:

  - A statement to select all the table attribute values for the categories having parent IDs as the given category ID is created in $stmt.

  - Using the DBI object $this->dbi, the $stmt statement is run via the $this->dbi->query() method in the DBI object, and the result is stored in the $result variable.

  - If there are more than zero rows in the $result object, each row is fetched in the $row variable.

  - For each category found, the category name and the category ID is stored in a single associative array.

  - The method returns the array if the result set is not empty; otherwise, it returns null.

◆ modifyCategory(): This method updates the category information for a given category. Update information is passed in an associative array as a parameter to this method. The method works as follows:

  - From the given parameter list, all the values that are of text type in the database are escaped for characters such as quotation marks and slashes using $this->dbi->quote(addslashes()) methods.

  - A SQL statement, $stmt, is created to update the given category data to the CONTACT_CATEGORY table using the associative array that has been passed as parameter.

  - The SQL statement is executed using $this->dbi->query().

  - The method returns TRUE on successful update operation; otherwise, it returns FALSE.

◆ getParentOf(): This method returns the parent of the given category. This is how it works:

  - setCatID()is called to set the given category ID.

  - A statement to select the parent category ID for the given category ID is created in $stmt.

- Using the DBI object ($this->dbi), the $stmt statement is run via the $this->dbi->query() method in the DBI object, and the result is stored in the $result variable.

- If there are more than zero rows in the $result object, each row is fetched in the $row variable.

- If there are no rows in the $result object, the method returns null. If the result set is not empty, the row is fetched in the $row variable, and the parent category ID from the row is returned.

Following are the rest of the methods for this class:

Method	Description
setCatID()	If the category ID is passed to this method, it sets the member variable cid to the given category ID. At the end, it returns the category ID.
getCategoryName()	Uses loadCatInfo() with the given category ID to set all the attributes for the category, and returns the name of the category.
getCategoryParent()	Uses loadCatInfo() with the given category ID to set all the attributes for the category, and returns the parent ID of the category.
getCategoryDesc()	Uses loadCatInfo() with the given category ID to set all the attributes for the category, and returns the description of the category.
deleteCategory()	Deletes the category from the database. It takes the category ID as input and returns TRUE or FALSE depending on the status of the deletion operation.
hasChild()	Determines if the given category has a child category under it and returns TRUE if it has at least one.
replaceParentCat()	This method will replace the parent ID for one more sub categories with a new parent ID. It returns TRUE or FALSE, depending on the status of the update operation.

The `Contact` class

This `Contact` class provides the contact object, which is used to add, modify, delete, or search contacts. The `ch9/apps/class/class.Contact.php` file in the CD-ROM is an implement of this class. Following are the methods available in this class:

- ◆ `Contact()`: This is the constructor method, which performs the following tasks:

    - Sets a member variable named `dbi` to point to the `class.DBI.php`-provided object, which is passed to the constructor by an application. `dbi` holds the DBI object that is used to communicate with the back-end database.

    - Sets a member variable called `cat_tbl` to `$CONTACT_CATEGORY_TBL`, which is loaded from the `contact.conf` file. `$CONTACT_CATEGORY_TBL` holds the name of the category table.

    - Sets a member variable called `contact_tbl` to `$CONTACT_INFO_TBL`, which is loaded from the `contact.conf` file. `$CONTACT_INFO_TBL` holds the name of the contact table.

    - Sets a member variable called `keyword_tbl` to `$CONTACT_KEYWORD_TBL`, which is loaded from the `contact.conf` file. `$CONTACT_KEYWORD_TBL` holds the name of the contact keyword table.

    - Sets a member variable called `reminder_tbl` to `$CONTACT_REMINDER_TBL`, which is loaded from the `contact.conf` file. `$CONTACT_REMINDER_TBL` holds the name of the contact reminder table.

    - Sets a member variable called `mail_tbl` to `$CONTACT_MAIL_TBL`, which is loaded from the `contact.conf` file. `$CONTACT_MAIL_TBL` holds the name of the mail table.

    - Sets a member variable named `'std_fields'`, which is an associative array to hold all the attributes (i.e. CAT_ID,CONTACT_FIRST, CONTACT_INITIAL,CONTACT_LAST,EMAIL,PHONE,FAX,URL, COMPANY_NAME,COMPANY_ADDRESS,HOME_ADDRESS,SOURCE, REFERENCE,FLAG) of the `CONTACT_INFO` table and their types.

    - Sets a member variable named `'fields'`, which is a comma-separated list of `CONTACT_INFO` table fields.

    - Calls `setContactID()` to set the contact ID of the object.

- ◆ `loadContactInfo()`: This is the constructor method. It performs the following functions:

    - It calls `setContactID()` to make sure that the passed contact ID (if any) is set to the member variable.

- It creates in `$stmt` a statement to select all the `CONTACT_INFO` table attribute values for the given contact ID.

- It uses the DBI object `$this->dbi` to run `$stmt` via the `$this->dbi->query()` method in the DBI object, and stores the result in `$result`.

- If there are more than zero rows in the `$result` object, each row is fetched in the `$row` variable.

- For each contact table field of type `text`, the data is stripped for embedded slash characters, which are used to escape quotation marks and slashes in the value of the field.

- Each contact field data is stored as member variable using the `$this->$fieldname` run-time variable.

◆ `searchContact()`: This method returns a set of contacts for the given criteria and/or keyword. This is how it works:

- It checks whether the method has been called with keywords in the criteria. The second parameter (`$keyword_exists`) to the method is responsible for checking this. When the method is called with `TRUE` value set for `$keyword_exists`, it knows that the criteria (the first parameter) supplied includes keywords.

- If it finds out that there is a keyword involved, the search query statement includes the `CONTACT_KEYWORD` table in it. Otherwise the query statement involves only the `CONTACT_INFO` table.

- The query statement is prepared with the `$criteria` parameter, and is run via the `$this->dbi->query()` method in the DBI object. The result is stored in the `$result` variable.

- If there are more than zero rows in the `$result` object, each row is fetched in the `$row` variable.

- For each contact found, the `CONTACT_INFO` table attributes are stored in a single associative array.

- The method returns the array if the result set is not empty; otherwise, it returns null.

◆ `getKeywords()`: This method returns keyword(s) for a given contact. It works the following way:

- It uses `setContactID()` to set the given contact ID

- It creates in `$stmt` a statement to select the keyword for the given contact ID.

- It uses the DBI object `$this->dbi` to run `$stmt` via the `$this->dbi->query()` method in the DBI object, and stores the result in `$result`.

- If there are more than zero rows in the $result object, each row is fetched in the $row variable.

- All keywords found in the result set are stored in an array.

- The method returns the array if the result set is not empty; otherwise, it returns null.

◆ addContact(): This method adds new contact information to the CONTACT_INFO table. The category number, first name, middle initial, last name, e-mail, phone, fax, URL, company name, company address, home address, source, reference, and flag are passed in an associative array as a parameter to the method. It works in the following manner:

- From the given parameter, all the values of text type in the database are escaped for characters such as quotation marks and slashes using $this->dbi->quote(addslashes()) methods.

- A variable called $values is assigned a comma-separated list of all the parameter values.

- A SQL statement, $stmt, is created to insert the new contact data into the contact table using the member variable 'fields' (contains attribute names) and $values.

- The SQL statement is executed using $this->dbi->query(), and the result of the query is stored in the $result object.

- If the $result status is not okay, the method returns FALSE to indicate an insert failure. Otherwise, it returns the newly created contact's ID by executing a second query.

◆ modifyContact(): This method updates the contact information for a given contact. Update information is passed in an associative array as parameter to this method. The method works as follows:

- From the given parameter, all the values that are supposed to be of text type in the database are escaped for characters such as quotation marks and slashes using $this->dbi->quote(addslashes()) methods.

- A SQL statement, $stmt, is created to update the given contact data to the contact table using the associative array that has been passed as a parameter.

- The SQL statement is executed using the $this->dbi->query() method.

- The method returns TRUE on successful update operation; otherwise, it returns FALSE.

◆ `deleteContact()`: This method deletes the contact from the database. It takes the ID of the contact to be deleted as a parameter. This is how it works:

- It sets the given contact ID by the `setContactID()` method.

- It executes the delete query statement to delete the given contact.

- After successful deletion, it calls the `deleteKeywordsByContactID()` method to delete all the related keywords, and the `deleteRemindersByContactID()` method to delete all the related reminders.

◆ `getContactsByCatID()`: This method returns all contacts that fall under the given category. This is how it works:

- A SQL statement, `$stmt`, is created to select the contacts that fall under the given category ID.

- The SQL statement is executed using `$this->dbi->query()`, and the result is stored in `$result`.

- If there are more than zero rows in the `$result` object, each row is fetched in the `$row` variable.

- All contacts found in the result set are stored in an array. The method returns the array if the result set is not empty; otherwise, it returns null.

◆ `getRelatedMOTDs()`: This method returns MOTDs related to the given contact. A MOTD message is only found for a contact when the administrator has set one or more reminders, which are displayed using MOTD feature of the intranet. In other words, if an administrator creates one or more reminders when adding a contact in the contact database, these MOTD messages are going to have to be removed if the contact is to be removed. The getRelatedMOTD method retrieves the ID(s) for such MOTD messages (if any). It works as follows:

- It sets the given contact ID using the `setContactID()` method.

- A SQL statement, `$stmt`, is created to select the related MOTDs for the given category ID.

- The SQL statement is executed using the `$this->dbi->query()` method and the result is stored in `$result`.

- If there are more than zero rows in the `$result` object, each row is fetched in the `$row` variable.

- All MOTD messages found in the result set are stored in an array.

- The method returns the array if the result set is not empty; otherwise, it returns null.

♦ getReminders(): This method returns all reminders for the given contact ID. It works as follows:

  ■ First it sets the given contact ID using the setContactID() method.

  ■ A SQL statement, $stmt, is created to select all the reminder information for the given contact ID.

  ■ The SQL statement is executed using $this->dbi->query(), and the result is stored in $result.

  ■ If there are more than zero rows in the $result object, each row is fetched in the $row variable.

  ■ All reminders found in the result set are stored in an array.

  ■ The method returns the array if the result set is not empty; otherwise, it returns null.

♦ getMails(): This method returns all e-mails for the given contact number. This is how it works:

  ■ It sets the given contact ID using the setContactID() method.

  ■ A SQL statement, $stmt, is created to select all the e-mails sent to the given contact.

  ■ The SQL statement is executed using $this->dbi->query(), and the result is stored in $result.

  ■ If there are more than zero rows in the $result object, each row is fetched in the $row variable.

  ■ All e-mails found in the result set are stored in an array.

  ■ The method returns the array if the result set is not empty; otherwise, it returns null.

Here are the other methods in this class:

Method	Description
addKeywords()	Adds new keywords for the given contact. It explodes the $keyword string passed as a parameter and stores the different keywords in an array; for each keyword in the array, it adds a new entry in the CONTACT_KEYWORD table.
deleteKeywords()	Deletes keywords for the given contact. It takes contact ID as the parameter.

Method	Description
modifyKeywords()	Updates keyword information for the given contact. It uses deleteKeywords() to delete the previous keywords, and then uses addKeywords() to add the new keywords. This method takes the contact ID and the new keywords array as parameters.
setContactID()	Sets the contact ID. If the contact ID is passed to this method, it sets the member variable cid to the given contact ID. At the end it returns the contact ID.
getColumnValue()	Returns the value of the given column from the database for the current contact object. It takes the column name as a parameter. This method uses loadContactInfo() with the given contact ID to set all the attributes for the contact, and then returns the formatted value of the specified column.
deleteRemindersByContactID()	Deletes all reminders from the reminder table for a given contact ID. It takes the contact ID as the input and returns TRUE or FALSE, depending on the deletion status.
deleteKeywordsByContactID()	Deletes all keywords from the keyword table for a given contact ID. So it takes contact ID as the input and returns TRUE or FALSE, depending on the deletion status.
addReminder()	Adds new reminders to the reminder table for the given contact. It takes the contact ID, author ID, the remind note, the publish date, and the message ID as a parameter. Then it returns TRUE or FALSE, depending on the status of the operation.
storeMail()	Stores new mail in the database. Attributes such as contact ID, CC To, subject, body, and send time stamp are passed as parameters to this method.
replaceCategory()	Replaces the old category with the given new one. It takes the old and new category IDs as parameters and returns TRUE or FALSE, depending on the status of the operation.
getMailDetails()	Returns detailed information of the given mail ID. It takes the mail ID as a parameter and returns the details of it.

The Application Configuration Files

Like all other applications we've developed in this book, the intranet contact manager applications also use a standard set of configuration, message, and error files. These files are discussed in the following sections.

The main configuration file

The primary configuration file for the contact manager is called `contact.conf`. Table 9-2 discusses each configuration variable.

TABLE 9-2 **THE** `CONTACT.CONF` **VARIABLES**

Variable	Purpose
`$PEAR_DIR`	Set to the directory containing the PEAR package; specifically the DB module needed for `class.DBI.php` in our application framework.
`$PHPLIB_DIR`	Set to the PHPLIB directory, which contains the PHPLIB packages; specifically the `template.inc` package needed for template manipulation.
`$APP_FRAMEWORK_DIR`	Set to our application framework directory.
`$PATH`	Set to the combined directory path consisting of the `$PEAR_DIR`, the `$PHPLIB_DIR`, and the `$APP_FRAMEWORK_DIR`. This path is used with the `ini_set()` method to redefine the `php.ini` entry for `include_path` to include `$PATH` ahead of the default path. This allows PHP to find our application framework, PHPLIB, and PEAR-related files.
`$AUTHENTICATION_URL`	Set to the central login application URL.
`$LOGOUT_URL`	Set to the central logout application URL.
`$HOME_URL`	Set to the top most URL of the site. If the URL redirection application does not find a valid URL in the e-campaign database to redirect to for a valid request, it uses this URL as a default.
`$APPLICATION_NAME`	Internal name of the application.
`$DEFAULT_LANGUAGE`	Set to the default two-character language code.

Variable	Purpose
$ROOT_PATH	Set to the root path of the application.
$REL_ROOT_PATH	Relative path to the root directory.
$REL_APP_PATH	Relative application path as seen from the web browser.
$TEMPLATE_DIR	The fully qualified path to the template directory.
$THEME_TEMPLATE_DIR	The fully qualified path to the theme template directory.
$REL_PHOTO_DIR	The Web-relative path to the photo directory used to store user photos.
$PHOTO_DIR	The fully qualified path to the photo directory.
$DEFAULT_PHOTO	Name of the default photo file, which is used when a user does not have a photo in the photo directory.
$CLASS_DIR	The fully qualified path to the class directory.
$REL_TEMPLATE_DIR	The Web-relative path to the template directory used.
$CATEGORY_CLASS	Name of the Category class file.
$CONTACT_CLASS	Name of the Contact class file.
$MESSAGE_CLASS	Name of the Message class file. This class was developed for the MOTD application discussed in Chapter 8.
$CONTACT_MNGR	Name of the application that shows the index page of the application with the contact search menu.
$CONTACT_CAT_MNGR	Name of the application that manipulates all functions related to contact category.
$INTRANET_DB_URL	The fully qualified URL for the database used to MOTD information.
$CONTACT_DB_URL	The fully qualified URL for the database used to store the contacts and categories.

Continued

TABLE 9-2 **THE** `CONTACT.CONF` **VARIABLES** *(Continued)*

Variable	Purpose
$CONTACT_CATEGORY_TBL	Name of the category table in the database.
$CONTACT_INFO_TBL	Name of the contact info table in the database.
$CONTACT_KEYWORD_TBL	Name of the contact keyword table in the database.
$USER_PREFERENCE_TBL	Name of the user preference table in the intranet database.
$MESSAGE_TBL	Name of the MOTD message table in the intranet database.
$CONTACT_MAIL_TBL	Name of the contact mail table in the database.
$MSG_VIEWER_TBL	Name of the message viewer list table in the intranet database.
$AUTH_DB_TBL	Name of the user authentication table in the auth database.
$STATUS_TEMPLATE	Name of the status template file used to display status messages.
$CONTACT_HOME_TEMPLATE	Name of the contact index template file.
$CONTACT_CAT_HOME_TEMPLATE	Name of the contact category index template file.
$CONTACT_INFO_ADD_MOD_TEMPLATE	Name of the add/modify contact entry form template file.
$CONTACT_CAT_ADD_MOD_TEMPLATE	Name of the add/modify category entry form template file.
$CONTACT_DETAILS_TEMPLATE	Name of the contact details template file.
ODD_COLOR	Color defined for odd rows when displaying tabular data.
EVEN_COLOR	Color defined for even rows when displaying tabular data.
USER_DB_URL	The fully qualified authentication database URL.

Variable	Purpose
$DEFAULT_THEME	The default theme index in the $THEME_TEMPLATE array.
$USER_DEFAULTS	A user's theme and auto tip default settings.
$TIP_SCRIPT	The name of the tip script.
$TIP_URL	The Web-relative path for the tip files.
$MAX_AVAILABLE_TIP	The maximum number of tips from which to display the tip.
$THEME_TEMPLATE[x]	The list of theme templates
$PRINT_TEMPLATE[x]	The list of print templates associated with the theme templates.

The directory structure used in the contact.conf file (in the ch09 directory on the CD-ROM) may need to be tailored to your own system's requirements. Here is how the current directory structure looks:

```
+---htdocs ($ROOT_PATH == %DocumentRoot%)
    |
    +---home (base intranet application discussed in chapter 7)
    |   |
    |   +--templates
    |   |   |
    |   |   +---themes (theme templates used by all intranet apps)
    |
    +---photos (user photos used by all intranet apps)
    |
    +---contact_mngr (Intranet Contact Manager Application)
        |
        +---apps (contact manager apps and configuration files)
            |
            +---class (contact manager apps and configuration)
            |
            +---templates (contact manager HTML templates)
                |
                +---themes (symbolic link to home/templates/themes)
```

By changing the following configuration parameters in `contact.conf`, you can modify the directory structure to fit your site requirements:

```
$APP_FRAMEWORK_DIR=$_SERVER['DOCUMENT_ROOT'] . '/framework';
$PEAR              =$_SERVER['DOCUMENT_ROOT'] . '/pear';
$PHPLIB            =$_SERVER['DOCUMENT_ROOT'] . '/phplib';
$ROOT_PATH         = $_SERVER['DOCUMENT_ROOT'];
$REL_ROOT_PATH     = '/contact_mngr';
$REL_APP_PATH      =  $REL_ROOT_PATH . '/apps';
$REL_PHOTO_DIR     = '/photos';
$PHOTO_DIR         = $ROOT_PATH . $REL_PHOTO_DIR;
$TEMPLATE_DIR        = $ROOT_PATH . $REL_APP_PATH . '/templates';
$THEME_TEMPLATE_DIR  = $TEMPLATE_DIR . '/themes';
$CLASS_DIR         = $ROOT_PATH . $REL_APP_PATH . '/class';
$REL_TEMPLATE_DIR  = $REL_APP_PATH . '/templates/';
```

The messages file

The messages displayed by the contact manager applications are stored in the `ch9/apps/contact.messages` file in the CDROM. You can change the messages using a text editor.

The errors file

The error messages displayed by the contact manager applications are stored in the `ch9/apps/contact.errors` file in the CDROM. You can modify the error messages using a text editor.

The Application Templates

The HTML interface templates needed for the contact manager system applications are included on the CD-ROM. These templates contain various template tags to display necessary information dynamically. They are named in the `contact.conf` file. These templates are discussed in Table 9-3.

TABLE 9-3 HTML TEMPLATES

Configuration Variable	Template File	Purpose
$STATUS_TEMPLATE	contact_status.html	Shows status message.
$CONTACT_HOME_TEMPLATE	contact_home.html	Contact index template.

Configuration Variable	Template File	Purpose
$CONTACT_CAT_HOME_ TEMPLATE	contact_cat_home.html	Category index template.
$CONTACT_INFO_ADD_ MOD_TEMPLATE	contact_info_add_ mod.html	Web form template to add or modify contacts.
$CONTACT_CAT_ADD_ MOD_TEMPLATE	contact_cat_add_ mod.html	Web form template to add or modify categories.
$CONTACT_DETAILS_ TEMPLATE	Contact_details.html	Contact details template.
$CONTACT_SEARCH_ INPUT_TEMPLATE	contact_search_ input.html	Shows the search options.
$CONTACT_SEARCH_ RESULT_TEMPLATE	contact_search_ result.html	Shows the search output.
$REMINDER_MSG_TEMPLATE	reminder_contents.html	Shows the reminder.
$CONTACT_MAIL_TEMPLATE	contact_mail.html	Takes input for the mail to contact.
$CONTACT_MAIL_ DETAIL_TEMPLATE	contact_mail_ detail.html	Shows details of each of the sent mails.

The Contact Category Manager Application

The application contact_category_mngr.php is responsible for managing contact categories. This application is included on the CD-ROM in the ch9/apps directory.
It implements the following functionality:

◆ Allows administrative users to create, modify, and delete categories.

◆ Does not allow non-administrative users to create, modify, or delete categories.

This application has the following methods:

◆ run(): When the application is run, this method is called. It decides which functionality is requested by the user and calls the appropriate driver method to perform the desired operations:

- Creates a theme object, $this->themeObj.

- The current user's theme choice is stored in $this->theme by calling the getUserTheme() method of the theme object created.

- Next, the appropriate driver is called according to the $cmd value. For example, if the $cmd is set to 'add', then addDriver() is called.

◆ setUserType(): This method sets $this->isAdmin to TRUE if the user is administrator; otherwise, it sets it to FALSE. Here is how it works:

- It checks whether the user has a valid user ID. If she does, then it gets the type of the user using the getType() method of the User class.

- If the type of the user is the same as CONTACT_ADMIN_TYPE, which is taken from the contact.conf, then it sets the isAdmin as TRUE. Otherwise, it sets isAdmin as False.

◆ deleteCategory(): This method controls how categories are deleted. It works as follows:

- If del_opt is set to 1, it deletes the category and everything related to that category, including subcategories and contacts, from the database.

- If del_opt is set to 2, then siblings or children of this category are assigned to the new given parent and only the category information is deleted.

- Whatever del_opt is, this method shows the appropriate confirmation message at the end of the operation.

◆ addCategory(): This method adds a new category or subcategory to the database. If it's adding a subcategory, it assigns a parent to the category. This is how it works:

- It checks whether the new category to be added is a parent or a subcategory. If it is chosen to be a subcategory, the method finds out the parent category for the category.

- Then it prepares an associative array with the necessary attribute name and the values to add the category to the CONTACT_CATEGORY table. The parent category ID is set to 0 if the new category is a parent; otherwise, the parent category ID that has been specified is set.

- The array is passed into the addCategory() method of the category class.

- The status (success/failure) of the add operation is shown to the user at the end.

◆ `displayDeleteOptions()`: This method is used to display deletion options (a deletion options page that contains two radio buttons and a list box/combo box) to the user. This is how it works:

- It checks whether there is a category ID supplied to the method. If there is no category ID, it shows an alert message and returns to the previous page.

- A delete option menu template (`$CONTACT_CAT_DEL_OPT_TEMPLATE`) is loaded in a template object called `$template`.

- This template includes a Web form with two radio buttons. One of the buttons is to delete all subcategories and contacts under the selected category. The other button is to transfer all its subcategories and contacts to some other category (to be selected from a combo box).

- If the category to be deleted is a parent category, then the combo box is loaded with all of the other parent categories.

- If the category to be deleted is a subcategory, then the combo box is loaded with the subcategories that fall under the subcategory's parent.

- The contents of the `$template` object are inserted into the `$themeTemplate` object's content block, and the results are printed on user's browser screen.

◆ `displayAddModifyMenu()`: This method displays the add or modify category Web form as needed. It works as follows:

- An add modify menu template (`$CONTACT_CAT_ADD_MOD_TEMPLATE`) is loaded in a template object called `$template`.

- The template includes a Web form that takes input such as category name, category description, and category hierarchy (parent/sub). The list of parent categories becomes enabled when the user chooses the category to be a parent category.

- Finally, the contents of the `$template` object are inserted into the `$themeTemplate` object's content block and the results are printed on the user's browser screen.

◆ `modifyCategory()`: This method is used to modify a given category. It works as follows:

- It checks whether there is category ID supplied to the method. If there is no category ID, it shows an alert message and returns to the previous page.

- If the request is to change a parent category to a subcategory, this method denies that if the parent (main) category already has subcategories (we're limited to one level of subcategory). Under this circumstance, it shows an alert method and takes the administrator back to previous page.

- It prepares an associative array with the necessary attribute name and the values to update the category table.

- The array is passed into the `modifyCategory()` method of the `Category` class.

- The status (success/failure) of the modify operation is shown to the user at the end.

◆ `showContents()`: This method displays the given contents according to the theme preferences of the user. This is how it works:

- The user's preferred theme template is loaded in a template object called `$themeTemplate`.

- The template contains a `contentBlock` that is to be filled by the parameter to this method.

- After the passed content is set into the `contentBlock`, it is rendered to the user.

The following are the other methods used by this application:

Method	Description
`authorize()`	Authorizes access to this application. It calls `setUserType()` to set the member variable `isAdmin` and returns the value of `isAdmin`. This means that only users only with administrative authority can access this application.
`deleteDriver()`	Controls how delete operations are performed on categories. If `step` is set to 1 or is not set, it calls `displayDeleteOptions()` to display delete options. If `step` is set to 2, it runs `deleteCategory()` to do the category-deletion process.
`modifyDriver()`	Controls how modify operations are performed on documents and categories. If `step` is set to 1 or is unset, it calls `displayAddModifyMenu()` with a `modify` parameter to display the modify category Web form. If `step` is set to 2, it runs `modifyCategory()` to start the category modification process.

Method	Description
addDriver()	Controls how add operations are performed on contacts and categories. If step is set to 1 or is unset, it calls displayAddModifyMenu() with an add parameter to display the new category Web form. If step is set to 2, it runs addCategory() to start the category-creation process.
deleteContactsByCatID()	Deletes all contacts for the given category. All information related to the contacts is also deleted. It takes the category ID as the parameter and uses the getContactsByCatID() and deleteContact() methods of the Contact class to find and delete the contacts, respectively.

The Contact Manager Application

The application contact_mngr.php is responsible for managing contacts. This application is included on the CD-ROM in the ch9/apps directory.

Let's take a look at its methods:

◆ run(): When the application is run, this method is called. It decides which functionality is requested by the user and calls the appropriate driver method to perform the desired operations:

■ Creates a theme object, $this->themeObj.

■ The current user's theme choice is stored in $this->theme by calling the getUserTheme() method of the theme object created. Remembers, themes are part of the intranet as they allow users see the intranet pages in a certain look and feel.

■ It decides which method to call depending on the value of cmd.

■ If no cmd is specified, it calls searchDriver() to show the search menu.

◆ mailToContact(): This method gets e-mail information for the given contact, such as e-mail address, CC To, subject, body, and so forth, and sends e-mail to the contact. This is how it works:

■ It checks whether the e-mail body has been supplied or not. If not, it shows an alert message and takes the user back to the previous page.

- The storeMail() method of the Contact class is used to store the e-mail information that includes the contact ID, CC address, subject of the mail, and mail send time.

- The PHP's mail API is used to send the e-mail with appropriate headers.

- The user receives a confirmation after the e-mail is sent successfully.

◆ showMail(): This method displays e-mail information of a previously sent e-mail. This is how it works:

- A mail content template (CONTACT_MAIL_DETAIL_TEMPLATE) is loaded in a template object called $template.

- The template contains different blocks for date, mail to, mail CC to, mail subject, mail body, and so forth.

- These blocks are set with appropriate values retrieved using the getMailDetails() method of the Contact class.

- The template is parsed and printed to the user.

◆ showDetail(): This method shows detailed information of the given contact. This is how it works:

- It checks whether the contact ID has been provided. If not, it shows an alert message and returns to previous page.

- A contact detail template (CONTACT_DETAILS_TEMPLATE) is loaded in a template object called $template.

- A new contact object is created and stored in $contactObj. The getKeywords() method of the Contact object is used to retrieve the keywords for the given contact and all keywords are stored into an array named $keywordArr.

- The values of $keywordArr are taken into a string after separating them with commas. This string is set into appropriate blocks in the template later.

- Reminders for the contact are also retrieved and set in the template.

- All the attribute values of the CONTACT_INFO table are retrieved using the getColumnValue() method of the Contact object, and are rendered in the template file.

- The sent e-mails are retrieved using getMails(). Sent e-mails are shown only to users having admin privilege. For non administrative users, this mail block is set to null to hide it from her.

- showContents() is called to show the output of this template in the preferred theme template of the user.

◆ `displayContactMngrHome()`: This method shows the administrator home page for the contact manager application. It shows all add, delete, and modify options for contacts and categories. This is how it works:

- A contact home template (`CONTACT_HOME_TEMPLATE`) is loaded in a template object called `$template`.

- The template includes combo boxes for category, subcategory, and contacts, and add, delete, modify links for both contacts and categories.

- When the user first comes to this page, she sees the subcategory and contact lists to be empty and the category list loaded with all the parent categories that are retrieved using the `getParentCategories()` method of category class.

- After she chooses a main category, the subcategory list loads with that category's subcategories, retrieved using the `getSubCategories()` method of the `Category` class. Similarly, all the contacts of a chosen subcategory are shown using the `getContactsByCatID()` method of the `Contact` class.

- Then `showContents()` is called to render the template with the appropriate theme.

◆ `deleteContact()`: This method deletes the given contact and all related information such as: e-mails, reminders, keywords, and so on from the database. This is how it works:

- It checks whether the category ID has been supplied. If not, it returns to previous page and shows an alert message.

- It finds the MOTDs related to this contact using the `getRelatedMOTDs()` method of the `Contact` class, and then uses the `deleteMessage()` and `deleteViewers()` methods of the `Message` class to delete the messages and their viewers.

- It calls the `deleteContact()` method of the `Contact` class to delete the contact.

- It shows a confirmation message to the user depending on the status of the delete operation.

◆ `addContact()`: This method s adds new contacts to the database. It works as follows:

- It creates an associative array with the given values such as first name, last name, phone, address, and so forth.

- It uses the `addContact()` method of the `Contact` class and passes the array as parameter to add the new contact to the contact table.

- It adds the keywords for this contact using the `addKeywords()` method of `Contact` class.

- It adds reminder messages in the MOTD table, using the `addMessage()` and `addViewer()` methods of the `Message` class, if there are any reminders for this contact. A reminder entry is also added in the reminder table in this case using `addReminder()` method of the `Contact` class.

◆ `modifyContact()`: This method updates the database with the modified information. It works as follows:

- It creates an associative array with the given values like contact ID, first name, last name, phone, address, and so on. The array contains all the attributes of the contact table as index and the modified contact information as values to those indexes.

- It uses the `modifyContact()` method of the `Contact` class with this array to add the new contact to the CONTACT_INFO table.

- It modifies the keywords for this contact using the `modifyKeywords()` method of the `Contact` class.

- It deletes the previous messages from the MESSAGE table in the INTRANET database and previous reminders from the CONTACT_REMINDER table in the CONTACT database using `deleteMessage()`, `deleteViewers()`, and `deleteRemindersByContactID()`.

- It adds the new reminder messages using the `addMessage()` and `addViewer()` methods of the `Message` class, if there are any reminders for this contact. The new reminder is also added in the CONTACT_REMINDER table in this case using the `addReminder()` method of the Contact class.

◆ `displayAddModifyMenu()`: This method displays the add or modify contact Web form, as needed. It works as follows:

- A contact add/modify template (`CONTACT_INFO_ADD_MOD_TEMPLATE`) is loaded in a template object called `$template`.

- The template includes a Web form to take personal information of the contact, the keywords for the contact, and the reminders for this contact.

- The template also includes category and subcategory lists from which the user has to choose the appropriate category and subcategory for this contact. The lists are loaded using the `getParentCategories()` and `getSubCategories()` methods of the `Category` class.

- Then the `showContents()` method is called to render the template with appropriate theme.

◆ `displaySearchResult()`: This method displays the result of the search performed according to the user's query. The result shows a list of contacts that matches the search criteria. This is how it works:

- A search result template (`CONTACT_SEARCH_RESULT_TEMPLATE`) is loaded in a template object called `$template`.

- The `'where'` clause of the search query is prepared using the information given by the user.

- The `'where'` clause is passed into the `searchContact()` method of the Contact class to search for the contact. `searchContact()` returns an array of contacts if it finds a match.

- The array of contacts is then fed into the contact block of the template. If no match is found, the array is empty, the contact block is set with a message indicating that no match was found.

- `showContents()` is called to render the template with the appropriate theme.

◆ `displaySearchMenu()`: This method displays the contact search Web form as needed. It works as follows:

- A search input template (`CONTACT_SEARCH_INPUT_TEMPLATE`) is loaded in a template object called `$template`.

- The template includes a Web form to take input such as company name, contact name, subcategory, category, and keywords to search for contacts.

- The subcategory list is empty until the user chooses a category.

- `showContents()` is called to render this template with the appropriate theme.

◆ `displayMailMenu()`: This method displays the e-mail menu where the user can write her e-mail to send to a contact. This is how it works:

- A mail template (`CONTACT_MAIL_TEMPLATE`) is loaded in a template object called `$template`.

- The template includes a Web form to take input (CC address, mail subject, mail body, and so forth).

- The ID of the contact that is the target of this mail is stored as hidden HTML field in this template for later use.

- `showContents()`is called to render this template with appropriate theme.

Here are the other methods used in this application:

Method	Description
authorize()	Authorizes the user access to this application. It authorizes all users only when the cmd value is search, detail, or null. (Other cmds (add/modify/delete) are available only to users with administrative privilege.) It returns TRUE if it finds the cmd to be one of the three. Otherwise, it depends on setUserType() to get the value of the isAdmin variable that identifies whether the user is an administrator or not and returns TRUE or FALSE depending on that value.
setUserType()	Sets $this->isAdmin to TRUE if the user is an administrator; otherwise, it sets it to FALSE. It checks whether the user has a valid user ID. If she does, it gets the type of the user using the getType() method of the User class. If the type of the user is the same as CONTACT_ADMIN_TYPE, which is taken from the conact.conf, then it sets the isAdmin to TRUE. Otherwise, it sets isAdmin to FALSE.
mailDriver()	Controls how e-mail operations are performed on contacts. If step is set to 1 or step is unset, it calls displayMailMenu() to show the e-mail input menu. If step is set to 2, it calls mailToContact() to send e-mail to the contact. If step is set to 3, it runs showMail() to display e-mail information.
addDriver()	Controls how new contacts are created. If step is set to 1 or step is unset, it calls displayAddModifyMenu() with mode as 'add' to display the create contact Web form. If step is set to 2, it runs addContact() to do the contact-creation process.
modifyDriver()	Controls how modify operations are performed on contacts. If step is set to 1 or step is unset, it calls displayAddModifyMenu() with mode as 'modify' to display the create contact Web form. If step is set to 2, it runs modifyContact() to do the contact creation process.

Method	Description
searchDriver()	Controls how search operations are performed on contacts. If step is set to 1 or step is unset, it calls displaySearchMenu() to display the search contact Web form. If step is set to 2, it runs displaySearchResult() to display search output.
showContents()	Displays the given contents according to the theme preferences of the user. The user's preferred theme template is loaded in a template object called $themeTemplate. The template contains a contentBlock that is to be filled by the parameter to this method. After the passed content is set into the contentBlock, it is rendered to the user.

Installing Intranet Contract Manager

Here I assume the following:

◆ You're using a Linux system with MySQL and Apache server installed.

◆ You've followed the instructions in Chapters 5, 6, and 7 to create a base intranet system with user home page applications.

◆ Your intranet web server document root directory is /evoknow/ intranet/htdocs. Of course, if you have a different path, which is likely, you should change this path whenever you see it in a configuration file or instruction in this chapter. During the installation process, I refer to this directory as %DocumentRoot%.

◆ You've installed the PHPLIB and PEAR library. Normally, these get installed during PHP installation. For your convenience, I've provided these in the lib/phplib.tar.gz and lib/pear.tar.gz directories on the CD-ROM. In these sample installation steps, I assume that these are installed in %DocumentRoot%/phplib and %DocumentRoot%/pear directories. Because your installation location for these libraries is likely to differ, make sure you replace these paths in the configuration files.

◆ You have installed the INTRANET database (see Chapter 7 for details).

Here is how you can get your contact manager applications up and running:

1. **Install base intranet applications.** If you haven't yet installed the base intranet user home application and the messaging system discussed in Chapter 7, you must do so before proceeding further.

2. **Install intranet contact database tables.** The `ch9/sql/contact.sql` file in the CDROM can be used to create the CONTACTS database. The quickest way to create this database is to run the following commands:

```
mysqladmin -u root -p create CONTACTS
mysql -u root -p -D CONTACTS < contact.sql
```

3. **Install intranet contact manager applications.** From the `ch9` directory of the CD-ROM, extract `ch9.tar.gz` in `%DocumentRoot%`. This will create `contact_mngr` in your document root. Configure `%DocumentRoot%/contact_mngr/apps/contact.conf` for path and database settings. The applications are installed in the `%DocumentRoot%/contact_mngr/apps` directory and the templates are stored in `%DocumentRoot%/contact_mngr/apps/templates`.

Your MySQL server is hosted on the intranet web server and, therefore, it can be accessed via localhost. However, if this is not the case, you can easily modify the database URLs in each application's configuration files. For example, the `contact.conf` file has a MySQL database access URLs such as:

```
$INTRANET_DB_URL= 'mysql://root:foobar@localhost/INTRANET';

$CONTACT_DB_URL = 'mysql://root:foobar@localhost/CONTACTS';

$USER_DB_URL = 'mysql://root:foobar@localhost/auth';
```

Say your database server is called `db.domain.com` and the user name and password to access the INTRANET and auth databases (which you will create during this installation process) are admin and db123. You would modify the database access URLs throughout each configuration file as

```
$INTRANET_DB_URL =
'mysql://admin:db123@db.domain.com/INTRANET';

$CONTACT_DB_URL=
'mysql://admin:db123@db.domain.com/CONTACTS';

$USER_DB_URL = 'mysql://admin:db123@db.domain.com auth';
```

4. **Set file/directory permissions.** Make sure you have changed file and directory permissions so that your intranet web server can access all the files.

The default theme template (std_blue) has links to the document publishing application. If you've installed the document publishing applications anywhere other than %DocumentRoot%/contact_mngr/apps directory (default), you'll need to modify the %DocumentRoot%/themes/std_blue/home_left_nav.html file. Similarly, you have to modify the other (std_aqua, std_wheat) themes.

After you've performed these steps, you're ready to test your contact manager applications.

Testing Contract Manager

Log in to your intranet via http://yourserver/index.php or http://yourserver/home/home.php using the user name and password you created in Chapter 6 and tested in Chapter 7.

Click on the Contact Manager link in the left navigation bar of your intranet home page or point your web browser to http://yourserver/contact_mngr/apps/contact_mngr.php after you're logged in to the intranet.

This displays the contact search interface, as shown in Figure 9-3.

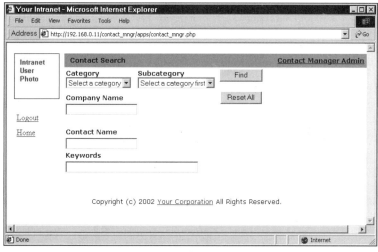

Figure 9-3: Contact manager search interface.

Because there are no contacts entered into the system yet, searching will result in no matches. Before contacts can be added, categories and subcategories have to be created. As an administrative user, you can create categories by clicking on the Contact Manager Admin link in the upper-left of the search interface. The interface shown in Figure 9-4 displays.

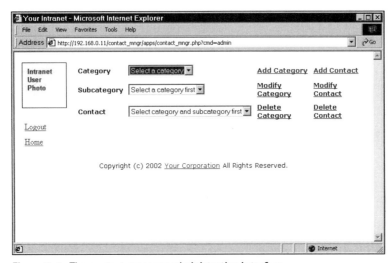

Figure 9-4: The contact manager administrative interface.

From here you can add, modify, and delete categories and contacts.

Adding categories

To add a new category, click the Add Category link, which brings up an interface as shown in Figure 9-5.

Filling out the new category information (name, description) and clicking the Add button creates the new category. Note that first you have to create a primary (parent) category to create a subcategory. Only subcategories hold contact information. The example in Figure 9-5 shows a category called Vendors being created. Create a new subcategory by clicking on the Add Category link from the administrative menu shown in Figure 9-4. Once again you will see a screen like Figure 9-5. Figure 9-6 shows that we are creating a sub-category called Communication Vendors as a sub-category of Vendors.

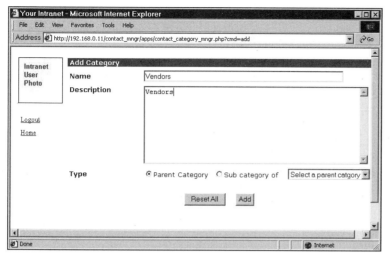

Figure 9-5: Adding a new category information.

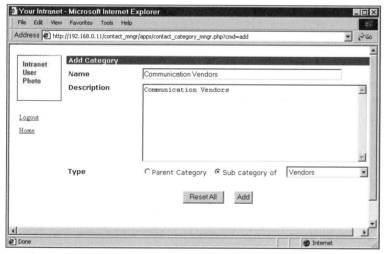

Figure 9-6: Adding a new subcategory (Communication Vendors) under a parent category (Vendors).

Adding a contact

To add a contact in a subcategory, do the following:

1. Go to the search interface as an administrative user and click on the Contact Manager Admin link.

2. Click on the Add Contact link, which shows a Web form similar to the one shown in Figure 9-7.

3. Select the category and then select the subcategory. Do not enter any information until you've selected the appropriate subcategory.

4. Enter all the contact information you have available in the data fields. If you want to find this contact via certain keywords, make sure you add the keywords in a comma-separated list in the appropriate keyword field in this form.

5. If you want to set reminders for yourself regarding future meetings or calls that you want to be reminded of via the intranet messaging system, add the reminders in the reminder fields with the appropriate data.

6. After you've filled in the contact's information, submit the contact data to be added in the database.

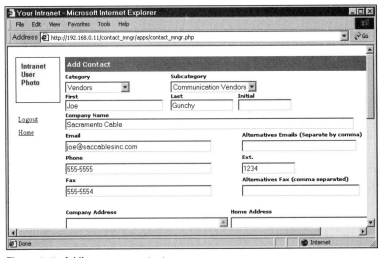

Figure 9-7: Adding a new contact.

Searching for a contact

To find a contact in your contact database, click on the Contact Manager link on your home page and enter the contact's first name or company name or select a category or keywords. Currently, the address fields (company/home) are not searchable but you should try to add search capability for these fields as a learning experience.

To find a contact by first name, for example, enter the name in the search interface's Contact Name field and click the Find button. Figure 9-8 shows a user entering **joe** as the name in the search interface.

The result of the search is shown in Figure 9-9.

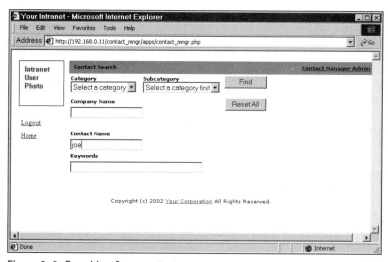

Figure 9-8: Searching for a contact.

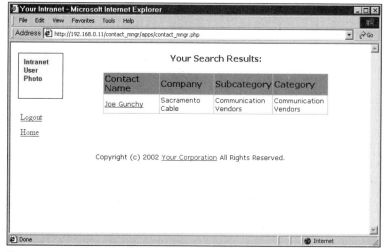

Figure 9-9: Brief search results.

To view a detailed version of the search results, click on the name of the contact. A detailed result screen displays, as shown in Figure 9-10.

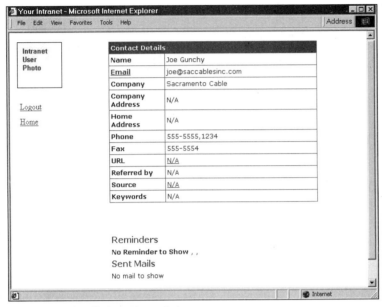

Figure 9-10: Detailed search results.

Sending e-mail to a contact

When you view detailed information about a contact, you can click on the Email link and send an e-mail to the contact, as shown in Figure 9-11.

The e-mail will be stored in the contact database along with the contact. When you search for this contact again, the e-mail will be available for review. This is a great way to keep in touch with leads in your contact database.

Searching for contacts in a subcategory

You can find all the contacts in a subcategory by selecting the subcategory on the Contact Search screen. For example, Figure 9-12 shows that a user wants to find all the contacts in Communication Vendors subcategory of the Vendors parent category.

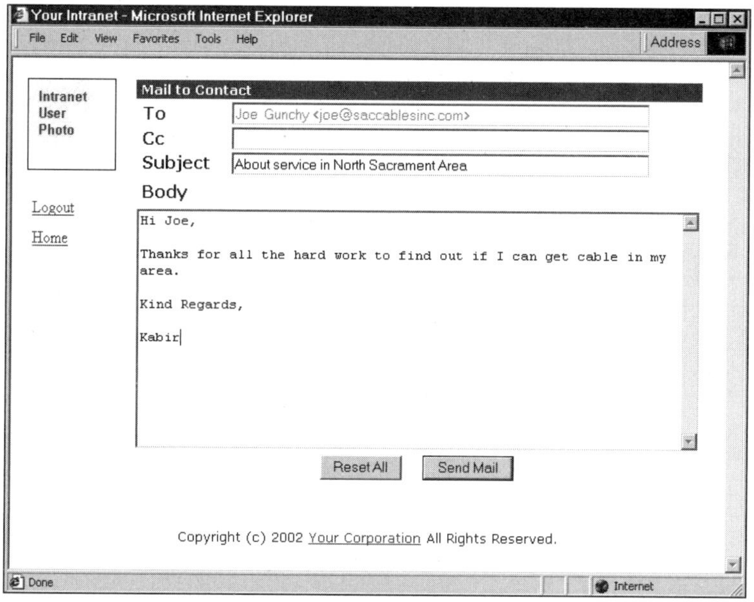

Figure 9-11: Sending e-mail to a contact.

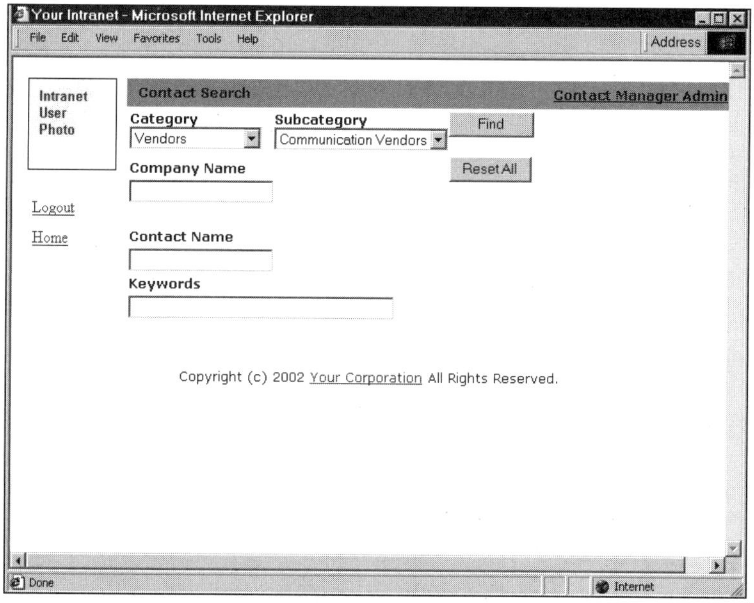

Figure 9-12: Searching for all contacts in a subcategory.

An abridged result of the search is shown in Figure 9-13.

Clicking on a contact name brings up the details as discussed earlier. Figure 9-14 shows a detailed contact information page that includes e-mail history.

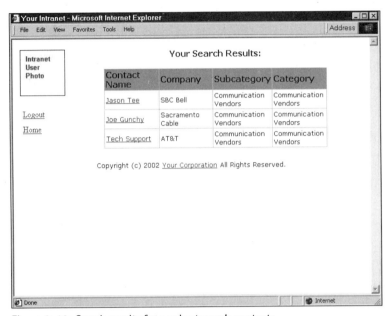

Figure 9-13: Search results for a subcategory's contacts.

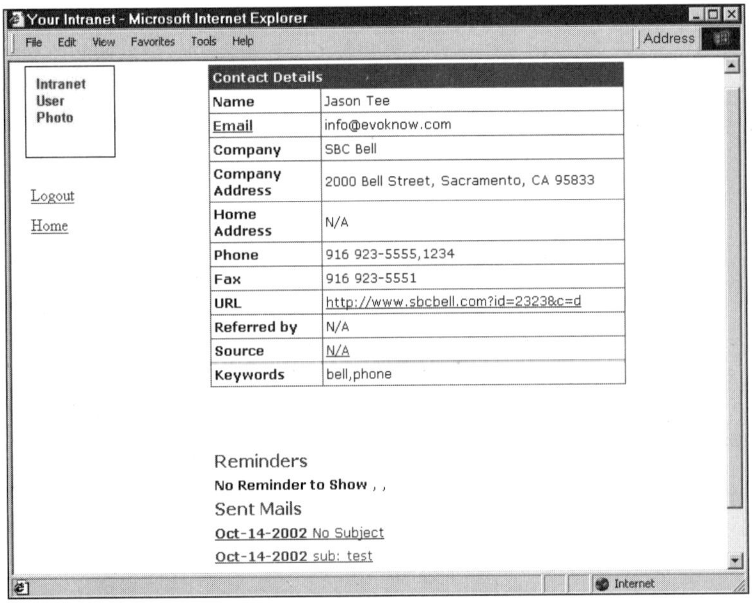

Figure 9-14: E-mail history of a contact.

Summary

In this chapter, you developed a central contact manager tool for your intranet. This tool enables your intranet users to search and manage contacts in a very efficient way compared to individual contact files. This application can be extended to include private and public contacts, or you can even consider extending it to allow groups of users to view a category (or prevent them from viewing a category).

Chapter 10

Intranet Calendar Manager

IN THIS CHAPTER

- ◆ Developing an intranet event calendar
- ◆ Installing an intranet event calendar
- ◆ Using an intranet event calendar

WORK MEANS SCHEDULES, and schedules mean important dates. Everyone has important family- and work-related dates that they need to remember. Many use a calendar as a tool to remind themselves of such events. In this chapter, we look at an intranet calendar system that enables a company to publish important events via a central calendar, and enables users to keep track of their personal events and dates.

Identifying Functionality Requirements

The calendar system that you'll put together in this chapter will have the following functionality:

- ◆ **Global events:** These events can be predefined in a configuration file to show up on the calendar every year. These may include annual company events.

- ◆ **Holiday events:** These events can be predefined in a configuration file to show up on the calendar every year. These are standard holidays with fixed dates, such as Independence Day, Christmas, New Year's Day, and so forth. Holidays that are not on a fixed date such as Thanksgiving, Labor Day, etc. will have to be set up manually.

- ◆ **Weekends:** Weekends can be configured to be any days and any number of days using a configuration file. Some parts of the world don't follow the Saturday-Sunday weekend system used in the U.S. and Europe.

- ◆ **Repeatable events:** Users can configure events to repeat weekly, monthly, or yearly.

335

♦ **Sharing and assigning events among users:** Users can create events for themselves or assign events to others or even share events with multiple users.

♦ **Automatic reminders:** Users can choose to be reminded about an event when they log in to the intranet on the day of the event.

Let's look at the prerequisites of the calendar system.

Understanding Prerequisites

The event calendar builds on the intranet classes discussed in the Chapters 4 through 7. For example, it uses the `Message` class (discussed in Chapter 7) to announce event reminders. That class enables the application to create and delete messages.

The intranet calendar applications that you'll develop require the central login/logout, user management, and intranet home applications discussed in those earlier chapters.

Now let's look at the database design and implementation needed for creating the intranet calendar manager.

Designing the Database

Figure 10-1 shows the database diagram for the intranet calendar manager. Here the CALENDAR_EVENT table holds the event data, CALENDAR_EVENT_VIEWER table holds the viewer list for an event in the CALENDAR_EVENT table. The CALENDAR_REPETITIVE_EVENTS table stores information about how an event is repeated.

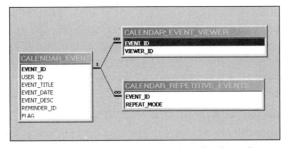

Figure 10-1: Intranet calendar manager database diagram.

Table 10-1 provides the details of the database tables.

TABLE 10-1 CALENDAR DATABASE TABLES

Table	Description
CALENDAR_EVENT	This table is the integral part of this database. It holds the event number (EVENT_ID), user ID (USER_ID), event title (EVENT_TITLE), event date (EVENT_DATE), event description (EVENT_DESC), reminder ID (REMINDER_ID), and a check flag (FLAG). The event number (EVENT_ID) is automatically generated by the database.
CALENDAR_EVENT_VIEWER	Holds the calendar event viewer information. The calendar event viewer consists of the EVENT_ID and VIEWER_ID.
CALENDAR_REPETITIVE_EVENTS	Holds the calendar repetitive event information. The calendar repetitive event consists of EVENT_ID and repeat mode (REPEAT_MODE).

The ch10/sql/calendar.sql file in the CDROM contains all the table creation statements for the CALENDAR database. You can create this CALENDAR database in your MySQL server by running the following commands.

```
mysqladmin -u root -p create CALENDAR
mysql -u root -p -D CALENDAR < calendar.sql
```

Make sure you change the user name (root) to whatever is appropriate for your system.

With the intranet calendar manager database established, it's time to look at the PHP classes that are needed to implement the applications.

The Intranet Calendar Application Event Class

We need only one new object, the Event object, to implement the intranet calendar manager, as you can see in Figure 10-2, which shows the system diagram. The Message object was discussed in Chapter 7.

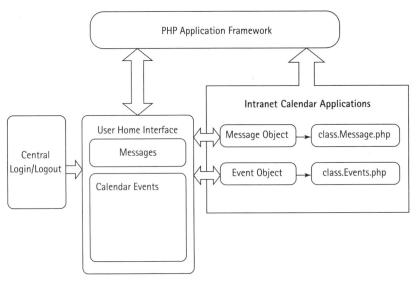

Figure 10-2: Intranet calendar manager system diagram.

The `Event` class provides the `Event` object. The class is used to manipulate each event. It allows an application to create and delete events. The ch10/apps/class/class.Event.php in the CDROM is an implementation of this class.

This class implements the following methods:

◆ `Event ()`: This is the constructor method. It performs the following functions:

■ Sets an object variable named `dbi` to point to the `class.DBI.php`-provided object, which is passed to the constructor by an application. `dbi` holds the DBI object that is used to communicate with the back-end database.

■ Sets a member variable named `event_tbl` to `$CALENDAR_EVENT_TBL`, which is loaded from the `calendar.conf` file. `$CALENDAR_EVENT_TBL` holds the name of the calendar event table.

■ Sets a member variable named `event_view_tbl` to `$CALENDAR_EVENT_VIEW_TBL`, which is loaded from the `calendar.conf` file. `$CALENDAR_EVENT_VIEW_TBL` holds the name of the event view table.

■ Sets a member variable named `event_repeat_tbl` to `$CALENDAR_EVENT_REPEAT_TBL`, which is loaded from the `calendar.conf` file. `$CALENDAR_EVENT_REPEAT_TBL` holds the name of the event repeat table.

■ Sets a member variable called `'std_fields'` as an associative array to hold the attributes of the calendar event table and their data types (text/number).

- Sets a member variable named 'fields', which is a comma-separated list of calendar event table fields.

- Calls setEventID() to set the given event ID to this object.

◆ loadEventInfo (): This method sets all the attribute values for a given event as member variables to this class. This is how it works:

  - The given event ID is set to a member variable called to eid using setEventID().

  - A statement to select all the event table fields for the given event ID is created in $stmt.

  - Using the DBI object $this->dbi, the $stmt statement is run via the $this->dbi->query() method in DBI object. The result of the query is stored in the $result variable.

  - If there are more than zero rows in the $result object, each row is fetched in the $row variable.

  - For each message field of type text, the data is stripped for embedded slash characters.

  - Each message field data is stored as object variable using $this->$fieldname run-time variable.

◆ getEvents (): This method returns all the events that are to be shown to the given user on a given date. It works as follows:

  - The date string (mm-dd-yyyy format) passed to this method is used to find out these three formats of the given date: the day of the week string, the day of the month string, and the month-day string. These formats are later used to check whether the given date is a weekly, monthly, or yearly repetitive date.

  - A statement to select all the events that are to be viewed by the given user on the given date is prepared. This statement also selects the events viewable by the given user that fall on this day because of the repetitive event feature. The statement is stored in a variable named $stmt.

  - Using the DBI object ($this->dbi), the $stmt statement is run via the $this->dbi->query() method in the DBI object. The result of the query is stored in the $result variable.

  - If there are more than zero rows in the $result object, each row is fetched in the $row variable.

  - An associative array is prepared using each row's event ID and Event Title.

  - The method returns the array. If the result set is found to be empty, the method returns null.

◆ getOwnEvents (): This method returns the events that are created by the given user for a given day. This is how it works:

- The date string parameter is formatted using addslashes and the quote() method of the DBI object.

- A statement to select all the events that are created by this user for the given date is prepared and stored in $stmt.

- Using the DBI object $this->dbi, the $stmt statement is run via the $this->dbi->query() method in the DBI object. The result of the query is stored in the $result variable.

- If there are more than zero rows in the $result object, each row is fetched in the $row variable.

- An associative array is prepared using each row's event ID and event title.

- The method returns the array. If the result set is empty, the method returns null.

◆ getViewers (): This method returns all viewer IDs for a given event. This is how it works:

- It sets the event ID using setEventID().

- A statement to select all the viewer IDs (user ID) of the event viewer table for the given event ID is prepared and stored in $stmt.

- Using the DBI object ($this->dbi), the $stmt statement is run via the $this->dbi->query() method in the DBI object. The result of the query is stored in the $result variable.

- If there are more than zero rows in the $result object, each row is fetched in the $row variable.

- An associative array is prepared using each row's event ID and event title.

- The method returns the array. In case the result set found is empty, the method returns null.

◆ addEvent (): This method adds a new event into to the CALENDAR_EVENT table. Attributes such as user ID, event title, event date, event description, reminder ID, and flag are passed as an associative array to this method. It works as follows:

- From the given parameter, all the values of text type in the database are escaped for characters such as quotation marks and slashes using $this->dbi->quote(addslashes()).

- A variable called $values is assigned a comma-separated list of all the parameter values.

- A SQL statement, $stmt, is created to insert the new event data into the event table using the member variable 'fields' (contains attribute names) and $values.

- The SQL statement is executed using $this->dbi->query(), and the result of the query is stored in the $result object.

- If the $result status is not okay, the method returns FALSE to indicate an insert failure. Otherwise, it returns the newly created event's ID by executing a second query.

◆ modifyEvent (): This method updates modified event information to the database. Attributes such as event ID, user ID, event title, event date, event description, reminder ID, and flag are passed as an associative array to this method. This is how it works:

- From the given parameter, all the values that of text type in the database are escaped for characters such as quotation marks and slashes using $this->dbi->quote(addslashes()).

- A SQL statement, $stmt, is created to update the event table using the parameter attributes and values.

- The SQL statement is executed using $this->dbi->query(), and the result of the query is stored in the $result object.

- If the $result status is not okay, the method returns FALSE to indicate an insert failure. Otherwise, it returns the newly created event's ID by executing a second query.

◆ addViewer (): This method adds a viewer to a given event. This is how it works:

- It takes the event ID and an array containing the viewer IDs (users ID) as a parameter.

- setEventID()is called to set the given event ID.

- It checks whether there is an entry of zero in the given array. If there is, it means that the event is viewable by all, and only a zero is added to the viewer table with the given event ID.

- When the array has all the entries greater than zero, each of the array entries is added to the event viewer table with the given event ID.

◆ `getRepeatMode ()`: This method returns the repeat mode for a given event. This is how it works:

- The given event ID is set using `setEventID()`.

- A statement is prepared to select the repeat mode for a given event from the repetitive event table. The statement is stored in a variable named `$stmt`.

- Using the DBI object `$this->dbi`, the `$stmt` statement is run via the `$this->dbi->query()` method in the DBI object, and the result is stored in the `$result` variable.

- If the result set is not empty, the row is fetched using the `fetchRow()` method of the DBI object, and `REPEAT_MODE` is returned from there. Otherwise, it returns null.

Here are the other methods of this class:

Method	Description
`setEventID()`	Sets the event ID (eid) of the event object. It takes the event ID from the user and, after setting it to member variable `'eid'`, returns the same. This setting is not done when the method is called without an event ID. In that case, the previously set event ID is returned.
`getEventTitle()`	Returns the title of the given event from the `CALENDAR_EVENT` table. It uses `loadEventInfo()` to set all the attribute members for the event, and returns the title of the event by getting the value from `$this->EVENT_TITLE`. This method takes the event ID as a parameter.
`getEventDate()`	Returns the date of the given event from the `CALENDAR_EVENT` table. It uses `loadEventInfo()` to set all the attribute members for the event, and returns the date of the event by getting the value from `$this->EVENT_DATE`. This method takes the event ID as a parameter.

Method	Description
getEventDesc()	Returns the description of the given event from the CALENDAR_EVENT table. It uses loadEventInfo() to set all the attribute members for the event, and returns the title of the event by getting the value from $this->EVENT_DESC. This method takes the event ID as a parameter.
getEventReminder()	Returns the reminder (MOTD) ID of the given event from the CALENDAR_EVENT table. It uses loadEventInfo() to set all the attribute members for the event, and returns the title of the event by getting the value from $this->REMINDER_ID. This method takes the event ID as a parameter.
deleteEvent()	Deletes the event from the CALENDAR_EVENT table. It takes the event ID as a parameter and returns TRUE or FALSE, depending on the status of the deletion operation.
deleteViewers()	Deletes all viewers for a given event. It takes the event ID as a parameter and returns TRUE or FALSE, depending on the status of the deletion operation.
addRepeatMode()	Adds repeat mode for a given event into the CALENDAR_REPETITIVE_EVENTS table. It takes the event ID and the event mode as parameters and returns TRUE or FALSE depending on the status of the insertion operation.
deleteRepeatMode()	Deletes all repeat modes for a given event. It takes the event ID as a parameter and returns TRUE or FALSE on the success or failure of the deletion operation.

The Application Configuration Files

Like all other applications we've developed in this book, the intranet calendar manager applications also use a standard set of configuration, message, and error files. These files are discussed in the following sections.

The main configuration file

The primary configuration file for the entire intranet calendar manager is called calendar.conf. Table 10-2 discusses each configuration variable.

TABLE 10-2 CALENDAR.CONF **VARIABLES**

Configuration Variable	Purpose
$PEAR_DIR	Set to the directory containing the PEAR package; specifically the DB module needed for class.DBI.php in our application framework.
$PHPLIB_DIR	Set to the PHPLIB directory, which contains the PHPLIB packages; specifically the template.inc package needed for template manipulation.
$APP_FRAMEWORK_DIR	Set to our application framework directory.
$PATH	Set to the combined directory path consisting of the $PEAR_DIR, $PHPLIB_DIR, and the $APP_FRAMEWORK_DIR. This path is used with ini_set() to redefine the php.ini entry for include_path to include $PATH ahead of the default path. This allows PHP to find our application framework, PHPLIB, and PEAR-related files.
$AUTHENTICATION_URL	Set to the central login application URL.
$LOGOUT_URL	Set to the central logout application URL.
$HOME_URL	Set to the topmost URL of the site. If the URL redirection application does not find a valid URL in the e-campaign database to redirect to for a valid request, it uses this URL as a default.
$APPLICATION_NAME	Internal name of the application.
$DEFAULT_LANGUAGE	Set to the default two-digit language code.
$ROOT_PATH	Set to the root path of the application.
$REL_ROOT_PATH	Relative path to the root directory.
$REL_APP_PATH	Relative application path as seen from the web browser.
$TEMPLATE_DIR	The fully qualified path to the template directory.

Configuration Variable	Purpose
$THEME_TEMPLATE_DIR	The fully qualified path to the theme template directory.
$REL_PHOTO_DIR	The Web-relative path to the photo directory used to store user photos.
$PHOTO_DIR	The fully qualified path to the photo directory.
$DEFAULT_PHOTO	Name of the default photo file, which is used when a user does not have a photo in the photo directory.
$CLASS_DIR	The fully qualified path to the class directory.
$REL_TEMPLATE_DIR	The Web-relative path to the template directory used.
$EVENT_CLASS	Name of the Event class file.
$MESSAGE_CLASS	Name of the Message class file. This class is developed for the MOTD application discussed in Chapter 9.
$CALENDAR_DB_URL	The fully qualified URL for the database used to store the calendar events.
$CALENDAR_EVENT_TBL	Name of the calendar event table in the database.
$CALENDAR_EVENT_VIEW_TBL	Name of the event viewer table in the database.
$CALENDAR_EVENT_REPEAT_TBL	Name of the event repeat table in the database.
$USER_PREFERENCE_TBL	Name of the user preference table in the database.
$MESSAGE_TBL	Name of the MOTD message table in the intranet database.
$MSG_VIEWER_TBL	Name of the message viewer list table in the intranet database.
$AUTH_DB_TBL	Name of the user authentication table in the auth database.
$STATUS_TEMPLATE	Name of the status template file used to display status messages.
$CALENDAR_HOME_TEMPLATE	Name of the calendar index template file.
$CALENDAR_EVENT_TEMPLATE	Name of the calendar event details template file.

Continued

TABLE 10-2 `CALENDAR.CONF` **VARIABLES** *(Continued)*

Configuration Variable	Purpose
`TODAY_COLOR`	Color defined for current day when displaying calendar.
`WEEKEND_COLOR`	Color defined for weekends when displaying calendar.
`HOLIDAY_COLOR`	Color defined for holidays when displaying calendar.
`GLOBAL_EVENT_COLOR`	Color defined for global events when displaying calendar.
`PERSONAL_EVENT_COLOR`	Color defined for personal events when displaying calendar.
`SECONDS_PER_DAY`	Defines amount of seconds per day.
`USER_DB_URL`	The fully qualified authentication database URL.
`$DEFAULT_THEME`	The default theme index in the `$THEME_TEMPLATE` array.
`$USER_DEFAULTS`	A user's theme and auto tip default settings.
`$TIP_SCRIPT`	The name of the tip script.
`$TIP_URL`	The Web-relative path for the tip files.
`$MAX_AVAILABLE_TIP`	The maximum number of tips from which to display the tip.
`$THEME_TEMPLATE[x]`	The list of theme templates.
`$PRINT_TEMPLATE[x]`	The list of print templates associated with the theme templates.

The directory structure used in the `calendar.conf` file supplied in `ch10` directory on the CD-ROM might need to be tailored to your own system's requirements. Here's how the current directory structure looks:

```
htdocs ($ROOT_PATH same as %DocumentRoot%)
|
+---home (base intranet application discussed in chapter 7)
|   |
|   +---templates
|       |
```

```
|          +---themes (theme templates used by all intranet apps)
|
+---photos (user photos used by all intranet apps)
|
+---calendar_mngr (Intranet Calendar Applications)
    |
    +---apps (calendar apps and configuration files)
        |
        +---class (calendar classes)
        |
        +---templates (publisher HTML templates)
           |
           +---themes (symlink to %DocumentRoot%/home/templates/themes)
```

By changing the following configuration parameters in `calendar.conf`, you can modify the directory structure to fit your site requirements:

```
$APP_FRAMEWORK_DIR=$_SERVER['DOCUMENT_ROOT'] . '/framework';
$PEAR             =$_SERVER['DOCUMENT_ROOT'] . '/pear';
$PHPLIB           =$_SERVER['DOCUMENT_ROOT'] . '/phplib';

$ROOT_PATH = $_SERVER['DOCUMENT_ROOT'];
$REL_ROOT_PATH       = '/calendar_mngr';
$REL_APP_PATH        =  $REL_ROOT_PATH . '/apps';
$REL_PHOTO_DIR       = '/photos';
$PHOTO_DIR           = $ROOT_PATH . $REL_PHOTO_DIR;
$TEMPLATE_DIR        = $ROOT_PATH . $REL_APP_PATH . '/templates';
$THEME_TEMPLATE_DIR = $TEMPLATE_DIR . '/themes';
$CLASS_DIR           = $ROOT_PATH . $REL_APP_PATH . '/class';
$REL_TEMPLATE_DIR    = $REL_APP_PATH . '/templates/';
```

The messages file

The messages displayed by the calendar manager applications are stored in the `ch10/apps/calendar.messages` file in the CDROM. You can change the messages using a text editor.

The errors file

The error messages displayed by the calendar manager applications are stored in the `ch10/apps/calendar.errors` file in the CDROM. You can modify the error messages using a text editor.

The Application Templates

The HTML interface templates needed for the applications are included in the ch10/apps/templates directory in the CD-ROM. These templates contain various template tags to display necessary information dynamically. The templates are named in the `calendar.conf` file. These templates are listed in Table 10-3.

TABLE 10-3 HTML TEMPLATES

Configuration Variable	Template File	Purpose
$STATUS_TEMPLATE	calendar_status.html	Used to show status message.
$CALENDAR_HOME_TEMPLATE	calendar_home.html	The calendar index template.
$CALENDAR_EVENT_TEMPLATE	calendar_events.html	The calendar event–related template.

The Calendar Manager Application

This calendar manager application is responsible for displaying an intranet calendar page to each user. The application, `calendar_mngr.php`, is included on the CD-ROM in the ch10/apps directory.

It implements the following functionality:

◆ When the user logs in, he is shown a calendar of the current month.

◆ Dates of the month are highlighted and colored according to events scheduled for those days.

◆ The user can use the navigator buttons to browse forward and backward through different months.

This application has the following methods:

◆ run(): This method is responsible for running this application. This is how it works:

■ It creates an object of the Theme class called $themeObj and sets it as a member variable.

- It finds out the preferred theme for the current user using the `getUserTheme()` method of the `Theme` class.

- It calls `displayCalendar()` to render the calendar along with all the events and holidays.

◆ `authorize()`: This method authorizes everyone on the intranet to view the page and, therefore, always returns `TRUE`.

◆ `displayCalendar()`: This method displays the calendar to the user. This is how it works:

- A calendar template (`$CALENDAR_HOME_TEMPLATE`) is loaded in a template object called `$template`.

- The method checks whether a time stamp has been supplied; if not, the current time stamp is stored in `$ts`. An array named `$date` is filled with the information of the time stamp using the `getDate()` API.

- A static array `$weekDays` is declared to store the weekdays and their indexes.

- For each day of the given time stamp's month, the events and holidays are retrieved from the database and the configuration file. Holidays and global events are loaded from the `calendar.conf` file.

- Each day is also checked if it's on weekend or not. (The weekend definition is configurable in the `calendar.conf` file.)

- Personal events are loaded into an array using the `getEvents()` method of the `Event` class.

- After getting all information of each day, the day of the month is set with events, holidays, weekend, cell color, and so on. If the total number of events to be shown for the day is less than or equal to four, they are set to the corners of the day cell. Otherwise, three corners are filled with the first three events and the fourth corner is set with a link to the other events.

- After the template is set with all the information for each day of the month, the template is parsed and the output is fed into `showContents()` to render it to the user.

◆ `showContents()`: This method is used to display the given contents according to the theme preferences of the user. This is how it works:

- The user's preferred theme template is loaded in a template object called `$themeTemplate`.

- The template contains a `contentBlock` that is to be filled by the parameter to this method.

- After the passed content is set into the `contentBlock`, it is rendered to the user.

The Calendar Event Manager Application

This application, `calendar_event_mngr.php`, is responsible for managing calendar events. This application is included on the CD-ROM in the `ch10/apps` directory.

The application has the following methods:

- ◆ `run()`: This method is responsible for running the application. It works as follows:

  - It creates an object of the `Theme` class called `$themeObj` and sets it as a member variable.

  - It finds out the preferred theme for the current user using the `getUserTheme()` method of the `Theme` class.

  - It calls `displayCalendarEventMngrHome()` to show the event manager menu with the given mode (add/modify).

- ◆ `authorize()`: This method authorizes everyone on the intranet to view the page and, therefore, always returns `TRUE`.

- ◆ `displayCalendarEventMngrHome()`: This method displays the calendar event manager menu, enabling users to add, delete, and modify calendar events. This is how it works:

  - The mode passed to this method decides which operation to perform. If the mode is `add` and `step` is set to 1, it only has to show an empty Web form to take the input from the user. When the step is set to 2, it calls `addEvent()` to add a new event.

  - If the mode is set to `modify` with step set as 1, it preloads the Web form with the event's previous information. When step is set to 2, it calls `modifyEvent()` to modify the event.

  - When the mode is `delete`, it calls `deleteEvent()` to delete the event.

  - It uses the `getOwnEvents()` method of the `Event` class to shows a list of the events created by the current user. Each event is followed by a delete link that allows the user to delete the event. There is also a radio button with each event that the user can select to start the modification process.

  - To show the contents of the event manager menu, a calendar event template (`CALENDAR_EVENT_TEMPLATE`) is loaded in a template object called `$template`.

- The template file includes a Web form that takes the input for a new event to be added or an old event to be modified.

- When the method is called with mode `modify`, it loads the Web form using the `getEventTitle()`, `getEventDesc()`, `getViewers()`, `getRepeatMode()`, and `getEventReminder()` methods of the `Event` class.

- After setting appropriate blocks and variables of the template, `showContents()` is called to render the output using the proper theme for the user.

◆ `deleteEvent()`: This method is responsible for deleting events when requested. This works in the following manner:

- It creates objects for the `Event` and `Message` classes.

- The message ID (MOTD ID) for the event is retrieved using the `getEventReminder()` method of the `Event` class, and fed into the `deleteMessage()` and `deleteViewers()` methods of the `Message` class to delete the message.

- All entries related to this event are eliminated from the `CALENDAR_EVENT_VIEWER` and `CALENDAR_REPETITIVE_EVENTS` tables using the `deleteViewers()` and `deleteRepeatMode()` methods of the `Event` class.

- After deleting all the related data, the event itself is deleted using the `deleteEvent()` method of the `Event` class.

- Depending on the outcome of the deletion process, a success or fail message is shown to the user.

◆ `modifyEvent()`: This event modifies a given event. Its functionalities are as follows:

- It checks whether the option to show the event to other users is turned on. If it's not, it takes only the current user's ID to add to the viewer table.

- It validates the user inputs by checking if the publish date and event title have been supplied. If not, it shows an alert message and returns null.

- If the event's reminder option is turned on, it checks for previous messages related to the event ID. If it finds a message, the message is modified using the `modifyMessage()` method of the `Message` class. Otherwise, the new message is added using `addMessage()` and `addViewer()`.

- If the event's reminder option is turned off, all the messages and message viewers related to the event are deleted using `deleteMessage()` and `deleteViewers()`.

- The event attributes are modified using the `modifyEvent()` method of the `Event` class.

- If the status of the `modifyEvent()` is successful, the new viewers and repeat mode (if any) are added for the event after deleting the previous ones.

- The user is shown the appropriate confirmation message on the basis of success or failure of the modification operation.

◆ `addEvent()`: This method adds a new event to the calendar. It works in the following way:

- It checks whether the option to show the event to other users is turned on. If it's not, it takes only the current user's ID to add to the viewer table.

- It validates the user inputs by checking if the publish date and event title have been supplied or not. If not, it shows an alert message and returns null.

- If the event's reminder option is turned on, a new message is added using the `addMessage()` and `addViewer()` methods of the `Message` class.

- The event attributes are added into the event table using the `addEvent()` method of the `Event` class.

- If the status of `addEvent()` is successful, the viewers and repeat mode (if any) are added for the event.

- The user is shown an appropriate confirmation message on the basis of the success or failure of the insertion operation.

◆ `showContents()`: This method displays the given contents according to the theme preferences of the user. This is how it works:

- The user's preferred theme template is loaded in a template object called `$themeTemplate`.

- The template contains a `contentBlock` that is to be filled by the parameter to this method.

- After the passed content is set into the `contentBlock`, it is rendered to the user.

Installing the Event Calendar on Your Intranet

The event calendar installation process assumes the following:

- ◆ You're using a Linux system with MySQL and Apache server installed.

- ◆ Your intranet web server document root directory is `/evoknow/intranet/htdocs`. Of course, if you have a different path, which is likely, you should change this path whenever you see it in a configuration file or instruction in this chapter. During the installation process, I refer to this directory as `%DocumentRoot%`.

- ◆ You've installed the PHPLIB and PEAR library. Normally, these get installed during PHP installation. For your convenience, I've provided these in the `lib/phplib.tar.gz` and `lib/pear.tar.gz` directories on the CD-ROM. In the example installation steps, I assume that these are installed in the `/%DocumentRoot%/phplib` and `/ %DocumentRoot%/pear` directories. Because your installation location for these libraries is likely to differ, make sure you replace these paths in the configuration files.

- ◆ You've installed the base intranet user home application, the messaging system, and the INTRANET database (see Chapter 7 for details).

Here is how you can get your intranet calendar applications up and running:

1. **Install intranet calendar database tables.** You need to create the CALENDAR database. The `ch10/sql/calendar.sql` file in the CDROM has all the create table scripts needed for the CALENDAR database. The quickest way to create the database is to run the following commands:

```
mysqladmin -u root -p create CALENDAR
mysql -u root -p -D CALENDAR < calendar.sql
```

2. **Install intranet calendar applications.** Now from the `ch10` directory of the CD-ROM, extract `ch10.tar.gz` in `%DocumentRoot%`. This will create `calendar_mngr` in your document root. Configure `%DocumentRoot%/calendar_mngr/apps/calendar.conf` for path and database settings. The applications are installed in the `%DocumentRoot%/calendar_mngr/apps` directory and the templates are stored in `%DocumentRoot%/calendar_mngr/apps/templates`.

Your MySQL server is hosted on the intranet web server and can be accessed via localhost. However, if this is not the case, you can easily modify the database URLs in each application's configuration files. For example, the `home.conf` file has MySQL database access URLs such as

```
$INTRANET_DB_URL  = 'mysql://root:foobar@localhost/INTRANET';

$CALENDAR_DB_URL = 'mysql://root:foobar@localhost/CALENDAR';

$USER_DB_URL  = 'mysql://root:foobar@localhost/auth';
```

Say your database server is called `db.domain.com` and the user name and password to access the INTRANET and auth databases (which you will create during this installation process) are admin and db123. You would modify the database access URLs throughout each configuration file as

```
$INTRANET_DB_URL  =
'mysql://admin:db123@db.domain.com/INTRANET';

$CALENDAR_DB_URL =
'mysql://admin:db123@db.domain.com/CALENDAR';

$USER_DB_URL  = 'mysql://admin:db123@db.domain.com/auth';
```

3. **Adding the calendar to theme navigation bar.** You need to update your theme navigation bar files stored in `%DocumentRoot%/themes/%theme%/home_left_nav.html` whenever you add a new application. For example, to update the `std_blue` theme, you need to update the `%DocumentRoot%/themes/std_blue/ home_left_nav.html` file to include the following line in the HTML table:

```
<tr><td width="100%"><font size=2><a
href="/calendar_mngr/apps/calendar_mngr.php">Calendar</a></fo
nt></td> </tr>
```

This creates a new HTML table row in the left navigation bar.

4. **Set file/directory permissions.** Make sure you've changed file and directory permissions such that your intranet web server can access all the files.

After you've performed these steps, you're ready to test your calendar applications.

Testing the Event Calendar

Log in to your intranet via `http://yourserver/index.php` or `http://yourserver/home/home.php` using the user name and password you created in Chapter 6 and tested in Chapter 7.

Click on the Calendar link in the left navigation bar of your intranet home page or point your web browser to `http://yourserver/calendar_mngr/apps/` `calendar_mngr.php`. This shows you the current month, like the example shown in Figure 10-3.

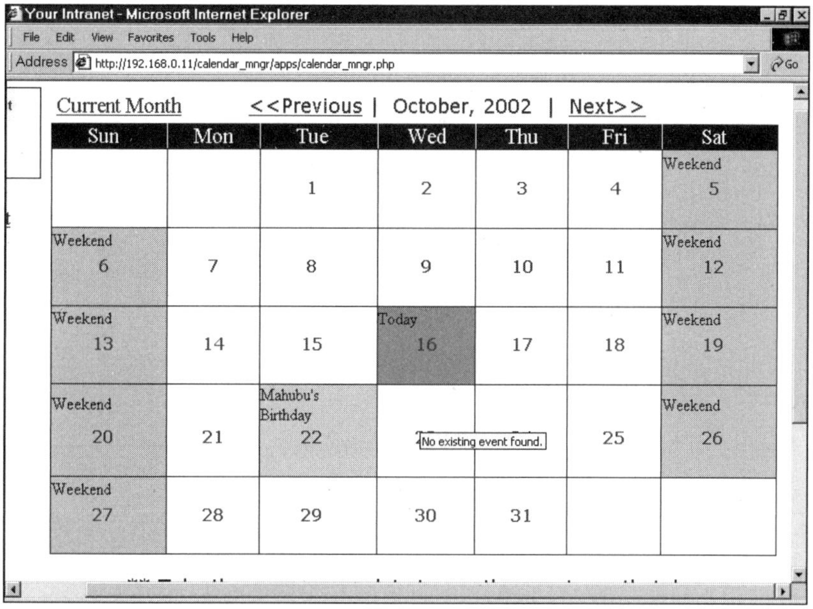

Figure 10-3: The current month calendar.

The current day (October 16, in my example) is shown is its own color (orange by default), weekends are shown in gray, and a global event (October 22) is shown in cream color. You can configure these colors using `calendar.conf` parameters such as

```
define('TODAY_COLOR', 'FF8800');
define('WEEKEND_COLOR', 'CCCCCC');
define('HOLIDAY_COLOR', 'ABCDEF');
define('GLOBAL_EVENT_COLOR', 'FFCC99');
define('PERSONAL_EVENT_COLOR', 'dfefcf');
```

The colors are stored in standard RGB format in hex numbers ranging from 000000 (black) to FFFFFF (white).

Adding a new event

To add an event, find the appropriate month using the Next or Previous links on the top, and then click on the day of the event. For example, to add an event on July 7, 2003, move forward to July 2003 using the Next button and click on the day (7). After you've clicked on a date, a screen similar to the one in Figure 10-4 displays.

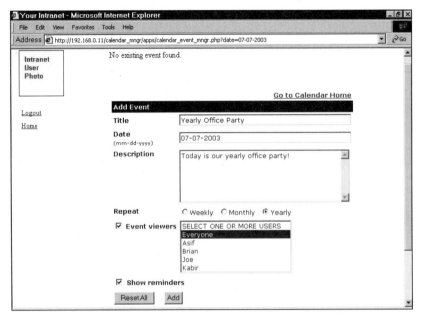

Figure 10-4: Adding an event.

To add a reminder, add an event title, description, frequency (weekly, monthly, yearly, default is once only), who can view the event, and also if you want to view a reminder on that day. After all these fields are entered, you can add the event by clicking the Add button.

Modifying an existing event

To modify an existing event, select the day of the event and you'll see a screen similar to the one in Figure 10-5.

A list of events on that day appears at the top. (There's only one event in this example.) Select the event you want to modify by clicking its radio button. When you select it, you can delete it by clicking the Delete button, or make changes to the event and resubmit it by clicking the Modify button.

Viewing an event reminder

When you log in, any reminder for an event that day shows up automatically because the Calendar system sets up the reminder using the central messaging mechanism that you developed earlier. Figure 10-6 shows an event reminder.

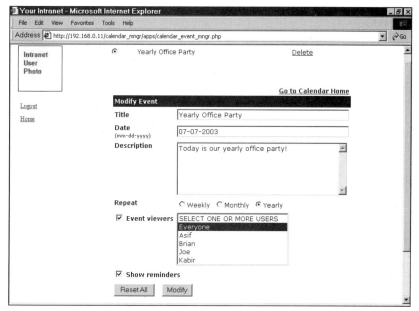

Figure 10-5: Modifying an event.

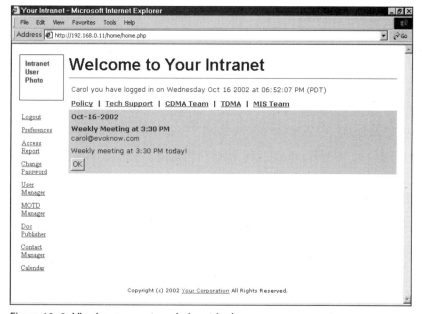

Figure 10-6: Viewing an event reminder at login.

Summary

In this chapter, you saw how to create a central event calendar for your intranet. This calendar tool allows users to remind themselves of important personal and shared events.

Chapter 11

Internet Resource Manager

IN THIS CHAPTER

♦ Developing an Internet Resource Manager system

♦ Installing an Internet Resource Manager system

♦ Using an Internet Resource Manager system

ALL OF US MAKE bookmarks of Web resources that are useful or entertaining to us. Storing useful bookmarks on desktop computers is helpful but often leads to a lots of e-mails among co-workers who need to share resources that they find on the Web or via FTP. In this case, a central Internet Resource (Web sites or FTP sites) Management (IRM) tool can be a great help. It can help organize the commonly needed resources on a central database, which all users can share and also search to locate sites by keywords. In this chapter, we'll design such a tool.

Functionality Requirements

The IRM tool will do the following:

♦ It will have a central database to store all Internet resources.

♦ It will allow administrators to organize resources in categories. All resources will be stored in subcategories of main categories.

♦ It will allow all users to add new resources without duplicating. The user can specify a rank (1 star to 5 stars) for the resource to indicate the value of the resource.

♦ It will allow all users to search resources by keywords entered during resource creation. It will also allow users to find resources by creator (user) name or resource visitor (user) name. This is very helpful in finding resources created and visited by people in an organization.

♦ It will track click-through to identify the most frequently requested resources. This is a great way to know which resources are most widely used.

Now let's look at the prerequisites of this system.

Understanding the Prerequisites

This Internet Resource Manager builds on the Intranet classes discussed in Chapters 4 through 7. It uses the message class to announce event reminders.

The intranet calendar applications that we will develop here require the central login/logout, user management, and home applications of the intranet discussed in the previous chapters in this section.

Now let's look at the database design and implementation needed for creating this Internet Resource Manager.

Designing the Database

Figure 11-1 shows the database diagram for the IRM. The central table in this database is RESOURCE, which stores the details of the Internet site. Each resource stored in this table can be created by a user. The user, who adds the resource, information is store din USER table. Each resource belongs to a resource category stored in CATEGORY table. Each category can have one or more resources in the RESOURCE table and therefore the CATEGORY table has a one to many relationship with the RESOURCE table. Each resource in the RESOURCE table can have one or more keywords, which are stored in the RESOURCE_KEYWORD table. Similarly, each resource can be visited by one or more visitors. The tracking information for the visitors are stored in the RESOURCE_VISITOR table.

In the following section I will describe each of these tables in details.

CATEGORY table

The CATEGORY table is an integral part of this database. This table holds the category number (CATEGORY_ID), category name (CATEGORY_NAME), parent category (P_CATEGORY_ID), created by (CREATED_BY), and creation timestamp (CREATE_TS). The category number (CATEGORY_ID) is automatically generated by the database.

RESOURCE table

The RESOURCE table contains the resource information. This table holds the resource number (RESOURCE_ID), resource title (RESOURCE_TITLE), resource location (RESOURCE_LOCATION), resource category (RESOURCE_CATEGORY), resource rating (RESOURCE_RATING), resource description (RESOURCE_DESCRIPTION), resource added by (RESOURCE_ADDED_BY), creation timestamp (CREATE_TS), and flag (FLAG). The resource number (RESOURCE_ID) is automatically generated by the database.

RESOURCE_KEYWORD table

The RESOURCE_KEYWORD table holds the resource keyword information. The resource keyword consists of resource number (RESOURCE_ID) and keyword (KEYWORD).

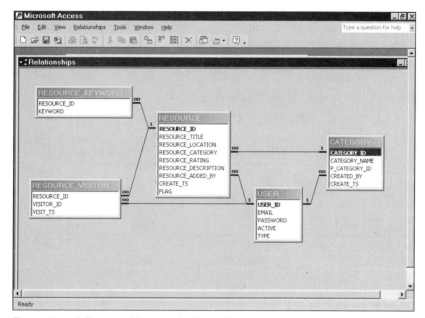

Figure 11-1: A Resource Manager database diagram.

RESOURCE_VISITOR table

The RESOURCE_VISITOR table contains visitor(s) of resources. This table holds the resource number (RESOURCE_ID), visitor ID (VISITOR_ID), and visit timestamp (VISIT_TS).

The ch11/sql/irm.sql file in the CDROM has a set of create table statements, which can be used to create the IRM database in MySQL. To create the IRM database and its tables run the following commands:

```
mysqladmin -u root -p create IRM
mysql -u root -p -D IRM < irm.sql
```

Make sure you change the user name (root) to whatever is appropriate for your system.

After you have the Resource Manager database designed, you need to design the PHP classes that will be needed to implement the applications. In the following sections, I discuss these classes.

Designing and Implementing the Internet Resource Manager Application Classes

As shown in the system diagram, Figure 11-2, there are three objects that are needed to implement the Internet Resource Manager.

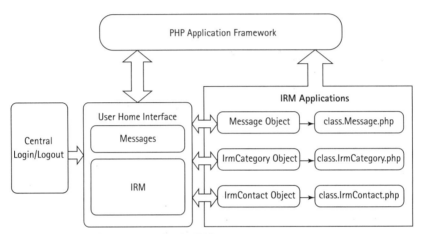

Figure 11-2: A system diagram for the IRM.

Here you will develop three classes that will provide these objects for your resource applications.

Designing and implementing the IrmCategory class

The `IrmCategory` class is used to manipulate each category. It allows an application to create and delete a category. The `ch11/apps/class/class.IrmCategory.php` file in the CDROM is an implementation of this class. This class implements the following methods.

IrmCategory()

This is the constructor method. It performs the following functions:

◆ Sets a member variable named `category_tbl` to `$IRM_CATEGORY_TBL`, which is loaded from the `irm.conf` file. The `$IRM_CATEGORY_TBL` holds the name of the category table.

◆ Sets a member variable named `dbi` to point to the `class.DBI.php`-provided object, which is passed to the constructor by an application. The `dbi` member variable holds the `DBI` object, which is used to communicate with the back-end database.

getCategoryList()

This method returns the list of main categories or categories that do not have any parent categories. It works as follows:

◆ First, it initializes an array named `$listArr`, which will be used for storing the category list.

◆ A SQL statement is created in `$stmt`, which queries the category table for the entire main category list. It returns all the names and IDs of the main category.

◆ Then It fetches the result of the query and return the `$listArr` array containing the list of category IDs and category names.

If the result of the query is empty, then it returns null.

getSubCategoryList()

This method returns the list of all subcategories for a given category. It works as follows:

◆ This method is called with category ID (`$p_id`).

◆ It initializes an array named `$listArr` for containing the list of subcategory ID and name.

◆ A SQL select statement, `$stmt`, is created to return all the category IDs and their names for which the parent category ID matches the given category ID (`$p_id`).

◆ If the result of the SQL query returns no rows, the method returns null.

◆ Otherwise, the list of subcategory IDs and names are returned in an array called `$listArr`.

getCategoryName()

This method returns the name of the category from the `CATEGORY` table. This method takes the category ID (`$catID`) as a parameter.

getParentCategory()

This method returns the parent category of the given category from the `CATEGORY` table. This function takes category ID (`$catID`) as a parameter.

existInList()

This method determines the existence of a category in the CATEGORY table. It takes category name ($catName) as a parameter. It returns the category ID if the given name matches with the existing category name in the CATEGORY table; otherwise, it return zero.

addCategory()

This method adds a new category into to the CATEGORY table. This method is called with category name ($name), parent category ID ($pcat), and created by ($uid). Along with this, information about the new category adding time is also entered into the database. If the category is successfully added, then it returns TRUE; otherwise, it returns FALSE.

deleteCategory()

This method deletes the category from the database. This method is called with category ID ($catID). If it successfully deletes the category, then it returns TRUE; otherwise, it returns FALSE.

modifyCategory()

This method updates the category information for a given category. This method is called with category ID ($catID), name ($newcategory), parent category ID ($pid) and the user ID ($uid). If it updates successfully, then it returns TRUE; otherwise, it returns FALSE.

Designing and implementing the IrmResource class

This class provides the Resource object. The Resource object is used to manipulate Internet resources. The ch11/apps/class/class.IrmResource.php file in the CDROM is an implementatio of this class. In the following section, I discuss the methods available in this class below.

IrmResource()

This is the constructor method, which performs the following tasks:

◆ Sets a member variable called resource_tbl to $IRM_RESOURCE_TBL, which is loaded from the irm.conf file. The $IRM_RESOURCE_TBL variable holds the name of the resource table.

◆ Sets a member variable called resource_track_tbl to $IRM_RESOURCE_VISITOR, which is loaded from the irm.conf file. The $IRM_RESOURCE_VISITOR variable holds the name of the resource visitor table.

- Sets a member variable called `resource_keyword_tbl` to `$IRM_RESOURCE_KEYWORD_TBL`, which is loaded from the `irm.conf` file. The `$IRM_RESOURCE_KEYWORD_TBL` variable holds the name of the resource keyword table.

- Sets a member variable named `dbi` to point to the `class.DBI.php`-provided object, which is passed to the constructor by an application. The `dbi` member variable holds the `DBI` object, which is used to communicate with the back-end database.

- Sets an object variable called `$std_map_fields` to field names of the `RESOURCE` table. The `std_map_fields` variable is an associative array, which contains both field names and field types in a `key = value` format.

- A comma-separated list of `RESOURCE` table field names are created in the `$fields` variable using the `$this->std_map_fields`.

- Sets an object variable called `$resource_track_map_fields` to field names of the `RESOURCE_VISITOR` table. The `std_map_fields` variable is an associative array, which contains both field names and field types in a `key = value` format.

- A comma-separated list of `RESOURCE_VISITOR` table field names are created in the `$resource_track_fields` variable using the `$this->resource_track_map_fields`.

addResource()

Called with an associative array (`$params`), which contain the field names of the table and the field value, the method adds new resource in the `RESOURCE` table. It works as follows:

- The given resource title (`$params[RESOURCE_TITLE]`), resource location (`$params[RESOURCE_LOCATION]`), and resource description (`$params[RESOURCE_DESCRIPTION]`) are escaped for characters such as quotation marks and slashes using `$this->dbi->quote(addslashes())` methods.

- A SQL statement, `$statement`, is created to insert the new resource data into the `RESOURCE` table.

- The SQL statement is executed using the `$this->dbi->query()` method and the result of the query is stored in the `$result` object.

- Another SQL statement, `$stmt`, is created to select the newly added resource from the `RESOURCE` table and execute the SQL statement in the `$this->dbi->query()` method.

- This method returns the resource ID if it inserts the resource successfully; otherwise, it return `FALSE`.

addKeywords()

This method inserts keywords in the RESOURCE_KEYWORD table. This method is called with resource ID ($rid) and an array ($params), which contains the keywords. Each keyword is inserted into the table using a foreach loop. It returns TRUE if it adds keywords successfully; otherwise, it returns FALSE.

deleteKeywords()

This method deletes all the keywords for the given resource from the database. This method is called with the resource ID ($rid). It returns TRUE if it successfully deletes all the keywords; otherwise, it returns FALSE.

getKeywords()

This method returns keyword(s) for the given resource. It works as follows:

- ◆ This method is called with the resource ID ($rid).

- ◆ A SQL statement, $stmt, is created which queries the RESOURCE_KEYWORD table for all keywords for the given resource ID.

- ◆ The SQL statement is executed using the $this->dbi->query() method and the result of the query is stored in the $result object.

- ◆ If no rows are returned in the $result object, the method returns null.

- ◆ On the other hand, it fetches the $result object and each row is stored in the $row object and the keyword is stored in the $retArr array. Then the array $retArr is returned.

searchResource()

This method searches resource in the RESOURCE table. This method works as follows:

- ◆ This method is called with an associative array ($params), which contains search criteria.

- ◆ If the resource category ($params[RESOURCE_CATEGORY]) is provided in the parameter, then the method checks whether the given category is the main category or not. If it is the main category, then it generates SQL conditions for each subcategory of the given category along with the main category. On the other hand, it generates the SQL condition only for the main category. These conditions are stored in a variable called $category.

- ◆ Then It checks whether the rating $params[RESOURCE_RATING] criteria is provided or not. If the rating criteria is provided, then the SQL condition is generated and stored in a variable called $rating.

- ◆ If the resource added by criteria $params[RESOURCE_ADDED_BY] is given, then it generates the SQL condition for the resources, which is added by a particular user.

- If the resource visited by criteria $params[RESOURCE_VISITED_BY] is given, then it generates the SQL condition for the resources, which is visited by a particular user.

- Next This method checks whether the keywords are provided for searching or not. If they are provided, then it generates the SQL condition that will search for resources that have the given keywords.

- A SQL statement, $stmt, is created which queries for the resources falling under all the given criterion.

- The SQL statement is executed using the $this->dbi->query() method and the result of the query is stored in the $result object.

- If no rows are returned in the $result object, the method returns null.

- On the other hand, it fetches the $result object and each row is stored in the $row object and the $row object is stored in the $retArr array. Then the array $retArr is returned.

modifyResource()

This method updates existing resource information in the database. It works as follows:

- The method is called with an associative array ($params), which contains the fields name of the RESOURCE table, its new value, and the resource ID ($resource_id) for which it will update.

- The given resource title ($params[RESOURCE_TITLE]), resource location ($params[RESOURCE_LOCATION]), and resource description ($params[RESOURCE_DESCRIPTION]) are escaped for characters such as quotation marks and slashes using $this->dbi->quote(addslashes()) methods.

- A SQL statement, $statement, is created to update the new resource data into the RESOURCE table.

- The SQL statement is executed using the $this->dbi->query() method and the result of the query is stored in the $result object.

- If the resource is successfully updated, then this method returns TRUE; otherwise, it returns FALSE.

trackResourceVisit()

When a user clicks on a URL for a resource displayed in a category or as a search result, the URL click event is tracked. This method is responsible for inserting a track record in the RESOURCE_TRACK table for such URL clicks.

deleteResource()

This method deletes a resource from RESOURCE table of the database. It deletes a resource by the given resource ID ($rid).

getNumOfResourceInCat()

This method returns the number of resources that reside in the given category. This method is called with a category ID ($catID) as parameter.

getResourceByCategory()

This method returns all the resources that fall under the given category. This method is called with a category ID ($catID).

getResourceUrl()

This method returns URL of the resource. This method is called with a resource ID ($rid).

getTotalResourceNum()

This method returns the total number of resources in the RESOURCE table.

getResourceInfo()

This method returns information related to the given resource. This method is called with resource ID ($rid).

getNewResource()

This method returns the number of newly added resources. This method is called with category ID ($catid) and time limit ($timeLimit). It finds the number of the resources that fall under the given category ID and are added after the given time limit.

getTopRankingList()

This method returns the top-ranking resource list. This method is called with a parameter that can be considered as the lower bound of the top ranking list (that is, this method finds all the resources that have ranking higher than or equal to this parameter). It returns an associative array, which contain the resource ID and its information.

Designing and implementing the Message class

The Message class is used to manipulate each message. It allows an application to create and delete messages. This class is discussed in Chapter 7.

Creating Application Configuration Files

Like all other applications we've developed in this book, the Internet Resource Manager applications also use a standard set of configuration, message, and error files. These files are discussed in the following sections.

Creating the main configuration file

The primary configuration file for the entire Internet Resource Manager is called irm.conf. Table 11-1 discusses each configuration variables.

TABLE 11-1 IRM.CONF VARIABLES

Configuration Variable	Purpose
$PEAR_DIR	Set to the directory containing the PEAR package; specifically the DB module needed for class.DBI.php in our application framework.
$PHPLIB_DIR	Set to the PHPLIB directory, which contains the PHPLIB packages; specifically the template.inc package needed for template manipulation.
$APP_FRAMEWORK_DIR	Set to our application framework directory.
$PATH	Set to the combined directory path consisting of the $PEAR_DIR, $PHPLIB_DIR, and $APP_FRAMEWORK_DIR. This path is used with the ini_set() method to redefine the php.ini entry for include_path to include $PATH ahead of the default path. This allows PHP to find our application framework, PHPLIB, and PEAR-related files.
$AUTHENTICATION_URL	Set to the central login application URL.
$LOGOUT_URL	Set to the central logout application URL.
$HOME_URL	Set to the topmost URL of the site. If the URL redirection application doesn't find a valid URL in the e-campaign database to redirect to for a valid request, it uses this URL as a default.
$APPLICATION_NAME	The internal name of the application.

Continued

TABLE 11-1 **IRM.CONF VARIABLES** *(Continued)*

Configuration Variable	Purpose
$DEFAULT_LANGUAGE	Set to the default (two characters) language code.
$ROOT_PATH	Set to the root path of the application.
$REL_ROOT_PATH	Relative path to the root directory.
$REL_APP_PATH	Relative application path as seen from Web browser.
$TEMPLATE_DIR	The fully qualified path to the template directory.
$THEME_TEMPLATE_DIR	The fully qualified path to the theme template directory.
$REL_PHOTO_DIR	The Web-relative path to the photo directory used to store user photos.
$PHOTO_DIR	The fully qualified path to the photo directory.
$DEFAULT_PHOTO	Name of the default photo file, which is used when a user does not have a photo in the photo directory.
$CLASS_DIR	The fully qualified path to the class directory.
$REL_TEMPLATE_DIR	The Web-relative path to the template directory used.
$IRM_CATEGORY_CLASS	Name of the Category class file.
$IRM_RESOURCE_CLASS	Name of the Resource class file.
$IRM_MESSAGE_CLASS	Name of the Message class file. This class is developed for the MOTD application discussed in Chapter 10.
$IRM_RESOURCE_MNGR	Name of the application that manages resources.
$IRM_SEARCH_MNGR	Name of the application that is used to search for resources.
$IRM_RESOURCE_TRACK_MNGR	Name of the application that tracks user visits to resources.
$IRM_CAT_MNGR	Name of the application that manages categories.
$IRM_DB_URL	The fully qualified URL for the database used to store the resources and categories.
$IRM_CATEGORY_TBL	Name of the category table in the database.
$IRM_RESOURCE_TBL	Name of the resource table in the database.
$IRM_RESOURCE_KEYWORD_TBL	Name of the resource keyword table in the database.

Configuration Variable	Purpose
$USER_PREFERENCE_TBL	Name of the user preference table in the database.
$MESSAGE_TBL	Name of the MOTD message table in the database.
$IRM_RESOURCE_VISITOR	Name of the resource visitor table in the database.
$MSG_VIEWER_TBL	Name of the message viewer list table in the database.
$AUTH_DB_TBL	Name of the user authentication table in the database.
$IRM_RESOURCE_DES_TEMPLATE	Name of the resource description template file.
$IRM_RESOURCE_MENU_TEMPLATE	Name of the resource menu template file.
$IRM_RESOURCE_MODIFY_MENU_TEMPLATE	Name of the resource modify form template file.
$IRM_MOTD_TEMPLATE	Name of the live note template file.
$IRM_CAT_HOME_TEMPLATE	Name of the category index template file.
$IRM_CAT_ADD_MODTEMPLATE	Name of the add/modify category entry form template file.
$IRM_SEARCH_RESULT_TEMPLATE	Name of the search result showing template file.
$IRM_SEARCH_TEMPLATE	Name of the resource searching template file.
$IRM_STATUS_TEMPLATE	Name of the status template file used to display status messages.
ODD_COLOR	Color defined for odd rows when displaying tabular data such as document track listing.
EVEN_COLOR	Color defined for even rows when displaying tabular data such as document track listing.
$RATINGS	Defines an associative array used to display response rating information.
USER_DB_URL	The fully qualified authentication database URL.
CAT_PER_LINE'	Number of categories per row to show in a navigation table, which is created in the navigation file.

Continued

TABLE 11-1 IRM.CONF VARIABLES *(Continued)*

Configuration Variable	Purpose
SEPARATOR	The characters that separate each navigation entry (category) in the navigation, which is created in the navigation file.
$DEFAULT_THEME	The default theme index in the $THEME_TEMPLATE array.
$USER_DEFAULTS	A user's theme and auto tip default settings.
$TIP_SCRIPT	The name of the tip script.
$TIP_URL	The Web-relative path for the tip files.
$MAX_AVAILABLE_TIP	The maximum number of tips from which to display the tip.
$THEME_TEMPLATE[x]	The list of theme templates.
$PRINT_TEMPLATE[x]	The list of print templates associative with the theme templates.

The directory structure used in the `irm.conf` file supplied in the `ch11` directory on the CD-ROM might need to be tailored to your own system's requirements. Here is how the current directory structure looks:

```
htdocs ($ROOT_PATH = %DocumentRoot%)
|
+---home (base intranet application discussed in chapter 7)
|   |
|   +---templates (templates used by intranet apps)
|       |
|       +---themes (theme templates used by all intranet apps)
|
+---photos (user photos used by all intranet apps)
|
+---irm (IRM Applications)
    |
    +---apps (IRM apps and configuration files)
        |
        +---class (IRM classes)
        |
```

```
+---templates (IRM HTML templates)
    |
    +---themes (symlink to %DocumentRoot%/home/templates/themes)
```

By changing the following configuration parameters in irm.conf, you can modify the directory structure to fit your site requirements:

```
$PEAR_DIR            = $_SERVER['DOCUMENT_ROOT'] . '/pear' ;
$PHPLIB_DIR          = $_SERVER['DOCUMENT_ROOT'] . '/phplib';
$APP_FRAMEWORK_DIR   = $_SERVER['DOCUMENT_ROOT'] . '/framework2';
$PATH                = $PEAR_DIR . ':' . $PHPLIB_DIR . ':' .
$APP_FRAMEWORK_DIR;

$ROOT_PATH           = $_SERVER['DOCUMENT_ROOT'];
$REL_ROOT_PATH       = '/irm';
$REL_APP_PATH        =  $REL_ROOT_PATH . '/apps';

$TEMPLATE_DIR        = $ROOT_PATH    . $REL_APP_PATH . '/templates';
$CLASS_DIR           = $ROOT_PATH    . $REL_APP_PATH . '/class';

$THEME_TEMPLATE_DIR  = $TEMPLATE_DIR   . '/themes';
$REL_PHOTO_DIR       = '/photos';
$PHOTO_DIR           = $ROOT_PATH    . $REL_PHOTO_DIR;
```

Creating a messages file

The messages displayed by the IRM applications are stored in the ch11/apps/
calendar.messages file in the CDROM. You can change the messages using a text
editor.

Creating an errors file

The error messages displayed by the IRM applications are stored in the /ch11/
apps/calendar.errors file in the CDROM. You can modify the error messages
using a text editor.

Creating Application Templates

The HTML interface templates needed for the applications are included in the
ch11/apps/templates directory in the CD-ROM. These templates contain various template tags to display necessary information dynamically. The templates are
named in the irm.conf file. These templates are discussed in Table 11-2.

TABLE 11-2 HTML TEMPLATES

Configuration Variable	Template File	Purpose
$IRM_STATUS_TEMPLATE	irm_status.html	This template is used to show status message.
$IRM_RESOURCE_DES_TEMPLATE	irm_resource_des.html	This template is used to display resource description.
$IRM_RESOURCE_MENU_TEMPLATE	irm_resource_mngr.html	This is the template used to show/create resources.
$IRM_RESOURCE_MODIFY_MENU_TEMPLATE	irm_resource_modify_mngr.html	This is the Web form template to modify resource information.
$IRM_CAT_HOME_TEMPLATE	irm_cat_home.html	This is the category index template.
$IRM_CAT_ADD_MODTEMPLATE	irm_cat_add_mod.html	This is the Web form template to add or modify a category.
$IRM_SEARCH_RESULT_TEMPLATE	irm_search_result.html	This template is used to show search results.
$IRM_SEARCH_TEMPLATE	irm_search.html	This template is used to show search options.
$IRM_MOTD_TEMPLATE	irm_motd.html	This template is used to generate the live note message.

Creating a Category Manager Application

This application, irm_cat_mngr.php, is responsible for managing categories. This application is included on the CD-ROM in the ch11/apps directory.

It implements the following functionality:

◆ Allows administrative users to create, modify, and delete categories.

◆ Allows non-administrative users to create categories. Non-administrative users cannot modify or delete categories.

The ch11/apps/irm_cat_mngr.php in the CDROM is an implementaiton of this application. This application has the following methods.

run()

When the application is run, this method is called. It does the following:

◆ Creates a theme object, $this->themeObj.

◆ The current user's theme choice is stored in $this->theme by calling the getUserTheme() method of the theme object created.

◆ Next, if the application is called with cmd set to add query parameter, the addDriver() method starts running. If cmd is set to modify then the modifyDriver() method is called. Similarly, if cmd is set to delete then it invokes deleteCategory() method. If the cmd is set to null then it calls the showMenu() method.

In other words, the run() method decides which functionality is requested by the user and calls the appropriate driver method to perform the desired operations.

addDriver()

This method controls how add operations are performed on categories. It works as follows:

◆ If step is set to 1 in the query parameter when the application is called, this method calls the displayAddCategoryMenu() method to show the category creation options.

◆ If step is set to 2 in the query parameter when this application is called, this method runs the addCategory() method to add the new category.

modifyDriver()

This method controls how modify operations are performed on categories. It works as follows:

◆ If step, query parameter, is set to 1, then it calls the displayModifyCategoryMenu() method to show the category modification options.

◆ If step, query parameter, is set to 2, then it runs the modifyCategory() method to start the category modification process.

addCategory()

This method adds new category to the database. It works as follows:

- First, this method checks whether the category name ($newcategory) is provided or not. If it is not provided, then an error message is shown and it returns null.

- Next it checks whether the category is already existing in the category list of the database or not. If it already exists in the database, then it gives an appropriate message. Otherwise, it follows the following processes.

- Next It creates a category object called $categoryObj and calls the addCategory() with the category name and parent category ID (if given) and the user ID.

- If the addCategory() method returns TRUE status, an appropriate status message is shown. The status message is created using the getMessage() method.

- In case of failure to add, a failure status message is shown.

- Finally, the showWithTheme() method is called with the status message embedded in the user theme template.

modifyCategory()

This method updates modified information to the database. It works as follows:

- First, this method checks whether the category name ($newcategory) is provided or not. If it is not provided, then an error message is shown and returns null.

- Next, it checks whether the name of the category is changed or not. If the name is changed, then it checks whether the new given name already exists in the CATEGORY table or not using the existInList() method. If the name exists, then it gives an appropriate message and returns null.

- Next, it creates a category object called $categoryObj and calls the modifyCategory() with the category ID, category name, parent category ID (if given), and the user ID.

- If the modifyCategory() method returns TRUE status, a successful modification massage is shown. The message is constructed using the getMessage() method.

- In case of failure to modify, a failure status message is shown.

- Finally the showWithTheme() method is called with the status message embedded in the user theme template.

deleteCategory()

This method deletes category information. It works as follows:

- ◆ This method first checks whether the category ID is provided or not. If it is not given, then it shows an error message and returns null.

- ◆ If the given category has resources or its subcategories have resources or more subcategories, then it shows an error message and returns null.

- ◆ Next it calls `deleteCategory()` method of the `Category` object with the given category ID. If it successfully deletes the category from the `CATEGORY` table, then it gives the category a successfully deleted message; otherwise, it gives the deletion failure message.

- ◆ Finally, it calls the `showWithTheme()` method to show the message with the user's theme.

displayModifyCategoryMenu()

This method displays the modify category Web form. It works as follows:

- ◆ This method first checks whether any category is selected by the user to modify or not. If it is not provided, then an error message is shown and returns null.

- ◆ A template object called `$menuTemplate` is created. To load the template file, `$templateFile` is passed to this method as input.

- ◆ Next it creates a `Category` object called `$catObj`.

- ◆ If the selected category is a main category, then it calls the `getCategoryName()` to get the selected main category name; otherwise, it calls `getCategoryName()` for getting the main category and the selected sub-category name.

- ◆ Next it calls the `populateCategory()` method to generate the main category names.

- ◆ Then it parses the main block of the template and calls the `showWithTheme()` method with the output template, which is embedded in the user's theme template.

displayAddCategoryMenu()

This method displays the add new category Web form. It works as follows:

- ◆ A template object called `$menuTemplate` is created. To load the template file, `$templateFile` is passed to this method as input.

- ◆ Then it calls the `populateCategory()` method to generate the list of parent (main) categories as an HTML drop-down list.

- ◆ Finally, parsing the main block, it calls the `showWithTheme()` method with the output template, which is embedded in the user's theme template.

populateCategory()

This method is used to populate the list of all available main categories. It works as follows:

- This method is called with the template name ($template), the block name ($blockName), and the default selected value ($selectValue).

- A new category object called $categoryObj is created and the getCategoryList() method of that object is called to generate the available main categories name and stored in a array named $categoryList.

- If the category list is not empty, then it sets the category ID and name for each category in the list; otherwise, it returns null.

- If $blockName is set to jsblock block, then it parses the jsCategoryBlock and sets the output into the $category variable. Otherwise, if the category ID is not equal to the $selectValue, it parses the categoryBlock block and sets the output in the $category variable.

- Finally, this method returns the value of the $category variable.

populateSubCategory()

This method is used to populate the subcategory list for the given category. It works as follows:

- This method is called with the template name ($template), category ID ($cat_id), and the HTML template block name ($blockName) in which block the subcategory will be populated.

- A new object of category class is created named $subcatagoryObj and from that class, the getSubCategoryList() method is called with the given category ID ($cat_id) as a parameter. The subcategory list is stored in the array named $subcategoryList.

- If the subcategory list is not there, it checks the given HTML template block name. Then it sets the subcategory name and ID in respective variables in the given block and sets the output in the $subCategory variable parsing the block.

- Finally, this method returns the subcategory list stored in the $subCategory.

showMenu()

This method displays add, delete, and modify category options. It works as follows:

- A template object called $menuTemplate is created. To load the template, a file named $IRM_CAT_HOME_TEMPLATE (configurable via irm.conf) is passed to the method.

- Then it defines all the HTML template block names using set_block() method of the $menuTemplate object and assigns values to the HTML template variables using set_var() method of the $menuTemplate object.

- Next it calls the populateCategory() and sets the return value in the required blocks.

- Finally it parses the main block and calls the showWithTheme() method to show output with the user's theme.

showWithTheme()

This method is used to show user's theme template. It works as follows:

- It creates a theme template object called $themeTemplate.

- The user's theme template is loaded into the $themeTemplate object.

- This method is called with a parameter called $output, which will be shown with the theme template. This $output is set into in the 'CONTENT_BLOCK' block.

- Then it parses all the blocks and shows the final output.

authorize()

This method authorizes everyone on the intranet to view the resource manager and, therefore, always returns TRUE.

Creating a Resource Manager Application

This application, irm_resource_mngr.php, is responsible for managing resources. This application is included on the CD-ROM in the ch11/apps directory. It implements the following functionality:

- It allows administrators to create, modify, and delete resources.

- Non-administrative users can only create resources.

The ch11/apps/irm_resource_mngr.php file in the CDROM is an implementation of this application. This application has the following methods.

run()

When the application is run, this method is called. It does the following:

- Creates a theme object, $this->themeObj.

- The current user's theme choice is stored in $this->theme by calling the getUserTheme() method of the theme object created.

- Next if the query parameter cmd is set to add, then it calls the addDriver() method; if $cmd is set to delete, then the delete() method starts running. If $cmd is set to modify, then it calls the modifyDriver() or if $cmd is set to the disdes (short for *display description*) then it calls the displayDescription() method.

In other words, the run() method decides which functionality is requested by the user and calls the appropriate driver method to perform the desired operations.

addDriver()

This method controls how add operations are performed on resources. It works as follows:

- If $step, query parameter, is set to 2, when called this method is called. It invokes the addResource() method to insert the resource then.

- Otherwise, this method calls the showAddMenu() method to show the resource creation options.

modifyDriver()

This method controls how modify operations are performed on categories. It works as follows:

- If query parameter, $step is set to 1, then it calls the selectResource() to show the option for selecting the resource to be modified.

- If $step is set to 2, then it calls the showModifyMenu() to show the selected resource property where the user is able to modify the resource.

- If the $step is set to 3, it calls the modifyResource() method to modify the resource property.

populateCategory()

This method is used to populate the list of all available main categories. It works as follows:

- ◆ This method is called with the template name ($template), HTML template block name ($blockName) and the default selected value ($selectValue).

- ◆ A new category object called $categoryObj is created and the getCategoryList() method of that object is called to generate the available main categories name and stored in a array named $categoryList.

- ◆ If the category list is not empty, then it sets the category ID and name for each category in the list; otherwise, it returns null.

- ◆ If $blockName is set to jsblock then it parses the jsCategoryBlock and sets the output into the $category variable. Otherwise, it parses the categoryBlock block to see whether the category ID is equal to the $selectValue or not and sets the output in the $category variable.

- ◆ Finally this method returns the value of $category variable.

populateSubCategory()

This method is used to populate the subcategory list for the given category. It works as follows:

- ◆ This method is called with the template name ($template), category ID ($cat_id), and block name ($blockName) where the subcategory will be populated.

- ◆ A new object of category class is created named $subcatagoryObj and the getSubCategoryList() method is called of the class with the given category ID ($cat_id) as the parameter. The subcategory list is stored in the array named $subcategoryList.

- ◆ If the subcategory list is not there, then it checks the given block name. Then it sets the subcategory name and ID in respective variables in the given block and parses the block and sets the output in the $subCategory variable.

- ◆ Finally, this method returns the subcategory list stored in the $subCategory.

showAddMenu()

This method displays the Web form to add new resources. It works as follows:

- ◆ A template object called $menuTemplate is created. To load the template, a file named $IRM_CAT_HOME_TEMPLATE (configurable via irm.conf) is passed to the method.

- ◆ Next this method creates an object of user class named $userObj. Then it calls the getUserList() method of that object to get all users' e-mail addresses. The user's name is taken from each e-mail address field.

- ◆ Then This method calls populateCategory to generate the category list.

- ◆ Finally, the showWithTheme() method is called with the output of parsing main block to embed the message in the user theme template.

addResource()

This method adds the new resource to the database. It works as follows:

- ◆ First, this method checks whether it is called with valid and required input or not. It checks where the category is provided or not. If it is not provided, then it gives an error message of "category name missing" and returns null.

- ◆ Next, it checks if the resource name and URL are given or not. If they are not given, then an error message is shown and returns immediately.

- ◆ It checks the validity of the given URL. If it is not valid, then it shows the appropriate error message to the user and returns from the method.

- ◆ If a new category name is provided by the user of his own, then it checks whether the category is already existing or not. If not, then it adds the new category in the CATEGORY table.

- ◆ Now it creates an object of resource class and call the addResource() method with the proper parameter in the RESOURCE table. If it can successfully add the resource, then it returns the resource ID. If it fails to add, then a message is shown that the resource could not be added.

- ◆ If the resource is added successfully, then it generates intranet MOTD messages for the requested users.

- ◆ Finally, it calls the displayWithTheme() method to show the message with the user's theme.

showModifyMenu()

This method displays the modify resource Web form. It works as follows:

- ◆ First, this method checks whether any resource name ($resource) is selected or not. If not, it gives an error message and returns from the method.

- ◆ A template object called $menuTemplate is created. To load the template, a file named $IRM_CAT_HOME_TEMPLATE (configurable via irm.conf) is passed to the method.

◆ Then an object of Resource class is created named $resourceObj. It calls getResourceInfo() with the resource ID to get the information about the selected resource and calls getKeywords() to get keywords for the resource.

◆ Next it sets the resource information in the template.

◆ It calls populateCategory() to generate the category list.

◆ Finally, the showWithTheme() method is called with the output of parsing the main block to embed the message with the user theme template.

modifyResource()

This method updates modified resource information to the database. It works as follows:

◆ First, this method checks whether the category is provided. If the category is not provided, then it gives an error message and returns null.

◆ Next, the method checks whether the resource name and URL is given. If the resource name is not given, then an error message is shown and it returns null.

◆ Then It checks the validity of a given URL. If the URL is not valid, then it shows the appropriate error message to the user ("incorrect URL given") and returns from the method.

◆ If a new category name is provided by the user of his own, then it checks whether the category already exists. If it doesn't exist, then it adds the new category in the CATEGORY table.

◆ Then It creates an object of Resource class and calls the modifyResource() method with the proper parameter to resource in the RESOURCE table. If it successfully modifies the resource, then it returns the resource ID. If it fails to modify, then a message is shown that the resource is not modified.

◆ If the resource is modified successfully, then it deletes all the previous keywords and adds new keywords in the RESOURCE_KEYWORD table.

◆ Finally, it calls the displayWithTheme() method to show the message with the user's theme.

delete()

This method deletes resource information. It works as follows:

◆ This method first checks whether any resource is selected to delete or not. If it is not given, then an error message is shown and returns null.

◆ Then it creates an object of `Resource` class and calls `deleteKeywords()` with the selected resource ID as a parameter.

◆ If it successfully deletes the keywords, then it calls the `deleteResource()` method to delete the resource information from the `RESOURCE` table.

◆ Finally, it calls the `displayWithTheme()` method to show the status message of deletion with the user's theme.

displayDescription()

This method is used to display the description of the given resource. It works as follows:

◆ A template object is created named `$menuTemplate`. This method then loads the `$IRM_RESOURCE_DES_TEMPLATE` template.

◆ Then It creates an object of `Resource` class and calls `getResourceInfo()` with the selected resource ID as a parameter, which returns the resource information.

◆ Next it sets the title and description in the template.

◆ Finally, it parses the main block and calls the `displayWithTheme()` method to show output with the user's theme.

selectResource()

This method is used to give the user an option to choose a resource for modification. The method works as follows:

◆ First, the method creates an object of `Category` class named `$catObj`.

◆ Next it populates the main category by calling the `populateCategory()` method.

◆ If the `$category` is assigned any value, then it finds the subcategory list by calling the `getSubCategoryList()`.

◆ Then It checks whether the variable `$change` is assigned any value or not. If `$change` has any value, then it generates the resource list according to the main category or the subcategory changes.

◆ Finally the `showWithTheme()` method is called with the output of parsing the main block to embed the message with the user theme template.

displayWithTheme()

This method is used to show the user's theme template. It works as follows:

◆ It creates a theme template object called $themeTemplate.

◆ The user's theme template is loaded into the $themeTemplate object.

◆ This method is called with a parameter called $output, which will be shown with the theme template. This $output is set into in the 'CONTENT_BLOCK' block.

◆ Then it parses all the blocks and shows the final output.

authorize()

This method authorizes everyone on the intranet to view the resource manager and, therefore, always returns TRUE.

Creating a Resource Tracking Application

This application, irm_resource_track_mngr.php, is responsible for resources tracking. This application is included on the CD-ROM in the ch11/apps directory. The application has the following methods.

run()

This method is responsible for running the application. First it sets the user ID into a variable named $uid. Then it calls the keepTrack() method.

keepTrack()

This method keeps track of resource visits and updates the database. It works as follows:

◆ First it defines an array named $params containing the resource ID, visitor ID (user ID), and current time.

◆ Then it creates an object of Resource class and calls the trackResourceVisit() method with the $params array to insert records in the RESOURCE_VISITOR table.

◆ If it successfully inserts the data, then it calls the getResourceUrl() method to get the URL of the resource.

◆ Finally, it redirects the page to the resource URL.

authorize()

This method authorizes everyone on the intranet to view the resource manager and, therefore, always returns TRUE.

Creating a Search Manager Application

This application, irm_search_mngr.php, is responsible for managing search operations. This application is included on the CD-ROM in the ch11/apps directory. This application has the following methods.

run()

When the application is run, this method is called. It does the following:

- ◆ It creates a theme object, $this->themeObj.

- ◆ The current user's theme choice is stored in $this->theme by calling the getUserTheme() method of the theme object created.

- ◆ Next, if the query parameter $cmd is set to search, it calls the displaySearchResult() method; if $cmd is set to previous or next, then it calls displaySearResultNextandPrevious(); if it is set to mostvisited, then it calls showMostVisitedResource() to show the most visited resources; if it is set to topranking, then it calls showTopRankingResource() to show the top-ranking resources; if the $cmd is set to title, rating, or addedby, then it calls sortAndDisplay(); and if $cmd is set to nothing then it calls showMenu().

In other words, the run() method decides which functionality is requested by the user and calls the appropriate driver method to perform the desired operations.

populateCategory()

This method is used to populate the list of all available main categories. It works as follows:

- ◆ This method is called with the template name ($template), the block name ($blockName), and the default selected value ($selectValue).

- ◆ A new Category object called $categoryObj is created and the getCategoryList() method of that object is called to generate the available main categories name and stored in an array named $categoryList.

- If the category list is not empty, then it sets the category ID and name for each category in the list; otherwise, it returns null.

- If $blockName is set to jsblock, then it parses the jsCategoryBlock and sets the output into the $category variable. Otherwise, it parses the categoryBlock block if the category ID is not equal to the $selectValue and sets the output in the $category variable.

- Finally, this method returns the value of $category variable.

populateSubCategory()

This method is used to populate the subcategory list for the given category. It works as follows:

- This method is called with the template name ($template), category ID ($cat_id), and block name ($blockName), where the subcategory will be populated.

- A new object of the Category class is created named $subcatagoryObj, and the getSubCategoryList() method is called from the class with the given category ID ($cat_id) as a parameter. The subcategory list is then stored in the array named $subcategoryList.

- If the subcategory list is not there, then it checks the given block name. Then it sets the subcategory name and ID in respective variables in the given block and sets the output in the $subCategory variable parsing the block.

- Finally, this method returns the subcategory list stored in the $subCategory.

populateResource()

This method is used to display resources to show the search result. It works as follows:

- This method is called with a template name ($template), resource display starting point ($startingPoint), and block name ($blockName) where the resource information is displayed.

- Next it sets the resource information in the template.

- Then It sets the alternative different colors in rows to display, parses each row, and stores it in the $resource variable.

- Finally, it returns the value of $resource.

showMenu()

This method is used to display the menu shown in the search index page. It works as follows:

- A template object is created named $menuTemplate. To load, the template file named $IRM_SEARCH_TEMPLATE (configurable via irm.conf) is passed to the method.

- It creates an object of the Category class named $catObj and shows the category and subcategory names with the number of resources belonging to respective categories.

- Then It calls the populateCategory() method to show the category list in the drop-down list in the template.

- It creates an object of the User class named $userObj and calls the getUserList() method to populate all the user lists.

- Next it checks whether the viewer is an administrator of the IRM application or not. If she is not an administrator, it gives only the add resource link. On the other hand, If she is an administrator, it gives the category and resource manager link along with the add resource.

- Finally, the showWithTheme() method is called with the output of parsing the main block to embed with the user's theme template.

displaySearchResult()

This method is used to display the results after executing a search operation. It works as follows:

- A template object is created named $menuTemplate. To load, the template file named $IRM_SEARCH_RESULT_TEMPLATE (configurable via irm.conf) is passed to the method.

- Then it creates a Resource class object named $resourceObj and calls the searchResource() method with the search criteria given by the user and stores it in the array named $resourceList.

- It creates a User class object named $userObj and calls the getUserInfo() method to get the name of the user who added the resource.

- Next, it assigns the search result in the SESSION_SEARCH_LIST session variable and assigns the value in the SESSION_PAGE_SIZE session variable if it is given by the user from the search interface. If it is not given by the user, then it assigns the default value (DEFAULT_PAGE_SIZE), which is configurable via irm.conf.

- Then It calls the populateResource() method to show the search result.

- Finally, the showWithTheme() method is called with the output of parsing the main block to embed with the user's theme template.

sortAndDisplay( )

This method is used to sort the search result according to user's criteria. This method works as follows:

◆ A template object is created named $menuTemplate. To load, the template file named $IRM_SEARCH_RESULT_TEMPLATE (configurable via irm.conf) is passed to the method.

◆ This method stores the value of the session variable in an array object named $data, which is used to sort the data.

◆ Next it checks the $cmd value, which contains sorting criteria. If $cmd is set to 'title', then it calls usort( ) with 'sortByResourceTitle' as the function parameter to sort the search result according to resource title and checks the $sorttype value. Depending on the value of $sorttype, array_reverse( ) is called to reverse the sorting result.

◆ If the $cmd is set to rating, then it calls usort( ) with sortByResourceRating as the function parameter to sort the result depending on the $sorttype value according to the resource rating.

◆ If the $cmd is set to addedby, then it calls usort( ) with 'sortByResourceAddedBy' as the function parameter.

◆ Then the method registers the SESSION_SEARCH_LIST session variable and assigns the sorted result in that variable.

◆ Next it calls the populateResource( ) method to show the sorted result.

◆ Finally, the showWithTheme( ) method is called with the output of parsing the main block to embed with the user's theme template.

displaySearResultNextandPrevious( )

This method is used to display the previous/next page results after executing a search operation. This method works as follows:

◆ A template object is created named $menuTemplate. To load, the template file named $IRM_SEARCH_RESULT_TEMPLATE (configurable via irm.conf) is passed to the method.

◆ Now it checks the $cmd value. If it is set to 'next', then it generates the next page resource starting point. If $cmd is set to 'previousBlock', then it generates the previous page starting point.

◆ Next it calls the populateResource( ) method to show the sorted result.

◆ Finally, the showWithTheme( ) method is called with the output of parsing the main HTML template block to embed with the user's theme template.

showTopRankingResource()

This method is used to display the top-ranked resources. It works as follows:

- ◆ A template object is created named $menuTemplate. To load, the template file named $IRM_SEARCH_RESULT_TEMPLATE (configurable via irm.conf) is passed to the method.

- ◆ Next it registers the session variables SESSION_SEARCH_LIST and SESSION_PAGE_SIZE to store the search output and number of resources that needs to be shown each page, respectively.

- ◆ Then it creates a Resource class object named $resourceObj and calls the getTopRankingList() method with the defined variable 'TOPRANKING' (which is configurable in the irm.conf) to get the top-ranking resource.

- ◆ It creates a User class object named $userObj and calls getUserInfo() method to get the name of the user who added the resource.

- ◆ It sets the result and parses the main block. Then it calls the showWithTheme() method to embed the output with the user's theme template.

showMostVisitedResource()

This method is used to display the most visited resources. It works as follows:

- ◆ A template object is created named $menuTemplate. To load, the template file named $IRM_SEARCH_RESULT_TEMPLATE (configurable via irm.conf) is passed to the method.

- ◆ Next it registers the session variables SESSION_SEARCH_LIST and SESSION_PAGE_SIZE to store the search output and number of resources to be shown in each page, respectively.

- ◆ Then It creates an object of Resource class named $resourceObj and calls the getMostVisitedResource() method with a arameter called MOSTVISITED, which specifies the number of the most visited resource to be shown (configurable in the irm.conf).

- ◆ It calls the getResourceInfo() method to get information for each resource and stores in the session variable SESSION_SEARCH_LIST and displays the search result.

- ◆ Finally the showWithTheme() method is called with the output of parsing the main block to embed with the user's theme template.

showWithTheme()

This method is use to show the user's theme template. It works as follows:

- It creates a theme template object called `$themeTemplate`.

- The user's theme template is loaded into the `$themeTemplate` object.

- This method is called with a parameter called `$output`, which will be shown with the theme template. This `$output` is set into in the `'CONTENT_BLOCK'` block.

- Then it parses all the blocks and shows the final output.

authorize()

This method authorizes everyone on the intranet to view the resource manager and, therefore, always returns `TRUE`.

sortByResourceTitle()

This method is used to sort resources by their titles according to alphabetical order. It takes two arrays as inputs and compares their `RESOURCE_TITLE` element using the `strcmp()` method.

sortByResourceAddedBy()

This method is used to sort resources by its creator name according to alphabetical order. It takes two arrays as input and compares their `'RESOURCE_ADDED_BY'` element using the `strcmp()` method.

sortByResourceRating()

This method is used to sort resources by their rating. It takes two arrays as input and compares their `'RESOURCE_RATING'` element. If the first array's resource rating is greater than the second one then it returns `-1`; if they are equal, it returns `0`; otherwise, it returns `1`.

sortByResourceVisitor()

This method is used to sort resources by their visitor numbers. It takes two arrays as input and compares them. If the first array's visitor number is greater than the second one, then it returns `-1`; if they are equal, then it returns `0`; otherwise, it returns `1`.

Installing an IRM on Your Intranet

Here we will assume that you're using a Linux system with MySQL and Apache server installed. The following installation process assumes the following:

◆ Your intranet Web server document root directory is /evoknow/intranet/ htdocs. Of course, if you have a different path, which is likely, you should change this path whenever you see it in a configuration file or instruction in this chapter. During the installation process, I will refer to this directory as %DocumentRoot%.

◆ Finally I also assume that You have installed the PHPLIB and PEAR library. Normally, these gets installed during PHP installation. For your convenience, I have provided these in the lib/phplib.tar.gz and lib/pear.tar.gz directories on the CD-ROM. In these sample installation steps, we will assume that these are installed in the /%DocumentRoot%/phplib and /%DocumentRoot%/pear directories. Because your installation locations for these libraries are likely to differ, make sure you replace these paths in the configuration files.

Here is how you can get your IRM applications up and running:

◆ **Install Base Intranet Applications.** If you haven't yet installed the base intranet user home application and the messaging system discussed in Chapter 7, you must do so before proceeding further.

◆ **Install Intranet Calendar Database Tables.** I make the assumption that you have already installed the INTRANET database (see Chapter 7 for details). You need to install the ch11/sql/irm.sql database. The quickest way to create the database is to run the following commands:

```
mysqladmin -u root -p create IRM
mysql -u root -p -D IRM < irm.sql
```

◆ **Install IRM Applications.** Now from the ch11 directory on the CD-ROM, extract ch11.tar.gz in %DocuemntRoot%. This will create irm in your document root. Configure %DocumentRoot%/irm/apps/irm.conf for path and database settings. The applications are installed in the %DocumentRoot%/ irm/apps directory and the templates are stored in %DocumentRoot%/irm/ apps/templates.

Your MySQL server is hosted on the intranet Web server and, therefore, it can be accessed via localhost. However, if this is not the case, you can easily modify the database URLs in each application's configuration files. For example, the home.conf file has a MySQL database access URLs such as the following:

```
$INTRA_DB_URL  = 'mysql://root:foobar@localhost/INTRANET';

$IRM_DB_URL = 'mysql://root:foobar@localhost/CALENDAR';

$APP_DB_URL  = 'mysql://root:foobar@localhost/auth';
```

Say your database server is called db.domain.com and the user name and password to access the INTRANET and auth databases (which you will create during this installation process) are admin and db123. In such a case, you would modify the database access URLs throughout each configuration file as follows:

```
$INTRA_DB_URL  = 'mysql://admin:db123@db.domain.com/INTRANET';

$IRM_DB_URL = 'mysql://admin:db123@db.domain.com/IRM';

$APP_DB_URL  = 'mysql://admin:db123@db.domain.com/auth';
```

◆ **Add IRM to the Theme Navigation Bar.** You need to update your theme navigation bar files stored in %DocumentRoot%/themes/%theme%/ home_left_nav.html, whenever you add a new application. For example, to update the std_blue theme, you need to update the %DocumentRoot%/ themes/std_blue/home_left_nav.html file to include the following line in the HTML table:

```
<tr><td width="100%"><font size=2><a href="/irm/apps/
irm_search_mngr.php">IRM</a></font></td> </tr>
```

This will create a new row in the left navigation bar created with the HTML table.

◆ **Set File/Directory Permissions.** Make sure you have changed file and directory permissions such that your intranet Web server can access all the files.

After you've performed the preceding steps, you're ready to test your IRM applications.

Testing IRM

Log in to your intranet via http://yourserver/index.php or http://yourserver/ home/home.php.

Click on the Calendar link on the left navigation bar of your intranet home page, or point your Web browser to http://yourserver/irm/apps/irm_search_mngr. php after you're logged in to the intranet.

This will show you the IRM search interface as shown in Figure 11-3.

You will notice that there are no resources set up, because we haven't yet set up categories.

To set up categories, click on the Category Manager as an administrative user. You will see a screen similar to Figure 11-4.

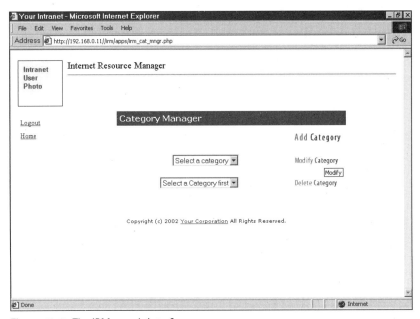

Figure 11-3: The IRM search interface.

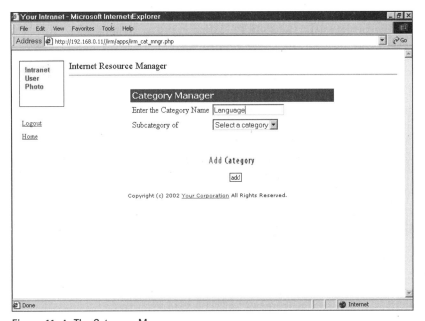

Figure 11-4: The Category Manager.

Click on the Add Category button and you will see a screen similar to Figure 11-5.

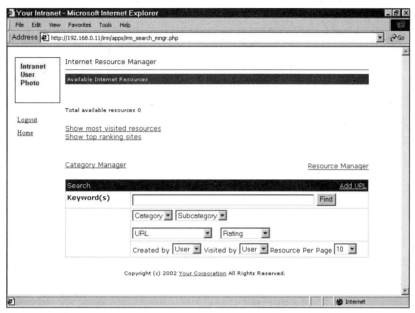

Figure 11-5: Adding a new category.

Enter a new category name. If this is a subcategory of an existing category, select the parent category from the available categories. Finally, click on the Add Category button to add the new category.

As mentioned in the functionality requirements, the Internet resources are only added in subcategories. There can be only one-level subcategories for each main category. So you should add at least one subcategory per main category. Figure 11-6 shows a new category called Languages with the PHP subcategory.

Keep adding categories and subcategories as you need. Figure 11-7 shows a list of categories with subcategories that we've created for this test.

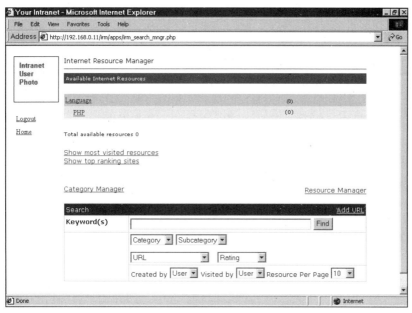

Figure 11-6: A category with a single subcategory.

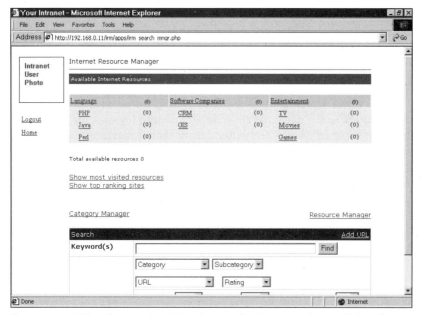

Figure 11-7: A list of categories with subcategories shown on the search interface.

To add a new resource, click on the Add URL link (`http://server//irm/apps/irm_resource_mngr.php?cmd=add&step=1`) shown on the title bar of the search interface. This brings up a screen similar to Figure 11-8.

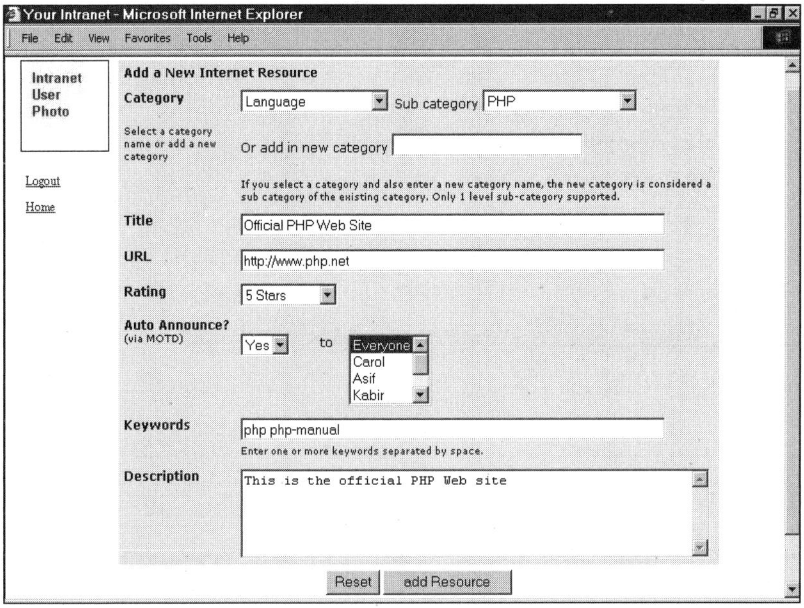

Figure 11-8: Adding a new Internet resource.

First, select the main category and subcategory before adding any data. Make sure you enter a valid URL, because the system will try to contact the URL and if it fails it will not add it in the database. Enter keywords, descriptions, titles, and rating as appropriate. If you want the resource to be announced to others via the intranet messaging system, you should select the Auto Announce option and select the users who should receive this announcements. Finally submit the form. The resource will be added to the appropriate subcategory.

After adding a resource, you can access it via the search interface by clicking on the subcategory or using keywords or other search parameters to locate it. Figure 11-9 show that we have added a new resource under the PHP subcategory in the Language category.

Clicking on the PHP subcategory shows what you see in Figure 11-10.

Figure 11-9: A new resource in the search interface.

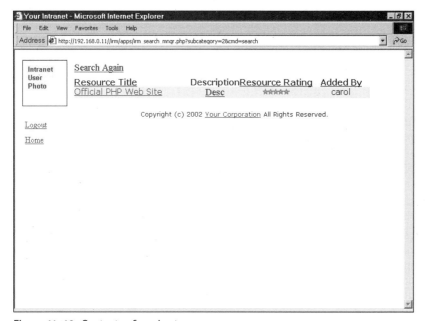

Figure 11-10: Contents of a subcategory.

You can use the result titles such as Resource Title, Resource Rating, and Added By User to sort the results. To view the description of the resource, click on the Desc link.

Figure 11-11 shows that the same resource can be found by entering a search parameter in the search interface.

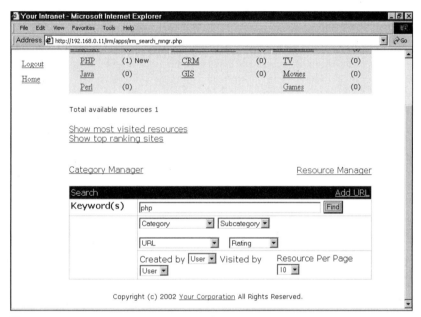

Figure 11-11: Using search parameters to find resources.

To find the most visited resources, click on the Show Most Visited Resources link on the search interface. You will see a screen similar to Figure 11-12.

Remember that whenever a user clicks on a resource, it is tracked and this information is used to generate the most-visit data.

To find the highest-ranking resources, click on the Show Top Ranking Sites on the Search interface. You will see a screen similar to Figure 11-13.

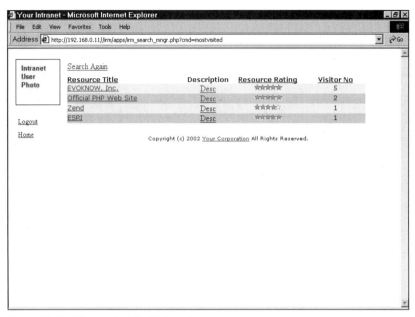

Figure 11-12: The most visited Internet resources.

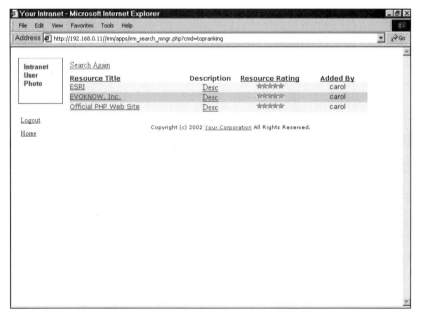

Figure 11-13: The top-ranking Internet resources.

Security Concerns

Now you have a set of intranet applications that allow you to add/modify/delete Internet site resources. Since these applications are run from your intranet they are only accessible to your intranet users who must authenticate using the central authentication system developed in Chapter 5. However, if you needed to restrict access to these applications even further using some other special schema such as IP subnet or time, you can incorporate such custom authorization requirements in the `authorize()` methods for each of these applications.

Summary

In this chapter, you learned to create an Internet Resource Manager for your intranet. This application allows users to organize the resources on a shareable and searchable central database.

Chapter 12

Online Help System

IN THIS CHAPTER

◆ Developing an online help system

◆ Installing an online help system

◆ Using an online help system

HAVING ONLINE HELP with your Web or intranet applications can be a great blessing, because it may reduce user support calls and, therefore, cost. In this chapter, you'll develop an online help system that can be used for any of the Web or intranet applications developed in this book.

First, let's look at the functionality you want the help system to offer.

Functionality Requirements

The help system will offer the following features.

◆ **Structured help contents:** The system will assume a structured help content design where help for an application will be divided into sections. Each section will be represented with one or more HTML pages, which may or may not have embedded images. Each section will have a number like x.y.z where x is the section number, y is the second level subsection number, and z is the third level subsection number. For example, 1.0.0.html, 1.1.0.html, and 1.1.1.html are pages for section 1. The images for all the help contents will be stored in an images directory.

◆ **Automatic table of contents page:** The system should generate the table of contents page automatically. This feature is very good to have because you can then add or remove sections.

◆ **Automatic navigation:** The system should generate automatic navigation links from section to section and also have a link to the table of contents from each page.

◆ **Keyword search:** The system will allow keyword-based searches using the logic operators AND and OR.

◆ **Template-based interface:** The system should support a central help template to display help pages but also allow individual sections to have their own templates to alter the look and feel of the help as needed.

Understanding the Prerequisites

The help system requires the application framework classes that were discussed in Chapter 4. You must have the application framework classes along with PHPLIB and PEAR packages installed.

Designing and Implementing the Help Application Classes

As shown in the system diagram, Figure 12-1, there is one new object, Help object, which is needed to implement the online help system.

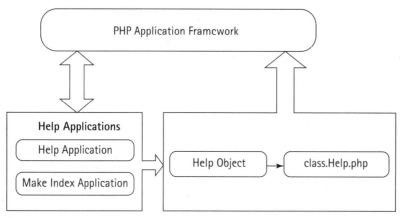

Figure 12-1: The help system diagram.

Here you will develop the class that will provide the help object for the online help applications.

Designing and implementing the Help class

The Help class is used by all help applications. It allows help applications to display, search, and index help contents. The `ch12/apps/class/class.Help.php` file on the CD-ROM implements this class. This class implements the following methods.

Help()

This is the constructor method. It works as follows:

♦ It sets the object `variable _APP` to the given application name. The name of the application for which help will be displayed is passed to this method using the `$params['app']` parameter.

♦ It sets the object variable `_MAP` to the given application's map file name. The name of the map file that will be used to locate help contents for the current application is passed to this method using the `$params['map']` parameter.

♦ The object variable `_FORCE` is set using the `$params['force']` parameter, which indicates if the help index should be forcefully created again even if the current index is up to date.

♦ The object variable `_OPERATORS` is set to an array of two logical operators: OR and AND. These are the logical operators that are supported in keyword search operations.

♦ The object variable `_LOADED` is set to false, which indicates that the object has not yet loaded the help map information from the named map file.

♦ If the application for which help contents is to be displayed, searched, indexed is named (that is, `$this->_APP` is set) and the map file name is given (that is, `$this->_MAP` is set), then the method calls the `loadMap()` method to load the map information for the named application. The map file contains help contents information for the named application.

getApp()

This method returns the value of the `_APP` object variable, which is the name of the application for which the help object is to display, search, or index the help contents.

getRelHelpDir()

This method returns the relative help directory path stored in the `_REL_HELP_DIR` object variable, which is set in the `loadMap()` method.

getSectionContents()

This method returns the contents of a section of the help contents. The section number is passed as a parameter (`$section`) to this method. The contents are stored in a hash called `$contents`. It works as follows:

♦ The `$contents['output']` is set to `show_section`, which indicates to the help display application (`help.php`) that it needs to show the help content for a given section.

♦ A local variable called `$tocLink` is created to store the table of contents link. The table of contents link is simply the path to the help application with the app=*current_application* query parameter. For example, if the application name is irm, then this link can be http://server/path/to/help.php?app=irm. The $tocLink value is stored in $contents hash using $contents['toc_link'].

◆ A local variable called $prevSection is used to store the previous section of the $section. The previous section number is retrieved by calling the getPreviousSection() method. If the previous section is available, then a URL is created to point to the previous section and the URL is stored in $contents['previous_section']. Otherwise, the $contents['previous_section'] is set to null. Similarly, a URL is created for the next section by calling the getNextSection() method and the value is stored in $contents['next_section'].

◆ The body of the help contents for the current section is stored in $contents['next_section'], which is populated using the contents returned by the _loadFile() method. The _loadFile() loads the help contents for the current section when it is given a fully qualified help file name using the $this->getFQPNofSection($section)) method.

◆ A local array variable called $search is set up with a set of regular expression (RE) patterns that identifies embedded image sources in HTML contents. Another local array variable called $replace is set up with a set of path replacements for RE patterns stored in $search. The idea is to replace image sources with relative paths such as src=images, src="images, background=images, background="images with the proper relative path generated using the getRelHelpDir() method. When the help contents are displayed by the help application, the relative paths of the HTML image sources must be modified this way to ensure that images are visible. The built-in preg_replace() function is used replace all $search patterns with $replace in $contents['body'].

◆ The template path for the current section is set to $contents['template'] using the getSectionTemplate() method.

◆ Similarly, the base URL path for the current section is set to $contents['base_url'] using the getBaseURL() method.

◆ Finally, the method returns the $contents associative array.

getPreviousSection()

This method returns the previous section number for a given section. It works as follows:

◆ First it stores the total number of sections, $totalSections, in the current help map by counting the entries in $this->_SECTIONS, which is the list of sections.

◆ Then it finds the array index of the current section ($section) in the $this->_SECTIONS array using the _indexOfSection() method. This array index is stored in $thisSectionIndex.

◆ If the current section's array index, $thisSectionIndex, is greater than zero, which means the current section is not the first section, than the method returns the previous section number by subtracting 1 from the current section's array index and calling the getSectionAtIndex() method to return the section number at this index.

◆ If the current section is the first section, the method returns null.

getNextSection()

This method returns the next section number for a given section. It works as follows:

◆ First it stores the total number of sections, $totalSections, in the current help map by counting the entries in $this->_SECTIONS, which is the list of sections.

◆ Then it finds the array index of the current section ($section) in the $this->_SECTIONS array using the _indexOfSection() method. This array index is stored in $thisSectionIndex.

◆ If the current section's array index, $thisSectionIndex, is less than the total index count, which means the current section is not the last section, then the method returns the next section number by adding 1 to the current section's array index and calling the getSectionAtIndex() method to return the section number at this index.

◆ If the current section is the last section, the method returns null.

getSectionAtIndex()

This method returns the section number from the $this->_SECTIONS hash for a given section array index. It works as follows:

◆ First it creates a list called $list, which stores the section names from the $this->_SECTIONS hash.

◆ If the given array index number, $index, is within the range of the $list array, it returns the section number at the index; otherwise, it returns null.

_indexOfSection()

This method returns the array index of a given section number. It works as follows:

◆ First it creates a list called $list, which stores the section names from the $this->_SECTIONS hash.

◆ A local variable called $index is initialized to null.

- Then it loops through the list of sections and checks whether the given section number matches with one in the list. If a match is found, the loop is stopped and the index of the matched section is stored in `$index`.

- The `$index` value is returned.

getTOCContents()
This method returns the table of contents in a hash. It works as follows:

- It sets a hash called `$contents` to an empty array.

- The `$contents['output']` is set to `show_toc`, which indicates to the help display application (`help.php`) that it needs to show the table of contents.

- It creates a hash called `$sections` with the list of sections using `getSectionHash`. If there are no sections, the method returns the empty `$contents`. Otherwise, the section hash is stored in `$contents['sections']`.

- For each section of the help contents, it creates a URL and stores the URL in `$sectionLinks`, which is later stored in `$contents['section_links']`.

- Then it gets the template for the table of contents using the `getTOCTempalte()` method and stores the template path in `$contents['template']`.

- Similarly, the base URL path for the current section is set to `$contents['base_url']` using the `getBaseURL()` method.

- Finally, the method returns the `$contents` hash.

isLoaded()
This method returns the value of object variable `_LOADED`, which indicates if the help map is loaded or not.

isSection()
This method returns `TRUE` if a given section name belongs to the current section list.

search()
This method performs a keyword search using the help index. It receives keywords as a parameter. It works as follows:

- It creates a keyword list called `$keywordList` using the `getKeywordList()` method. Note that the given keyword parameter, `$kwords`, might contain duplicates; the `getKeywordList()` method removes these duplicates and also removes the OR operator, because whenever multiple words are searched, the default operation is logical OR.

- It creates a list of sections, `$allSections`, using the `getSectionList()` method.

◆ It initializes an array called $matchedSections to an empty list.

◆ It sets $keywordCount to the number of keywords in $keywordList.

◆ For each keyword in the list, it runs through a while loop to find matching sections. When looping through the list of keywords, each keyword is compared with 'and' (for an AND operation). If the current keyword is 'and', the next keyword is searched only in the section list of already matched sections for all previous keywords. If the keyword is not 'and', then the keyword is searched in all sections ($allSections). This effectively creates the AND operation.

◆ All found matches are consolidated in the $matchedSections list. If the $matchedSections array has a size greater than zero, that indicates that a match for the given keywords was found. In such a case, the matched sections are stored in an object variable called _SEARCH_RESULT and the match count is stored in another object variable called _SEARCH_MATCH_COUNT.

◆ Based on whether a match was found or not, the method returns TRUE or FALSE.

getSearchMatchCount()

This method returns the number of matches found in a search. The number of matches is stored in the _SEARCH_MATCH_COUNT object variable.

getSearchResults()

This method returns the match results in a hash. It works as follows:

◆ An associative array variable called $contents is initialized to an empty array.

◆ The $contents['output'] is set to search_result, which indicates to the help display application (help.php) that it needs to show the search results.

◆ A string version of the keyword array is stored in $contents['keyword_string'].

◆ The $contents['sections'] is assigned to a hash that represents the matching sections stored in $this->_SEARCH_RESULT. This hash is created by passing $this->_SEARCH_RESULT to the getSectionHash() method.

◆ A local variable called $linkPrefix is set to the URL prefix needed to access the help for the current application. This URL has a syntax such as http://server/path/to/help.php?app=current_application.

◆ For each matching section in the search result, a link is created in the $sectionLinks array using the $linkPrefix and section ID information

so that the URL has a syntax of `http://server/path/to/help.`
`php?app=`*`current_application`*`&section=`*`section_number`*.

♦ The list of matched section links is stored in `$contents['section_links']`. The total match count is stored in `$contents['match_count']`.

♦ The template for showing the results is retrieved by the `getSearchResultTempalte()` method and stored in `$contents ['template']`.

♦ The base URL path for the current section is set to `$contents['base_url']` using the `getBaseURL()` method.

♦ The most recent search history hash is retrieved using the `getRecentSearchList()` method and stored in `$contents ['recent_search']`.

♦ Finally, the `updateRecentSearchList()` method is used to update the recent search history using the current keyword string returned by the `getKeywordString()` method.

getRecentSearchList()

This method returns a hash with recent search history. It works as follows:

♦ It creates an empty hash called `$hash`.

♦ The fully qualified history file name for the current help content is retrieved using the `getFQPNSearchHistoryFile()` method and stored in the `$historyFile` variable.

♦ The serialized contents of the history file, `$historyFile`, is loaded in `$serializedHistory` using the `_loadFile()` method.

♦ If the history is not empty, then the `$asis` parameter is checked to see how the data should be returned. If `$asis` is set to `FALSE`, then the history data is unserialized in the `$history` variable and, using a loop, each history element is parsed. The key of each history hash element is the search keyword; the value consists of a time stamp and relative URL link that can be used to search for the keyword. The `$hash` is populated with search keywords from the history, and the relative URL is stored as a value.

♦ On the other hand, if `$asis` is `TRUE`, then the unserialized history hash is returned as is.

updateRecentSearchList()

This method adds the given keywords to the recent search history if they aren't already in the history. It works as follows:

◆ If no keyword is passed as a parameter to the method, it returns FALSE.

◆ If the keywords have been supplied, it reads the recent search history as a hash in $hash using the getRecentSearchList() method. The getRecentSearchList() is called with TRUE as a $asis parameter so that it returns the search history as an unmodified hash.

◆ If the current keywords already exist in $hash, then the method returns FALSE since there is no need to add duplicate keywords in the history.

◆ If the current history does not exceed the SEARCH_HISTORY_SIZE size specified in the configuration file (help.conf), then the current keywords are inserted into the a new hash called $outHash along with the existing history data.

◆ Finally, the new $outHash is written to the history file using the writeSearchHistory() method, and the method returns TRUE.

getKeywordMatch()

This method checks to see whether the given keyword ($keyword) exists in the keyword index of the given sections ($sections) and returns the matching section list. It works as follows:

◆ The given keyword is lowercased because the keyword index stores all keywords in lowercase format.

◆ A list called $matchedSections is initialized as an empty array.

◆ For each given section, the given keyword is searched in the keyword index cache stored in the keyword index file.

◆ In the loop, for each given section, a keyword index cache file called $keywordCacheFile is set using the getKeywordFile() method.

◆ A hash object (that is, keyword index cache) called $cache is loaded using the readKeywordCacheFile() method.

◆ If the current keyword is found in the $cache object, the current section is stored in $matchedSections.

◆ Finally, the matched section list is returned.

getSectionNumberList()

This method returns the section numbers from the current section hash.

getSectionHash()

This method returns a hash that has section numbers as keys and section names as values. If a section list is given, the method only returns the hash for the given section list. Otherwise, it returns the entire list of sections for the current help contents.

getSectionList()
This method returns the list of sections.

getKeywordString()
This method creates a string out of the list of keywords and returns the string.

getKeywordList()
This method sets the object variable _KEYWORDS with given keywords. However, it removes duplicates and any instance of the word 'or'. The 'or' operator is implied automatically when multiple keywords exist in the keyword list and, therefore, it is removed.

getSections()
This method returns the section hash stored in the object variable _SECTIONS.

getHelpDir()
This method returns the help directory path stored in _HELP_DIR. If _HELP_DIR is empty, it returns null.

makeKeywordIndex()
This method creates the keyword index cache object for a given section and stores the cache as a serialized hash object in a file. It works as follows:

◆ First, it creates a local variable called $helpFile that is set to the fully qualified pathname of the given section's ($section) help file returned by the getFQPNofSection() method.

◆ If the help file (that is, the help contents) does not exist for the current section, the method returns FALSE.

◆ If the help file exists, a local variable called $keywordCacheFile is set to the fully qualified pathname of the current section's keyword index cache file returned by the getKeywordFile() method.

◆ If this keyword index cache exists, the help file's modification time ($helpFileModifyTimeStamp) is compared with the modification time ($keywordIndexCreateTimeStamp) of the keyword index. If the help file modification time is older than the keyword index file modification time, the keyword index is up to date and therefore not needed to be re-created, unless the object variable _FORCE is set to true. When the keyword index is up to date and the index doesn't need to be forcefully re-created, the method returns TRUE, indicating that index creation was a success.

◆ On the other hand, if the keyword index doesn't exist or the modification time of the help file is newer than the existing keyword index file, then the method must continue and create the index cache from the help contents.

◆ The _getWords() is called with the help file ($helpFile) and the returned word list is stored in the $words variable.

◆ The _removeExcludedWords() method is called with the $words to remove words that need to be excluded. The words are compared to words stored in the EXCLUDED_WORD_FILE file and matching words are removed from the $words list.

◆ The resulting $words list and the $keywordCacheFile file name are passed as a parameter to the writeKeywordCacheFile() method to write the cache file.

◆ If the file is written successfully, the method returns TRUE; otherwise, it returns FALSE.

getFQPNSearchHistoryFile()
This method returns the fully qualified search history file name.

getFQPNofSection()
This method returns the fully qualified section file name.

getHelpTemplateDir()
This method returns the fully qualified help template directory path.

getDefaultSectionTemplatc()
This method returns the default section template path.

getTOCTempalte()
This method returns the table of contents template path.

getSearchResultTempalte()
This method returns the search result template path.

getSectionTemplate()
This method returns the template path for a given section if it exists; otherwise, it returns the default section template path.

getBaseURL()
This method returns the base URL.

loadMap()
This method loads the help map file, which defines all the information needed to provide help for an application. It works as follows:

◆ First, it sets $mapFile to the fully qualified pathname of the map file returned by the getMapFile() method.

◆ If the map file does not exist, the method returns FALSE.

- ◆ The method then uses the built-in `require_once()` function to load the map file, which is a PHP script.

- ◆ If the `$HELP_DIR` variable in the map file has a value that does not start with leading slash character, the `$HELP_DIR` is a relative path and `ROOT_PATH` from `help.conf` is added as a prefix to this path; finally, it is stored in the object's `_HELP_DIR` variable. Similarly, `_REL_HELP_DIR` is constructed using `REL_ROOT_PATH` (from `help.conf`) and the current application's name.

  On the other hand, if the `$HEL_DIR` value does start with a leading slash, it is stored as is along with `$REL_HELP_DIR` in `_HELP_DIR` and the `_REL_HELP_DIR` object variables, respectively.

- ◆ The other variables in the map file — `$REL_TEMPLATE_DIR`, `$DEFAULT_SECTION_TEMPLATE`, `$TOC_TEMPLATE`, `$SEARCH_RESULT_TEMPLATE`, `$TEMPLATES`, and `$SECTIONS` — are assigned to `_REL_TEMPLATE_DIR`, `_DEFAULT_SECTION_TEMPLATE`, `_TOC_TEMPLATE`, `_SEARCH_RESULT_TEMPLATE`, `_TEMPLATES`, and `_SECTIONS`, respectively.

getMapFile()

This method returns the fully qualified pathname of the map file.

readKeywordCacheFile()

This method returns the named keyword file (`$file`), unserializes the contents, and returns the hash object.

writeKeywordCacheFile()

This methods writes the given word list, `$words`, in the named keyword file, `$file`. It first creates a hash called `$cache` using each of the keywords in the `$words` list and serializes the `$cache` object before writing to the file.

writeSearchHistory()

This method writes the keyword history hash (`$hash`) into the keyword search history file returned by the `getFQPNSearchHistoryFile()` method. The `$hash` is serialized before writing to the file.

getKeywordFile()

This method returns the fully qualified keyword index cache file name for the given section.

_removeExcludedWords()

This method removes words from the `$words` list if they are found in the `EXCLUDED_WORD_FILE` file.

_getWords()

This method reads the named file (`$file`), parses out text from HTML tags, creates a list of unique words, and returns the list.

_getUniqueWords()

This method removes duplicates from the given word list ($words) and returns the duplicate-free word list.

_loadFile()

This method loads the given file ($file) if it exists and returns the contents as a string.

HTMLtoText()

This method removes HTML tags from the given string ($contents) and returns the HTML tag–free contents.

Creating Application Configuration Files

Like all other applications you've developed in this book, the online help applications also use a standard set of configuration, message, and error files. These files are discussed in the following sections.

Creating a main configuration file

The primary configuration file for the entire system is called help.conf. Table 12-1 discusses each configuration variables.

TABLE 12-1 THE help.conf VARIABLES NEED TO BE CHANGED

Configuration Variable	Purpose
$PEAR_DIR	Set to the directory containing the PEAR package; specifically the DB module needed for class.DBI.php in our application framework. By default, this is set to the %DocumentRoot%/pear.
$PHPLIB_DIR	Set to the PHPLIB directory, which contains the PHPLIB packages; specifically the template.inc package needed for template manipulation. By default this is set to the %DocumentRoot%/phplib.
$APP_FRAMEWORK_DIR	Set to our application framework directory. By default this is set to the %DocumentRoot%/framework.

Continued

TABLE 12-1 THE `help.conf` VARIABLES NEED TO BE CHANGED *(Continued)*

Configuration Variable	Purpose
$PATH	Set to the combined directory path consisting of the $PEAR_DIR, the $PHPLIB_DIR, and the $APP_FRAMEWORK_DIR. This path is used with the ini_set() method to redefine the php.ini entry for include_path to include $PATH ahead of the default path. This allows PHP to find our application framework, PHPLIB, and PEAR-related files.
$APPLICATION_NAME	Internal name of the application.
$DEFAULT_LANGUAGE	Set to the default (two-character) language code.
ROOT_PATH	Set to the root path of the application. By default this is set to the %DocumentRoot%.
REL_ROOT_PATH	Relative path to the root directory. By default this is set to the %DocumentRoot%/help.
REL_APP_PATH	Relative application path as seen from the Web browser.
TEMPLATE_DIR	The fully qualified path to the template directory.
CLASS_DIR	The fully qualified path to the class directory.
REL_TEMPLATE_DIR	The Web-relative path to the template directory used.
HELP_MAP_DIR	The fully qualified pathname of the help map directory where application-specific help map files are stored.
EXCLUDED_WORD_FILE	The fully qualified pathname of the word file, which contains the words that are to be excluded from help index caching.

The directory structure used in the help.conf file supplied in the ch12 directory on the CD-ROM may need to be tailored to your own system's requirements. Here is what the current directory structure looks like:

```
+---%DocumentRoot%  (Your Web document Root)
    |
    +---help (Help Applications)
        |
        +---apps (apps and configuration files)
```

```
|   |
|   +---class (class files)
|   |
|   +---templates (HTML templates)
|   |
|   +---maps (help maps for your applications)
|
+--self (the help on help system itself)
```

By changing the following configuration parameters in ld.conf, you can modify the directory structure to fit your site requirements:

```
define(ROOT_PATH          , $_SERVER['DOCUMENT_ROOT']);
define(REL_ROOT_PATH      , '/help');
define(REL_APP_PATH       , REL_ROOT_PATH . '/apps');
define(TEMPLATE_DIR       , ROOT_PATH    . REL_APP_PATH .
'/templates');
define(CLASS_DIR          , ROOT_PATH    . REL_APP_PATH .
'/class');
define(REL_TEMPLATE_DIR   , REL_APP_PATH . '/templates/');
define('HELP_MAP_DIR'     , ROOT_PATH    . REL_APP_PATH . '/maps');
```

Creating a messages file

The messages displayed by the help applications are stored in the CDROM/ch12/apps/help.messages file. You can change the messages using a text editor.

Creating an error message file

The error messages displayed by the help applications are stored in the CDROM/ch12/apps/help.errors file. You can modify the error messages using a text editor.

Creating Application Templates

The HTML interface templates needed for the applications are included on the CD-ROM. These templates contain various template tags to display the necessary information dynamically. The templates are named in the help.conf file. These templates are discussed in Table 12-2.

TABLE 12-2 HTML TEMPLATES

Configuration Variable	Template File	Purpose
GLOBAL_DEFAULT_TOC_ TEMPLATE_FQPN	toc.html	This template is used to display the table of contents when an application-specific TOC template is not found. The application-specific TOC template is specified using $TOC_TEMPLATE in the application help map file.
GLOBAL_DEFAULT_SECTION_ TEMPLATE_FQPN	section.html	This template is used to display section contents when an application-specific section template is not found. The application-specific section template is specified using $TEMPLATES in the application help map file.
GLOBAL_DEFAULT_SEARCH_ RESULT_TEMPLATE_FQPN	search_result.html	This template is used to display search results contents when an application-specific search result template is not found. The application-specific section template is specified using $SEARCH_RESULT_ TEMPLATE in the application help map file.

Creating the Help Indexing Application

This application, makeindex.php, is responsible for creating keyword indexes for each help section of an application's help contents. This application is included on the CD-ROM in the ch12/apps directory.

It implements the following functionality:

◆ Automatically generates keyword indexes for each section of a given application

◆ Automatically excludes given keywords from adding into a help index

This application has the following methods.

run()

When the application is run, this method is called. It calls the makeIndex() method to create a keyword index cache.

makeIndex()

This method is the heart of this application. It creates the keyword index cache. Here's how it works:

◆ A hash called $mapHash is loaded with the map file and application name for the given application or all the applications whose map files are known in the $APP_HELP_MAP configuration variable. If the user wants to create an index for only a single application, she must call the makeindex.php application with app=*application_name* per $APP_HELP_MAP stored in help.conf. If the app parameter is not provided in the query string, when this application is called, all the applications in $APP_HELP_MAP are indexed.

◆ For each application in the $mapHash, a message is displayed showing which application is being indexed.

◆ A help object, $helpObj, is created and if the object was not successful in loading the current application map (that is, $helpObj->isLoaded() returns FALSE), then the current application is not indexed. If the map cannot be loaded, a message is shown and the application is skipped.

◆ For an application whose map is successfully loaded by $helpObj, the keyword index cache is created for each section using the $helpObj->makeKeywordIndex() method.

◆ Status messages are shown onscreen based on the success or failure of the index creation process for each section. Errors are stored in the $errors array.

◆ If there are errors, the method returns FALSE; otherwise, it returns TRUE.

getMapHash()

This method returns a hash with application names as keys and map file names as values. If the method is called with an application list, it only returns the hash appropriate for the given application list. If the application list is empty, it returns the hash for all the known applications based on the $APP_HELP_MAP configuration variable.

authorize()

This method decides if the makeindex.php application can be run by the requesting user. The IP address of the user is compared against the ACL_ALLOW_FROM and ACL_DENY_FROM lists stored in the configuration file using an ACL object.

The ACL object is created using the current IP address of the request, as well as the ACL_ALLOW_FROM and ACL_DENY_FROM information. Once created, the $aclObj is used to call its isAllowed() method, which returns TRUE only if the requesting IP is allowed access to the application.

Note that by default, access is allowed.

Creating the Help Application

This application, help.php, is responsible for displaying help contents and search operations. This application is included on the CD-ROM in the ch12/apps directory.

It implements the following functionality:

◆ Automatically generates a table of contents page based on the help map for a given application.

◆ Displays help contents for each section and provides automatic navigation from one section to another.

◆ Performs search operations on the help contents using the keyword index generated by the makeindex.php application.

This application has the following methods.

run()

When the application is run, this method is called. It does the following:

◆ It calls the getCommand() method to determine what the application is to do. Based on the given command ($cmd), it calls the appropriate method dynamically using a $this->$cmd() call.

◆ If no command is given by the user, the application displays an alert message and terminates.

authorize()

This method is used to authorize access to this application. Because we want everyone to access the help file, the method simply returns TRUE.

getCommand()

This method's purpose is to determine what the user wants to do with the help application. There are two operations user can request: show help or perform search on an application's help contents.

However, for both operations, the user must supply the application name, because without an application name, the help system does not know what to show or what to search on. The application name is passed as a query parameter (for example, `http://server/path/help.php?app=app_name`) and, therefore, must be found as an entry called `$_REQUEST['app']` in the associative array called `$_REQUEST` provided by PHP. If the application name is not found, the method returns null.

If the application name is found, the method checks to see whether the user has provided any keyword in the query string (`http://server/path/help.php?app=app_name&keyword=keywords`). If a keyword is found in `$_REQUEST['keyword']`, then the method returns `'doSearch'` as the command because the user wants to do a search operation on the named application help contents. If no keyword is found, the method returns `'showHelp'` as the default command, which makes the help application display help contents.

getAppInfo()

This method returns a hash object with user-supplied information.

showHelp()

This method displays help contents. It works as follows:

- The user-supplied keyword and application name are stored in `$info` hash by retrieving them using the `getAppInfo()` method.
- A help object, `$helpObj`, is created.
- If a valid section number is supplied by the user, the method retrieves the section contents using the `$helpObj->getSectionContents()` method and stores the contents in `$contents` hash.
- If no valid section number is given, the method retrieves the table of contents information using the `$helpObj->getTOCContents()` method and stores the contents in `$contents` hash.
- It displays the contents in `$contents` hash using the `displayOutput()` method.

displayOutput()

This method displays a page, be it a section contents page, search results, or a table of contents based on the `contents['output']` field information in the `$contents` hash. It works as follows:

♦ It creates a template object called `$template` and loads the `$contents ['template']` template. It then sends the base URL and app parameter.

♦ If the content to be displayed is the search result (that is, the `$contents ['output']` is set to `'search_result'`), the history block of the template is configured.

♦ If the content to be displayed is help section contents (that is, the `$contents['output']` is set to `'show_section'`), the navigation blocks (`prevBlock`, `nextBlock`) of the template are configured.

♦ If there are URL links to sections to be displayed (that is, `$contents ['section_links']` is not empty), then each section to be displayed is inserted and parsed into the template from the data stored in `$contents ['section_links']`.

♦ If the recent search history is to be displayed (that is, `$contents ['recent_search']`) is not empty), then each recent keyword to be displayed is inserted and parsed into the template from the data stored in `$contents['recent_search']`. Otherwise, the history block is set to null, which is appropriate since only the search result page has the history block data.

♦ If the page to be displayed is search results (that is, match count, `$contents['match_count']`, not empty), then match count data is entered into the template by replacing the `MATCH_COUNT` tag.

♦ If the body of the contents, `$contents['body']`, is not empty, the body is inserted into the template. Otherwise, an appropriate message is inserted to indicate the body is missing.

♦ The previous and next blocks (`prevBlock`, `nextBlock`) are populated with URL links using `$contents['previous_section']` and `$contents ['next_section']`, respectively. This is needed for the section contents page. If the current page to be displayed is not a section contents page, these blocks are set to null.

♦ The template is parsed and the resulting page is stored in the `$documents` variable as a string.

♦ Now if the $documents page has embedded links to other sections using the `<a href="`*`section_number`*`.html">label</a>` HTML tags, they are replaced using appropriate relative URLs built-in using the `preg_replace()` function.

♦ Finally, the contents of the $documents page are displayed.

doSearch()

This method performs a keyword search and displays the output. It works as follows:

♦ The user-supplied keyword and application name are stored in $info hash by retrieving them using the `getAppInfo()` method.

♦ A help object, $helpObj, is created.

♦ The user-supplied keywords are stored in $keyword. The keywords are lowercased and stripped of any slashes, if there are any.

♦ The `$helpObj->search()` method is called using the keywords, and if the search results in any matches the results are retrieved using the `$helpObj->getSearchResults()` method into a hash called $contents and displayed using `displayOutput()`.

♦ On the other hand, if no match is found, an alert window is shown.

Installing Help Applications

Here we'll assume that you're using a Linux system with MySQL and Apache server installed. During the installation process, I refer to this directory as `%DocumentRoot%`.

I also assume that you have installed the PHPLIB and PEAR library. Normally, these get installed during PHP installation. For your convenience, I've provided these in the `lib/phplib.tar.gz` and `lib/pear.tar.gz` directories on the CD-ROM. In these sample installation steps, we'll assume that these are installed in the `/evoknow/phplib` and `/evoknow/pear` directories. Because your installation locations for these libraries are likely to differ, make sure you replace these paths in the configuration files.

Here is how you can get your help applications up and running:

♦ **Install the applications framework.** If you haven't yet installed the application framework discussed in Chapter 4, you must do so before proceeding further.

♦ **Install help applications.** From the `ch12` directory on the CD-ROM, extract `ch12.tar.gz` in `%DocumentRoot%`. This will create a help directory in your document root.

◆ **Set file/directory permissions.** Make sure you've changed the file and directory permissions such that your intranet Web server can access all the files. The `makeindex.php` script must write to the help contents directory to store the generated help indexes. Make sure your Web server has write access to the help contents directory you create for your application-specific help files.

After you've performed the preceding steps, you're ready to test your online help applications.

Testing the Help System

If you've installed the applications properly, it came with help on itself. Therefore, you can run it immediately without needing to create help contents first.

Run `http://yourserver/help/apps/help.php?app=self`

You should see a screen similar to Figure 12-2.

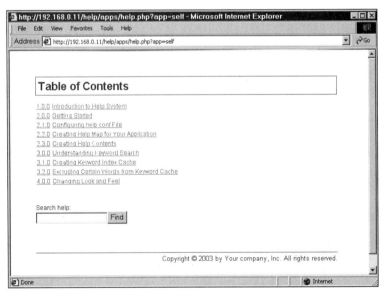

Figure 12-2: The table of contents page for the help system itself.

Now click on any of the sections and you'll see the sections page. For example, Figure 12-3 shows the section that introduces the help system to you.

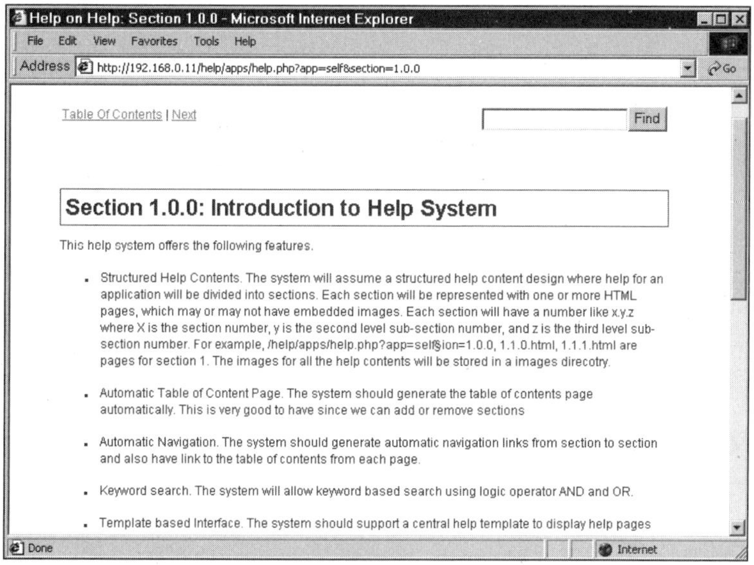

Figure 12-3: A section page.

Now you can enter search key words in any of the screens to see if there is any match. For example, I entered the keyword "built-in" in the search keyword entry and clicked on the GO button. The result is shown in Figure 12-4.

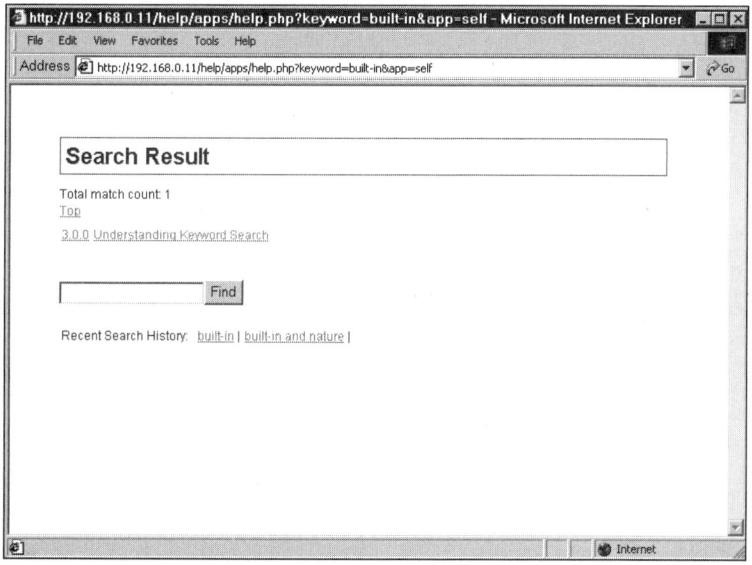

Figure 12-4: A sample search output.

As you can see, you can easily click on the appropriate links to view the matching sections. Now let's try a more complex search using the AND operator, as shown in Figure 12-5.

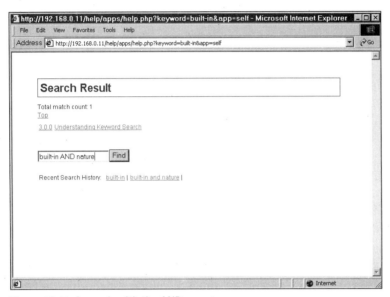

Figure 12-5: A search with the AND operator.

The search for "built-in and nature" found the results shown in Figure 12-6.

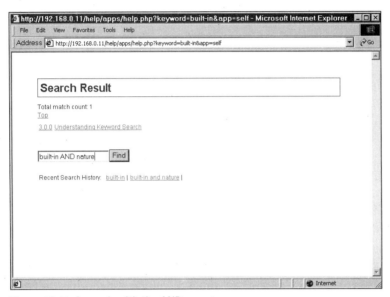

Figure 12-6: Search results for "built-in and nature."

Notice that previous searches are shown as recent search links. This allows you to view a previous search result without reentering the keywords. Also, if the application is used by other users, this will show you what are the most recent keywords that have been searched by other users.

 The help provided as the Help on Help System serves as a guide to how you can set up help for your own application.

If you update your help files and want to regenerate the keyword index, you can run the `makeindex.php` script. This will update all applications. For example, Figure 12-7 shows a sample run of `makeindex.php`.

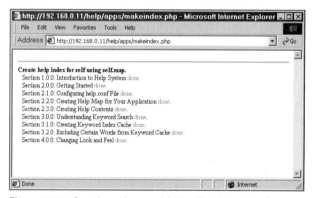

Figure 12-7: Creating a keyword index for all applications.

To limit creating an index to a single application, use `app=application_name` in the query string. For example, `http://yourserver/help/apps/makeindex.php?app=self` will only create an index for the help application itself. To create keyword indices for multiple but not all applications, use the URL calls such as:

```
http://yourserver/help/apps/makeindex.php?app[]=app_name1&app[]=app_name2
```

Security Considerations

Like all other applications you've developed in this book, the online help system has some security considerations that you need to be aware of. They are discussed here.

Restricting access to makeindex.php script

The makeindex.php writes keyword index cache files in each application's help directory. Therefore, you must make this directory writable by the Web server.

Any time you have an application that is writing new files to your Web site, you need to ensure that this isn't going be abused in any way. One of the best ways to protect against abuse is to make sure the application has limited access.

You can limit the use of the makeindex.php to your own network by utilizing the following help.conf parameters: ACL_ALLOW_FROM and ACL_DENY_FROM.

For example

```
define('ACL_ALLOW_FROM', '192.168.0.10');
define('ACL_DENY_FROM',  '0.0.0.0');
```

Here, the allow list specifies that access to makeindex.php is allowed from 192.168.0.10 and denied from every host of every network. The 0 octet in the network address in ACL_DENY_FROM can be thought of as "don't care." Because I specified 0.0.0.0, I stated that I deny all hosts, and then I opened the access for 192.168.0.11.

Similarly, if you want to allow everyone but deny one IP address, you can make configuration such as:

```
define('ACL_ALLOW_FROM', '0.0.0.0');
define('ACL_DENY_FROM',  '192.168.0.11,192.168.0.12');
```

Here access is allowed to everyone but 192.168.0.11 and 192.168.0.12. You can also specify network IP addresses when defining these rules. For example:

```
define('ACL_ALLOW_FROM', '192.168.0');
define('ACL_DENY_FROM',  '0.0.0.0');
```

Here access is granted for all hosts in the 198.168.0.x network. That means 192.168.0.1 to 192.168.0.254 can access the makeindex.php script.

Summary

In this chapter, you learned to develop an online help system that allows you to provide a central help facility for all your Web or intranet applications. It gives you a structured approach to designing online help for your applications, which is great for developers who are often reluctant to write help for the users.

Part III

Developing E-mail Solutions

Chapter 13

Tell-a-Friend System

IN THIS CHAPTER

◆ Developing a tell-a-friend system

◆ Installing a tell-a-friend system

◆ Using a tell-a-friend system

SENDING E-MAILS TO EXISTING customers or prospective customers has become standard business practice among modern companies. After all, e-mail is cheap and more reliable than direct mail, especially when you consider the entire world as your market. Marketing departments have been coming up with creative ways of using e-mail to increase companies' exposure and customer base via e-mail. In this process, the Tell-a-Friend concept was invented. This process involves embedding a small HTML form within HTML messages that are sent out to customers or leads and encouraging them to tell their friends about the company's product and/or services. This viral marketing technique is widely used to increase Web site visits and even sell new products and services.

In this chapter, you'll develop a Tell-a-Friend system that you can use with your in-house or outsourced e-mail campaign solution.

Let's look at the functionality requirements of this system.

Functionality Requirements

The Tell-a-Friend that we will build in this chapter will have the following features:

◆ **Central Tell-a-Friend database:** A single database will be used to store all Tell-a-Friend information. The database will store Tell-a-Friend forms, a friends list (name, e-mail) submitted per form by each user who fills out the forms, and subscription information (each friend who subscribes via a link embedded in the e-mail sent by the system).

♦ **Central Tell-a-Form form management application:** The system will have a form-management application that will allow valid users (who make requests from a set of given IP addresses, which is configured in a central configuration file) to register an HTML form name to a form ID and a message ID along with other information, such as maximum individual submissions, score per friend's e-mail, and score per subscription by a friend. The user will also define which message to send to friends and which message to send to the submission originator (that is, the friend forwarder).

♦ **Central Tell-a-Friend form processor application:** A single application will process all registered forms. The form data will be stored in the central Tell-a-Friend database. Each submission will also track the request IP, time stamp, and user agent (that is, the web browser) preferences.

♦ **Central message editor:** The user can add, modify, and delete HTML messages that can be used as automatic responses to a Tell-a-Friend submission request or Tell-a-Friend introductory/forward message (that is, a message sent to a friend).

♦ **Friend subscription application:** Each friend receiving an e-mail due to another friend's submission of her name in the Tell-a-Friend database has a choice to subscribe or not subscribe for future mailing. She will be given a link embedded in the automatic e-mail she received that allows her to say yes or no to the future mailing. When she clicks this link, she'll be shown an interface where she will select yes or no for future e-mailing along with other information such as the frequency of e-mail she prefers and the type of mail she prefers (HTML or Text).

♦ **Easy reporting:** For each Tell-a-Friend form, there will be a report showing how many e-mail recipients have submitted their friends' names and e-mail addresses. This report can only be accessed by IP addresses listed in central configuration files.

♦ **Score-card reporting:** Each person who signs up friends using the Tell-a-Friend receives a thank-you mail whenever a new friend is added to the database. This thank-you message includes a link that allows the user to view her total score per form. In other words, she'll know how many of her forms she has submitted via the Tell-a-Friend form, as well as how many of her friends have actually subscribed. There are two scores: the score related to each friend submission (which is limited to a maximum value set per form) and the score related to each friend subscription. The report also tells her where she stands among other users who have submitted friends using this same form.

Understanding Prerequisites

This is an Internet application and does not require central authentication techniques. Therefore, it is not dependent on intranet tools discussed in earlier chapters.

However, it does require the application framework classes that are discussed in Chapter 4. You must have the application framework classes installed, along with PHPLIB and PEAR packages.

Designing the Database

Figure 13-1 shows the database diagram for the Tell-a-Friend system. Here I will describe each table in detail.

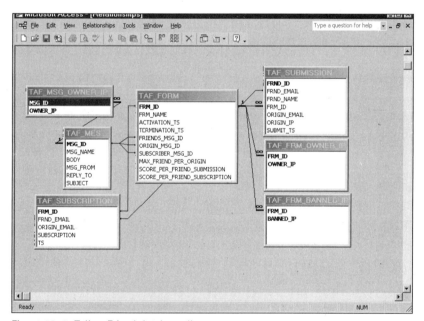

Figure 13-1: Tell-a-Friend database diagram.

TAF_FORM Table

This table is the integral part of this application. It holds the form number (FRM_ID), form name (FRM_NAME), form activation time stamp (ACTIVATION_TS), form termination time stamp (TERMINATION_TS), ID of the message to be sent to the friends (FRIENDS_MSG_ID), ID of the message to be sent to the user (ORIGIN_MSG_ID), ID of the message to be sent to the friend who subscribes (SUBSCRIBER_MSG_ID), maximum number of friends allowed per user (MAX_FRIEND_PER_ORIGIN), score per friend submission (SCORE_PER_FRIEND_SUBMISSION), and score per friend subscription (SCORE_PER_FRIEND_SUBSCRIPTION). The form number (FRM_ID) is the primary key for this table.

TAF_FRM_BANNED_IP Table

This table is used to store the IP addresses that are banned from viewing a form report or modifying a form configuration. This has two attributes: the form number (FRM_ID) and the banned IP address (BANNED_IP). Both the attributes are used as primary keys.

TAF_FRM_OWNER_IP Table

This table is used to store the IP addresses that are authorized to view a form report or modify a form configuration. This has two attributes: the form number (FRM_ID) and the authorized IP address (OWNER_IP). Both the attributes are used as primary keys because we want to allow multiple IP addresses to be allowed for a single form.

TAF_MESSAGE Table

This is the table that stores all kinds of message needed to operate the Tell-a-Friend application. This holds the message number (MSG_ID), message name (MSG_NAME), message content (BODY), from address (FROM), reply-to address (REPLY_TO), and message subject (SUBJECT). The message number (MSG_ID) is the primary key in this table.

TAF_MSG_OWNER_IP Table

This table contains the IP addresses that are allowed to modify a message. The message number (MSG_ID) and the authorized IP (OWNER_IP) are the two attributes of this table. Both of them are also the primary keys of the table.

TAF_SUBMISSION Table

This table holds information about friend submission. It has friend number (FRND_ID), friend e-mail (FRND_EMAIL), friend name (FRND_NAME), form number (FRM_ID), originator e-mail (ORIGIN_EMAIL), originator IP Address (ORIGIN_IP), and submission time stamp (SUBMIT_TS). The friend number (FRND_ID) is the primary key and the friend's e-mail (FRND_EMAIL) and form number (FRM_ID) are the unique fields for this table.

TAF_SUBSCRIPTION Table

This table contains information about the friend subscription. It has the form number (FRM_ID), friend e-mail (FRND_EMAIL), originator e-mail (ORIGIN_EMAIL), subscription type (SUBSCRIPTION), and subscription time stamp (TS). The form number (FRM_ID) and friend e-mail (FRND_EMAIL) are the primary keys for the table.

The `taf.sql` file in the `ch13/sql` directory of the CD-ROM shows an implementation of the Tell-a-Friend database in MySQL. To implement this Tell-a-Friend database in MySQL, you can create a database called `TELL_A_FRIEND` in your database server and run the following command:

```
mysql -u root -p -D TELL_A_FRIEND < taf.sql
```

Make sure you change the user name (`root`) to whatever is appropriate for your system.

Designing and Implementing the Tell-a-Friend Application Classes

As shown in the system diagram, Figure 13-2, there are three new objects that are needed to implement the Tell-a-Friend application.

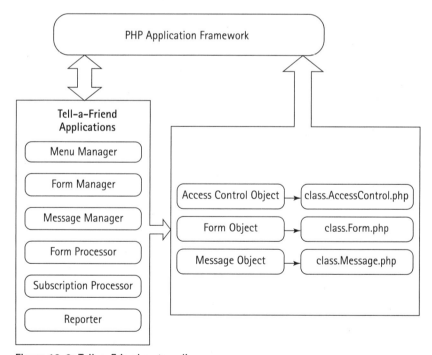

Figure 13-2: Tell-a-Friend system diagram.

Here you will develop some classes that will provide these objects for your Tell-a-Friend applications.

Designing and implementing the Form class

The Form class is used to manipulate each form. It allows an application to create, modify, and delete a form. The ch13/apps/class/class.Form.php file on the CD-ROM implements this class. This class implements the following methods.

Form()

This is the constructor method. It works as follows:

- ◆ First it sets a member variable named dbi to point to the class.DBI.php-provided object, which is passed to the constructor by an application. The dbi member variable holds the DBI object, which is used to communicate with the back-end database.

- ◆ Then it sets member variables named frm_tbl, submtn_tbl, and subscr_tbl to store the names of the form table, submission table, and subscription table, respectively.

- ◆ It also sets member variables named field_arr (to store the form table attributes and their type as an array) and fields (to hold the attributes as a comma-separated string).

- ◆ Then it calls the setFormID() method to set the Form ID that has been passed as a parameter.

setFormID()

This method is used to set the form ID as member variable fid. It takes the ID as a parameter and returns it after setting it to the member variable if the ID is not empty.

getFormInfo()

This method is used to retrieve all the information for a given form. This is how it works:

- ◆ First it calls the setFormID() method to set the given form ID.

- ◆ Then it builds a query statement to retrieve all the attribute values of the form and stores the statement $stmt.

- ◆ Using the DBI object ($this->dbi), the $stmt statement is run via the $this->dbi->query() method in the DBI object. The result of the query is stored in the $result variable.

- ◆ The method directly returns null when it finds out, using the numRows() method, that the $result object has no rows.

- ◆ Otherwise, the row is fetched using the fetchRow() method and stored in $row.

◆ Then the member variable `field_arr` is looped through to store each column value of the `$row` object into the `$retArr` array with the respective field name as the key for each value. The values are formatted using the `stripslashes()` method before storing them in the array.

◆ Then the `$retArr` array is returned from this method.

getAllForms()

This method is used to retrieve all the forms from the database. This is how it works:

◆ First a query statement is prepared and stored in `$stmt` to retrieve the form number and form name of all the forms.

◆ Using the DBI object (`$this->dbi`), the `$stmt` statement is run via the `$this->dbi->query()` method in the DBI object. The result of the query is stored in the `$result` variable.

◆ The method directly returns null when it finds out, using the `numRows()` method, that the `$result` object has no rows.

◆ Otherwise, each row of the `$result` object is fetched using the `fetchRow()` method and `$retArr` is prepared with all the form IDs and form names.

◆ At the end, the `$retArr` array is returned.

addForm()

This method is used to add new forms to the database. It works as follows:

◆ From the given parameter, all the values that are supposed to be of text type in the database are escaped for characters such as quotation marks and slashes using `$this->dbi->quote(addslashes())` methods.

◆ Then all the parameter values are taken into a string named `$paramValueStr` by imploding a comma among them.

◆ A SQL statement, `$stmt`, is created to insert the new form data into the form table using the member variable `fields` (contains attribute names) and `$paramValueStr`.

◆ The SQL statement is executed using the `$this->dbi->query()` method and the result of the query is stored in the `$result` object.

◆ If the `$result` status is not okay, the method returns false.

◆ Otherwise, another query statement is prepared to retrieve the form ID of the newly added form by using the form name, which is a unique field, in the `where` condition.

◆ The statement is executed as usual and the form ID is returned from the method.

modifyForm()

This method is used to modify forms. This is how it works:

◆ From the given parameter, all the values that are supposed to be of text type in the database are escaped for characters such as quotation marks and slashes using `$this->dbi->quote(addslashes())` methods.

◆ Then a string named `$keyValue` is prepared that contains all the attribute names and values as $attr1 = value1, attr2 = value2, \ldots$ format

◆ A SQL statement, `$stmt`, is created to update the form data using `$keyValue`.

◆ The SQL statement is executed using the `$this->dbi->query()` method and the result of the query is stored in the `$result` object.

◆ The method returns TRUE or FALSE depending on the status of the `$result`.

deleteForm()

This method is used to delete a given form. It takes form ID as the parameter and returns TRUE or FALSE depending on the status of the deletion operation.

isMaximumSubmitted()

This method identifies whether the maximum number of friends allowed has exceeded or not for the given originator according to the form configuration. This is how it works:

◆ First it sets the given form ID using the `setFormID()` method.

◆ Then the given originator e-mail is formatted using `$this->dbi->quote(addslashes())` methods.

◆ Then a query statement is prepared to retrieve the number of friends submitted by the given originator for the given form.

◆ Then the number of maximum allowed friends is retrieved using the `getFormInfo()` method.

◆ Then the two numbers are compared to return TRUE when the number of friends submitted is already equal to or greater than the maximum allowed; otherwise, it returns FALSE.

addSubmissionData()

This method is used to add friend submission data in to the database. It works as follows:

◆ First it sets `$field_arr` (to store the submission table attributes and their type as an array) and `$fields` (to hold the attributes as a comma-separated string).

- From the given parameter, all the values that are supposed to be of text type in the database are escaped for characters such as quotation marks and slashes using $this->dbi->quote(addslashes()) methods.

- Then all the parameter values are taken into a string named $paramValueStr by imploding comma among them.

- A SQL statement, $stmt, is created to insert the new submission data into the submission table using $fields and $paramValueStr.

- The SQL statement is executed using the $this->dbi->query() method and the result of the query is stored in $result object.

- If the $result status is not okay, the method returns false.

- Otherwise, another query statement is prepared to retrieve the friend ID of the newly submitted friend by using the friend e-mail and form ID, which are the unique fields, in the where condition.

- The statement is executed as usual and the friend ID is returned from the method.

getFriendList()

This method returns the list of all friends for a given form. This is how it works:

- First it sets the given form ID using the setFormID() method.

- Then it prepares a query to retrieve the friend ID and e-mail from the submission table for the given form.

- The SQL statement is executed using the $this->dbi->query() method and the result of the query is stored in the $result object.

- The method directly returns null when it finds out, using the numRows() method, that the $result object has no rows.

- Otherwise, each row of the $result object is fetched using the fetchRow() method and $retArr is prepared with all the friend IDs and e-mails.

- At the end the $retArr array is returned.

addSubscriptionData()

This method is used to add subscription data after a friend decides to subscribe or unsubscribe. It works in the following manner:

- First it sets $field_arr (to store the subscription table attributes and their type as an array) and $fields (to hold the attributes as a comma-separated string).

◆ From the given parameter, all the values that are supposed to be of text type in the database are escaped for characters such as quotation marks and slashes using $this->dbi->quote(addslashes()) methods.

◆ Then all the parameter values are taken into a string named $paramValueStr by imploding a comma among them.

◆ A SQL statement, $stmt, is created to insert the new subscription data into the submission table using $fields and $paramValueStr.

◆ The SQL statement is executed using the $this->dbi->query() method and the result of the query is stored in the $result object.

◆ The method returns TRUE or FALSE depending on the status of $result.

This method is used to determine whether the given friend has already unsubscribed. It takes the friend's e-mail as the parameter and checks whether the e-mail is already unsubscribed or not.

getNumberOfSubscriber()
This method returns the number of friends that have subscribed for a given form. It takes the form ID as a parameter and returns the number of subscribers for that form.

getNumberOfUnsubscriber()
This method returns the number of friends that have unsubscribed for a given form. It takes the form ID as a parameter and returns the number of unsubscriber for that form.

getOriginSubmissions()
This method returns the originator information for a given form. This is how it works:

◆ First it sets the form ID using the setFormID() method.

◆ Then it prepares a query statement to retrieve the originator e-mails and number of submission by each of them.

◆ The SQL statement is executed using the $this->dbi->query() method and the result of the query is stored in the $result object.

◆ The method directly returns null when it finds out, using the numRows() method, that the $result object has no rows.

◆ Otherwise, each row of the $result object is fetched using the fetchRow() method and $retArr is prepared with all the originator e-mails and number of submissions by each of them.

◆ At the end, the $retArr array is returned.

getNumSubscriptionPerOrigin()

This method returns the number of friends that have subscribed for a given originator and form. It takes the form ID and the originator e-mail as the parameter and returns the number of subscriber.

getFriendsByOrigin()

This method is used to retrieve the list of friends for a given originator and form. This is how it works:

♦ First the originator e-mail is formatted using `$this->dbi->quote (addslashes())` methods for use in the SQL query.

♦ Then the `setFormID()` method is called to set the given form ID.

♦ Then it prepares a query statement to retrieve the friend e-mails and names for the given form and originator.

♦ The SQL statement is executed using the `$this->dbi->query()` method and the result of the query is stored in the `$result` object.

♦ The method directly returns null when it finds out, using the `numRows()` method, that the `$result` object has no rows.

♦ Otherwise, each row of the `$result` object is fetched using the `fetchRow()` method and `$retArr` is prepared with all the friend e-mails and names.

♦ At the end, the `$retArr` array is returned.

getSubscriptionStatus

This method is used to find out the subscription status for a given form and friend e-mail. It works in the following manner:

♦ First the friend e-mail is formatted using `$this->dbi->quote (addslashes())` methods for use in the SQL query.

♦ Then the `setFormID()` method is called to set the given form ID.

♦ Then it prepares a query statement to retrieve the subscription status for the given form and friend.

♦ The SQL statement is executed using the `$this->dbi->query()` method and the result of the query is stored in the `$result` object.

♦ The method directly returns null when it finds out, using the `numRows()` method, that the `$result` object has no rows.

♦ Otherwise, the row containing the subscription status is fetched, using the `fetchRow()` method.

♦ The method returns 1 or -1 depending on the subscription/unsubscription status of the friend.

Designing and implementing the Message class

The Message class is used to manipulate each message. It allows an application to create, modify, and delete a message. The ch13/apps/class/class.Message.php file on the CD-ROM implements this class. This class implements the following methods.

Message()
This is the constructor method. It works as follows:

- ◆ First, it sets a member variable named dbi to point to the class.DBI.php-provided object, which is passed to the constructor by an application. The dbi member variable holds the DBI object, which is used to communicate with the back-end database.

- ◆ Then it sets member variable named msg_tbl to store the name of the message table.

- ◆ It also sets member variables named field_arr (to store the message table attributes and their type as an array) and fields (to hold the attributes as a comma-separated string).

- ◆ Then it calls the setMessageID() method to set the Message ID that has been passed as parameter.

setMessageID()
This method is used to set the message ID as member variable mid. It takes the ID as a parameter and returns it after setting it to the member variable if the ID is not empty.

getMessageInfo()
This method is used to retrieve all the information for a given message. This is how it works:

- ◆ First it calls the setMessageID() method to set the given message ID.

- ◆ Then it builds a query statement to retrieve all the attribute values of the message and stores the statement, $stmt.

- ◆ Using the DBI object ($this->dbi), the $stmt statement is run via the $this->dbi->query() method in the DBI object. The result of the query is stored in the $result variable.

- ◆ The method directly returns null when it finds out, using the numRows() method, that the $result object has no rows.

- ◆ Otherwise, the row is fetched using the fetchRow() method and is stored in $row.

- ◆ Then the member variable field_arr is looped through to store each column value of the $row object into the $retArr array with the respective field name as the key for each value. The values are formatted using the stripslashes() method before storing into the array.

◆ Then the $retArr array is returned from this method.

getAllMessages()

This method is used to retrieve all the messages from the database. This is how it works:

◆ First, a query statement is prepared and stored in $stmt to retrieve the message number and message name of all the messages.

◆ Using the DBI object ($this->dbi) the $stmt statement is run via the $this->dbi->query() method in the DBI object. The result of the query is stored in the $result variable.

◆ The method directly returns null when it finds out, using the numRows() method, that the $result object has no rows.

◆ Otherwise, each row of the $result object is fetched using the fetchRow() method and $retArr is prepared with all the message IDs and message names.

◆ At the end, the $retArr array is returned.

addMessage()

This method is used to add a new message to the database. It works as follows:

◆ From the given parameter, all the values that are supposed to be of text type in the database are escaped for characters such as quotation marks and slashes using $this->dbi->quote(addslashes()) methods.

◆ Then all the parameter values are taken into a string named $paramValueStr by imploding a comma among them.

◆ A SQL statement, $stmt, is created to insert the new message data into the message table using the member variable fields (which contains attribute names) and $paramValueStr.

◆ The SQL statement is executed using the $this->dbi->query() method and the result of the query is stored in $result object.

◆ If the $result status is not okay, the method returns false.

◆ Otherwise, another query statement is prepared to retrieve the message ID of the newly added message by using the message name, which is a unique field, in the where condition.

◆ The statement is executed as usual and the message ID is returned from the method.

modifyMessage()

This method is used to modify messages. This is how it works:

- ◆ From the given parameter, all the values that are supposed to be of text type in the database are escaped for characters such as quotation marks and slashes using `$this->dbi->quote(addslashes())` methods.

- ◆ Then a string named `$keyValue` is prepared that contains all the attribute names and values as `attr1 = value1, attr2 = value2,...` format

- ◆ A SQL statement, `$stmt`, is created to update the message data using `$keyValue`.

- ◆ The SQL statement is executed using the `$this->dbi->query()` method and the result of the query is stored in the `$result` object.

- ◆ The method returns `TRUE` or `FALSE` depending on the status of the `$result`.

deleteMessage()

This method is used to delete a given message. It takes message ID as the parameter and returns `TRUE` or `FALSE` depending on the status of the deletion operation.

Designing and implementing the AccessControl class

The `AccessControl` class is used to control access to objects (Messages, Forms). The `ch13/apps/class/class.AccessControl.php` file on the CD-ROM implements this class. This class implements the following methods.

AccessControl()

This is the constructor method. This is how it works:

- ◆ First, it sets a member variable named `dbi` to point to the `class.DBI.php`-provided object, which is passed to the constructor by an application. The `dbi` member variable holds the DBI object, which is used to communicate with the back-end database.

- ◆ Then it sets the member variable named `access_obj` to store the type of the object (Message or Form) for access control. The type of object is passed as parameter in an array named `$ACInfo`.

- ◆ The member variables `allow_tbl` and `deny_tbl` are set with the table names of the authorized and denied tables of the given object. These are also passed as a parameter through the `$ACInfo` array.

- ◆ Then the `setAccessObjectID()` and `setCurrentIP()` is called to set the object ID and the IP address that are provided in the `$ACInfo`.

setCurrentIP()

This method is used to set the current IP address that is to be authorized. It takes the IP address as a parameter and returns it after setting it to the member variable request_ip.

setAccessObjectID()

This method is used to set the ID of the object for access control. It takes the ID as a parameter and returns the same after binding it to the member variable access_obj_id.

isAccessAllowed()

This method determines whether the current IP is authorized to access the current object (Message or Form). It uses getAccessIPs() to retrieve the list of authorized IPs to match with the current IP and returns TRUE or FALSE depending on the matching outcome.

isAccessDenied()

This method determines whether the current IP is banned from accessing the current object (Message or Form). It uses getDeniedIPs() to retrieve the list of banned IPs to match with current IP and returns TRUE or FALSE depending on the matching outcome.

getAccessIPs()

This method returns the list of IPs that are authorized to access the current given object. This is how it works:

- ◆ First it prepares a SQL query statement to retrieve the authorized IP addresses for the current object ID.

- ◆ The SQL statement is executed using the $this->dbi->query() method and the result of the query is stored in $result object.

- ◆ The method directly returns null when it finds out, using the numRows() method, that $result object has no rows.

- ◆ Otherwise $retArr array is prepared with all the authorized IPs.

- ◆ At the end, the $retArr is returned from the method.

getDeniedIPs()

This method returns the list of IPs that are banned from accessing the current given object. This is how it works:

- ◆ First, it prepares a SQL query statement to retrieve the banned IP addresses for the current object ID.

- ◆ The SQL statement is executed using the $this->dbi->query() method and the result of the query is stored in the $result object.

◆ The method directly returns null when it finds out, using the numRows() method, that $result object has no rows.

◆ Otherwise $retArr array is prepared with all the banned IPs.

◆ At the end, the $retArr is returned from the method.

addAccessIPs()

This method inserts IP addresses to the authorized table for the given object. It takes an array of IP addresses as a parameter and adds them one by one into the authorized table.

deleteAccessIP()

This method deletes all the IP addresses from the authorized table for a given object ID. It takes the object ID as parameter and returns TRUE or FALSE depending on the status of the deletion operation.

addDeniedIPs()

This method inserts IP addresses to the denied table for the given object. It takes an array of IP addresses as a parameter and adds them one by one into the denied table.

deleteDeniedIP()

This method deletes all the IP addresses from the denied table for a given object ID. It takes the object ID as parameter and returns TRUE or FALSE depending on the status of the deletion operation.

Creating Application Configuration Files

Like all other applications you've developed in this book, Tell-a-Friend applications also use a standard set of configuration, message, and error files. These files are discussed in the following sections.

Creating the main configuration file

The primary configuration file for the entire system is called taf.conf. Table 13-1 discusses each configuration variables.

TABLE 13-1 THE `taf.conf` **VARIABLES NEED TO BE CHANGED**

Configuration Variable	Purpose
$PEAR_DIR	Set to the directory containing the PEAR package; specifically the DB module needed for `class.DBI.php` in our application framework.
$PHPLIB_DIR	Set to the PHPLIB directory, which contains the PHPLIB packages; specifically the `template.inc` package needed for template manipulation.
$APP_FRAMEWORK_DIR	Set to our application framework directory.
$PATH	Set to the combined directory path consisting of the $PEAR_DIR, the $PHPLIB_DIR, and the $APP_FRAMEWORK_DIR. This path is used with the `ini_set()` method to redefine the `php.ini` entry for `include_path` to include $PATH ahead of the default path. This allows PHP to find our application framework, PHPLIB, and PEAR-related files.
$AUTHENTICATION_URL	Set to the central login application URL.
$LOGOUT_URI	Set to the central logout application URL.
$HOME_URL	Set to the topmost URL of the site. If the URL redirection application does not find a valid URL in the e-campaign database to redirect to for a valid request, it uses this URL as a default.
$APPLICATION_NAME	Internal name of the application.
$DEFAULT_LANGUAGE	Set to the default (two characters) language code.
$ROOT_PATH	Set to the root path of the application.
$REL_ROOT_PATH	Relative path to the root directory.
$REL_APP_PATH	Relative application path as seen from the web browser.
$TEMPLATE_DIR	The fully qualified path to the template directory.
$CLASS_DIR	The fully qualified path to the class directory.
$REL_TEMPLATE_DIR	The Web-relative path to the template directory used.

Continued

TABLE 13-1 THE `taf.conf` VARIABLES NEED TO BE CHANGED *(Continued)*

Configuration Variable	Purpose
ACCESS_CONTROL_CLASS	Name of the AccessControl class file.
MSG_CLASS	Name of the Message class file.
FRM_CLASS	Name of the Form class file.
$TAF_DB_URL	The fully qualified URL for the database used to store the Tell-A-Friend information.
TAF_FRM_TBL	Name of the form table in the database.
TAF_FRM_OWNER_IP_TBL	Name of the table that stores authorized IPs for forms in the database.
TAF_FRM_RESTRICT_IP_TBL	Name of the table that stores banned IPs for forms in the database.
TAF_MSG_OWNER_IP_TBL	Name of the table that stores authorized IPs for messages in the database.
TAF_MSG_TBL	Name of the message table in the database.
TAF_FRM_SUBMTN_TBL	Name of the form submission table in the database.
TAF_SUBSCRIPTION_TBL	Name of the friend subscription table in the database.
$STATUS_TEMPLATE	Name of the status template file used to display status messages.
TAF_MENU_TEMPLATE	Name of the Tell-A-Friend index template file.
TAF_CREATOR_REPORT_TEMPLATE	Name of the report template for the form creator.
TAF_FRM_SETUP_TEMPLATE	Name of the Tell-A-Friend form setup template file.
TAF_MSG_SETUP_TEMPLATE	Name of the Tell-A-Friend message setup template file.
TAF_FRIEND_MSG_TEMPLATE	Name of the Tell-A-Friend "mail to the friend" template file.
TAF_ORIGIN_MSG_TEMPLATE	Name of the Tell-A-Friend "mail to the originator" template file.
TAF_ORIGIN_REPORT_TEMPLATE	Name of the report template for the originator.
MIN_YEAR	The earliest year to be shown in different year lists.
MAX_YEAR	The latest year to be shown in different year lists.
TOP	The number of originators to be shown in the top user list in the form creator report.

The directory structure used in the `taf.conf` file supplied in the `ch13` directory on the CD-ROM might need to be tailored to your own system's requirements. Here is what the current directory structure looks like:

```
htdocs ($ROOT_PATH == %DocumentRoot%)
 |
 +---taf (Tell-a-Friend Applications)
     |
     +---apps (apps and configuration files)
         |
         +---class (class files)
         |
         +---templates (HTML templates)
)
```

By changing the following configuration parameters in `taf.conf`, you can modify the directory structure to fit your site requirements:

```
$PEAR_DIR           = $_SERVER['DOCUMENT_ROOT'] . '/pear' ;
$PHPLIB_DIR         = $_SERVER['DOCUMENT_ROOT'] . '/phplib';
$APP_FRAMEWORK_DIR  = $_SERVER['DOCUMENT_ROOT'] . '/framework';
$ROOT_PATH          = $_SERVER['DOCUMENT_ROOT'];
$REL_ROOT_PATH      = '/taf';
$REL_APP_PATH       = $REL_ROOT_PATH . '/apps';
$TEMPLATE_DIR       = $ROOT_PATH    . $REL_APP_PATH . '/templates';
$CLASS_DIR          = $ROOT_PATH    . $REL_APP_PATH . '/class';
$REL_TEMPLATE_DIR   = $REL_APP_PATH . '/templates/';
```

Creating a Messages file

The messages displayed by the Tell-a-Friend applications are stored in the `ch13/apps/taf.messages` file in the CDROM. You can change the messages using a text editor.

Creating an Errors file

The error messages displayed by the Tell-a-Friend applications are stored in the `ch13/apps/taf.errors` file in the CD-ROM. You can modify the error messages using a text editor.

Creating Application Templates

The HTML interface templates needed for the applications are included on the CD-ROM. These templates contain various template tags to display necessary information dynamically. The templates are named in the `taf.conf` file. These templates are discussed in Table 13-2.

TABLE 13-2 HTML TEMPLATES

Configuration Variable	Template File	Purpose
$STATUS_TEMPLATE	taf_status.html	This template is used to show the status message.
TAF_MENU_TEMPLATE	taf_menu.html	This template is used to show the index page of the application.
TAF_CREATOR_REPORT_ TEMPLATE	taf_report_creator .html	This template is used for the report to be shown to the form creator.
TAF_FRM_SETUP_TEMPLATE	taf_setup.html	This template is used to show the form setup menu.
TAF_MSG_SETUP_TEMPLATE	taf_add_modify_ msg.html	This template is used for the message add/modify menu.
TAF_FRIEND_MSG_TEMPLATE	taf_frnd_msg.html	This template is used while sending mail to the friend.
TAF_ORIGIN_MSG_TEMPLATE	taf_orig_msg.html	This template is used while sending mail to the originator.
TAF_ORIGIN_REPORT_ TEMPLATE	taf_report_origin .html	This template is used for the report to be shown to the originator.

Creating the Tell-a-Friend Main Menu Manager Application

This application, `taf_mngr.php`, is responsible for managing the main menu of the system. This application is included on the CD-ROM in the `ch13/apps` directory.

It implements the following functionality:

◆ Allows every user to create messages and forms.

◆ Allows users from authenticated IP addresses to delete or modify forms or messages.

◆ Allows users from authenticated IP addresses to view the form report.

This application has the following methods.

run()

When the application is run, this method is called. It simply calls the `displayTAFMenu()` method to render the main menu for the system.

displayTAFMenu()

This method is responsible for showing the main menu according to the privileges based on the IP address of the client. It works in the following manner:

◆ A menu template (`TAF_MENU_TEMPLATE`) is loaded in a template object called `$template`.

◆ All the form names and form IDs of the database are loaded in the array `$frms`.

◆ For each of those forms the `AccessControl` object is used to check whether the request IP is allowed to access the form. If the check result is yes, then the form name is showed in the list to the user for him to modify, delete, or view a report.

◆ Similarly, all the messages are loaded in an array and the `AccessControl` object is again used to verify the request IP's eligibility to access the message and the message list is prepared thereby.

◆ After preparing the message list and the form list and setting all the links for deletion, modification, and report for the messages or forms, the template is parsed and printed to the user.

Creating a Tell-a-Friend Form Manager Application

This application, `taf_form_mngr.php`, is responsible for managing forms. This application is included on the CD-ROM in the `ch13/apps` directory.

It implements the following functionality:

- Allows any user to add a new form.

- Allows users from authenticated IP addresses to delete or modify selected forms.

This application has the following methods.

run()

When the application is run, this method is called. It does the following:

- First it retrieves the `$cmd` value from the user request.

- Depending on the `$cmd` value, different methods are called.

- When the `$cmd` is add or `modify`, it calls the `addModifyDriver()` method with the appropriate mode (add or `modify`).

- And when the `$cmd` is `delete`, it calls the `deleteForm()` method to delete the form.

authorize()

This method checks whether the IP address from where the user is accessing the application is an authorized one. This is how it works:

- This application allows everyone to add forms. So when the request `$cmd` is add, it directly returns true.

- In case of `modify` and `delete`, the `AccessControl` object is used to verify whether the request IP is allowed to access the given form. It returns `TRUE` or `FALSE` depending on the verification result.

addModifyDriver()

This method is responsible for driving the add/modify procedure. Depending on the hidden form value `$step`, it decides whether to call the add/modify menu rendering method, `displayAddModifyMenu()`, or the add/modify method, `addModifyForm()`. Both the methods are called with the proper mode (add or `modify`).

displayAddModifyMenu()

This method is used to show the menu for adding or modifying forms. It works as follows:

- If the method is called with mode `modify`, it first checks whether the form ID has been supplied or not. In case of no form ID, the method shows an alert message and returns null.

- Otherwise, all the previous information of the given form is retrieved and loaded in variables for later usage, to preload the modification Web form while showing to the user. In this case, the `AccessControl` object is used to retrieve the authorized and banned IPs for the form.

- Then a form setup template (`TAF_FRM_SETUP_TEMPLATE`) is loaded in a template object called `$template`.

- For loading different message lists in the Web form, the `Message` object's `getAllMessages()` is used and then filtered using the `AccessControl` object's `isAccessAllowed()` method.

- At the end, the template is parsed and printed to the user to give her a Web form to add or modify forms.

addModifyForm()

This method is used to add or modify forms. It works as follows:

- First, it checks whether the date range given for the form (the activation and termination date) is a valid one or not. If not, the method shows an alert message and returns null.

- Then it prepares the `$params` array with all the form field values from the user request.

- Then it creates an object of `AccessControl` to add or modify the access to the form.

- When the mode for the method is `add` the `params` array is fed into the `addForm()` method of the `Form` class to add the new form. If the addition fails, the method shows a failure message and returns.

- If the addition operation is successful, the authorized and denied IPs are added to the database using the `addAccessIPs()` and `addDeniedIPs()` methods of the `AccessControl` class. Then a successful addition message is shown to the user.

- When the mode for the method is `modify`, the `$params` array is fed into the `modifyForm()` method of the `Form` class to update the given form. If the update fails, the method shows a failure message.

◆ If the update operation is successful, the authorized and denied IPs are added to the database using the `addAccessIPs()` and `addDeniedIPs()` methods of the `AccessControl` class after deleting the previous IPs. And then a successful update message is shown to the user.

deleteForm()

This method is used for deleting forms. This works as follows:

◆ First, it checks whether the form ID has been supplied or not. If not, it shows an alert message and returns null.

◆ Then a new `Form` object, `$frmObj`, is created and the `deleteForm()` method of `$frmObj` is used to delete the form.

◆ If the deletion succeeds, the `AccessControl` class is used to delete the related IPs from the authorized and banned tables for the form.

◆ At the end, a status message is shown depending on the outcome of the deletion operation.

Creating a Tell-a-Friend Message Manager Application

This application, `taf_msg_mngr.php`, is responsible for managing all messages for the system. This application is included on the CD-ROM in the `ch13/apps` directory. It implements the following functionality:

◆ Allows any user to add a new message.

◆ Allows users from authenticated IP addresses to delete or modify the selected message.

This application has the following methods.

run()

When the application is run, this method is called. It does the following:

◆ First, it retrieves the `$cmd` value from the user request.

◆ Depending on the `$cmd` value, different methods are called.

◆ When the $cmd is add or modify, it calls the addModifyDriver() method with the appropriate mode (add or modify).

◆ And when the $cmd is delete, it calls the deleteForm() method to delete the form.

authorize()

This method checks whether the IP address (where the user is accessing the application from) is an authorized one. This is how it works:

◆ This application allows everyone to add messages. So when the request $cmd is add, it directly returns true.

◆ In case of modify and delete, the AccessControl object is used to verify whether the request IP is allowed to access the given message. It returns TRUE or FALSE depending on the verification result.

addModifyDriver()

This method is responsible for driving the add/modify procedure. Depending on the hidden form value $step, it decides whether to call the add/modify menu rendering method, displayAddModifyMenu(), or the add/modify method, addModifyMessage(). Both the methods are called with proper mode (add or modify).

displayAddModifyMenu()

This method is used to show the Web form for adding or modifying forms. It works as follows:

◆ If the method is called with mode modify, it first checks whether the message ID has been supplied or not. In case of no message ID, the method shows an alert message and returns null.

◆ Otherwise, all the previous information of the given message is retrieved and loaded in variables for later usage, to preload the modification Web form while showing to the user. In this case, the AccessControl object is used to retrieve the authorized IPs for the message.

◆ Then a message setup template (TAF_MSG_SETUP_TEMPLATE) is loaded in a template object called $template.

◆ The different form fields required for adding or modifying a message are prepared.

◆ At the end, the template is parsed and printed to the user to give her a Web form to add or modify messages.

addModifyMessage()

This method is used to add or modify messages. It works as follows:

- ◆ First, it prepares the $params array with all the message field values from the user request.

- ◆ Then it creates an object of AccessControl to add or modify the access to the message.

- ◆ When the mode for the method is add, the $params array is fed into the addMessage() method of the Message class to add the new message. If the addition fails, the method shows a failure message and returns.

- ◆ If the addition operation is successful, the authorized IPs are added to the database using the addAccessIPs() method of the AccessControl class. And then a successful addition message is shown to the user.

- ◆ When the mode for the method is modify, the $params array is fed into the modifyMessage() method of Message class to update the given message. If the update fails, the method shows a failure message and returns.

- ◆ If the update operation is successful, the authorized IP addresses are added to the database using addAccessIPs() method of the AccessControl class after deleting the previous IPs. And then a successful update message is shown to the user.

deleteMessage()

This method is used for deleting messages. This works as follows:

- ◆ First, it checks whether the message ID has been supplied or not. If not, it shows an alert message and returns null.

- ◆ Then a new Message object $msgObj is created and the deleteMessage() method of $msgObj is used to delete the message.

- ◆ If deletion succeeds, the AccessControl class is used to delete the related IPs from the authorized table for the message.

- ◆ At the end, a status message is shown depending on the outcome of the deletion operation.

Creating a Tell-a-Friend Form Processor Application

This application, `taf.php`, is the core part of the system that is responsible for handling the form submission requests from users. This application is included on the CD-ROM in the `ch13/apps` directory.

It implements the following functionalities:

◆ Processes the form submitted by the users and updates the database accordingly.

◆ Sends appropriate mails to newly added friends and the originator of those friends.

To achieve those functionalities, it uses the following methods.

run()

When the application is run, this method is called. It simply calls the `processRequest()` method to process the submit request from the user.

processRequest()

This method is responsible for handling the request and takes the action thereby. This is how it works:

◆ First, it checks whether the form ID is supplied or not. If not, it shows an alert message and returns null.

◆ Then it verifies if the originator e-mail has been provided from the form or not. If not, it returns null after showing an alert.

◆ Then it uses the `AccessControl` class to check whether the request IP address is banned from submitting friends for this form. If it is banned, then it shows the appropriate alert and returns null.

◆ Then an object of the `Form` class, named `$frmObj`, is created.

◆ `$frmObj` retrieves the activation date and termination date for the form and checks whether the current time falls into a valid time range. If not, it shows an alert message and returns null.

♦ Then the campaign message ID is retrieved (the one to be sent to the new friends for this form) and $msgObj, an object of Message class, is used to get and store the information on that message.

♦ For each friend supplied by the user request, the method first checks whether the friend e-mail is already unsubscribed. If not, the friend's submission data is added in to the submission table and the friend is sent the campaign message along with links for subscription and unsubscription.

♦ Then the message ID to be sent to the originator is retrieved using $frmObj and given to $msgObj for information on that message. That message along with information on the successfully submitted friends is sent to the originator. This also contains a link to the scorecard for the originator.

♦ At the end, a status message is shown to the user saying that her submission has been granted and a mail has been sent to her with details.

Creating a Tell-a-Friend Subscriber Application

This application, taf_subscribe.php, is responsible for handling the subscription requests from friends. This application is included on the CD-ROM in the ch13/apps directory.

It implements the following functionalities:

♦ Checks whether the request is valid via the authorize() method.

♦ Updates database according to the subscription request.

To achieve those functionalities it uses the following methods.

run()

When the application is run, this method is called. It simply calls the processRequest() method to process the subscription request from the friend.

authorize()

This method is used to verify the authenticity of the request. This is how it works:

♦ Ideally, friends access this application through the link provided by the Form Handler application. And that link contains a check flag that is used here to verify.

- The encrypted check flag is decrypted and matched with the other parameters from the link. If the matching fails, the method returns false.

- Even after the matching succeeds, a second checking is done using the friend ID that was hidden in the check flag. This friend ID is matched with all the friend IDs of the database and checked to see whether the corresponding e-mail is same as the e-mail hidden in the check flag. The method returns TRUE or FALSE depending on this matching result.

processRequest()

This method is used to process the subscription data and update the database thereby. It works as follows:

- First it creates an array named $param with the form ID, friend e-mail, subscription status (sub or unsub), originator e-mail, and subscription time stamp.

- Then the array is passed into the addSubscriptionData() method of the Form class to add the subscription data.

- If the addition is successful and the subscription type is sub (which means the friend agreed to subscribe to the system), an e-mail is sent to the friend.

- The e-mail to be sent to the friend is decided from the subscription message ID specified while setting up the form. This ID is retrieved using the Form class and then fed into the Message class to get its details.

- At the end, the friend is shown a status message depending on the subscription data addition status.

Creating a Tell-a-Friend Reporter Application

This application, taf_reporter.php, is responsible for generating reports for the system. This application included on the CD-ROM in the ch13/apps directory.

It implements the following functionalities:

- Produces a report for form creator with subscription ratio and other details.

- Produces a scorecard report for friend originator.

These are the methods used by the application.

run()

This method is called when the application is run. It decides, from the cmd value of the request, which report to generate (form creator or originator). And then it either calls generateFormCreatorReport() for the form creator report or generateOriginReport() for the originator report.

generateFormCreatorReport()

This method is used for showing a report to the form creator for her form. It works as follows:

- ◆ First, it takes the form ID and checks whether the form is accessible by the request IP. If not, it shows an alert message and returns null.

- ◆ Then a creator report template (TAF_CREATOR_REPORT_TEMPLATE) is loaded in a template object called $template.

- ◆ On the top of the template, the form summary is displayed using the methods getFormInfo(), getFriendList(), getNumberOfSubscriber(), and getNumberOfUnsubscriber() of the Form class.

- ◆ In the lower part of the template, a block for top originators is set using the getOriginSubmissions() and getNumSubscriptionPerOrigin() methods of the Form class.

- ◆ At the end, the template is parsed and printed to the form creator to give her a complete report on the form.

generateOriginReport()

This method is used for showing the report to the friend originator for a given form. It works as follows:

- ◆ First, it validates the check flag from the user request that is given from the form handler application. It shows an alert message and returns null if the validation fails.

- ◆ Then an originator report template (TAF_ORIGIN_REPORT_TEMPLATE) is loaded in a template object called $template.

- ◆ Then the getFriendsByOrigin() method of the Form class is used to retrieve the list of friends originated by this user.

- ◆ Then the status of each friend is retrieved using the getSubscriptionStatus() method of the Form class. This status along with different scores (like score per subscription and score per submission) is used to set the score per friend for the originator.

◆ After setting the score per each friend, the total score for the originator is calculated and set at the bottom of the template.

◆ At the end, the template is parsed and printed to the user to give her a scorecard report.

Installing a Tell-a-Friend System

Here I assume that you're using a Linux system with MySQL and Apache server installed. Your Internet web server document root directory is /evoknow/ intranet/htdocs. Of course, if you have a different path, which is likely, you should change this path whenever you see it in a configuration file or instruction in this chapter. During the installation process, I refer to this directory as %DocumentRoot%.

I also assume that you've installed the PHPLIB and PEAR library. Normally, these get installed during PHP installation. For your convenience, I've provided these in the lib/phplib.tar.gz and lib/pear.tar.gz directories on the CD-ROM. In these sample installation steps, I assume that these are installed in the /%DocumentRoot%/phplib and /%DocumentRoot%/pear directories. Because your installation locations for these libraries are likely to differ, make sure you replace these paths in the configuration files.

Here is how you can get your Tell-a-Friend applications up and running:

1. **Install the application framework.** If you have not yet installed the application framework discussed in Chapter 4, you must do so before proceeding further.

2. **Install the Tell-a-Friend Database.** The quickest way to create the Tell-a-Friend database is to run the following commands:

```
mysqladmin -u root -p create TELL_A_FRIEND
mysql -u root -p -D TAF < taf.sql
```

3. **Install the Tell-a-Friend applications.** Now from the ch13 directory on the CD-ROM, extract ch13.tar.gz in %DocuemntRoot%. This will create taf in your document root. Configure %DocumentRoot%/taf/apps/ contact.conf for path and database settings. The applications are installed in the %DocumentRoot%/taf/apps directory and the templates are stored in %DocumentRoot%/taf/apps/templates.

   If your MySQL server is hosted on the web server, it can be accessed via localhost. However, if this is not the case, you can easily modify the database URLs in each application's configuration files. For example, the contact.conf file has a MySQL database access URLs such as the following:

```
define('TAF_DB_URL','mysql://root:foobar@localhost/TELL_A_FRI
END');
```

Say your database server is called db.domain.com and the user name and password to access the TELL_A_FRIEND databases (which you will create during this installation process) are admin and db123. In such a case, you would modify the database access URLs throughout each configuration file as:

```
define('TAF_DB_URL','mysql://admin:db132@db.domain.com/TELL_A
_FRIEND');
```

If you change the database name from TELL_A_FRIEND to some other name make sure the database prefix in the following configuration lines are changed accordingly:

```
/*  ----- DEFINE TABLE NAMES -----------  */
define('TAF_FRM_TBL',
       'TELL_A_FRIEND.TAF_FORM');

define('TAF_FRM_OWNER_IP_TBL',
       'TELL_A_FRIEND.TAF_FRM_OWNER_IP');

define('TAF_FRM_RESTRICT_IP_TBL',
       'TELL_A_FRIEND.TAF_FRM_BANNED_IP');

define('TAF_MSG_OWNER_IP_TBL',
       'TELL_A_FRIEND.TAF_MSG_OWNER_IP');

define('TAF_MSG_TBL',
       'TELL_A_FRIEND.TAF_MESSAGE');

define('TAF_FRM_SUBMTN_TBL',
       'TELL_A_FRIEND.TAF_SUBMISSION');

define('TAF_SUBSCRIPTION_TBL',
       'TELL_A_FRIEND.TAF_SUBSCRIPTION');
```

4. **Set file/directory permissions.** Make sure you've changed the file and directory permissions such that your intranet web server can access (read) all the files.

After you've performed the preceding steps, you're ready to test your Tell-a-Friend applications.

Testing the Tell-a-Friend System

Now that you're ready to test your system, the very first step is to create a Tell-a-Friend form. I've supplied two sample Tell-a-Friend forms called sample_taf_form1.html and sample_taf_form2.html in the taf directory.

To set up a Tell-a-Friend form, you need to do the following:

◆ **Create three messages using Tell-a-Friend message manager.**

- One message is for friends who get e-mail because another friend gives their name and information to your Tell-a-Friend system. This e-mail should introduce the friend to what you have to offer. For example, if you're interested in signing up people for a newsletter, you should state what the newsletter has to offer in this message. This message is created using the `taf_frnd_msg.html` template file in the `template` directory. So if you want to control the look and feel of this message, you should modify this template. Make sure if you use any images in the template, the images are directly accessible from your Web site. In other words, use fully qualified path names for images. For example, instead of using `<img src=images/space.gif">` use `<img src="http://yourserver/images/space.gif">`. **Remember:** This is a message template for all messages to friends, so don't customize it for a single campaign. Your actual content of the message is entered via the form manager application. The content is inserted dynamically into the message template by replacing the `{FRND_MSG}` tag in the template.

- The second message you need to set up is for the originator who submits the friend's name. This is usually a thank-you message for helping you market your product/services/information. This message is sent using the `taf_frnd_msg.html` template. The actual content of the message is entered via the form manager like the friend's message.

- The third message is the subscription message and it's sent when a friend actually clicks on the subscription link (in the introduction mail generated by `taf_frnd_msg.html`) and subscribes to your offer. Note that when a friend decides to unsubscribe, she does not receive an e-mail, but a confirmation of her unsubscription status is shown on the web browser when she clicks on the remove or unsubscription link from the introduction mail.

◆ **Create the form with a form action that runs the Tell-a-Friend form processor application.** When you set up the form with the Tell-a-Friend form manager, the form action is given to you at the end of the process, so you can simply copy and paste the form action from there.

After you've set up the messages and the Tell-a-Friend form, you can use your form in e-mail campaigns.

In the following section, I discuss a Tell-a-Friend campaign from setup to execution.

Creating Msg for Friend (Introduction Msg)

The first step is to create an introductory message for the friends who would be referred by other friends filling out the Tell-a-Friend form.

Run `http://yourserver/taf/apps/taf_mngr.php`, which should bring up a menu interface as shown in Figure 13-3.

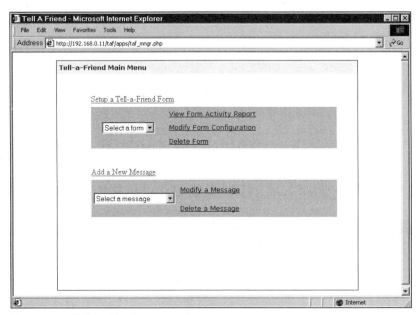

Figure 13-3: Tell-a-Friend system main menu.

Click on the Add a New Message link, which will show the screen shown in Figure 13-4.

Fill out this form and decide if you want to restrict access to this message by IP/network. For example, if you don't want anyone to modify or delete this message from somewhere else, and you have a static IP network (most offices do), you can enter the IP address of your PC or the network in the Restrict Message Setup to IP Networks field. For your convenience, your current IP address is shown on the top of the form.

Similarly, add two other messages: one for the originator who refers friends via the Tell-a-Friend form and the other for the friend who decides to subscribe by clicking on the subscription link shown by the very first message she gets from your Tell-a-Friend system.

When you have three messages set up, you're ready to set up a Tell-a-Friend form.

From the main menu, click on the Setup a Tell-a-Friend Form link, which shows a screen similar to Figure 13-5.

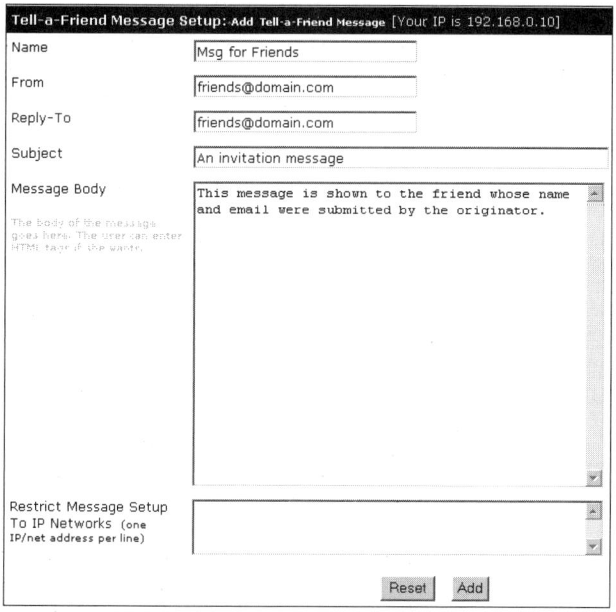

Figure 13-4: Adding the message for friends.

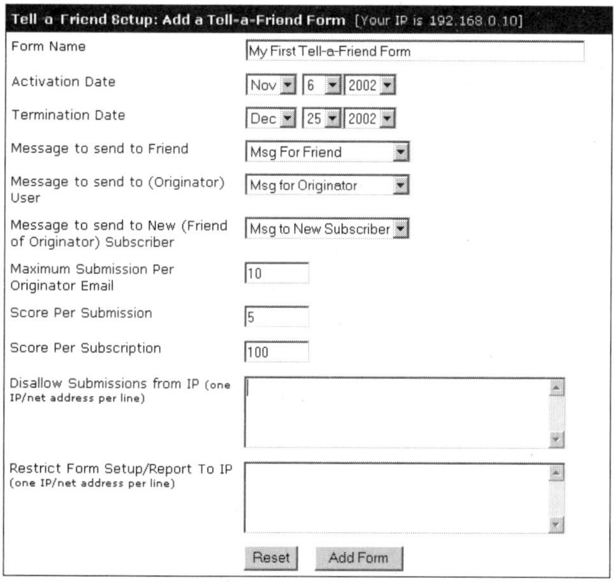

Figure 13-5: Setting up a Tell-a-Friend form.

Give a name to your form; select the date you want the data submission to be activated. This is the date when the Tell-a-Friend system will start accepting data requests for this form. Select a suitable termination date, which is when the Tell-a-Friend system will stop accepting data for this form. The termination date is very useful if you tie the Tell-a-Friend form with a limited-time promotional activity.

Select the messages that you created earlier as appropriate. Enter the maximum number of submissions (friend referrals) that a person (the originator who received your e-mail campaign message) can make. This limit is needed to protect your system against people who would try to add many friends' addresses if there is any promotion attached to the Tell-a-Friend campaign. For example, if you offered the top 100 people with the most friends submitted and/or friend subscriptions some prizes, some people would submit too many e-mail addresses.

For each submission, assign a score for the originator by setting the Score Per Submission field. This score is given to the originator every time she fills out the Tell-a-Friend form received via an e-mail campaign or other means.

Whenever a friend referred by the originator opts into become a subscriber by clicking on the subscription link in the e-mail she receives, the originator can get another score for delivering a new lead or customer. This score is set by Score Per Subscription field.

If you have any reason to disallow one or more IP address or IP networks from submitting Tell-a-Friend referrals, you can ban them using the Disallow Submissions from IP field. Enter a single IP such as 192.168.1.123 or partial IP (network address) such as 192.168 per line. If you want to restrict access to the form setup or report scripts, use the Restrict Form Setup/Report to IP field.

Click on the Add Form button and you'll see a screen similar to Figure 13-6.

Figure 13-6: Form information.

Copy the information given in the textarea box; you need this for your actual HTML Tell-a-Friend form. The form action of your HTML Tell-a-Friend form has to be exactly as shown in this screen. Also, the hidden field set stores the formid needed in your form. Each Tell-a-Friend form must include

- ◆ A valid form action that points to the Tell-a-Friend form processor application.

- ◆ A hidden field that has the formid assigned during form setup.

- ◆ An originator e-mail field. Typically, this will be a hidden field if the form is used in an e-mail campaign. It can be an input field as well if you want the user to enter his e-mail address or your e-mail campaign software cannot customize a message with e-mail fields.

I've provided two sample Tell-a-Friend forms in the `taf` directory. You can modify these forms to fit your requirements. For example, say you want to use `sample_taf_form1.html` in an e-mail campaign where the message will embed this form. In this case, you need to make sure that the following hidden field is set up correctly:

```
<input type=hidden name=origin value='nobody@domain.com '>
```

Change the value to a personalization tag that your e-mail campaign software will replace with the e-mail address of the person who is receiving the campaign. For example:

```
<input type=hidden name=origin value="{EMAIL}">
```

If your campaign software will personalize the message where `{EMAIL}` will be replaced with the e-mail address of the recipient of the campaign, then you can use this tag. For testing purposes, you can hardcode this value to your own e-mail address for now.

After you have the messages and form set up, you're ready to test the Tell-a-Friend system. Send the Tell-a-Friend form via e-mail to yourself or use your web browser to load it on your browser. Figure 13-7 is a Tell-a-Friend form received by a user as part of an e-mail campaign.

When the user fills out the form and clicks on the button to submit, she will be entering the friends into the Tell-a-Friend system. The friends she enters will receive an e-mail message that introduces the product or service to them. Such a message can look like the one shown in Figure 13-8.

Remember: This message is created using the `taf/apps/templates/taf_frnd_msg.html` file and the message body contents you entered via the message manager application.

If the friend decides to subscribe, she can click on the subscription link; or she can choose to remove herself from any mailing in the future. By default, you should never include any of the friends who do not respond either way in any future mailing.

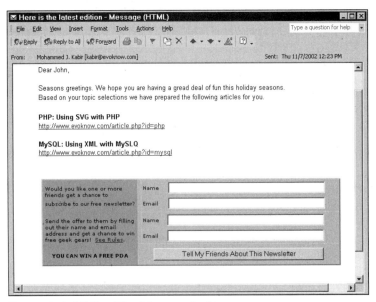

Figure 13-7: A Tell-a-Friend form received by a user.

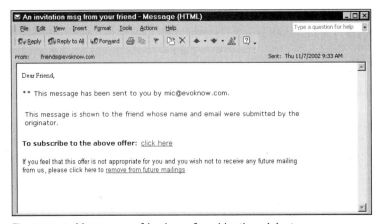

Figure 13-8: Message to a friend as referred by the originator.

If the friend decides to subscribe by clicking on the subscription link, she will get another mail confirming that she has been subscribed. This message look like what you see in Figure 13-9.

Figure 13-9: A message to friend who subscribes.

Remember: This message is created in the message body contents you entered via the message manager application.

Whenever a user (originator) submits friends via the Tell-a-Friend form, she gets a message as well. This message can look as shown in Figure 13-10.

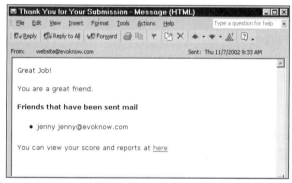

Figure 13-10: A message to the originator who referred friends.

The originator can view her score report by clicking on the appropriate link. **Remember:** This message is created using the `taf/apps/templates/ taf_orig_msg.html` file and the message body contents you entered via the message manager application.

If the originator wants to see the clicks on the link to view the score report, she'll see a screen similar to Figure 13-11.

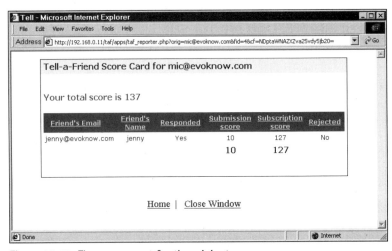

Figure 13-11: The score report for the originator.

You can also view the activity report of a Tell-a-Friend form by selecting the form from the Main Menu (`http://yourserver/taf/apps/taf_mngr.php`) and clicking on the View Form Activity Report. A sample report is shown in Figure 13-12.

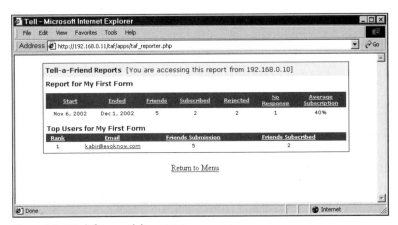

Figure 13-12: A form activity report.

As you can see, as a Tell-a-Friend system owner, you can see how many friends have been sent e-mails by the system (in the Friends column), how many subscribed (in the Subscribed column), how many rejected subscription request by unsubscribing (in the Rejected columns), and so on.

You can also see the top users who've given you new leads or possibly customers. If you use promotions such as giveaways for the top ten originators, you can simply review this report from time to time and see who your top customers are who referred you to their friends.

Security Considerations

Here we decided to allow anyone to add Tell-a-Friend forms using the `taf_form_mngr.php` application and restricted modify and delete privileges. However, you might want to restrict add form privilege to a certain list of IP addresses, in such case you have to modify the `authorize ()` method in the `taf_form_mngr.php` application.

Summary

In this chapter, you learned to develop a Tell-a-Friend system that you can use with your e-mail campaign system, whether it's in-house or outsourced via Internet service providers. This tool can increase exposures and potentially increase customers for your organization; it's widely used by both large and small companies around the world.

Chapter 14

E-mail Survey System

IN THIS CHAPTER

- ◆ Designing a survey system
- ◆ Implementing a survey system
- ◆ Testing a survey system

BEING ABLE TO SURVEY your customers frequently is an important requirement for business today. Thanks to the pervasiveness of e-mail, you can now perform most of your surveys via e-mail.

Customers provide valuable information when they participate, which benefits both the company and the customers.

In this section, you'll design a simple yet powerful survey system that can be managed by marketing personnel with a bit of HTML form knowledge. The system functionality is shown in Figure 14-1.

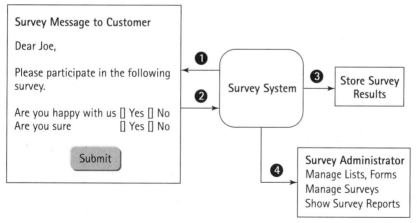

Figure 14-1: Survey system functional diagram.

A typical survey process can be described as follows:

1. The survey system sends an e-mail survey to the customer.

2. The customer fills out the survey from within the e-mail client program and submits the results by clicking on the Submit button.

3. The customer survey results are stored in the survey database.

4. The survey administrator views the compiled survey result as a report.

In the following sections, you'll develop a survey system that has the following features.

Functionality Requirements

◆ **Unlimited number of survey email (target) lists:** Supports unlimited number of survey email (target) lists. The survey administrator can create many survey target lists.

◆ **Comma-separated value (CSV) file support:** Survey target lists can be created from CSV files.

◆ **Duplicate entry protection per list:** When a list is added to the system, the system should automatically detect duplicate entries within a list and should only add one instance of any e-mail address. This will ensure that when a survey is executed no user ever gets two or more survey forms.

◆ **Unlimited number of questions:** Supports an unlimited number of questions. However, questions can be only multiple-choice or text data not exceeding the size limit used in the database. The survey must support: text data, checkboxes, radio buttons, and drop-down menu selections as answers for questions.

◆ **Personalized survey form:** Each survey form can be personalized using the survey target's first and last name.

◆ **Simple reporting:** A simple tabular report to allow the survey administrator to collect valuable insight into the customer's understanding and perception of the company.

Now let's look at the architecture of such a survey system.

Architecture of the Survey System

Figure 14-2 shows the system diagram for the survey system you're going to develop in this section.

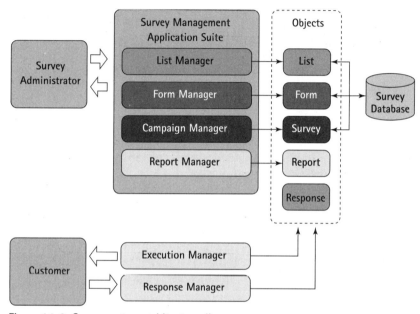

Figure 14-2: Survey system architecture diagram.

There are two types of users in the system: the survey administrator and the customers who are the survey participants. The survey system administrator user is able to perform the following tasks:

◆ **Add or delete survey target lists.** The survey administrator can add a new survey target list using the list-management component of the survey-management application suite.

◆ **Add or delete survey forms.** The survey administrator can add a new survey form that can be used in a survey campaign. A survey form is an HTML document that has all the survey questions in it. This form is sent as an e-mail to the target list and the response is collected using the response-management application.

◆ **Add or delete survey campaigns.** The survey administrator can add or delete a survey campaign. Each survey campaign consists of an existing survey form and a target list. In other words, each survey campaign can only be sent to a single target predefined target list using a predefined survey form in the system.

◆ **View survey reports.** The survey administrator can access automatically generated survey reports via the management application suite.

The customer, the survey participant, can receive a survey form via e-mail and respond to the survey questions. The result is not accessible by the customer.

As shown in Figure 14-1, there are six applications in the survey system:

◆ **List Manager:** Responsible for creating simple survey lists from comma-separated value (CSV) files that have three fields — EMAIL, FIRSTNAME, and LASTNAME — in the previously mentioned order. When a new list is added to the system, the List Manager application automatically creates one user ID per e-mail address entered into the new list from the CSV file. It automatically protects the list against duplicate entries, and it can also apply filters on all the data fields. This application also allows the user to remove existing lists from the database.

◆ **Form Manager:** This application is responsible for adding new survey forms in the system. The survey forms must follow a specific HTML form development guideline, which is specified in a later section.

◆ **Campaign Manager:** This application is responsible for creating new survey campaigns using existing survey forms and target lists. It also allows the user to delete old surveys.

◆ **Report Manager:** This application is responsible for displaying the survey response report.

◆ **Execution Manager:** This application executes a given survey by sending e-mails using the appropriate survey form to the appropriate survey target list.

◆ **Response Manager:** When a customer fills out a survey form, this application writes the survey response data to the survey database.

The system diagram also shows that all the applications use five objects: list, form, survey, report, and response. These objects are described in the "Designing and Implementing the Survey Classes" section of this chapter in detail. Before the classes providing the objects can be defined, you need to implement the database needed to support the features discussed earlier.

Designing the Database

Figure 14-3 shows the database diagram for the survey system. In the following sections, I describe each table in details.

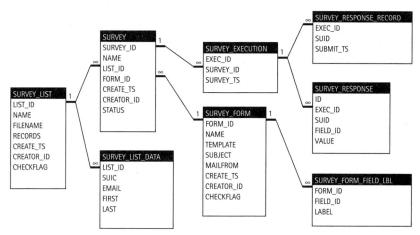

Figure 14-3: Survey system database diagram.

SURVEY Table

This table is the integral part of this database. This table holds the survey name (NAME), survey list number (LIST_ID), survey form number (FORM_ID), execution status (STATUS), survey creation time (CREATE_TS), and user ID of the user who created the survey (CREATOR_ID). The survey number (SURVEY_ID) is automatically generated by the database.

SURVEY_LIST Table

This table contains the survey list information. The survey list consists of a list number (LIST_ID), which is automatically generated when the list is created. It contains the list name (NAME), the user's uploaded data file name (FILENAME) used to create the list, the number of records (RECORDS), the survey creation time (CREATE_TS), and the user ID of the user who created the survey (CREATOR_ID).

SURVEY_LIST_DATA Table

This table holds the list data. The list is identified by the LIST_ID field from the SURVEY_LIST table. Each list contains survey user ID (SUID), e-mail address (EMAIL), first name (FIRST), and last name (LAST) fields. The FIRST and the LAST fields can be used to personalize the survey form sent out by the system. These fields are accessed in the survey form as {FIRST} and {LAST} tags.

SURVEY_FORM Table

This table holds information about the survey form that is uploaded by the user. It contains the name of the form (NAME), form template (that is, file name) name (TEMPLATE), subject (SUBJECT) of the survey, from address (MAILFROM), survey creation time (CREATE_TS), and user ID of the user who created the survey (CREATOR_ID).

The form ID (FORM_ID) is automatically generated when a new survey form is added to the system. The CHECKFLAG field is used to protect the system against multiple uploading of the same form if the user accidentally refreshes the browser during the form upload process.

SURVEY_FORM_FIELD_LBL Table

This table contains labels for questions asked in a survey form. Each survey form consists of a set of questions, which are stored in this table to allow the reporting of the collected survey data. The FORM_ID identifies a form in the SURVEY_FORM table, the FIELD_ID identifies a field in the survey form and the LABEL field holds the question or label to identify the form data.

SURVEY_EXECUTION Table

This table is used to store information about how many times each survey is executed. The EXEC_ID is automatically generated per new execution of the survey. The SURVEY_ID identifies the survey being executed, the SURVEY_TS is used to store the execution time of the survey.

SURVEY_RESPONSE Table

This table holds the survey response data per survey participant. The ID field is used to create an automatic sequence number, which is unique per row. The EXEC_ID identifies the execution number of the survey, which is identified by SURVEY_ID. The SUID field is the user ID for the participant, the FIELD_ID identifies the question, and the VALUE field stores the response data.

SURVEY_RESPONSE_RECORD Table

This table is used to control how many times a user participating in a single survey posts data. Currently, one survey response per user is allowed. The EXEC_ID identifies the survey response being recorded for a given survey, the SUID identifies the participant, and the SUBMIT_TS stores the survey response time.

The ch14/sql/survey_tool.sql file in the CDROM is an implementation of the survey database. To implement this survey database in MySQL you can create a database called SURVEY in your database server and run the following command:

```
mysql -u root -p -D SURVEY < survey_tool.sql
```

Make sure you change the user name (root) to whatever is appropriate for your system. When you have the survey database designed you need to design the PHP classes that will be needed to implement the applications. In the following sections, I discuss these classes.

Designing and Implementing the Survey Classes

As shown in the system diagram (Figure 14-2) five objects are needed to implement the survey system. Here you will develop five classes that will provide these objects for your survey applications.

Designing and implementing the Survey Class

The `Survey` class is used to manipulate each survey. It allows an application to create and delete a survey and its execution data. The `ch14/apps/class/class. Survey.php` in the CDROM is an implementation of this class. This class implements the following methods.

SURVEY()   This is the constructor method. It performs the following functions:

- Sets a member variable named `survey_tbl` to `$SURVEY_TBL`, which is loaded from the `survey.conf` file. The `$SURVEY_TBL` holds the name of the survey table.

- Sets a member variable named `survey_execution_tbl` to `$SURVEY_EXECUTION_TBL`, which is loaded from the `survey.conf` file. The `$SURVEY_EXECUTION_TBL` holds the name of the survey execution table.

- Sets a member variable named `response_tbl` to `$SURVEY_RESPONSE_TBL`, which is loaded from the `survey.conf` file. The `$SURVEY_RESPONSE_TBL` holds the name of the survey response table.

- Sets a member variable named `response_rec_tbl` to `$SURVEY_RESPONSE_RECORD_TBL`, which is loaded from the `survey.conf` file. The `$SURVEY_RESPONSE_RECORD_TBL` holds the name of the survey response record table.

- Sets a member variable named dbi to point to the `class.DBI.php`-provided object, which is passed to the constructor by an application. The dbi member variable holds the `DBI` object, which is used to communicate with the back-end database.

- Sets a member variable called `SURVEY_ID` to the given survey ID, if any.

GETSURVEYID()   This method returns the current survey ID of the `Survey` object.

SETSURVEYID()   This method sets the survey ID of the `Survey` object.

GETSTATUS()   This method returns the status (`STATUS` field) of the survey from the `SURVEY` table.

SETSTATUS()   This method updates the status (STATUS field) of the survey in the SURVEY table.

GETSURVEYINFO()   This method returns all the information about the survey from the SURVEY table.

GETLISTID()   This method returns the list ID that is used for a survey.

GETFORMID()   This method returns the form ID for a given survey.

ADDSURVEY()   This method adds a new survey into to the SURVEY table. The survey name, list ID, form ID, and the creator ID (user ID) are passed as parameters to the method.

DELETESURVEY()   This method deletes the named survey from the database. It will delete all data related to the survey from the survey database. This includes the response data as well.

DELETEEXECUTIONRECORDS()   This method deletes all execution records related to a survey.

DELETERESPONSESBYEXECID()   This method deletes all responses related to an execution of a survey.

GETEXECUTIONRECORDLIST()   This method returns the execution records for a given survey. The execution records are returned an associative array, with execution ID (EXEC_ID) being the key and the full execution record as a row object.

ADDEXECUTIONRECORD()   This method adds an execution record for a given survey in the SURVEY_EXECUTION table and returns the newly created EXEC_ID for the survey.

   The method first inserts the new execution record in the SURVEY_EXECUTION table and then selects the EXEC_ID from the same table.

GETAVAILABLESURVEYS()   This method returns a list of available surveys in the database. It returns an associative array, which uses the SURVEY_ID as the key and survey name (NAME) as the value.

GETRETURNVALUE()   This is a utility method that returns TRUE if the DBI returned result is set to DB_OK, which notifies that the SQL operation was successful; otherwise, it returns FALSE.

Designing and implementing the SurveyList Class

This class provides the survey List object. The List object is used to manipulate survey lists. It allows an application to create and delete survey lists. Survey lists are created from external comma-separated value (CSV) files that are uploaded by the survey administrator. The ch14/apps/class/class.SurveyList.php file in the CDROM is an implementation of this class. I will discuss the methods available in this class.

SURVEYLIST( )   This is the constructor method, which performs the following tasks:

◆ Sets a member variable called `list_tbl` to `$SURVEY_LIST_TBL`, which is loaded from the `survey.conf` file. The `$SURVEY_LIST_TBL` variable holds the name of the survey list table.

◆ Sets a member variable called `list_data_tbl` to `$SURVEY_LIST_DATA_TBL`, which is loaded from the `survey.conf` file. The `$SURVEY_LIST_DATA_TBL` variable holds the name of the list data table.

◆ Sets a member variable named `dbi` to point to the `class.DBI.php`-provided object, which is passed to the constructor by an application. The `dbi` member variable holds the `DBI` object, which is used to communicate with the back-end database.

◆ This method calls the `setSurveyListID( )` method to set the list ID of the object.

SETSURVEYLISTID( )   This method sets the survey list ID. If the list ID is provided as a parameter, it is set as the object's list ID; otherwise, the current list ID is returned.

SETRETURNVALUE( )   This is a utility method that returns `TRUE` if the DBI returned result is set to `DB_OK`, which notifies that the SQL operation was successful; otherwise, it returns `FALSE`.

ADDNEWSURVEYLIST( )   This method creates a list using user uploaded CSV data. The method does the following:

◆ Creates a unique check flag called `$checkflag` using the user's ID (`$uid`) and current time stamp (`$today`) supplied from the calling application.

◆ It then inserts a new row in the survey list (`SURVEY_LIST`) table and gets the newly created list id (`LIST_ID`), which is needed to insert the list data in the list data table (`SURVEY_LIST_DATA`).

◆ For each line in the user uploaded file, it creates a record set consisting of `$email` (`EMAIL`), `$fname` (`FIRST`), and `$lname` (`LAST`) fields.

◆ If the filter options are enabled for filtering the name fields (`FIRST`, `LAST`) and/or the e-mail field (`EMAIL`), the method applies fields. Currently, the name fields are filtered such that each word in a name is first lower-cased and then only the first character is uppercased. The e-mail field is lowercased.

◆ The filtered (or not filtered) data is then inserted into the list data table (SURVEY_LIST_DATA).

◆ When all data is inserted, the RECORDS field in the list table (SURVEY_LIST) is updated to reflect the data inserted in the list table.

GETTOTALRECORDCOUNT()   This method returns the total record count for a given list. In other words, it returns the number of survey recipients in a list.

 Since the EMAIL address is unique in the list table per list, each list can only contain a single instance of an e-mail address. This ensures that a survey is not sent to the same user twice from the same execution of the survey.

GETAVAILABLELISTS()   This method returns a list of available survey lists in the database. The returned list is an array, which is indexed with LIST_ID, and the value of each element is the corresponding name of the list.

DELETELIST()   This method removes a list from the database.

GETTARGETDATA()   This method returns a list of records from the survey list data table (SURVEY_LIST_DATA) using LIST_ID. It limits the returned list of records using SUID and delivery chunk size stored in the survey.conf file.

In other words, this method returns a list of records as an associative array, which has SUID as key and row object per record as value. The returned record set is limited by the SUID and specified record size ($deliverySize).

For example, to get a list of 100 records that have SUID greater than 5,000 from the SURVEY_LIST_DATA, you can call this method as follows:

```
$surveyListObject->getTargetData(5000, 100);
```

Designing and implementing the SurveyForm Class

This class provides the survey Form object. The survey form object is used to manipulate survey form data. Applications can add or remove survey forms using the survey Form object. The methods provided by the class are discussed below. The ch14/apps/class/class.SurveyForm.php file in the CDROM is an implementation of this class

SURVEYFORM()   This is the constructor method, which creates the survey form object. This method sets member variables survey_form_tbl to $SURVEY_FORM, survey_form_field_tbl to $SURVEY_FORM_FIELD_LBL_TBL, dbi to $dbi and fid to $fid.

SETSURVEYFORMID()   This method sets the survey form ID.

SETRETURNVALUE()   This is an utility method that returns NULL if the passed parameter is null else returns the value passed to it.

ADDNEWSURVEYFORM()   This method adds a new survey form in the database. It inserts the survey form information in the SURVEY_FORM after making sure text data is properly quoted. Then it returns the new form's FORM_ID from the database.

GETAVAILABLEFORMS()   This method returns a list of all available forms in the SURVEY_FORM in an associative array, which has FORM_ID as the index and form name (NAME) as the value.

DELETEFORM()   This method deletes a form with the given FORM_ID from the SURVEY_FORM.

ADDLABEL()   This method inserts a field label for a given form field in a given form.

GETTEMPLATE()   This method returns the form template (TEMPALTE) from the SURVEY_FORM for a form with the given FORM_ID field.

GETFORMINFO()   This method returns the NAME, TEMPLATE, MAILFROM, SUBJECT, CREATE_TS, and CREATOR_ID fields of a form with given FORM_ID. If the given form is not found in the SURVEY_FORM, the method returns FALSE.

Designing and implementing the SurveyResponse Class

This class provides the survey form Response object, which is used to manipulate the survey response. An application can use the survey Response object to add a new response or check whether a user has already submitted a survey or not. The methods in this class are discussed in the following sections. The ch14/apps/class/class.SurveyResponse.php file in the CDROM is an implementation of this class.

SURVEYRESPONSE() This is the construtor method used to create the SurveyResponse object. It initializes member variables: dbi to $dbi, survey_id to $sid, form_id to $fid, response_tbl to $SURVEY_RESPONSE_TBL and response_rec_tbl to $SURVEY_RESPONSE_RECORD_TBL.

ISSUBMITTED() This method returns TRUE if a given user has already submitted her response for a given survey. It performs a SELECT query for the given run of the survey ($EXEC_ID) using the user's ID ($SUID) in the SURVEY_RESPONSE_RECORD. If a row is found in the user's table, she has already responded, and the query returns TRUE, otherwise it returns FALSE.

ADDSUBMITRECORD()   This method adds a submission record in the SURVEY_ RESPONSE_RECORD table for a given run ($EXEC_ID) of a survey for a given user ID ($SUID). The method returns TRUE if the submission record is added successfully else it returns FALSE.

ADD()   This method adds survey response data for a given survey run ($EXEC_ID) for a given user ($SUID).

Designing and implementing the SurveyReport Class

This class provides the survey Report object. Using the survey Report object, an application can perform queries on survey response data stored in the database. The following methods are needed to implement the class, which can be found in the ch14/apps/class/class.SurveyReport.php file in the CDROM.

SURVEYREPORT()   This is the constructor method that is used to create the SurveyReport object. It initializes member variables: dbi to $dbi, execid to execid, response_tbl to $SURVEY_RESPONSE_TBL, execution_tbl to $SURVEY_ EXECUTION_TBL, survey_tbl to $SURVEY_TBL, survey_response_rec_tbl to $SURVEY_RESPONSE_RECORD_TBL, form_field_tbl to $SURVEY_FORM_FIELD_ LBL_TBL

SETSURVEYEXECID()   This method sets the survey execution (i.e. run) ID.

GETSURVEYRESPONSE()   This method returns the responses for a given survey execution in an array.

GETRESPONSEDATERANGE()   This method returns the start and the last date of recorded response for a given survey execution.

GETTOTALRESPONSECOUNT()   This method returns the total responses for a given survey run.

GETLABELSBYFIELDANDEXECID()   This method returns the field label for a given field ID of a survey.

Designing and Implementing the Survey Applications

According to the system diagram shown in Figure 14-2, the survey system consists of six applications, which are discussed in the following sections.

Developing Survey Manager

This application is responsible for displaying the administrative menu to manage the survey application suite. It allows the survey administrator user to add and delete surveys. The ch14/apps/survey_mngr.php file in the CDROM is an implementation of a survey manager.

As usual, this application extends the PHPApplication class to create the surveyMngr class, which has the following four methods.

run()

This method overrides the run() method provided by the PHPApplication class as required by the application framework. It performs the following tasks:

◆ Uses the check_session() method to see if the user has an authenticated session. If not, the user is redirected to the authentication application.

◆ If the user is authenticated, it then checks to see if the user has authorization to access this application. This check is done using the authorize() method, which is also overridden in this application to replace the empty (abstract) one provided by the PHPApplication class.

◆ A global variable called $cmd is used to control how business logic is chosen in this application. This variable is set automatically by PHP when cmd=*command* is passed from the interface. The acceptable command values are create or delete.

◆ When both authentication and authorization checks pass the global variable, $cmd is used to implement a select business logic selection driver. If the $cmd is set to create, the createSurveyDriver() method is called to handle the survey creation process. If the $cmd variable is set to delete, the delSurvey() method is called to handle the survey deletion process. Otherwise, the displayMenu() method is called to load the survey management menu.

createSurveyDriver()

When the global variable $cmd is set to create from the GUI, the application runs this method. This method uses another global variable called $step to determine the appropriate step for the survey creation process.

When a user first enters the survey creation process, the $step is not set in the GUI and, therefore, the method runs the displayMenu() method with the appropriate interface template ($SURVEY_ADD_TEMPLATE). The displayMenu() method loads the survey add interface. This interface has a hidden field called step, which is set to 2 to indicate that the next time createSurveyDriver() is called it should call the saveSurvey() method.

delSurvey( )

This method is called when the run( ) method is passed $cmd='delete' from the user interface. This method uses the deleteSurvey( ) method of a Survey object to delete the chosen survey (indicated by $survey_id, which is also passed from user interface).

saveSurvey( )

This method saves a new survey with the data given from the survey add interface. It uses the addSurvey( ) method of a Survey object to perform the actual add survey operation.

The method displays a status message based on the success or failure of the add operation.

displayMenu( )

This method displays a user interface. It can display either the survey management menu interface or the survey add interface.

When this method is called from the run( ) method, it displays the survey menu interface ($SURVEY_MENU_TEMPLATE) and when it is called from the create SurveyDriver( ) it displays the survey add interface ($SURVEY_ADD_TEMPLATE).

authorize( )

This method is responsible for authorizing the user to run the application. In this version, this method always returns TRUE. If you want to implement a user-level access control for the survey management application, you'll have to change the current implementation of the authorize( ) method. For example, if you want to allow only a known group of users to administer surveys, you can store their user ID in a new table within the survey database and perform a query to see if the current user is a member of such a group.

Developing Survey List Manager

This application is responsible for managing the survey list. It performs the following tasks:

- Allows the user to add a new list from a CSV file. The user uploads a CSV file via the Web interface and assigns it a list name.

- Allows the user to delete an existing list.

- The ch14/apps/survey_list_mngr.php file in the CDROM is an implementation of the Survey List Manager application. This application creates an instance of the PHPApplication class and uses the following methods.

run( )

The run method performs the usual checks for authenticated and authorized users and then uses the global $cmd variable to select either the addDriver( ) or the delList( ) method. The value of the $cmd is set in the user interface displayed by the Survey Manager application. If the $cmd variable is set to upload or empty the addDriver() method is called to add a new list. If the $cmd variable is set to anything else, the delList() method is called to delete a list.

addDriver()

This method uses a global variable called $step to determine which phase of the add list process the user is currently at and selects the next step in the process.

For example, if the $step variable is empty, the first step in the add list process is assumed and the displayAddListMenu() method is called to display the add list interface.

If the $step value is anything but empty, the addList() method is called to add the list in the database.

authorize()

See the authorize() method in the "Developing Survey Manager" section in this chapter for details.

displayAddListMenu()

This method displays the add list interface. The interface HTML file name is retrieved from the survey.conf file using the $SURVEY_ADD_LIST_TEMPLATE variable.

The current time stamp is embedded in the add list interface as a hidden field called today to ensure that the user cannot enter the same list multiple times. Because there is no accidental way for the user to generate the same time stamp in submitting multiple lists, this field serves as the unique flag associated with the list in the database.

delList()

This method is used to delete a chosen list. The chosen list is identified using a global variable called $list_id, which is passed to the application via the user interface as part of the request.

The actual delete operation is implemented using the deleteList() method found in the SurveyList object.

The delList() method displays a success or failure status message based on the status of the delete operation.

addList()

This method adds a list, for which data has been collected via the displayAddList Menu() method. This method performs the following tasks:

◆ It first checks to see if the upload has been successful and if the list name is given. If any of these checks fails, the method returns an error message.

- It then copies the uploaded file in the list upload directory pointed by the $UPLOAD_DIR variable found in survey.conf file.

- Next it creates a SurveyList object and uses the addNewSurveyList() method to add all records in the uploaded CSV file in the new list.

- Finally, it displays a status message stating the success or failure of the list upload.

Developing Survey Form Manager

This application is responsible for managing survey forms. It allows the user to add or delete survey forms. The following methods are implemented in this application, which can be found in ch14/apps/survey_form_mngr.php file in the CDROM.

run()

The run method performs the usual checks for authenticated and authorized users and then uses the global $cmd variable to select either the addDriver() or the delForm() method. The value of the $cmd is set in the user interface displayed by the Survey Manager application. If the $cmd variable is set to anything other than delete or empty, then the addDriver() method is called to add a new survey form. Otherwise, the delForm() method is called to delete an existing survey form.

addDriver()

Using a global variable $step, which is set in the user interface, this method controls the add survey form process.
When the $step variable is empty, the displayAddFormMenu() method is called to display the initial add form interface, which collects the form data.

The next time the $step variable is set to 2 in the initial form data entry interface displayed by displayAddFormMenu(), the addForm() method is called.

Finally, the addDriver() method calls the addLabels() method to collect data about the question labels in Step 3.

authorize()

See the authorize() method in the "Developing Survey Manager" section for details.

displayAddFormMenu()

This method displays the add form interface. The interface HTML file name is retrieved from the survey.conf file using the $SURVEY_ADD_FORM_TEMPLATE variable.

addForm()

This method adds the uploaded form to the survey system using the following steps:

◆ Checks to see if the user has entered the required subject ($subject) and from address ($from) fields.

◆ Checks to see if the form is uploaded or the form name ($formname) is empty.

◆ Checks to see if the user has entered the number of questions ($num_fields) data.

◆ If all of the preceding checks passes, the uploaded file is copied into the forms directory from the $UPLOAD_DIR (set in survey.conf) and renamed with the .ihtml extension.

◆ A SurveyForm object is created and its addNewSurveyForm() method is called to create the form data in the database.

◆ Next, the addForm() method calls the takeFormLabels() method to display the label entry page for each questions unless the survey form could not be added to the database. In case of insert failure, a status message is displayed to notify the user.

takeFormLabels()

This method displays the interface to collect the question labels. It shows text entry boxes per question so that the user can define question labels that are needed to display the survey report.

addLabels()

This method adds the question labels entered in the interface displayed by the takeFormLabels() method. The labels are added using the addLabel() method of the SurveyForm object.

A status message is displayed to notify the status of the label addition in the database.

delForm()

This method deletes a survey form from the database. The form ID is selected from the interface shown by the Survey Manager interface.

The actual delete operation is implemented using the SurveyForm object's deleteForm() method.

Developing Survey Execution Manager

This application executes a survey. Because this execution of each survey is done via the Web, it's important that this application doesn't run continuously until the survey finishes. Because web browsers can mistake the long time it takes to process large campaigns as a timeout, I've implemented this method such that it will execute a set of records in the given campaign and then create an automatic refresh using meta tags in HTML interface to call itself back after a configurable period of time.

This allows the application to continue with small interruptions and also allows it to report the status of the campaign using a status message after each chunk of records has been processed for e-mail delivery. Therefore, the base algorithm of this method can be written in the following pseudo code:

```
Get Last Record Executed
If No Last Record then
BEGIN
  Set LastRecord = 0
END

Get a Chunk of Records > Last Record
       Ordered by Record ID (SUID) AND
       Limit By Maxmimum Records
       Per Run

Get Message Template

For Each Record in Current Record List
BEGIN
  Process for Mail using a Copy of the Message Template
  Send Mail
END

Set LastRecord in Database to Current Last Record

Set Refresh Meta Tag

Terminate
```

The ch14/apps/survey_exec_mngr.php file in the CDROM implements this application. This application has the following methods.

run()

The run method performs the usual checks for authenticated and authorized users and then calls the executeSurvey() method to run the survey.

executeSurvey()

This method executes the chosen campaign. It works as follows:

♦ First it checks to see if the user has chosen a survey ID ($survey_id) or not. If not, it displays an error message and exits.

♦ If the survey ID is found, the method then creates a Survey object using the given survey ID ($survey_id) and gets the details of the survey using the getSurveyInfo() method. The STATUS field of the survey is stored in the $status variable. If the given survey does not exist in the database, the method exists with an error message.

♦ When the survey information is located, the method determines if this was being called before. If it was called before, the $lastrow information is set to the last row processed for this campaign.

♦ If the $lastrow is empty then the executeSurvey() method creates an execution record in the SURVEY_EXECUTION table using the addExecution Record() method of the Survey object. This record is used to identify that the current survey was executed at the current time. The newly created execution record ID (EXEC_ID) is returned by the addExecutionRecord() method, and it is used as a hidden field within the survey form to allow the survey response manager to identify which survey execution the user is responding to.

♦ Using the $lastrow and maximum delivery per run ($MAX_DELIVERY_ AT_A_TIME) value, the getTargetData() method is used to get the list of target records for the current run of the executeSurvey() method.

♦ The survey form is loaded into an HTML template, and it is personalized per the survey recipient and sent via e-mail.

♦ Once the current set of records is processed and delivered, a status message is displayed on the screen using an HTML template. This template has a meta tag to refresh the screen automatically after $MAX_WAIT_PER_DELIVERY delay, which is configurable form the survey.conf file.

♦ The application is automatically called from the status message page and it restarts the entire process automatically and starts exactly where it left off. This allows the application to run large campaigns without having to deal with web browser timeout.

authorize()

See the authorize() method in the "Developing Survey Manager" section for details.

Developing Survey Response Manager

This application is responsible for submitting survey responses to the survey database. When an end user who received a survey via e-mail clicks on the Submit button, this application is called and it stores the result in the database. The ch14/ apps/survey.php file in the CDROM implements this application, which uses the following methods.

run( )

The `run` method performs the usual checks for authenticated and authorized users and then calls the `addRecord()` method to add the survey response.

addRecord( )

This method is responsible for adding the response record in the database. It works as follows:

♦ A `SurveyResponse` object is created with the user ID (`$SUID`) and survey execution ID (`$EXEC_ID`) that are collected from the submitted survey response. Note that the values are supplied as hidden data when the survey form is mailed out.

♦ After the `SurveyResponse` object is created, the `isSubmitted()` method is called to see if this participant has already submitted this particular survey response or not. If she has submitted a response for this particular execution of the survey, a status message is shown to inform her that the survey has already been submitted earlier. No data is added to the database.

♦ On the other hand, if this is the first time she is submitting the response data, the `addSubmitRecord()` is used to create a submission record for this survey execution in the `SURVEY_RESPONSE_RECORD` table.

♦ Then the response data is added to the appropriate table (`SURVEY_RESPONSE`) using the `add()` method for the `SurveyResponse` object.

Developing Survey Report Manager

This application displays the survey report. The `ch14/apps/survey_rpt_mngr.php` file in the CDROM is an implementation of this application. It uses the following methods.

run( )

The `run` method performs the usual checks for authenticated and authorized user and then calls the `showSurveyReport()` method to display the survey report.

showSurveyReport( )

This method shows the survey report. It works as follows:

♦ First, it checks to see if the user chose the survey's execution ID (`$exec_id`) from the Survey Manager interface. The execution ID is used to create the report.

♦ A report template is loaded and a `SurveyReport` object is created.

♦ The report column ordering is set using the `$orderid` field, which is stored in the report column heading.

- ◆ Using the SurveyReport object's getSurveyResponse() method, a list of responses are retrieved from the database for the chosen execution of the survey.

- ◆ Each response is then displayed.

- ◆ The getResponseDateRage() and getTotalResponseCount() methods are used to display the range of date and the total response record count.

toggleDescField()

This is a utility method that toggles the DESC value from desc to null. The DESC value is used in creating ascending or descending order for the displayed columns in the report table.

authorize()

See the authorize() method in the "Developing Survey Manager" section for details.

Setting Up the Central Survey Configuration File

Each of the applications in the survey system uses a central configuration file called survey.conf, which is shown in Listing 14-1.

Listing 14-1: survey.conf

```php
<?php

    error_reporting(E_ALL);

    $PEAR_DIR          = $_SERVER['DOCUMENT_ROOT'] . '/pear' ;
    $PHPLIB_DIR        = $_SERVER['DOCUMENT_ROOT'] . '/phplib';
    $APP_FRAMEWORK_DIR = $_SERVER['DOCUMENT_ROOT'] . '/framework';
    $PATH              = $PEAR_DIR . ':' . $PHPLIB_DIR . ':' .
$APP_FRAMEWORK_DIR;

    ini_set( 'include_path', ':' . $PATH . ':' . ini_get('include_path'));

    $AUTHENTICATION_URL = "/login/login.php";
    $LOGOUT_URL         = "/logout/logout.php";

    $APPLICATION_NAME  = 'SURVEY';
    $XMAILER_ID        = 'Survey System Version 1.0';
    $DEFAULT_LANGUAGE  = 'US';
```

Continued

Listing 14-1 *(Continued)*

```
$ROOT_PATH            = $_SERVER['DOCUMENT_ROOT'];
$REL_ROOT_PATH        = '/survey_tool';
$REL_APP_PATH         =  $REL_ROOT_PATH . '/apps';

$REL_FORMS_DIR        = $REL_ROOT_PATH . '/forms';
$UPLOAD_DIR           = $ROOT_PATH      . $REL_ROOT_PATH . '/uploads';
$FORMS_DIR            = $ROOT_PATH      . $REL_FORMS_DIR;

$TEMPLATE_DIR         = $ROOT_PATH      . $REL_APP_PATH . '/templates';
$CLASS_DIR            = $ROOT_PATH      . $REL_APP_PATH . '/class';

//Classes
$SURVEY_LIST_CLASS     = $CLASS_DIR . '/' . 'class.SurveyList.php';
$SURVEY_FORM_CLASS     = $CLASS_DIR . '/' . 'class.SurveyForm.php';
$SURVEY_CLASS          = $CLASS_DIR . '/' . 'class.Survey.php';
$SURVEY_RESPONSE_CLASS = $CLASS_DIR . '/' . 'class.SurveyResponse.php';
$SURVEY_REPORT_CLASS   = $CLASS_DIR . '/' . 'class.SurveyReport.php';


require_once "survey.errors";
require_once "survey.messages";
require_once 'DB.php';
require_once $APP_FRAMEWORK_DIR . '/' . 'constants.php';
require_once $APP_FRAMEWORK_DIR . '/' . $APPLICATION_CLASS;
require_once $APP_FRAMEWORK_DIR . '/' . $ERROR_HANDLER_CLASS;
require_once $APP_FRAMEWORK_DIR . '/' . $AUTHENTICATION_CLASS;
require_once $APP_FRAMEWORK_DIR . '/' . $DBI_CLASS;
require_once $TEMPLATE_CLASS;

// Application names

$SURVEY_MNGR          =  'survey_mngr.php';
$SURVEY_FORM_MNGR     =  'survey_form_mngr.php';
$SURVEY_LIST_MNGR     =  'survey_list_mngr.php';
$SURVEY_RPT_MNGR      =  'survey_rpt_mngr.php';
$SURVEY_EXEC_MNGR     =  'survey_exec_mngr.php';
$SURVEY_RESPONSE_MNGR =  'survey.php';

$SURVEY_CLASS       = $CLASS_DIR . '/class.Survey.php';
$REL_TEMPLATE_DIR   = $REL_APP_PATH . '/templates/';

$SURVEY_DB_URL        = 'mysql://root:foobar@localhost/SURVEY';
$MAX_DELIVERY_AT_A_TIME = 1;
```

```
    $MAX_WAIT_PER_DELIVERY   = 5;


    /*  -------------START TABLE NAMES -------------------- */


    $SURVEY_TBL                 = 'SURVEY';
    $SURVEY_LIST_TBL            = 'SURVEY_LIST';
    $SURVEY_LIST_DATA_TBL       = 'SURVEY_LIST_DATA';
    $SURVEY_FORM_TBL            = 'SURVEY_FORM';
    $SURVEY_RESPONSE_TBL        = 'SURVEY_RESPONSE';
    $SURVEY_FORM_FIELD_LBL_TBL  = 'SURVEY_FORM_FIELD_LBL';
    $SURVEY_RESPONSE_RECORD_TBL = 'SURVEY_RESPONSE_RECORD';
    $SURVEY_EXECUTION_TBL       = 'SURVEY_EXECUTION';



    /*  -------------END TABLE NAMES -------------------- */


    $STATUS_TEMPLATE            = 'survey_status.ihtml';
    $SURVEY_MENU_TEMPLATE       = 'survey_menu.ihtml';

    $SURVEY_ADD_LIST_TEMPLATE   = 'survey_add_list.ihtml';
    $SURVEY_ADD_FORM_TEMPLATE   = 'survey_add_form.ihtml';

    $SURVEY_ADD_LABEL_TEMPLATE  = 'survey_add_label.ihtml';

    $SURVEY_ADD_TEMPLATE        = 'survey_add.ihtml';
    $SURVEY_EXECUTION_TEMPLATE  = 'survey_execute.ihtml';

    $SURVEY_REPORT_TEMPLATE     = 'survey_report.ihtml';
    $SURVEY_POWERED_BY_TEMPLATE = 'powered_by.html';

    /* -------------------- REPORT --------------------*/
    $REPORT_EVEN_ROW_COLOR = '#ffccff';
    $REPORT_ODD_ROW_COLOR  = '#ccccff';
?>
```

For the preceding sample configuration file, the directory structure is shown here:

```
htdocs ($ROOT_PATH = %DocumentRoot%)
 |
+--survey_tool
   |
   +---uploads
```

Continued

Listing 14-1 *(Continued)*

```
|
+---forms
|
+---apps
    |
    +---class
    |
    +---templates
        |
        +---images
```

To configure the applications for your directory structure, you'll have to change the settings shown in Table 14-1.

TABLE 14-1 THE survey.conf SETTINGS THAT YOU NEED TO CHANGE

Fields	Explanation
$PEAR_DIR	This should be set to the directory where you have installed the PEAR packages. This is needed because the DB class needed for class.DBI.php is part of the PEAR packages.
$PHPLIB_DIR	This should be set to the directory where the PHPLIB packages are stored. This is needed because the Template class (template.inc) is part of the PHPLIB packages.
$APP_FRAMEWORK_DIR	This directory should point to our application framework class directory.
$AUTHENTICATION_URL	This URL should point the central authentication application (login.php), which is part of the application framework.
$LOGOUT_URL	This URL should point to the central logout application (logout.php), which is part of the application framework.
$ROOT_PATH	This directory point to the document root directory of your Web site where you host this application.
$REL_ROOT_PATH	This should point to the relative path, which is the parent of the apps directory.

Fields	Explanation
$SURVEY_DB_URL	This URL should be configured to allow you to connect to the survey database via the named host using the named user name and password.
$MAX_DELIVERY_AT_A_TIME	This should be set to the maximum number of e-mail deliveries per run by the Survey Execution Manager. You should not set this number to a very large number.
$MAX_WAIT_PER_DELIVERY	This number sets how many seconds are past before the Survey Execution Manager is recalled via the meta refresh tag.

Setting Up the Interface Template Files

The applications use a number of template files that are provided in the ch14/apps/templates directory in the CD-ROM. These files are discussed in Table 14-2.

TABLE 14-2 INTERFACE TEMPLATES

File Name	Purpose
survey_menu.ihtml	This is the Survey Menu template.
survey_add.ihtml	This template is used to add surveys.
survey_add_form.ihtml	This template is used to add survey forms.
survey_add_label.ihtml	This template is used to add survey form labels.
survey_add_list.ihtml	This template is used for adding survey lists.
survey_execute.ihtml	This template is used for executing a survey. It shows the execution status information.
survey_report.ihtml	This template is used for showing the survey report.
survey_status.ihtml	This template is used to show status messages. This template is used by the PHPApplication's show_status() method.
powered_by.html	This HTML file contains the footer that is added to the survey sent to the end user.

These templates also use images that are stored in an image directory called images within the template directory pointed by the $TEMPLATE_DIR variable in the survey.conf file.

Setting Up the Central Survey Messages File

All the applications in the survey suite use a central messages file called survey.messages, which is shown in Listing 14-2.

Listing 14-2: survey.messages

```php
<?php

   $MESSAGES['US']['LIST_DELETE_SUCCESSFUL']     = "List deleted.";
   $MESSAGES['US']['LIST_DELETE_FAILED']         = "List not deleted.";
   $MESSAGES['US']['LIST_UPLOAD_SUCCESSFUL']     = "List upload successful.";
   $MESSAGES['US']['LIST_UPLOAD_FAILED']         = "List upload failed.";
   $MESSAGES['US']['FORM_UPLOAD_SUCCESSFUL']     = "Form upload successful.";
   $MESSAGES['US']['FORM_UPLOAD_FAILED']         = "Form upload failed.";
   $MESSAGES['US']['FORM_DELETED']               = "Form deleted.";
   $MESSAGES['US']['FORM_NOT_DELETED']           = "Form not deleted.";
   $MESSAGES['US']['SURVEY_ADD_FAILED']          = "Survey not added.";
   $MESSAGES['US']['SURVEY_ADD_SUCCESSFUL']      = "Survey added.";
   $MESSAGES['US']['SURVEY_DELETE_SUCCESSFUL']   = "Survey deleted.";
   $MESSAGES['US']['SURVEY_DELETE_FAILED']       = "Survey not deleted.";
   $MESSAGES['US']['SURVEY_SENT']                = "Survey sent.";

?>
```

The default language of the messages is set in the survey.conf file using the $DEFAULT_LANGUAGE parameter. If you want to port this application to a different language, copy the above messages at the end of this file and change US to your two-digit language name and replace the English error messages with the appropriate translation.

 TIP   Google has a translation tool that can be used to translate simple messages to other languages such as Spanish, Italian, German, and so on. See www.google.com for details.

Setting Up the Central Survey Errors File

Like the central messages file, all the applications in the survey system use the survey.errors file for error messages, as shown in Listing 14-3.

Listing 14-3: survey.errors

```php
<?php

  // Errors for survey apps

  $ERRORS['US']['APP_FAILURE']                    = "Application failure";
  $ERRORS['US']['ADD_SURVEY_LIST_REQ_MISSING'] = "Please enter list and file
name";
  $ERRORS['US']['ADD_SURVEY_FORM_REQ_MISSING'] = "Please enter form and file
name";
  $ERRORS['US']['IHTML_REQUIRED']                = "IHTML file expected";
  $ERRORS['US']['FIELD_NUM_INVALID']             = "Number of fields has to be a
number greater than zero";
  $ERRORS['US']['LIST_NO_LIST_CHOSEN']           = "Please select a list.";
  $ERRORS['US']['FORM_NOT_SELECTED']             = "Please select a form.";
  $ERRORS['US']['ADD_SURVEY_NAME_MISSING']       = "Please enter a survey name.";
  $ERRORS['US']['ADD_SURVEY_LIST_MISSING']       = "Please select a survey list.";
  $ERRORS['US']['ADD_SURVEY_FORM_MISSING']       = "Please select a survey form.";
  $ERRORS['US']['DEL_SURVEY_ID_MISSING']         = "Please select a survey.";
  $ERRORS['US']['RUN_SURVEY_ID_MISSING']         = "Please select a survey.";
  $ERRORS['US']['ADD_FORM_MISSING_SUBJECT']      = "Please enter a subject line.";
  $ERRORS['US']['ADD_FORM_MISSING_FROM']         = "Please enter a from address.";
  $ERRORS['US']['SURVEY_EXECUTION FAILED']       = "Survey execution failed.";
  $ERRORS['US']['SURVEY_ALREADY_SUBMITTED']      = "Survey already submitted.";
  $ERRORS['US']['SURVEY_SUBMITTED']              = "Survey submitted. \\n\\nThank
you.";
  $ERRORS['US']['REPORT_NOT_SELECTED']           = "Please select a report.";

?>
```

Creating Survey Forms

The survey forms that are used in the survey system are HTML files that have a few specific requirements. They are listed here:

◆ Form action value should be set to {SERVER_URL}{APP_PATH}/
{SURVEY_RESPONSE} as shown here:

```
<form action="{SERVER_URL}{APP_PATH}/{SURVEY_RESPONSE}">
```

◆ The form must contain the mainBlock comments as shown here:

```
<!-- BEGIN mainBlock -->
 Your form data goes here
<!-- ENDBEGIN mainBlock -->
```

◆ You can only personalize the form using the {FIRST} and {LAST} tags.

◆ Each field in the HTML form must be named using numbers.

◆ Each question can be either a text box (the maximum size is limited by the database, currently set to 50 characters), a checkbox, a radio button, or a drop-down select list.

◆ A set of hidden fields are a must to allow proper handing of the form. These fields are shown here:

```
<input type=hidden name="SURVEY_ID" value="{SURVEY_ID}">
<input type=hidden name="SUID" value="{SUID}">
<input type=hidden name="EXEC_ID" value="{EXEC_ID}">
<input type=hidden name="EXEC_TS" value="{EXEC_TS}">
```

A sample form is available in ch14/forms directory in the CDROM.

The {POWERED_BY_LOGO} tag is optional.

Testing the Survey System

When you've configured the application using survey.conf and installed it per the configuration under your web server's document root, you can test the system.

To test the system you need to create a CSV file with the following format:

```
EMAIL, FIRST, LAST
```

A sample CSV file called mycustomers.csv is shown in Listing 14-4.

Listing 14-4: mycustomers.csv

```
KABIR@evoknow.com,MOHAMMED,KABIR
joe@evoknow.COM,Joe,Gunchy
jennifer@evoknow.com,JENNIFER,GUNCHY
abe@EVOKNOW.COM,ABE,NONE
rome@EvoKnow.Com,rome,ahead
```

Notice that this list has badly formatted e-mails and names. Because the List Manager can filter name and e-mail for case issues, you can fix these during list creation.

In the following section, I assume that you'll use the preceding list and the sample survey form (`ch14/forms/sample_form.html` file in the CDROM) to test your installation as follows:

1. Run the `survey_mngr.php` application using the appropriate URL. For the given `survey.conf` file used by my system this URL is `http://php.evoknow.com/phpbook/survey_tool/apps/survey_mngr.php`.

   When this URL is requested, the application automatically detects that is not an authenticated user session and redirects the user to the login application. When the user supplies the appropriate user name/password pair, she is logged in to the application and the Survey Manager menu is displayed (Figure 14-4).

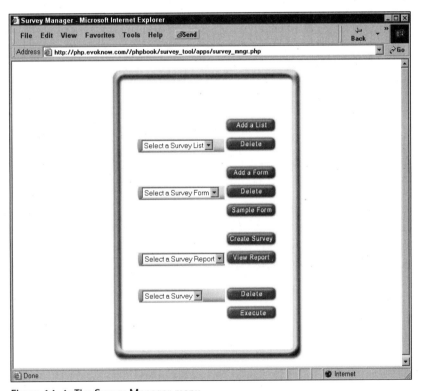

Figure 14-4: The Survey Manager menu.

2. To add a new list, click on the Add a List button, which shows the add list interface as shown in Figure 14-5.

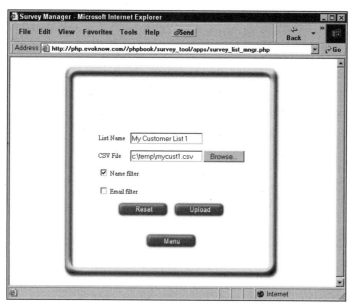

Figure 14-5: Adding a survey list.

3. Enter the local file name for the CSV file and give the list a unique name. If you want to fix the name and the e-mail problem, use the appropriate filters. Note that you should always use these filters to be safe.

4. After you've entered all the required fields, click on the Upload button to create the new list.

5. After creating the list, you should add a new form (the sample form shown earlier) using the Add a Form button. Like adding a list, you will have to give a name, local file path of the survey form you want to upload, subject of the survey message, from address of the e-mail that will be sent, and number of question fields in the form as shown in Figure 14-6.

6. After you've entered all these fields, you should click on Upload, and if the upload is successful, you will be asked to add question labels as shown in Figure 14-7.

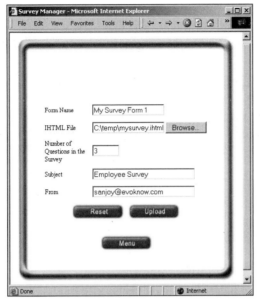

Figure 14-6: Adding a survey form.

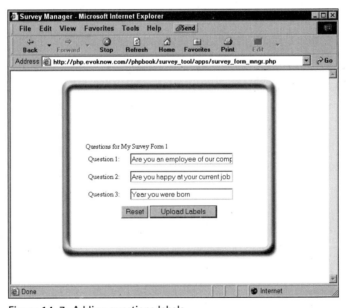

Figure 14-7: Adding questions labels.

7. When the question labels have been added, you can create a survey by clicking on the Create Survey button, which shows the user interface shown in Figure 14-8.

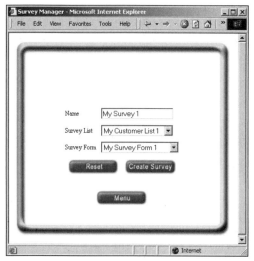

Figure 14-8: Adding a survey.

8. Select the appropriate survey list and form, name the survey, and save it.

9. When it's saved, you can execute the survey immediately using the Execute button. Just select the survey from the list and click on the Execute button.

10. When the survey starts executing, you'll see a status screen such as Figure 14-9.

11. When the survey recipients submit the responses, the report can be viewed from the Survey menu using the View Report button by selecting a survey. A sample report is shown in Figure 14-10.

Note that you can execute the same survey as many times as you want. However, it would be unwise to send the same survey to the same people too frequently.

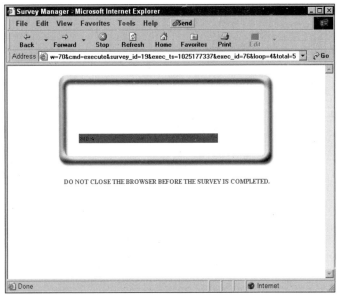

Figure 14-9: Survey status while being executed.

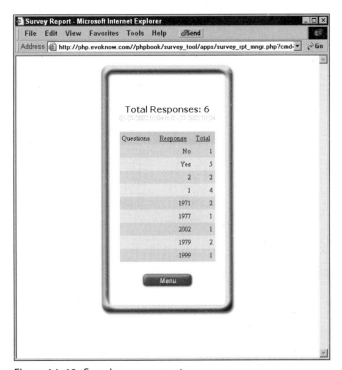

Figure 14-10: Sample survey report.

Security Considerations

This survey system by default does not offer any control on who can run the survey applications. However, that does not mean you cannot easily change the authorization process in each application to fit your security needs. For example, say you would like to limit access to `survey_form_mngr.php`, `survey_exec_mngr.php`, `survey_list_mngr.php`, and `survey_mngr.php` to a limited set of IP addresses. In such case you would need to replace the given `authorize()` method (shown below) to handle IP restrictions.

```
function authorize()
{
    return TRUE;
}
```

For example, say that you want to control access to this application such that only 192.168.1.1 to 192.168.1.5 IP addresses are allowed to run them. In such case you can change the authorization method to be:

```
function authorize()
{
  $safeIPs = array('192.168.1.1',
                   '192.168.1.2',
                   '192.168.1.3',
                   '192.168.1.4',
                   '192.168.1.5');

  return (in_array($_SERVER['REMOTE_ADDR'], $safeIPs,) ? TRUE:
FALSE;

}
```

By replacing the default `authorize()` method in these applications with the new one, you have customized the applications with your site's security needs.

Summary

In this chapter you learned to design an email based survey system that sends HTML forms to target email lists and collects responses in the database. This creates an effective tool for small- to medium-scale surveys that can be done quickly and quite easily via the Web interface.

Chapter 15

E-campaign System

IN THIS CHAPTER

- ◆ Architecting an e-campaign system
- ◆ Designing e-campaign classes
- ◆ Creating a list manager application
- ◆ Creating a URL manager application
- ◆ Creating a message manager application
- ◆ Creating a campaign manager application
- ◆ Creating a URL tracking and redirection application
- ◆ Creating a unsubscription tracking application
- ◆ Creating a campaign reporting application

WHEN COMMUNICATING WITH LARGE groups of professionals, friends, or customers, e-mail is a very effective medium. E-mail campaigns are frequently used to communicate with groups of people. An company can remain in close contacts with its customers via e-mail by frequently engaging the customer in providing electronic feedback, informing the customer about new products and services, and providing valuable complementary and socially responsible information. A company that interacts with its existing customer base using e-mail can reduce marketing cost by effectively turning existing customers into repeat customers. To achieve such goals, a company needs an effective e-mail campaign (e-campaign) tool. In this chapter, I discuss the features, design, and implementation of such a tool.

First, let's look at the feature set for an effective e-campaign system.

Features of an E-campaign System

An effective e-campaign system allows a company to communicate with groups of customers with ease. It must have the following features:

- ◆ **Live database list management:** Allows the company to create mailing lists from existing customer databases. The list management capability should be such that the customer database need not be copied or exported into external files or other databases before use. This is very important because a customer database is typically the repository of other business-specific applications, which are responsible for adding, modifying, and removing customers. If the e-campaign system requires that customer data be exported, then there is always the issue of being out of sync with the customer database over time and, therefore, it would create a great deal of work for the database administrator. This is why an ideal e-campaign system directly accesses a live customer database in a read-only manner to retrieve customer information needed for e-mail campaigns. This ensures that the ever-growing customer database is always used in future campaigns.

◆ **Effective message management:** Messages must be personalized and rich in content formatting. Because HTML messages are most appealing when the appropriate amount of care is used in designing the look and feel of the message, the e-campaign tool must support HTML messages. Each message must be trackable.

◆ **Personalization:** Each message should be personalized using customer data available in a customer database located anyone within the company.

◆ **Easy campaign execution:** E-campaign execution should be so simple that it doesn't require programming or the help of the IS department. Marketing personnel can execute e-campaigns via a Web interface.

◆ **Duplication-free campaigns:** Each campaign must be automatically free from duplicate e-mails. When sending an e-campaign to customers, it's vital that the same customer is never sent the same message more then once in the same campaign. If a customer exists in a database multiple times because she bought two or more products, she should not receive the same message multiple times. Customers will get extremely disappointed or annoyed if their mailboxes are flooded with the same message from the same campaign. They're likely to consider the company unprofessional and take their business to a competitor. Therefore, it is essential that an e-campaign system never sends duplicate e-mails for any campaign.

◆ **Automatic unsubscription filtering:** An e-campaign system must automatically filter out the previously unsubscribed recipients before sending a new campaign to the same list. This is not only vital for maintaining responsible, professional business image for a company but also likely to be a legal requirement in many parts of the world.

◆ **Click-through and unsubscription tracking:** A good e-campaign system must be able to track click-through and unsubscription requests. Such tracking ability is the most important aspect of the e-campaign system. Being able to track the click-through can be very important in understanding customer interests. Tracking unsubscription requests is a must, because if someone does not want to receive the type of campaign you're sending to her, it's important to remove her from future campaigns of a similar type. In many parts of the world, unsubscription tracking is a legal requirement of e-mail communication.

◆ **Easy report generation:** A good e-campaign system must produce a report of each campaign such that the company personnel can access it quickly and without needing programming or database expertise.

Architecting an E-campaign System

Figure 15-1 shows the system diagram of the e-campaign system that you will develop in this chapter.

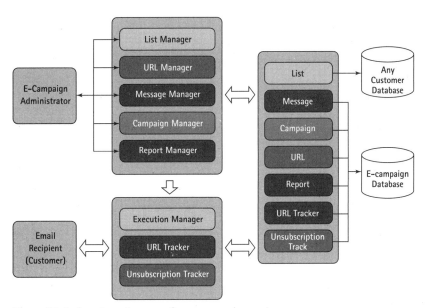

Figure 15-1: A system diagram of an e-campaign system.

The system has two types of users: the e-campaign administrator and e-mail recipients who are the customers. An e-campaign administrator can manage lists, URLs, messages, campaigns, and reports. The end-user receives campaign-executed campaign messages and interacts by clicking on trackable URLs or unsubscribing from future campaigns via unsubscription links.

To implement these functionalities the system requires a set of objects: list, URLs, messages, campaigns, URL tracks, unsubscription tracks, and reports. These objects are stored in a system database with the exception that list data is stored in existing databases within the company.

For example, a company with this e-campaign system can have its customer databases in multiple database hosts and e-campaign system on a different database server. In such a case, the list objects point to data stored in customer databases in other database hosts throughout the company. This is a very powerful feature because customer data need to be exported and loaded in the e-campaign system via any manual or scheduled synchronization glue logic.

When the customer executes a campaign, the appropriate customer data is temporarily copied to the e-campaign system and removed after the execution. During the execution, each message is personalized if the standard tag fields shown in Table 15-1 are mapped to data fields in the customer table.

TABLE 15-1 STANDARD PERSONALIZATION TAG FIELDS

Standard Personalization Tag Field	Meaning
{REC_ID}	Record ID. This is a required field, which should be mapped to the numeric record ID field in the customer database.
{FIRST}	First name. This field should be mapped to the first name field in the customer database (if any).
{LAST}	Last name. This field should be mapped to the last name field in the customer database (if any).
{AGE}	Age. This field should be mapped to the age field in the customer database (if any).
{INCOME}	Income. This field should be mapped to the income field in the customer database (if any).
{SEX}	Gender. This field should be mapped to the gender (sex) field in the customer database (if any).

Also during the execution, each trackable URL tag within a message is replaced with a redirection link that can track and redirect the user via the URL tracking and redirection application. The unsubscription tag, {UNSUB}, is replaced with an unsubscription link.

When the end-user clicks on a URL, she is tracked and redirected. The tracking data is stored in the e-campaign database. Similarly, if she unsubscribes, the request is stored in the e-campaign database for future exclusion of her e-mail from a list in any campaign.

Designing an E-campaign Database

The e-campaign database consists of 11 tables. Figure 15-2 shows the entity relationship (ER) diagram for the entire e-campaign database.

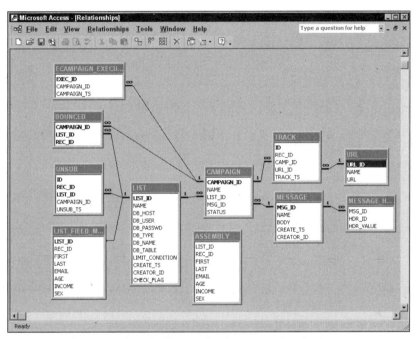

Figure 15-2: Entity relationship diagram for the e-campaign database

Listing 15-1 shows a script that you can use to create this database in MySQL.

Listing 15-1: ecampaign.sql

```
# phpMyAdmin MySQL-Dump
# version 2.2.5
# http://phpwizard.net/phpMyAdmin/
# http://phpmyadmin.sourceforge.net/ (download page)
#
# Host: localhost
# Generation Time: Jun 07, 2002 at 09:16 PM
# Server version: 3.23.35
# PHP Version: 4.1.0
# Database : `ECAMPAIGN`
```

Continued

Listing 15-1 *(Continued)*

```
# ---------------------------------------------------------

#
# Table structure for table `ASSEMBLY`
#

CREATE TABLE ASSEMBLY (
  LIST_ID int(11) NOT NULL default '0',
  REC_ID int(11) NOT NULL default '0',
  FIRST varchar(255) default NULL,
  LAST varchar(255) default NULL,
  EMAIL varchar(255) NOT NULL default '',
  AGE varchar(255) default NULL,
  INCOME varchar(255) default NULL,
  SEX varchar(255) default NULL
) TYPE=MyISAM;
# ---------------------------------------------------------

#
# Table structure for table `BOUNCED`
#

CREATE TABLE BOUNCED (
  CAMPAIGN_ID tinyint(4) NOT NULL default '0',
  LIST_ID tinyint(4) NOT NULL default '0',
  REC_ID tinyint(4) NOT NULL default '0',
  PRIMARY KEY  (LIST_ID,REC_ID,CAMPAIGN_ID)
) TYPE=MyISAM;
# ---------------------------------------------------------

#
# Table structure for table `CAMPAIGN`
#

CREATE TABLE CAMPAIGN (
  CAMPAIGN_ID int(11) NOT NULL auto_increment,
  NAME varchar(127) NOT NULL default '',
  LIST_ID int(11) NOT NULL default '0',
  MSG_ID int(11) NOT NULL default '0',
  STATUS int(4) NOT NULL default '0',
  PRIMARY KEY  (CAMPAIGN_ID)
) TYPE=MyISAM;
```

```
# ---------------------------------------------------------

#
# Table structure for table `ECAMPAIGN_EXECUTION`
#

CREATE TABLE ECAMPAIGN_EXECUTION (
  EXEC_ID int(11) NOT NULL auto_increment,
  CAMPAIGN_ID int(11) NOT NULL default '0',
  CAMPAIGN_TS timestamp(14) NOT NULL,
  PRIMARY KEY  (EXEC_ID),
  UNIQUE KEY CAMPAIGN_TS (CAMPAIGN_TS)
) TYPE=MyISAM;
# ---------------------------------------------------------

#
# Table structure for table `LIST`
#

CREATE TABLE LIST (
  LIST_ID int(11) NOT NULL auto_increment,
  NAME varchar(127) NOT NULL default '',
  DB_HOST varchar(127) NOT NULL default '',
  DB_USER varchar(127) NOT NULL default '',
  DB_PASSWD varchar(127) NOT NULL default '',
  DB_TYPE varchar(127) NOT NULL default '',
  DB_NAME varchar(127) NOT NULL default '',
  DB_TABLE varchar(127) NOT NULL default '',
  LIMIT_CONDITION varchar(255) default NULL,
  CREATE_TS bigint(20) NOT NULL default '0',
  CREATOR_ID int(11) NOT NULL default '0',
  CHECK_FLAG bigint(20) NOT NULL default '0',
  PRIMARY KEY  (LIST_ID),
  UNIQUE KEY CHECK_FLAG (CHECK_FLAG),
  UNIQUE KEY NAME (NAME)
) TYPE=MyISAM;
# ---------------------------------------------------------

#
# Table structure for table `LIST_FIELD_MAP`
#

CREATE TABLE LIST_FIELD_MAP (
```

Continued

Listing 15-1 *(Continued)*

```
    LIST_ID int(11) NOT NULL default '0',
    REC_ID varchar(127) NOT NULL default '',
    FIRST varchar(127) default NULL,
    LAST varchar(127) default NULL,
    EMAIL varchar(127) NOT NULL default '',
    AGE varchar(127) default NULL,
    INCOME varchar(127) default NULL,
    SEX varchar(127) default NULL,
    PRIMARY KEY  (LIST_ID)
) TYPE=MyISAM;
# ---------------------------------------------------------


#
# Table structure for table `MESSAGE`
#

CREATE TABLE MESSAGE (
    MSG_ID tinyint(4) NOT NULL auto_increment,
    NAME varchar(127) NOT NULL default '',
    BODY text NOT NULL,
    CREATE_TS bigint(20) NOT NULL default '0',
    CREATOR_ID int(11) NOT NULL default '0',
    PRIMARY KEY  (MSG_ID),
    UNIQUE KEY NAME (NAME)
) TYPE=MyISAM;
# ---------------------------------------------------------


#
# Table structure for table `MESSAGE_HDRS`
#

CREATE TABLE MESSAGE_HDRS (
    MSG_ID int(11) NOT NULL default '0',
    HDR_ID int(11) NOT NULL default '0',
    HDR_VALUE varchar(127) NOT NULL default ''
) TYPE=MyISAM;
# ---------------------------------------------------------


#
# Table structure for table `TRACK`
#

CREATE TABLE TRACK (
```

```
    ID int(11) NOT NULL auto_increment,
    USER_ID int(11) NOT NULL default '0',
    CAMP_ID int(11) NOT NULL default '0',
    URL_ID int(11) NOT NULL default '0',
    TRACK_TS bigint(20) NOT NULL default '0',
    PRIMARY KEY  (ID)
) TYPE=MyISAM;
# -------------------------------------------------------


#
# Table structure for table `UNSUB`
#

CREATE TABLE UNSUB (
    ID int(11) NOT NULL auto_increment,
    REC_ID int(11) NOT NULL default '0',
    LIST_ID int(11) NOT NULL default '0',
    CAMPAIGN_ID int(11) NOT NULL default '0',
    UNSUB_TS bigint(20) NOT NULL default '0',
    PRIMARY KEY  (ID,REC_ID,LIST_ID),
    UNIQUE KEY REC_ID (REC_ID,LIST_ID)
) TYPE=MyISAM;
# -------------------------------------------------------


#
# Table structure for table `URL`
#

CREATE TABLE URL (
    URL_ID int(11) NOT NULL auto_increment,
    NAME varchar(127) NOT NULL default '',
    URL varchar(255) NOT NULL default '',
    PRIMARY KEY  (URL_ID),
    UNIQUE KEY NAME (NAME)
) TYPE=MyISAM;
```

Understanding Customer Database Requirements

Each customer database that you want to use in e-campaigns must have the following data fields:

- ◆ **Record ID:** A numeric record ID must be in the target list table to identify the customer record.

- ◆ **E-mail field:** An e-mail field must be there in the target list table.

The field names can be anything. These two fields must be mapped during the list-creation process using the list management application.

The e-campaign system allows you to map all the standard personalization fields shown in Table 15-1 during list creation so that you can use them in message personalization.

Designing E-campaign Classes

Based on the system diagram shown in Figure 15-1, you need to create a set of classes to provide the objects needed to implement the e-campaign system. In the following sections, I discuss the necessary classes in details.

Creating a List class

The purpose of this class is to provide the List object, which is needed to manipulate the lists. An implementation of this class can be found in the ch15/apps/class/class.EcampaignList.php file in the CDROM. This class implements the methods discussed in the following sections.

EcampaignList()
This is the constructor method. It does the following:

- ◆ Sets member variables list_tbl, list_field_map, assembly_tbl, unsub_tbl, and bounced_tbl to global configuration variables $ECAMPAIGN_LIST_TBL, $LIST_FIELD_MAP_TBL, $ECAMPAIGN_ASSEMBLY_TBL, $ECAMPAIGN_UNSUB_TBL, and $ECAMPAIGN_BOUNCED_TBL, respectively.

- ◆ A member variable called dbi is set to $dbi, which is a DBI object passed from the application.

- ◆ A member variable called std_map_fields is set to an associative array that holds the field and field type for standard personalization fields supported by the e-campaign system.

- ◆ Finally, this method calls the setEcampaignListID() method to set the list ID, which can also be passed from the application when creating an object.

setEcampaignListID()
This method sets the current object's list ID to the given list ID, which is passed as a parameter. It always returns the current list ID.

getEcampaignListInfo()

This method returns all the information about a given list. Information is returned as a standard row object. If no information is found about a list, null is returned.

addNewEcampaignList()

This method adds a new list to the database.

modEcampaignList()

This method updates an existing list.

addMapping()

This method stores standard personalization fields (FIRST, LAST, EMAIL, and so on) mapping information that is used to identify which customer database field matches with which standard personalization fields.

getAvailableLists()

This method returns a list of available lists. The method returns an associative array where LIST_ID is the key and NAME is the value.

deleteList()

This method deletes an existing list.

prepareLocalList()

This method creates a local copy of the list data necessary to execute a campaign. It does the following:

- ◆ Determines the list of mapped fields.

- ◆ Makes a SQL statement to get the mapped field data from the customer database table.

- ◆ Queries the customer database with the prepared statement.

- ◆ Inserts the data in the assembly table.

- ◆ Removes the customers who have previously unsubscribed from this list.

- ◆ Returns the total number of records inserted in the assembly table.

pushMappedFields()

This is a utility method that pushes a field name into an array if the field name is not null.

map()

This is a utility method that returns the field name for a given standard contact field name.

getClientDBURL()

This method returns the database URL for a given list. It retrieves the database information from the list record and constructs a `database_type://user:password↓tabase_hostname/database_name` URL, which can be used to retrieve customer data.

getTargetData()

This method returns a list of row objects from the assembly table and then deletes the records from the assembly table. This method is used to fetch a specific number of rows from the assembly table for mail delivery. The returned array of rows uses `REC_ID` as the key and the row object as the value.

addToBounced()

This method inserts a record in the bounce e-mail table. This record is used in the report to determine how many e-mails bounced during delivery.

When an e-mail is not bounced during delivery, it can still be bounced later after delivery by the recipient's target mail server, which may try to delivery it to an internal mail server within an organization. Therefore, the bounce tracking done in the e-campaign is not 100-percent accurate. In fact, if e-mail addresses aren't local to the mail server being used, the bounces usually aren't right away. This problem can be avoided in a future version of the e-campaign system.

modifyMapList()

This method allows you to modify the standard personalization field map for a given list.

Creating a URL class

The purpose of this class is to provide the `URL` object, which is needed to manipulate the URL. An implementation of this class can be found in `ch15/apps/class/class.EcampaignURL.php` . This class implements the methods discussed in the following sections.

EcampaignURL()

This is the constructor method. It does the following:

- Sets the `url_tbl` variable to the configuration variable called `$ECAMPAIGN_URL_TBL`, which holds the name of the URL table in the campaign database.

- Sets the `home_url` variable to configuration variable called `$HOME_URL`, which holds the home URL.

- Sets the `dbi` variable to the `DBI` object, which is passed to the `URL` object from the caller application.

addURL()

This method inserts a new URL in the URL table within the e-campaign database.

getURL()

This method gets the URL for a given URL ID.

getURLInfo()

This method returns the name and URL for a given URL ID from the URL table in the e-campaign database.

modURL()

This method updates an existing URL in the URL table in the e-campaign database.

getURLList()

This method returns a list of URLs in an associative array (`key = URL_ID, value = name`) from the URL table in the e-campaign database.

getURLLocationList()

This method returns a list of URLs in an associative array (`key = URL_ID, value = URL`) from the URL table in the e-campaign database.

deleteURL()

This method deletes an existing URL from the URL table in the e-campaign database.

Creating a Message class

The purpose of this class is to provide the `Message` object, which is needed to manipulate the message. An implementation of this class can be found in `ch15/ apps/class/class.EcampaignMessage.php`. This class implements the methods discussed in the following sections.

EcampaignMessage()

This is the constructor method for the `Message` class. It does the following:

- Sets `message_tbl` to `$ECAMPAIGN_MESSAGE_TBL`, which holds the name of the message table. The `$ECAMPAIGN_MESSAGE_TBL` is set in the `ecampaign. conf` configuration file.

- Sets `header_tbl` to `$MESSAGE_HDRS_TBL`, which holds the name of the header table. The `$MESSAGE_HDRS_TBL` is set in the `ecampaign.conf` configuration file.

- ◆ Sets `msg_fields` to an associative array, which contains the message table field names and their types (text or number). This associative array is used in other methods to determine which field value needs to be quoted and protected from embedded slashes using the `addslashes()` method.

- ◆ Sets `hdr_fields` to an associative array, which contains the message header table field names and their types (text or number). This associative array is used in other methods to determine which field value needs to be quoted and protected from embedded slashes using the `addslashes()` method.

- ◆ Calls `setEcampaignMessageID()` to set the campaign ID, which is passed to the constructor method from the application.

setEcampaignMessageID()
This method sets the message ID.

getEcampaignMessageInfo()
This method returns the message information for a given message ID or the current message ID.

getEcampaignHeaderInfo()
This method returns message header information for a given message ID or the current message ID.

addNewEcampaignMessage()
This method adds a new message in the message table and its headers in the header table.

getAvailableMessages()
This returns a list of messages in the current e-campaign database. The returned list is an associative array with the message ID (`MSG_ID`) being the key and the message name (`NAME`) as the value.

deleteMessage()
This method deletes a message and its header.

UpdateEcampaignMessage()
This method updates a message.

UpdateEcampaignMessageHdr()
This method updates headers of a message.

Creating a Campaign class

The purpose of this class is to provide the `Campaign` object, which is needed to manipulate the campaign. An implementation of this class can be found in `ch15/apps/class/class.EcampaignCampaign.php` file in the CDROM. This class implements the methods discussed in the following sections.

EcampaignCampaign()

This method sets the member variable, `ecampaign_tbl`, to the `$ECAMPAIGN_TBL` configuration variable. The member variable, `dbi`, is set to `$dbi`, which is passed from the application. This method also sets the current campaign ID using the `setCampaignID()` method.

setCampaignID()

This method sets the current campaign ID to the campaign ID supplied. If no campaign ID is supplied as a parameter, the current campaign ID is returned.

getCampaignInfo()

This method returns campaign information about a given campaign or the current campaign.

getAvailableCampaigns()

This method returns the list of campaigns from the e-campaign database. The returned associative array is keyed with the campaign ID (`CAMPAIGN_ID`), and the values are set to campaign name (`NAME`).

addCampaign()

This method adds a campaign in the e-campaign database.

deleteCampaign()

This method deletes a campaign from the e-campaign database.

modifyCampaign()

This method updates a campaign in the e-campaign database.

Creating a URL Tracking class

The purpose of this class is to provide the URL `Track` object, which is needed to manipulate the URL track information. An implementation of this class can be found in `ch15/apps/class/class.EcampaignTrack.php` file in the CDROM. This class implements the methods discussed in the following sections.

EcampaignTrack()

This is the constructor method that sets a member variable, track_tbl, to e-campaign configuration variable $ECAMPAIGN_TRACK_TBL, which holds the URL track table name. This method also sets another member variable, dbi, to the DBI ($dbi) object, which is passed from the application.

storeTrack()

This method stores a URL track record in the URL track table.

Creating an Unsubscription Tracking class

The purpose of this class is to provide the Unsubscription Track object, which is needed to manipulate the unsubscription track information. An implementation of this class can be found in ch15/apps/class/class.EcampaignUnsub.php. This class implements the methods discussed in the following sections.

EcampaignUnsub()

This is the constructor method that sets a member variable, unsub_tbl, to $ECAMPAIGN_UNSUB_TBL, which is an ecampaign.conf configuration variable set to hold the unsubscription table name. This method also sets another member variable, dbi, to the DBI ($dbi) object, which is passed from the application.

storeUnsub()

This method stores an unsubscription record in the unsubscription track table.

Creating a Report class

The purpose of this class is to provide the Report object, which is needed to manipulate the report information. An implementation of this class can be found in ch15/apps/class/class.EcampaignReport.php file in the CDROM. This class implements the methods discussed in the following sections.

EcampaignReport()

This constructor method sets member variables ecampaign_tbl, track_tbl, unsub_tbl, and bounced_tbl to e-campaign configuration variables $ECAMPAIGN_TBL, $ECAMPAIGN_TRACK_TBL, $ECAMPAIGN_UNSUB_TBL, and $ECAMPAIGN_BOUNCED_TBL, respectively.

The member variable, dbi, is set to the DBI object ($dbi), which is passed as a parameter from an application. Another member variable, campaign_id, is set to the campaign ID passed as a parameter from an application creating the report object.

setEcampaignCampaignID()

This method sets the current campaign ID to the campaign ID parameter if it is not null and returns the current campaign ID.

getURLResponse()

This method returns URL click-through count for each tracked URL in a campaign.

getUnsubResponse()

This method returns the total unsubscription track for a campaign.

getBounceResponse()

This method returns the total number of immediate bounces for a given campaign.

Creating Common Configuration and Resource Files

Like all other applications you've developed in this book, the e-campaign applications also use a standard set of configuration, message, and error files. These files are discussed in the following sections.

Creating an e-campaign configuration file

The primary configuration file for the entire e-campaign system is called `ecampaign.conf`, which can be found in `ch15/apps` directory in the CDROM. Table 15-2 discusses each configuration variable.

TABLE 15-2 `ecampaign.conf` **VARIABLES**

Configuration Variable	Purpose
$PEAR_DIR	Set to the directory containing the PEAR package; specifically the DB module needed for class.DBI.php in the application framework.
$PHPLIB_DIR	Set to the PHPLIB directory, which contains the PHPLIB packages; specifically the template.inc package needed for template manipulation.
$APP_FRAMEWORK_DIR	Set to the application framework directory.

Continued

TABLE 15-2 `ecampaign.conf` **VARIABLES** *(Continued)*

Configuration Variable	Purpose
$PATH	Set to the combined directory path consisting of the $PEAR_DIR, the $PHPLIB_DIR, and the $APP_FRAMEWORK_DIR. This path is used with the ini_set() method to redefine the php.ini entry for include_path to include $PATH ahead of the default path. This allows PHP to find the application framework, PHPLIB, and PEAR-related files.
$AUTHENTICATION_URL	Set to the central login application URL.
$LOGOUT_URL	Set to the central logout application URL.
$HOME_URL	Set to the topmost URL of the site. If the URL redirection application does not find a valid URL in the e-campaign database to redirect to for a valid request, it uses this URL as a default.
$APPLICATION_NAME	Internal name of the application.
$XMAILER_ID	This is the X-Mailer mail header sent with each mail to identify what program was used to send mail.
$DEFAULT_LANGUAGE	Set to the default (two- digit) language code.
$ROOT_PATH	Set to the default (two-digit) language code.
$REL_ROOT_PATH	Relative path to the root directory.
$REL_APP_PATH	Relative application path as seen from the Web browser.
$ECAMPAIGN_MENU_URL	Relative URL path to the campaign manager interface application.
$TEMPLATE_DIR	Set to the template directory containing the ihtml template files needed for the user-management applications.
$CLASS_DIR	Set to the class directory where user-management-related class files are stored.
$ECAMPAIGN_LIST_CLASS	Name of the List class.
$ECAMPAIGN_URL_CLASS	Name of the URL class.

Configuration Variable	Purpose
$ECAMPAIGN_TRACK_CLASS	Name of the `URL Track` class.
$ECAMPAIGN_UNSUB_CLASS	Name of the `Unsubscription` class.
$ECAMPAIGN_CAMPAIGN_CLASS	Name of the `Campaign` class.
$ECAMPAIGN_MESSAGE_CLASS	Name of the `Message` class.
$ECAMPAIGN_REPORT_CLASS	Name of the `Report` class.
$ECAMPAIGN_MNGR	Name of the campaign manager interface application. This application displays the primary user interface.
$ECAMPAIGN_URL_MNGR	Name of the URL manager application.
$ECAMPAIGN_CAMPAIGN_MNGR	Name of the campaign manager application.
$ECAMPAIGN_LIST_MNGR	Name of the list manager application.
$ECAMPAIGN_MESSAGE_MNGR	Name of the message manager application.
$ECAMPAIGN_EXEC_MNGR	Name of the campaign execution application.
$ECAMPAIGN_REPORT_MNGR	Name of the report manager application.
$ECAMPAIGN_REDIR_MNGR	Name of the URL redirection application.
$ECAMPAIGN_UNSUB_MNGR	Name of the unsubscription application.
$REL_TEMPLATE_DIR	Set to relative template directory.
$ECAMPAIGN_DB_URL	Set to campaign database URL.
$MAX_DELIVERY_AT_A_TIME	Set to maximum e-mail delivery count per run. Because the execution application cannot run the entire campaign in one shot due to browser timeout issues, it executes this number of e-mails at a time. The execution application calls itself after each run using the meta refresh method.
$MAX_WAIT_PER_DELIVERY	The number of seconds the campaign execution application waits before it restarts via the meta refresh tag.
$SECRET	A random number used in the `checksum` algorithm.
$ECAMPAIGN_LIST_TBL	Name of the list table.
$ECAMPAIGN_URL_TBL	Name of the URL table.

Continued

TABLE 15-2 `ecampaign.conf` **VARIABLES** *(Continued)*

`$LIST_FIELD_MAP_TBL`	Name of the list map table.
`$ECAMPAIGN_TBL`	Name of the campaign table.
`$ECAMPAIGN_MESSAGE_TBL`	Name of the message table.
`$MESSAGE_HDRS_TBL`	Name of the message header table.
`$ECAMPAIGN_EXECUTION_TBL`	Name of the execution table.
`$ECAMPAIGN_ASSEMBLY_TBL`	Name of the assembly table.
`$ECAMPAIGN_TRACK_TBL`	Name of the URL track table.
`$ECAMPAIGN_UNSUB_TBL`	Name of the unsubscription table.
`$ECAMPAIGN_BOUNCED_TBL`	Name of the bounced e-mail table.
`$REPORT_EVEN_ROW_COLOR`	HTML color code for even rows in a report table.
`$REPORT_ODD_ROW_COLOR`	HTML color code for odd rows in a report table.
`$FROM_HEADER`	Header ID for the From header.
`$REPLY_HEADER`	Header ID for the Reply-to header.
`$PRIORITY_HEADER`	Header ID for the Priority header.
`$SUBJECT_HEADER`	Header ID for the Subject header.

Creating an e-campaign messages file

The messages displayed by the e-campaign applications are stored in an e-campaign messages file called `ecampaign.messages`, which can be found in `ch15/apps` directory in the CDROM.

Creating an e-campaign errors file

The error messages displayed by the e-campaign applications are stored in an e-campaign error messages file called `ecampaign.errors`, which can be found in `ch15/apps` directory in the CDROM.

Creating Interface Template Files

The HTML interface templates needed for the e-campaign applications are included on the CD-ROM. These templates contain various template tags to dynamically display necessary information. Table 15-3 shows which template file is used for what purpose.

TABLE **15-3** INTERFACE TEMPLATE FILES

Configuration Variable	File Name and Purpose
$ECAMPAIGN_ADD_TEMPLATE	ecampaign_add.ihtml
$ECAMPAIGN_MENU_TEMPLATE	ecampaign_menu.ihtml
$ECAMPAIGN_ADD_URL_TEMPLATE	ecampaign_add_url.ihtml
$ECAMPAIGN_EXECUTION_TEMPLATE	ecampaign_execute.ihtml
$ECAMPAIGN_ADD_LIST_TEMPLATE	ecampaign_add_list.ihtml
$STATUS_TEMPLATE	ecampaign_status.ihtml
$ECAMPAIGN_MAPPING_TEMPLATE	ecampaign_take_map.ihtml
$ECAMPAIGN_ADD_CAMPAIGN_TEMPLATE	ecampaign_add_campaign.ihtml
$ECAMPAIGN_ADD_LABEL_TEMPLATE	ecampaign_add_label.ihtml
$ECAMPAIGN_REPORT_TEMPLATE	ecampaign_report.ihtml
$ECAMPAIGN_MOD_URL_TEMPLATE	ecampaign_modify_url.ihtml
$ECAMPAIGN_ADD_MESSAGE_TEMPLATE	ecampaign_add_message.ihtml
$ECAMPAIGN_PREVIEW_MESSAGE_TEMPLATE	ecampaign_preview_message
$ECAMPAIGN_MOD_LIST_TEMPLATE	ecampaign_mod_list.ihtml
$ECAMPAIGN_UNSUB_TEMPLATE	ecampaign_unsub.ihtml
$MAIL_TEMPLATE	ecampaign_mail.ihtml
$ECAMPAIGN_PREVIEW_MESSAGE_ INPUT_TEMPLATE	ecampaign_preview_message_ input.ihtml
$ECAMPAIGN_PREVIEW_MESSAGE_ SHOW_TEMPLATE	ecampaign_preview_message_ show.ihtml
$ECAMPAIGN_PREVIEW_MESSAGE_TEMPLATE	ecampaign_preview_ message.ihtml
$ECAMPAIGN_UNSUB_CONFIRM_TEMPLATE	ecampaign_unsub_ confirmation.ihtml

---

Now you're ready to create the e-campaign applications.

Creating an E-campaign User Interface Application

This application displays the main user interface for the e-campaign applications. The main user interface application called ecampaign_mngr.php can be found in ch15/apps directory in the CDROM. The methods implemented by this user interface application are discussed in the following sections.

run()

This method calls the displayMenu() method to display the user interface.

displayMenu()

This method displays the main user interface. This method creates a List object, a URL object, and a Campaign object to get lists of lists, URLs, and campaigns to display in the interface.

authorize()

This method returns TRUE since, in the current version everyone is allowed to view the campaign report. If you want to restrict access to the report to a specific user or group of users, you'll have to modify this method to implement your restrictions.

Creating a List Manager Application

The list-management application manipulates lists. The list-creation process is shown in Figure 15-3.

The ecampaign_list_mngr.php application that can be found in ch15/apps directory in the CDROM, which implements the list creation, modification, and deletion process. This application has the following methods.

run()

This method uses a form variable called the $cmd variable, which is set in the user interface displayed by ecampaign_mngr.php, to select the appropriate function to implement the list operation.

When $cmd is set to add, it calls the addDriver() method to add a list. When $cmd is set to modify, it calls the modDriver() method to modify a list; otherwise, it calls the delList() method to delete a list.

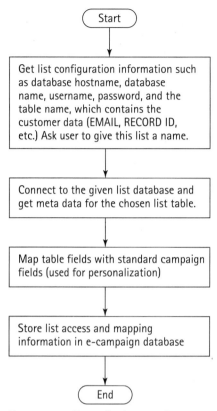

Figure 15-3: How a list is created.

addDriver()

This method uses $step, a variable set in the add list interface forms, to control which method is called. The $step variable is used to select the appropriate method for the appropriate stage of the list adding process. Here is how the addDriver() works:

♦ If $step is not set, then the first step of the add list process is started by calling displayAddListMenu(), which shows the add list interface. This interface sets the $step to 2, using a hidden HTML field.

♦ If $step is set to 2, then the second step of the add list process is started by calling the addList() method. This method stores the list configuration data collected in the previous step and displays the database field mapping interface by calling the takeMap() method. This interface sets the $step value to 3.

◆ If $step is set to 3, then the database field map that maps the standard personalization fields such as REC_ID, FIRST, LAST, AGE, SEX, INCOME, and EMAIL is stored in the database using the addDatabaseFieldMap method.

modifyDriver()

This method uses $step, a variable set in the modify list interface forms, to control which method is called. The $step variable is used to select the appropriate method for the appropriate stage of the list modification process. Here is how the modifyDriver() method works:

◆ If $step is not set, then the first step of the modify list process is started by calling displayModifyListMenu(), which shows the modify list interface. This interface sets the $step to 2, using a hidden HTML field.

◆ If $step is set to 2, then the second step of the modify list process is started by calling the modifyList() method. This method stores the list configuration data collected in the previous step and displays the database field mapping interface by calling the takeMap() method. This interface sets the $step value to 3.

◆ If $step is set to 3, then the database field map that maps the standard personalization fields such as REC_ID, FIRST, LAST, AGE, SEX, INCOME, and EMAIL are stored in the database using the modifyDatabaseFieldMap method.

authorize()

See the authorize() method in the e-campaign user interface application called ecampaign_mngr.php for details.

displayAddListMenu()

This method displays the add list interface.

displayModListMenu()

This method displays the modify list interface.

modifyList()

This method is called when a user makes changes in the modify interface shown by displayModListMenu(). The modifyList() method creates a list object and calls its modEcampaignList() method to update the list in the database.

If the database is successfully updated, the `modifyList()` method calls `takeMap()` to show the database and personalization field map interface. If the update fails, it shows an appropriate status message.

modifyDatabaseFieldMap()

This method uses a `list` object to call its `modifyMapList()` method to update the map data in the database. The map interface is displayed by the `takeMap()` method.

delList()

This method uses a `list` object to call its `deleteList()` method to delete the list. It displays an appropriate status message based on the success or failure of the `deleteList()` method.

takeMap()

This method allows you to map the database fields to the standard personalization fields `REC_ID`, `EMAIL`, `FIRST`, `LAST`, `AGE`, `INCOME`, and `SEX`. It works as follows:

◆ It connects to the list database using a `DBI` object called `$dbiObj`.

◆ If the connection to the list database is successful, it performs a select query to detect if the list table exists in the list database. If the table does not exist, the list is deleted from the database.

◆ If the table exists, the `takeMap()` method uses the `tableInfo()` method on the query result object, `$result`, to get the list table's meta data – field name and type.

◆ Then it shows an interface that allows the user to map each standard personalization field to a database field. The user must map at least `REC_ID` (record ID) and the `EMAIL` (email address).

addList()

This method is called when a user makes changes in the add interface shown by `displayAddListMenu()`. It works as follows:

◆ First, it checks to see if the user supplied all the required fields: list name (`$listname`), database host name (`$db_host`), database user name (`$db_user`), database type (`$db_type`), database table name (`$db_table`). If these fields are empty, then an alert message is shown and the user is returned to the previous screen.

◆ If the required fields are supplied, a `list` object called `$ecampaignListObj` is created and its `addNewEcampaignList()` is called to add the list in the database.

- ◆ If the list is successfully added, the takeMap() method is called to display the map interface.

- ◆ If the list is not added due to database failure, an appropriate failure message is displayed.

addDatabaseFieldMap()

This method adds database fields to standard personalization field mapping to the database using a list object's addMapping() method.

Creating a URL Manager Application

The URL manager allows you to add, delete, and modify trackable URLs. Figure 15-4 shows how URLs are added to the database using a simple user interface, how it's used in a message template using the {URLx} tag and replaced with a redirection URL in the message received by end-users, and how the redirection URL is finally resolved in the final target URL being tracked.

The ecampaign_url_mngr.php, which can be found in ch15/apps directory in the CDROM implements the URL manager application using the methods discussed in the following sections.

run()

This method uses a form variable called $cmd variable, which is set in the user interface displayed by ecampaign_mngr.php, to select the appropriate function to implement the list operation.

When $cmd is set to delete, it calls the delList() method to delete a URL. When $cmd is set to modify, it calls the modifyURL() method to modify a URL; otherwise, it calls the addURL() method to add a URL.

addURLDriver()

This method controls the add URL process using the interface variable $step. Here's how it works:

- ◆ If $step is not set, then displayAddURLMenu() is called to display the add URL interface. This interface sets $step to 2, using a hidden HTML field.

- ◆ If $step is set to 2, then addURL() is called to add the URL in the database.

authorize()

See the authorize() method in the e-campaign user interface application called ecampaign_mngr.php for details.

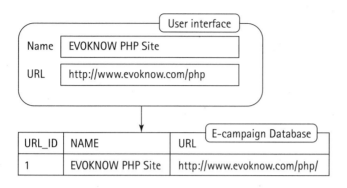

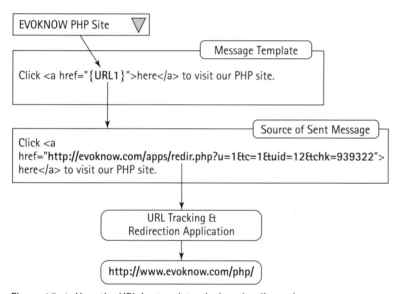

Figure 15-4: How the URL is stored, tracked, and redirected.

modifyURLDriver()

This method controls the modify URL process using the interface variable $step. Here's how it works:

- If $step is not set, then displayModifyURLMenu() is called to display the add URL interface. This interface sets $step to 2, using a hidden HTML field.

- If $step is set to 2, then modifyURL() is called to modify the URL in the database.

delURL()

This method deletes a URL from the database. It works as follows:

◆ If the URL is not selected from the e-campaign main interface, then an alert message is shown and the user is returned to the main interface.

◆ It creates a URL object and calls its deleteURL() method to delete the selected URL from the database.

◆ Finally, it shows a status message that reflects the status of the database delete operation.

displayAddURLMenu()

This method displays the add URL interface.

addURL()

This method adds a URL in the database. It works as follows:

◆ If the required fields — URL ($url) and URL name ($name) — are missing, then an alert message is shown and the user is returned to the previous screen.

◆ A URL object is created and its addURL() method is called to store the URL in the database.

◆ Finally, the status of the add operation is displayed.

displayModifyURLMenu()

This method displays the modify URL interface.

modifyURL()

This method modifies a URL in the database. It works as follows:

◆ If the required fields — URL ($url) and URL name ($name) — are missing, then an alert message is shown and the user is returned to the previous screen.

◆ A URL object is created and its modURL() method is called to update the URL in the database.

◆ Finally, the status of the modify operation is displayed.

Creating a Message Manager Application

The message is the central element of the e-campaign system. Figure 15-5 shows a simple message that is stored in the database. It contains personalization tag {FIRST}, multiple URL tags {URL1} and {URL99}, and the unsubscription tag {UNSUB}.

When this message is executed by the message execution application, a sample of the resulting end-user message is also shown in Figure 15-5.

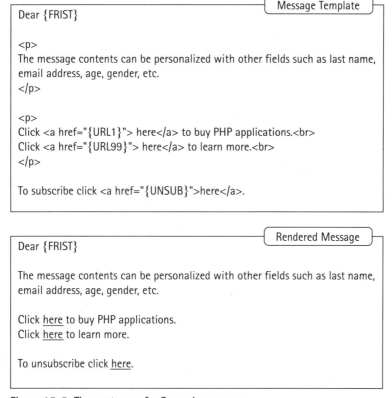

Figure 15-5: The anatomy of a Campaign message.

A message manager application called ecampaign_message_mngr.php, which can be found in ch15/apps directory in the CDROM, provides the message addition, modification, deletion, and preview functionality using the methods discussed in the following sections.

run()

This method selects the appropriate driver to manage messages. It works as follows:

◆ If the $cmd variable is set to add or is empty, then the addDriver() is called to manage the message addition process.

◆ If the $cmd variable is set to modify, then the modifyDriver() is called to manage the message modification process.

◆ If the $cmd variable is set to delete, then the deleteDriver() is called to manage the message deletion process.

◆ If the $cmd variable is set to preview, then the doPreview() is called to manage the message previewing process.

addDriver()

This method uses the $step variable to control the message addition process as follows:

◆ If $step is not set, then the displayAddMessageMenu() is called to display the message interface to allow the user to add a new message. This interface sets $step to 2 to move the control to the next phase of the message addition process.

◆ If $step is 2, then addMessage() is called to store the message in the database.

◆ If $step is 3, then getMsgPreviewInput() is called to get the preview data needed to personalize the preview message.

◆ If $step is 4, then showMsgPreview() is called to show the preview message. This method loads an interface template that runs a JavaScript, which calls the message management application with $cmd set to preview.

modifyDriver()

This method uses the $step variable to control the message modification process as follows:

◆ If $step is not set, then the displayModMessageMenu () is called to display the message interface to allow the user to modify an existing message selected from the main user interface. This interface sets $step to 2 to move the control to the next phase of the message modification process.

◆ If $step is 2, then updateMessage () is called to update the message in the database.

◆ If `$step` is 3, then `getMsgPreviewInput()` is called to get the preview data needed to personalize the preview message.

◆ If `$step` is 4, then `showMsgPreview()` is called to show the preview message. This method loads an interface template that runs a JavaScript, which calls the message management application with `$cmd` set to `preview`.

authorize()

See the `authorize()` method in the e-campaign user interface application called `ecampaign_mngr.php` for details.

displayAddMessageMenu()

This method displays the add message interface.

displayModMessageMenu()

This method displays the message modification interface.

updateMessage()

This method updates a modified message as follows:

◆ If any of the required fields — message name, from address, priority, or message text — is missing, an alert message is shown and the user is returned to the previous page.

◆ A message object is created and its `UpdateEcampaignMessage()` method is called to update the message data in the message table.

◆ The `Message` object's `UpdateEcampaignMessageHdr()` is called to update the message header data in the message header table.

◆ Finally, an appropriate status message is displayed.

deleteMessage()

This message deletes a message from the database. It works as follows:

◆ If the required message ID is not supplied from the main user interface, the method alerts the user and returns to the main interface.

◆ If the message ID is supplied, it creates a message object and deletes the message by calling the object's `deleteMessage()` method.

◆ Finally, an appropriate status message is displayed.

addMessage()

This message adds a message in the database. It works as follows:

- ◆ If any of the required fields – message name, from address, priority, or message text – is missing, an alert message is shown and the user is returned to the previous page.

- ◆ A `Message` object is created and the message is added by calling the object's `addNewEcampaignMessage()` method.

- ◆ Finally, an appropriate status message is displayed.

getMsgPreviewInput()

This method displays a user interface to collect the personalization data needed to display the preview message.

doPreview()

This method displays a message in preview mode using the data collected by the `getMsgPreviewInput()` method.

showMsgPreview()

This method displays a screen, which loads a JavaScript. This JavaScript loads a pop-up window, which automatically calls the message management application with `$cmd` set to `preview` to call the `doPreview()` method to display a preview message.

appendHashes()

This is a utility method that concats two associative arrays together to create a single associative array.

Creating a Campaign Manager Application

The campaign management application adds, deletes, and modifies campaigns. Figure 15-6 shows how a campaign is created using the existing list and message from a simple user interface and stored in the database.

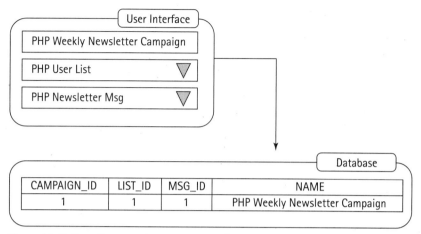

Figure 15-6: How the campaign manager works.

The `ecampaign_campaign_mngr.php` which can be found in the `ch15/apps` directory in the CDROM, implements the campaign management application using the methods discussed in the following sections.

run()

This method is used to select the appropriate method to perform add, modify, and delete operations on campaign as follows:

- If the `$cmd` variable is not set or is set to `create` from the main user interface shown by `ecmapaign_mngr.php`, then the `createCampaign()` method is called to handle the campaign addition process.

- If the `$cmd` variable is set to `delete`, then the `delCampaign()` method is called to delete the campaign.

- If the `$cmd` variable is set to `modify`, then the `modifyCampaign()` method is called to handle the campaign modify process.

createCampaign()

This method is used to manage the campaign creation process using the `$step` variable set in the user interface as follows:

- If `$step` is not set, then the `displayCampaignMenu()` method is called to display the campaign addition interface, which sets `$step` to 2 using hidden HTML form field.

- If `$step` is set to 2, then the `addCampaign()` is called to add the campaign in the database.

delCampaign()

This method is used to delete a campaign as follows:

- ◆ If campaign ID (`$campaign_id`) is not supplied from the main user interface, then an alert message is displayed and the user is returned to the previous screen.

- ◆ If campaign ID is supplied, a `Campaign` object is created. The `deleteCampaign()` of this object is called to delete the campaign from the database.

- ◆ Finally, an appropriate status message reflecting the success or failure of the delete operation is displayed.

modifyCampaign()

This method is used to manage the campaign modification process using the `$step` variable set in the user interface as follows:

- ◆ If the campaign ID (`$campaign_id`) is not supplied from the main user interface, then an alert message is displayed and the user is returned to the previous screen.

- ◆ If `$step` is not set, then the `displayCampaignMenu()` method is called to display the campaign modification interface, which sets `$step` to 2 using a hidden HTML form field.

- ◆ If `$step` is set to 2, then the `updateCampaign()` is called to update the campaign in the database.

authorize()

See the `authorize()` method in the e-campaign user interface application called `ecampaign_mngr.php` for details.

displayCampaignMenu()

This method displays the campaign interface menu.

addCampaign()

This method adds the new campaign in the database as follows:

◆ First, it checks to see if all required fields – campaign name ($name), list ID ($lid), and message ID ($mid) – are provided. If not, error messages are displayed and the user is returned to the previous screen.

◆ A Campaign object is created and its addCampaign() is called to add the campaign in the database.

◆ Finally, an appropriate status message reflecting the success or failure of the add operation is displayed.

updateCampaign()

This method updates an existing campaign in the database as follows:

◆ First, it checks to see if all required fields – campaign name ($name), list ID ($lid), and message ID ($mid) – are provided. If not, error messages are displayed and the user is returned to the previous screen.

◆ A Campaign object is created and its modifyCampaign() is called to modify the campaign in the database.

◆ Finally, an appropriate status message reflecting the success or failure of the modification operation is displayed.

Creating a Campaign Execution Application

The campaign execution application delivers e-mails by fetching the appropriate list data and localizing them in the assembly table and then delivering e-mails to them.

Because large e-mail campaigns require a great deal of time, performing them in one shot is not possible via the Web due to the potential for browser timeout. This is why this execution application performs a chunk-size number of delivery and then calls itself from the Web status screen using an HTTP meta refresh trick.

The entire execution process is shown in Figure 15-7.

The campaign execution application called ecampaign_execution.php, which can be found in ch15/apps directory in the CDROM, performs the e-mail delivery using the methods discussed in the following sections.

run()

This method calls the executeCampaign() method to perform the e-mail delivery task.

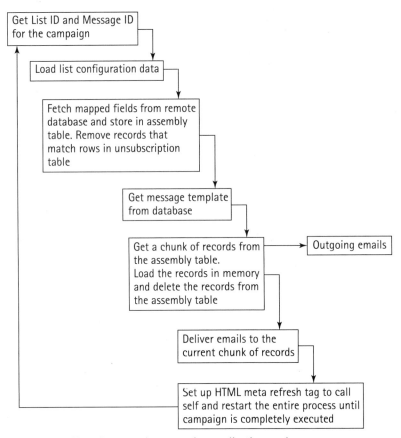

Figure 15-7: How the campaign execution application works.

executeCampaign()

This method performs all the tasks necessary to execute the campaign. It works as follows:

- ◆ If the user has not selected a campaign ID ($campaign_id) from the main user interface to execute, an alert message is displayed and user is returned to the main interface.

- ◆ A Campaign object is created, and the selected campaign data is loaded.

- ◆ If the selected campaign is loaded, its status is checked using the getStatus() method. If the status is -1, then the campaign execution has already finished. The status value is stored in the $lastrow variable.

- ◆ The campaign's message ID is retrieved via the Campaign object's getMessageID().

- The campaign's list ID is retrieved via the `Campaign` object's `getListID()`.

- The server name and the application path are stored in `$server` and `$appPath` variables, respectively.

- If `$lastrow` is empty, then this is the first time the campaign is being run. In other words, the `executeCampaign()` method is running for the first time for this campaign. So it needs to assemble the campaign data in the e-campaign database by fetching the required data from the remote table in the database pointed by the list configuration.

- A `List` object is used to retrieve the client database URL using the `getClientDBURL()` method. A connection to the client database holding the list is made using a `DBI` object called `$client_dbi`.

- The `prepareLocalList()` of the `List` object is called to prepare the assembly table.

- If the `prepareLocalList()` method returns 0, then there are no data to pump out via e-mail and, therefore, an error message is shown.

- The `getTargetData()` method is used to retrieve chunk-size (set by `$MAX_DELIVERY_AT_A_TIME` in the `ecampaign.conf` configuration file) records to execute.

- A `Message` object is created and message data is retrieved using the `getEcampaignMessageInfo()` of the object. If message data is not found, the execution halts with an error message.

- The body of the message is retrieved from the `Message` object and it is inserted into a message template.

- The message headers are retrieved using the `getEcampaignHeaderInfo()`. E-mail is sent via the built-in `mail()` method.

- For each record in the current chunk or rows, the message is personalized using the data retrieved from the assembly table, the URL tags are replaced with redirection URL, and the `UNSUB` tag is replaced with a personalized unsubscription link.

- The campaign status field is set to indicate where the next chunk should start.

- A status template is shown after each chunk size of message is sent. This template has a meta refresh tag, which recalls the execution application after `$MAX_WAIT_PER_DELIVERY` (configuration variable) seconds to continue with the next chunk of messages.

authorize()

See the `authorize()` method in the e-campaign user interface application called `ecampaign_mngr.php` for details.

Creating a URL Tracking and Redirection Application

When the campaign execution application sends e-mail, the URLs are transformed into the redirection URL. Figure 15-8 shows how such redirection URLs are tracked and redirected using the URL tracking application.

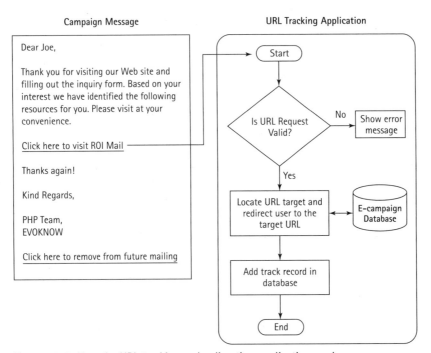

Figure 15-8: How the URL tracking and redirection application works.

The redir.php, which can be found in the ch15/apps directory in the CDROM, implements the tracking and URL redirection using the following methods.

run()

This method first determines if the redirection request mode is test or not. If the redirection mode is test, which is true during message preview, the redirectTest() method is called to redirect the tester to the target URL without recording the track in the database.

If the mode is not test, the checksum value of the redirection request is compared with the calculated checksum. If both checksum values match, the redirection request is considered valid and the `keepTrackAndRedirect()` method is called to track and redirect the end-user to the target URL.

computeCheckSum()

This method implements a simple checksum algorithm using the URL ID (`$u`), USER ID (`$uid`), campaign ID (`$c`), and a random number stored in configuration file called `$SECRET`.

This checksum value is compared with the campaign-execution-application-generated checksum stored in the redirection link to check the validity of the redirection request.

Using this checksum technique, we can avoid invalid requests from unfriendly users who want to distort the tracking data.

keepTrackAndRedirect()

This method tracks the URL request in the database and redirects the user to the target URL. It creates a URL `Track` object and calls the `storeTrack()` method to store the track data.

It also creates a `URL` object and gets the URL for the given URL ID (`$u`) and redirects the user to the target URL via the HTTP location header.

redirectTest()

This method creates a `URL` object and redirects the user to the target URL by finding the target URL using the `getURL()` method and redirecting using the HTTP location header.

Creating an Unsubscription Tracking Application

When an end-user clicks on the unsubscription link sent by the campaign execution application, it is processed by the unsubscription process shown in Figure 15-9.

The `unsub.php`, which can be found in `ch15/apps` directory in the CDROM, implements the unsubscription application using the following methods.

run()

This method first determines if the unsubscription redirection request mode is `test` or not. If the mode is `test`, which is true during message preview, the `alert()` method is used to display a message stating that the unsubscription request is a test and therefore it isn't tracked and stored in the database.

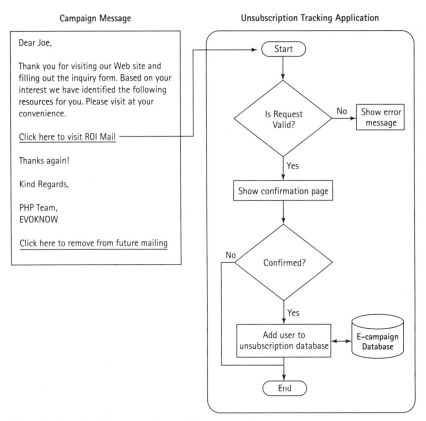

Figure 15-9: How the unsubscription tracking application works.

If the mode is not test, the checksum value of the request is compared with the calculated checksum. If both checksum values match, the unsubscription request is considered valid and the `askForConfirmation()` method is called to confirm the unsubscription request.

If the user confirms the unsubscription request by continuing forward, the `unsubUser()` method is called to store the unsubscription request in the database.

computeCheckSum()

This method implements a simple checksum algorithm using USER ID ($uid), campaign ID ($c), and a random number stored in the configuration file called $SECRET.

This checksum value is compared with the campaign-execution-application-generated checksum stored in the unsubscription link to check the validity of the request.

Using this checksum technique, you can avoid invalid requests from unfriendly users who want to distort the unsubscription tracking data.

askForConfirmation()

This method displays a confirmation screen to allow the user to confirm that she wants to unsubscribe from this e-mail list.

unsubUser()

This method uses an unsubscription object, which calls the `storeUnsub()` method to unsubscribe the user from this list in the database.

This user will not receive an e-mail from this list again.

Creating a Campaign Reporting Application

The campaign report application displays the data collected for each campaign. The user selects the campaign from the main e-campaign interface displayed by the e-campaign user interface application. A sample report is shown in Figure 15-10.

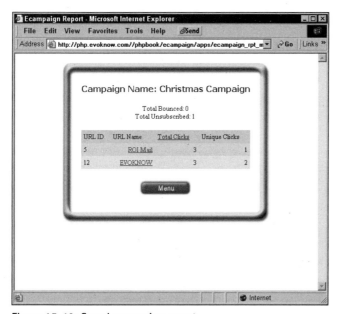

Figure 15-10: Sample campaign report.

The campaign report application, `ecampaign_rpt_mngr.php`, can be found in `ch15/apps` directory in the CDROM, which implements the following methods.

run()

This method calls the `showEcampaignReport()` to show the report.

showEcampaignReport()

This method shows the campaign report. It works as follows:

◆ If the campaign ID (`$ecampaign_id`) is not supplied from the e-campaign user interface, displayed by the e-campaign interface application, the method shows an alert message and returns the user to the user interface page.

◆ By default, it sets the column order of the report to URL ID (`$url_id`) if the user does not supply any order by clicking on any column heading after the report is shown.

◆ Next, the method creates a `Report` object, a `URL` object, and a `Campaign` object.

◆ The `getURLResponse()` method of the `Report` object is called to get the total and unique URL track (click-through) number.

◆ The `getUnsubResponse()` method of the `Report` object is called to get the total number of unsubscribers for the current campaign.

◆ The `getBounceResponse()` method of the `Report` object is called to get the total number of bounced e-mails for the current campaign.

◆ Finally, the report is displayed using an HTML template.

authorize()

See the `authorize()` method in the e-campaign user-interface application called `ecampaign_mngr.php` for details.

toggleDescField()

This is a utility method that toggles the DESC option used in the report column title links to toggle the column's ascending or descending order.

Testing the E-Campaign System

Now that you have all the e-campaign applications built, you're ready to test them. You'll need a database with a table that has numeric record ID (to be mapped to REC_ID), an e-mail address field (to be mapped to EMAIL), and, optionally, the first name field (to be mapped to FIRST) and last name field (to be mapped to LAST). Of course, you can have additional fields that map to AGE, SEX, INCOME, and so on, as well as standard personalization fields.

In this test, I assume that you have a test database called PRODDB, which has a table called PHPCustomers with fields called custid (REC_ID), fname (FIRST), lname (LNAME), and e-mail (EMAIL). I also assume that this database is on a host called diablo.evoknow.com and the user name and password needed to access this MySQL database are scott and tiger, respectively. Also, make sure that you have some valid data in the table to be able to test the campaign.

TIP If you have a PHP MyAdmin application installed on a system, you can easily add sample data via its interface.

We also assume that the e-campaign applications can be accessible via the http://www.evoknow.com/php/ecampaign/ecampaign_mngr.php main interface application.

Creating a list

To create the previously mentioned list, run the ecampaign_mngr.php application and click on the Add List button. This will show the interface shown in Figure 15-11.

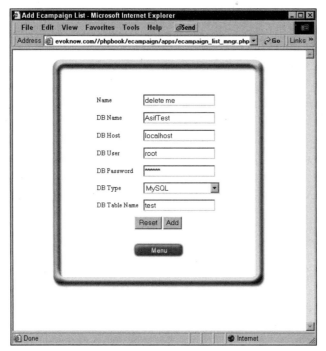

Figure 15-11: Configuring a list.

Enter the necessary information as assumed earlier and submit the information. If the `ecampaign_list_mngr.php` application is able to connect to the given database using the user name and password, it will retrieve the metadata for the given table and display a mapping interface, as shown in Figure 15-12.

Map the fields as shown and save the list. After the list is created, you can modify or delete it as you please. Keep the list for the time being so that you can continue with the test.

Creating a target URL

Now create one or more URLs that you can use in your e-mail campaign. Click on the Add URL button from the main user interface shown by the `ecampaign_mngr.php` application. This will show a screen like the one in Figure 15-13.

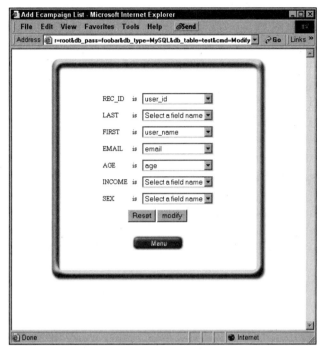

Figure 15-12: Mapping database fields.

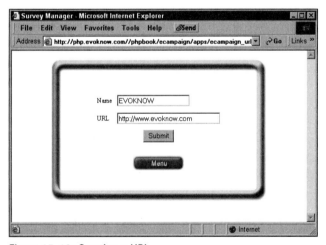

Figure 15-13: Creating a URL.

Add a URL of your choice and give a name to the URL. Submit the URL and it should be stored in the database. Repeat this process as many times as you want, to create multiple URLs. These URLs will be trackable.

Creating a message

Next create a message by clicking on the Add Msg button. You'll see a screen like the one in Figure 15-14. Create a message to your liking by filling out the form. You can enter the same information as shown in the screen if you want.

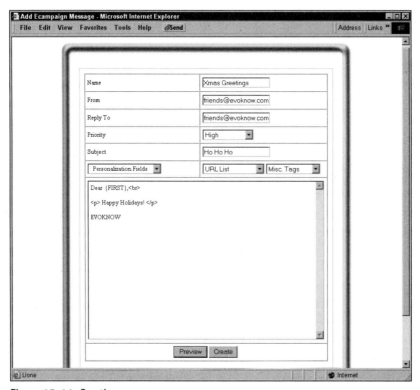

Figure 15-14: Creating a message.

You can personalize the message, as shown in Figure 15-14, by selecting the personalization menu and inserting the appropriate tags.

Due to JavaScript limitations, the personalization tag is always appended to the message at the end. You can simply copy and paste it in the designed location. The same is also true for URLs.

If you want to track URLs, you can insert one or more trackable URLs from the URL list. If you enter the URL directly in the message, it will not be tracked by the redirection application. Only URLs that are inserted from the URL list are tracked.

TIP When inserting URLs in the message, consider using `<a   href="">` `label</a>` instead of inserting raw URL in the message. The automatically generated redirection URLs are not pretty to look at, so they're best kept somewhat invisible from the average user by using the HTML anchor link tag.

After you've created the message, you can preview it or save it. If you decided to preview it, you'll be asked to fill out the standard personalization field values once, because during preview no real list data from the database is fetched.

Save the message after you have previewed. Remember that this e-campaign system only sends an HTML message, so you must use proper HTML tags to format your message so it's rendered properly in modern e-mail clients such as Outlook Express.

Creating a campaign

After you've created a list, one or more URLs (if you want to add URLs in the message), and a message, you're ready to create a campaign. Click on the Add Campaign button in the main user interface shown by `ecampaign_mngr.php` to add a campaign from an interface similar to Figure 15-15.

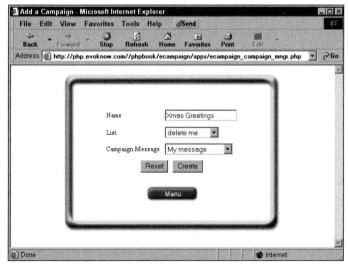

Figure 15-15: Creating a campaign.

Give a name to your campaign, select a list and a message, and save the campaign. That's all there is to creating a campaign!

Now you're ready to execute this test campaign.

Executing a campaign

Select the campaign from the bottom of the main user interface shown by ecmapaign_mngr.php, and click on the red Execute button. The campaign will be executed and a status message will be shown as shown in Figure 15-16.

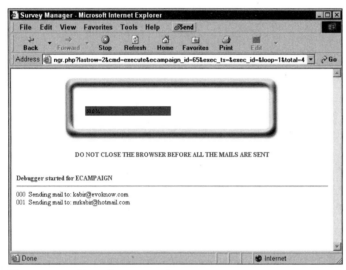

Figure 15-16: Executing a campaign.

Now access the campaign e-mail in your e-mail client program.

Viewing a campaign report

After you've executed the campaign, the campaign report becomes available immediately. You can view the campaign report by selecting the campaign name from the main user interface shown by ecampaign_mngr.php and clicking on the Show Report button.

If you view the report before any URL is clicked by any user, the report will show no URL track. If you click on a tracked URL in a message and then check the report, you'll see your track being reported. You can click on the URL in your message as many times as you want, and you'll notice that the report accurately reports the unique and total URL clicks. Figure 15-10 shows a sample report. Like URL clicks, the unsubscription tracks are also reported in the report.

Security Considerations

The checksum algorithm used in making trackable URL links and unsubscription URL needs to be modified before you start using the redir.php and unsub.php applications in real-world email campaign scenarios. At the least, you should change the value of $SECRET in the configuration file.

Because the current algorithms are published in the book, someone can easily guess how to defeat them. For example, the computeCheckSum() method in the redir.php application can be changed to:

```
function computeCheckSum()
{
    global $SECRET;

    $u = $this->getRequestField('u');
    $uid = $this->getRequestField('uid');
    $c = $this->getRequestField('c');

    return ($u << 4) + ($uid << 3) +  ($c << 7) + $SECRET;
}
```

Here this version uses different bit shifts for $u, $uid, and $c. Of course you should choose your own values to make sure they are not known to anyone. The best approach would be to come up with a completely new algorithm that does not use even the same bit shifting technique. I will leave that to you to develop.

Summary

In this chapter you learned to develop a simple email campaign system that allows you to send personalized, URL tracked HTML messages to email addresses found in MySQL databases. Note that since the email campaign system uses your default mail transport agent (i.e. mail server), the performance will very based on your mail server's abilities.

Part IV

Using PHP for Sysadmin Tasks

Chapter 16

Command-Line PHP Utilities

IN THIS CHAPTER

- ♦ Writing command-line PHP utilities
- ♦ How to create a cron-based reminder
- ♦ How to develop a geographic location query tool for IP
- ♦ Developing a spam-busting utility for POP3 mailboxes
- ♦ How to develop a hard disk monitoring tool
- ♦ Creating a CPU load monitoring tool

PHP STARTED OUT AS A SIMPLE Web scripting tool written in Perl and later became the most popular Web application development language. Because of its strong ties with the Web, it has lagged behind as an all-purpose programming language. Especially for command-line users, PHP is considered a newcomer, because not many command-line PHP utilities are floating around on the Internet just yet. In this chapter, you develop a few command-line utilities to get you started in command-line PHP development.

 Most of the scripts discussed here might not work on a Windows platform. They have been tested on the Linux platform only.

Working with the Command-Line Interpreter

The command-line version of PHP is installed when you enable CGI support during the PHP installation process. The command-line PHP interpreter can be found by running the following:

```
which php
```

This will show the full path of the PHP command-line interpreter. Sample output appears as follows:

```
/usr/bin/php
```

In most cases, you should find the PHP binary in the /usr/bin directory, which is typically in your path, so you can run the following:

```
php -h
```

The 4.3.x version of the PHP command-line interpreter will display output similar to following:

```
Usage: php [options] [-f] <file> [args...]
       php [options] -r <code> [args...]
       php [options] [-- args...]
  -s              Display color syntax highlighted source.
  -w              Display source with stripped comments and
whitespace.
  -f <file>       Parse <file>.
  -v              Version number
  -c <path>|<file> Look for php.ini file in this directory
  -a              Run interactively
  -d foo[=bar]    Define INI entry foo with value 'bar'
  -e              Generate extended information for
debugger/profiler
  -z <file>       Load Zend extension <file>.
  -l              Syntax check only (lint)
  -m              Show compiled in modules
  -i              PHP information
  -r <code>       Run PHP <code> without using script tags <?..?>
  -h              This help

  args...         Arguments passed to script. Use -- args when
first argument

                  starts with - or script is read from stdin
```

These options are not necessary for running command-line scripts because most command-line scripts under a Linux/UNIX system are run by adding the interpreter path as the first line. For example, Listing 16-1 shows a simple PHP script called helloworld.php.

Listing 16-1: helloworld.php

```
#!/usr/bin/php -q
<?php

    echo "Hello World\n";

?>
```

 In PHP Version 4.3.x, the -q option is not needed if the PHP binary is compiled with the --enable-cli option, which enables Command Line Interface (CLI) support and automatically suppresses HTTP headers. Earlier versions of PHP supported multiple options, but only one option would actually work.

In the preceding code, the first line starts with #! and is followed by the fully qualified path name of the PHP command-line interpreter. The next line is the starting tag for the PHP script.

After making the file executable by running the `chmod 755 helloworld.php` command, you can run it from the script's current directory as follows:

```
./helloworld.php
```

Following is sample output:

```
Hello World
```

When the helloworld.php script is run from the shell, the shell loads this file and locates the first line (#!, called the *bang line*) and runs the script using the named interpreter. All the scripts discussed in this chapter run this way. However, you can also run PHP scripts as follows:

```
php -q filename.php
```

where *filename*.php is your script.

It's good practice to get in the habit of using the –q option when running PHP from the command line to suppress the HTML headers. That way you are sure to suppress the headers.

In the 4.3.x version of PHP (compiled with the --enable-cli option), you can also run the following:

```
php -q -r 'echo "Your PHP Code";'
```

Here, the echo statement will be executed as if it were in a script. This type of execution is not suitable for most real problem-solving work. It is most useful when you want to write a quick and dirty script for one-time use.

Reading standard input

Reading input from the shell is a common task performed by a command-line script. Listing 16-2 shows a simple script called ask.php, which reads user input from a command-line prompt.

Listing 16-2: ask.php

```
#!/usr/bin/php -q
<?php

    $name = prompt('Enter your name: ');

    echo "Hello $name\n";

    exit;

    function prompt($label = null)
    {
        echo $label;
        return getSTDIN();
    }

    function getSTDIN()
    {

        // In PHP 4.3.x with --enable-cli option
        // you can use STDIN constant which replaces
        // the following fopen() line.
        $STDIN =fopen("/dev/stdin","r");
```

```php
        $keyboardBuffer = null;

        if ($STDIN)
        {
            while(($ch = fgetc($STDIN)) != "\n")
            {
                $keyboardBuffer .= $ch;
            }

            fclose($STDIN);
        }

        return $keyboardBuffer;

    }

?>
```

The script calls a function called `prompt()`, which takes a string message and displays it on the shell screen. The `prompt()` function calls another function called `getSTDIN()`, which opens a file handle called `$STDIN` to /dev/stdin (i.e., php://stdin) and reads characters from it until a newline (\n) character is entered by the user. This effectively gives us the command line entered by the user. The user-entered data is stored in a string buffer called `$keyboardBuffer`, which is returned to the caller of `getSTDIN()`.

 The PHP 4.3.x version of the command-line PHP binary with CLI enabled (--enable-cli) has STDIN, STDOUT, and STDERR constants predefined. These constants replace the following code:

```php
// STDIN constant replaces:
$stdin = fopen('php://stdin', 'r');
// STDOUT constant replaces:
$stdout = fopen('php://stdout', 'w');
// STDERR constant replaceS:
$stderr = fopen('php://stderr', 'w');
```

Getting into arguments

You will often need to get command-line arguments from the user. Listing 16-3 shows a simple script called arg.php, which prints out an array called `$argv`.

Listing 16-3: arg.php

```php
#!/usr/bin/php -q
<?php

  print_r($argv);

?>
```

When this script is run as follows:

```
./args.php -h -k -x 100
```

it prints the following:

```
Array
(
    [0] => ./arg.php
    [1] => -h
    [2] => -k
    [3] => -x
    [4] => 100
)
```

The $argv array is created by PHP, which stores all the command-line arguments as shown in the preceding output. However, it is not the most efficient way to deal with command arguments. Listing 16-4 shows a script called cmd_options.php, which uses the Console/Getopt.php class from the PEAR package.

Listing 16-4: cmd_options.php

```php
#!/usr/bin/php -q
<?php

    $CMD_SHORT_OPTIONS = 'hs:';
    $CMD_LONG_OPTIONS  = array('help', 'size=');

    // Set this to the PEAR directory
    $PEAR_DIR = '/evoknow/intranet/htdocs/pear' ;

    ini_set( 'include_path', ':' .
             $PEAR_DIR . ':' .
             ini_get('include_path'));

    require_once "Console/Getopt.php";

    $cmd = getCommandLineOptions(
```

```php
                          Console_Getopt::getopt
                          (
                          $GLOBALS['argv'],
                          $CMD_SHORT_OPTIONS,
                          $CMD_LONG_OPTIONS
                          )
                  );

if ($cmd == null)
{
    syntax();
}
else if (isset($cmd['h']) ||
        isset($cmd['help']))
{
    echo "You selected help option.\n";

}

if (isset($cmd['s']) ||
    isset($cmd['size']))
{

    echo "You selected size option. Chosen size is " .
        $cmd['s'] . ' ' . $cmd['size'] . "\n";

}

exit;

function syntax()
{
    $script = basename($GLOBALS['argv'][0]);

    echo<<<HELP

    Syntax $script [-h | --help] [-s bytes | --size=bytes]

    More help will be added later.

HELP;

    }
```

Continued

Listing 16-4 *(Continued)*

```php
function getCommandLineOptions($options)
{

    $type = gettype($options);

    if (gettype($options) != "array")
    {
        // Error in command line
        echo "$options->message \n";
        return null;
    }

    $cmd = array();

    foreach ($options[0] as $argArray)
    {

        $argName = preg_replace('/[^\w]/' ,
                                '' ,
                                $argArray[0]);

        $argValue = $argArray[1];

        $cmd[$argName] = ($argValue != '') ? $argValue : TRUE;
    }

    return (count($cmd) > 0) ? $cmd : null;

}

?>
```

Here, getCommandLineOptions() is passed the output of the Console_Getopt::getopt() function. The Console_Getopt::getopt() function takes $GLOBALS['argv'], $CMD_SHORT_OPTIONS, and $CMD_LONG_OPTIONS as arguments. The $GLOBALS['argv'] argument is same as $argv, which holds the user-supplied command-line arguments. The second argument, $CMD_SHORT_OPTIONS, is a list of short argument options such as 'hs:'. These are the options that a user can enter as -h and -s *size*. The -s option takes a value and therefore ':' is added in the $CMD_SHORT_OPTIONS string to indicate that. The $CMD_LONG_OPTIONS is set to an array such as array('help', 'size='). These arguments can be entered by the user as -help and --size=*size*.

The syntax for short arguments in `Console_Getopt::getopt()` is fairly simple. List each short argument, order doesn't matter. If an argument requires a parameter (like "s" in the listing above) you follow it with a colon (as we did above). If the parameter is optional, you add two colons.

The short and the long argument lists are the expected lists of arguments. The `Console_Getopt::getopt()` function returns an error object if the user enters an invalid argument that is not listed in the short or long expected argument list passed to it.

If the user enters valid arguments and argument options, the `getopt()` method returns the list of options supplied by the user in an array. The `getCommandLineOptions()` function goes through the valid list of user-entered arguments, removes - characters from each argument, and makes an associative array called `$cmd`, using the argument name as the key and the argument value as the value. For example, if the user runs this script as follows:

```
./cmd_options.php -h -s 100
```

the `$cmd` array looks like the following:

```
Array
(
    [h] => 1
    [s] => 100
)
```

Similarly, if the user runs it as

```
./cmd_options.php -h --size 100 --king=burger
```

the `$cmd` array looks like the following:

```
Array
(
    [h] => 1
    [size] => 100
    [king] => burger
)
```

Notice that arguments that do not have a value (such as -h) have a value of "1" in the $cmd array. Since "1" evaluates to TRUE in Boolean expressions, when this array is returned, you can easily find out which command-line arguments were selected. In this script, it uses the built-in isset() function to determine whether a known argument is set, and prints a message indicating the result. For example:

```
./cmd_options.php -h
```

Returns:

```
You selected help option.
```

```
This shows that -h has been supplied.
```

To add a new short argument called -z, we can simply update the $CMD_SHORT_OPTIONS list. Similarly, to add a long argument called -zero, we can add this argument in $CMD_LONG_OPTIONS. For example, to allow a new long argument called -count that expects a value, we can add 'count=' in the following array:

```
$CMD_LONG_OPTIONS  = array('help', 'size=', 'count=');
```

Then we can write code to determine whether the user has chosen this argument or not. For example:

```
if (isset($cmd['count']))
{
    echo "You entered count value of ". $cmd['count'] . "\n";
}
```

Now that you know how to deal with command line PHP scripting along with argument handling, let's develop some interesting command-line scripts. In the following section, you will develop a simple reminder tool.

 Most chapters in this book refer you to the accompanying CD-ROM for source listings. Because the tools discussed in this chapter are very small, we include the source listing so that you can see the entire code while reading the chapters.

Building a Simple Reminder Tool

In this day and age, who does not need to be reminded of something? In this section, you will develop a reminder utility that runs on a Linux system as a daily cron job. A cron job is simply another name for a scheduled task. Linux and other UNIX systems have a daemon program called *cron*, which runs other programs at given intervals. Linux contains predefined cron directories in the main system configuration /etc directory, including the following:

- **/etc/cron.daily:** scripts and programs that are run once a day

- **cron.hourly:** scripts and programs that are run once every hour

- **cron.monthly:** scripts and programs that are run once a month

- **cron.weekly:** scripts and programs that are run once a week

You can generally create a symbolic link (symlink) from the program you want to run via cron to one of these directories and get it run on the predefined schedule.

If you want to know when an hourly, daily, weekly, or monthly cron job is run from the aforementioned scripts, look at /etc/crontab, which shows the time when these directories are processed by the cron daemon. You might have to consult the crontab manual pages (man crontab) to understand the cryptic time assignments. The user who needs more information on cron should start with the man 5 crontab command, which describes the basic syntax of the crontab file and operation of cron in general.

Note that if you are not a privileged user, you will want to explore the cron -l and cron -e commands for dealing with cron and crontab. Although this section deals mainly with Linux and cron, Windows users can use the Windows Scheduler application to schedule tasks to run at preset time(s).

We will develop this reminder tool and symbolically link it inside the /etc/cron.daily so that the reminder tool is run once a day automatically. In most systems, daily tasks are run very early in the morning (for example, 4:00 A.M.). First, let's examine what our reminder system will offer.

Features of the reminder tool

The reminder tool will offer the following features:

- ◆ It will process reminders for all users on the system.

- ◆ All users can have their own set of reminders, which they can manage using configuration files and message templates.

- ◆ Each reminder can be sent using a separate message template.

- ◆ Types of reminders supported are daily, weekly, monthly, and yearly.

- ◆ For each type of reminder, there can be an unlimited number of reminders per user.

Now let's implement this tool.

Implementing the reminder tool

Listing 16-5 shows a configuration file that we will use for our reminder tool. The DEBUG constant will be used for enabling and disabling debug messages.

The PASSWD_FILE constant points to the system's password file. You can use a different file, but two fields are required by the reminder system: *username* and home directory. If you use a custom user list file, make sure it mimics the /etc/passwd file in terms of the formatting and placement of *username*, and the home directory field.

 Reading man htpasswd and/or man passwd will help with managing and mimicking the /etc/passwd file.

The $XMAILER variable is used to name the reminder in an X-header for each mail message sent. This can be set to anything.

The USER_REMINDER_DIR constant is used to store the expected name of the user's reminder directory. Each user can have a reminder directory inside the home directory as ~*username*/%USER_REMINDER_DIR/. For example, ~kabir/reminders is the default reminder directory per the following configuration for the user kabir.

Each user's reminder configuration is stored in the reminders.txt file pointed to by the USER_REMINDER_FILE constant. This file must reside in a directory specified by USER_REMINDER_DIR, within a user's home directory. For example, the user sheila, whose home directory is /home/sheila (i.e., ~sheila), can have /home/sheila/reminders/reminders.txt as the full path for her reminder configuration file. The configuration file is as follows:

Listing 16-5: reminder.conf

```php
<?php

    define(DEBUG, TRUE);
    define(PASSWD_FILE, '/etc/passwd');

    $XMAILER = 'Reminder Version 1.0';

    // Reminder directory for users
    // Default: ~username/reminders
    define(USER_REMINDER_DIR, 'reminders');

    // Reminder configuration file for user
    // in user's reminder directory
    // (%USER_REMINDER_DIR%/filename)
    // Default: %USER_REMINDER_DIR%/reminders.txt
    define(USER_REMINDER_FILE, 'reminders.txt');

?>
```

Listing 16-6 shows a sample configuration file for a user. This configuration file can be altered by the user to add, delete, and modify reminders as desired.

Listing 16-6: ~username/reminders/reminders.txt

```
# User Reminder Configuration Format
#
# Lines starting with # are ignored
# Lines that are blank are ignored

# Format
# FREQUENCY:

#daily:todo.txt

weekly:mon:monday_plans.txt
#weekly:tue:tuesday.txt
weekly:tue:foo.txt
weekly:wed:wednesday_plans.txt
weekly:fri:friday_prayer.txt

monthly:10:groupmtg10th.txt
monthly:30:payroll.txt
```

Continued

Listing 16-6 *(Continued)*

```
yearly:12-10:12-10.txt
yearly:07-22:ak_birthday.txt
yearly:07-23:ak_birthday.txt

yearly:07-02:mk_birthday.txt
yearly:07-03:mk_birthday.txt
```

As you can see, this is a plain-text reminder configuration file. The lines that are blank or start with the # character are ignored by the reminder tool, so a user can use them to keep the reminder configuration readable and commented. There are four types of configuration lines:

```
daily:reminder_mail_file.txt
weekly:week_day:reminder_mail_file.txt
monthly:MM:reminder_mail_file.txt
yearly:MM-DD:reminder_mail_file.txt
```

The first line (daily) defines a daily reminder. Whenever such a line is processed by the reminder system, it reads the named file (reminder_mail_file.txt) and sends e-mail to the user or anyone else specified (in the To: field) within the file.

The second line (weekly) defines a weekly reminder. The reminder is sent only if the weekday (mon, tue, wed, thu, fri, sat, sun) reminder tool running corresponds with the same day as the current day. For example, if the reminder tool is running on a Saturday (sat) and a line such as the following is found:

```
weekly:sat:myweekend_plan.txt
```

the reminder system will load the myweekend_plan.txt file and e-mail the user (or whomever else is listed in the To:, Bcc:, and Cc: fields in the file).

Similarly, the third line (monthly) is used for monthly reminders. The MM field is simply the two-digit day of the month. For example, to send a reminder on the 27th of each month, a user can set up the following:

```
monthly:27:oh_no_its_27th_already.txt
```

Finally, the yearly reminder is set by the last line. The yearly reminder requires both the MM and DD part of a (MM-DD-YYYY) date. For example, if you want to send a reminder to yourself about a friend's birthday on July 23, you can set up the following:

```
yearly:07-23:sheila_birthday.txt
```

Now let's look at a message file to understand how users can set up the actual reminder message sent to themselves or anyone they choose. Listing 16-7 shows an example reminder message file that can be used in any daily, weekly, monthly, or yearly reminders.

Listing 16-7: ~username/reminders/todo.txt

```
From: Reminder <reminder@evoknow.com>
To: Alter Ego <kabir@evoknow.com>
Cc: mrkabir@hotmail.com
Bcc: kabir@sac-home.evoknow.com
Content-Type: text/plain
Subject: My TODO for <%TODAY%>

I need to accomplish the following tasks today:

1. Check and respond to all my pending emails (on going)
2. Call Andrew @ 10:30 AM to discuss remote mgmt contract
3. Call Chad  @ 11:30 PM to discuss security contract
4. Lunch with TLT @ 1:00 PM (Geek)
5. Write rest of the article for CMP (2 Hrs)
6. Finish spec for Metrocomia
7. Buy holiday gifts

Too much to do, too little time!

-alter-ego
```

This is a text reminder file. The From:, To:, Cc:, Bcc:, Content-Type:, and Subject: lines correspond to standard e-mail headers. They are used in sending e-mail messages. For example, if you wanted to send an HTML message as a reminder, you could set Content-Type: text/html instead of text/plain. The message is sent to recipients listed in the To:, Cc:, and Bcc: fields. You do not have to have Cc: or Bcc: fields.

Listing 16-8 shows the reminder.php script that implements the reminder tool.

Listing 16-8: reminder.php

```php
#!/usr/bin/php -q
<?php

    require_once('reminder.conf');

    define(USER_FILE_MISSING, 1);
```

Continued

Listing 16-8 *(Continued)*

```php
$userList = getUsers(PASSWD_FILE);

foreach($userList as $username => $homeDir)
{
    doRemind(USER_REMINDER_DIR,
             USER_REMINDER_FILE,
             $username,
             $homeDir);
}

exit;

function doRemind($userDir = null,
                  $userFile = null,
                  $username = null,
                  $homeDir = null)
{
    $userReminderDir = sprintf("%s/%s",
                               $homeDir,
                               $userDir);

    $userReminderFile = sprintf("%s/%s",
                                $userReminderDir,
                                $userFile);

    $userReminderLogFile = sprintf("%s/%s.log",
                                   $userReminderDir,
                                   $username);

    $logEntries = array();

    if (!file_exists($userReminderFile))
    {
        return USER_FILE_MISSING;
    }

    if (DEBUG)
        echo "Processing reminders for $username ...\n";

    if (DEBUG)
        echo "Reminder File $userReminderFile \n";

    $mailings =  getRemindersForToday(
                     file($userReminderFile),
```

```php
                    $userReminderLogFile
                    );

    foreach ($mailings as $mail)
    {
        $mail = sprintf("%s/%s", $userReminderDir, $mail);

        if (file_exists($mail))
        {
            if (! doMail($mail, $username))
                array_push($logEntries,
                    "mail failed!");;

        } else
        {
            array_push($logEntries,
                    "cannot find or open $mail");
        }
    }

    writeLog($userReminderLogFile, $logEntries);

}

function doMail($file = null, $user = null)
{
    $lines = file($file);
    $lines = str_replace("\r\n", "\n", $lines);
    $lines = str_replace("\r", "\n", $lines);
    $lines = str_replace("\n", "\r\n", $lines);


    $today = date('M-d-Y h:i:s A');

    $contentTypeSet = FALSE;

    $message = array();

    $headers = array("X-Mailer: " .
                    $ XMAILER . "\r\n");

    $to = $user;
```

Continued

Listing 16-8 *(Continued)*

```
foreach ($lines as $str)
{
    $index++;
    if (preg_match('/To:\s*(.+)/i',
                    $str,
                    $match
                    )
        )
    {
        $to = $match[1];
    }
    else if (preg_match('/From:\s*(.+)/i',
                          $str,
                          $match
                          )
            )
    {
        array_push($headers, "From: $match[1] \r\n");
    }
    else if (preg_match('/Subject:\s*(.+)/i',
                          $str,
                          $match
                          )
            )
    {
        $subject = $match[1];
    }
    else if (preg_match('/^CC:\s*(.+)/i', $str, $match))
    {
        array_push($headers, "Cc: $match[1] \r\n");
    }
    else if (preg_match('/Bcc:\s*(.+)/i', $str, $match))
    {
        array_push($headers, "Bcc: $match[1] \r\n");
    }
    else if (preg_match('/Content-Type:\s*(.+)/i',
                          $str,
                          $match
                          )
            )
    {
        if (preg_match('/html/', $match[1]))
        {
            array_push($headers,
```

```
                             "Content-Type: text/html\r\n");
            } else {
                array_push($headers,
                           "Content-Type: text/plain\n");
            }

            $contentTypeSet = TRUE;
        }
        else if (preg_match('/MIME-Version:\s*(.+)/i',
                            $str,
                            $match
                            )
                 )
        {
            array_push($headers,
                       "MIME-Version: $match[1] \r\n");

        } else {
            array_push($message, $str);
        }
    }

    if (! $contentTypeSet)
        array_push($headers,
                   "Content-Type: text/plain\r\n");

    $subject = preg_replace( '/<%TODAY%>/i',
                             $today,
                             $subject);

    $body = implode('', $message);
    $body = preg_replace('/<%TODAY%>/i', $today, $body);

    $headerStr = implode('', $headers);

    if (DEBUG)
        echo "Sending mail to: $to (subject: $subject)\n";

    return mail($to, $subject, $body, $headerStr);
}

function getRemindersForToday($list = null,
                             $logFile = null)
{
```

Continued

Listing 16-8 *(Continued)*

```php
$reminders = array();
$logEntries = array();

// Get today's date
$thisMonth = date('M');
$thisMM = date('m');

$thisDay = strtolower(date('D'));
$thisDD = date('d');

$MMDD = sprintf("%02d-%02d", $thisMM, $thisDD);

$lineNumber = 0;

// Parse each line in the user's reminder file
foreach ($list as $line)
{

    // Count line number (needed for error reporting)
    $lineNumber++;

    // Ignore lines starting with # as comments
    if (preg_match('/^#/', $line)) continue;

    // Ignore lines that are blank
    $line = ltrim($line);
    if (preg_match('/^$/', $line)) continue;

    $line = substr($line,0, strlen($line)-1);
    list ($type,$when,$what) = explode(':', $line);

    if (preg_match('/daily/i', $type))
    {
        // daily reminders have only 2 parts daily:file
        // so $when will have what we want in $what

        // Daily reminder
        array_push($reminders, $when);
    }
    else if ( preg_match('/weekly/i', $type) &&
                !strcmp($thisDay, strtolower($when)) &&
                !empty($what)
            )
    {
```

```php
        // Weekly reminder
        array_push($reminders, $what);
    }
    else if ( preg_match('/monthly/i', $type) &&
              ($thisDD == $when) &&
              !empty($what)
            )
    {
        // Monthly reminder
        array_push($reminders, $what);
    }
    else if ( preg_match('/yearly/i', $type) &&
              (!strcmp($MMDD, $when)) &&
              !empty($what)
            )
    {
        // Yearly reminder
        array_push($reminders, $what);

    }
    else if (empty($what))
    {
        array_push($logEntries,
                   "error in line $lineNumber ($line)");
    }
}

// Write log entries
writeLog($logFile, $logEntries);

// Remove duplicates from reminder list
return array_values(array_unique($reminders));
}

function writeLog($logFile = null, $entries = null)
{

    if (count($entries) <1) return FALSE;

    $logFD = fopen($logFile, 'a+');

    $today = date('M-d-Y h:i:s A');

    if (! $logFD) return FALSE;
```

Continued

Listing 16-8 *(Continued)*

```
    foreach ($entries as $logRecord)
    {
        fputs($logFD, "$today: $logRecord\n");
    }

    fclose($logFD);

    return TRUE;
}

function getUsers($userFile = null)
{
    $users = array();

    if (!file_exists($userFile))
    {
        return $users;
    }

    // For each line in the file
    // create a entry in users array
    // as:  $users[username] = home_dir
    foreach ( file($userFile) as $line)
    {
        $userInfo = explode(':',$line);

        $users[$userInfo[0]] = $userInfo[5];
    }

    return $users;
}

?>
```

Here is how this script works:

◆ It first gets a list of users by calling the getUsers() function. This function is given the PASSWD_FILE file name, which is configured in reminder.conf. The user list is returned into $userList.

◆ For each user in $userList, the script calls the doRemind() function, which processes the reminders for the user.

Now let's examine each of the functions used in this script.

doRemind()

This function obtains four things: the user's reminder directory ($userDir, which is USER_REMINDER_DIR set in reminder.conf), the user reminder file name ($userFile, which is USER_REMINDER_FILE set in reminder.conf), $username, and the user's home directory ($homeDir).

It first determines whether the user has a reminder file in the reminder directory inside the user's home directory. If there is no reminder configuration (reminders.txt) file, the function returns. That ends the user's reminder processing.

However, because the user does have a reminders.txt file in the reminders directory, the getRemindersForToday() function is called see if any of the reminders are meant for the current day.

The getRemindersForToday() method parses the reminders.txt file and if any reminder matches, it returns the associated reminder mail file. For example, suppose a user has the following configuration in reminders.txt:

```
weekly:mon:my_monday_tasklist.txt
weekly:tue:my_tuesday_tasklist.txt
weekly:wed:my_wednesday_tasklist.txt
weekly:thu:my_thursday_tasklist.txt
weekly:fri:my_friday_tasklist.txt
weekly:sat:my_saturday_plans.txt
weekly:sun:my_sunday_plans.txt
```

Whenever the reminder is run, one of the weekly reminders will match, as the user has a weekly reminder for each day. The matching reminder mail file will be returned in an array called $mailings by the getRemindersForToday() function.

For each of the entries in $mailings, the doMail() method is called only if the mail file exists. In other words, if it is Monday, the preceding configuration will return $mailings = array('monday_tasklist.txt'). If ~*username*/reminders/monday_tasklist.txt exists, then doMail() will send out the mail.

In the case of a missing file, log entries will be created. The log is later written to the ~*username*/reminders/*username*.log file so that the user can review it and fix the configuration file or create missing mail files.

doMail()

This function sends the mail out. It receives a reminder mail filename, which exists in the ~*username*/reminders directory. The function loads the file into an array called $lines using the file() function.

Each line is parsed for mail headers, such as To:, From:, Cc:, Bcc:, Subject:, and Content-Type:. These headers are stored in appropriate format in the $headers array.

The other lines are considered part of the body of the message, and are stored in the $messages array.

The default content type is set to text/plain in this function.

Then the $body string is created by concatenating the lines in the $messages array using the implode() function. Both the $body and the $subject line are parsed for the <%TODAY%> tag, which is replaced with the current date and time. The $subject line is stored outside the $headers array even though it is a header too. This is done because the PHP mail() function requires the subject as a separate argument from the other headers. The same is true for the To: header, which is also stored outside $headers in $to .

Finally, the $headers are imploded into $headerString, and the mail() function is called with all the necessary arguments. The mail is sent out. If the actual mail() function encounters any errors a log entry is added to that effect.

getRemindersForToday ()

This function receives a list of lines (the contents of the reminders.txt file), and parses through each line to determine whether the line is a reminder configuration or should be ignored (blank or a comment line starting with the # character).

Each reminder configuration line is compared against the current date (MM, DD, and weekday) values to determine whether any of the lines match a reminder for today.

If a match is found, the reminder mail filename is added into the $reminders array, which is returned by the function.

writeLog ()

This function writes a log file as ~*username*/reminders/*username*.log. The log entries are generated by other functions in the script.

getUsers ()

This function loads the user list file (/etc/passwd) in an array, loops through each record, and finds the *username* (field position 0) and home directory (field position 5) from each line separated by colons.

It stores each username and home directory in an associative array called $user and returns it.

Installing the reminder tool as a cron job

To set up reminder.php as a cron job under Linux, do the following:

1. As root, create a symbolic link in /etc/cron.daily as follows:

   ```
   ln -s /path/to/reminder.php
   ```

For example, say you kept `reminder.php` and reminder.conf in `/usr/local/src/reminder` directory, you can run the following commands as root to create the link:

```
cd /etc/cron.daily
ln -s /usr/local/src/reminder/reminder.php
```

2. Once the symlink is created, run: `/etc/cron.daily/reminder.php` as a test. If you get an error message about `reminder.conf` not being found, you need to edit the `reminder.php` to change `require_once ('reminder.conf')` to `require_once('/path/to/reminder/reminder.conf')`. For our example case, this would be `require_once('/usr/local/src/reminder/reminder.conf')`.

3. Make sure reminder.php is executable. You can run

```
chown root:root reminder.*
chmod 700 reminder.php
```

from the directory of the script to allow root to own and be able to execute the reminder scripts. If your cron daemon does not run as root, make sure you replace root:root with the appropriate user and group names that enable cron to execute the script.

4. Now you can set up reminders in one or more user reminder directories (`~username/remidners/reminders.txt`) and create necessary mail files in the reminders directory.

5. Let cron run the job at the regularly scheduled time and you should receive reminders if you have set any for yourself. If you do not receive a reminder you expect to receive, check the `~usernmame/reminders/username.log` file. Also check `/var/log/cron` for possible file execute permission issues

Building a Geo Location Finder Tool for IP

Ever find an IP address in a log file that looked suspicious or interesting and you wanted to know from which part of the world that IP came? A trace route might give you clues but it is too much work to find geographic locations of an IP address.

In this section, we will develop a simple script called geolocator.php using the `netgeo.php` class, which you can download from `http://www.phpclasses.org/netgeoclass`.

This class uses The Internet Geographic Database, which maps IP addresses to physical world locations. To learn more about this, visit http://www.caida.org/tools/utilities/netgeo.

Listing 16-9 shows the geolocator.php script.

Listing 16-9: geolocator.php

```php
#!/usr/bin/php -q
<?php

    require_once("netgeo.php");

    // Get a list of hosts/ip from command line
    $hostList = getHostList();

    // if no host/ip was given show syntax msg
    if (count($hostList) < 1)
    {
        echo "Syntax: " . basename($GLOBALS['argv'][0]) .
            " host | ip_address\n";
        exit;
    }

    // For each host/ip find geo location
    foreach ($hostList as $host)
    {
        findLocation($host);
        echo "-------------------------\n";
    }

    exit;

function findLocation($hostname = null)
{

    // Create a netgeo class object
    $netgeo=new netgeo_class;

    // Find location for the given host/ip
    if($netgeo->GetAddressLocation($hostname,$location))
    {

        // Set longitude and latitude from retrieved data
        $longitude=doubleval($location["LONG"]);
        $latitude=doubleval($location["LAT"]);
```

```php
      // Show output
      echo $host": Approximate location:\n";

      if(IsSet($location["CITY"]) ||
         IsSet($location["STATE"]) ||
         IsSet($location["COUNTRY"]))
      {
         if(IsSet($location['CITY']))
            echo "City    : " . $location['CITY'] . "\n";

         if(IsSet($location['STATE']))
            echo "State   :" . $location['STATE'] . "\n";

         if(IsSet($location['COUNTRY']))
            echo "Country :".  $location['COUNTRY'] . "\n";
      }

      echo "Longitude:" .
          ($longitude>=0.0 ? $longitude .
          "degree East" : (-$longitude)."degree West")."\n";

      echo "Latitude:".
          ($latitude>=0.0 ? $latitude .
          "degree North" : (-$latitude)."degree South")."\n";
   }
   else
   {
      echo "Cannot find location.\n";
      echo "Error: ".$netgeo->error."\n";
   }
}

   function getHostList()
   {
      $arr = array();

      // Except for the first argument in the command
      // line, insert all in a list as host/ip
      // Note: first argument is the name of the script.
      foreach($GLOBALS['argv'] as $key => $value)
      {
         if ($key) array_push($arr, $value);
      }

      return $arr;
   }
?>
```

This script requires the `netgeo.php` class. It works as follows:

◆ It gets a list of IP addresses or host names from the command line using the `getHostList()` function.

◆ For each given IP or host name, it performs netgeo lookup using `findLocation()`, which prints the geographic data available for the given IP or host name. Note that not all IP addresses or host names are in the netgeo database, so a result might not always be available.

Here are some example runs of this script:

```
$ ./geolocator.php www.yahoo.com
www.yahoo.com: Approximate location:
City     : SUNNYVALE
State    :CALIFORNIA
Country :US
Longitude:122degree West
Latitude:37.4degree North
------------------------
```

You can see that www.yahoo.com appears to be located in Sunnyvale, CA, U.S. Following is another example:

```
$./geolocator.php www.amazon.com
www.amazon.com:Approximate location:
City     : SEATTLE
State    :WASHINGTON
Country :US
Longitude:122.31degree West
Latitude:47.55degree North
------------------------
```

In the preceding example, you can see that www.amazon.com appears to be located in Seattle, Washington, U.S.

One last example:

```
$./geolocator.php www.csus.edu
www.csus.edu: Approximate location:
City     : SACRAMENTO
State    :CALIFORNIA
Country :US
Longitude:121.44degree West
Latitude:38.57degree North
------------------------
```

You can see www.csus.com (California State University, Sacramento) appears to be located in Sacramento, CA, U.S., which makes sense.

This script should be used from the command line as needed. However, if you wish to make it available to everyone, you can install it in /usr/bin, which is typically in any user's path. Here is how:

1. Make a directory called `/usr/local/src/php/gelocator` and copy the `netgeo.php` class into that directory. Make sure the directory is r+x by all users. In addition, make sure `netgeo.php` is readable by all users, but neither should be writable.

2. Copy `geolocator.php` into `/usr/bin` as `geolocator`. We remove the php extension because executable scripts typically do not need extensions.

3. Modify `/usr/bin/geolocator` such that `require_once("netgeo.php")` now is `require_once("/usr/local/src/php/geolocator/netgeo.php")`. This will ensure that when users run `geolocator` from the command line, the `/usr/bin/geolocator` script will find the `netgeo.php` class.

Now you and your users can run `geolocator` from anywhere.

Note that the geolocator script is fairly accurate, but its output should not be used as a final (and perhaps critical) determination of a particular host's location.

Building a Hard Disk Usage Monitoring Utility

Now we will develop a hard disk usage monitoring tool that uses Linux proc file system information to determine hard disk usage, and if usage for a given mounted file system exceeds a specified percentage, the utility sends an e-mail message to the administrator.

The script we will develop here requires the `classLinux.inc.php` and `common_functions.php` classes from the `phpSysInfo` project, which is located at `http://phpsysinfo.sourceforge.net/project`.

Download the phpSysInfo project and you will find the `common_functions.php` in the main distribution directory; the `class.Linux.inc.php` can be found in the os subdirectory within the includes directory.

Listing 16-10 shows an example configuration file for this script.

Listing 16–10: hdmonitor.conf

```php
<?php

    define(DEBUG, FALSE);

    // Send email when mounted filesystem reaches
    // percentage or more as given here
    $MAXSIZE['/'] = 30;
    $MAXSIZE['/usr'] = 50;
    $MAXSIZE['/mnt/win'] = 90;

    $MAIL_TEMPLATE = 'hdmonitor_mail.txt';

?>
```

Defined in the $MAXSIZE array are three mount points (partitions), which can be also written as follows:

```php
$MAXSIZE = array ( '/' => 30,
                   '/usr' => 50,
                   '/mnt/win' => 90
                 );
```

These three mount points will be monitored by the script when it is run daily via cron. Whenever any of these mount points exceed the usage percentage stated here, the $MAIL_TEMPLATE file is used to send mail to the e-mail addresses listed in this mail template. Listing 16-11 shows the monitoring script called hdmonitor.php.

Listing 16–11: hdmonitor.php

```php
#!/usr/bin/php -q
<?php

    require_once('hdmonitor.conf');
    require_once('class.Linux.inc.php');
    require_once('common_functions.php');

    $alertInfo = array();

    $system = new sysinfo;
    $alertInfo['/<%HOST%>/']    = $system->chostname();
    $alertInfo['/<%IP_ADDR%>/'] = $system->ip_addr();
    $alertInfo['/<%KERNEL%>/']  = $system->kernel();
    $alertInfo['/<%TODAY%>/']   = date('M-d-Y h:i:s A');
```

```php
$diskInfo = getDiskInfo($system->filesystems());

$alert = 0;

foreach ($diskInfo as $mount => $currentPercent)
{
  if (!empty($MAXSIZE[$mount]) &&
      $MAXSIZE[$mount] <= $currentPercent
    )
  {
    $alert++;
    $alertInfo['/<%DISK_STATUS%>/'] .=
        "Filesystem: $mount exceeds limit. " .
        "Currently used: $currentPercent%\n";

    if (DEBUG)
      echo "Filesystem: $mount exceeds limits.\n";
  }
}

if ($alert) sendAlert($alertInfo);

exit;

function sendAlert($info = null)
{
  $lines = file($GLOBALS['MAIL_TEMPLATE']);

  $contentTypeSet = FALSE;

  $message = array();

  $headers = array();

  foreach ($lines as $str)
  {
    $index++;
    if (preg_match('/To:\s*(.+)/i',
                   $str, $match))
    {
        $to = $match[1];
    }
    else if (preg_match('/From:\s*(.+)/i',
                   $str, $match))
```

Continued

Listing 16-11 *(Continued)*

```php
      {
          array_push($headers, "From: $match[1] \r\n");
      }
      else if (preg_match('/Subject:\s*(.+)/i',
                          $str, $match))
      {
          $subject = $match[1];
      }
      else if (preg_match('/^CC:\s*(.+)/i',
                          $str, $match))
      {
          array_push($headers, "Cc: $match[1] \r\n");
      }
      else if (preg_match('/Bcc:\s*(.+)/i',
                          $str, $match))
      {
          array_push($headers, "Bcc: $match[1] \r\n");
      }
      else if (preg_match('/Content-Type:\s*(.+)/i',
                          $str, $match))
      {
        if (preg_match('/html/', $match[1]))
        {
            array_push($headers,
                      "Content-Type: text/html\r\n");
        } else {
            array_push($headers,
                      "Content-Type: text/plain\n");
        }

        $contentTypeSet = TRUE;
      }
      else if (preg_match('/MIME-Version:\s*(.+)/i',
                          $str, $match))
      {
        array_push($headers,
                  "MIME-Version: $match[1] \r\n");

      } else {
        array_push($message, $str);
      }
    }

    if (! $contentTypeSet)
```

```php
       array_push($headers,
                 "Content-Type: text/plain\r\n");

   $body = implode('', $message);

   $search  = array_keys($info);

   $replace = array_values($info);

   $body = preg_replace($search,
                        $replace,
                        $body);

   $subject = preg_replace($search,
                           $replace,
                           $subject);

   $headerStr = implode('', $headers);

   if (DEBUG)
      echo "Sending mail to: $to ($subject)\n";

   mail($to, $subject, $body, $headerStr);
}


function getDiskInfo($fs = null)
{
   $info = array();

   foreach($fs as $disk)
   {
      $mountPoint = $disk['mount'];
      $percent = $disk['percent'];

      // remove % sign
      $info[$mountPoint] = substr($percent,
                                  0,
                                  strlen($percent) -1);

   }

   return $info;
}
?>
```

This script works as follows:

1. It requires the `class.Linux.inc.php` and `common_functions.php` classes.

2. It creates a `sysinfo` object called `$system`, which is used to retrieve host name, IP address, and kernel information, using the `chostname()`, `ip_addr()`, and `kernel()` methods.

3. It calls the `getDiskInfo()` function with an array of disk information returned by the `filesystems()` method of the `$system` object.

4. The `getDiskInfo()` function returns an array called `$diskInfo`, which returns each mount point (file system) in the system and the usage percentage.

5. For each mount point returned in `$diskInfo`, the usage percentage is compared against the maximum allowed usage percentage stored in `$MAX-SIZE` (from the hdmonitor.conf file).

6. If current usage is greater than or equal to the `$MAXSIZE` usage specified for that mount point, an alert record is appended in `$alertInfo['/<%DISK_STATUS%>/']`. The alert count `$alert` is incremented.

7. If disk usage alerts (i.e., `$alert > 0`) are found, then `sendAlert()` is called to e-mail the alert information stored in the `$alertInfo` array.

Listing 16-12 shows the alert message template. The To:, From:, Subject:, and Content-Type: headers are used in creating the e-mail message headers. There are custom tags such as `<%HOST%>`, `<%IP_ADDR%>`, `<%KERNEL%>`, and `<%DISK_STATUS%>`. These are replaced with the `$alertInfo` contents. The following message is in HTML, but you can use plain text as well by setting the Content-Type: header to text/plain and removing HTML tags from the message body as needed.

Listing 16-12: hdmonitor_mail.txt

```
To: kabir@example.com
From: THE REDEYE GROUP <admin@example.com>
Subject: Disk(s) on <%HOST%> need your attention
Content-Type: text/html

<html>
<body>
The following disk(s) have exceeded set limit in hdmonitor.conf:
<br> <br>
```

```
<table border=0 cellpadding=1 cellspacing=0 width="400"
bgcolor="#000000">
<tr>
<td>
<table border=0 cellpadding=3 cellspacing=0 width="400"
bgcolor="red">
<tr> <td> <font color="black"> <strong> Disk Information
</strong> </font> </td> </tr>
<tr> <td> <font color="black"><%DISK_STATUS%> </font> </td> </tr>
</table>
</td>
</tr>
</table>

<br>

<table border=0 cellpadding=1 cellspacing=0 width="400"
bgcolor="#000000">
<tr>
<td>
<table border=0 cellpadding=3 cellspacing=0 width="400"
bgcolor="#cccccc">
<tr> <td colspan=2> System Information </td></tr>
<tr> <td>Hostname </td><td> <%HOST%></td></tr>
<tr> <td>IP Addr   </td><td> <%IP_ADDR%></td></tr>
<tr> <td>Kernel    </td><td> <%KERNEL%></td></tr>
</table>
</td>
</tr>
</table>

<br>

Thanks,
<br>

The Wheel Group
<br>

</body>
</html>
```

The hdmonitor.php script contains the following functions.

sendAlert()

This function sends an e-mail message by loading the message template from the hdmonitor.conf configuration variable $GLOBALS['MAIL_TEMPLATE']. Each line of this message is parsed for e-mail headers such as To:, From:, Cc:, Bcc:, Subject:, and Content-Type:, which are stored in variables needed for the mail() function. The lines constituting the body of the message are stored in $messages, which is later imploded into the $body string.

The $body string is searched for special tags stored in $alertInfo, which is passed to the sendAlert() function as an associative array called $info. The keys of the $info array are stored in $search using the array_keys() function, and the values are stored in $replace using the array_values() function. The $search array contains tags such as <%HOST%>, <%IP_ADDR%>, <%DISK_STATUS%>, and so on, which were inserted into $info (i.e., $alertInfo) prior to calling the sendAlert() function.

These tags are replaced with their values in the $body string using the preg_replace() function. The fully expanded template body is e-mailed along with the $headers using mail().

getDiskInfo()

This function returns an associative array called $info with mount points as keys and their usage percentage as values. The function is called with disk statistics as a parameter.

Installing the hdmonitor tool as a cron job

To set up hdmonitor.php as a cron job under Linux, do the following:

1. As root, create a symbolic link in /etc/cron.daily as follows:

   ```
   ln -s /path/to/hdmonitor.php
   ```

   For example, if you kept hdmonitor.php and hdmonitor.conf in the /usr/local/src/hdmonitor directory, you could run the following commands as root to create the link:

   ```
   cd /etc/cron.daily
   ln -s /usr/local/src/hdmonitor/hdmonitor.php
   ```

2. Once the symlink is created, run /etc/cron.daily/*hdmonitor.php* as a test. If you get an error message that *hdmonitor.conf* was not found, or that any of the classes were not found (class.Linux.inc.php or common_functions.php), you need to edit *hdmonitor.php* to change require_once('*hdmonitor*.conf'), require_once('class. Linux.inc.php'), and require_once('common_functions.php'); to require_once('/path/to/hdmonitor/hdmonitor.conf'),

```
require_once('/path/to/hdmonitor/class.Linux.inc.php'),
```
and `require_once('/path/to/hdmonitor/common_functions.php')`,
respectively. For our example case, this would be `require_once('/usr/`
`local/src/hdmonitor/hdmonitor.conf')`, `require_once('/usr/`
`local/src/hdmonitor/class.Linux.inc.php')`, and `require_once`
`('/usr/local/src/hdmonitor/common_functions.php ')`.

3. Make sure `hdmonitor.php` is executable. You can run

```
chown root:root hdmonitor.*   \
                class.Linux.inc.php \
                common_functions.php
chmod 700 hdmonitor.php
```

from the directory of the script to allow root to own and be able to execute the `hdmonitor` scripts. If your cron daemon does not run as root,
make sure you replace `root:root` with the appropriate user and group
names that enable cron to execute the script.

4. Configure the hdmonitor.conf file to reflect what mount points you want
to monitor and at what level. In addition, customize the mail template as
needed.

5. Let cron run the job at the regularly scheduled time and you should
receive disk alert messages when any of your mount points exceeds the
`$MAXSIZE` limit.

6. To test your installation, you can set the `$MAXSIZE` limits to a very low
number, which will trigger an alert the next time `hdmonitor.php` is run
by cron. If you do not receive an alert that you expect to receive, check
the `var/log/cron` file for possible file execute permission issues.

Building a CPU Load Monitoring Utility

In this section, we will develop a system load-average monitoring tool that will
enable us to monitor a Linux system's load average automatically, and when the load
average exceeds a specified limit, an alert message will be sent out to administrators.
We define multiple levels of alert so that an administrator can take appropriate
actions based on the alert levels indicated.

Like the hdmonitor script, this script requires the class.Linux.inc.php and
common_functions.php classes from the phpSysInfo project, which is located at
`http://phpsysinfo.sourceforge.net/project`.

Listing 16-13 shows a sample configuration file for the load monitoring tool.

Listing 16-13: loadmonitor.conf

```php
<?php

    define(DEBUG, TRUE);

    $ALERT_CONDITIONS = array('RED', 'YELLOW', 'BLUE');

    // When system load has been in any of the following
    // alert condition for at least last 15 minutes
    // system is said to be at that alert level
    // Note: the order does not matter as loadmonitor
    // automatically chooses the highest alert level
    $ALERT['RED']     = 25;
    $ALERT['YELLOW']  = 15;
    $ALERT['BLUE']    = 5;

    $MAIL_TEMPLATE = 'loadmonitor_mail.txt';

    // Mail every n seconds when alert condition exists
    // Mail is sent only if the loadmonitor is run
    // every n-1 seconds. Recommend running loadmonitor
    // every 5 min and mail frequency 30 min (30 * 60 sec)
    // 0 = always send mail
    $MAIL_FREQUENCY = 30 * 60;

    // Store when was the last time mail was sent
    // in a file so that we don't mail bomb the
    // admin
    $MAIL_CONTROL_FILE = '/tmp/loadmonitor.out';

    // Include this program output in mail
    $PS_BIN = 'top';
    $PS_OPT = ' -b -n 1';

?>
```

Here we have defined $ALERT_CONDITIONS as an array of alerts. Currently, there are three alert conditions: RED, YELLOW, BLUE. These names are arbitrary and you can choose any name you like.

An associative array called $ALERT defines the load average associated with each alert level. For example, alert condition RED is set to load average 25. This means that a RED alert is sent out when the system is experiencing a load average of 25 for at least the last 15 minutes until the current time.

Similarly, a load average of 15 triggers an alert condition YELLOW, and a load average of 5 triggers a BLUE alert.

Whenever an alert condition is reached, the $MAIL_TEMPLATE file is used to send out the alert message. However, we do not want to bombard an administrator about an alert condition that exists among multiple runs of the loadmonitor script. For example, if loadmonitor were run every minute, it could note an alert condition and message the administrator every minute. This would be bad, so we can use $MAIL_FREQUENCY to control how frequently an administrator is notified when an alert condition is identified. The sample setting is 1800, which is 30 minutes. Therefore, we only resend notification about an alert condition if the last message was sent at least 30 minutes ago. The $MAIL_CONTROL_FILE keeps the timestamp information for each notification sent. This information is used to determine the last delivery time of the alert mail. The $PS_BIN and $PS_OPT are set to the top command and its argument -b and -n 1. The output of the top command is appended in the mail message to enable an administrator get a glimpse of the troubled system just from the e-mail. This is very useful if the main administrator receives the alert from a remote location; he or she can guide on-site junior administrators to appropriately deal with the situation based on the information provided by the top command.

Listing 16-14 shows the loadmonitor script.

Listing 16-14: loadmonitor.php

```
#!/usr/bin/php -q
<?php

    require_once('loadmonitor.conf');
    require_once('class.Linux.inc.php');
    require_once('common_functions.php');

    $alertInfo = array();

    $system = new sysinfo;
    $alertInfo['/<%HOST%>/']    = $system->chostname();
    $alertInfo['/<%IP_ADDR%>/'] = $system->ip_addr();
    $alertInfo['/<%KERNEL%>/']  = $system->kernel();
    $alertInfo['/<%TODAY%>/']   = date('M-d-Y h:i:s A');

    $loadInfo = $system->loadavg();

    $load0  = $loadInfo[0];
    $load5  = $loadInfo[1];
    $load15 = $loadInfo[2];
    $alertInfo['/<%LOAD%>/'] = "Now: $load0 ".
                               "Last 5 Min: $load5".
                               "Last 15 Min: $load15";
```

Continued

Listing 16-14 *(Continued)*

```php
$highestAlertRange = 0;
$highestAlert = null;

foreach ($ALERT_CONDITIONS as $alertType)
{
    $alertRange = $ALERT[$alertType];

    if (DEBUG)
        echo "Alert: $alertRange => ".
            "Current $load0 $load5 $load15\n";

    if (
        ($alertRange <= $load0) &&
        ($alertRange <= $load5) &&
        ($alertRange <= $load15)
    )
    {
        if (DEBUG)
            echo "Alert: $alertType ($alertRange)".
                " as load for last 15 min till ".
                " now is $load15 $load0 \n";

        if ($alertRange > $highestAlertRange)
        {
            $highestAlertRange =  $alertRange;
            $highestAlert      =  $alertType;
        }
    }
}

if ($highestAlert != null)
{
    if (DEBUG)
        echo "Highest alert $highestAlert \n";

    $alertInfo['/<%ALERT%>/'] = $highestAlert;
    $ps =execute_program($PS_BIN, $PS_OPT);
    $alertInfo['/<%PSAUX%>/'] = $ps;

    // Find out if last mail sent was
    // within mail frequency range
    // or not, if not send mail
    if (isOKtoSendMail($MAIL_CONTROL_FILE,
                       $MAIL_FREQUENCY))
    {
```

```php
            sendAlert($alertInfo);
        }
    }

exit;

function isOKtoSendMail($ctrlFile = null,
                        $interval = null)
{
    $now = time();
    if (DEBUG)
        echo "Now: " . date('M-d-Y h:i:s A', $now) . "\n";

    if (file_exists($ctrlFile))
    {
        // Read file
        $lastTime = file($ctrlFile);
        if (DEBUG)
            echo "Last time mail sent: " .
                    date('M-d-Y h:i:s A', $lastTime[0]) . "\n";

    } else {
        // If control file does not exist
        // Create one and yes we can send mail
        if (DEBUG)
            echo "Create new control file.\n";

        writeControlFile($ctrlFile);

        return TRUE;
    }

    // If current time - last time is greater than
    // or equal to the mail interval, we can send mail
    if ($now - $lastTime[0] >= $interval)
    {
        // Update file
        if (DEBUG)
            echo "$now - $lastTime[0] => $interval\n";

        writeControlFile($ctrlFile);

        return TRUE;
    }
```

Continued

Listing 16-14 *(Continued)*

```php
        // No cannot send mail as we already
        // did not too long ago.
        return FALSE;
    }

    function writeControlFile($file = null)
    {
        $now = time();
        $fp = fopen($file, 'w');
        if ($fp)
        {
            if (DEBUG)
                echo "Writing control $file: $now\n";

            fputs($fp, $now);

            fclose($fp);

            return TRUE;

        } else {

            echo "Error: could not create ".
                "control file $file \n";
        }


        return FALSE;
    }

    function sendAlert($info = null)
    {
        $lines = file($GLOBALS['MAIL_TEMPLATE']);

        $contentTypeSet = FALSE;

        $message = array();

        $headers = array();

        foreach ($lines as $str)
        {
            $index++;
```

```php
if (preg_match('/To:\s*(.+)/i',
               $str,
               $match))
{
    $to = $match[1];
}
else if (preg_match('/From:\s*(.+)/i',
                     $str,
                     $match))
{
    array_push($headers, "From: $match[1] \r\n");
}
else if (preg_match('/Subject:\s*(.+)/i',
                     $str,
                     $match))
{
    $subject = $match[1];
}
else if (preg_match('/^CC:\s*(.+)/i',
                     $str,
                     $match))
{
    array_push($headers, "Cc: $match[1] \r\n");
}
else if (preg_match('/Bcc:\s*(.+)/i',
                     $str,
                     $match))
{
    array_push($headers, "Bcc: $match[1] \r\n");
}
else if (preg_match('/Content-Type:\s*(.+)/i',
                     $str,
                     $match))
{
    if (preg_match('/html/', $match[1]))
    {
        array_push($headers,
                   "Content-Type: text/html\r\n");
    } else {
        array_push($headers,
                   "Content-Type: text/plain\n");
    }
```

Continued

Listing 16-14 *(Continued)*

```
                $contentTypeSet = TRUE;
            }
            else if (preg_match('/MIME-Version:\s*(.+)/i',
                                 $str,
                                 $match))
            {
                array_push($headers,
                        "MIME-Version: $match[1] \r\n");

            } else {
                array_push($message, $str);
            }
        }

        if (! $contentTypeSet)
            array_push($headers,
                        "Content-Type: text/plain\r\n");

        $body = implode('', $message);

        $search  = array_keys($info);
        $replace = array_values($info);
        $body = preg_replace($search, $replace, $body);
        $subject = preg_replace($search,
                                $replace,
                                $subject);

        $headerStr = implode('', $headers);

        if (DEBUG)
            echo "Sending mail to: $to ".
                "(subject: $subject)\n";

        mail($to, $subject, $body, $headerStr);
    }

?>
```

The loadmonitor script works as follows:

1. It creates a `sysinfo` object called `$system`.

2. The `$system` object is used to retrieve host name, IP address, and kernel information into an associative array called `$alertInfo`. The `$alertInfo`

stores the information using custom tags as keys. For example, `<%HOST%>` stores the host name returned by the `$system->chostname()` method.

3. The load average information is retrieved by calling the `loadavg()` method of the `$system` object. The returned load average array is stored in the `$loadInfo` array. The current load `$loadInfo[0]`, the 5-minute-old load average `$loadInfo[5]`, and the 15-minute-old load average `$loadInfo[15]` are stored separately in `$load0`, `$load5`, and `$load15`, respectively.

4. For each known alert condition, the script compares the current, 5-minute-old, and 15-minute-old loads against the alert condition's maximum load average, stored in `$alertRange`. If the alert condition's maximum load is less than or equal to the current, last 5-minute, and last 15-minute load average, the system can be said to be in that alert status for the last 15 minutes. The three points in time serve as three samples of time in that 15-minute interval, which is sufficient for our purposes to make the assumption that the system has entered an alert condition.

5. However, to find the highest alert condition met by the system, the system keeps track of matched alert conditions using the `$highestAlert` and `$highestAlertRange` variables. These variables are set only if the current alert condition is higher than the last one.

6. Finally, if there is an alert condition set in `$highestAlert`, the `$alertInfo['/<%ALERT%>/']` entry is set to `$highestAlert`; and the PS_BIN program is run with PS_OPT options using the `execute_program()` method found in the common_functions.php script.

7. The output of the PS_BIN (i.e., the top command) is stored in `$alertInfo['/<%PSAUX%>/']`.

8. Finally, the `isOKtoSendMail ()` function is called to determine whether the current alert condition has been already reported within the alert mail control interval. If it has not been reported yet or was reported before the interval expired, the `sendAlert()` method is called to send the e-mail alert.

The loadmonitor tool has the following methods.

isOKtoSendMail ()

This function determines if an alert mail message should be sent in the event of an alert condition. This check is performed to ensure that the administrator is not sent repetitive alert messages too frequently if the loadmonitor is run frequently via cron or other means.

This function is passed the mail control file name and the alert mail frequency, both of which are configured in loadmonitor.conf. The `isOKtoSendMail()` function loads the previous mailing's timestamp stored in the mail control file (if any) and compares it against the current time.

If the difference between the current time and the last alert message timestamp is greater than or equal to the allowed interval, it returns TRUE and updates the mail control file with the current time. Otherwise, it returns FALSE.

writeControlFile ()

This function writes the mail control file. The mail control file stores the last time an alert mail was sent. This timestamp is used to ensure that alert messages do not bombard the administrator's mailbox if the loadmonitor is run frequently.

sendAlert()

See the sendAlert() function details in the hdmonitor section above.

Listing 16-15 shows the default e-mail template:

Listing 16-15: loadmonitor_mail.txt

```
To: kabir@example.com
From: THE LOAD WATCHER <admin@example.com>
Subject: [ALERT-<%ALERT%>] load on <%HOST%> need your attention
Content-Type: text/html

<html>
<body>
The <%HOST%> is experiencing <%ALERT%> level load.
<br> <br>
Current load averages are <%LOAD%>
<br> <br>
Here is the output of the top command:
<br>
<pre>
<font color="<%ALERT%>">
<%PSAUX%>
</font>
</pre>
<br>

Thanks,
<br>

The Wheel Group
<br>

</body>
</html>
```

Installing the loadmonitor tool as a cron job

To set up `loadmonitor.php` as a cron job under Linux, do the following:

1. As root, create a symbolic link in `/etc/cron.daily` as follows:

   ```
   ln -s /path/to/loadmonitor.php
   ```

   For example, if you kept `loadmonitor.php` and `loadmonitor.conf` in the `/usr/local/src/loadmonitor` directory, you could run the following commands as root to create the link:

   ```
   cd /etc/cron.daily
   ln -s /usr/local/src/loadmonitor/loadmonitor.php
   ```

2. Once the symlink is created, run `/etc/cron.daily/loadmonitor.php` as a test. If you get an error message that *loadmonitor*.conf was not found or that any of the classes (`class.Linux.inc.php` or `common_functions.php`) were not found, you need to edit `loadmonitor.php` to change `require_once('loadmonitor.conf')`, `require_once('class.Linux.inc.php')`, and `require_once('common_functions.php')`; to `require_once('/path/to/loadmonitor/loadmonitor.conf')`, `require_once('/path/to/loadmonitor/class.Linux.inc.php')`, `require_once('/path/to/loadmonitor/common_functions.php')`, respectively. For our example case, this would be `require_once('/usr/local/src/loadmonitor/loadmonitor.conf')`, `require_once('/usr/local/src/loadmonitor/class.Linux.inc.php')`, and `require_once('/usr/local/src/loadmonitor/common_functions.php ')`.

3. Make sure `loadmonitor.php` is executable. You can run:

   ```
   chown root:root loadmonitor.*        \
                   class.Linux.inc.php \
                   common_functions.php
   chmod 700 loadmonitor.php
   ```

   from the directory of the script to allow root own and be able to execute the loadmonitor scripts. If your cron daemon does not run as root, make sure you replace root:root with the appropriate user and group names that enable cron to execute the script.

4. Configure the loadmonitor.conf file to set the load averages that you want to consider as RED, YELLOW, and BLUE. Set the mail frequency you want to use.

5. Let cron run the job at the regularly scheduled time; you should receive excessive load alert messages when the load average exceeds the specified alert condition level.

Summary

In this chapter, you learned how to develop command-line PHP scripts that can be run via a cron job to automate user reminders, to monitor system resources, and to protect your POP3 user mailboxes from SPAM and other unwanted e-mail.

Chapter 17

Apache Virtual Host Maker

IN THIS CHAPTER

♦ Learning the basics of an Apache Virtual Host

♦ Developing an Apache Virtual Host Maker

♦ Configuring Apache for virtual hosts

♦ Deploying virtual hosts using an Apache Virtual Host Maker

APACHE IS THE MOST POPULAR Web server in the world. Approximately 60 percent of the Web servers available on the Internet are running Apache or Apache-like (e.g., Zeus) Web servers. Not only is it Open Source software, but Apache is capable of hosting multiple Web sites on a single physical Web server system. These *virtual* hosts make Apache a great platform to deploy in organizations of any size. Internet service providers and large organizations often prefer Apache because they can deploy tens to hundreds of Web sites on a single system. In this chapter, you will develop a command-line PHP script to help you manage Apache virtual hosts for a Linux system. The script should work on other UNIX-like platforms as well.

The following section outlines the basics of Apache virtual hosts.

Understanding an Apache Virtual Host

To understand how Apache virtual hosts work, first assume that you have a Linux server running the latest stable version of Apache. Furthermore, assume that your server's IP address is 192.168.1.100 and that Apache is installed in the /usr/local/httpd directory.

To create a virtual host called www.mynewsite.com manually, you have to edit the httpd.conf file (usually stored in the /usr/local/httpd/conf/ directory) by adding lines such as the following:

```
NameVirtualHosts *

<VirtualHost 192.168.1.100>
    ServerName www.mynewsite.com
    DocumentRoot /www/mynewsite/htdocs
    ErrorLog  /www/mynewsite/logs/errors.log
    CustomLog /www/mynewsite/logs/access.log common
</VirtualHost>
```

The first line tells Apache that the name-based virtual host feature should be enabled – and should appear only once in the config file. This means that a single IP address can represent multiple Web server names, and that Apache should find a name in a specific HTTP (HOST) header from Web browser requests.

The configuration enclosed in the <VirtualHost ...> container defines www.mynewsite.com as a virtual host. Each of these lines represents an Apache directive. For example, the ServerName directive defines the name of the virtual host. The DocumentRoot directive defines the path to the Web site's document tree. The ErrorLog and CustomLog directives define the paths to the error and access log file, respectively.

You can add many directives within a virtual host container to define the virtual hosts as needed. To add a second virtual host called www.mysecondsite.com, duplicate the <VirtualHost ...> container for the new site with any appropriate site-specific changes, as shown in the following example:

```
NameVirtualHosts *

# defines www.mynewsite.com
<VirtualHost 192.168.1.100>
    ServerName www.mynewsite.com
    DocumentRoot /www/mynewsite/htdocs
    ErrorLog  /www/mynewsite/logs/errors.log
    CustomLog /www/mynewsite/logs/access.log common
</VirtualHost>

# defines www.mysecondsite.com
<VirtualHost 192.168.1.100>
    ServerName www. mysecondsite.com
    DocumentRoot /www/ mysecondsite /htdocs
    ErrorLog  /www/ mysecondsite /logs/errors.log
    CustomLog /www/ mysecondsite /logs/access.log common
</VirtualHost>
```

Visit www.apache.org for documentation on Apache and more directives for use with virtual hosts.

After a new configuration is added to httpd.conf, the Web server needs to be restarted so that it can reload the new configuration. This is done using the following command:

```
/usr/local/httpd/bin/apachectl restart
```

The location of the script to control the Apache server is dependent upon the version of Linux you are running.

Once restarted, the virtual Web sites become available via http://www.mynewsite.com/ and http://www.mysecondsite.com/ as long as the domains have the appropriate DNS records defined on the server.

Name server configuration management is covered in Chapter 17, so this discussion will assume that the DNS configuration points virtual host names to their respective Web server hosts.

Defining Configuration Tasks

In most cases, adding a new virtual host to a system involves the following tasks:

1. Creating a DNS address (A) record for the new host in the name server configuration for that domain.

   This chapter assumes that you have the appropriate DNS configuration. Chapter 18 shows you how to manage DNS configuration using another tool.

2. Creating a virtual host configuration in the httpd.conf file. This can be complex or very simple depending on your needs.

3. Creating appropriate directory structure and permission settings so that the virtual host configuration you created in httpd.conf has a physical document tree in your Web server's disk.

4. Creating a user account to enable someone to manage Web contents via FTP or a shell.

5. Installing default access control (.htaccess) or other site-specific files, such as missing file handler (404 error handler) pages.

6. Copying default Web contents (if any) to the new site.

7. Optionally, creating a MySQL database account for the Web site.

8. Restarting the Web server to make the site accessible via the Web.

9. Testing the new site using a Web browser to ensure that it is accessible.

As you can see, this is quite a list. If these tasks are undertaken manually, there are many places where an administrator could make a mistake, and spend hours to retrace steps and fix problems.

Therefore, we want to build a tool (called makesite) that will enable administrators to perform most of these operations using a single command line such as the following:

```
./makesite -add \
        --user username \
        --pass password \
        --vhost www.example.com \
        --type gold \
        --restart \
        --test \
        --notify_email username@example.com
```

This application is built as a command-line tool instead of a Web form for security reasons. With the correct permissions (namely 700), this script can only be run by a privileged user. If constructed as a Web form, the application would be far less secure due to it being much easier to access remotely. Despite taking various precautions to secure critical Web pages, making them accessible via the standard Web server is just a bad idea.

The preceding command line will do the following:

1. Create a user account, called username, with a password.

2. Create an Apache virtual host configuration for www.example.com.

3. Create all the necessary Web and user account configurations and copy appropriate contents based on account type "gold." In other words, all the "gold" account features will be implemented. This may include enabling PHP, CGI, SSI, and other Web features, or the installation of custom software such as phpMyAdmin, and so on.

4. Automatically restart Apache server.

5. Automatically test the new Web site by making requests to see if the site is operational.

6. Automatically notify the account owner via e-mail that the site is operational, and provide necessary instructions to access and manage the Web site.

Clearly, this script reduces quite a bit of work for a Web administrator, and therefore it is well worth developing. However, before we can make such an interesting script, we need to define a set of standard account types for the system.

Creating a Configuration Script

The makesite script uses the -type=account_type command-line argument to determine numerous tasks that need to be performed in the virtual host setup process. For example, we can define the following accounts:

```
$ACCOUNT_TYPE['standard'] = array(
                              vhost_template => 'std_vhost.conf',
                              master_contents =>'std_contents.conf',
                              mail_template  => 'std_vhost.mail',
                              shell => '/bin/true'
                              );


$ACCOUNT_TYPE['gold'] = array(
                              vhost_template => 'gold_vhost.conf',
                              master_contents =>'gold_contents.conf',
                              mail_template  => 'gold_vhost.mail',
                              shell => '/bin/tcsh'
                              );


$ACCOUNT_TYPE['platinum'] = array(
                              vhost_template => 'platinum_vhost.conf',
                              master_contents =>'platinum_contents.conf',
                              mail_template  => 'platinum_vhost.mail',
                              shell => '/bin/bash',
                              );
```

This script defines three types of Web site accounts: standard, gold, and platinum. These names are arbitrary, of course. You can choose whatever names you like. For example, a university administrator might choose: coursesite, deptsite, studentsite, and so on, as account types. Now let's examine one of the account configurations. The standard account type defines that the virtual host configuration (vhost_template) template is std_vhost.conf. This is a PHP-based virtual host configuration generator script. The std_contents.conf script is another PHP-based contents configuration script. The mail template is simply a text file with special tags that are replaced before it is sent to the account owner.

When creating a standard account, the makesite script does the following:

1. It uses the vhost_template (std_vhost.conf) to create the Apache configuration.

2. It uses the master_contents (std_contents.conf) to do content-specific configuration.

3. Optionally (if told to do so), it uses the mail_template (std_vhost.mail) to send an e-mail to the account owner.

Note that there is no restriction governing how many types of accounts you can define as long as you also create the necessary configuration templates.

Developing makesite

As you have seen, the makesite script has several pieces that must be created and fit together for the script to operate. The following sections will cover the development of the various pieces.

Creating the makesite.conf file

The makesite script uses the makesite.conf file, as shown in Listing 17-1. The makesite configuration file is the central configuration file for the application.

Listing 17-1: makesite.conf

```php
<?php

    // Set this to the PEAR directory
    $PEAR_DIR            = '/example/intranet/htdocs/pear' ;

    ini_set( 'include_path', ':' . $PEAR_DIR . ':' . ini_get('include_path'));

    require_once "Console/Getopt.php";

    define(DEBUG, FALSE);
```

```php
$APACHE_INFO = array(
                    'user'        => 'httpd',
                    'group'       => 'httpd',
                    'path'        => '/usr/local/apache',
                    'bin_dir'     => 'bin',
                    'conf_dir'    => 'conf',
                    'conf_flie'   => 'httpd.conf',
                    'server_bin'  => 'httpd',
                    'config_chk_opt'  => '-t -f',
                    'restart_opt'    => '-k restart',
                    'vhost_conf_dir' => 'conf/vhosts'
                );


$SYSTEM_INFO = array(
                    'passwd_file'    => '/etc/passwd',
                    'home_dir'       => '/home',
                    'min_passwd_length'   => 5,
                    'group_file'    => '/etc/group',
                    'server_ip'      => '192.168.0.11',
                    'useradd_bin'    => '/usr/sbin/useradd',
                    'www_partition' => '/www',
                    'permission'     => '0755',
                    'symlink_bin'    => '/bin/ln',
                    'symlink_opt'    => '-s',
                    'cp_bin'         => '/bin/cp',
                    'cp_opt'         => '-r',
                    'mkdir_bin'      => '/bin/mkdir',
                    'chmod_bin'      => '/bin/chmod',
                    'chown_bin'      => '/bin/chown'
                );

define(DEFAULT_ACCOUNT_TYPE , 'standard');
define(DEFAULT_SYMLINK_USER_TO_WEBSITE , TRUE);

//$TEMPLATE_DIR = '/www/vhosts';
$TEMPLATE_DIR = 'vhosts';

$ACCOUNT_TYPE['standard'] = array(
                              vhost_template => 'std_vhost.conf',
                              master_contents =>'std_contents.conf',
                              mail_template  => 'std_vhost.mail',
                              shell => '/bin/true'
                            );
```

Continued

Listing 17-1 *(Continued)*

```
$ACCOUNT_TYPE['gold'] = array(
                                vhost_template => 'gold_vhost.conf',
                                master_contents =>'gold_contents.conf',
                                mail_template  => 'gold_vhost.mail',
                                shell => '/bin/tcsh'
                                );

$ACCOUNT_TYPE['platinum'] = array(
                                vhost_template => 'platinum_vhost.conf',
                                master_contents =>'platinum_contents.conf',
                                mail_template  => 'platinum_vhost.mail',
                                shell => '/bin/bash',
                                );
?>
```

This configuration file defines a set of the `$ACCOUNT_TYPE` associative array as discussed previously and also defines the following:

- ◆ `$APACHE_INFO` is an associative array that holds information about various Apache-specific configurations. For example, the sample configuration indicates that the Apache server is run as the 'httpd' user, as `$APACHE_INFO[user]` is set to 'httpd'. Similarly, it indicates that Apache is installed in `$APACHE_INFO[path]`, which is set to /usr/local/apache. Numerous other configuration parameters specify options to check, options for restarting the server, and locations of configuration files.

- ◆ `$SYSTEM_INFO` is an associative array that holds information specific to the system on which the Apache server is running. For example, `$SYSTEM_INFO[passwd_file]` points to the password file used by the system, which is /etc/passwd. Similarly, it defines `$SYSTEM_INFO[server_ip]`, the IP address Apache server listens on. Numerous other configuration parameters specify paths to system commands, the main path to the www directory, and the value of various options to be set by the script.

- ◆ The `DEFAULT_ACCOUNT_TYPE` constant defines the default account type.

- ◆ The `DEFAULT_SYMLINK_USER_TO_WEBSITE` constant is set to `TRUE` if a symbolic soft link is to be created from the user's home directory to his or her Web server's directory.

- ◆ The `$TEMPLATE_DIR` constant points to the subdirectory in the makesite script directory, which holds the account-specific templates. For example, the standard account templates (std_vhost.conf, std_contents.conf, and std_vhost.mail) are stored in the vhosts directory.

The makesite script uses the Console/Getopt.php class from PEAR; therefore, the makesite.conf script loads this script in the beginning of the configuration file. Make sure that the $PEAR_DIR variable in makesite.conf is set properly to point to your PEAR installation.

Creating the virtual host configuration

Listing 17-2 shows the standard account's virtual host configuration, std_vhosts.conf. This is loaded by the makesite script and processed by calling the makeVirtualHost() function within the configuration file.

Listing 17-2: vhosts/std_vhost.conf

```php
<?php

    function makeVirtualHost()
    {

        $www     = $GLOBALS[SYSTEM_INFO][www_partition];
        $ipAddr  = $GLOBALS[SYSTEM_INFO][server_ip];
        $server  = $GLOBALS[SERVER_NAME];

        $serverRoot = sprintf("%s/%s", $www, $server);
        $docRoot = sprintf("%s/%s/htdocs", $www, $server);
        $logDir  = sprintf("%s/%s/logs", $www, $server);

        $vhostConfig = <<<STD_VHOST_CONF


#
# Automated virtual host configuration for $GLOBALS[SERVER_NAME]
#
# Account Type: standard
#
<VirtualHost $ipAddr>

    ServerName      $server
    DocumentRoot    "$docRoot"
    ErrorLog        "$logDir/errors.log"
    CustomLog       "$logDir/access.log" common
```

Continued

Listing 17-2 *(Continued)*

```
        <Directory />
          <Files "*.conf">
            deny from all
          </Files>
        </Directory>

      </VirtualHost>


STD_VHOST_CONF;

    $output['config'] = $vhostConfig;

    $output['makedir'] = array(
                              'SERVER_ROOT' => $serverRoot,
                              'DOCUMENT_ROOT' => $docRoot,
                              'LOG_DIR' => $logDir);

    return $output;

  }
?>
```

The makesite script loads this file if the account type is specified as standard. The standard template can be selected by either explicitly selecting --type standard or not specifying any account type, as the standard type is set as the default in make-site.conf (DEFAULT_ACCOUNT_TYPE). Of course, you can specify any account type as the default. When the std_vhost.conf file is loaded, the makeVirtualHost() function is called from makesite, which must return an Apache virtual server configuration enclosed in a <VirtualHost ..> container.

In this sample configuration, a virtual host configuration is returned. That defines the server name, using the ServerName directive; the Web document root, using the DocumentRoot directive; and the error and access logs, using the ErrorLog and CustomLog directives, respectively. It also specifies that any files with .conf extensions are not allowed for Web browsing. You can create highly customizable configurations using PHP in the makeVirtualHost() function. The sample configuration is simply a basic example.

 To learn more about Apache 2 configurations, visit http://httpd.
apache.org to review online documentation.

Creating the contents configuration file

Listing 17-3 shows the contents configuration file, std_contents.conf, which is stored in the vhosts subdirectory pointed to by $TEMPLATE_DIR in makesite.conf.

This configuration file is loaded once the new user account, the virtual host configuration, and the necessary directory structure have been created. The purpose of this configuration file is to enable you to install contents.

Listing 17-3: vhosts/std_contents.conf

```php
<?php


   // Master contents for standard account


   function copyContentsToSite($site = null)
   {

      $MASTER_CONTENTS_DIR = "vhosts/standard/htdocs/*";

      $CP_BIN = $GLOBALS[SYSTEM_INFO][cp_bin];
      $CP_OPT = $GLOBALS[SYSTEM_INFO][cp_opt];

      $CHOWN_BIN = $GLOBALS[SYSTEM_INFO][chown_bin];
      $CHMOD_BIN = $GLOBALS[SYSTEM_INFO][chmod_bin];

      $user = $site[user];
      $group = $site[group];

      $docRoot = $site[DOCUMENT_ROOT];

      $cmd = "$CP_BIN $CP_OPT $MASTER_CONTENTS_DIR $docRoot";

      echo "$cmd\n";
      exec($cmd, $output, $status);

      $cmd = "$CHOWN_BIN -R $user:$group $docRoot";
      exec($cmd, $output, $status);

      $cmd = "$CHMOD_BIN -R 755 $docRoot";
      exec($cmd, $output, $status);

      return TRUE;
   }

?>
```

In the sample version, once the configuration file is loaded, the copyContentsToSite() function is run by the makesite script. This function performs a copy operation that copies all files in vhosts/standard/htdocs/* (including subdirectories) to the newly created Web site's document root directory. Then it sets the directory ownership and file permissions for the entire document root so that files can be both accessible by the owner of the account and read by the Apache server.

Of course, you can do much more using this configuration file. For example, you can install any specific applications you want to offer users of this account type.

Creating the e-mail template

Listing 17-4 shows the e-mail template, which is also stored in the vhosts directory pointed to by the $TEMPLATE_DIR variable in makesite.conf. This is a simple text file that stores e-mail headers and a message body containing a set of custom tags. These tags are parsed and replaced before mail is sent out. The mail is sent to the email address specified by the --notify_email=email_address command-line argument for makesite.

Listing 17-4: vhosts/std_vhost.mail

```
From: Your Friendly ISP  <admin@examplep.net>
Content-Type: text/html
Subject: Your <%VHOST%> is now ready [Account Type: <%TYPE%>]

Dear Customer,

Your web site <%VHOST%> is now ready.

You can access it via http://<%VHOST%>

Your account information is as follows:

Shell account: <%USER%> [GROUP: <%GROUP%>]
     Password: <%PASSWD%>

Your Web site information is as follows:

[ ] PHP
[ ] CGI
[ ] SSI

Server Root: <%SERVER_ROOT%>
Document Root: <%DOCUMENT_ROOT%>
Log dir: <%LOG_DIR%>
```

Thanks.

Account Team,
Your ISP

Ideally, this e-mail is sent with enough instructions for the new account owner to be able to start using the Web site account.

Creating the makesite script

Listing 17-5 shows the makesite script.

Listing 17-5: makesite

```php
#!/usr/bin/php -q
<?php

    require_once('makesite.conf');

    $CMD_SHORT_OPTIONS = 'hu:p:v:t:rtn:g:';

    $CMD_LONG_OPTIONS  = array('help',
                               'add',
                               'enable',
                               'disable',
                               'user=',
                               'group=',
                               'pass=',
                               'vhost=',
                               'type=',
                               'restart',
                               'test',
                               'notify_email='
                               );

    $cmd = getCommandLineOptions(Console_Getopt::getopt($GLOBALS['argv'],
                           $CMD_SHORT_OPTIONS,
                           $CMD_LONG_OPTIONS)
                          );


    $SITE_INFO = null;
```

Continued

Listing 17-5 *(Continued)*

```php
if (empty($cmd) || (getValue($cmd, 'v', 'vhost')) == null )
{
    syntax();
    exit;
}


if (isset($cmd['add']))
{
    $request = makeAddRequest($cmd);
    if ($request != null)
    {

        $type = $request[type];
        $account = $GLOBALS[ACCOUNT_TYPE][$type];

        // See if user account already exists or not
        // if new, create
        if(! userExists($request[user]) &&
           ! createUser($request[user], $request[passwd], $account[shell]))
        {
            echo "User $request[user] does not exist\n";
            echo "User $request[user] could not be created.\n";
            return FALSE;
        }


        // See if group already exists or not
        // If new, create
        if(! groupExists($request[group]))
        {
            echo "Group $request[group] does not exist\n";
            return FALSE;
        }


        $addOK = addSite($request);

        // If site was added successfully see if we need to
        // restart or test
        if ($addOK && (isset($request[restart]) ||
                       isset($request[test])
                      )
           )
        {
            if (!restartApache())
            {
```

```
                echo "Error: Apache could not be restarted!\n";
                return FALSE;
            }

            if (isset($request[test]) && !testNewSite($request[vhost]))
            {
                echo "Error: site test failed!\n";
                return FALSE;
            }
        }

        // Now link the user account to the web site document root
        if ($addOK &&
            DEFAULT_SYMLINK_USER_TO_WEBSITE  &&
            ! createSymLink($request[user], $request[vhost]))
        {
            echo "Error: could not create symbolic link to site in user
account!\n";
            return FALSE;
        }

        // Now process content configuration
        if ($addOK && ! addContents($SITE_INFO, $account[master_contents]))
        {
            echo "Error: could not add contents!\n";
            return FALSE;
        }
        // Now process content configuration
        if ($addOK && isset($request[notify_email]) &&
            ! sendMail($SITE_INFO, $request, $account[mail_template]))
        {
            echo "Error: could not send mail!\n";
            return FALSE;
        }
    }
}

if (isset($cmd['enable']))
{
    echo "Enable named site \n";
    enableSite($siteName);
}
```

Continued

Listing 17-5 *(Continued)*

```php
    if (isset($cmd['disable']))
    {
        echo "Disable named site \n";
    }

    //print_r($cmd);

    exit;

    function createUser($user = null, $pass = null, $shell =null)
    {

        echo "Creating user account: $user  with password $pass shell=$shell\n";
        if (empty($pass) || strlen($pass) <
$GLOBALS[SYSTEM_INFO][min_passwd_length])
        {
            echo "Error: Password is missing or too short.\n";
            return FALSE;
        }

        if ($shell != null)
        {
            $shell = "-s $shell";
        }

        $cmd = $GLOBALS[SYSTEM_INFO][useradd_bin];
        exec("$cmd -p $pass $shell $user");
        return TRUE;
    }

    function userExists($user = null)
    {
        $passwdFile = $GLOBALS[SYSTEM_INFO][passwd_file];

        $lines = file($passwdFile);
        foreach($lines as $record)
        {
            $str = explode(':', $record);
            if (!strcmp($str[0], $user)) return TRUE;
        }

        return FALSE;
    }
```

```
    function groupExists($group = null)
    {
        $groupFile = $GLOBALS[SYSTEM_INFO][group_file];

        $lines = file($groupFile);
        foreach($lines as $record)
        {
          $str = explode(':', $record);
          if (!strcmp($str[0], $group)) return TRUE;
        }

        return FALSE;
    }

    function addSite($request = null)
    {
        $vhost = $request[vhost];
        $type = $request[type];
        $user = $request[user];
        $group = $request[group];

        echo "Creating $vhost configuration\n";

        // config file
        $vhostConfigFile = sprintf("%s/%s/%s", $GLOBALS['APACHE_INFO']['path'],

$GLOBALS['APACHE_INFO']['vhost_conf_dir'],
                                        $vhost);

        // See if this virtual host already exists or not
        if (file_exists($vhostConfigFile))
        {
            echo "Error: $vhostConfigFile already exists. Cannot add site!\n";
            return FALSE;
        }

        $account = $GLOBALS['ACCOUNT_TYPE'][$type];

        if (!isset($account))
        {
            echo "Error: given account type ($type) not defined in
makesite.conf\n";
            return FALSE;
        }
```

Continued

Listing 17-5 *(Continued)*

```php
        // Configure Apache Virtual Host
        $GLOBALS[SERVER_NAME] = $vhost;
        $results = loadVhostTemplate($account[vhost_template]);

        if ($results == null) return FALSE;

        $success = writeVirtualConfigFile($results[config], $vhostConfigFile);
        if (! $success) return FALSE;

        // Create directories
        if (DEBUG) echo "Create directories\n";
        foreach($results[makedir] as $dirName => $dirPath)
        {
            makeDirectory($GLOBALS[SYSTEM_INFO][permission],$dirPath);
            setOwnerAndGroup($user, $group, $dirPath);
            setPermissions($GLOBALS[SYSTEM_INFO][permission], $dirPath);
            $GLOBALS[SITE_INFO][$dirName] = $dirPath;
        }

        // Perform apache syntax check for vhost configuration
        $success = checkApacheSyntax($vhostConfigFile);
        if (! $success) return FALSE;

        $success = appendVhostConfigToApacheConfig($vhostConfigFile);
        if (! $success) return FALSE;

        return TRUE;
    }

    function checkApacheSyntax($file = null)
    {
        $serverBin = sprintf("%s/%s/%s", $GLOBALS[APACHE_INFO][path],
                                         $GLOBALS[APACHE_INFO][bin_dir],
                                         $GLOBALS[APACHE_INFO][server_bin]
                            );

        if (! file_exists($serverBin))
        {
            echo "Error: could not find $serverBin\n";
            return FALSE;
        }

        $cmd = "$serverBin " . $GLOBALS[APACHE_INFO][config_chk_opt] . " " .
$file ;
```

```
        echo "Checking syntax: $file\n";

        exec($cmd, $output, $status);

        return ($status) ? FALSE : TRUE;

}

function restartApache()
{

        $serverBin = sprintf("%s/%s/%s", $GLOBALS[APACHE_INFO][path],
                                        $GLOBALS[APACHE_INFO][bin_dir],
                                        $GLOBALS[APACHE_INFO][server_bin]
                        );

        if (! file_exists($serverBin))
        {
            echo "Error: could not find $serverBin\n";
            return FALSE;
        }

        $cmd = "$serverBin " . $GLOBALS[APACHE_INFO][restart_opt];

        echo "Restarting Apache: $cmd\n";

        exec($cmd, $output, $status);

        return ($status) ? FALSE : TRUE;

}

function writeTestPage()
{
    $testFile = sprintf("%s/test.txt", $GLOBALS[SITE_INFO][DOCUMENT_ROOT]);

    echo "Writing test page: $testFile \n";

    $fp = fopen($testFile, 'w');
    if ($fp)
    {
      fputs($fp, "SUCCESS");
      fclose($fp);
```

Continued

Listing 17-5 *(Continued)*

```php
        return TRUE;
    }
    return FALSE;
}


function createSymLink($user = null, $vhost = null)
{

    $link = sprintf("%s/%s/%s", $GLOBALS[SYSTEM_INFO][home_dir],$user, $vhost);


    $cmd = sprintf("%s %s %s %s", $GLOBALS[SYSTEM_INFO][symlink_bin],
                                  $GLOBALS[SYSTEM_INFO][symlink_opt],
                                  $GLOBALS[SITE_INFO][SERVER_ROOT],
                                  $link
                    );

    echo "Creating symbolic link using $cmd\n";

    if (file_exists($link))
    {
        echo "Warning! Symlink: $link already exists.\n";
        return TRUE;
    }

    exec($cmd, $output, $status);
    if ($status)
    {
        echo "Error: could not make symbolic link: $cmd\n";
        return FALSE;
    }
    return TRUE;
}

function removeTestPage()
{
    $testFile = sprintf("%s/test.txt", $GLOBALS[SITE_INFO][DOCUMENT_ROOT]);

    if (! file_exists($testFile))
    {
        return FALSE;
```

```
    }

    $status = unlink($testFile);

    return $status;
}


function testNewSite($host = null)
{

    // Write a test page in document root
    // of the new site
    if (! writeTestPage())
    {
        echo "Could not write test page in $GLOBALS[SITE_INFO][DOCUMENT_ROOT]
\n";

        return FALSE;
    }

    $url = sprintf("http://%s/test.txt", $host);

    echo "Testing: requesting $url ...";

    $fp = fopen($url, 'r');

     if ($fp)
     {
        while(!feof($fp))
        {
            $buffer .= fgets($fp, 1024);
        }

        removeTestPage();

        if (preg_match('/SUCCESS/', $buffer))
        {
            echo "successful.\n";
            return TRUE;
        } else {
            echo "failed.\n";
        }
     }
```

Continued

Listing 17-5 *(Continued)*

```php
        return FALSE;

    }


    function appendVhostConfigToApacheConfig($vhostFile = null)
    {
        $httpdConf = sprintf("%s/%s/%s", $GLOBALS[APACHE_INFO][path],
                                        $GLOBALS[APACHE_INFO][conf_dir],
                                        $GLOBALS[APACHE_INFO][conf_flie]
                        );

        if (! file_exists($httpdConf))
        {
            echo "Error: could not find $httpdConf\n";
            return FALSE;
        }

        $newDirective  = "#\n#\n# Following line loads configuration\n";
        $newDirective .= "# for the ". basename($vhostFile) . " virtual host\n";
        $newDirective .= "Include $vhostFile \n\n\n";

        echo "Appending Include $vhostFile in $httpdConf\n";

        if (DEBUG) echo $newDirective;

        $fp = fopen($httpdConf, 'a');
        if (! $fp)
        {
            echo "Error: could not open $httpdConf in append mode.\n";
            return FALSE;
        }

        fputs($fp, $newDirective);

        fclose($fp);

        return TRUE;

    }


    function makeDirectory($mode = '0750', $path = null)
    {
        $cmd = $GLOBALS[SYSTEM_INFO][mkdir_bin] . " -m $mode -p $path";
```

```
    if (DEBUG) echo "$cmd\n";
    exec($cmd);
}

function setPermissions($mode = null, $path = null)
{
    $cmd = $GLOBALS[SYSTEM_INFO][chmod_bin] . " -R $mode $path";
    if (DEBUG) echo "$cmd\n";
    exec($cmd);
}

function setOwnerAndGroup($user = null, $group = null, $path = null)
{
    $cmd = $GLOBALS[SYSTEM_INFO][chown_bin] . " -R $user:$group $path";
    if (DEBUG) echo "$cmd\n";
    exec($cmd);
}

function writeVirtualConfigFile($contents = null, $file = null)
{
    $fp = fopen($file, 'w');
    if (! $fp)
    {
        echo "Cannot write $file !\n";
        return FALSE;
    }

    fputs($fp, $contents);
    fclose($fp);

    return TRUE;
}

function loadVhostTemplate($template = null)
{
    $file = sprintf("%s/%s", $GLOBALS[TEMPLATE_DIR], $template);

    $contents = null;

    if (!file_exists($file))
    {
        echo "Virtual host template $file does not exists!\n";
        return null;
    }
```

Continued

Listing 17-5 *(Continued)*

```php
        // Load template
        require_once($file);

        $contents = makeVirtualHost();
        return $contents;
    }


    function checkVhostName($host = null)
    {
        $hostParts = explode('.', $host);

        // host must be at least:  domain.tld
        return (count($hostParts) <= 1) ? FALSE : TRUE;
    }


    function makeAddRequest($cmd = null)
    {
        $request = array();
        $request[vhost] = strtolower(getValue($cmd, 'v', 'vhost'));
        $request[user] = strtolower(getValue($cmd, 'u', 'user'));
        $request[group] = strtolower(getValue($cmd, 'g', 'group'));
        $request[restart] = getValue($cmd, 'r', 'restart');
        $request[test] = $cmd[test];
        $request[passwd] = getValue($cmd, 'p', 'pass');
        $request[type] = getValue($cmd, 't', 'type');
        $request[type] = ($request[type] != null) ?
            $request[type] : DEFAULT_ACCOUNT_TYPE;
        $request[notify_email] = (isset($cmd[notify_email])) ?
            strtolower($cmd[notify_email]) : null;

        if (empty($request[vhost]) ||
            empty($request[user]) ||
            empty($request[type])
          )
        {
            echo "You must provide --vhost --user --type ".
                "values to create a new virtual host.\n";

            return null;
        }

        // Remove leading or trailing dots from hostname
        $request[vhost] = preg_replace('/\.$/', '', $request[vhost]);
        $request[vhost] = preg_replace('/^\./', '', $request[vhost]);
```

```
    // Copy in to SITE_INFO
    $GLOBALS[SITE_INFO][user] = $request[user];
    $GLOBALS[SITE_INFO][group] = $request[group];
    $GLOBALS[SITE_INFO][vhost] = $request[vhost];

    // Check to see if given vhost is a hostname
    if (!checkVhostName($request[vhost]))
    {
        echo "Error: virtual hostname $request[vhost] is not valid.\n";
        return null;
    }


    if (empty($request[group]))
    {
        $request[group] = $request[user];
    }

    return $request;
}


function getValue($cmd = null, $short, $long)
{
    return (isset($cmd[$short])) ? $cmd[$short] : $cmd[$long];
}



function syntax()
{
    $script = basename($GLOBALS['argv'][0]);

    echo<<<HELP

    Syntax $script [options]

     -h
     --help shows this help

     -u username
     --user username the name of the user account
```

Continued

Listing 17-5 *(Continued)*

```
        -p password
        --pass password the password for the user account

        -v hostname
        --vhost hostname the virtual hostname

        -t account_type
        --type account_type sets type of account

        -r
        --restart  restarts Apache after configuration test OK

        -t
        --test  runs test to access http://hostname

HELP;

    }

    function getCommandLineOptions($options)
    {

        $type = gettype($options);

        if (gettype($options) != "array")
        {
            // Error in command line
            echo "$options->message \n";
            return null;
        }

        $cmd = array();

        foreach ($options[0] as $argArray)
        {

          $argName = preg_replace('/[^\w]/' , '', $argArray[0]);

          $argValue = $argArray[1];

          if ($argValue[0] == '-')
          {
              echo "$argName cannot have $argValue\n";
              return array();
          }
```

```php
        $cmd[$argName] = ($argValue != '') ? $argValue : TRUE;
    }

    return (count($cmd) > 0) ? $cmd : null;

}

function addContents($site = null, $template = null)
{

    $file = sprintf("%s/%s", $GLOBALS[TEMPLATE_DIR], $template);

    if (!file_exists($file))
    {
        echo "Virtual host content template $file does not exists!\n";
        return null;
    }

    // Load template
    require_once($file);

    $results = copyContentsToSite($site);
    return $results;
}

function sendMail($info = null, $request = null, $template = null)
{
    $mailTemplate = sprintf("%s/%s", $GLOBALS[TEMPLATE_DIR], $template);

    echo "Sending mail to $to using $mailTemplate\n";

    $to = $request[notify_email];

    if (! file_exists($mailTemplate))
    {
        echo "Error: mail template $mailTemplate not found! \n";
        return FALSE;
    }

    $lines = file($mailTemplate);

    $contentTypeSet = FALSE;

    $message = array();
```

Continued

Listing 17-5 *(Continued)*

```php
        $headers = array();

        foreach ($lines as $str)
        {
            $index++;
            if (preg_match('/From:\s*(.+)/i', $str, $match))
            {
                array_push($headers, "From: $match[1] \r\n");
            }
            else if (preg_match('/Subject:\s*(.+)/i', $str, $match))
            {
                $subject = $match[1];
            }
            else if (preg_match('/^CC:\s*(.+)/i', $str, $match))
            {
                array_push($headers, "Cc: $match[1] \r\n");
            }
            else if (preg_match('/Bcc:\s*(.+)/i', $str, $match))
            {
                array_push($headers, "Bcc: $match[1] \r\n");
            }
            else if (preg_match('/Content-Type:\s*(.+)/i', $str, $match))
            {
                if (preg_match('/html/', $match[1]))
                {
                    array_push($headers, "Content-Type: text/html\r\n");
                } else {
                    array_push($headers, "Content-Type: text/plain\n");
                }

                $contentTypeSet = TRUE;
            }
            else if (preg_match('/MIME-Version:\s*(.+)/i', $str, $match))
            {
                array_push($headers, "MIME-Version: $match[1] \r\n");

            } else {
                array_push($message, $str);
            }
        }

        if (! $contentTypeSet) array_push($headers, "Content-Type:
text/plain\r\n");

        $body = implode('', $message);
```

```
$search = array();
$replace = array();

foreach ($info as $key => $value)
{
    array_push($search, '/<%' . strtoupper($key) . '%>/');
    array_push($replace, $value);
}

foreach ($request as $key => $value)
{
    array_push($search, '/<%' . strtoupper($key) . '%>/');
    array_push($replace, $value);
}

$body = preg_replace($search, $replace, $body);
$subject = preg_replace($search, $replace, $subject);

$headerStr = implode('', $headers);

mail($to, $subject, $body, $headerStr);

return TRUE;
}

?>
```

This makesite script builds on the command-line examples discussed throughout this portion of the book. The makesite script uses the two types of command-line arguments, short and long.

The short arguments that are allowed are defined in the `$CMD_SHORT_OPTIONS` string, and the long ones are defined in `$CMD_LONG_OPTIONS`. These strings are needed for the `Console_Getopt::getopt()` function, which is available from the Console/Getopt.php class in the PEAR package.

The makesite script works as follows:

1. It retrieves all the command-line arguments using the `getCommandLine Options()` function and stores them in the `$cmd` array.

2. If –add is included as a command-line argument then the script performs the actual task of adding the new virtual Web site.

3. It calls the `makeAddRequest()` method to create an array called `$request` with user-supplied information such as virtual host name (supplied using the `--vhost` host name or the `-v` hostname), account type (`-t` account_type or `--type` account_type), username (`--user` username), password (`-p` password or `--pass` password), and so on.

4. It determines whether the named user account in the command line already exists, using the `userExists()` function. If the user account does not exists, it creates the account using the `createUser()` function.

5. Similarly, the script determines whether the user-supplied group name exists, using the `groupExists()` function. Note that if the user does not supply a group name using the `--group` option, the username is assumed as the default group name. This is possible because in popular Linux systems such as Red Hat Linux, each user is assigned to his or her own group when the user account is created using a standard account-creation tool like useradd. If your system does not create a group corresponding to the username, you should supply the `--group` option with an appropriate group name.

6. Once usernames and groups are checked and/or created as needed, the script calls `addSite()` to create the virtual site configuration along with the actual directory structure of the site on the disk.

7. Once the configuration is created, the script checks to see if the user wants to restart Apache (`--restart`) or test (`--test`) the configuration. If either case is true, the Web server is restarted using the `restartApache()` function.

8. If the test option (`--test`) was provided in the command line, the `testNewSite()` function is called to test the new site. The test is performed by adding a test.txt file in the site and retrieving it as an HTTL get request. If the test.txt can be retrieved via an HTTP get request, the site is assumed to be installed and operating properly.

9. If `DEFAULT_SYMLINK_USER_TO_WEBSITE` is set to `TRUE`, a symbolic soft link is created from the user's home directory to the new Web site using the `createSymLink()` function.

10. Next, the `addContents()` function is called to optionally add any contents using the master_content template for the current account type.

11. Finally, if the `--notify_email` option was provided with an e-mail address, the `sendMail()` function is called to send an e-mail message to the given e-mail address using the mail template specified for the current account type.

Installing makesite on Your System

The complete makesite package is provided in the CDROM/ch17 directory in `makesite.tar.gz`. Extract this package on your Linux system and modify the configuration files as needed. The makesite.conf file has two path settings that are likely to differ from your system:

```
$PEAR_DIR          = '/example/intranet/htdocs/pear' ;
```

The $PEAR_DIR must point to the directory in which you installed PEAR, or at least the Console/Getopt.php package from PEAR:

```
$APACHE_INFO[path] = '/usr/local/apache',
```

The preceding path should point to the top directory of your Apache Web server. For example, if you have installed Apache in /home/httpd, you should change it.
The makesite script assumes that your Apache directory structure is as follows:

```
Top Apache Directory: /usr/local/apache
Apache Binary Directory: /usr/local/apache/bin
Apache Configuration Directory: /usr/local/apache/conf
Apache Virtual Host Configuration Directory: /usr/local/apache/conf/vhosts
```

You will have to create the virtual host configuration directory manually, as it is not standard in the Apache installer.
In addition, the makesite.conf file has a few other system-dependent configurations, such as server_ip and www_partition, in $SYSTEM_INFO. You should review all the configurations in makesite.conf to ensure that the paths and values reflect your system as closely as possible.
The www_partition should point to the top directory of your system, where you want to create the actual virtual host sites. For example, the sample configuration assumes /www as the www_partition, and therefore a –virtual host www.example.com is created as follows:

```
/www
Site directory: /www/www.example.com
Site's document root: /www/www.example.com/htdocs
Site's log directory: /www/www.example.com/logs
```

If this is now the directory structure you want to implement, you have to change www_partition to reflect the top directory, and then you have to change each account's vhost_template code to reflect your requirements.
For example, the std_vhost.conf file (used for standard account) creates the following:

```
$serverRoot = sprintf("%s/%s", $www, $server);
$docRoot = sprintf("%s/%s/htdocs", $www, $server);
$logDir  = sprintf("%s/%s/logs", $www, $server);
```

These can be changed to reflect your directory structure.

Testing makesite

Once you have installed and configured makesite in a directory, you can run it as root from the script directory.

For example:

```
./makesite --add  --user mrfrog  -p 12345  -v r2d2.exampleexample.com --type
gold -test
```

Here, the makesite script is asked to create a virtual host configuration for a host called r2d2.exampleexample.com using the account type of gold. The script also indicates that the host will be owned by the user mrfrog, with the password 12345.

Here is the sample output:

```
Creating user account: mrfrog with password 12345 shell=/bin/tcsh
Creating r2d2.exampleexample.com configuration
Checking syntax: /usr/local/apache/conf/vhosts/r2d2.examplexample.com
Syntax OK
Appending Include /usr/local/apache/conf/vhosts/r2d2.exampleexample.com in
/usr/local/apache/conf/httpd.conf
Restarting Apache: /usr/local/apache/bin/httpd -k restart
Writing test page: /www/r2d2.exampleexample.com/htdocs/test.txt
Testing: requesting http://r2d2.exampleexample.com/test.txt ...successful.
Creating symbolic link using /bin/ln -s /www/r2d2.exampleexample.com
~mrfrog/r2d2.exampleexample.com
```

The actual virtual host configuration used by Apache is stored in the conf/vhosts/r2d2.exampleexample.com file, which looks like the following:

```
    #
    # Automated virtual host configuration for
r2d2.exampleexample.com
    #
    # Account Type: standard
    #
    <VirtualHost 192.168.0.11>

        ServerName     r2d2.exampleexample.com
        DocumentRoot   "/www/r2d2.exampleexample.com/htdocs"
        ErrorLog
"/www/r2d2.exampleexample.com/logs/errors.log"
        CustomLog
"/www/r2d2.exampleexample.com/logs/access.log" common
```

```
<Directory />
   <Files "*.conf">
      deny from all
   </Files>
</Directory>

</VirtualHost>
```

The httpd.conf file is appended with the following lines:

```
#
#
# Following line loads configuration
# for the r2d2.exampleexample.com virtual host
Include /usr/local/apache/conf/vhosts/r2d2.exampleexample.com
```

When the Apache server restarts, it loads the virtual host configuration for r2d2.exampleexample.com host from /usr/local/apache/conf/vhosts/r2d2.example-example.com.

This ensures that your httpd.conf file is not cluttered with numerous virtual host configurations, as the Include directive enables you to keep the virtual host configuration outside the main httpd.conf file.

You must have a NameVirtualHost directive specified in httpd.conf before any "name virtual hosts" configurations are added. For example:

```
NameVirtualHost *
   Include /usr/local/apache/conf/vhosts/
r2d2.exampleexample.com
   Include /usr/local/apache/conf/vhosts/
diablo.exampleexample.com
```

To better understand the tasks that are performed by makesite, you can set DEBUG to TRUE in makesite.conf to see what gets done. For example:

```
./makesite --add --user mrfrog  --vhost r2d2.exampleexample.com -p 12345 --
notify_email=kabir
```

Here is a sample output:

```
Creating user account: mrfrog  with password 12345 shell=/bin/true
Creating r2d2.example.com configuration
Create directories
/bin/mkdir -m 0755 -p /www/r2d2.example.com
/bin/chown -R mrfrog:mrfrog /www/r2d2.example.com
/bin/chmod -R 0755 /www/r2d2.example.com
/bin/mkdir -m 0755 -p /www/r2d2.example.com/htdocs
/bin/chown -R mrfrog:mrfrog /www/r2d2.example.com/htdocs
/bin/chmod -R 0755 /www/r2d2.example.com/htdocs
/bin/mkdir -m 0755 -p /www/r2d2.example.com/logs
/bin/chown -R mrfrog:mrfrog /www/r2d2.example.com/logs
/bin/chmod -R 0755 /www/r2d2.example.com/logs
Checking syntax: /usr/local/apache/conf/vhosts/r2d2.example.com
Syntax OK
Appending Include /usr/local/apache/conf/vhosts/r2d2.example.com in
/usr/local/apache/conf/httpd.conf
#
#
# Following line loads configuration
# for the r2d2.example.com virtual host
Include /usr/local/apache/conf/vhosts/r2d2.example.com

Creating symbolic link using /bin/ln -s /www/r2d2.example.com
/home/mrfrog/r2d2.example.com
/bin/cp -r vhosts/standard/htdocs/* /www/r2d2.example.com/htdocs
Sending mail to  using vhosts/std_vhost.mail
```

Summary

In this chapter, you learned how to develop a command-line PHP script that helps you manage Apache virtual hosts on your Linux system. Using this script creating, changing, and removing virtual servers becomes almost easy.

 Remember to visit www.apache.org for documentation on Apache and more directives for use with virtual hosts.

Chapter 18

BIND Domain Manager

IN THIS CHAPTER

♦ Developing a BIND administrator tool

♦ Using the BIND administrator tool

IN THIS CHAPTER, we will develop a simple DNS management application that runs via the command line and creates DNS configurations for domains that you can host on your Linux-based BIND server. BIND is the most widely used DNS server on the Linux/UNIX platform. The script developed here creates only forward domain configuration, as reverse DNS domain management is the primary task of ISPs.

Features of makezone

The DNS administration tool we will develop is called makezone. The makezone utility has the following features:

♦ It is a command-line tool that can be run by the root user to create new DNS configurations for domains that are primarily used for Web service.

♦ It uses a template-based configuration that enables an administrator to create classes of DNS configurations. For example, an administrator can create a DNS configuration template that creates a new DNS domain with the bare minimum number of entries, namely the name server entries, a Web server entry, an FTP server entry, and two mail (MX) server records (with differing priorities). The administrator can also create another configuration template that creates multiple round-robin Web server configurations.

♦ The utility works only with forward domains, as reverse DNS is primarily handed by ISPs, and requires a fair amount of knowledge of DNS and IP addresses to implement. Our focus is to create a Web server host DNS configuration, which can often work without any reverse DNS setup.

Note that this utility assumes you are running on a Linux server and running a suitable version of BIND. If you are using another DNS server application you can still use this application, but significant editing of the templates, file names, and configuration files. Also note that some versions of Linux store their BIND files in other locations – edit the configuration for this application according to your version of BIND.

To determine if your machine is running BIND, use the following command:

```
ps -A | grep "named"
```

If the system replies with something similar to the following, you are running BIND:

```
15314 ?        00:00:04 named
```

If nothing is returned, `named` (the BIND server) is not running.

Following is a sample command line of makezone. Here, makezone is instructed to add a new zone called example.com using the standard template.

```
./makezone --add=zone --name=example.com  --template=standard
```

Creating the Configuration File

Listing 18-1 shows the makezone.conf configuration file. This is the primary configuration file for the makezone script.

The makezone script uses the `Console/Getopt.php` package from the PEAR package; therefore, the PEAR path must be added using `$PEAR_DIR`. The sample PEAR path `/www/pear` is not likely to be the same as yours, so you should change it and any other paths to reflect your system configuration.

The `NAMED_CONF` constant points to the central BIND configuration file `/etc/named.conf`. The `ZONE_DIR` constant points to the standard BIND zone directory `/var/named`. The `ZONE_TEMPLATE_DIR` constant points to the template directory, which is a subdirectory of the makezone script directory. The makezone script looks for two types of templates: one to create the `/etc/named.conf` configuration and another to create the actual zone configuration.

The `DEFAULT_TEMPLATE` constant specifies the name of the default template. The rest of the configuration defines various host name and IP addresses that are used in the zone configuration, and will be discussed later in this section when we cover the standard template.

Listing 18-1: makezone.conf

```php
<?php

    // Set this to the PEAR directory
    $PEAR_DIR = '/www/pear' ;
```

```
ini_set( 'include_path', ':' .
        $PEAR_DIR . ':' . ini_get('include_path'));

require_once "Console/Getopt.php";

define(DEBUG, TRUE);

define(NAMED_CONF, '/etc/named.conf');
define(ZONE_DIR, '/var/named');
define(ZONE_TEMPLATE_DIR, 'templates');
define(ZONE_MASTER_TEMPLATE, 'named.master_zone.conf');
define(DEFAULT_TEMPLATE, 'standard');

$DOMAIN                 = 'example.com';
$PRIMARY_NAME_SERVER    = '192.168.0.11';
$SECONDARY_NAME_SERVER  = '192.168.1.254';
$PRI05_MAIL_SERVER      = '192.168.0.100';
$PRI10_MAIL_SERVER      = '192.168.0.101';
$WWW_SERVER_IP_ADDR     = '192.168.0.12';
$FTP_SERVER_IP_ADDR     = '192.168.0.12';
$WWW_SERVER_ALIAS       = 'apache.example.com';

?>
```

As mentioned before, the makezone script uses two types of template, one of which is used to create the zone. There can be many different zone templates. Listing 18-2 shows a zone template called standard.template. This template is used to create a new zone when the option --template=standard is provided.

The DEFAULT_TEMPLATE is set to standard; therefore, in the absence of a --template option, the standard template is used. If you wish to use a different template as the default, change the value of the DEFAULT_TEMPLATE constant.

For example, if you specify --template=advanced, makezone will use the templates/advanced.template file as the zone template. Now let's look at the standard.template in detail.

Listing 18-2: standard.template

```php
<?php


function getZoneConfiguration()
{

    $output = <<<DNS
;
; This zone file is generated automatically by makezone script
; If you edit this file manually, the changes will be lost
; if you regenerate the zone again using makezone
;
\$TTL    86400
\$ORIGIN $GLOBALS[ZONE].
@                       1D IN SOA       @ root (
                                        01              ; serial
                                        3H              ; refresh
                                        15M             ; retry
                                        1W              ; expiry
                                        1D )            ; minimum

                        1D IN NS        $GLOBALS[PRIMARY_NAME_SERVER]
                        1D IN NS        $GLOBALS[SECONDARY_NAME_SERVER]
                        1D IN MX 5      $GLOBALS[PRI05_MAIL_SERVER]
                        1D IN MX 10     $GLOBALS[PRI10_MAIL_SERVER]

ns                      1D IN A         $GLOBALS[PRIMARY_NAME_SERVER]

www                     1D IN A         $GLOBALS[WWW_SERVER_IP_ADDR]
www                     IN CNAME        $GLOBALS[WWW_SERVER_ALIAS].

ftp                     1D IN A         $GLOBALS[FTP SERVER IP_ADDR]

DNS;


    return $output;

}

?>
```

As you can see, the standard template is a PHP script, which means you can do anything you want in this template using the power of PHP. The standard template defines a zone that has a Start of Authority (SOA) record, two name servers (NS) records, two mail exchanger (MX) records, three address (A) records, and a CNAME alias.

The configuration shown here (number of records and types) is simply a solution. Feel free to edit the template according to your own needs, adding or removing records as you see fit.

If you need more information about BIND, pick up a copy of....

When this zone template is loaded, the makezone script calls the getZoneConfiguration() function, which returns a complete zone configuration. Listing 18-3 shows a sample configuration created using the standard.template.

Listing 18-3: Sample Output of standard.template

```
;
; This zone file is generated automatically by makezone script
; If you edit this file manually, the changes will be lost
; if you regenerate the zone again using makezone
;
$TTL    86400
$ORIGIN example.com.
@                       1D IN SOA       @ root (
                                        01              ; serial
                                        3H              ; refresh
                                        15M             ; retry
                                        1W              ; expiry
                                        1D )            ; minimum

                        1D IN NS        192.168.0.11
                        1D IN NS        192.168.1.254
                        1D IN MX 5      192.168.0.100
                        1D IN MX 10     192.168.0.101

ns                      1D IN A         192.168.0.11

www                     1D IN A         192.168.0.12
www                     IN CNAME        apache.example.com.

ftp                     1D IN A         192.168.0.12
```

All the IP addresses and host names are inserted using various $GLOBALS set from the makezone script and makezone.conf file.

You can create as many zone templates as you wish. To use them, just call the desired zone template using the --template=*zone_template* option. Remember to place your zone template in the templates directory pointed to by the ZONE_TEMPLATE_DIR constant in makezone.conf.

 Make sure your template is a PHP script containing the getZone Configuration() function, which returns the full zone configuration.

The zone template produced configuration is stored in the ZONE_DIR directory as a separate zone file.

There is one other kind of template that makezone uses for creating the configuration needed to add a new zone configuration to /etc/named.conf. This template is shown in Listing 18-4.

Listing 18-4: named.master_zone.conf

```php
<?php

function getNamedZoneConfig()
{

    $output = <<<MASTER_ZONE_NAMED_CONF

//
// Master zone configuration for $GLOBALS[ZONE]
//
zone "$GLOBALS[ZONE]" IN {
        type master;
        file "$GLOBALS[ZONE_FILE]";
        allow-update { none; };
};


MASTER_ZONE_NAMED_CONF;

    return $output;
}

?>
```

Like the zone template, this is also a PHP script. It has a function called getNamedZoneConfig(), which is called by makezone. This function returns the configuration that is appended to the /etc/named.conf file to hook up the new zone to the DNS server. The following code shows sample output of this template:

```
//
// Master zone configuration for example.com
//
zone "example.com" IN {
        type master;
        file "example.com.zone";
        allow-update { none; };
};
```

This configuration is appended to /etc/named.conf. Notice that we only create a master configuration for the new forward domain.

When makezone is run successfully to create a new zone, a zone file is created in the location specified by ZONE_DIR, and the appropriate configuration is appended to the file specified by NAMED_CONF to enable the DNS server to find the new zone configuration.

Once makezone is successful, you can restart the BIND name server using the following:

```
/etc/rc.d/init.d/named restart
```

This will load the new zone, and you can test your new zone data using the dig command, which is discussed in the section, " Testing makezone."

Understanding makezone

The makezone utility is implemented in Listing 18-5. This script works as follows:

- ◆ It expects the command-line arguments and options defined in $CMD_SHORT_OPTIONS and $CMD_LONG_OPTIONS.

- ◆ It retrieves the command-line arguments and options into $cmd using the getCommandLineOptions() function, which is called with Console_Getopt::getopt() output, which returns valid command-line arguments and options or an error object.

- ◆ If no command-line argument is provided, the syntax() function is called to display syntax.

- ◆ If the --add option is specified, the addZone() function is called to create the new zone.

Listing 18-5: makezone

```php
#!/usr/bin/php -q
<?php

    require_once('makezone.conf');

    $CMD_SHORT_OPTIONS = 'h';

    $CMD_LONG_OPTIONS  = array('help',
                               'add=',
                               'name=',
                               'template=',
                               'enable',
                               'disable',
                               'test'
                               );

    $cmd = getCommandLineOptions(
           Console_Getopt::getopt($GLOBALS['argv'],
                                  $CMD_SHORT_OPTIONS,
                                  $CMD_LONG_OPTIONS)
                                  );

    if (empty($cmd)) syntax();

    if ($cmd[add] == 'zone')
    {
        addZone($cmd[name], $cmd[template]);
    }

    exit;

    function addZone($zone =null, $template = null)
    {

        // First check if zone is already created
        $zoneFile = getFQPNZoneFile($zone);

        if (zoneExists($zoneFile))
        {
            echo "Error: $zoneFile exists.\n";
            return FALSE;
```

```
}

$zoneTemplate = getFQPNZoneTemplate($template);

if (empty($zoneTemplate)) return FALSE;

echo "Adding $zone using $zoneTemplate \n";

require_once($zoneTemplate);

$GLOBALS[ZONE] = $zone;

$config = getZoneConfiguration();

echo $config;

$status = writeZoneFile($zoneFile, $config);

$namedMasterZoneTemplate =
    getFQPNNamedMasterZoneTemplate();

if ( ! file_exists($namedMasterZoneTemplate))
{
    echo "Error: $namedMasterZoneTemplate is missing\n";
    return FALSE;
}

echo "Loading $namedMasterZoneTemplate ...";

require_once($namedMasterZoneTemplate);

echo "OK.\n";

$GLOBALS[ZONE_FILE] = basename($zoneFile);

$baseZoneFile = basename($zoneFile);

if (! zoneInNamedConf($baseZoneFile))
{
    $namedConf = getNamedZoneConfig();

    $status = appendNamedConfFile($namedConf);
```

Continued

Listing 18-5 *(Continued)*

```
        echo $namedConf;

    } else {

        echo "Warning: $baseZoneFile ".
            "already used in " . NAMED_CONF . "\n";
    }

    return TRUE;
}

function zoneInNamedConf($file = null)
{
    $lines = file(NAMED_CONF);

    if (count($lines) <1) return FALSE;

     $search = '/' . $file . '/';

    foreach ($lines as $named_conf)
    {
        if (preg_match($search, $named_conf)) return TRUE;
    }

    return FALSE;
}

function appendNamedConfFile($config = null)
{
    $fp - fopen(NAMED_CONF, 'a');
    if (! $fp)
    {
        echo "Error: could not open " .
            NAMED_CONF . " for update.\n";

        return FALSE;
    }

    fputs($fp, $config);
    fclose($fp);

    return TRUE;
```

```
}


function getFQPNNamedMasterZoneTemplate()
{
    return sprintf("%s/%s",
                    ZONE_TEMPLATE_DIR,
                    ZONE_MASTER_TEMPLATE);
}

function writeZoneFile($file = null, $config = null)
{
    $fp = fopen($file, 'w+');
    if (! $fp)
    {
        echo "Error: $file could ".
            " not be open for writing!\n";
        return FALSE;
    }

    echo "Writing zone file ($file)....\n";
    fputs($fp, $config);
    fclose($fp);
    echo "OK.\n";
}

function getFQPNZoneFile($zone = null)
{
    return sprintf("%s/%s.zone", ZONE_DIR, $zone);
}

function zoneExists($file = null)
{
    echo "Looking for zone file: $file ... ";

    if (!file_exists($file))
    {
        echo "not found\n";
        return null;
    }

    echo "OK.\n";
```

Continued

Listing 18-5 *(Continued)*

```
        return $file;
    }

    function getFQPNZoneTemplate($template = null)
    {
        $file = sprintf("%s/%s.template", ZONE_TEMPLATE_DIR,
$template);

        echo "Looking for zone template file: $file ... ";

        if (!file_exists($file))
        {
            echo "not found\n";
            return null;
        }

        echo "OK.\n";

        return $file;
    }

    function syntax()
    {
        $script = basename($GLOBALS['argv'][0]);

        echo<<<HELP

        Syntax $script [options]

        --add-zone
        --name=name of zone e.g --name=example.com
        --template=template_name e.g --template=standard

HELP;

    }

    function getCommandLineOptions($options)
    {

        $type = gettype($options);

        if (gettype($options) != "array")
```

```
{
    // Error in command line
    echo "$options->message \n";
    return null;
}

$cmd = array();

foreach ($options[0] as $argArray)
{

    $argName = preg_replace('/[^\w]/' , '', $argArray[0]);

    $argValue = $argArray[1];

    if ($argValue[0] == '-')
    {
        echo "$argName cannot have $argValue\n";
        return array();
    }

    $cmd[$argName] = ($argValue != '') ? $argValue : TRUE;
}

return (count($cmd) > 0) ? $cmd : null;

}

?>
```

The makezone Functions

The makezone script has the following functions:

addZone()

This function adds a new zone in the DNS configuration. Here is how it works:

1. It first creates a variable called $zoneFile using getFQPNZoneFile().
   This variable stores the fully qualified path name of the new zone file.
   The zone name is specified by the user, using the --name option in the
   command line.

2. If the zone file already exists, the function displays an error message and
   returns FALSE.

3. A `$zoneTemplate` variable is used to store the fully qualified path name of the zone template using `getFQPNZoneTemplate()`. The zone template is selected by the user, using the `--template` option in the command line.

4. The zone template is loaded using `require_once()` and the `$GLOBALS[ZONE]` value is set to the new zone. The `getZoneConfiguration()` function found in the zone template is called to return the complete zone configuration in `$config`.

5. The new zone configuration is then written to the zone file using the `writeZoneFile()` function.

6. The fully qualified master zone template is retrieved using `getFQPNNamed MasterZoneTemplate()`, and the path is stored in `$namedMasterZone Template`. If the `$namedMasterZoneTemplate` is missing, the function displays an error and returns FALSE.

7. The master template is loaded using `require_once()`. The `$GLOBALS [ZONE_FILE]` value is set to the zone file created earlier. The base name of the zone file is stored in `$baseZoneFile`. If the `$baseZone File` value is found in NAMED_CONF (/etc/named.conf) using the `zoneInNamedConf()` function, then the zone is already added to the NAMED_CONF file and the function displays a warning message. Otherwise, it appends the master zone configuration in NAMED_CONF using `appendNamedConfFile()`.

8. Finally, the function returns TRUE to indicate success.

zoneInNamedConf()
This function returns TRUE if a given zone already exists in NAMED_CONF (/etc/named.conf). Otherwise, it returns FALSE.

appendNamedConfFile()
This function appends the given configuration to the NAMED_CONF (/etc/named. conf) file.

getFQPNNamedMasterZoneTemplate()
This function returns the fully qualified master zone file template path.

writeZoneFile()
This function writes the zone file in the ZONE_DIR directory.

getFQPNZoneFile()
This function returns the fully qualified name of the zone file.

zoneExists( )
This function returns TRUE if the given zone file already exists. Otherwise, it returns FALSE.

getFQPNZoneTemplate( )
This function returns the fully qualified zone template path. If the zone template does not exist, it displays an error message and returns null. If it does exist, it returns the zone file path.

syntax( )
This function provides syntax help.

getCommandLineOptions( )
This function returns the command-line arguments as an array if valid arguments were entered by the user. If an invalid argument is entered, the function displays an error message and returns null.

Installing makezone

To install this script, you need to extract CDROM/ch18/ch18.tar.gz in a suitable directory. You will see makezone, makezone.conf, and a template directory with two files named.master_zone.conf and standard.template.

If you wish to run makezone from any directory, you should do the following:

1. Install makezone in /usr/bin, which is typically in the root user's path.

2. Store makezone and the template directory with the files in the /usr/local/makezone directory.

3. Edit makezone.conf to change $PEAR_DIR to point to your PEAR installation directory, and ZONE_TEMPLATE_DIR to point to /usr/local/makezone/templates.

4. Change the file ownership of makezone to be readable and executable by only the root user as follows:

```
chown root:root /usr/bin/makezone
chown -R root:root /usr/local/makezone
chmod -R 700 /usr/bin/makezone
chmod -R 700 /usr/local/makezone
```

5. Now you should be able to run makezone from anywhere. To create new zone templates, copy the standard template to another file and modify it to fit your needs. Make sure new template file name ends with the .template extension.

Testing makezone

Running makezone is simple. Here is a test run:

```
./makezone --add=zone --name=example.com --template=standard
```

This creates the `/var/named/example.com.zone` zone file for example.com using the standard zone template. The contents of this zone file look like the following:

```
;
; This zone file is generated automatically by makezone script
; If you edit this file manually, the changes will be lost
; if you regenerate the zone again using makezone
;
$TTL    86400
$ORIGIN example.com.
@                       1D IN SOA       @ root (
                                        01              ; serial
                                        3H              ; refresh
                                        15M             ; retry
                                        1W              ; expiry
                                        1D )            ; minimum

                        1D IN NS        192.168.0.11
                        1D IN NS        192.168.1.254
                        1D IN MX 5      192.168.0.100
                        1D IN MX 10     192.168.0.101

ns                      1D IN A         192.168.0.11

www                     1D IN A         192.168.0.12
www                     IN CNAME        apache.example.com.

ftp                     1D IN A         192.168.0.12

the /etc/named.conf has the following lines appended:
//
// Master zone configuration for example.com
//
zone "example.com" IN {
        type master;
        file "example.com.zone";
        allow-update { none; };
};
```

Now, if the BIND server is restarted using the /etc/rc.d/init.d/named restart command, it loads the new zone.

 On some systems the named control script will be located in a different directory.

You can test the new zone using the dig command.
For example:

```
dig www.example.com A
```

outputs something like the following:

```
; <<>> DiG 9.2.1 <<>> www.example.com A
;; global options:  printcmd
;; Got answer:
;; ->>HEADER<<- opcode: QUERY, status: NOERROR, id: 50838
;; flags: qr rd ra; QUERY: 1, ANSWER: 2, AUTHORITY: 3, ADDITIONAL: 0

;; QUESTION SECTION:
;www.example.com.                IN      A

;; ANSWER SECTION:
www.example.com.        26922   IN      A       192.168.0.12


;; AUTHORITY SECTION:
example.com.            86400   IN      NS      ns.example.com.


;; Query time: 3469 msec
;; SERVER: 192.168.0.11#53(192.168.0.11)
;; WHEN: Sat Dec 14 03:03:58 2002
;; MSG SIZE  rcvd: 127
```

Similarly, you can query about other records, as shown here:
The following will show mail exchanger (MX) records:

```
dig example.com MX
```

The following will show name server (NS) records:

```
dig example.com NS
```

Summary

In this chapter, you learned how to develop a command-line PHP script that helps you manage DNS configuration on your Linux system. Such scripts can take the tedium out of administering the several files that need updating when you add a domain. Scripts such as this also maintain the integrity of the configuration by helping omit typos and other mistakes.

Part V

Internet Applications

Chapter 19

Web Forms Manager

WEB FORMS ARE COMMON in virtually any commercial Web site. Using Web forms, you can collect data from users and perform business operations such as sending a quotation or brochures or soliciting feedback. In this chapter, you will design a general-purpose Web Forms Management application that enables you to manage virtually any single-page Web form. The virtue of managing all your Web forms by using a central general-purpose Web forms application suite is that you can control and manage your data security from a single point, thus eliminating a great deal of the time and effort that goes into managing multiple form scripts for security and other issues.

Functionality Requirements

Our general-purpose Web Forms Management application suite offers the following feature set:

◆ **A single application for Web form processing.** All single-page Web forms can be managed by a single application.

◆ **Central, smart CSV downloading.** A central CSV export application enables a site administrator to download new data at any time. The application enables the administrator to export data from the form database by using either a range of dates or the last download. This is a nice feature if, for example, your business has a department that retrieves data from your Web forms and sends out brochures or other documents to potential customers.

◆ **Central form data reporting.** A single interface to view form data as stored in a database.

◆ **Inbound and outbound e-mail.** When a form is submitted, the Web form processor can send e-mail to both the submitter and the Web administrator or to anyone else to whom inbound e-mail should be directed. The e-mail messages sent are created by using mail templates and are, therefore, very flexible.

◆ **A template-driven interface.** Each form should have its own thank-you page template and inbound and outbound message template.

◆ **Automatic return to the referred page.** If the Web form provides a return URL, the form processing application should return the user to the return URL once processing is completed.

Understanding Prerequisites

This is an Internet application and does not require central authentication techniques. Therefore, it is not dependent on intranet tools discussed in earlier chapters.

However, it does require the application framework classes discussed in Chapter 4. You must install the application framework classes along with the PHPLIB and PEAR packages.

Designing the Database

Figure 19-1 shows the database diagram for the Web Forms Manager. Here, I will describe the only table (WEBFORMS_DL_TBL) of the database. Furthermore, there will be one or more tables, depending on the number of forms. This means that each form to be managed will have its own table. For your convenience, I will describe a sample form table along with WEBFORMS_DL_TBL.

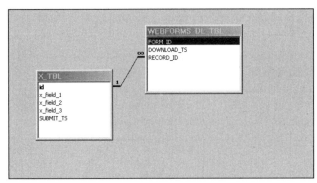

Figure 19-1: The WEBFORMS database diagram.

WEBFORMS_DL_TBL table

This table is responsible for storing the track of record ID for each form up to which the user has downloaded the data. This helps the user download the latest data for a form. This table stores the form code (FORM_ID), timestamp of download (DOWNLOAD_TS), and the record ID (RECORD_ID) up to which the form data have been downloaded.

X_TBL table (a sample form table)

This is a form-specific table. X_TBL stores the data collected from the X form. The two fields of this table that are common to all form tables are the record ID (id) and the time of form submission (SUBMIT_TS). The record ID is auto-incremented with each insertion. Depending on the particular form, you can have many other fields in each of the form tables. These fields are used to store the data collected from the form.

Listing 19-1 shows an implementation of the WEBFORMS database in MySQL. To implement this WEBFORMS database in MySQL, you can create a database called WEBFORMS in your MySQL database server and run the following command:

```
mysql -u root -p -D WEBFORMS < webforms.sql
```

Make sure that you change the username (root) to whatever is appropriate for your system.

Listing 19-1: WEBFORMS.mysql

```
# phpMyAdmin MySQL-Dump
# version 2.2.5
# http://phpwizard.net/phpMyAdmin/
# http://phpmyadmin.sourceforge.net/ (download page)
#
# Host: localhost
# Generation Time: Dec 13, 2002 at 07:50 PM
# Server version: 3.23.35
# PHP Version: 4.1.0
# Database : `WEBFORMS`
# -------------------------------------------------------

#
# Table structure for table `WEBFORMS_DL_TBL`
#

CREATE TABLE WEBFORMS_DL_TBL (
```

Continued

Listing 19-1 *(Continued)*

```
   FORM_ID varchar(255) NOT NULL default '0',
   DOWNLOAD_TS bigint(20) NOT NULL default '0',
   RECORD_ID int(11) NOT NULL default '0'
) TYPE=MyISAM;
# ---------------------------------------------------------


#
# Table structure for table `X_TBL`
#

CREATE TABLE X_TBL (
   id int(11) NOT NULL auto_increment,
   x_field_1 varchar(255) NOT NULL default '',
   x_field_2 text NOT NULL,
   x_field_3 int(11) NOT NULL default '0',
   SUBMIT_TS bigint(20) NOT NULL default '0',
   PRIMARY KEY  (id)
) TYPE=MyISAM;
```

Note that the X_TBL is really an example table; you should rename it to match your form name. For example, if you have a form called ASK.php or ASK.html, with three fields named first, last, and e-mail, you can create it as follows:

```
CREATE TABLE ASK_TBL (
   id int(11) NOT NULL auto_increment,
   first varchar(25) NOT NULL default '',
   last  varchar(25) NOT NULL,
   email varchar(60) NOT NULL,
   SUBMIT_TS bigint(20) NOT NULL default '0',
   PRIMARY KEY  (id)
) TYPE=MyISAM;
```

Notice that the id and SUBMIT_TS fields are required for managing the forms.

Designing and Implementing the Web Forms Manager Application Classes

As shown in the system diagram (see Figure 19-2), five objects are needed to implement the Web Forms Manager application.

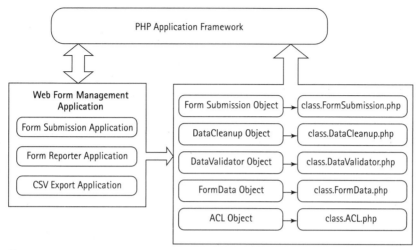

Figure 19-2: System diagram of the Web Forms Manager.

In this section, you will develop the class that provides the objects needed for your Web Forms Manager application.

Designing and implementing the ACL class

The ACL (Access Control List) class is used to control access to the application. The `ch19/apps/class/class.ACL.php` file on the CD-ROM implements this class, which implements the methods described in the following sections.

ACL()

This is the constructor method. It sets the member variables `$IP`, `$ALLOW`, and `$DENY` from the given parameter `$param`. `$IP` holds the IP address of the current machine; `$ALLOW` holds the comma-separated list of allowed IP addresses; and `$DENY` holds the list of denied IP addresses.

isAllowed()

This method identifies whether the current IP is allowed to access the application. If the list of denied IPs is not empty, this method matches the current IP with each of the denied IPs. It uses the `isNetworkAddr()` method and the `isNodeOf()` method to ensure that the current IP is not part of any denied network address. The method returns `TRUE` or `FALSE` depending on the match result.

isDenied()

This method uses the `isAllowed()` method to decide whether the current IP is denied access to the application. It returns exactly the opposite value (`TRUE`/`FALSE`) of the result of the `isAllowed()` method.

isNodeOf()

This method determines whether the current IP is a part of the given network. This is how it works:

- It first takes the octets of both IPs (the current IP and the network IP) into two arrays named $currentOctets and $networkOctets.

- It removes the fourth octet of the network IP (if it exists) and the current IP.

- Each octet (three in total) of the current IP is matched with the octets of the network IP. The match counter $matchCount is incremented with each successful match.

- The method returns TRUE if the match counter is exactly equal to the number of octets of the network; otherwise, it returns FALSE.

isNetworkAddr()

This method determines whether the given IP is a network address. It first takes the octets of the IP in an array. Then it determines whether the given IP is a network address by matching it with any of the following three conditions: whether the length of the array is less than four; whether the second to last element of the octet array is a zero; and whether the second to last element of the octet array is an "x".

Designing and implementing the DataCleanup class

The DataCleanup class is used to clean up form data collected from the user. The ch19/apps/class/class.DataCleanup.php file on the CD-ROM implements this class, which implements the methods described in the following sections.

DataCleanup()

This is the constructor method. Basically, it is used by the caller application to instantiate the class.

cleanup_none()

This is the basic cleanup method, which does the simple job of returning the string passed to the method as a parameter without any formatting.

cleanup_ucwords()

This method takes a string as a parameter and returns it after formatting the first character of each word into an uppercase character.

cleanup_ltrim()

This method returns the given string after removing all whitespace from the left of it.

cleanup_rtrim()

This method returns the given string after removing all whitespace from the right of it.

cleanup_trim()

This method returns the given string after removing all whitespace around it.

cleanup_lower()

This method takes a string as a parameter and returns it after converting all the characters to lowercase characters.

Designing and implementing the DataValidator class

The `DataValidator` class is used to validate form data collected from the user. The `ch19/apps/class/class.DataValidator.php` file on the CD-ROM implements this class, which implements the methods described in the following sections.

DataValidator()

This is the constructor method. Basically, it is used by the caller application to instantiate the class.

validate_size()

This method validates the size of the input. This is how it works:

- It takes as parameters the data to be validated (`$str`), the size permitted (`$size`), and the type of the data (`$type`).

- The `$size` parameter is provided as a string that has `"size="` at the beginning. Therefore, the method first gets the actual permitted size by removing the string `"size="` from the given `$size`.

- The method directly returns `TRUE` if it finds that the permitted size is `"any"`.

- Otherwise, `$size` is passed into the `get_size()` method to find the minimum and maximum allowed size.

- Depending on the type (text/number) of the data, the `validate_string_size()` method or the `validate_number_range()` method is called to validate the size of the data.

get_size()

This method takes the permitted size as a string and returns an array with information about the minimum and maximum allowed size. This is how it works:

- ◆ It first checks whether there is a ' - ' in the given size string, which means that two sizes are provided on either side of the ' - ', indicating both a minimum and a maximum. Otherwise, the method assumes that the given size is the only size allowed, and hence it returns the given size as both minimum and maximum size.

- ◆ If there is a ' - ' in the given parameter, the method explodes the string and determines the minimum and maximum allowed size.

- ◆ It then looks for a 'KB' or 'MB' in the string that identifies the maximum size. If it finds such a string, this method converts the sizes accordingly (it multiplies by 1024 in the case of 'KB') and keeps them in the associative array.

- ◆ Finally, the array indicating the minimum and maximum allowed size is returned.

validate_number_range()

This method takes three numbers as input (the number to be validated, the upper bound, and the lower bound) and determines whether the first number falls within the other two numbers.

validate_string_size()

This method validates the length of the string. It takes the string and the two bounds (minimum and maximum length) and determines whether the string length is within the boundary allowed.

validate_name()

This method determines whether the given string is a valid name by checking it for numbers and unusual characters (anything other than the alphabets).

validate_org_name()

This method determines whether the given string is a valid organization name by checking it for unusual characters (anything other than the alphabet, numeric characters, or the comma, period, and hyphen).

validate_number()

This method determines whether the given string is a valid number by allowing only numeric characters and the period (".").

validate_any_string()
This method takes a string as input and always returns TRUE.

validate_email()
This method takes a string as input and determines whether it is a valid e-mail address by using a complex regular expression taken from http://www.php.net/manual/en/function.preg-match.php.

validate_url()
This method validates the given string by checking it for valid schemes (http, https, or ftp).

validate_file_size()
This method determines whether the given file size falls within the specified allowed size. This method uses the get_size() method to determine the allowed maximum and minimum size.

Designing and implementing the FormSubmission class

The FormSubmission class is used to process the submission of the form. The ch19/apps/class/class.FormSubmission.php file on the CD-ROM implements this class, which implements the methods described in the following sections.

FormSubmission()
This is the constructor method. It sets member variables $DBI (to hold the DBI object), $ID (to hold the form ID), $KNOWN_FORMS (to hold the array of known forms), and $ERRORS (to hold the array of errors).

hasError()
This method determines whether the array for holding the errors is empty, returning either TRUE or FALSE.

getErrors()
This method returns the member variable $ERROR, which is an array of the errors.

getErrorMessage()
This method is used to retrieve the form-specific error messages. This is how it works:

◆ This method takes two parameters: $lang (for the language of the error message) and $err (for the error/array of errors).

◆ If $err is not supplied, this method takes $ERROR, the member variable of the class.

◆ If $err is given as a string and not an array, this method gets the single error message from the member variable $FORM_ERRORS, which is set in the loadConfigFile() method.

◆ If $err is an array, each of the error messages is retrieved from $FORM_ERRORS and returned as one string (by imploding a line break among them).

setupForm()

This method is used for the form setup. This is how it works:

◆ It uses the member variable $FORM_FIELDS, which is set in the loadConfigFile() method.

◆ $FORM_FIELDS is an associative array that holds all the field names of the form and their configurations. This method breaks down each of the field's configurations and sets them as member variables to be used later.

isKnownForm()

This method determines whether the current form is one of the known and configured forms by matching its ID with IDs of the $KNOWN_FORMS array.

loadConfigFile()

This method is responsible for loading the configuration file specific to the form. Every form to be managed has its own configuration file. Therefore, this method identifies the configuration file for the current form and includes it for later usage. It sets member variables $FORM_FIELDS, $FORM_ERRORS, and $FILE_LOAD_FIELDS from that configuration file.

processForm()

This method takes care of the entire processing of the form submission. This is how it works:

◆ It first calls the haveRequiredData() method to determine whether all of the form's required data has been submitted. If not, it returns with the proper error signal.

◆ It then calls the validateData() method to validate the given data. If it fails, it returns with the proper failure signal.

◆ The cleanupData() method is called to clean up the given data.

◆ After that, submitData() is invoked to insert the data into the database.

◆ The uploadFile() method is called to manage any file uploads.

◆ The method then sends outbound (to user) and/or inbound (to admin) e-mails, if specified in the form configuration.

haveRequiredData()

This method determines whether the required fields for the form are provided. It uses the member variable $REQUIRED, which is set in the setupForm() method.

validateData()

This method validates all the fields for the form. This is how it works:

◆ It first creates an object of class DataValidator.

◆ Then the method validate() of DataValidator is called, with type, size, and validation methods for each field of the form. If data validation fails, the field is pushed into the $ERRORS array.

◆ The method returns TRUE if none of the fields fail during data validation.

cleanupData()

This method is responsible for cleaning up the given data as prescribed in the form configuration file. This is how it works:

◆ It first creates an object of the DataCleanup class.

◆ For each field, the list of clean-up methods is retrieved. Those methods are called from the DataCleanup class.

◆ All the field data is returned after cleanup.

submitData()

This method is responsible for adding the given data into the form table in the database. This is how it works:

◆ First, the fields with type text are escaped for characters such as quotation marks and slashes by using the $this->_DBI->quote(addslashes()) methods.

◆ The common field for all forms, SUBMIT_TS (to store the time of form submission), is prepared from the current time and added to the insert query statement.

◆ The insert query statement is executed using the query() method of the DBI object.

◆ The method returns TRUE or FALSE depending on the success of the insertion process.

uploadFile()

This method is responsible for uploading any attachments from the user. This is how it works:

♦ It first creates an object of the `DataValidator` class to validate the size of the file(s) to be uploaded.

♦ For each upload field retrieved from the form configuration file, the method determines whether it is a required upload. If the upload is required but not supplied, it returns with a proper failure signal.

♦ The method moves the uploaded file to the appropriate destination directory as specified in the form configuration file.

sendMail()

This method is responsible for sending the form-specific inbound or outbound e-mail to the user or the administrator. This is how it works:

♦ It takes the list of recipients, the message template file name, and the subject as parameters.

♦ It immediately returns `FALSE` if the list of recipients is empty.

♦ It determines whether a form-specific template for the message exists. If not, it uses the default template directory of the application to instantiate the template class.

♦ Data received from the form is sent to the message template. Then the template is parsed and sent as the body to the recipient(s) using the `mail()` API with the given subject.

Designing and implementing the FormData class

The `FormData` class manipulates the submitted form data. For example, it is used in a report generation application to show the report to administrative users. The `ch19/apps/class/class.FormData.php` file on the CD-ROM implements this class, which implements the methods described in the following sections.

FormData()

This is the constructor method. It sets the member variables `$DBI` and `$DL_TBl` to hold the `DBI` object and the name of the download track table, respectively. Then it calls the `setFormID()` method to set the form ID.

setFormID()

This method first sets the given form ID as the member variable `$fid`. Then it includes the configuration file for the form. Two more member variables — `$fieldArr` (an array of form fields and their configurations) and `$fields` (a comma-separated list of the fields) – are set by retrieving the list of fields from the form configuration file.

getFormData( )

This method is used to retrieve form data from the database. This is how it works:

- ◆ The `setFormID( )` method is called to set the given form ID.

- ◆ If no sort criteria are supplied, the default sort criteria is set to the ID field.

- ◆ If no lower bound for submission time is given, it is assumed to be zero. Similarly, if no upper bound is supplied, it is assumed to be the current time.

- ◆ The `SELECT` query statement is prepared with the help of the member variable `$fields`.

- ◆ The name of the table is taken from the form configuration file, which has already been included.

- ◆ The `SELECT` query is executed using the `query( )` method of the `DBI` object, and all rows of the query result are returned as an array.

getDataAfterRecordID( )

This method returns all the data of a form that has a record ID greater than the given record ID. This is how it works:

- ◆ It first calls `setFormID( )` to set the given form ID.

- ◆ The query statement is prepared using the member variable `$fields` and the given record ID.

- ◆ The name of the table is taken from the form configuration file, which has already been included.

- ◆ The `SELECT` query is executed using the `query( )` method of the `DBI` object, and all rows of the query result are returned as an array.

getLastDLRecordID( )

This method returns the largest record ID number for a given form that has been tracked in the download track table. This is how it works:

- ◆ First, it calls `setFormID( )` to set the given form ID.

- ◆ The query statement is prepared.

- ◆ The name of the table is taken from the form configuration file, which has already been included.

- ◆ Finally, the `SELECT` query is executed using the `query( )` method of the `DBI` object, and the maximum record ID is returned after retrieving it from the query result.

updateDownloadTrack()
This method updates the download track table whenever a download is performed by the user. It takes the form ID and the top record ID up to the time at which the data was downloaded. Then it inserts them along with the current timestamp into the download track table. It returns TRUE or FALSE depending on the status of the insertion operation.

Creating the Application Configuration Files

Like all other applications we have developed in this book, the Web Forms Manager application also uses a standard set of configuration and error files. These files are discussed in the following sections.

Creating the main configuration file

The primary configuration file for the entire system is called webforms.conf. Table 19-1 describes each configuration variable.

TABLE 19-1 THE WEBFORMS.CONF VARIABLES THAT NEED TO BE CHANGED

Configuration Variable	Purpose
$PEAR_DIR	Set to the directory containing the PEAR package; specifically, the DB module needed for class.DBI.php in our application framework.
$PHPLIB_DIR	Set to the PHPLIB directory, which contains the PHPLIB packages; specifically, the template.inc package needed for template manipulation.
$APP_FRAMEWORK_DIR	Set to our application framework directory.
$PATH	Set to the combined directory path consisting of the $PEAR_DIR, $PHPLIB_DIR, and the $APP_FRAMEWORK_DIR. This path is used with the ini_set() method to redefine the php.ini entry for include_path to include $PATH ahead of the default path. This enables PHP to find our application framework, PHPLIB, and PEAR-related files.
$APPLICATION_NAME	Internal name of the application.

Configuration Variable	Purpose
$DEFAULT_LANGUAGE	Set to the two-digit default characterslanguage code.
$ROOT_PATH	Set to the root path of the application.
$REL_ROOT_PATH	Relative path to the root directory.
$REL_APP_PATH	Relative application path as seen from a Web browser.
$TEMPLATE_DIR	The fully qualified path to the template directory.
$CLASS_DIR	The fully qualified path to the class directory.
$ACL_CLASS	Name of the ACL class file.
$DATA_VALIDATOR_CLASS	Name of the DataValidator class file.
$FORM_SUBMISSION_CLASS	Name of the FormSubmission class file.
$DATA_CLEANUP_CLASS	Name of the DataCleanup class file.
$FORMDATA_CLASS	Name of the FormData class file.
$FORM_DB_URL	The fully qualified URL for the database used to store the form information.
$MISSING_REQUIRED_VALUES	Code for identifying the signal that required data is missing.
$BAD_DATA	Code for identifying the signal that the data is invalid.
$DATABASE_FAILURE	Code for identifying the signal that the form table does not exist.
$INVALID_FILE_SIZE	Code for identifying the signal that the file size is invalid.
$KNOWN_FORMS	The associative array of forms holding the form ID, along with its configuration file name.
$FORM_CONF_FILE_DIR	The directory that holds the configuration files of different forms.
$REPORT_TEMPLATE	The template used for showing the form data report.
$ODD_COLOR	Color used as background in odd-numbered rows in the report.
$EVEN_COLOR	Color used as background in even-numbered rows in the report.

Continued

TABLE **19-1** THE WEBFORMS.CONF VARIABLES THAT NEED TO BE CHANGED
(Continued)

Configuration Variable	Purpose
$DEFAULT_COLOR	Default color used as background in any row in the report.
$MAX_YEAR	The maximum year to be used in the report prompt.
$MIN_YEAR	The minimum year to be used in the report prompt.
$REPORTER	The name of the application that manages the report.
$CSV_EXPORTER	The name of the application that exports form data as CSV.
$DOWNLOAD_TRACK_TBL	The name of the table that tracks download information.
$DOWNLOAD_TYPE_LATEST	The code for identifying the type of download for which only the latest data is downloaded.
$DOWNLOAD_TYPE_ALL	The code for identifying the type of download for which all data is downloaded.

The directory structure used in the webforms.conf file supplied in the ch19 directory on the CD-ROM might need to be tailored to your own system's requirements. The current directory structure looks like the following:

```
htdocs ($ROOT_PATH == %DocumentRoot%)
|
+---webforms (Web Forms Manager Applications)
    |
    +---apps (apps and configuration files)
        |
        +---class (class files)
        |
        +---templates (HTML templates)
        |
        +---temp (Temporary folder to store the files to be downloaded)
        |
        +---site_forms (form configuration files)
            |
            +---x (configuration file for x form)
```

By changing the following configuration parameters in `webforms.conf`, you can modify the directory structure to fit your site requirements:

```
$PEAR_DIR           = $_SERVER['DOCUMENT_ROOT'] . '/pear' ;
$PHPLIB_DIR         = $_SERVER['DOCUMENT_ROOT'] . '/phplib';
$APP_FRAMEWORK_DIR  = $_SERVER['DOCUMENT_ROOT'] . '/framework';
$ROOT_PATH          = $_SERVER['DOCUMENT_ROOT'];
$REL_ROOT_PATH      = '/webforms';
$REL_APP_PATH       = $REL_ROOT_PATH . '/apps';
$TEMPLATE_DIR       = $ROOT_PATH     . $REL_APP_PATH . '/templates';
$CLASS_DIR          = $ROOT_PATH     . $REL_APP_PATH . '/class';
```

Creating a sample form configuration file

Now to examine a sample form configuration file. Assuming the name of the form is *x*, the configuration file name should be `x.conf`. Table 19-2 describes the configuration variables of `x.conf`, a typical form configuration file.

TABLE 19-2 THE X.CONF CONFIGURATION VARIABLES

Configuration Variable	Purpose
$ FORM_NAME	The name of the form to be configured.
$FORM_TABLE	The name of the table in which the form data will be stored.
$ACL_ALLOW_FROM	Comma-separated list of IP addresses that are allowed to access this form.
$ACL_DENY_FROM	Comma-separated list of IP addresses that are denied access to this form.
$FORM_LOG_FILE	The name and path of the log file for the form.
$FORM_FIELDS_ARRAY	The array of form fields, along with their configurations.
$UPLOAD_FILE	The code to identify whether there is an upload for this form or not.
$UPLOAD_FILE_DIR	The name and path of the directory to store the uploaded file.

Continued

TABLE 19-2 **THE X.CONF CONFIGURATION VARIABLES** *(Continued)*

Configuration Variable	Purpose
$FRM_TEMPLATE_DIR	Form-specific template directory. Whenever a template is required, the application first searches for it here. If it doesn't find it here, it searches the default application template directory.
$UPLOAD_FILE_FIELDS_ARRAY	The array to identify any upload-related field names and their configurations.
$SEND_OUTBOUND_MAIL	The code to identify whether there should be outbound mail or not.
$OUTBOUND_MAIL_TEMPLATE	The template file used to send outbound mail.
$OUTBOUND_MAIL_SUBJECT	The subject line to be used in outbound mail.
$EMAIL_FIELD	The name of the form field containing the e-mail address of the user.
$SEND_INBOUND_MAIL	The code to identify whether there should be inbound mail or not.
$INBOUND_MAIL_TEMPLATE	The template file used to send outbound mail.
$INBOUND_MAIL_TO	The e-mail address to which inbound mail will be sent.
$INBOUND_MAIL_SUBJECT	The subject line to be used in outbound mail.
$SHOW_THANKYOU_TEMPLATE	The name of the template file used to thank the user after filling out the form.
$AUTO_REDIRECT	The code to identify whether the page should be redirected after the form is submitted.
$AUTO_REDIRECT_URL	The URL to which the page should be redirected after form submission.
$ERRORS	The array of error messages related to different fields.

Creating the errors file

The error messages displayed by the Web Forms Manager applications are stored in the ch19/apps/webforms.errors file on the CD-ROM. You can modify the error messages by using a text editor.

Creating Application Templates

The HTML interface templates needed for the applications are included on the CD-ROM. These templates contain various template tags for displaying necessary information dynamically. These templates are described in Table 19-3.

TABLE 19-3 HTML TEMPLATES

Configuration Variable	Template File	Purpose
$REPORT_TEMPLATE	report.html	This template is used to show reports data collected via Web forms.
$OUTBOUND_MAIL_TEMPLATE	Outbound_mail.html	This template is used to send mail to the user who fills out the form.
$INBOUND_MAIL_TEMPLATE	Inbound_mail.html	This template is used to send mail to the form owner or the administrator.
$SHOW_THANKYOU_TEMPLATE	thanks.html	This template is used to thank the user after the form has been filled out.

Creating the Web Forms Submission Manager Application

This application, submit.php, is responsible for managing the entire form-submission process. This application is included on the CD-ROM in the ch19/apps directory.

It implements the following functionality:

♦ Adds submitted data to the database

♦ Sends mail to the appropriate recipient

♦ Shows error messages in case of invalid data

♦ Displays a thank-you page or redirects the user to a specified URL after form submission

This application contains the methods described in the following sections.

run()

When the application is run, this method is called. This is how it works:

◆ First, it creates a `FormSubmission` object. Then it determines whether the `id` of the form for which the request is being made is configured. If it isn't, it displays an error alert and returns null.

◆ Otherwise, the `loadConfigFile()` method of the `FormSubmission` class is called to load the configuration file for the form. Then the `setupForm()` method of the same class is called to set up the form variables.

◆ Next, the `authorize()` method is called to authorize the request. If authorization is successful, the `processForm()` method is called to process the form data.

◆ If `processForm()` returns a positive status, this method determines whether an auto redirect for this form exists. If yes, the user is redirected to the specified URL; otherwise, a thank-you message for submitting the form is displayed to the user by calling the `showPage()` method.

◆ If `processForm` returns a negative status, the error message is prepared using the `getErrorMessage()` method of the `Formsubmission` class. Then the exact violation issue is retrieved, and the error message is displayed as an alert to the user.

showPage()

This method renders the given template on the user's browser. This is how it works:

◆ It first determines whether the requested template exists in the form-specific template directory. If it does, the template directory for the template class is assumed to be the form template directory; otherwise, the default application template directory is assumed to be the template directory for the template class.

◆ After the template class is instantiated with the appropriate template directory, all the data posted by the user is set to the template.

◆ Finally, the template is parsed and printed to the user's browser.

authorize()

This method authorizes the client IP in the following way:

- First, it determines the client IP.

- Then it creates an object of class ACL (Access Control List) with the client IP, the allowed IP(s), and the denied IP(s).

- Finally, the isAllowed() method of the ACL class is used to determine whether the client is allowed to access the application.

Creating the Web Forms Reporter Application

This application, webformsreporter.php, is responsible for showing the form report to the administrator. This application included is on the CD-ROM in the ch19/apps directory.

This application has the methods described in the following sections.

run()

When the application is run, this method is called. This is how it works:

- It calls the showReport() method with the form id, the range of the report (start and end date), the sorting criteria, and the toggle flag.

- Form id, sort criteria, and toggle flag values are taken directly from the client request. If no starting or ending range is given, it assumes the start of the current day as the starting timestamp and the end of the current day as the ending timestamp.

showReport()

This method is responsible for showing the form report. This is how it works:

- First, the template class is created with the report template file of the default template directory. All the blocks of the templates are set accordingly.

- Then it determines whether the form id is valid. If it is empty, an error message is stored in $msg and the block to show the link for a data download for a specific form is set to null.

◆ It determines whether the given range for the report is valid. If not, an error message is stored in $msg, to be shown later.

◆ If both of the preceding checks pass, an object of the FormData class is created and the getFormData() method is called to get the data submitted within that range of time from the given form. This data is stored in an array named $dataArr.

◆ Dynamic contents of the report template are set. The form names and IDs are set to the select combo box for the forms. The starting date and ending date are set to the combo boxes accordingly.

◆ Then the $dataArr array is checked to determine whether it has any data. If not, $msg is checked for any error messages. If there is an error message, it is set to the template to be parsed and printed to the user. Otherwise, it means that the requested range doesn't have any data for the given form. Therefore, a message is set and printed accordingly.

◆ If $dataArr has any data in it, the headings of the data are set to the heading block of the template. Then the data block is set with the rows of data. The row colors are maintained according to the odd and even colors prescribed in the configuration file.

◆ If the form id is selected and it is a valid and known form, the links for data download are set to the template.

◆ Finally, the template is parsed and printed to the user's browser.

Creating the CSV Data Exporter Application

This application, CSVExporter.php, is responsible for allowing form administrators to download the data for a form. This application is included on the CD-ROM in the ch19/apps directory.

This application has the methods described in the following sections.

run()

When the application is run, this method is called. It calls the processRequest() method with the form ID and the type of download (all records or latest records) to enable users to download data.

processRequest()

This method is responsible for the entire process of enabling a user to download the form data. This is how it works:

◆ First, it determines whether the passed form ID is valid. If it is empty, it displays an alert message and returns null.

◆ Next, an object of FormData is created. Depending on the type of download (all records or latest records), the getFormData() or getData AfterRecordID() method is called to retrieve the appropriate data and then store it in the $dataArr array. In the case of the latest data download, the getLastDLRecordID() method is called to retrieve the top record id of the previously downloaded data so that the new download can start after it.

◆ If $dataArr is not empty, a CSV file is created and opened in the temp directory of the application, and the $dataArr values are written in it, separated by commas.

◆ After the data writing in the CSV file is done, the updateDownloadTrack() method is called to store the record id of the row that was last written in the CSV file.

◆ Finally, the user is redirected to the CSV file, from which he can download the data as a CSV file.

◆ If $dataArr is empty, the user is shown an alert message stating that the requested dataset is empty.

Installing the Web Forms Manager

In this section, it is assumed that you are using a Linux system with MySQL and the Apache server installed. During the installation process for the Web Forms Manager, we will refer to the Web document root directory as %DocumentRoot%.

It is also assumed that you have installed the PHPLIB and PEAR libraries. Normally, these are installed during PHP installation. For your convenience, these are provided in the lib/phplib.tar.gz and lib/pear.tar.gz directories on the CD-ROM. In the following sample installation steps, it is further assumed that these are installed in the %DocumentRoot/phplib and %DocumentRoot/pear directories. Because your installation locations for these libraries are likely to differ, make sure that you replace these paths in the configuration files.

Here is how you can get your Web Forms Manager application up and running:

♦ **Install the application framework.** If you have not yet installed the application framework discussed in Chapter 4, you must do so before proceeding further.

♦ **Install the WEBFORMS database.** The quickest way to create the WEBFORMS database is to run the following commands:

```
mysqladmin -u root -p create WEBFORMS
mysql -u root -p -D WEBFORMS < webforms.sql
```

♦ The WEBFORMS.mysql script can be found on the accompanying CD-ROM in the ch19/sql directory. The second command in the preceding listing will create two tables, X_TBL and ASK_TBL, in your WEBFORMS database. The X_TBL is not really used, as it is a generic table that explains how a form X can be configured. However, ASK_TBL can be used by the ask.php form.

♦ Note that if you cannot create a new database called WEBFORMS, you can use an existing one. Just make sure that you change the database URL in webforms.conf to reflect your database name as discussed in the following step.

♦ **Install the WEBFORMS applications.** Now, from the ch19 directory of the CD-ROM, extract ch19.tar.gz in %DocumentRoot%. This will create WEBFORMS in your document root. Configure %DocumentRoot%/webforms/apps/webforms.conf for the path and database settings. The applications are installed in the %DocumentRoot%/webforms/apps directory, and the templates are stored in %DocumentRoot%/webforms/apps/templates. You will have to keep your form-specific files (configuration files and upload directories) in different form directories in %DocumentRoot%/webforms/apps/site_forms.

If your MySQL server is hosted on the Internet Web server, it can be accessed via localhost. However, if your MySQL database is on a different server than your Web server, you can easily modify the database URLs in each application's configuration files. For example, the webforms.conf file has a database URL as follows:

```
define('FORM_DB_URL',
        'mysql://root:foobar@localhost/WEBFORMS');
```

Suppose that your database server is called db.domain.com and the username and password to access the WEBFORMS database (which you will create during this installation process) are admin and db123, respectively. In such a case, you would modify the database access URLs throughout each configuration file as follows:

```
define('FORM_DB_URL',
        'mysql://admin:db132@db.domain.com/WEBFORMS');
```

◆ **Set file/directory permissions.** Make sure that you have changed the file and directory permissions so that your intranet Web server can access all the files.

Once you have performed the preceding steps, you are ready to test your Web Forms Manager applications.

Testing the Web Forms Manager

Once everything is installed, make a copy of one of your existing Web forms and rename it *oldname*.php. Here, we will rename a Web form called ask.html to ask.|php. The ask.php form can be found on the CD-ROM that accompanies this book in the ch19/webforms/example_forms directory. It is already configured for the setup discussed here.

The changes in the Web form that we need to make are as follows:

◆ Change the FORM ACTION line as shown here:

```
<form action="/webforms/apps/submit.php" method="POST">
```

The action line should be pointing at the submit.php location. The preceding line shows the recommended location and what we used for this test.

◆ Add the following two hidden fields

```
<input type=hidden name="form_id"
value="X9393948482339292929">
```

```
<input type=hidden name="return_url" value="<?php echo
$_SERVER['HTTP_REFERER']; ?>">
```

The form_id value is something you choose arbitrarily. This value must be used in webforms.conf as follows:

```
$KNOWN_FORMS = array(
        'X9393948482339290000' => "contact.conf",
        'X9393948482339295000' => "newsletter.conf",
        'X9393948482339292929' => "askform.conf"
        );
```

Here, the form_id 'X9393948482339292929' is associated with a configuration file called askform.conf. This configuration file must reside in the /webforms/apps/site_forms/askform directory. A sample configuration is shown in Listing 19-2. This configuration defines the form-specific database table name using FORM_TABLE.

♦ Create a database table in your WEBFORMS database using the name given (FORM_TABLE) in askform.conf. This table should have all the fields in your Web form and the ID and SUBMIT_TS fields. The following CREATE TABLE statement is used for our sample ask.php form:

```
#
# Table structure for table `ASK_TBL`
#

CREATE TABLE ASK_TBL (
    id bigint(20) NOT NULL auto_increment,
    fname varchar(30) NOT NULL default '',
    lname varchar(30) NOT NULL default '',
    company varchar(30) NOT NULL default '',
    email varchar(70) NOT NULL default '',
    url varchar(127) NOT NULL default '',
    about tinytext NOT NULL,
    subject tinytext NOT NULL,
    details text NOT NULL,
    SUBMIT_TS bigint(20) NOT NULL default '0',
    PRIMARY KEY (id,email)
) TYPE=MyISAM
```

♦ Once you have created the appropriate database table, you are ready to submit requests. Make sure that you configure the rest of askform.conf to match your requirements. For example, to control access to your Web form via an IP address, you can use the ACL_ALLOW_FROM and ACL_DENY_FROM lists.

The $FORM_FIELDS_ARRAY should be used to define the fields that you have in your Web form (exactly as they appear in your Web form), whether they are required or not; and the type of validation and clean-up operations you want to perform on them before submission is stored in the database. For example, the askform.conf shown in Listing 19-2 shows the following:

```
'fname'    => '1:text:size=3-30:name:trim|lower|ucwords',
```

Here, the Web form has a field called fname. The above configuration line states that this field is required and can be of size 3 to 30 characters long. The field is to be validated using the validate_name() method. If the field is valid, the value of the field is to be cleaned up using trim, lower, and ucwords functions. This means that a valid fname field value will be trimmed for whitespaces and lowercases and, finally, each word of the value will be uppercased before storing in the WEBFORMS database. Similarly, the URL field (url) is defined using the following:

```
'url'      => '0:text:size=3-60:url:trim|lower',
```

However, it is not required (0), and it is considered text data; it is considered to be of size 3 to 60 and validated using validate_url() method. Once validated, the field data is trimmed and lowercased before being stored in a database.

As you can see, each field is defined in terms of required/not required, type (text, number, name, e-mail, and so on), size requirements, validation method, and cleanup functions.

◆ If you have a file upload field, make sure that you create the UPLOAD_FILE_DIR directory (/webforms/apps/site_forms/askform/ uploadfile) and make it writable by the Web server user. You also have to define $UPLOAD_FILE_FIELDS_ARRAY to list the Web form fields that are file names. For example, the sample ask form configuration shows a field called attachment as the file upload field, as follows:

'attachment'   => '0:size=0-60KB',

The uploaded file is not required (0) and cannot exceed size 60 kilobytes.

◆ If you do not want to use the default templates used for the thank-you response and inbound (to whomever you wish) and outbound mail (to the submitter), you can store your own templates per form in the FRM_ TEMPLATE_DIR directory. Make sure that this directory is stored in /webforms/apps/site_forms/askform/templates for the current example.

◆ If you want to send an e-mail message to the submitter upon submission, set SEND_OUTBOUND_MAIL to 1 as done in askform.conf. Set EMAIL_FIELD to point to the e-mail field in your Web form. The OUTBOUND_MAIL_ TEMPLATE template is used for mailing the message. You should customize this message as needed. The OUTBOUND_MAIL_SUBJECT defines the subject line used in the message. Note that if you do not supply a custom mail template, the default mail template from /webforms/apps/templates is used.

◆ To receive an e-mail for each successful form submission, set SEND_ INBOUND_MAIL to 1 as done in askform.conf. The INBOUND_MAIL_ TEMPLATE template is used for mailing this message to you. You should customize this message as needed. The INBOUND_MAIL_SUBJECT defines the subject line used in the message. Note that if you do not supply a custom mail template, the default mail template from /webforms/apps/ templates is used. The users who can receive inbound messages are listed in INBOUND_MAIL_TO.

◆ The thank-you template is specified using SHOW_THANKYOU_TEMPLATE. If you do not have a Web form–specific thank-you template in the form's own template directory, the default template is used.

◆ Upon successful completion of a Web form, if you want to automatically redirect users to an URL other than the one from which they came, you can set AUTO_REDIRECT to 1 and specify a value for AUTO_REDIRECT_URL. Note that if your Web form is a PHP script, you can redirect users to the URL from which they clicked the Web form by incorporating the following lines in the Web form:

```
<input type=hidden name="return_url" value="<?php echo
$_SERVER['HTTP_REFERER']; ?>">
```

◆ Finally, define the error messages that you want to show when a required field is missing. This is done using the following lines in askform.conf:

```
$ERRORS['US']['ERROR_FNAME'] = "First name -  missing.";
$ERRORS['US']['ERROR_LNAME'] = "Last name -  missing.";
$ERRORS['US']['ERROR_EMAIL'] = "Email address -  missing.";
$ERRORS['US']['ERROR_COMPANY'] = "Company name -  missing.";
$ERRORS['US']['ERROR_SUBJECT'] = "Subject of your question -
missing.";
$ERRORS['US']['ERROR_DETAILS'] = "Details of your question -
missing.";
```

Here, when the fname field is required but missing, the $ERRORS[ERROR_FNAME] value is displayed using a JavaScript alert window. You can customize these messages as you see fit.

Now you are ready to test the ask.php form.

Listing 19-2: askform.conf

```php
<?php

// Name of the Web form
define(FORM_NAME, 'Ask Form');

// Name of the table used
define(FORM_TABLE,     'ASK_TBL');

define('ACL_ALLOW_FROM', '');
define('ACL_DENY_FROM', '192.168.0.11');
define('FORM_LOG_FILE',  $_SERVER['DOCUMENT_ROOT'] .
       '/webforms/askform.log');

$FORM_FIELDS_ARRAY = array(
'fname'   => '1:text:size=3-30:name:trim|lower|ucwords',
```

```
'lname'   => '1:text:size=3-30:name:trim|lower|ucwords',
'company' => '1:text:size=2-60:org_name:trim|lower|ucwords',
'email'   => '1:text:size=5-60:email:trim|lower',
'url'     => '0:text:size=3-60:url:trim|lower',
'about'   => '0:text:size=3-60:any_string:trim|lower|ucwords',
'subject' => '1:text:size=3-60:any_string:trim|lower|ucwords',
'details' => '1:text:size=0-20KB:any_string:none'
);

//Do we need to upload file from the form    0 - not, 1 - yes
define(UPLOAD_FILE, 0);

//directory name for storing file
define(UPLOAD_FILE_DIR, 'site_forms/askform/uploadfile/');

//form relative template directory
define(FRM_TEMPLATE_DIR, 'site_forms/askform/templates/');

$UPLOAD_FILE_FIELDS_ARRAY = array(
'attachment'      => '0:size=0-60KB',
);

// Do we send email to person submitting the form? 1= yes 0 = no
define(SEND_OUTBOUND_MAIL, 1);
define(OUTBOUND_MAIL_TEMPLATE, 'outbound_mail.html');
define(OUTBOUND_MAIL_SUBJECT, 'Thank you');
define(EMAIL_FIELD,'email');


// Do we send email to inbound (company hosting the form) per
submission? 1= yes 0 = no
define(SEND_INBOUND_MAIL, 1);
define(INBOUND_MAIL_TEMPLATE, 'inbound_mail.html');

define(INBOUND_MAIL_TO, 'you@yourdomain.com,sales@yourdomain.com');

define(INBOUND_MAIL_SUBJECT, 'Inbound mail for new request');

// If auto redirect is not TRUE then we show a thank you template
define(SHOW_THANKYOU_TEMPLATE, 'thanks.html');

// Should we automatically redirect once form is submitted
define(AUTO_REDIRECT, FALSE);
```

Continued

Listing 19-2 *(Continued)*

```
define(AUTO_REDIRECT_URL, 'http://www.yourdomain.com');


$ERRORS['US']['ERROR_FNAME'] = "First name -  missing.";
$ERRORS['US']['ERROR_LNAME'] = "Last name -  missing.";
$ERRORS['US']['ERROR_EMAIL'] = "Email address -  missing.";
$ERRORS['US']['ERROR_COMPANY'] = "Company name -  missing.";
$ERRORS['US']['ERROR_SUBJECT'] = "Subject of your question -
missing.";
$ERRORS['US']['ERROR_DETAILS'] = "Details of your question -
missing.";

?>
```

Now on Your Web browser make a request for `http://yourserver/ask.php`. Figure 19-3 shows one such request.

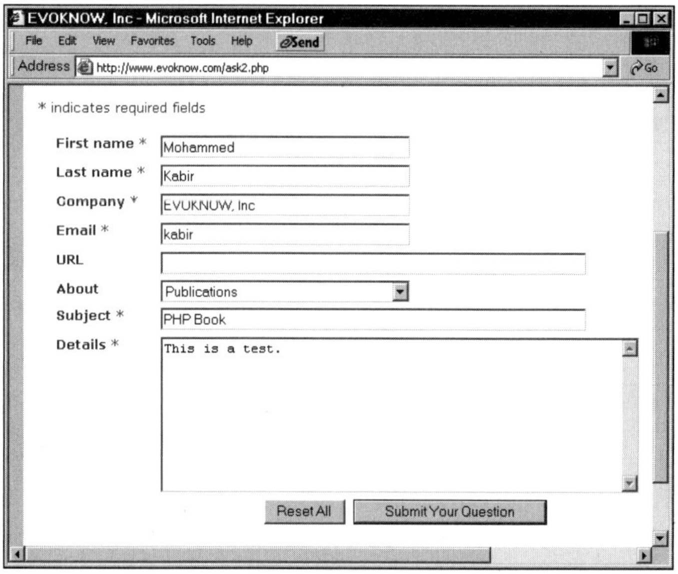

Figure 19-3: A simple Web form called ask.php.

This form is managed by the `submit.php` application developed in this chapter, but that can be noted only if you review the source code, which contains the following lines:

```
<form action="/webforms/apps/submit.php" method="POST">

<input type=hidden name="form_id" value="X9393948482339292929">

<input type=hidden
       name="return_url"
       value="<?php echo $_SERVER['HTTP_REFERER']; ?>">
```

If we don't enter all the required data and submit the form, the data entry dialog box shown in Figure 19-4 appears.

Figure 19-4: Data entry error dialog box.

After submitting valid data, submit.php shows the thank-you message shown in Figure 19-5. Clicking the Continue button takes us to the page from which the form originated. Note that if you directly called the form, as we did in this case, the form cannot redirect. Ideally, you will link the form using <a href="/path/ to/ask.php"> in a page within your site or another affiliate site. In such a case, submit.php can return you to the referring page.

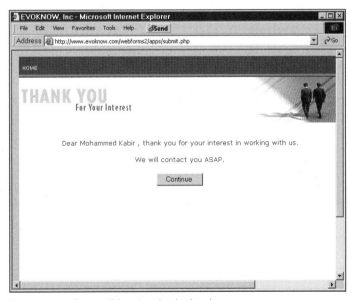

Figure 19-5: Data validated and submitted.

After submitting two requests as test data, we access the reporter application using `http://server/webforms/apps/webformsreporter.php`. It displays the interface shown in Figure 19-6.

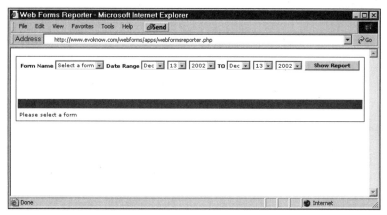

Figure 19-6: Selecting a form in the reporter interface.

Select a Web form such as the Ask Form and click the Show Report button, which displays a report, as shown in Figure 19-7.

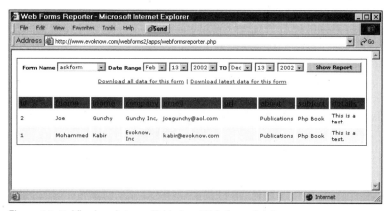

Figure 19-7: Viewing data available in a Web form database.

Downloading data from the form is as easy as clicking the `Download all data from this form` link shown in the report. Figure 19-8 shows the dialog box that appears after you click the link.

Figure 19-8: Downloading CSV data from the Web form.

When you click the Save button, the exporter-supplied file name will be given. For example, because the ASK form is named using FORM_NAME in askform.conf as "ASK_FORM", the default filename is askform.csv. Therefore, if your form names are unique, the file names will also be unique.

Figure 19-9 shows how the downloaded data file appears in MS Excel.

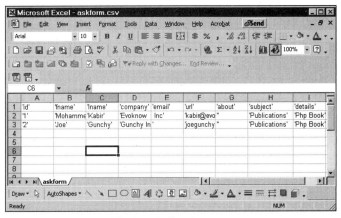

Figure 19-9: Viewing CSV data in Excel.

Security Considerations

The webformsreporter.php application and the CSVExporter.php application should be restricted using your Web server's username/password authentication scheme. In our example, we installed the Web forms application in %DocumentRoot%/webforms/apps. We can create a directory called %DocumentRoot/webforms/restricted and move CSVExporter.php and webformsreporter.php from the /webforms/apps directory to this new directory.

In the restricted directory, we can create symbolic links to `apps/class`, `apps/site_forms`, `apps/templates`, `webforms.conf`, and `webforms.error` files and directories, as shown here:

```
ln -s ../apps/webforms.conf webforms.conf
ln -s ../apps/webforms.errors webforms.errors
ln -s ../apps/templates templates
ln -s ../apps/class class
ln -s ../apps/site_forms site_forms
```

The preceding code should produce the following results using the `ls -l` command:

```
bash-2.03$ ls -l
total 32
-rw-r--r--  CSVExporter.php
lrwxrwxrwx  class -> ../apps/class
lrwxrwxrwx  site_forms -> ../apps/site_forms
lrwxrwxrwx  templates -> ../apps/templates
lrwxrwxrwx  webforms.conf -> ../apps/webforms.conf
lrwxrwxrwx  webforms.errors -> ../apps/webforms.errors
-rw-r--r--  webformsreporter.php
```

In the restricted directory, create an `.htaccess` file such as the following:

```
AuthType Basic
AuthName "WebForm Administration "
AuthUserFile /path/to/.users
Require valid-user
```

Make sure that you change the `AuthUserFile` from `/path/to/.users` to a path that's outside your Web document tree but still readable by the Apache user. In this file, create users using the `htpasswd` utility that comes with the Apache Web server. For example, to create a user named `joe` in the nonexistent `/path/to/.users` file, you can run the following:

```
htpasswd -c /path/to/.users joe
```

You will be asked to enter Joe's new password twice, after which Joe can access the reporter and CSV Export applications of the Web Forms Management application suite, using the `http://server/webforms/restricted/webformsreporter.php` and `http://server/webforms/restricted/CSVExporter.php` URLs, respectively.

Summary

In this chapter, you developed a set of Web applications that can manage single-page Web forms that do not have complex requirements. The application discussed in this chapter also offers you a way to download data collected by using the Web forms or view reports on collected data.

Chapter 20

Web Site Tools

IN THIS CHAPTER, WE WILL develop a simple voting tool that enables your visitors to cast votes on a topic of your choice. Such votes are typically gathered to review user preferences. The following section describes the voting application's functionality requirements.

Functionality Requirements

The vote application will have the following features:

♦ A **single database table**. It will store all vote data in a single table.

♦ An **unlimited number of surveys/polls**. You can set up as many surveys or polls as you want.

♦ An **unlimited number of polling options**. Users can select as many options as needed to generate the poll data. The options can be either radio buttons or checkboxes. However, each option value must be numeric.

♦ A **customizable results page.** The results page is displayed using a custom template for each poll/survey; therefore, this page can be customized as needed.

♦ **Control over multiple votes.** You can decide if you want to allow multiple votes from the same person or not. For example, you can set a time limit for the cookie used to identify Web visitors who have already voted. This time limit is configurable, so you can allow a visitor to vote on every visit, or disallow voting until a specified amount of time has passed. For example, you can set the expiration time such that a visitor can vote once per month.

Note that there are several prefab voting tools available online. However, sometimes it's better to create a simple, but custom application from scratch than modify an existing application.

Understanding Prerequisites

This is an Internet application and does not require central authentication techniques. Therefore, it is not dependent on the intranet tools discussed in earlier chapters.

However, it does require the application framework classes discussed in Chapter 4. You must install the application framework classes along with the PHPLIB and PEAR packages.

Designing the Database

Figure 20-1 shows the VOTE database diagram for the voting tool. This section describes the only table of the database.

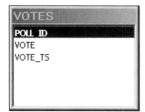

Figure 20-1: VOTE database diagram.

VOTES Table

This table is the integral part of the application. It holds the Poll ID (POLL_ID), the vote value (VOTE), and the submission timestamp of the vote (VOTE_TS).

Listing 20-1 shows an implementation of the VOTE database in MySQL. To implement this survey database in MySQL, you can create a database called VOTE in your MySQL database server by saving the code in Listing 20-1 in a text file (named VOTE.mysql) and running the following command:

Listing 20-1: VOTE.mysql

```
mysql -u root -p -D VOTE < VOTE.mysql
```

Make sure you change the username (root) to whatever is appropriate for your system.

Designing and Implementing the Voting Tool Application Class

As illustrated in the system diagram shown in Figure 20-2, only one object is needed to implement the voting tool application.

   In this section, you will develop the class that provides the only object needed for your voting tool application.

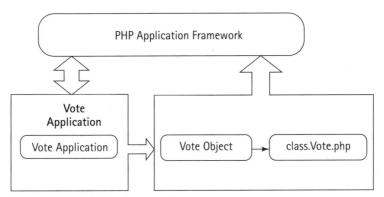

Figure 20-2: Voting tool system diagram.

Designing and implementing the Vote class

The Vote class is used to manipulate each poll. It enables the application to add votes and retrieve poll results. The ch20/apps/class/class.Vote.php file on the accompanying CD-ROM implements this class, which implements the following methods:

Vote()

This is the constructor method. It works as follows:

1. It sets a member variable named dbi to point to the object provided by the class.DBI.php, which is passed to the constructor by an application. The dbi member variable holds the DBI object, which is used to communicate with the back-end database.

2. It sets a member variable named vote_tbl to store the name of the vote table.

3. It calls the setPollID() method to set the Poll ID that has been passed as a parameter.

setPollID()

This method is used to set the Poll ID as the member variable "pid." It takes the ID as a parameter and returns it after setting it to the member variable if the ID is not empty.

addVote()
This method is used to add a vote to the database. This is how it works:

♦ It calls the `setPollID()` method to set the given poll ID to the member variable `pid`.

♦ It stores the current time in a variable named `$curTime`.

♦ It builds a query statement, `$stmt`, to insert the poll ID, the given vote, and the current timestamp into the database.

♦ Using the DBI object (`$this->dbi`), the `$stmt` statement is run via the `$this->dbi->query()` method in the DBI object.

♦ The method returns `TRUE` or `FALSE` depending on the status of the insertion operation.

getVoteCountByChoice()
This method is used to retrieve the number of votes per option for a given poll. This is how it works:

1. It first calls the `setPollID()` method to set the given poll ID to the member variable `pid`.

2. It builds a query statement, `$stmt`, to retrieve the number of votes posted for the given option and poll ID.

3. Using the DBI object (`$this->dbi`), the `$stmt` statement is run via the `$this->dbi->query()` method in the DBI object. The result of the query is stored in the `$result` object.

4. The row containing the number of votes is retrieved by fetching it from the `$result` variable using the `fetchRow()` method.

5. Finally, the number of votes is returned from this method.

getTotalVoteCount()
This method is used to retrieve the total number of votes posted for a given poll. This is how it works:

1. It calls the `setPollID()` method to set the given poll ID to the member variable pid.

2. It builds a query statement, `$stmt`, to retrieve the total number of votes posted for the given poll ID.

3. Using the DBI object (`$this->dbi`), the `$stmt` statement is run via the `$this->dbi->query()` method in the DBI object. The result of the query is stored in the `$result` object.

4. The row containing the number of votes is retrieved by fetching it from the $result variable using the fetchRow() method.

5. Finally, the number of votes is returned from this method.

Creating the Application Configuration Files

Like every other application developed in this book, the voting tool application also uses a standard set of configuration and error files. These files are discussed in the following sections.

Creating the main configuration file

The primary configuration file for the entire system is called vote.conf. Table 20-1 describes each configuration variable.

TABLE 20-1 VOTE.CONF VARIABLES

Configuration Variable	Purpose
$PEAR_DIR	Set to the directory containing the PEAR package; specifically, the DB module needed for class.DBI.php in our application framework.
$PHPLIB_DIR	Set to the PHPLIB directory, which contains the PHPLIB packages; specifically, the template.inc package needed for template manipulation.
$APP_FRAMEWORK_DIR	Set to our application framework directory.
$PATH	Set to the combined directory path consisting of $PEAR_DIR, $PHPLIB_DIR, and $APP_FRAMEWORK_DIR. This path is used with the ini_set() method to redefine the php.ini entry for include_path to include $PATH ahead of the default path. This enables PHP to find our application framework, PHPLIB, and PEAR-related files.
$APPLICATION_NAME	Internal name of the application.
$DEFAULT_LANGUAGE	Set to the two-digit default language code.

Continued

TABLE **20-1** **VOTE.CONF VARIABLES** *(Continued)*

Configuration Variable	Purpose
$ROOT_PATH	Set to the root path of the application.
$REL_ROOT_PATH	Relative path to the root directory.
$REL_APP_PATH	Relative application path as seen from a Web browser.
$TEMPLATE_DIR	The fully qualified path to the template directory.
$CLASS_DIR	The fully qualified path to the class directory.
$REL_TEMPLATE_DIR	The Web-relative path to the template directory used.
$VOTE_CLASS	Name of the Vote class file.
$VOTE_DB_URL	The fully qualified URL for the database used to store the VOTE information.
$VOTE_TBL	Name of the VOTES table in the database.
$COOKIE_EXPIRATION_TIME	The amount of time, in seconds, that specifies the cookie expiration time for a vote.

You may need to tailor to your own system's requirements the directory structure used in the `vote.conf` file supplied in the `ch20` directory on the CD-ROM. Here is what the current directory structure looks like:

```
/---evoknow
    |
    +---intranet
        |
        +---htdocs ($ROOT_PATH)
            |
            +---vote (Voting Tool Applications)
                |
                +---apps (apps and configuration files)
                    |
                    +---class (class files)
                    |
                    +---templates (HTML templates)
                    |
                +---images (images for the templates)
```

By changing the following configuration parameters in vote.conf, you can modify the directory structure to fit your site requirements:

```
$PEAR_DIR          = $_SERVER['DOCUMENT_ROOT'] . '/pear' ;
$PHPLIB_DIR        = $_SERVER['DOCUMENT_ROOT'] . '/phplib';
$APP_FRAMEWORK_DIR = $_SERVER['DOCUMENT_ROOT'] . '/framework';
$ROOT_PATH         = $_SERVER['DOCUMENT_ROOT'];
$REL_ROOT_PATH     = '/vote';
$REL_APP_PATH      = $REL_ROOT_PATH . '/apps';
$TEMPLATE_DIR      = $ROOT_PATH     . $REL_APP_PATH . '/templates';
$CLASS_DIR         = $ROOT_PATH     . $REL_APP_PATH . '/class';
$REL_TEMPLATE_DIR  = $REL_APP_PATH  . '/templates/';
```

Creating an errors file

The error messages displayed by the contact manager applications are stored on the CD-ROM in the ch20/apps/vote.errors file. You can modify the error messages using a text editor.

Creating the Application Templates

The templates used in this application are poll-specific. Every poll will have an output template that will be prepared by the user who initiates the poll. You can find an example poll output template on the CD-ROM in the ch20/apps/templates directory. These templates must be named according to the poll ID. For example, a poll with an ID of 99 should have an output template named 099.html.

Creating the Vote Application

This application, vote.php, is responsible for managing the entire process of the voting system. The application is included on the CD-ROM in the ch20/apps directory. It implements the following functionality:

◆ Allows a user to submit a vote

◆ Displays the poll result

This application has the following methods.

run()

When the application is run, this method is called. It first calls the `setPollID()` method to set the given poll ID to a member variable. Then it creates a member variable named "_voteObj" to hold an object of the Vote class with the member poll ID. It determines whether a cookie has been set, which indicates that the user has already voted for this poll. If it finds the cookie, it directly calls `displayVoteResult()` to show the vote result instead of adding the vote to the database.

setPollID()

This method sets the given poll ID from the user request. It displays an alert message when it determines that the poll ID has not been supplied from the user form.

getPollID()

This method is used to retrieve the current poll ID from the member variable `_pollID`. It simply returns `$this->_pollID`.

addVote()

This method is responsible for adding the user vote to the database by using the Vote class. This is how it works:

1. It first determines whether the user has selected a voting option. If not, it displays an alert message and returns null.

2. Next, the `addVote()` method of the Vote class is used to add the given vote to the database. The vote class object is instantiated with the member poll ID in the `run()` method, so it is not necessary to pass the poll ID to the `addVote()` method here.

3. If the vote addition status is successful, this method sets a cookie for the user, indicating that the user submitted a vote for this poll; otherwise, it displays an alert message indicating the failure of the addition operation.

4. Finally, the `displayVoteResult()` method is called to show the vote result.

displayVoteResult()

This method shows the poll result to the user. It works as follows:

1. It first determines whether the total number of options for the poll has been supplied. If it hasn't, it displays an error message and returns null, as a result cannot be found unless the method can ascertain the total number of options available.

2. Next, the output template for the poll is loaded in a template object called
   $template. The output template file name is determined from the poll ID.
   If the output template file does not exist in the template directory, it displays an alert message and returns null.

3. Then it calls the getTotalVoteCount() method of the Vote class to
   retrieve the total number of votes posted for this poll, and sets the number
   to the appropriate variable in the template.

4. For each of the poll options, the getVoteCountByChoice() method is
   called to retrieve the number of votes cast. This number, along with the
   total number of votes for the poll, is used to determine the percentage of
   votes for this option. These numbers are set to appropriate variables in the
   template.

5. Finally, the entire template is parsed and printed to the user to provide a
   full poll result.

Installing the Voting Tool

In this section, it is assumed that you are using a Linux system with MySQL and an
Apache server installed. Your Internet Web server document root directory is
%DocumentRoot%. Of course, if you have a different path, which is likely, you
should change this path whenever you see it in a configuration file or instruction in
this chapter.

It is further assumed that you have installed the PHPLIB and PEAR libraries.
Normally, these are installed during PHP installation. For your convenience, we
have provided these in the lib/phplib.tar.gz and lib/pear.tar.gz directories on the
CD-ROM. In these sample installation steps, it is assumed that these are installed in
the %DocumentRoot%/phplib and %DocumentRoot%/pear directories. Because
your installation locations for these libraries are likely to be different, make sure
you replace these paths in the configuration files.

Here is how you can get your voting tool applications up and running:

1. **Install the application framework.** If you have not yet installed the application framework discussed in Chapter 4, you must do so before proceeding further.

2. **Install the VOTE database.** The quickest way to create the VOTE database
   is to run the following commands:

```
mysqladmin -u root -p create VOTE
mysql -u root -p -D VOTE < VOTE.mysql
```

   The VOTE.mysql can be found in the vote/sql directory created from
   ch20.tar.gz or you can get it from the CD-ROM's ch20/sql directory.

3. **Install the VOTE applications.** From the `ch20` directory of the CD-ROM, extract `ch20.tar.gz` in %DocumentRoot%. This will create a directory called vote in your document root. Configure `%DocumentRoot%/vote/apps/vote.conf` for path and database settings. The applications are installed in the `%DocumentRoot%/vote/apps` directory, and the templates are stored in `%DocumentRoot%/vote/apps/templates`.

Your MySQL server is hosted on the intranet Web server; therefore, it can be accessed via localhost. However, if this is not the case, you can easily modify the database URLs in each application's configuration files. For example, the vote.conf file has a MySQL database access URL such as the following:

```
$VOTE_DB_URL          = 'mysql://root:foobar@localhost/VOTE';
```

Suppose, for example, that your database server is called `db.domain.com`, and that the username and password for accessing the VOTE database are `admin` and `db123`, respectively. (You will create both during this installation process.) In such a case, you would modify the database access URL in the `vote.conf` configuration file as follows:

```
$VOTE_DB_URL          =
'mysql://admin:db132@db.domain.com/VOTE';
```

4. **Set file/directory permissions.** Make sure you have changed file and directory permissions such that your internet Web server can access all the files.

Once you have performed the preceding steps, you are ready to test your application.

Testing the Voting Tool

The first step in testing y our vote application is to develop a poll form. In this sample case, we will develop a simple poll form that asks voters whether they like the current Web site. This form, which is provided on the CD-ROM in (`ch20/apps/vote/sample_polls/website_poll.html`), is shown in Figure 20-3.

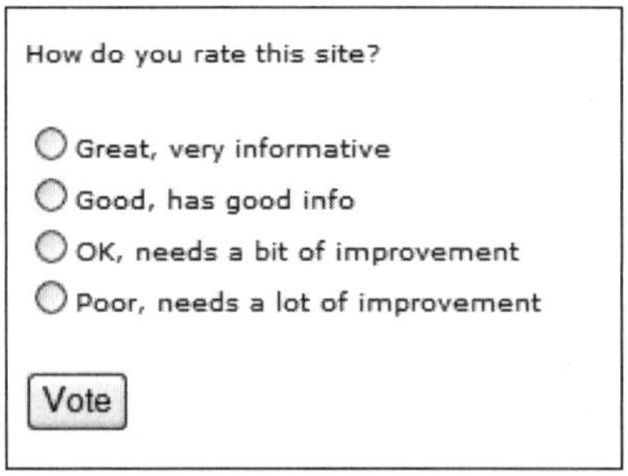

Figure 20-3: A sample Web site poll form.

If you examine the source of this Web form, you will notice the following HTML form code:

```
<form action="/vote/apps/vote.php" target=_blank method="POST">

<font face="Verdana" size="1">How do you rate this site? <p>

<input type=radio name="vote" value="1">Great, very informative<br>
<input type=radio name="vote" value="2">Good, has good info <br>
<input type=radio name="vote" value="3">OK, needs a bit of improvement<br>
<input type=radio name="vote" value="4">Poor, needs a lot of improvement
<p>



<input type=submit value="Vote">
<input type=hidden name="poll_id" value="1">
</font>
</form>
```

Notice that the form action line is set to /vote/apps/vote.php, as it is needed to call the vote application. In addition, note that each vote radio button is called "vote" and has a numeric value (1–4). This is needed to collect vote data. Finally, note a hidden form field called poll_id, which is set to 1. This number identifies the form in the vote.conf file's $choicesPerPoll array, which is shown here:

```
$choicesPerPoll = array(
                    //POLL ID       => NUMBER OF CHOICES
                         1          =>     4,
                         2          =>     7
                );
```

This array in vote.conf determines the maximum number of options per polling form. Here, our Web site polling form (poll_id 1) has four options, as shown in the aforementioned HTML form, so the $choicesPerPoll array has the same number specified.

Now, if you select any of the voting options for the Web site form and click the Vote button, your vote will be stored in the VOTES table in the VOTE database. You will be given a cookie so that you cannot vote again until the COOKIE_ EXPIRATION_TIME time specified in vote.conf expires.

As soon as you click the Vote button, you will see a pop-up window that shows the current poll results (i.e., including your vote). This page is shown using a results template stored in the templates directory (%DocumentRoot%/vote/ apps/templates). The name of the template is specific to each poll_id. For example, a poll form with poll_id must have a template called 001.html in the %DocumentRoot/%vote/apps/templates directory. Because each poll has its own results template, you can customize each poll's results as desired.

The basic structure of a results template is as follows:

```
<!-- BEGIN mainBlock -->
 {1_VOTE_COUNT}  {1_VOTE_PERCENT}
 {2_VOTE_COUNT}  {2_VOTE_PERCENT}


 ...


 {n_VOTE_COUNT}  {n_VOTE_PERCENT}

{TOTAL_VOTES}
<!-- END mainBlock -->
```

Each of the tags within the braces is replaced with respective vote data. For example, {1_VOTE_COUNT} is replaced with the total number of votes cast for option #1 in a poll. The {1_VOTE_PERCENT} tag is replaced with the percentage of votes cast for option #1 in a poll. The {TOTAL_VOTES} tag is replaced with the grand total of votes cast in a poll. Figure 20-4 shows a sample results page for the Web site poll described in the preceding example.

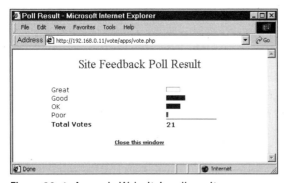

Figure 20-4: A sample Web site's poll results.

So far, our example poll form has used multiple radio button options. However, the vote tool also supports multiple checkbox options, for polls in which you want visitors to cast multiple votes that identify their preferences from a group of items. For example, Figure 20-5 shows a poll form that asks users to select one or more languages. This form can be found in the sample_polls directory as language_poll.html.

Figure 20-5: A sample language poll form using checkboxes.

The source for this form looks as follows:

```
<form action="/vote/apps/vote.php" target=_blank method="POST">
What languages do you write code? (check all that applies)<p>

<input type=checkbox name="vote[]" value="1">PHP<br>
<input type=checkbox name="vote[]" value="2">Perl<br>
<input type=checkbox name="vote[]" value="3">C<br>
<input type=checkbox name="vote[]" value="4">C++<br>
<input type=checkbox name="vote[]" value="5">Java<br>
<input type=checkbox name="vote[]" value="6">Python<br>
<input type=checkbox name="vote[]" value="7">Smalltalk<br>

<input type=submit value="Vote"<br>
<input type=hidden name="poll_id" value="2">
```

Here, notice that the vote field name is not `vote` but `vote[]`, to indicate that we are returning an array of options. The values are still numeric.

When this poll form is submitted with multiple selections, each vote is added in the database. Figure 20-6 shows an example results page (displayed using `templates/002.html`).

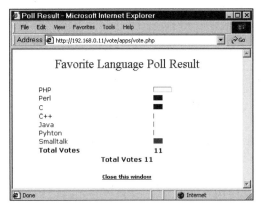

Figure 20-6: A favorite language poll results page.

Summary

In this chapter, you learned how to develop a vote application that could be used to poll your Web site visitors about issues related to your Web site or other matters about which you are interested to know their opinions. This is a nifty tool to have for most Web sites.

Part VI

Tuning and Securing PHP Applications

Chapter 21

Speeding Up PHP Applications

IN THIS CHAPTER

- Benchmarking your PHP application

- Stress-testing your PHP application

- Compressing your PHP application output

- Using output caching using jpcache

- Using output caching using the PEAR cache

- Using function caching using the PEAR cache

- Using PHP opcode caching techniques

THIS CHAPTER DESCRIBES HOW YOU can speed up your PHP applications using various techniques, including fine-tuning code, output buffering, output compression, output caching, and code caching. These techniques will enable you to turbocharge your application for the high-volume access scenarios usually present in heavy-traffic Web sites with PHP applications.

 Optimization isn't a task that should be undertaken on every piece of code. You must ask yourself, before starting to optimize code, "is this code fast enough?" If the answer is "yes," optimization probably isn't necessary. Spending time optimizing existing code could be time wasted if you neglect other tasks for the optimization time. The best advice is to use good techniques while constructing the code in the first place and only optimize code that actually needs it.

Benchmarking Your PHP Application

Most Web programming is done quickly, and often carelessly. When someone needs a new Web application, notifying the developers is often the last priority. Once the developers are notified, the application gets the "was needed yesterday" status. Therefore, developers design quick-and-dirty applications, and lack the necessary time to fine-tune the code.

When you plan to develop a new application, try to allocate one-third of your project time to fine-tuning your code. The first step in fine-tuning your code is identifying the most commonly used code segments. You can easily do this by adding spurious print statements to your code or enabling logging/debugging for critical segments of your applications.

Once you have identified the segments of code that are most commonly required to service a request, you need to identify any elements that are not operating at optimal speed.

To identify slow code, you should review your code as frequently as possible, using the benchmarking techniques described in the following section.

Note that optimizing code won't always improve performance. It's important to consider the whole picture when you are experiencing performance problems — if your database is maxed out, your bandwidth not adequate for your traffic, or hardware not keeping up with the demand, optimizing code won't improve a thing.

Benchmarking your code

The PEAR package discussed in Chapter 4 includes a set of benchmark classes that you can use to benchmark your code without writing a lot of new code. For example, Listing 21-1 shows a PHP script that benchmarks a function called myFunction.

Listing 21-1: bench1.php

```php
<?php

    // If you have installed PEAR packages in
    // a different directory than %DocumentRoot%/pear
    // change the setting below.
    $PEAR_DIR = $_SERVER['DOCUMENT_ROOT'] . '/pear' ;

    $PATH = $PEAR_DIR;
```

```
ini_set( 'include_path', ':' .
        $PATH . ':' . ini_get('include_path'));

require_once 'Benchmark/Iterate.php';

$benchmark = new Benchmark_Iterate;

$benchmark->run(10, 'myFunction', $argument);

$result = $benchmark->get();

echo "<pre>";
print_r($result);
echo "</pre>";
exit;

function myFunction($var) {
    // do something
    echo 'x ';
}

?>
```

The $PEAR_DIR variable points to the PEAR directory, which in this case is installed in %DocumentRoot%/pear. The $PEAR_DIR variable is included in the include_path using the ini_set() call. Then the Benchmark/Iterate.php class is loaded into the application.

A benchmark Iterate object called $benchmark is created. This object is used to run the myFunction function 10 times. The $argument variable is passed to myFunction each time it is called. The profiling result of the multiple execution, $result, is retrieved using the get() method of the benchmark object. The result is output to the screen using the print_r() function. A sample of typical output looks as follows:

```
x x x x x x x x x
Array
(
    [1] => 0.00074100494384766
    [2] => 0.00013399124145508
    [3] => 0.00013101100921631
    [4] => 0.0001380443572998
    [5] => 0.00014901161193848
    [6] => 0.00013506412506104
    [7] => 0.00013101100921631
    [8] => 0.00013399124145508
```

```
[9] => 0.00014710426330566
[10] => 0.00013601779937744
[mean] => 0.00019762516021729
[iterations] => 10
)
```

Notice that for each execution of myFunction, the benchmark object has tracked the execution time. It has also calculated the mean (average) time needed by myFunction, which is 0.00019762516021729 seconds (approximately 0.20 ms).

By running the target functions (slow functions) multiple times, you can determine the mean execution speed and start fine-tuning the code using the benchmark method described.

Now let's look at another method of benchmarking your code. Listing 21-2 shows a PHP script that uses the Benchmark/Timer.php class from PEAR's benchmark classes to time execution of a function named myFunction().

Listing 21-2: bench2php

```php
<?php

    // If you have installed PEAR packages in
    // a different directory than %DocumentRoot%/pear
    // change the setting below.
    $PEAR_DIR = $_SERVER['DOCUMENT_ROOT'] . '/pear' ;

    $PATH = $PEAR_DIR;
    ini_set( 'include_path', ':' . $PATH . ':' .
            ini_get('include_path'));

    require_once 'Benchmark/Timer.php';

    $timer = new Benchmark_Timer();

    $timer >start();

    $timer->setMarker('start_myFunction');

    for($i=0; $i<10; $i++)
    {
        myFunction($argument);
    }

    $timer->setMarker('end_myFunction');
    $timer->stop();
    $profiling = $timer->getProfiling();
```

```
echo '<p>Time elapsed: ' .
    $timer->timeElapsed('start_myFunction',
                        'end_myFunction') .
    '</p>';

echo '<pre>';
print_r($profiling);
echo '</pre>';

exit;

function myFunction($var) {

  static $counter = 0;
  // do something
  echo $counter++ . ' ';
}


?>
```

First, a benchmark timer object, $timer, is created. The timer is started using the start() method. To mark a section of code for benchmarking, the setMarker() method of the timer is used. The myFunction() function is called in a loop to retrieve a sample set of executions. Then an end marker is created using the setMarker() method of the $timer object.. The profiling data is retrieved using the getProfiling() method of the timer. The elapsed time is calculated between the markers (i.e., for the entire duration of the loop) using the timeElapsed() method of the $timer object. The profiling data is dumped using print_r(). Here is a sample of typical output:

```
0 1 2 3 4 5 6 7 8 9
Time elapsed: 0.00094497203826904
Array
(
    [0] => Array
        (
            [name] => Start
            [time] => 1039292459.17705900
            [diff] => -
            [total] => 0
        )

    [1] => Array
        (
            [name] => start_myFunction
            [time] => 1039292459.17758700
```

```
                      [diff] => 0.00052797794342041
                      [total] => 0.00052797794342041
                  )

          [2] => Array
              (
                      [name] => end_myFunction
                      [time] => 1039292459.17853200
                      [diff] => 0.00094497203826904
                      [total] => 0.0014729499816895
                  )

          [3] => Array
              (
                      [name] => Stop
                      [time] => 1039292459.17860700
                      [diff] => 7.4982643127441E-05
                      [total] => 0.0015479326248169
                  )

  )
```

Using this type of benchmarking, you can create numerous markers in your code, gathering profiling data for the marked code to analyze where your code is slow. You can then refine the code by rewriting as needed. The following section describes the most common cause of speed problems.

Avoiding bad loops

The most common PHP problem with speed comes from badly written loops. Listing 21-3 shows a PHP script that demonstrates both inefficiently written loops and efficiently written loops.

Listing 21–3: loops.php

```php
<?php

    // If you have installed PEAR packages in a different
    // directory than %DocumentRoot%/pear change
    // the setting below.
    $PEAR_DIR = $_SERVER['DOCUMENT_ROOT'] . '/pear' ;

    $PATH = $PEAR_DIR;

    ini_set( 'include_path', ':' . $PATH . ':' .
            ini_get('include_path'));
```

```php
require_once 'Benchmark/Iterate.php';

define(MAX_RUN, 100);

$data   = array(1, 2, 3, 4, 5);

doBenchmark('v1', $data);
doBenchmark('v2', $data);
doBenchmark('v3', $data);
doBenchmark('v4', $data);

function doBenchmark($functionName = null, $arr = null)
{
  reset($arr);

  $benchmark = new Benchmark_Iterate;
  $benchmark->run(MAX_RUN, $functionName, $arr);
  $result = $benchmark->get();

  echo '<br>';
  printf("%s ran %d times where average exec time %.5f ms",
         $functionName,
         $result['iterations'],
         $result['mean'] * 1000);

}

function v1($myArray = null) {

  // Do bad loop
  for ($i =0; $i < sizeof($myArray); $i++)
  {
      echo '<!--' . $myArray[$i] . ' --> ';
  }
}

function v2($myArray = null) {

  // Do better loop

  // Get the size of array
  $max = sizeof($myArray);
```

Continued

Listing 21-3 *(Continued)*

```php
    for ($i =0; $i < $max  ; $i++)
    {
        echo '<!--' . $myArray[$i] . ' --> ';
    }
}


function v3($myArray = null) {

  // Do much better loop

  // Get the size of array
  $max = sizeof($myArray);

  for ($i =0; $i < $max  ; $i++)
  {
      // Store the output in a string
      $output .= '<!--' . $myArray[$i] . ' --> ';
  }

  // Echo the output string
  echo $output;
}

function v4($myArray = null) {

  // Do much better loop

  // Get the size of array
  $max - sizeof($myArray);

  $output = array();

  for ($i =0; $i < $max  ; $i++)
  {
      // Store the output in a string
      array_push($output,  '<!--' .
                $myArray[$i] .
                ' --> '
                );
  }
```

```
    // Echo the output string
    echo implode('', $output);
  }


?>
```

This script demonstrates four versions of a method (v1, v2, v3, and v4), each of which performs the same task, but with progressive efficiency.

The script calls a method called doBenchmark(), which runs each version of the function under benchmark conditions using the Benchmark/Iterate.php class for MAX_RUN times. The result of each benchmark is printed using a printf() statement. Following is a sample of output from the script:

```
v1 ran 100 times where average exec time 1.60087 ms
v2 ran 100 times where average exec time 1.05392 ms
v3 ran 100 times where average exec time 0.55139 ms
v4 ran 100 times where average exec time 0.27371 ms
```

Here, you can see that v1() ran the slowest. Lets look at what v1() does. This function receives an array as an argument and loops through each element of the array using a for loop. Notice that the loop uses the sizeof() function to determine the size of the array. The sizeof() function is called each time the loop iterates. This degrades the speed of the loop substantially, as function calls are expensive in terms of execution time. Inside the loop, only an echo() function prints an HTML comment statement.

Now let's look at the v2() function. This function does the same task of v1(), but it is a bit faster (0.54695 ms), as it stores the size of the $myArray in the $max variable outside the loop and therefore avoids the penalty of calling sizeof() for each iteration.

Looking at the v3() version of the same function, you can see that this version is significantly faster than v2() because it not only does what v2() does, it also removes from the loop the iterative call to the expensive I/O function echo() by storing the output in a variable called $output. This improves its performance greatly, as it uses only a single echo() call to print the contents stored in $output as the last statement of the function.

Finally, v4() does everything v3() does except that instead of storing output in a $output string variable that is appended using the dot operator (as done in v4), it uses a faster array_push() function to store output as a series of sequential array elements in $output array. Finally, it appends the contents of the $output array using the implode() function, which is passed to a single echo() function. This appears to be the fastest of the four implementations.

How do you learn to make such improvements to your own code? The simple answer is experimentation and lots of practice. Study PHP's built-in functions in great detail, as they are faster than anything you will write in PHP. Use of built-in functions in comparable situations can improve your code speed significantly. For example, consider this listing:

```
function v5($myArray = null){
  echo "<!--", implode(" --> <!--", $myArray), " --> ";
}
```

Stress-testing your PHP applications using ApacheBench

The Apache server comes with a tool called ApacheBench (ab), which is installed by default in the bin directory of your Apache installation directory. By using this nifty tool, you can stress-test your application to see how it behaves under heavy load conditions.

Make an estimate of how many requests you want your application to be able to service from your Web server. Write it down in a goal statement such as "I wish to service N requests per second."

Restart your Web server and from a system other than the Web server, run the ab command as follows:

```
./ab -n number_of_total_requests \
    -c number_of_simultaneous_requests \
    http://your_web_server/your_php_app.php
```

For example:

```
./ab -n 1000 -c 50 http://www.domain.com/myapp.php
```

The ApacheBench tool will make 50 concurrent requests, and a total of 1,000 requests. Sample output is shown here:

```
Server Software:        Apache/2.0.16
Server Hostname:        localhost
Server Port:            80

Document Path:          /myapp.php
Document Length:        1311 bytes

Concurrency Level:      50
Time taken for tests:   8.794 seconds
Complete requests:      1000
Failed requests:        0
```

```
Total transferred:      1754000 bytes
HTML transferred:       1311000 bytes
Requests per second:    113.71
Transfer rate:          199.45 kb/s received

Connection Times (ms)
              min   avg   max
Connect:        0     0     5
Processing:   111   427   550
Total:        111   427   555
```

Notice that Requests per second is 113.71 for accessing the myapp.php PHP script. Change the concurrent request count to a higher number and see how the server handles additional concurrent load.

Tune your application as finely as possible using the techniques discussed earlier. You might have to also tune Apache using MaxClients, ThreadsPerChild, MaxThreadsPerChild, and so on, based on your MPM module choice in httpd.conf.

Visit www.apache.org for in-depth documentation on Apache, including modules and third-party applications to improve performance.

If you make changes to the Apache configuration file (httpd.conf), make sure you restart Apache, and apply the same benchmark tests by using ab as before.

You should see your Requests per second increase or decrease based on the numbers you try. As you tweak the numbers by changing the directive values, make sure you record the values and the performance so that you can determine the best setting for you.

Buffering Your PHP Application Output

Once you are sure that you have optimized your application to the best of your abilities, it is time to consider other techniques, such as *output buffering.*

Output buffering is very effective for scripts that use numerous I/O functions such as echo(), print, printf(), and so on. If you use these functions often, you might find output buffering to be a speed booster. For example, Listing 21-4 shows a script called buffer.php that benchmarks (using the PEAR Benchmark/Timer discussed earlier in the section, " Benchmarking your code") a function called doSomething(), which prints the 'x' character in a loop, using the echo() function.

Listing 21-4: buffer.php

```php
<?php

  define(MAX, 1024 * 10);


  // If you have installed PEAR packages in a different
  // directory than %DocumentRoot%/pear change the
  // setting below.
  $PEAR_DIR = $_SERVER['DOCUMENT_ROOT'] . '/pear' ;

  $PATH = $PEAR_DIR;
  ini_set( 'include_path', ':' . $PATH . ':' .
           ini_get('include_path'));

  require_once 'Benchmark/Timer.php';

  $timer = new Benchmark_Timer();

  $kb = MAX / 1024;

  // No output buffering
  $timer->start();
  doSomething();
  $timer->stop();
  printf("Buffer: OFF Size: %d KB Time elapsed: %.3f<br>",
          $kb,
          $timer->timeElapsed());

  // Enable output buffering
  ob_start();
  $timer->start();
  doSomething();
  $timer->stop();
  printf("Buffer: ON Size: %d KB Time elapsed: %.3f<br>" ,
          $kb,
          $timer->timeElapsed());

  exit;

  function doSomething()
  {
     $output = '';
```

```
    for($i=0;$i<=MAX;$i++)
    {
        echo 'x';
    }
  }

?>
```

The first call to doSomething() in the script is made without output buffering, whereas the second call is made after output buffering is enabled using the ob_start() function. Sample benchmark results of the two calls to doSomething() are shown here:

```
xxxxxxxxxxxxxx [ shortened for brevity] xxxxxxxxxxxxxxxxxxxxxx
Buffer: OFF Size: 10 KB Time elapsed: 10.939
xxxxxxxxxxxxxx [ shortened for brevity] xxxxxxxxxxxxxxxxxxxxxx
Buffer: ON Size: 10 KB Time elapsed: 0.071
```

As you can see, the unbuffered call to doSomething(), which uses echo() in a loop, required a significant amount of time vs. the buffered call. This means that ob_start() is an excellent choice to improve performance of this script.

Therefore, whenever it is possible for you to enable output buffering, try it and measure the performance gain. If the gain is significant, you can use ob_start() in your code.

Compressing Your PHP Application Output

You can also compress your PHP-generated HTML output or image output using GZIP compression. You must enable GZIP compression while compiling PHP. This is done using the option --with-zlib-dir=/usr/local/lib in the source code configuration step.

Not all Web browsers can handle compressed output. Therefore, this method might not be applicable for all situations. You can take advantage of compression when you know that the Web browsers used by your visitors support compression. Because Microsoft Internet Explorer is a popular Web browser that supports compression, it is often worth trying.

Listing 21-5 shows a simple script that enables output buffering using the `ob_start()` function, but it also enables gzip-based compression by providing the `ob_gzhandler` parameter to the `ob_start()` function.

Listing 21-5: compress.php

```php
<?php

    define(MAX, 100);

    ob_start("ob_gzhandler");

    $output = '';

    for($i=0;$i<=MAX;$i++)
    {
        $output .= "This is line $i <br>";
    }

    echo $output;
?>
```

The following code highlights the extra HTTP headers that are sent when compression is enabled:

```
lynx -head -dump http://www.evoknow.com/ch21/gzip/compress.php


HTTP/1.1 200 OK
Server: Apache/2.0.43 (Unix) PHP/4.1.2
Date: Sat, 07 Dec 2002 20:50:47 GMT
Connection: close
Content Encoding: gzip
Content-Length: 270
Content-Type: text/html
Vary: Accept-Encoding
X-Powered-By: PHP/4.1.2
```

The same script without compression enabled sends the following headers:

```
lynx -head -dump http://www.evoknow.com/ch21/gzip/compress.php


HTTP/1.1 200 OK
Server: Apache/2.0.43 (Unix) PHP/4.1.2
Date: Sat, 07 Dec 2002 20:52:20 GMT
Connection: close
Content-Type: text/html
X-Powered-By: PHP/4.1.2
```

Keep in mind that GZIP is only one practical option in improving your code. Also, the overhead in calling the ZIP function, hit on server RAM, etc., must be carefully weighed.

Caching Your PHP Applications

Using the benchmark and compression techniques described in this chapter, you can identify slow code and rewrite it to execute faster if possible. However, another popular method of enhancing the end user's experience of "speed" is to use *caching* techniques. By caching the output of your PHP application or caching the generation of PHP opcode, you can achieve higher performance. The following sections discuss these caching techniques in detail.

Caching PHP contents using the jpcache cache

The `jpcache` package is a lightweight page caching solution for PHP that reduces server load as PHP-generated pages are cached on the file system or database. It also uses compression (GZIP content-encoding) and ETag-headers, which can result in approximately 80 percent bandwidth savings.

When a jpcache-enabled page is requested for the first time, it is run as usual and the generated content is cached in a file or database per the jpcache configuration. The cached data is transmitted for any subsequent requests for a configurable amount of time. This means that pages that do not change often on your site can use this caching technique to reduce server load by avoiding running the same script for each request.

Configuring jpcache

Download the latest jpcache package from `http://www.jpcache.com/`. Once downloaded, extract the package under your Web server's document tree. Here is how you configure jpcache for database-based caching:

 Although you can configure jpcache for file-based caching, file-based caching requires a centralized file system (using NFS or SAMBA) when multiple Web servers are serving your contents in a Web server farm. Again, remember the tradeoffs associated with various solutions. For example, although NFS and SAMBA improve caching, their overhead also contributes to slower system functionality.

1. Edit the jpcache.php file to change the $includedir variable to point to the directory in which you have installed jpcache. In the following example, $includedir points to the %DocumentRoot%/ch21/cache/jpcache/ path.

```
// Set the includedir to the jpcache-directory
// ORIG: $includedir = "/path/to/jpcache-files";
$includedir = $_SERVER['DOCUMENT_ROOT'] .
                '/ch21/cache/jpcache/';
```

2. Create a database called jpcache in your MySQL database server. If you want to use an existing database name, skip to the next step.

3. Create a table called CACHEDATA in the jpcache database (or your existing database) using script.sql. For example:

```
mysql -u root -p -D jpcache < script.sql
```

The above command will create CACHEDATA table per script.sql in a database called jpcache in localhost. If your MySQL database server is not localhost, you can use -h *hostname* option. Also, if you are using an existing database replace -D jpcache with -D *your_existing_database* name.

4. Edit the jpcache-config.php file to include the following lines:

```
$JPCACHE_TYPE = "mysql";
$JPCACHE_TIME          =    900;

$JPCACHE_DB_HOST       = "localhost";
$JPCACHE_DB_DATABASE   = "jpcache";
$JPCACHE_DB_USERNAME   = "sqluser";
$JPCACHE_DB_PASSWORD   = "passwd";
$JPCACHE_DB_TABLE      = "CACHEDATA";
$JPCACHE_OPTIMIZE      = 1;
```

Here, the cached data will be stored in a table called CACHEDATA in a database called jpcache in the localhost. Access to the database will be allowed using a username called sqluser and the password "passwd".

5. Now create the following test script called test.php:

```
<?php

require "/path/to/jpcache/jpcache.php";
echo time();
phpinfo();

?>
```

Make sure that /path/to/jpcache in the require() line points to the appropriate directory in which jpcache.php is installed.

6. Now run this script via a Web browser using `http://server/path/to/jpcache/test.php`. You should see a page with a timestamp on top. Keep accessing this script by refreshing the request a few times. Notice that the timestamp shown as the output does not change. This means that caching is working, as the page will be cached for the duration of `$JPCACHE_TIME` specified in the jpcache-config.php.

That's all that is required to configure jpcache. Now you are ready to use it with your existing PHP applications.

Deploying jpcache

The jpcache caching should be used only for applications that do not generate their own headers (such as cookies) and are not user-level personalized. You should use this caching technique for pages that generate data from a database or external files unless you are comfortable with the lag that results from non-cache hits. To use jpcache in your existing PHP application, do the following:

1. Edit your application to include the following lines at the very beginning of your PHP application:

```
$cachetimeout=900;

require_once($_SERVER['DOCUMENT_ROOT'] .
            '/jpcache/jpcache.php');
```

The preceding code assumes that jpcache is installed in the `%DocumentRoot/jpcache` directory. If you install it somewhere else, make sure the path reflects the change.

2. If you wish to cache the output more or less than every 900 seconds, change the value of `$cachetimeout`. Setting `$cachetimeout` to -1 will disable caching for the current application. Setting `$cachetimeout` to 0 will enable a cache that does not expire automatically.

Caching PHP contents using the PEAR cache

PEAR cache support comes with the PEAR package found at `http://pear.php.net`. For more information about installing PEAR, refer to Chapter 4.

PEAR caching can store cached data in files, shared memory, or a database. Because you are already familiar with jpcache as a database-based caching method, here we will use a file as the cache storage. This section shows you how a simple PHP script (shown in Listing 21-6) can be converted to use the PEAR output caching feature.

Listing 21-6: non_cached.php

```php
<?php

    echo "This is the contents<P>";
    echo "Time is " . date('M-d-Y H:i:s A', time()) . "<BR>";

?>
```

To use the PEAR output cache for the preceding PHP script, you need to do the following:

1. Include PEAR in the path of this script using the following:

   ```php
   $PEAR_DIR = $_SERVER['DOCUMENT_ROOT'] . '/pear' ;

   $PATH = $PEAR_DIR;

   ini_set( 'include_path', ':' . $PATH . ':' .
               ini_get('include_path'));
   ```

2. Include the Output.php cache subclass from PEAR using the following:

   ```php
   require_once 'Cache/Output.php';
   ```

3. Create a cache directory variable as follows:

   ```php
   $cacheDir = '/tmp/pear_cache';
   ```

   Make sure this directory is writable by the Web server user. The caching scheme will write cache data in subdirectories within this directory.

4. Create an Output cache object as follows:

   ```php
   $cache = new Cache_Output('file',
                           array('cache_dir' => $cacheDir)
                           );
   ```

   The first argument states that we are choosing file-based caching, and the second argument is an associative array with the cache directory path defined as cache_dir.

5. Generate a unique cache ID for this page as follows:

   ```php
   $cache_id = $cache->generateID(
                   array('url' => $REQUEST_URI,
                         'post' => $HTTP_POST_VARS,
                         'cookies' => $HTTP_COOKIE_VARS
                         )
                   );
   ```

Here, the generateID() method of the $cache object is called by supplying an array of information (URL, HTTP POST data, and HTTP cookie) that can uniquely identify the request.

6. Add a conditional statement to see if cached data already exists for the created cached ID ($cache_id) and if so, retrieve the cached data and terminate the script as follows:

```
if ($content = $cache->start($cache_id))
    {
        // Cache has contents, display and terminate
        echo $content;
        die();
    }
```

7. Keep the content generation code after the preceding conditional statement and close the cache object using the following:

```
echo $cache->end();
```

Listing 21-7 shows the new PEAR output–cached version of non_cached.php as pear_content_cache.php.

Listing 21-7: pear_content_cache.php

```php
<?php



// If you have installed PEAR packages in a different
// directory than %DocumentRoot%/pear change the
// setting below.
$PEAR_DIR = $_SERVER['DOCUMENT_ROOT'] . '/pear' ;

$PATH = $PEAR_DIR;
ini_set( 'include_path', ':' . $PATH . ':' .
        ini_get('include_path'));

require_once 'Cache/Output.php';

// Set cache directory path
// This directory has to be writable
// by the Web server.
$cacheDir = '/tmp/pear_cache';

$cache = new Cache_Output('file',
                        array('cache_dir' => $cacheDir)
                        );
```

Continued

Listing 21-7 *(Continued)*

```
// If user does not want to view cached version
// she has to give ?nocache=anyvalue to view fresh contents
if (empty($_REQUEST['nocache']))
{
  // Create a unique cache identifier based on
  // the request + cookie information

   $cache_id = $cache->generateID(
              array('url' => $REQUEST_URI,
                    'post' => $HTTP_POST_VARS,
                    'cookies' => $HTTP_COOKIE_VARS
                   )
               );
} else {

    // User wants fresh contents so set cache ID to null
    $cache_id = null;

}

// See if cached contents is available for the cache ID
if ($content = $cache->start($cache_id))
{
    // Cache has contents, display and terminate
    echo $content;
    die();
}

// Cache does not have contents
// Generate content and write cache

echo "This is the contents<P>";
echo "Time is " . date('M-d-Y H:i:s A', time()) . "<BR>";

// write contents to cache file
echo $cache->end();

?>
```

Note that in the preceding script, when users do not want the cached version of
the page, they can specify nocache=1 in the request as a query parameter as follows:

```
http://server/path/to/pear_content_cache.php?nocache=1
```

This will ensure that users are served fresh contents. PEAR's cache package can also cache PHP function calls. Listing 21-8 shows a script called pear_func_cache.php that enables function caching for a function named slowFunction().

Listing 21-8: pear_func_cache.php

```php
<?php

   // If you have installed PEAR packages in a different
   // directory than %DocumentRoot%/pear change the
   // setting below.
   $PEAR_DIR  = $_SERVER['DOCUMENT_ROOT'] . '/pear' ;

   $PATH = $PEAR_DIR;
   ini_set( 'include_path', ':' . $PATH . ':' .
              ini_get('include_path'));

   require_once 'Cache/Function.php';

   // This directory has to be writable
   // by the Web server.
   $cacheDir = '/tmp/pear_cache/';

   $cache = new Cache_Function('file',
                                  array('cache_dir' => $cacheDir)
                                  );

   $arr = array('apple', 'orange');

   $cache->call('slowFunction', $arr);

   echo '<p>';

   $arr = array('banana', 'grapes');
   slowFunction($arr);

   function slowFunction($arr = null)
   {
      echo "Very slow function <br>";
      echo "Time is " . date('M-d-Y H:i:s A', time()) . '<br>';
      foreach ($arr as $fruit)
      {
         echo "Got $fruit <br>";
      }
   }

?>
```

The Cache/Function.php class from the PEAR Cache classes is used to enable function caching. The $cache variable is a new Cache_Function object that uses file-based caching of function data, which is cached into the $cacheDir directory.

To cache a function call, the call() method of the Cache_Function object, $cache, is used as follows:

```
$cache->call('slowFunction', $arr);
```

Here, the slowFunction() function is called with the argument $arr, and it is cached in a file in the $cacheDir directory. Any subsequent call to this function using $cache->call() will return the cached function result for the given argument. Sample output of this script is shown here:

```
Very slow function
Time is Dec-07-2002 21:37:21 PM
Got apple
Got orange

Very slow function
Time is Dec-07-2002 21:39:23 PM
Got banana
Got grapes
```

The first four lines are produced by the $cache->call('slowFunction', $arr) call, which has the cached version of the function call. However, the next four lines are generated by a direct call to the slowFunction() function using a different argument array. Therefore, the output of the two calls differs. If you were to make another call to showFunction() using $cache->call('slowFunction', $arr), the first set of output shown above will be returned. In other words, the cached output is returned only when calls to the cached function are made using the $cache->call() method. This enables you to make cached or uncached calls from the same script as desired.

Using PHP opcode caching techniques

So far, you have learned how you can improve your code through analysis by using benchmark techniques, and speed up your code delivery by various caching methods. However, there is another area of optimization that you can consider, which does not involve changing your code but your PHP execution environment.

Whenever a PHP script is run, it goes through parsing and opcode generation phases that are internal to PHP. You can use tools that optimize and even cache opcode of your scripts so that they do not go through the same parsing and opcode generation steps, which are the slowest.

Of course just reading the code off the disk also creates quite a bit of over-head.

The following sections describe alternatives to the available opcode caching solutions.

Alternative PHP Opcode cache

The Alternative PHP opcode Cache (APC) is open-source software that you can download as source distribution from `http://apc.communityconnect.com`.

The APC cache stores parsed, PHP opcode in shared memory (using either System V shared memory or memory-mapped files). When APC detects a request for a cached script, it reads the previously compiled opcode instead of going through the file load, parsing, and opcode generation process, as performed for noncached scripts.

The APC cache is available in two implementations: shared memory (shm) and a memory-mapped file (mmap). The shared memory implementation is more suitable, as it does not use a file handle per cached object per Web server process.

When APC caches a script, it keeps serving the cached version for all future requests unless the cache is manually reset using the `apc_reset_cache` command or the `apc_rm filename` command to expire the specific cache for the given file name. However, you can configure APC to reload a script upon modification if APC detects apc.check_mtime =1 in the php.ini configuration file.

APC has been known to work under PHP 4.0.3 or later versions, and currently compiles under Linux and FreeBSD. The developers claim a 50 percent to 400 per-cent increase in performance of scripts under their test conditions or production environment.

Note that the code is still being executed on each hit so you never get stale pages or data.

PHPA: the PHP Accelerator

This is also a very popular, free PHP opcode cache that features a built-in code optimizer as well. You can download PHPA from `http://www.php-accelerator.co.uk/`.

The PHPA does not currently have an official license to make it free. In addition, the source code is not yet released; therefore, be aware of these facts, as
they might (or might not) become a restriction for commercial use in the
future.

PHPA is currently available for Linux, FreeBSD, OpenBSD, BSDi, and Solaris.

Zend Tools for optimization and caching opcode

As the developer of the Zend opcode engine used in PHP, Zend has an edge
over other open-source or commercial efforts in building PHP-friendly, high-
performance tools. The commercial tools available from `http://www.zend.com` are
often the current state-of-the-art in PHP and therefore worth a look if you have the
budget for it.

Summary

In this chapter, you learned how to benchmark, stress-test, and improve your PHP
applications for speed. You also learned how to buffer output, how to compress
output, and how to cache output for faster response time. Finally, you learned
about tools that can optimize PHP itself.

Chapter 22

Securing PHP Applications

IN THIS CHAPTER

◆ Protecting your application-related files

◆ Controlling access to your applications

◆ Using MD5-based login

◆ Using MD5 encoding in your PHP application

◆ How to securely upload files

◆ Running PHP in safe mode

THIS CHAPTER DISCUSSES A SET of security issues that you should know about when deploying your applications in the real world. Here I will discuss how you can control access to your applications and related files, which is a big step in ensuring security. When you write applications there are various reasons for not allowing everyone access to your applications. This can be because of the fact that the application is needed for internal business or for external partners or customers or anyone. For example, a Web application that allows you to access your corporate e-mail from the Internet should have restricted access control vs. a Web application that allows potential customers to generate an automated quotation request or response for your products and services. This chapter will show you how to control access to applications that are not to be used by the masses but rather a defined set of users or systems.

Controlling Access to Your PHP Applications

When you deploy your application on the Web, it becomes available to everyone. Malicious hackers will try to find holes in your application to attack your data, your site, other sites, or all of the above. Therefore, you must take all the precautions necessary to ensure that all known risks are minimized or eliminated. This section describes how to control access to your application and related files using various Web server configurations. It is assumed that you are using Apache or an Apache-like Web server (such as Zeus).

Restricting access to your PHP application-related files

When you create a large PHP application, many files might contain sensitive information. For example, the configuration files used in many of the applications in this book contain database connection information, paths, and so on, that are sensitive. You need to protect these files from visibility on the Web. You have two ways in which you can do so.

Keep sensitive files outside your Web document tree

This method requires that you keep your sensitive files in directories outside the Web directory tree and access them with explicit paths. For example:

```
require_once 'app_name.conf';
```

can be changed to

```
require_once "/path/not/inside/docroot/app_name.conf";
```

Make it impossible to retrieve files with certain extensions

If you are using Apache or an Apache-like Web server such as Zeus, you can restrict access to configuration files or any other files using Web server configuration directives. For example, if your Web site supports the use of .htaccess files that contain per-directory configuration information, you can create an .htaccess file in the top directory of your Web site as follows:

```
# for .htaccess
<Files "*.conf">
   Order deny,allow
   Deny all
</Files>
```

This ensures that whenever your Apache server gets a request for a file that ends with a .conf extension, it denies access to that file. If you have access to the primary Apache server configuration file, httpd.conf, you can create a global configuration such as the following, which applies to all Web sites served by the Apache server:

```
# for httpd.conf
<Directory />
   <Files "*.conf">
     Order deny,allow
     Deny all
   </Files>
</Directory>
```

This tells Apache that it cannot serve any files with .conf extensions from any directories within the Web document root (pointed to by the `DocumentRoot` directive).

Using Web server–based authentication

Often, you will find it necessary to restrict access to your Web applications. In such cases, you can use your Web server's basic authentication scheme quite easily. For example, to require user authentication for an application stored in `http://yours-erver/yourapp/`, you can create or edit the following .htaccess file in the %DocumentRoot%/yourapp directory:

```
AuthType Basic
AuthName "Restricted Access"
AuthUserFile /path/to/yourapp.users
Require valid-user
```

You can also put the preceding configuration in your httpd.conf file using a `Location` container, as shown here:

```
<Location "/your_app/">
   AuthType Basic
   AuthName "Restricted Access"
   AuthUserFile /path/to/yourapp.users
   Require valid-user
</Location>
```

Don't forget to change your_app and /path/to/yourapp.users with the appropriate directory and file names.

Once you have created this configuration, you need to use Apache's htpasswd utility to create users. For example, to create a user called joegunchy, you can run the following:

```
htpasswd -c /path/to/yourapp.users joegunchy
```

If htpasswd is not in your path, you need to provide the path name. For example, if you store htpasswd in /usr/local/apache/bin, you can run the following:

```
/usr/local/apache/bin/htpasswd -c /path/to/yourapp.users joegunchy
```

 Creating a subsequent user does not require the `-c` option. Use this option only for the first user. In addition, make sure that the /path/to/yourapp.users file is accessible by the Apache Web server.

When creating a user, you will be asked to enter a new password for the user. Enter the desired password and try to access your application via `http://yourserver/yourapp/`. You will be promoted for a username and password. Use the newly created username and password to log in and access your application.

If you need to know the username in your PHP application, use the `$_SERVER['REMOTE_USER']` value, as shown in the following example:

```php
<?php

    $thisUser = $_SERVER['REMOTE_USER'];

    if (empty($thisUser))
    {
        // Your Web server authentication is
        // not working.
        exit;
    }

    echo "Hello $thisUser";

?>
```

When this script is accessed from a Web server–authenticated directory, the script will contain the username that successfully logged in. You can also use $_SERVER['PHP_AUTH_USER'] in place of $_SERVER['REMOTE_USER'].

 One of the problems with Web server authentication is that you have no way to log out the user by force. The Web browser always resends the authentication credentials (username/password) upon each request, and therefore the Web server keeps re-authenticating the user. If you need to allow logout, you should use application-level authentication, as discussed in Chapters 4 and 5 of this book.

Using the MD5 message digest for login

When you use a Web-based login form to log in a user, the username and password are transmitted as plain text. This is a major weakness if high security is desired. Unfortunately, because PHP cannot be implemented on the client side, there is no PHP solution that you can use to turn the plain-text data into encrypted or encoded form.

The best alternative for a high-grade Web login solution is to use a Secure Socket Layer (SSL)-based Web server, which encrypts all communication between the client and the server. In the absence of that, you can consider the following solution.

The client-side scripting language JavaScript provides a solution. You can use JavaScript to create a MD5 message digest of the password and transmit only the digest, rather than the real password. This means that the user's password never travels over the network.

On the server side, you can use a PHP script to compare the user-supplied MD5 of a password with the user's real password's MD5 digest. If both digests match, you have a user that knows his or her password and therefore should be given access.

Now let's look at this process using an example. Listing 22-1 shows a Web form with two JavaScripts. The first script simply loads an external JavaScript MD5 library called md5.js. You can also download it from the Internet via http://www.publicator.no/includes/script/md5.js.

Listing 22-1: md5_login.html

```html
<html>
<head>
<script language="JavaScript" src="md5.js"></script>

<script language="JavaScript">

function processForm() {
    document.loginForm.password.value =
    MD5(document.loginForm.password.value);

    document.loginForm.submit();
}

</script>
</head>
<body>

<center>
<form name="loginForm" method="post" action="md5_login.php">

<table border=0 cellpadding=3 cellspacing=0>
<tr>
<td> Name </td>
<td> <input type="text" name="username" size="10"> </td>
</tr>

<tr>
<td> Password </td>
<td> <input type="password" name="password" size="15" ></td>
</tr>
```

```
<tr>
<td colspan=2>
<input onclick="processForm(); return true;"
       type="button" value="Login">
</td>
</tr>
</table>

</form>
</center>

</body>
</html>
```

The second JavaScript has a single function called processForm(). This function is called when the login form's Login button is clicked. This function creates an MD5 digest of the user-supplied password and replaces the password value with the MD5 digest, and then submits the data to the md5_login.php PHP script, shown in Listing 22-2.

Listing 22-2: md5_login.php

```
<?php

    error_reporting(E_ALL);

    define('PASSWORD', '2manysecrets');

    $user = (! empty($_REQUEST['username'])) ? $_REQUEST['username'] : null;

    $givenMD5Hash = (! empty($_REQUEST['password'])) ? $_REQUEST['password'] :
null;

    // If user given MD5 of password does not match
    // with the md5(PASSWORD) then redirect
    // user to login page again

    if (strcmp($givenMD5Hash , md5(PASSWORD)))
    {
        header("Location: md5_login.html");

    }

    // User knows password so login successful
    echo "Welcome to PHP.";

?>
```

This PHP script creates an MD5 digest of the real password stored as a constant called PASSWORD and compares it against the user-supplied MD5 digest of the password. If they do not match, the user is redirected to the md5_login.html page. Otherwise, a welcome message is shown. Note that the password is hard-coded in the example code for demonstration only. In real application, the password will be stored in a database.

As the real password never travels the network, this method of login is more secure, as guessing the original password for an MD5 digest is very difficult.

Using Web server–based authorization

If you must limit the network or IP address from which users can access your application, you can create an .htaccess conf configuration as follows:

```
Order deny,allow
Deny all
Allow from 192.168.
```

You can also put this in your httpd.conf file by putting the preceding configuration in a directory container, as shown here:

```
<Directory "/path/to/your_app">
   Order deny,allow
   Deny all
   Allow from 192.168.
</Directory>
```

If you want to use the Location container, you can use a relative path:

```
<Location "/your_app">
   Order deny,allow
   Deny all
   Allow from 192.168.
</Location>
```

In any of the preceding three cases, all access to the /your_app directory under the Web document root is restricted to hosts with IP addresses that belong to 192.168.x.x networks. In other words, an IP address such as 192.168.0.1 or 192.168.254.1 can access the application. You can allow specific IP addresses as well, as shown in the following example:

```
<Location "/your_app">
   Order deny,allow
   Deny all
   Allow from 192.168.1.100 130.86.1.2
</Location>
```

In the preceding example, access is restricted to only the two named IP addresses.

If you want to exclude a particular IP or network, simply use Deny from, as shown here:

```
<Location "/your_app">
   Order allow,deny
   Deny from 130.86.
   Allow all
</Location>
```

Your Web application always has access to the user's IP address as $_SERVER['REMOTE_ADDR']. However, note that a block of users can have the same IP address if their requests are sent via a caching proxy server.

Restricting write access to directories

When your PHP applications need to write to a certain directory, be very careful about the directory permissions. Your PHP applications typically run as the Web server, so you must allow it to write to the directory in which you want to allow your application to create new files or update existing ones. Never make your directories world readable. In other words, never run commands such as chmod -R 777 on a directory that is accessible via the Web or your applications.

Securely Uploading Files

PHP makes uploading files easy, but with ease comes danger. Let's look at a simple scenario. Listing 22-3 shows a simple file upload form that calls bad_upload.html script to upload a file. The uploaded file is processed by a script called bad_uploader.php.

Listing 22-3: bad_upload.html

```
<html>
<head><title>Upload Form Using Bad Uploader Script</title>
<body>
<form method="POST"  enctype="multipart/form-data"
action="bad_uploader.php">
File: <input type="file" name="picfile">
<input type=submit value="Upload Picture">
</form>
</body>
</html>
```

The bad_uploader.php, shown in Listing 22-4, copies the Web browser–uploaded file to a directory called images. Before copying the uploaded temporary file (which is created automatically by PHP) to the images directory, it checks whether the file size is less than five thousands bytes, and whether the file is a GIF image or not. When both of these conditions are met, the file is copied to the images directory. Otherwise, it displays a message stating that the upload was unsuccessful.

Listing 22-4: bad_uploader.php

```php
<?php

    // This script will not work
    // if register_globals is OFF
    // This is here to make a point only

    define('MAX_FILE_SIZE', 5000);
    define('FILE_TYPE', 'image/gif');

    echo "File name : $picfile_name <br>";
    echo "File size : $picfile_size <br>";
    echo "File type : $picfile_type <br>";

    if ( ($picfile_size < MAX_FILE_SIZE) &&
         ($picfile_type == FILE_TYPE))
    {
        copy($picfile, "images/$picfile_name");

    } else {
        echo "Your file $picfile_name was not uploaded. <br>";
    }
?>
```

The Web form in Listing 22-4 has a file field called picfile. When processed by PHP, it creates `$picfile_name` as the file name, `$picfile_size` as the size of the file, and `$picfile_type` as the file's MIME type. The script uses these variables to perform its job. For many programmers, there is nothing wrong with the way the preceding script works. However, consider the Web form, hacked_bad_upload_ form.html, shown in Listing 22-5.

Listing 22-5: hacked_bad_upload_form.html

```html
<html>
<head><title>Hacker's Upload Form Attacking Bad Uploader
Script</title>
<body>
```

Continued

Listing 22-5 *(Continued)*

```
<form method="POST" enctype="multipart/form-data"
action="bad_uploader.php">
File: <input type="file" name="picfile">
<input type=hidden name="picfile_size" value="1">
<input type=submit value="Upload Picture">
</form>
</body>
</html>
```

A malicious hacker can easily create a Web form duplicating the bad_upload.html form, adding additional hidden fields, such as picfile_size=1 to populate the value for PHP's automatic variable $picfile_size to bypass the size requirements. This means that a hacker can upload a large file and thus take up huge amounts of disk space using this trick.

To prevent this problem, a better version of bad_uploader.php can be written as shown in Listing 22-6.

Listing 22-6: good_uploader.php

```php
<?php

    error_reporting(E_ALL);

    define('MAX_FILE_SIZE', 5000);
    define('FILE_TYPE', 'image/gif');


    // Get file name from the $_FILES array
    $picfile_name = (! empty($_FILES['picfile']['name'])) ?
                    $_FILES['picfile']['name'] : null;

    // Get file type from the $_FILES array
    $picfile_type = (! empty($_FILES['picfile']['type'])) ?
                    $_FILES['picfile']['name'] : null;

    // Get file size from the $_FILES array
    $picfile_size = (! empty($_FILES['picfile']['size'])) ?
                    $_FILES['picfile']['name'] : null;

    // Get temp file from the $_FILES array
    $tmp_picfile = (! empty($_FILES['picfile']['tmp_name'])) ?
                    $_FILES['picfile']['tmp_name'] : null;

    echo "File name : $picfile_name <br>";
    echo "File size : $picfile_size <br>";
    echo "File type : $picfile_type <br>";
```

```
    if ( ($picfile_size < MAX_FILE_SIZE) &&
        ($picfile_type == FILE_TYPE))
    {
       move_uploaded_file($tmp_picfile,
                           "images/$picfile_name");
    } else {

       echo "Your file $picfile_name was not uploaded. <br>";

    }

?>
```

The difference between good_uploader.php and bad_uploader.php is that the good script does not rely on PHP's automatic variables, instead using a $_FILES superglobal associative array, which ensures that malicious users cannot extract file-related information from the Web form.

Therefore, when dealing with uploads, make sure you use a $_FILES associative array for file information and do not rely on automatically created variables.

Using Safe Database Access

When using user data in a database query, always be careful, as a user might supply SQL commands to engage in unwanted activities, such as creating an account in your database or running an external program. User input validation is the key to avoiding most security issues. For example:

```
$stmt = "SELECT * FROM YOUR_TBL WHERE USER_ID > $where";
```
if the $where variable is created using $_REQUEST['where'] than a malicious user can get information from database that should not be available to him. For example:

```
http://phpbook.evoknow.com/ch22/bad_sql.php?where=a;select+count(USE
R_ID)+from+YOUR_TBL;
```

The above request makes the $stmt become:

```
SELECT * FROM YOUR_TBL WHERE USER_ID > a;select count(USER_ID) from
YOUR_TBL;
```

As you can see the user has tricked the script to give count of data in YOUR_TBL. Therefore you should ensure that direct user input is not used in SQL statements. Furthermore, when writing text data to a database, use the addslashes() function to quote data.

Recommended php.ini Settings for a Production Environment

When using PHP in a production environment, you should have the following settings in php.ini:

```
register_globals off
```

The preceding line will disable automatic variable creation. This means that all PHP script must use the $_REQUEST, $_GET, or $_POST superglobal associative arrays to retrieve user-provided data via GET/POST, GET, or POST, respectively.

When working on production server you should disable PHP error messages display so that malicious hackers do not learn about your system environment from badly written scripts.

```
display_errors off
```

The preceding line will disable the displaying of error messages onscreen. This is very important, as PHP error messages might reveal information that should not be shown to potential hackers. However, the following two settings will ensure that errors are logged in a safe log file called /var/log/php.errors:

```
log_errors on
```

```
error_log /var/log/php.errors
```

You should also consider using the set_error_handler function found in PHP. You can learn more about it at http://www.php.net/set_error_handler.

Limiting File System Access for PHP Scripts

If you do not want to allow a PHP application to access any file on your file system, you can control it using the open_basedir configuration option. For example, suppose you want to prevent an Apache-run virtual host called www.myvirtualhost.com from accessing any files beyond its document root tree using PHP. You can have a configuration such as the following:

```
<VirtualHost www.myvirtualhost.com>

  ServerName www.myvirtualhost.com
  DocumentRoot /www/my/htdocs
```

```
<Directory />
    php_admin_value open_basedir "/www/my/htdocs"
  </Directory>

</VirtualHost>
```

The preceding configuration restricts any PHP script in www.myvirtualhost.com from accessing any file outside the /www/my/htdocs directory.

 If a symbolic link is encountered by a PHP script that leads to a file or directory outside the specified open_basedir, PHP will refuse to access it.

In addition, if you wish to restrict the PHP include path, you can define the include path in the httpd.conf file. For example, if we want to limit the include path for www.myvirtualhost.com to be the current directory of the script and to /usr/local/lib/php, we can add the following line to the virtual host configuration after the DocumentRoot directive:

```
php_value include_path ".:/usr/local/lib/php"
```

Running PHP Applications in Safe Mode

PHP provides a mode called *safe mode,* which enables you to restrict how PHP works with user scripts. Safe mode can be turned on for virtual hosts in Apache configuration.

Here, www.myvirtualhost.com runs PHP in safe mode due to the php_admin_flag settings that enable safe_mode. The preceding configuration also prevents PHP from accessing any file beyond the specified document root (/www/my/htdocs). For example:

```
<VirtualHost www.myvirtualhost.com>

  ServerName www.myvirtualhost.com
  DocumentRoot /www/my/htdocs

  php_admin_flag safe_mode on

  <Directory />
```

```
        php_admin_value open_basedir "/www/my/htdocs"
    </Directory>
```

```
</VirtualHost>
```

In safe mode, you can limit sensitive configurations. For example, if you wanted users of www.myvirtualhost.com to only be able to run external programs (via system calls) from a directory called /www/my/safe/bin, then you can use the following:

```
php_admin_value safe_mode_exec_dir "/www/my/safe/bin"
```

You can also limit how much memory a PHP script can use:

```
php_admin_value memory_limit = 8388608
```

The preceding line of code limits any PHP script to 8 MB of RAM. Similarly, you can limit how long a PHP script can run:

```
php_admin_value max_execution_time = 30
```

The preceding line limits all PHP scripts to 30 seconds of execution time.

You can disable security-sensitive functions such as system(), readfile(), and so on, as follows:

```
php_admin_value disable_functions system:readfile
```

Summary

In this chapter, you learned various methods of securing your PHP environment. You learned that using Apache configuration you can restrict access to sensitive files containing PHP configuration. You can use Apache Web server's built-in authentication along with PHP to allow users access to your applications. Similarly, you can use Apache's authorization configuration to control which host name or IP address can access any of your applications. You also learned that using PHP configuration parameters you can control how it behaves.

Part VII

Appendixes

Appendix A

What's on the CD-ROM

THIS APPENDIX CONTAINS INFORMATION about the contents of the CD that accompanies this book. For the latest and greatest information, please refer to the ReadMe file located at the root of the CD. Here is what you will find:

- ◆ System Requirements
- ◆ What's on the CD
- ◆ Troubleshooting

System Requirements

Make sure that your computer meets the minimum system requirements listed in this section. If your computer doesn't meet most of these requirements, you may have a problem using the contents of the CD.

- ◆ A PC with a Pentium processor running at 266 MHz or faster
- ◆ At least 32MB of total RAM; for best performance, we recommend at least 256MB
- ◆ An Ethernet network interface card (NIC)
- ◆ A CD-ROM drive
- ◆ A high-speed Internet connection if you wish to serve requests from the Internet

What's on the CD

The following sections provide a summary of the software and other materials you'll find on the CD.

Author-created materials

All author-created material from the book, including code listings and samples, are on the CD. Each chapter's files are stored in the ch*XX* directory, where *XX* is a number from 01 to 22. For example, source code and other files for Chapter 20 are stored in the CH20 directory.

Each chapter has the following directory structure:

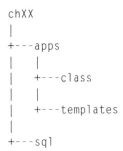

```
chXX
|
+---apps
|   |
|   +---class
|   |
|   +---templates
|
+---sql
```

The sql directory stores the SQL script needed to create any database tables. The apps directory contains the applications. The apps/class director contains the class files needed for the application. The apps/templates directory contains the HTML templates needed for the applications in the given chapter.

In addition to chapter directories, a directory called framework exists in the CD, which contains all the classes needed for all the application framework used in almost all applications in the book.

Applications

The following applications are included on the CD:

Apache Web Server
The latest version of the Apache Web server source distribution

PHP
The latest version of the PHP source distribution

PHPLIB
The latest version of the PHPLIB source distribution

MySQL
The latest version of the MySQL database server binary distribution in the RPM package

Adobe Acrobat Reader
The latest version of the Adobe Acrobat Reader used to read the Portable Document Format (PDF) files

Shareware programs are fully functional, trial versions of copyrighted programs. If you like particular programs, register with their authors for a nominal fee and receive licenses, enhanced versions, and technical support. *Freeware programs* are copyrighted games, applications, and utilities that are free for personal use. Unlike shareware, these programs do not require a fee or provide technical support. *GNU software* is governed by its own license, which is included inside the folder of the GNU product. See the GNU license for more details.

Trial, demo, or evaluation versions are usually limited by either time or functionality (such as the capability to save projects). Some trial versions are very sensitive to system date changes. If you alter your computer's date, the programs will "time out" and no longer be functional.

eBook version of Secure PHP Development

The complete text of this book is on the CD in Adobe's Portable Document Format (PDF). You can read and search through the file with the Adobe Acrobat Reader (also included on the CD).

Troubleshooting

If you have difficulty installing or using any of the materials on the companion CD, try the following solutions:

◆ **Reference the README or INSTALL file.** Please refer to the README or INSTALL file located in each source package, which is provided by the package developer.

If you still have trouble with the CD, please call the Wiley Customer Care telephone number: (800) 762-2974. Outside the United States, call 1 (317) 572-3994. You can also contact Wiley Customer Service by e-mail at techsupdum@wiley.com. Wiley Publishing, Inc. provides technical support only for installation and other general quality-control items; for technical support on the applications themselves, consult the program's vendor or author.

Appendix B

PHP Primer

THIS BOOK ASSUMES THAT READERS have PHP programming experience, and therefore does not cover the basics of PHP in any of the chapters. This appendix provides some fundamentals of PHP programming and especially object-oriented PHP development, which is used heavily throughout the book.

Object-Oriented PHP

Numerous books and publications are available that explain the benefits of object-oriented programming (OOP). Three of the main advantages include the following:

◆ Reusability of the existing code base

◆ Efficient organization

◆ Easy maintenance of the code base

By writing reusable objects, you can often reduce project development time. Moreover, using existing proven code is always a good idea in the effort to reduce bugs.

To use OOP in PHP, you define a class for your object. A skeleton of a class looks as follows:

```php
<?php

class CLASS_NAME {

    function CLASS_NAME ()
    {
        // Constructor method
    }

    function set_method_X($param = null)
    {
        // Set value
    }
```

```
function get_method_X()
{
   // Return value


}
}

?>
```

For example, if you want to develop an object called computer, you can define a class file as follows:

```
<?php

class Computer {

   function Computer($params = null)
   {
      $this->_CPU      = $params['CPU'];
      $this->_ROM      = $params['ROM'];
      $this->_RAM      = $params['RAM'];
      $this->_TYPE     = $params['TYPE'];
   }

   function getCPU()
   {
      // Return CPU
      return $this->_CPU;
   }

   function setCPU( $cpu = null)
   {
      // Set CPU
      $this->_CPU = $cpu;
   }

   function getRAM()
   {
      // Return RAM
      return $this->_RAM;
   }
```

```php
    function setRAM($ram = null)
    {
        // Set RAM
        $this->_RAM = $ram;
    }

    function getType()
    {
        return $this->_TYPE;
    }

    function setType($type = null)
    {
        // Set Type
        $this->_TYPE = $type;
    }
}

?>
```

This simple class has a set of set and get methods that retrieve or store information about the object. For cxample the `getRAM()` method returns the RAM value stored in an object's _RAM variable. Similarly, `setRAM()` sets the given RAM value (`$ram`) in an object's _RAM variable.

One special method, `Computer()` (the same name as the class), is called the *constructor*. This constructor method is automatically called whenever a new `Computer` object is created.

You can create another class by extending the `Computer` class as shown here:

```php
<?php

require_once 'class.Computer.php';

class PDA extends Computer {

    function printSpec($type = null)
    {
        echo "CPU  : " . $this->getCPU() . "<br>";
        echo "RAM  : " . $this->getRAM() . "<br>";
        echo "TYPE : " . $this->getType() . "<br>";
    }
}

?>
```

Here, the new class, PDA, extends Computer, since a PDA is a simple computer. This class simply creates a new method called printSpec() to print the computer's specifications. Now let's look at a simple application that uses the PDA class:

```php
<?php

    require_once 'class.PDA.php';

    $info['CPU']  = 'StrongArm 400 Mhz';
    $info['RAM']  = '512 GB';
    $info['TYPE'] = 'PDA';

    $myPDA = new PDA($info);

    $myPDA->printSpec();
?>
```

When run, this application prints the following:

```
CPU : StrongArm 400 Mhz
RAM : 512 GB
TYPE : PDA
```

This simple application demonstrates the power of reusable objects. Note that this application required only the PDA class, as we were interested in working only with PDA. This application creates a hash ($info) with information about the CPU, RAM, and the TYPE of the PDA, and creates a PDA object called $myPDA using the following line:

```
$myPDA = new PDA($info);
```

When the PDA object is created, PHP calls the Computer() constructor automatically, as the PDA class extends the Computer class and PDA does not have its own constructor PDA() defined. This enables the $info data to be set by the Computer's constructor method. Another way of explaining this is as follows.

When PDA object is created, PHP does not find the object's default constructor, PDA(), so it calls the constructor of the object that the PDA extends. In this case, that constructor is Computer(), and therefore the $info data is passed to the Computer() method.

Once the PDA object is created, the application calls the printSpec() method found in the PDA class to print the specification of the PDA.

Notice that our real application is very small. We simply created a printSpec() method and inherited all others from the parent class (Computer).

Now suppose we want to create another application that deals with PocketPCs. Because PocketPCs are really PDAs with specific operating system (Windows CE) requirements, we can easily inherit the PDA class and define a new class called PocketPC as follows:

```php
<?php

require_once 'class.PDA.php';

class PocketPC extends PDA {

    function printSpec($type = null)
    {
        echo "CPU  : " . $this->getCPU() . "<br>";
        echo "RAM  : " . $this->getRAM() . "<br>";
        echo "TYPE : " . $this->getType() . "<br>";
        echo "Windows CE Only System <br>";
    }
}

?>
```

In the preceding example, we have extended PDA and overridden the printSpec() method, as we want to print the fact that PocketPCs only run the Windows CE operating system. Therefore, an application such as the following can use this class:

```php
<?php

require_once 'class.PocketPC.php';

    $info['CPU']  = 'StrongArm 400 Mhz';
    $info['RAM']  = '512 GB';
    $info['TYPE'] = 'PDA';

    $myGizmo = new PocketPC($info);

    $myGizmo->printSpec();
?>
```

This will output the following:

```
CPU : StrongArm 400 Mhz
RAM : 512 GB
TYPE : PDA
Windows CE Only System
```

The classes discussed so far clearly show the power of OOP. Notice how we override the PDA's `printSpec()` method in the PocketPC class, but retain all the other benefits of the PDA, which happens to be a Computer object.

Appendix C

MySQL Primer

MYSQL IS THE MOST POPULAR open-source database in the world. Its popularity stems from the following:

◆ MySQL is free as long as you don't sell it to someone, sell a product that is bundled with it, or install and maintain it at a client site. If you're in doubt about whether you fit within the license parameters, please see the Web site at `http://www.mysql.com/`.

◆ MySQL supports many programming interfaces, including PHP, C, C++, Java, Perl, and Python. The possibilities it offers to tailor programs to fit your needs are virtually limitless.

◆ MySQL uses very fast methods of relating tables of information to one another. Using a method called a *one-sweep multijoin*, MySQL is very efficient at gathering the information you request from many different tables at once.

◆ MySQL is widely used. Chances are good that many other people have done something similar to what you are doing. If you have questions or problems, you have a wide group of people to consult. Not only can you get advice from others about what to do, you can also get valuable information about what *not* to do. This prevents you from making the same mistakes others have made.

MySQL is available all over the Internet. The best way to get MySQL is to go to `http://www.mysql.com/` and find a mirror site close to you. You can find out how to install MySQL on a Linux platform in Appendix D.

Using MySQL from the Command-Line

You can start the MySQL client program by typing the following:

```
mysql -u username -p
```

In this example, username is the username you are using to access the SQL server. If a password is required, you are prompted for it. You should now see something like the following:

```
Welcome to the MySQL monitor.  Commands end with ; or \g.
Your MySQL connection id is 143 to server version: 3.23.52
Type 'help;' or '\h' for help. Type '\c' to clear the buffer.
mysql>
```

Creating a database

When you install MySQL, you have no data. In fact, you don't even have a database defined, other than the ones provided by MySQL itself.   In this section, we will create a database called store. The syntax for this, at the mysql> prompt is simply

```
create database store;
```

You should get a response similar to the following:

```
Query OK, 1 row affected (0.02 sec)
```

This generic response indicates that your command has executed. You can confirm this by issuing the following command:

```
show databases;
```

 Your rights to create, change, or delete databases depends on your account and the rights associated with it. If you have root access you can (of course) do just about anything, including set parameters for other accounts. This chapter assumes that you have enough access to create and change databases. If you do have root access to MySQL, be sure to set/change the root password after installing MySQL!

If this is the first database you create, you see the following:

```
+----------+
| Database |
+----------+
| mysql    |
| test     |
| store    |
+----------+
1 row in set (0.00 sec)
```

Make sure you terminate each SQL query with a semicolon. Without a semicolon terminator, you will see another prompt line and your query will not be executed.

There it is. You now have a database named `store` that contains no data. Now it is up to you to create the tables that store the data. You need to define not only the names of all the columns, but also the types of data they store. Begin by identifying the database you're going to use by issuing the following command:

```
Use store;
```

Then issue the following command to make the first table:

```
create table customers (
   id INT AUTO_INCREMENT PRIMARY KEY,
   name CHAR(40) NOT NULL,
   address CHAR(80),
   telephone CHAR(13));
```

Let's examine each of these lines to see what it does, beginning with the first:

```
id INT AUTO_INCREMENT PRIMARY KEY,
```

This line is the meat of the table. In it, you are creating a column named `id` that holds whole numbers (`int` stands for *integer*). Additionally, this column is the primary key. A primary key provides a convenient element to access the data in an orderly fashion. For example, in our database the records will be stored with unique integers as their primary key. Later, to access a record you could use a query to specify what record(s) to return by using that key. Searching for matches with a primary key is significantly faster than other fields.

Following is the second line:

```
create table customers (
```

The preceding line tells the SQL server you are trying to create a table called customers. Following is the third line:

```
name CHAR(40) NOT NULL,
```

The preceding line creates a column named name that contains 40 characters of data per item. Additionally, it specifies that this column can never be null, or without data. Following is the fourth line:

```
address CHAR(80),
```

The preceding line creates a column called address that holds 80 characters of data per item. Following is the fifth line:

```
telephone CHAR(13));
```

The preceding line creates a column called telephone that holds 13 characters. This is set up as a character field instead of a numeric field because you would rarely, if ever, need to add telephone numbers or perform mathematical functions with them. You can just treat the telephone number as you would any other character data. Moreover, this makes it easier to deal with the dashes people put in telephone numbers.

Listing tables in a database

To see a list of tables in a database, you can run the following command:

```
show tables;
```

This command is run from the MySQL command-line client. Make sure you run this command after you have run the use command to change to the database. For example:

```
mysql> use store;
mysql> show tables;
```

The preceding commands display the following:

```
mysql> show tables;
+----------------+
| Tables_in_store |
+----------------+
| customers      |
+----------------+
1 row in set (0.00 sec)
```

Viewing table descriptions

To find out information about a table, run the following command:

```
desc table_name;
```

For example:

```
mysql> use store;
mysql> desc customers;
```

The preceding commands display the following:

```
+-----------+----------+------+-----+---------+----------------+
| Field     | Type     | Null | Key | Default | Extra          |
+-----------+----------+------+-----+---------+----------------+
| name      | char(40) |      |     |         |                |
| address   | char(80) | YES  |     | NULL    |                |
| telephone | char(13) | YES  |     | NULL    |                |
| id        | int(11)  |      | PRI | NULL    | auto_increment |
+-----------+----------+------+-----+---------+----------------+
4 rows in set (0.00 sec)
```

Inserting data into a database

To insert data in a table, you need to know the field names and their types, and then use the INSERT statement. Use the desc table_name command to find this information, and then you can run the following:

```
insert into table_name (comma separated field list)
         values(properly quoted and comma separated value list);
```

For example, to add data to the customers table in the store database, you can run the following:

```
mysql> insert into customers (name,address,telephone)
values('Mohammed Kabir','2904 Wead Way, Sacramento, CA 95833',
'555-5555');
Query OK, 1 row affected (0.33 sec)
```

> Note that the values should be properly quoted if the values contain any characters that could confuse the statement. Such characters include the comma (","), a space (" "), a quote ("'"), etc. If you must use a quote character of any type in the data, be sure to use the opposite quote to surround the values. For example, if you use an apostrophe (which is a single-quote), surround the data with a double-quote.

The preceding command inserts a row in the customers table. Notice that we do not use the id field in the insert statement because it is set to auto_increment and therefore is automatically inserted as the next available value. Note that you do not have to ever explicitly deal with setting an auto_increment field, nor do you have to worry about multiple clients causing an error — the MySQL developers have taken care of almost any contingencies.

Querying data from a database

To find data in a table, you need to use SELECT statements, as shown here:

```
select field_list FROM table_name WHERE conditions;
```

This statement enables you to find field_list data from a table called table_name, where the data meets the given conditions. For example:

```
mysql> select name from customers where id = 1;
+----------------+
| name           |
+----------------+
| Mohammed Kabir |
+----------------+
1 row in set (0.01 sec)
```

In the preceding example, the record matching ID = 1 condition is returned from the customers table. Another example is as follows:

```
mysql> select * from customers;
+----------------+------------------------------------------+-----------
+----+
| name           | address                                  | telephone |
id |
+----------------+------------------------------------------+-----------
+----+
| Mohammed Kabir | 2904 Wead Way, Sacramento, CA 95833 | 555-5555  |
1 |
| Sheila Kabir   | 2904 Wead Way, Sacramento, CA 95833 | 555-5555  |
2 |
+----------------+------------------------------------------+-----------
+----+
2 rows in set (0.01 sec)
```

Here, the field_list is set to the asterisk (*), to indicate all data. Because this statement did not use any conditions, all records were returned. (The "Sheila" data was not explicitly entered in this chapter, but is shown to further this example.)

You can also limit the number of records returned in a query:

```
mysql> select * from customers limit 3;
+----------------+------------------------------------------+-----------
+----+
| name           | address                                  | telephone |
id |
+----------------+------------------------------------------+-----------
+----+
| Mohammed Kabir | 2904 Wead Way, Sacramento, CA 95833 | 555-5555  |
1 |
| Sheila Kabir   | 2904 Wead Way, Sacramento, CA 95833 | 555-5555  |
2 |
| Joe Public     | 6000 J St, Sacramento, CA 95822      | 555-5555  |
3 |
+----------------+------------------------------------------+-----------
+----+
3 rows in set (0.00 sec)
```

Here, only three records were returned from the query results because of the given LIMIT condition. (Again, the extra data is implicitly added for this example.)

Limit actually takes an optional second argument, an offset for the record to start with. For example, if you specify LIMIT 10,3 in a SELECT statement, the data returned will start with the tenth record of the return set and return only three records from there. This option can be used to step through data an arbitrary number of records at a time—supposing that you uniquely order the data with each SELECT.

Updating data in a database

To update a record in a table within a database, you need to use the UPDATE statement, as shown in the following example:

```
UPDATE table_name SET field=value list WHERE condition;
```

This statement will update records in a table that matches the given condition. Only the given fields in the field=value list will be updated with new values. For example:

```
mysql> update customers set telephone = '555-444' where ID = 1;
Query OK, 1 row affected (0.32 sec)
Rows matched: 1  Changed: 1  Warnings: 0
```

Note the use of the WHERE clause. This clause specifies how to select the records to update and is usually a field (or two) and data to match. Here, the record #1 is updated with a new telephone number. Forgetting to use a condition will update all records!

Removing data from a database

To remove records from a table, you can use the DELETE statement, as shown in the following example:

```
DELETE from table_name WHERE condition;
```

This statement will delete all rows that match the given condition, as shown here:

```
mysql> delete from customers where ID > 1;
Query OK, 4 rows affected (0.01 sec)
```

Here, all records with an ID greater than 1 are deleted from the table. Use the DELETE statement very carefully, as you cannot undo a delete operation. If you don't use a WHERE clause you risk deleting all records!

Using phpMyAdmin to Manage MySQL Database

Managing MySQL databases via the command line is simple but often cumbersome for people new to SQL syntax. There is an easier way to manage MySQL, and it involves PHP. An open-source PHP tool called phpMyAdmin enables you to manage MySQL databases via the Web. This tool makes it very easy to manage a MySQL database without knowing a great deal about SQL syntax. It can perform all of the following database operations:

◆ Create and drop databases

◆ Create, copy, drop, and alter tables

◆ Delete, edit, and add fields

◆ Execute any SQL statement, even batch queries

◆ Manage keys on fields

◆ Load text files into tables

◆ Create and read dumps of tables

◆ Export and import CSV data

◆ Administer databases

Installing and configuring phpMyAdmin

To install and configure phpMyAdmin, do the following:

1. Download and extract the latest version of phpMyAdmin from `http://www.phpmyadmin.net` to a directory of your choice, preferably one under your Web server's document root directory.

2. Read the installation notes in the Documentation.txt file–specific installation instructions.

3. Typically, installation and configuration simply involves editing config.inc.php for your site-specific requirements, such as database host name, username and password, installed directory URL, and so on. For example:

```
$cfg['Servers'][$i]['host']        = 'localhost';
$cfg['Servers'][$i]['auth_type']   = 'config';
$cfg['Servers'][$i]['user']        = 'root';
$cfg['Servers'][$i]['password']    = 'foobar';
```

Configuring the preceding parameters in config.inc.php enables us to run phpMyAdmin on a Web server that also runs MySQL (hence, host is set to localhost) with the username/password pair set as root and foobar, respectively. Of course, your actual host name, username, and password parameters will be different, so you should change these accordingly.

4. Because this tool enables you to manage a database over the Web, you should restrict access to this tool so that no one else can run it without first being authorized in some manner. The simplest way to restrict access to this tool is to set up your Web server to require username/password authentication for the installed directory.

 Visit www.apache.org for more information about securing a Web site including the use of .htaccess files and configuration parameters.

Once you have configured phpMyAdmin, you can access it via the Web using http://yourserver/path/to/phpMyAdmin. You will see a welcome screen similar to what is shown in Figure C-1.

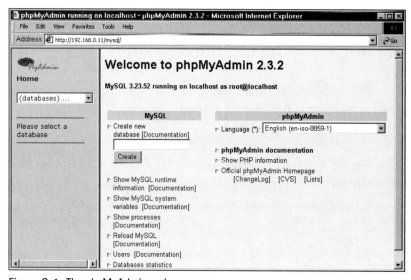

Figure C-1: The phpMyAdmin welcome screen.

Creating a database

Creating a database using phpMyAdmin is very easy. Just enter the database name in the Create New Database field and click the Create button. For example, Figure C-2 shows a newly created database called campaign.

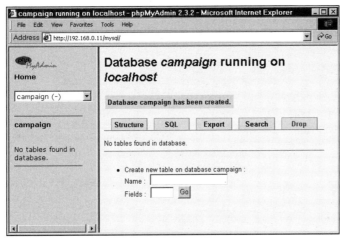

Figure C-2: The newly created database campaign.

Creating a table

Creating a table in a new or existing database is quite simple as well. Simply select the database from the database list (shown as a drop-down combo box on the left-hand side of the screen), and enter the new table name in the appropriate text box, along with number of fields in the table, as shown in Figure C-3.

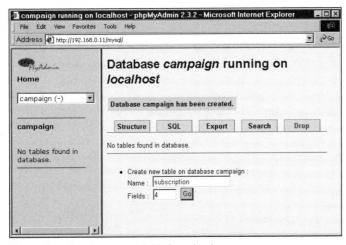

Figure C-3: Creating a new table in a database.

The example shown in Figure C-3 creates a new table called subscription with four fields. Click the Go button to start the table creation process. Now you will see a screen similar to the one shown in Figure C-4.

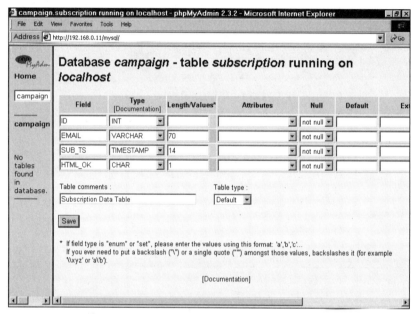

Figure C-4: Specifying fields for new table in a database.

Enter the parameters for each field name – Type, Length/Values, Attributes, Null, Default, and so on – by selecting appropriate options or entering values as needed. Figure C-4 indicates that four fields are created: an ID field as an integer (INT), an EMAIL field as a VARCHAR(70), a SUB_TS field as a TIMESTAMP(14), and an HTML_OK field as CHAR(1). You can also enter comments about the table in the appropriate text box.

Once you have configured the table fields as needed, click the Save button to save the table. You will be shown a status screen, as shown in Figure C-5.

Note that it shows the entire CREATE TABLE statement, which you can copy and store if you ever want to create this table using the command-line client.

In addition, clicking the Create PHP Code link will generate PHP code that is needed to create this table. This can also be very handy for use in configuration scripts.

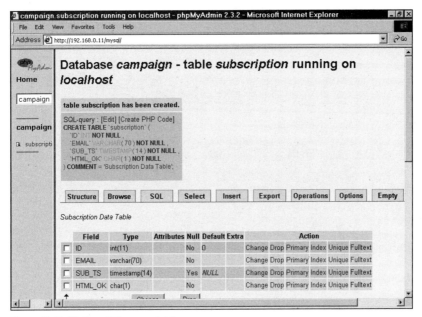

Figure C-5: Status of the new table.

Inserting data into a database

To insert new data in a table, select the database from the drop-down menu on the left side. Click on the table name as it appears on the left-hand side of the screen under the database name. For example, to add a new row in the subscription table in the campaign database, we can select campaign from the drop-down list and then click on subscription table, which displays the screen shown in Figure C-6.

Click the Insert link below the database name. This will bring up the actual insert form into which you can insert data. For our sample case, this form looks like the one shown in Figure C-7.

Figure C-7 shows that we entered 1 as the ID field value, kabir@evoknow.com as the EMAIL field value, the function NOW as the value for SUB_TS (timestamp), and 'Y' for the value of the HTML_OK field.

To submit the new data for this table, click the Go button. However, if you wish to add more records, you can select the *Insert another new row* option so that this form will be returned after the new data in entered. This saves some mouse clicks.

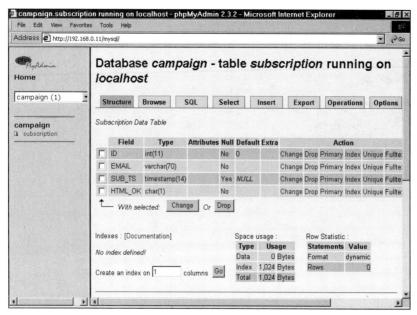

Figure C-6: Adding new rows to the database.

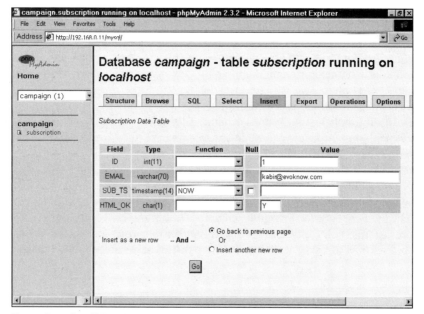

Figure C-7: Specifying data for new rows in the database.

Querying data from a database

To query data in a table, you can select the database and the table from the left-hand side of the screen as discussed before. Once you have selected the table, you can click the Browse button to view available data.

You can also click the SELECT link to define a `SELECT` query. For example, Figure C-8 shows that we are querying the subscription table in the campaign database for all records that have EMAIL fields `LIKE %kabir%`.

The LIKE directive, in its simplest form, simply does a substring match of fields. You can use "%" for wildcards, which will match 0 or many characters. For example, `LIKE   "%kabir%"` would match `kabir@evoknow.com`, `nobody@kabir.evoknow.com`, and simply `kabir`.

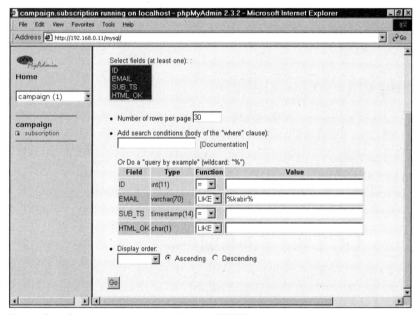

Figure C-8: Querying a database using the SELECT statement.

Define your query as needed using the conditions available. Then click the Go button to perform the query. In our sample case, the output is shown in Figure C-9. This output indicates that one record matched the query.

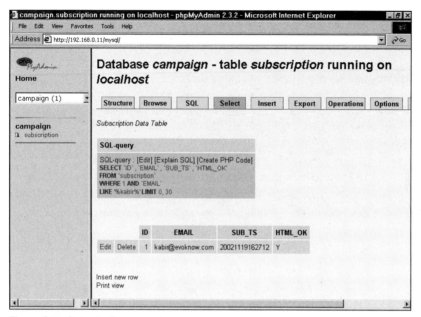

Figure C-9: Output of our sample query.

Updating data in a database

To update a record, simply query the database to locate the record or use the Browse option to find the record manually in the table. Once you have identified the record, click the Edit button to edit the data. For example, clicking the Edit button for the ouput of the last query (see Figure C-9) returns a screen similar to the one shown in Figure C-10.

Once you are done modifying the data, click the Go button to complete the update.

Removing data from a database

To remove a record, simply query the database to locate the record or use the Browse option to find the record manually in the table. Once you have identified the record, click the Delete button to delete the data. You will be alerted that you are about to perform a delete operation; select OK to delete or Cancel to abort the delete operation.

If you wish to empty the table completely, you can click the Empty link. You can also remove the table using the Drop link.

Exporting data from a database

To create an export copy of your database, you can select the database from the left menu and then click the Export link. This will show a screen similar to the one shown in Figure C-11.

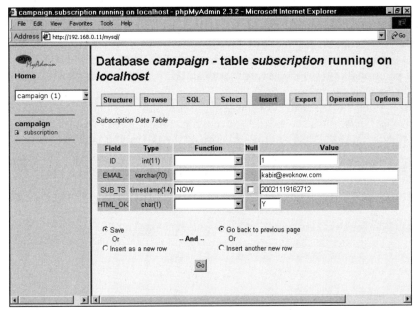

Figure C-10: Editing data from a previous query.

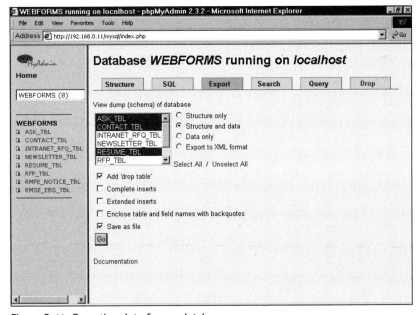

Figure C-11: Exporting data from a database.

Choose the tables you want to export. If you want to export the entire database, click Select All to select all the tables. Then choose whether you want to export both data and structure or just one of these two.

Once you have chosen the tables and what to export (data and/or structure), select any additional options that apply. For example, to export to a file, you need to select the Save as file option.

Once all options are selected, click the Go button to start the export. If you have chosen Save as file, you will be asked to save a file. Save the file in your local system. This file contains the data and/or structure of the tables you have selected.

In Figure C-11, both structure and data for three tables (ASK_TBL, CONTACT_TBL, RESUME_TBL) are selected for export from the WEBFORMS database as a file.

Appendix D

Linux Primer

LINUX IS ONE OF THE MOST POPULAR PHP platforms. This appendix describes how you can install PHP and related tools on a Linux platform.

Most people run the Apache Web server with Linux. Because Apache works very well with PHP and MySQL, it is the platform of choice for most sites. In this appendix, we will assume that you have a Red Hat Linux 8 system.

Installing and Configuring Apache 2.0

You can install Apache 2.0 either by using an RPM binary distribution or by compiling it from the source distributions. This section describes how to install Apache using both of these methods.

Installing Apache using an RPM binary

Your official Red Hat Linux distribution comes with the Apache server RPM package. You can install it using the following command:

```
rpm -ivh apache-version.i386.rpm
```

Once it is installed, you can access it from the /usr/local/apache directory.

Building a custom Apache from source

Although the official copy of Red Hat Linux comes with an RPM-packaged version of a pre-built Apache Web server, you may still want to download the latest version from the official Apache Web site at the following URL: http://www.apache.org/.

If you are not in the United States, it might be faster to get Apache source and binaries from a nearby Apache mirror site. Use the URL http://www.apache.org/dyn/closer.cgi to locate a good mirror site near you. Here we assume that you are getting the software from the official Apache Web site. The software (both source and binaries) can be found at http://www.apache.org/dist/httpd/.

You will find many recent versions of Apache distributions archived using various compression programs. For example:

```
Apache_2.0.43.tar.gz
Apache_2.0.43.tar.Z
```

These are both Apache Version 2.0.42 source distributions. They differ in size, due to differences in compression technique. Download one of these files. Regardless of which format you choose to download, you need the `tar` utility and the `gnuzip` or `gzip` utility to decompress the files. For example, to decompress the Apache `2.0.43.tar.gz` file on a Red Hat 8.0 system, use the following command:

```
tar xvzf apache_2.0.43.tar.gz
```

Alternately, you could use the following:

```
gzip -d apache_2.0.43.tar.gz
tar xvf apache_2.0.43.tar
```

These commands decompress and extract all the files in a subdirectory while keeping the relative path for each file intact.

Once you have extracted the source into a directory of your choice, you are ready to configure and compile your custom copy of Apache. You can configure Apache manually, or you can use the new Autoconf-style interface called *APACI*. We prefer the APACI method because it is quicker and requires less knowledge of Apache configuration details; in other words, you have to read fewer README and INSTALL files to get the job done.

In the top-level directory of the source distribution, you will find a script called `configure`, which is what you need for configuring Apache using APACI. You can run this script as follows:

```
./configure --help
```

This enables you to see all the available options.

The first step in configuring Apache is to determine where you want to install it. For example, to install Apache in a directory called `/usr/local/apache`, you can run the configuration script as follows:

```
./configure --prefix=/usr/local/apache
```

Apache 2.0 offers three different multiprocessing modules under Linux, each of which is described in Table D-1.

TABLE D-1 **MULTIPROCESSING MODULES UNDER LINUX**

MPM	Description
perfork	This makes Apache 2.0 behave very much like Apache 1.3.
	A parent Apache server launches an initial number of child processes. Each child process services a single request. Therefore, the maximum number of simultaneous requests that can be served is limited by the value of MaxClients directives.
	When a single child dies due to error, only a single request is lost.
worker	This MPM enables Apache to perform better with fewer resources than the perfork model.
	In this MPM model, Apache launches a set of child processes whereby each child runs ThreadsPerChild number of threads.
	Max Simultaneous Clients = MaxClients x ThreadsPerChild
	This is more scalable than the pre_fork model. However, when a single thread within a child dies, any requests serviced by the threads within that child also die along with the child. This means that if one child dies, multiple requests are lost.
perchild	In this model, Apache launches a set number of processes with a set number of threads.
	Max Simultaneous Clients =
	NumServer x MaxThreadsPerChild
	The number of child processes started depends on the value set for the NumServer directive.
	Each child process creates threads as specified in the StartThreads directive.
	Each child process maintains a pool of idle threads, ready to service requests. The number of idle threads per child process is controlled by MinSpareThreads and maxSpareThreads.

We recommend the worker model because the `perchild` MPM is still under test. You can use the worker MPM using the `--with-mpm=worker` option for the `configure` script.

Compiling and installing Apache

Compiling and installing Apache is very simple once you have run the `configure` script. Just run the `make` command from the top-level directory of your Apache source distribution. If everything goes well, you will not see any error messages. In such a case, you can install Apache by running the `make install` command. If you get error(s) when running `make`, note the error message(s) and repeat the configuration steps.

If you still have problems, go to the Apache Web site and read the FAQs to determine whether you need to do something else to get Apache running. In my experience, the standard Apache source distribution compiles on Red Hat without a single hitch. Therefore, if Apache is not working at this point, double-check your steps before you seek help from Usenet newsgroups such as `comp.infosystems.www.servers.unix` and `linux.redhat`.

Once you have compiled and installed Apache, you can run `make clean` to remove all the object files that are created during compilation.

Compiling and installing Apache support tools

When you configure Apache with the `configure` (or `config.status`) script, it automatically installs a set of support tools. You do not need to do anything extra to install any of the support tools. The only exception to this is the `logresolve.pl` Perl script, which you need to install manually. This section describes these support tools.

apachectl
Using this script, you can now control Apache. To learn about the command-line options it accepts, just run it without any command-line options or use the help option, For example, if you installed Apache in /usr/local/apache, you can run:

*/usr/local/apache/bin/*apachectl help

To start the server, run the script as follows:

*/usr/local/apache/bin/*apachectl start

To stop the server, run the script shown here:

*/usr/local/apache/bin/*apachectl stop

To restart the server, run the following:

*/usr/local/apache/bin/*apachectl restart

To test the server configuration files for syntax errors, you can run the apachectl script as follows:

*/usr/local/apache/bin/*apachectl configtest

ab
This utility enables you to run benchmarks on your Web server. Just run the program without any options to find out about the command-line options it takes.

apxs2
This utility helps in compiling modules for dynamic loading. It is not useful unless you have Dynamic Module Support (DSO) enabled on your Apache server, and your operating system supports DSO.

logresolve.pl
This Perl script is not installed automatically, but you can manually copy it to an appropriate place from the src/support directory of your Apache source distribution. This script resolves IP addresses found in an Apache log file to their host names. This script also spawns child processes and uses the parent process to provide caching support to speed up DNS lookups, which are often very slow.

logresolve
This utility works practically the same way as the logresolve.pl script. However, this executable program is installed by default. To learn about the command-line syntax, just run it with -h option.

htpasswd
This utility enables you to create username/password pairs for per-directory authentication schemes. To see the usage syntax, run the program without any arguments. Unlike the previously mentioned support tools, this utility is installed in the bin directory of your Apache server installation directory.

dbmmanage
This utility enables you to manage DBM-based username/password pairs for DBM-based authentication schemes. To see the usage syntax, run the program without any arguments. This utility also is installed in the bin directory of your Apache server installation directory.

htdigest
This utility enables you to create username/password pairs for MD5 digest-based authentication schemes. To see the usage syntax, run the program without any arguments. This utility also is installed in the bin directory of your Apache server installation directory.

Configuring Apache

By default, Apache reads a single configuration file called `httpd.conf`. Every Apache source distribution comes with a set of sample configuration files. In the standard Apache source distribution, you will find a directory called `conf`, which contains sample configuration files with the `-dist` extension.

The first step you need to take before you modify this file is to create a backup copy of the original. The `httpd.conf` file contains two types of information: comments and server directives. Lines starting with a leading # character are treated as comment lines; these comments have no purpose for the server software, but they serve as a form of documentation for the server administrator. You can add as many comments as you want; the server simply ignores all comments when it parses the file.

Except for the comments and blank lines, the server treats all other lines as either complete or partial directives. A *directive* is like a command for the server. It tells the server to perform a certain task in a particular fashion. While editing the `httpd.conf` file, you need to make certain decisions regarding how you want the server to behave. The following sections describe what these directives mean and how you can use them to customize your server.

Listing D-1 shows the default `httpd.conf` file created in the `conf` directory of your Apache installation. Most of the comments have been removed, and the code has been edited slightly for brevity.

Listing D-1: Default httpd.conf Created from httpd.conf-dist

```
ServerRoot "/usr/local/apache"

<IfModule !mpm_netware.c>
PidFile logs/httpd.pid
</IfModule>

Timeout 300
KeepAlive On
MaxKeepAliveRequests 100
KeepAliveTimeout 15

<IfModule prefork.c>
StartServers          5
MinSpareServers       5
MaxSpareServers      10
MaxClients          150
MaxRequestsPerChild   0
ServerLimit          16
</IfModule>

<IfModule worker.c>
StartServers          2
```

```
MaxClients          150
MinSpareThreads      25
MaxSpareThreads      75
ThreadsPerChild      25
MaxRequestsPerChild   0
ServerLimit          16
</IfModule>

<IfModule perchild.c>
NumServers            5
StartThreads          5
MinSpareThreads       5
MaxSpareThreads      10
MaxThreadsPerChild   20
MaxRequestsPerChild   0
ServerLimit          16
</IfModule>

Listen 80

<IfModule !mpm_winnt.c>
<IfModule !mpm_netware.c>
User nobody
Group #-1
</IfModule>
</IfModule>

ServerAdmin you@your.address

UseCanonicalName Off

DocumentRoot "/usr/local/apache/htdocs"

<Directory />
    Options FollowSymLinks
    AllowOverride None
</Directory>

<Directory "/usr/local/apache/htdocs">
    Options Indexes FollowSymLinks
    AllowOverride None
    Order allow,deny
    Allow from all
```

Continued

Listing D-1 *(Continued)*

```
</Directory>

UserDir public_html
DirectoryIndex index.html index.html.var
AccessFileName .htaccess

<Files ~ "^\.ht">
    Order allow,deny
    Deny from all
</Files>

TypesConfig conf/mime.types
DefaultType text/plain

<IfModule mod_mime_magic.c>
    MIMEMagicFile conf/magic
</IfModule>

HostnameLookups Off
ErrorLog logs/error_log
LogLevel warn
LogFormat "%h %l %u %t \"%r\" %>s %b \"%{Referer}i\" \"%{User-Agent}i\""
combined
LogFormat "%h %l %u %t \"%r\" %>s %b" common
LogFormat "%{Referer}i -> %U" referer
LogFormat "%{User-agent}i" agent
CustomLog logs/access_log combined
ServerSignature On
Alias /icons/ "/usr/local/apache/icons/"

<Directory "/usr/local/apache/icons">
    Options Indexes MultiViews
    AllowOverride None
    Order allow,deny
    Allow from all
</Directory>

Alias /manual "/usr/local/apache/manual"

<Directory "/usr/local/apache/manual">
    Options Indexes FollowSymLinks MultiViews IncludesNoExec
    AddOutputFilter Includes html
    AllowOverride None
```

```
    Order allow,deny
    Allow from all
</Directory>

ScriptAlias /cgi-bin/ "/usr/local/apache/cgi-bin/"

<IfModule mod_cgid.c>
</IfModule>

<Directory "/usr/local/apache/cgi-bin">
    AllowOverride None
    Options None
    Order allow,deny
    Allow from all
</Directory>

IndexOptions FancyIndexing VersionSort

AddIconByEncoding (CMP,/icons/compressed.gif) x-compress x-gzip
AddIconByType (TXT,/icons/text.gif) text/*
AddIconByType (IMG,/icons/image2.gif) image/*

AddIcon /icons/binary.gif .bin .exe
AddIcon /icons/binhex.gif .hqx
# Many AddIcon directives are removed
# to keep the listing short

DefaultIcon /icons/unknown.gif
ReadmeName README.html
HeaderName HEADER.html

IndexIgnore .??* *~ *# HEADER* README* RCS CVS *,v *,t

AddEncoding x-compress Z
AddEncoding x-gzip gz tgz

AddLanguage en .en
AddLanguage fr .fr
AddLanguage de .de
# Other AddLanguage directives are removed
# to keep the listing short

LanguagePriority en da nl et fr de el it ja ko no pl pt pt-br ltz ca es sv tw
ForceLanguagePriority Prefer Fallback
```

Continued

Listing D-1 *(Continued)*

```
AddDefaultCharset ISO-8859-1
AddCharset ISO-8859-1  .iso8859-1  .latin1
AddCharset ISO-8859-2  .iso8859-2  .latin2 .cen
# Other AddCharset removed to reduce the size
# of this listing

AddType application/x-tar .tgz
AddHandler type-map var

<IfModule mod_negotiation.c>
<IfModule mod_include.c>
    Alias /error/ "/usr/local/apache/error/"

    <Directory "/usr/local/apache/error">
        AllowOverride None
        Options IncludesNoExec
        AddOutputFilter Includes html
        AddHandler type-map var
        Order allow,deny
        Allow from all
        LanguagePriority en es de fr
        ForceLanguagePriority Prefer Fallback
    </Directory>

    ErrorDocument 400 /error/HTTP_BAD_REQUEST.html.var
    ErrorDocument 401 /error/HTTP_UNAUTHORIZED.html.var
    ErrorDocument 403 /error/HTTP_FORBIDDEN.html.var
    ErrorDocument 404 /error/HTTP_NOT_FOUND.html.var
    # Other ErrorDocument directives have been removed
    # to keep the listing short.

</IfModule>
</IfModule>

BrowserMatch "Mozilla/2" nokeepalive
BrowserMatch "MSIE 4\.0b2;" nokeepalive downgrade-1.0 force-response-1.0
BrowserMatch "RealPlayer 4\.0" force-response-1.0
# Other BrowserMatch directives have been removed
# to keep the listing short.

<IfModule mod_ssl.c>
    Include conf/ssl.conf
</IfModule>
```

Configuring the global environment for Apache

The directives discussed in this section create the global environment for the Apache server. The directives are described in the order in which they appear in the httpd.conf file.

 Whenever we refer to %directive%, we are referring to the value of the directive set in the configuration file. For example, if a directive called ServerAdmin is set to kabir@domain.com, a reference to %ServerAdmin% means "kabir@domain.com". Therefore, if we ask you to change %ServerAdmin%, you are being asked to change the e-mail address in question.

The first directive is ServerRoot, which appears as follows:

```
ServerRoot "/usr/local/apache"
```

This directive specifies the top-level directory of the Web server. The specified directory is not where you keep your Web contents. It is the directory where the Web server program (httpd) and the files/directories that control Apache are on your hard disk. It is really a directory, which normally has the following subdirectories:

```
{ServerRoot Directory}
    |
    |----bin
    |----conf
    |----htdocs
    |
    +---manual
    |       |----developer
    |       |----howto
    |       |----images
    |       |----misc
    |       |----mod
    |       |----platform
    |       |----programs
    |       |----search
    |       +----vhosts
    |
    |----icons
    |       |
    |       +---small
    |
```

```
|----logs
|----cgi-bin
+----include
```

/usr/local/apache is the parent directory for all server-related files. The default value for ServerRoot is set to whatever you choose for the --prefix option during source configuration using the configure script. By default, the make install command executed during server installation copies all the server binaries in %ServerRoot%/bin, server configuration files in %ServerRoot%/conf, and so on.

 You should change the value of this directive only if you have manually moved the entire directory from the installation location to another location. For example, if you simply run cp -r /usr/local/apache/home/ apache and want to configure the Apache server to work from the new location, you will change this directive to ServerRoot/home/apache. Note that in such a case, you must also change other direct references from /usr/local/apache to /home/apache.

Also note that whenever you see a relative directory name in the configuration file, Apache will prefix %ServerRoot% to the path to construct the actual path. You will see an example of this in the directive in the following section.

PidFile

The PidFile directive is encapsulated within an if condition by using the <IfModule . . .> container, as shown here:

```
<IfModule !mpm netware.c>
PidFile logs/httpd.pid
</IfModule>
```

This tells Apache to set the PidFile to %ServerRoot%/logs/httpd.pid file only if you have chosen a multiprocessing module (MPM) other than mpm_netware.c.

The PidFile directive sets the process ID (PID) file path. By default, it is set to logs/httpd.pid, which translates to %ServerRoot%/logs/httpd.pid (that is, /usr/local/apache/logs/httpd.pid). Whenever you want to find the PID of the main Apache process that runs as root and spawns child processes, you can run the cat %ServerRoot/logs/httpd.pid command. Don't forget to replace %ServerRoot% with an appropriate value.

If you change the %PidFile% value to point to a different location, make sure the directory in which the httpd.pid file resides is not writable by anyone but the root user, for security reasons

Timeout, KeepAlive, MaxKeepAliveRequests, and KeepAliveTimeout

Timeout sets the server timeout in seconds. The default should be left alone. The next three directives KeepAlive, MaxKeepAliveRequests, and KeepAliveTimeout are used to control the keep-alive behavior of the server.

IfModule containers

Apache will use one of three <IfModule . . .> containers depending on which MPM you chose. For example, if you configured Apache using the --with-mpm=worker, multi-threaded MPM (worker), the following <IfModule . . .> container will be used:

```
<IfModule worker.c>
StartServers          2
MaxClients          150
MinSpareThreads      25
MaxSpareThreads      75
ThreadsPerChild      25
MaxRequestsPerChild   0
ServerLimit          16
</IfModule>
```

If you kept the default prefork MPM during source configuration by using the configure script, the following <IfModule . . .> container will be used:

```
<IfModule prefork.c>
StartServers          5
MinSpareServers       5
MaxSpareServers      10
MaxClients          150
MaxRequestsPerChild   0
ServerLimit          16

</IfModule>
```

Similarly, the --with-mpm=perchild option forces Apache to use the last <IfModule . . .> container.

Because we recommend the worker MPM here, the following sections describe the directives used for this MPM.

StartServers

StartServers tells Apache to start two child servers as it starts. You can start more servers if you want, but Apache is pretty good at increasing the number of child processes as needed based on load. For that reason, changing this directive is not required.

MaxClients

In threaded (worker) MPM, this directive represents the maximum number of simultaneous threads that can be serving requests. In prefork MPM, it represents the maximum number of simultaneous processes that can be serving the requests. In worker MPM, when MaxClient is set to 150 and ThreadPerChild is set to 25, six processes are needed to service 150 simultaneous requests. If you wish to raise this limit, set ServerLimit accordingly. Suppose you want to service 400 simultaneous requests per second with 25 threads per process in worker MPM; in such a case, you need MaxClient set to 400 and ThreadPerChild set to 25, and ServerLimit = MaxClient / ThreadPerChild = 16.

MinSpareThreads

The MinSpareThreads directive specifies the minimum number of idle threads. These spare threads are used to service requests, and new spare threads are created to maintain the minimum spare thread pool size. You can leave the default settings alone.

MaxSpareThreads

The MaxSpareThreads directive specifies the maximum number of idle threads; leave the default as is. In the default threaded mode, Apache kills child processes to control minimum and maximum thread count.

ThreadsPerChild

This directive defines how many threads are created per child process.

MaxRequestPerChild

The final directive for the global environment is MaxRequestPerChild, which sets the number of requests a child process can serve before getting killed. The default value of zero makes the child process serve requests forever. We do not like to use the default value because it enables Apache processes to slowly consume large amounts of memory when a faulty mod_perl script, or even a faulty third-party Apache module, leaks memory. Thus, we prefer to set this to 30.

TIP   If you do not plan to run any third-party Apache modules or mod_perl scripts, you can keep the default or set it to a reasonable number. A setting of 30 ensures that the child process is killed after processing 30 requests. Of course, a new child process is created as needed.

Configuring the main server

The main server configuration applies to the default Web site Apache serves. This is the site that will come up when you run Apache and use the server's IP address or host name on a Web browser.

LISTEN   The first directive in this section is the `Listen` directive, which sets the TCP port that Apache listens to for connections. The default value of 80 is the standard HTTP port. If you change this to another number, such as 8080, you can access the server only using a URL such as `http://hostname:8080/`. You must specify the port number in the URL if the server runs on a nonstandard port.

There are many reasons for running Apache on nonstandard ports, but the only good one we can think of is that you do not have permission to run Apache on the standard HTTP port. As a non-root user, you can run Apache only on ports higher than 1024.

After you have decided to run Apache by using a port, you need to tell Apache what its user and group names are.

USER AND GROUP DIRECTIVES   The `User` and `Group` directives tell Apache which user (UID) and group (GID) names to use. These two directives are very important for security reasons. When the parent Web server process launches a child server process to fulfill a request, it changes the child's UID and GID according to the values set for these directives.

If the child processes are run as root user processes, a potential security hole will be opened for attack by hackers. Enabling the capability to interact with a root user process maximizes a potential breach of security in the system; hence, this is not recommended. Rather, we highly recommend that you choose to run the child server processes as a very low privileged user belonging to a very low privileged group. In most UNIX systems, the user named `nobody` (usually UID = -1) and the group named `nogroup` (usually GID = -1) are low-privileged. You should consult your `/etc/group` and `/etc/passwd` files to determine these settings.

If you plan to run the parent Web server as a nonroot (regular) user, it will not be able to change the UID and GID of child processes, because only root user processes can change the UID or GID of other processes. Therefore, if you run your parent server as the user named `ironsheik`, all child processes will have the same privileges as `ironsheik`. Similarly, whatever group ID you have also will be the group ID for the child processes.

 If you plan to use the numeric format for user and/or group ID, you need to insert a # symbol before the numeric value, which can be found in `/etc/passwd` and `/etc/group` files.

SERVERADMIN `ServerAdmin` defines the e-mail address that is shown when the server generates an error page. Set this to your e-mail address.

SERVERNAME Now you need to set the host name for the server using the `ServerName` directive. This directive is commented out by default because the Apache install cannot guess what host name to use for your system. Therefore, if the host name is called `www.domain.com`, set the `ServerName` directive accordingly.

Ensure, however, that the host name you enter here has proper domain name server records that point it to your server machine.

USECANONICALNAME The next directive is `UseCanonicalName`, which is set to On. It tells Apache to create all self-referencing URLs using `%ServerName%:%Port%` format. Leaving it on is a good idea.

DOCUMENTROOT Like all other Web servers, Apache needs to know the path of the top-level directory in which Web pages will be kept. This directory is typically called the *document root directory*. Apache provides a directive called `DocumentRoot`, which can be used to specify the path of the top-level Web directory.

This directive instructs the server to treat the supplied directory as the root directory for all documents. Consider this decision carefully. For example, if the directive is set as follows:

```
DocumentRoot /
```

Every file on the system becomes accessible by the Web server. Of course, you can protect files by providing proper file permission settings, but setting the document root to the physical root directory of your system is definitely a major security risk. Instead, you should point the document root to a specific subdirectory of your file system. If you have used the `--prefix=/usr/local/apache` option in configuring the Apache source, this directive will be as follows:

```
DocumentRoot "/usr/local/apache/htdocs"
```

Note that just because your document root points to a particular directory, this does not mean the Web server cannot access directories outside your document tree. You can easily enable it to do so by using symbolic links (with proper file permission) or by using aliases.

From an organization and security perspective, we don't recommend using a lot of symbolic links or aliases to access files and directories outside your document tree. Nonetheless, it is sometimes necessary to keep a certain type of information outside the document tree, even if you need to keep the contents of such a directory accessible to the server on a regular basis. If you have to add symbolic links to other directory locations outside the document tree, make sure that when you back up your files, your backup program backs up symbolic links properly.

DIRECTORY CONTAINER DIRECTIVES   The next set of directives are enclosed in a `<Directory . . .>` container, as shown here:

```
<Directory />
    Options FollowSymLinks
    AllowOverride None
</Directory>
```

The scope of the enclosed directives is limited to the named directory (with any subdirectories); however, you may use only directives that are allowed in a directory context.

The `Options` and the `AllowOverride` directives apply to `%DocumentRoot%`, which is the top-level directory of the main Web site. Because directives enclosed within a directory container apply to any subdirectories of the named directory, the directives apply to all directories within `%DocumentRoot%`.

The `Options` directive is set to `FollowSymLinks`, which tells Apache to allow itself to traverse any symbolic link within `%DocumentRoot%`. Because the `Options` directive is set to follow only symbolic links, no other options are available to any of the directories within `%DocumentRoot%`. Effectively, the `Options` directive is as follows:

```
Options FollowSymLinks  -ExecCGI -Includes -Indexes -MultiViews
```

The main intent here is to create a very closed server. Because only symbolic link traversal is allowed, you must explicitly enable other options as needed on a per-directory basis. This is very good thing from a security perspective. The next directory container opens up the `%DocumentRoot%` directory, as shown here:

```
<Directory "/usr/local/apache/htdocs">
    Options Indexes FollowSymLinks MultiViews
    AllowOverride None
    Order allow,deny
    Allow from all
</Directory>
```

If your %DocumentRoot% is different, change the named directory path. Here is what the preceding configuration means to Apache:

◆ The named directory and its subdirectories can be indexed. If there is an index file, it will be displayed; in the absence of an index file, the server will create a dynamic index for the directory. The Options directive specifies this.

◆ The named directory and all its subdirectories can have symbolic links that the server can follow (that is, use as a path) to access information. The Options directive also specifies this.

◆ The named directory and all its subdirectories can be part of content negotiations. The MultiViews option for the Options directive sets this. We are not a fan of this option, but do not dislike it enough to remove it. For example, when the given Options directive is enabled within the %DocumentRoot% directory as shown previously, a request for http://www.domain.com/ratecard.html can be answered by a file called ratecard.html.bak, ratecard.bak, ratecard.old, and the like if ratecard.html is missing. This may or may not be desirable.

◆ No options specified here can be overridden by a local access control file (specified by the AccessFileName directive in httpd.conf; the default is .htaccess). This is specified using the AllowOverride directive.

◆ The Allow directives are evaluated before the Deny directives. Access is denied by default. Any client that does not match an Allow directive or that does match a Deny directive is denied access to the server.

◆ Access is permitted for all.

The default settings should be sufficient.

If your server is going to be on the Internet, you may want to remove the FollowSymLinks option from the Options directive line. Leaving this option creates a potential security risk. For example, if a directory in your Web site does not have an index page, the server displays an automated index that shows any symbolic links you may have in that directory. This could cause sensitive information to be displayed or may even allow anyone to run an executable that resides in a carelessly linked directory.

USERDIR   The UserDir directive tells Apache to consider %UserDir% as document root (~username/%UserDir%) of each user Web site. This makes sense only if you have multiple users on the system and want to allow each user to have his or her own Web directory. The default setting is shown here:

```
UserDir public_html
```

This command means that if you set up your Web server's name to be www.yourcompany.com and you have two users (joe and jenny), their personal Web site URLs would be as follows:

```
http://www.yourcompany.com/~joe    Physical directory:
~joe/public_html
http://www.yourcompany.com/~jenny Physical directory:
~jenny/public_html
```

Note that on Red Hat Linux systems, the ~ (tilde) expands to a user's home directory. The directory specified by the UserDir directive resides in each user's home directory, and Apache must have read and execute permissions to read files and directories within the public_html directory. This can be accomplished using the following commands on your system:

```
chown -R <user>.<Apache server's group name>
  ~<user>/<directory assigned in UserDir>
chmod -R 2770 ~<user>/<directory assigned in UserDir>
```

For example, if the username is joe and Apache's group is called httpd, and public_html is assigned in the UserDir directive, the preceding commands will look like this:

```
chown -R joe.httpd  ~joe/public_html
chmod -R 2770 ~joe/public_html
```

The first command, chown, changes ownership of the ~joe/public_html directory (and that of all files and subdirectories within it) to joe.httpd. In other words, it gives the user joe and the group httpd full ownership of all the files and directories in the public_html directory. The next command, chmod, sets the access rights to 2770, meaning that only the user (joe) and the group (httpd) have full read, write, and execute privileges in public_html and all files and subdirectories under it. It also ensures that when a new file or subdirectory is created in the public_html directory, the newly created file has the group ID set. This enables the Web server to access the new file without the user's intervention.

TIP

If you create user accounts on your system using a script (such as the /usr/sbin/adduser script on Linux systems), you may want to incorporate the Web site creation process in this script. Just add a mkdir command to create a default public_html directory (if that's what you assign to the UserDir directive) to create the Web directory. Add the chmod and chown commands to give the Web server user permission to read and execute files and directories under this public directory.

DIRECTORYINDEX   Next, you need to configure the `DirectoryIndex` directive, which has the following syntax:

```
DirectoryIndex [filename1, filename2, filename3, ? ]
```

This directive specifies which file the Apache server should consider as the index for the directory being requested. For example, when a URL such as `www.yourcompany.com/` is requested, the Apache server determines that this is a request to access the / (document root) directory of the Web site. If the `DocumentRoot` directive is set as follows:

```
DocumentRoot "/www/www.yourcompany.com/public/htdocs"
```

the Apache server looks for a file named `/www/www.yourcompany.com/public/htdocs/index.html`; if it finds the file, Apache services the request by returning the content of the file to the requesting Web browser. If the `DirectoryIndex` is assigned `welcome.html` instead of the default `index.html`, however, the Web server will look for `/www/www.yourcompany.com/public/htdocs/welcome.html`. If the file is absent, Apache returns the directory listing by creating a dynamic HTML page.

You can specify multiple index file names in the `DirectoryIndex` directive:

```
DirectoryIndex index.html index.htm welcome.htm
```

This command tells the Web server that it should check for the existence of any of the three files, and if any one file is found, it should be returned to the requesting Web client.

Listing many files as the index may create two problems. First, the server will now have to check for the existence of many files per directory request; this could make it slower than usual. Second, having multiple files as indexes could make your site difficult to manage from an organizational point of view. If your Web site content developers use various systems to create files, however, it might be practical to keep both `index.html` and `index.htm` as index files. For example, an older Windows machine is unable to create file names with extensions longer than three characters, so a user working on such a machine may need to manually update all of the user's `index.htm` files on the Web server. Using the recommended index file names eliminates this hassle.

ACCESSFILENAME   The `AccessFileName` directive defines the name of the per-directory access control configuration file. The default name `.htaccess` has a leading period to hide the file in a normal directory listing under UNIX systems. The only reason to change the name to something else is to increase security by obscurity, which is not much of a reason. However, if you do change the file name to something else, make sure that you change the regular expression `"^\.ht"` to `"^\.whatever"`, where `.whatever` is the first view character of what you set `AccessFileName` to.

FILES CONTAINER   The following `<Files . . .>` container tells Apache to disallow access to any file that starts with a `.ht` (that is, the `.htaccess` or `.htpasswd`). This corresponds to the default `%AccessFileName%`:

```
<Files ~ "^\.ht">
    Order allow,deny
    Deny from all
</Files>
```

TYPESCONFIG   The `TypesConfig` directive points to the mime configuration file `mime.types` that resides in the default `conf` directory. You do not need to change it unless you have relocated this file.

DEFAULTTYPE   The `DefaultType` directive sets the `Content-Type` header for any file whose MIME type cannot be determined from the file extension. For example, if you have a file `%DocumentRoot%/myfile`, Apache uses the `%DefaultType`, which is set to `text/plain`, as the content type for the file. This means that when the Web browser requests and receives such a file in response, it will display the contents in the same way it displays a plain-text file. If you think most of your unknown file contents should be treated as HTML, use `text/html` in place of `text/plain`.

IFMODULE CONTAINER   The next `<IfModule . . .>` container tells Apache to enable the MIME magic module (`mod_mime_magic`) if it exists, and to use the `%MIMEMagicFile%` file as the magic information (bytes patterns) needed to identify MIME-type files. The default should be left alone unless you want to change the path of the magic file. Here's an example:

```
<IfModule mod_mime_magic.c>
    MIMEMagicFile conf/magic
</IfModule>
```

HOSTNAMELOOKUPS   The `HostnameLookups` directive tells Apache to enable DNS lookup per request if it is set to `On`. However, the default setting is `Off`, and therefore no DNS lookup is performed to process a request, which speeds up response time. Performing a DNS lookup to resolve an IP address to the host name is a time-consuming step for a busy server and should be done only using the `logresolve` utility. Leave the default as it is.

ERRORLOG   The `ErrorLog` directive is very important. It points to the log file dedicated to recording server errors. The default value of logs/errors translates to `%ServerRoot%/logs/error_log`, which should work for you, unless you want to write a log in a different place. Generally, it is a good idea to create a log partition for keeping your logs. It also is preferable that your log partition be on one or more dedicated log disks. If you have such a hardware configuration, you might want to change the directive to point to a new log path.

LOGLEVEL   The `LogLevel` directive sets the level of logging that will be done. The default value of `warn` is sufficient for getting started. The `LogFormat` directives dictate what is logged and in what format it is logged. In most cases, you should be able to live with the defaults.

CUSTOMLOG   The `CustomLog` directive sets the path for the access log, which stores your server hits. By default, it uses the common log format (CLF), which is defined in the preceding `LogFormat` directive. Consider the advice about keeping logs on their own disk and partition, and make changes to the path if necessary.

 A good bit of advice for all logs, regardless of which directory you keep the logs in, is to make sure that only the parent server process has write access in that directory. This is a major security issue, because allowing other users or processes to write to the log directory can potentially enable someone unauthorized to take over your parent Web server process UID, which is normally the root account.

SERVERSIGNATURE   The next directive is `ServerSignature`, which displays server name and version number and is a server-generated page such as dynamic directory index pages, error pages, and the like. If you feel uncomfortable about displaying your server information so readily to everyone, set it to `Off`. We do.

ALIAS   The `Alias` directive defines a new directory alias called `/icons/` to point to `/usr/local/apache/icons/` (that is, `%ServerRoot%/icons/`). The icon images stored in this directory are used to display dynamic directory listings when no `%DirectoryIndex%`-specified files are found in that directory. You should leave the alias alone unless you changed the path of the `icons` directory. The directory container that follows the alias definition sets the permission for this `icon` directory. We do not like the idea that it enables directory browsing (that is, dynamic directory indexing) by setting `Options` to `Indexes`. You should change `Options Indexes` to `Options -Indexes` and not worry about the `MultiViews` option.

SCRIPTALIAS   The `ScriptAlias` directive is used to set a widely used CGI script alias directory `/cgi-bin/` to point to `/usr/local/apache/cgi-bin/` (that is, `%ServerRoot%/cgi-bin/`). If you plan to use CGI scripts from the main server, keep it; otherwise, remove this directive. Alternately, if you want to change the CGI script directory to another location, change the physical path given in the directive to match yours.

> Never set a CGI script path to a directory within your document root — that is, `%DocumentRoot%/somepath` — because keeping CGI scripts in your document root directory opens it to various security issues. Set your CGI script path and `DocumentRoot` at the same level. In other words, if you set `DocumentRoot` to `/a/b/c/htdocs`, then set `ScriptAlias` to point to `/a/b/c/cgi-bin`, not to `/a/b/c/htdocs/cgi-bin` or to `/a/b/c/htdocs/d/cgi-bin`.

Next, a directory container places a restriction on the `%ScriptAlias%` directory to ensure that no directory-level options are allowed. Here, the `Options` directive is set to `None`, which means that the contents of `%ScriptAlias%` cannot be browsed for security reasons and that symbolic links within the `%ScriptAlias%` directory are not followed.

OTHER DIRECTIVES   The rest of the directives — `IndexOptions`, `AddIconByEncoding`, `AddIconByType`, `AddIcon`, `DefaultIcon`, `ReadmeName`, `HeaderName`, `IndexIgnore`, `AddEncoding`, `AddLanguage`, `AddCharset`, `BrowserMatch`, are not required to get up and running, so they are ignored for now. You may want to consider changing two additional directives if necessary: `LanguagePriority` and `AddDefaultCharset`.

AddType
This directive allows you to add or override MIME configuration information stored in mime.types file. For example:

```
AddType application/x-httpd-php .php
```
Here the .php extension is associated with PHP scripts.

LanguagePriority

By default, the `LanguagePriority` directive sets the default language to be `en` (English), which might not work for everyone in the world. You might want to change the default language to your native language, if it is supported.

AddDefaultCharset

`AddDefaultCharset` should be set to the character set that best suits your local needs. If you do not know which character set you should use, you can leave the default alone, find out which character set you should use, and change the default later.

Starting and stopping Apache

After you have customized `httpd.conf`, you are ready to run the server. For this section, we assume that you installed Apache in `/usr/local/apache`. If you did not, make sure that you replace all references to `/usr/local/apache` to whatever is appropriate for your system in the following discussion.

Starting Apache

Run the `/usr/local/apache/bin/apachectl start` command to start the Apache Web server. If `apachectl` complains about syntax errors, fix the errors in the `httpd.conf` file and retry.

Check the `%ErrorLog%` log file (that is, `/usr/local/apache/logs/error_log`) for error messages (if any). If you see errors in the log file, you need to fix them first. Following are the most common errors:

- ◆ **Not running the server as the root user.** You must start Apache as the root user. After Apache is started, it will spawn child processes that will use the `User` and `Group` directives, specified UID and GID. Most people are confused by this issue and try to start the server using the user account specified in the `User` directive.

- ◆ **Apache complains about being unable to "bind" to an address.** Either another process is already using the port that you have configured Apache to use, or you are running `httpd` as a normal user but are trying to use a port below 1024 (such as the default port 80).

- ◆ **Missing log file paths.** Make sure that both the `%ErrorLog%` and `%CustomLog%` paths exist and are not writable by anyone but the Apache server.

- ◆ **Configuration typo.** Anytime you change the `httpd.conf` configuration file, run `/usr/local/apache/apachectl configtest` to verify that you do not have a syntax error in the configuration file.

TIP The quickest way to check whether the server is running is to try the following command:

```
ps auxww | grep httpd
```

This command uses the `ps` utility to list all the processes in the process queue and then pipes this output to the `grep` program. `grep` searches the output for lines that match the keyword `httpd`, and then displays each matching line. If you see one line with the word root in it, that's your parent Apache server process.

Note that when the server starts, it creates a number of child processes to handle the requests. If you started Apache as the root user, the parent process continues to run as `root`, while the children change to the user as instructed in the `httpd.conf` file. If you are running Apache on Linux, you can create the script shown in Listing D-2 and keep it in `/etc/rc.d/init.d/` directory. This script allows you to automatically start and stop Apache when you reboot the system.

Listing D-2: The httpd Script

```sh
#!/bin/sh
#
# httpd   This shell script starts and stops the Apache server
# It takes an argument 'start' or 'stop' to receptively start and
# stop the server process.
#
# Notes: You might have to change the path information used
# in the script to reflect your system's configuration.
#

APACHECTL=/usr/local/apache/bin/apachectl

[ -f $APACHECTL ] || exit 0

# See how the script was called.
case "$1" in
  start)
        # Start daemons.
        echo -n "Starting httpd: "
        $APACHECTL start
        touch /var/lock/subsys/httpd
        echo
        ;;
  restart)
```

Continued

Listing D-2 *(Continued)*

```
        # Restart daemons.
        echo -n "Restarting httpd: "
        $APACHECTL restart

        echo "done"
        rm -f /var/lock/subsys/httpd
        ;;

  stop)
        # Stop daemons.
        echo -n "Shutting down httpd: "
        $APACHECTL stop

        echo "done"
        rm -f /var/lock/subsys/httpd
        ;;
  *)
        echo "Usage: httpd {start|stop|restart}"
        exit 1
esac
exit 0
```

 To start Apache automatically when you boot up your Red Hat Linux system, simply run the following command once:

`ln -s /etc/rc.d/init.d/httpd /etc/rc.d/rc3.d/S99httpd`

This command creates a special link called S99httpd in the /etc/rc.d/ rc3.d (run-level 3) directory that links to the /etc/rc.d/init.d/httpd script. When your system boots up, this script will be executed with the start argument and Apache will start automatically.

Restarting Apache

To restart the Apache server, run the /usr/local/apache/bin/apachectl restart command. You also can use the kill command as follows:

`kill -USR1 'cat /usr/local/apache/logs/httpd.pid'`

When restarted with apachectl restart or by using the HUP signal with kill, the parent Apache process (run as root user) kills all its children, reads the configuration file, and restarts a new generation of children as needed.

This type of restart is sudden to the Web clients that were promised service by the then-alive child processes. Therefore, you might want to consider using graceful with apachectl instead of the restart option, and WINCH instead of HUP signal with the kill command. In both cases, the parent Apache process will advise its child processes to finish the current request and then terminate so that it can reread the configuration file and restart a new batch of children. This might take some time on a busy site.

Stopping Apache

You can automatically stop Apache when the system reboots, or manually stop it at any time. These two methods of stopping Apache are discussed in the following sections.

STOPPING APACHE AUTOMATICALLY   To terminate Apache automatically when the system is being rebooted, run the following command once:

```
ln -s /etc/rc.d/init.d/httpd /etc/rc.d/rc3.d/K99httpd
```

This command ensures that the httpd script is run with the stop argument when the system shuts down.

STOPPING THE APACHE SERVER MANUALLY   To stop the Apache server manually, run the /usr/local/apache/bin/apachectl stop command.

The Apache server also makes it convenient for you to find the PID of the root Web server process. The PID is written to a file assigned to the PidFile directive. This PID is for the parent httpd process. Do not attempt to kill the child processes manually one by one because the parent process will re-create them as needed. Another way to stop the Apache server is to run the following:

```
kill -TERM 'cat /usr/local/apache/logs/httpd.pid'
```

This command runs the kill command with a -TERM signal (that is, -15) for the process ID returned by the cat /usr/local/apache/logs/httpd.pid (that is, cat %PidFile%) command.

Testing Apache

After you have started the Apache server, access it via a Web browser using the appropriate host name. For example, if you are running the Web browser on the server itself, use http://localhost/ to access the server. If you want to access the server from a remote host, however, use the fully qualified host name of the server.

For example, to access a server called `apache.pcnltd.com`, use `http://apache.pcnltd.com`. If you set the `Port` directive to a nonstandard port (that is, to a port other than 80), remember to include the `:port` in the URL. For example, `http://localhost:8080` will access the Apache server on port 8080.

Finally, you want to ensure that the log files are updated properly. To check your log files, enter the `log` directory and run the following command:

```
tail -f path_to_access_log
```

The `tail` part of the command is a UNIX utility that enables viewing of a growing file (when the `-f` option is specified). Make sure that you change the `path_to_access_log` to a fully qualified path name for the access log. Now use a Web browser to access the site; if you are already at the site, simply reload the page you currently have on the browser. You should see an entry added to the listing on the screen. Click the reload button a few more times to ensure that the access file is updated appropriately. If you see the updated records, your access log file is working. Press Ctrl+C to exit from the `tail` command session. If you do not see any new records in the file, check the permission settings for the log files and the directory in which they are kept. Another log to check is the error log file. Use the following command:

```
tail -f path_to_error_log
```

This allows you to view the error log entries as they come in. Simply request nonexistent resources (such as a file you don't have) to view on your Web browser, and you should see entries being added. If you can observe entries being added, the error log file is properly configured.

If all of these tests were successful, you have successfully configured your Apache server. Congratulations!

Installing and Configuring MySQL Server

Many SQL servers are available for Red Hat, including Oracle, DB2, Postgres, and MySQL. We chose to explore MySQL for a number of reasons:

◆ MySQL is free as long as you don't sell it to someone, sell a product that is bundled with MySQL, or install and maintain MySQL at a client site. If you're unsure whether you fit within the license parameters, please visit the Web site at `http://www.mysql.com/`.

◆ MySQL supports many programming interfaces, including C, C++, Java, Perl, and Python. You can tailor programs to fit your needs in nearly infinite ways.

◆ MySQL uses very fast methods of relating tables of information to each other. Using a method called a *one-sweep multijoin*, MySQL is very efficient at gathering the information you request from many different tables at once.

◆ MySQL is widely used. Chances are good that many other people have done something similar to what you are doing. If you have questions or problems, you can consult with a large group of people. Not only can you get advice from others about how to solve your problems and what to do, you can also get information about what *not* to do. This saves you from making the same mistakes others have made.

Where to get MySQL

MySQL is available all over the Internet. The best way to get MySQL is to go to `http://www.mysql.com/` and find a mirror site close to you.

During your Red Hat server installation, you can choose to install MySQL. However, if you missed that chance, you have two options: you can compile a custom copy of MySQL from the source RPM packages, or you can simply download the binary distribution. Here we assume that you will use the binary distribution. You want to get both the RPM package containing the MySQL server program and the RPM package containing the client programs and libraries. You also need the RPM package containing the include files and libraries, from `http://www.mysql.org/download.html`.

Installing the MySQL RPM packages

Installing the MySQL RPM package is simple. Just run `rpm -i` *mysql-version.rpm*, where *mysql-version.rpm* is the name of the RPM package containing the MySQL server. Next, run `rpm -i` *mysql-client-version.rpm* again, substituting the name of the RPM package you have. Do the same for the RPM package, with the `include` files and library binaries.

Accessing the MySQL server

After you install the MySQL server RPM package, the server starts automatically every time you boot your system. You will find a file called `mysql` in `/etc/rc.d/init.d` that you can use to start and stop the MySQL server by using the following commands:

```
/etc/rc.d/init.d/mysqld start
/etc/rc.d/init.d/mysqld stop
```

The RPM installation automatically starts the server for you. To ensure that the MySQL server is running, you can ping it by using the following command:

```
/usr/bin/mysqladmin ping
```

You should get a response such as mysqld is alive when the server is up and running. If you don't get such a response, use the /etc/rc.d/init.d/mysql start command to start the server.

After the server starts, you need to run the following command to create some required tables:

```
/usr/bin/mysql_install_db
```

By default, the password for the server's administrative account (root) is not set, so use the following command to set the password:

```
/usr/bin/mysqladmin -u root password newpassword
```

Now you are ready to run the MySQL client. You can start the MySQL client program by typing the following:

```
mysql -u username -p
```

In this example, *username* is the username you are using to access the SQL server. If a password is required, you are prompted for it. You should now see something like the following:

```
Welcome to the MySQL monitor.  Commands end with ; or \g.
Your MySQL connection id is 3 to server version: 3.22.15
Type 'help' for help.
mysql>
```

You are now ready to start laying the framework of your database.

Installing and Configuring PHP for Apache 2.0

The current version of PHP is 4.x. You can download PHP source or binary distributions from www.php.net. This section assumes that you have downloaded the latest source distribution of PHP, php-4.3.1tar.gz.

After downloading the source distribution, extract the source in a directory by using the `tar xvzf php-4.3.1tar.gz` command. We recommend that you install it in the same directory as you installed the Apache source. For example, if you installed the Apache source in the `/usr/local/src/httpd-2.0.16` directory, then extract PHP into the `/usr/local/src` directory. A new subdirectory, called `php-4.2.3`, will be created.

At this point, you have to decide how you plan to run PHP. PHP can be run as an Apache module (embedded in the server itself or as a DSO module) or as a CGI solution. The CGI solution means that you will not have any performance advantage over regular CGI scripts with PHP scripts because a PHP interpreter will be loaded each time to process a CGI-mode PHP script.

Building PHP as a CGI solution

Like Perl, PHP can be used in standalone scripts as well as embedded in Web pages. To build the PHP interpreter for CGI-mode operations, do the following:

1. As root, change to the PHP source distribution directory and run the following:

   ```
   ./configure --enable-discard-path --with-mysql
   ```

2. Now run `make && make install` to compile and install the PHP interpreter on your system.

Building PHP as an Apache module

This is the preferred way of using PHP with Apache. You can either store the PHP module within the Apache binary or install it as a DSO module for Apache. An advantage of a DSO module is that it can be unloaded by just commenting out a configuration line in `httpd.conf`, thus saving some memory. Here we will show you how to create PHP as a DSO module for Apache.

You must have DSO support enabled in Apache before you can use PHP as a DSO module. To recompile Apache with DSO support, do the following:

1. From the Apache source distribution directory, run the following command as root:

   ```
   ./configure --prefix=/usr/local/apache --enable-so
   ```

   You can also add other options as necessary.

2. Compile and install Apache using the `make && make install` command.

After you have a DSO support–enabled Apache server, perform the following steps to create a DSO module for PHP:

1. From the PHP source distribution directory, run the following command as root:

```
./configure --with-apxs2=/usr/local/apache/bin/apxs \
            --enable-track-vars \
            --with-zlib \
            --with-mysql=/usr
```

Here, the `--with-mysql` option is set to `/usr` because MySQL RPM packages install the include files in the `/usr/include/mysql` directory. If your system has MySQL includes in a different location, you should use a different directory name. You can find out where MySQL includes are kept by using the `locate mysql.h` command, which is available on most UNIX systems with the locate database feature.

2. Run `make && make install` to compile and install the DSO version of the PHP module for Apache.

3. Run the `/usr/local/apache/bin/apachectl restart` command to restart (or start) Apache.

Configuring Apache for PHP

After you have installed the `mod_php` module for Apache and configured `php.ini` as discussed earlier, you are ready to configure Apache for PHP as follows:

1. Add the following line to the `httpd.conf` file:

```
AddType application/x-httpd-php .php
```

This tells Apache that any file with a `.php` extension must be treated as an `application/x-httpd-php` application and processed by the `mod_php` module.

There is no reason to use a different extension for PHP scripts. For example, you can set the preceding AddType directive to AddType application/x-httpd-php .html and have all your HTML pages treated as PHP script. We don't recommend using the .html extension because chances are good that many of your HTML pages are not PHP scripts, and you simply do not want to slow down your Web server by having it parse each page for PHP scripts.

2. Save the `httpd.conf` file and restart the Apache Web server as usual.

Now you are ready to create PHP scripts for your Web site. You can create PHP scripts and store them anywhere in your Web site's document tree and Apache will automatically process them as PHP scripts.

Configuring PHP by using php.ini

The PHP configuration file is called `php.ini`, and it is stored in the `/usr/local/lib` directory by default unless you specified a different path during PHP source configuration using the configure utility. When a PHP module is loaded, it reads the `php.ini` file. The module looks for `php.ini` in the current working directory, the path designated by the environmental variable `PHPRC`, and in `/usr/local/lib`.

If you use PHP as a CGI solution, the `php.ini` file is read every time a PHP CGI is run. Conversely, when PHP is loaded as an Apache module, it is read once. You must restart the Apache server by using the `/usr/local/apache/bin/apachectl restart` command to reload any changes that you make in the `php.ini` file.

PHP directives in httpd.conf

With Version PHP 4, only four `mod_php`-specific directives, as outlined in the following sections, are allowed in `httpd.conf`. All other PHP directives must be in the `php.ini` file.

php_admin_flag

The `php_flag` directive enables you to set a Boolean value (On or Off) for a configuration parameter. This directive cannot appear in directory containers or per-directory `.htaccess` files.

Syntax: `php_admin_flag` *name* `On | Off`

Context: Server config, virtual host

php_admin_value

The `php_admin_value` directive enables you to set a value for a configuration parameter. This directive cannot appear in directory containers or per-directory `.htaccess` files.

Syntax: `php_admin_value` *name value*

Context: Server config, virtual host

php_flag

The `php_flag` directive enables you to set a Boolean value (On or Off) for a configuration parameter.

Syntax: `php_flag name On | Off`

Context: Server config, virtual host, directory, per-directory (`.htaccess`)

For example:
```
php_flag display_errors On
```

php_value

The `php_value` directive enables you to set a value for a configuration parameter.

Syntax: `php_value name value`

Context: Server config, virtual host, directory, per-directory (`.htaccess`)

For example:
```
php_value error_reporting 15
```

PHP directives in php.ini

The `php.ini` file has a simple *directive = value* structure syntax. Lines consisting of leading semicolons or lines with only whitespace are ignored. Section names are enclosed in brackets. You can learn about all the directives that go in `php.ini` at `www.php.net/manual/en/configuration.php`. The following sections discuss the most useful directives.

auto_prepend_file

The `auto_prepend_file` directive enables you to set a header document with each PHP-parsed page.
Syntax: `auto_prepend_file filename`

The following example `preload.php` page will be loaded before each PHP page is processed (this page is a good place to establish database connections if all the pages in the site use the same database connection.):

```
auto_prepend_file preload.php
```

default_charset

The `default_charset` directive sets the default character set.
Syntax: `default_charset char_set`

The following example sets the default character set to 8-bit UTF:
```
default_charset = "UTF-8"
```

disable_functions

The `disable_functions` directive enables you to disable one or more functions for security reasons.

Syntax: `disable_functions` *function_name* [*function_name*]

You can specify a comma-delimited list of PHP functions as follows:
`disable_functions = fopen, fwrite, popen`

In the preceding example, the functions responsible for opening, writing file or pipes are disabled.

 This directive is not affected by the `safe_mode` directive.

display_errors

The `display_errors` directive enables or disables printing of error message onscreen. This is recommended only for use on development systems and not for use on production servers. For production systems, you should use `log_errors` along with `error_log` directives to log error messages to files or to a syslog server so that malicious users cannot break your applications to glean information about them.

Syntax: `display_errors On | Off`

enable_dl

The `enable_dl` directive enables or disables the capability to dynamically load a PHP extension.

Syntax: `enable_dl On | Off`

Default setting: `enable_dl On`

error_append_string

The `error_append_string` directive sets the string that is appended to the error message. See the `error_prepend_string` directive above.

Syntax: `error_append_string` *string*

error_log

The `error_log` directive sets the PHP error log path. You can specify a fully qualified pathname of the log file, or you can specify the keyword `syslog` on Unix systems to log using the syslog facility. On Windows systems, setting this directive to `syslog` writes log entries in the Windows Event log.

Syntax: `error_log` *fqpn*

error_prepend_string

The `error_prepend_string` directive sets the string that is prepended to an error message. This directive is used with the `error_append_string`.

Syntax: `error_prepend_string` *string*

If you do not log errors, error messages are shown onscreen if display_errors is turned on. For example, by using the following two directives, you can print error messages in red:

```
error_prepend_string = "<font color=red>"
error_append_string = "</font>"
```

error_reporting

The `error_reporting` directive enables you to specify a bit field to specify an error reporting level. The bit field can be constructed using the predefined constants shown in Table D-2.

Syntax: `error_reporting [bit field] [predefined_ constant]`

TABLE **D-2** CONSTANTS FOR THE ERROR_REPORTING DIRECTIVE

Constant	**Meaning**
`E_ALL`	Displays all errors, warnings, and notices
`E_ERROR`	Displays only fatal run-time errors
`E_WARNING`	Displays run-time warnings
`E_PARSE`	Displays parse errors
`E_NOTICE`	Displays notices of likely problems in code
`E_CORE_ERROR`	Displays fatal errors that occur during PHP's initial startup
`E_CORE_WARNING`	Displays warnings that occur during PHP's initial startup
`E_COMPILE_ERROR`	Displays fatal compile-time errors
`E_COMPILE_WARNING`	Displays compile-time warnings (nonfatal errors)
`E_USER_ERROR`	User-generated error message
`E_USER_WARNING`	User-generated warning message
`E_USER_NOTICE`	User-generated notice message

You can use bit field operators such as ~ (inverts), & (bitwise meaning "AND"), and | (bitwise meaning "OR") to create a custom error-reporting level. For example:

```
Error_reporting = E_ALL & ~E_WARNING & ~E_NOTICE
```

This tells the PHP engine to display all errors except warnings and notices. Displaying error messages on a production server is not recommended. You should display errors only on your development system or during the development phase of your production server. On production servers, use log_errors and error_log directives to write logs to files or to a syslog facility.

extension

The extension directive enables you to load a dynamic extension module for PHP itself.

Syntax: extension *module_name*

For example, the following directive loads the graphics library GD extension for PHP for Windows via the extension directive. The PHP engine loads such dynamic modules at server startup.

```
extension=php_gd.dll
```

Similarly, the following directive loads the MySQL DSO module for Apache on the Unix platform with DSO support:

```
extension=mysql.so
```

You can repeat extension as many times as needed to load different modules.

extension_dir

The extension_dir directive defines the directory in which dynamically loadable PHP modules are stored. The default value is appropriate for most PHP installations.

Syntax: extension_dir *directory*

Default setting: extension_dir ./

implicit_flush

The implicit_flush directive enables or disables implicit flushing of script output as it uses print, echo, and HTML blocks for output. When turned on, this directive will issue the flush() call after every print(), echo, or HTML block output. This is extremely useful for debugging purposes, but a major performance drain on the production environment. It is only recommended for development systems.

Syntax: implicit_flush On | Off

Default setting: implicit_flush Off

include_path

The `include_path` directive sets the path for `include()` and `require()` functions. You can list multiple directories.

Unix Syntax: `include_path path[:path]`

Windows Syntax: include_path *path*[;*path*]

For example, the following specifies that PHP should first look for include files in the `/usr/local/lib/php` directory and then in the current directory:

```
include_path = /usr/local/lib/php:.
```

On Windows, this directive is set as follows:

```
include_path = "c:\php;."
```

log_errors

The `log_errors` directive enables or disables logging of PHP errors. You must use the `error_log` directive to specify a log path or a `syslog` file.
Syntax: `log_errors On | Off`

magic_quotes_gpc

The `magic_quotes_gpc` directive enables or disables escaping of quotes (single quotes, double quotes, null, and backslash characters) for GET, POST, and cookie data.

Syntax: `magic_quotes_gpc On | Off`

Default setting: `magic_quotes_gpc On`

magic_quotes_runtime

The `magic_quotes_runtime` directive enables or disables automatic quoting of internally generated text. In other words, if you retrieve a record from a database that has the `<?php anything goes here ?>` type of tag embedded in it, the contents within the tags (which is part of the data) will be escaped (i.e., not processed) and not treated as PHP code.

Syntax: `magic_quotes_runtime On | Off`

Default setting: `magic_quotes_runtime = Off`

max_execution_time

The `max_execution_time` directive sets the maximum time that a script can run to produce output. After a script exceeds the specified amount of seconds, PHP times out the script. Unless you plan to run PHP scripts that take a lot of time, the default value should be acceptable for most situations.

Syntax: `max_execution_time seconds`

Default setting: `max_execution_time 30`

memory_limit

The `memory_limit` directive sets the maximum RAM a PHP script can consume. The default, 8MB, should be more than adequate for small-to-modest PHP scripts. You can specify memory in bytes as well.

Syntax: `memory_limit bytes [nM]`

Default setting: `memory_limit 8M`

For example, the following are equivalent:

```
memory_limit 8M
memory_limit 8388608
```

output_buffering

The `output_buffering` directive allows you to enable or disable output buffering. When it is set to `On`, you can print HTTP headers anywhere in a PHP script. Being able to output a header in the middle of a script even after printing other contents means that a script can display an error page even if it was partially successful earlier.

Syntax: `output_buffering On | Off`

Default setting: `output_buffering On`

You can also use the built-in `ob_start()` and `ob_end_flush()` directives to start and end flushing of the contents directly, as shown in the following example:

```php
<?php

ob_start();  // Buffer all output

echo "Buffered contents \n";

ob_end_flush(); // Page rendered, flush the output buffer.

?>
```

Here the output is buffered.

safe_mode

The `safe_mode` directive sets the safe mode for PHP when it is used as a CGI solution. Do not use this mode when using PHP as an Apache module. When set to On, this directive ensures that PHP scripts run by the PHP interpreter in CGI mode are not allowed any access beyond the document root directory of the Web site.

Syntax: `safe_mode On | Off`

Default setting: `safe_mode Off`

safe_mode_allowed_env_vars

The `safe_mode_allowed_env_vars` directive enables you to set a prefix for all the environment variables that a user can change by using the `putenv()` function. The default value enables users to change any environment variable that starts with the `PHP_` prefix.

Syntax: `safe_mode_allowed_env_vars prefix`

Default setting: `safe_mode_allowed_env_vars PHP_`

safe_mode_protected_env_vars

The `safe_mode_protected_env_vars` directive enables you to set a comma-delimited list of environment variables that cannot be changed by any PHP script that uses the `putenv()` function.

Syntax: `safe_mode_protected_env_vars environment_variable [environment_variable ...]`

Default setting: `safe_mode_protected_env_vars = LD_LIBRARY_PATH`

If you wish to protect all the environment variables that start with the HTTP_ prefix, you can use the following:

```
safe_mode_protected_env_vars = HTTP_
```

track_errors

The `track_errors` directive enables or disables the storing of error message in a PHP variable called `$php_errormsg`.
Syntax: `track_errors On | Off`

upload_max_filesize

The `upload_max_filesize` directive sets the maximum size of a file that can be uploaded via PHP. The default limit is 2MB (2M). Alternatively, you can specify just the kilobyte number.

Syntax: `upload_max_filesize kilobytes`

Default setting: `upload_max_filesize 2M`

For example, the following are equivalent:

```
upload_max_filesize = 2M
upload_max_filesize = 2097152
```

upload_tmp_dir

The `load_tmp_dir` directive defines the temporary directory location for files uploaded via PHP. It is customary to set this to `/tmp` on UNIX systems; on Windows systems, this is typically set to `/temp` or left alone, in which case, PHP uses the system default.

Syntax: `load_tmp_dir` *directory*

Common File/Directory Commands

This section describes a few commonly used Linux file and directory commands.

chmod

Syntax:

```
chmod  [-R] permission-mode   file or directory
```

Use this command to change the permission mode of a file or directory. The permission mode is specified as a three- or four-digit octal number. For example:

```
chmod 755  myscript.pl
```

The preceding command changes the permission of `myscript.pl script` to 755 (`rwxr-xr-x`), which allows the file owner to read, write, and execute, and allows only read and execute privileges for everyone else. Here is another example:

```
chmod -R 744 public_html
```

The preceding command changes the permissions of the `public_html` directory and all its contents (files and subdirectories) to 744 (`rwxr-r-`), which is a typical permission setting for the personal Web directories you access using `http://server/~username` URLs under Apache Server. The `-R` option tells `chmod` to recursively change permissions for all files and directories under the named directory.

chown

Syntax:

```
chown [ -fhR ] Owner [ :Group ] { File . . . | Directory. . . }
```

The `chown` command changes the owner of a file or directory. The value of the
`Owner` parameter can be a user ID or a login name in the `/etc/passwd` file.
Optionally, you also can specify a group. The value of the `Group` parameter can be
a group ID or a group name in the `/etc/group` file.

Only the root user can change the owner of a file. You can change the group of
a file only if you are a root user or you own the file. If you own the file but are not
a root user, you can change the group only to a group of which you are a member.
Table D-3 describes the `chown` options.

TABLE D-3 CHOWN OPTIONS

Option	Description
-f	Suppresses all error messages except usage messages.
-h	Changes the ownership of an encountered symbolic link but not that of the file or directory to which the symbolic link points.
-R	Descends directories recursively, changing the ownership for each file. When a symbolic link is encountered and the link points to a directory, the ownership of that directory is changed, but the directory is not further traversed.

The following example changes the owner of the file to another user:

```
chown bert hisfile.txt
```

cp

Syntax:

```
cp [-r] source destination
```

Use the `cp` command to make an exact copy of a file. The `cp` command requires
at least two arguments. The first argument is the file you want to copy, and the second argument is the location or file name of the new file. If the second argument is

an existing directory, cp copies the source file into the directory. The -r parameter recursively copies a directory.

```
cp main.c main.c.bak
```

The preceding example copies the existing file main.c and creates a new file called main.c.bak in the same directory. These two files are identical, bit for bit.

grep

Syntax:

```
grep [-viw] pattern file(s)
```

The grep command enables you to search for one or more files for particular character patterns. Every line of each file that contains the pattern is displayed at the terminal. The grep command is useful when you have numerous files and you want to find out which ones contain certain words or phrases.

Using the -v option, you can display the inverse of a pattern. Perhaps you want to select the lines in data.txt that do not contain the word the:

```
grep -vw 'the' data.txt
```

If you do not specify the -w option, any word containing the matches, such as toge[the]r. The -w option specifies that the pattern must be a whole word. Finally, the -i option ignores the difference between uppercase and lowercase letters when searching for the pattern.

Much of the flexibility of grep comes from the fact that you can specify not only exact characters but also a more general search pattern. To do this, you use what are described as *regular expressions.*

find

Syntax:

```
find [path] [-type fdl] [-name pattern] [-atime [+-]number of days] [-exec command {} \;] [-empty]
```

The find command finds files and directories, as shown in the following example:

```
find . -type d
```

The find command returns all subdirectory names under the current directory. The -type option is typically set to d (for directory), f (for file), or l (for links):

```
find . -type f -name "*.txt"
```

The preceding command finds all text files (ending with a .txt extension) in the current directory, including all its subdirectories.

```
find  .  -type f -name "*.txt" -exec grep -l "magic" {} \;
```

The preceding command searches all text files (ending with the .txt extension) in the current directory, including all its subdirectories for the keyword magic, and returns their names (because -l is used with grep):

```
find . -name ?*.gif? -atime -1 -exec ls -l {} \;
```

The preceding command finds all GIF files that have been accessed in the past 24 hours (one day) and displays their details using the ls -l command.

```
find . -type f -empty
```

The preceding command displays all empty files in the current directory hierarchy.

head

Syntax:

```
head [-count | -n number] filename
```

This command displays the first few lines of a file. By default, it displays the first 10 lines of a file. However, you can use the preceding options to specify a different number of lines, as follows:

```
head -2 doc.txt
# Outline of future projects
# Last modified:   02/02/99
```

The preceding example illustrates how to view the first two lines of the text file doc.txt.

ln

Syntax:

```
ln [-s] sourcefile target
```

ln creates two types of links: hard and soft. Think of a link as two names for the same file. Once you create a link, you cannot distinguish it from the original file.

You cannot remove a file that has hard links from the hard disk until you remove all links. You create hard links without the -s option:

```
ln ./www ./public_html
```

A hard link does have limitations, however. A hard link cannot link to another directory, and a hard link cannot link to a file on another file system. Using the -s option, you can create a soft link, which eliminates these restrictions:

```
ln -s /dev/fs02/jack/www /dev/fs01/foo/public_html
```

Here you create a soft link between the directory www on file system 2 and a newly created file public_html on file system 1.

locate

Syntax:

```
locate keyword
```

The locate command finds the path of a particular file or command if updated script was run at an earlier time using cron job or manually. locate finds an exact or substring match. For example:

```
locate foo
/usr/lib/texmf/tex/latex/misc/footnpag.sty
/usr/share/automake/footer.am
/usr/share/games/fortunes/food
/usr/share/games/fortunes/food.dat
/usr/share/gimp/patterns/moonfoot.pat
```

The output that locate produces contains the keyword foo in the absolute path or does not have any output.

ls

Syntax:

```
ls [-1aRl] file or directory
```

The ls command allows you to list files (and subdirectories) in a directory. It is one of the most popular programs. When you use it with the -1 option, it displays only the file and directory names in the current directory. When you use the -1 option, a long listing containing file/directory permission information, size, modification date, and so on, are displayed. The `-a` option allows you to view all files and directories (including the ones that have a leading period in their names) within the current directory. The `-R` option allows the command to recursively display contents of the subdirectories (if any).

mkdir

Syntax:

```
mkdir directory . . .
```

To make a directory, use the `mkdir` command. You have only two restrictions when choosing a directory name: (1) File names can be up to 255 characters long, and (2) directory names can contain any character except the slash (/). For example,

```
mkdir dir1 dir2 dir3
```

The preceding example creates three subdirectories in the current directory.

mv

Syntax:

```
mv [ if] sourcefile targetfile
```

Use the `mv` command to move or rename directories and files. The command performs a move or rename depending on whether the `targetfile` is an existing directory. To illustrate, suppose you would like to give a directory called `foo` the new name of foobar:

```
mv foo foobar
```

Because `foobar` does not already exist as a directory, `foo` becomes `foobar`. If you issue the following command:

```
mv doc.txt foobar
```

and `foobar` is an existing directory, you perform a move. The file `doc.txt` now resides in the directory `foobar`.

The `-f` option removes existing destination files and never prompts the user. The `-i` option prompts the user whether to overwrite each destination file that exists. If the response does not begin with `y` or `Y`, the file is skipped.

pwd

Syntax:

```
pwd
```

This command prints the current working directory. The directories displayed are the absolute path. None of the directories displayed are hard or soft symbolic links.

```
pwd
/home/usr/charmaine
```

rm

Syntax:

```
rm [-rif] directory/file
```

To remove a file or directory, use the rm command, as shown in the following examples:

```
rm doc.txt
rm ~/doc.txt
rm /tmp/foobar.txt
```

To remove multiple files with rm, you can use wildcards or type each file individually. For example,

```
rm doc1.txt doc2.txt doc3.txt
```

is equivalent to

```
rm doc[1-3].txt
```

rm is a powerful command that can cause chaos if you use it incorrectly. For instance, suppose that you have been working on your thesis for the last six months. You decide to rm all of your docs, thinking you are in another directory. After finding out that a backup file does not exist (and you are no longer in denial), you wonder whether there was any way you could have prevented this.

The rm command has the -i option, which allows rm to be interactive. This tells rm to ask your permission before removing each file:

```
rm -i *.doc
rm: remove thesis.doc (yes/no)? n
```

The -i option gives you a parachute. It's up to you to either pull the cord (answer no) or suffer the consequences (answer yes). The -f option is completely the opposite. The -f (force) option tells rm to remove all the files you specify, regardless of the file permissions. Use the -f option only when you are 100 percent sure that you are removing the correct file(s).

To remove a directory and all files and subdirectories within it, use the -r option. rm -r will remove an entire subtree, as shown here:

```
rm -r documents
```

If you are not sure what you are doing, combine the -r option with the -i option:

```
rm -ri documents
```

The preceding example asks for your permission before it removes every file and directory.

sort

Syntax:

```
sort [-rndu] [-o outfile] [infile/sortedfile]
```

The obvious task this command performs is to sort. However, sort also merges files. The sort command reads files that contain previously sorted data and merges them into one large, sorted file.

The simplest way to use sort is to sort a single file and display the results on your screen. As an example, suppose that a.txt contains the following:

```
b
c
a
d
```

To sort a.txt and display the results to the screen, use the following:

```
sort a.txt
a
b
c
d
```

To save the sorted results, use the `-o` option: `sort -o sorted.txt a.txt` saves the sorted `a.txt` file in `sorted.txt`. To use `sort` to merge existing sorted files and to save the output in `sorted.txt`, use

```
sort -o sorted.txt a.txt b.txt c.txt
```

The `-r` option for this command reverses the sort order. Therefore, a file that contains the letters of the alphabet on a line is sorted from z to a if you use the `-r` option.

The `-d` option sorts files based on dictionary order. The `sort` command considers only letters, numerals, and spaces, ignoring other characters.

The `-u` option looks for identical lines and suppresses all but one. Therefore, `sort` produces only unique lines.

stat

Syntax:

```
stat file
```

This program displays various statistics on a file or directory, as shown in the following example:

```
stat foo.txt
```

This command displays the following output:

```
  File: 'foo.txt'
  Size: 4447232      Filetype: Regular File
  Mode: (0644/-rw-r--r--)  Uid: ( 0/root)  Gid: (0/root)
Device:  3,0   Inode: 16332     Links: 1
Access: Fri Aug  2 21:39:43 2002(00000.02:32:30)
Modify: Fri Aug  2 22:14:26 2002(00000.01:57:47)
Change: Fri Aug  2 22:14:26 2002(00000.01:57:47
```

You can see the following displayed: file access; modification; change date; size; owner and group information; permission mode; and so on.

strings

Syntax:

```
strings filename
```

The `strings` command prints character sequences at least four characters long. You use this utility mainly to describe the contents of nontext files.

tail

Syntax:

```
tail [-count | -fr] filename
```

The `tail` command displays the end of a file. By default, `tail` displays the last 10 lines of a file. To display the last 50 lines of the file `doc.txt`, you issue the following command:

```
tail -50 doc.txt
```

The `-r` option displays the output in reverse order. By default, `-r` displays all lines in the file, not just 10 lines. For instance, use the following to display the entire contents of the file `doc.txt` in reverse order:

```
tail -r doc.txt
```

To display the last 10 lines of the file `doc.txt` in reverse order, use this:

```
tail -10 -r doc.txt
```

Finally, the `-f` option is useful when you are monitoring a file. With this option, `tail` waits for new data to be written to the file by some other program. As new data is added to the file by some other program, `tail` displays the data on the screen. To stop `tail` from monitoring a file, press Ctrl+C (the intr key) because the `tail` command does not stop on its own.

touch

Syntax:

```
touch file or directory
```

This command updates the timestamp of a file or directory. If the named file does not exist, this command creates it as an empty file.

uniq

Syntax:

```
uniq [-c] filename
```

The `uniq` command compares adjacent lines and displays only one unique line. When used with the `-c` option, `uniq` counts the number of occurrences. For example, a file with the following contents:

```
a
a
a
b
a
```

produces the following result when you use it with `uniq`:

```
uniq test.txt
a
b
a
```

Notice that you remove the adjacent letter as, but not all as in the file. This is an important detail to remember when using `uniq`. If you would like to find all the unique lines in a file called `test.txt`, you can run the following command:

```
sort  test.txt  | uniq
```

This command sorts the `test.txt` file and puts all similar lines next to each other, allowing `uniq` to display only unique lines. For example, to quickly determine how many unique visitors come to your Web site, you can run the following command:

```
awk '{print $1}' access.log | sort | uniq
```

This displays the unique IP addresses in a CLF log file, which is what the Apache Web server uses.

Index

Symbols & Numerics

continued

continued

continued

continued

continued

continued

Wiley Publishing, Inc.
End-User License Agreement

5. <u>Limited Warranty</u>.

   (a) WPI warrants that the Software and Software Media are free from defects in materials and workmanship under normal use for a period of sixty (60) days from the date of purchase of this Book. If WPI receives notification within the warranty period of defects in materials or workmanship, WPI will replace the defective Software Media.

   (b) WPI AND THE AUTHOR OF THE BOOK DISCLAIM ALL OTHER WARRANTIES, EXPRESS OR IMPLIED, INCLUDING WITHOUT LIMITATION IMPLIED WARRANTIES OF MERCHANTABILITY AND FITNESS FOR A PARTICULAR PURPOSE, WITH RESPECT TO THE SOFTWARE, THE PROGRAMS, THE SOURCE CODE CONTAINED THEREIN, AND/OR THE TECHNIQUES DESCRIBED IN THIS BOOK. WPI DOES NOT WARRANT THAT THE FUNCTIONS CONTAINED IN THE SOFTWARE WILL MEET YOUR REQUIREMENTS OR THAT THE OPERATION OF THE SOFTWARE WILL BE ERROR FREE.

   (c) This limited warranty gives you specific legal rights, and you may have other rights that vary from jurisdiction to jurisdiction.

6. <u>Remedies</u>.

   (a) WPI's entire liability and your exclusive remedy for defects in materials and workmanship shall be limited to replacement of the Software Media, which may be returned to WPI with a copy of your receipt at the following address: Software Media Fulfillment Department, Attn.: *Secure PHP Development: Building 50 Practical Applications*, Wiley Publishing, Inc., 10475 Crosspoint Blvd., Indianapolis, IN 46256, or call 1-800-762-2974. Please allow four to six weeks for delivery. This Limited Warranty is void if failure of the Software Media has resulted from accident, abuse, or misapplication. Any replacement Software Media will be warranted for the remainder of the original warranty period or thirty (30) days, whichever is longer.

   (b) In no event shall WPI or the author be liable for any damages whatsoever (including without limitation damages for loss of business profits, business interruption, loss of business information, or any other pecuniary loss) arising from the use of or inability to use the Book or the Software, even if WPI has been advised of the possibility of such damages.

   (c) Because some jurisdictions do not allow the exclusion or limitation of liability for consequential or incidental damages, the above limitation or exclusion may not apply to you.

7. <u>U.S. Government Restricted Rights</u>. Use, duplication, or disclosure of the Software for or on behalf of the United States of America, its agencies and/or instrumentalities "U.S. Government" is subject to restrictions as stated in paragraph (c)(1)(ii) of the Rights in Technical Data and Computer Software clause of DFARS 252.227-7013, or subparagraphs (c) (1) and (2) of the Commercial Computer Software - Restricted Rights clause at FAR 52.227-19, and in similar clauses in the NASA FAR supplement, as applicable.

8. <u>General</u>. This Agreement constitutes the entire understanding of the parties and revokes and supersedes all prior agreements, oral or written, between them and may not be modified or amended except in a writing signed by both parties hereto that specifically refers to this Agreement. This Agreement shall take precedence over any other documents that may be in conflict herewith. If any one or more provisions contained in this Agreement are held by any court or tribunal to be invalid, illegal, or otherwise unenforceable, each and every other provision shall remain in full force and effect.